FREE Study Skills DVD Offer

Dear Customer,

Thank you for your purchase from Mometrix! We consider it an honor and a privilege that you have purchased our product and we want to ensure your satisfaction.

As a way of showing our appreciation and to help us better serve you, we have developed a Study Skills DVD that we would like to give you for <u>FREE</u>. This DVD covers our *best practices* for getting ready for your exam, from how to use our study materials to how to best prepare for the day of the test.

All that we ask is that you email us with feedback that would describe your experience so far with our product. Good, bad, or indifferent, we want to know what you think!

To get your FREE Study Skills DVD, email <u>freedvd@mometrix.com</u> with *FREE STUDY SKILLS DVD* in the subject line and the following information in the body of the email:

- The name of the product you purchased.
- Your product rating on a scale of 1-5, with 5 being the highest rating.
- Your feedback. It can be long, short, or anything in between. We just want to know your impressions and experience so far with our product. (Good feedback might include how our study material met your needs and ways we might be able to make it even better. You could highlight features that you found helpful or features that you think we should add.)
- Your full name and shipping address where you would like us to send your free DVD.

If you have any questions or concerns, please don't hesitate to contact me directly.

Thanks again!

Sincerely,

Jay Willis
Vice President
<u>jay.willis@mometrix.com</u>
1-800-673-8175

MTTC®

Elementary Education (103)

Secrets Study Guide

Exam Review and MTTC® Practice Test for the Michigan Test for Teacher Certification

Written and edited by Mometrix Test Prep

Printed in the United States of America

This paper meets the requirements of ANSI/NISO Z39.48-1992 (Permanence of Paper).

Mometrix offers volume discount pricing to institutions. For more information or a price quote, please contact our sales department at sales@mometrix.com or 888-248-1219.

Mometrix Media LLC is not affiliated with or endorsed by any official testing organization. All organizational and test names are trademarks of their respective owners.

Paperback
ISBN 13: 978-1-5167-3008-7
ISBN 10: 1-5167-3008-9

DEAR FUTURE EXAM SUCCESS STORY

First of all, **THANK YOU** for purchasing Mometrix study materials!

Second, congratulations! You are one of the few determined test-takers who are committed to doing whatever it takes to excel on your exam. **You have come to the right place.** We developed these study materials with one goal in mind: to deliver you the information you need in a format that's concise and easy to use.

In addition to optimizing your guide for the content of the test, we've outlined our recommended steps for breaking down the preparation process into small, attainable goals so you can make sure you stay on track.

We've also analyzed the entire test-taking process, identifying the most common pitfalls and showing how you can overcome them and be ready for any curveball the test throws you.

Standardized testing is one of the biggest obstacles on your road to success, which only increases the importance of doing well in the high-pressure, high-stakes environment of test day. Your results on this test could have a significant impact on your future, and this guide provides the information and practical advice to help you achieve your full potential on test day.

Your success is our success

We would love to hear from you! If you would like to share the story of your exam success or if you have any questions or comments in regard to our products, please contact us at **800-673-8175** or **support@mometrix.com**.

Thanks again for your business and we wish you continued success!

Sincerely,
The Mometrix Test Preparation Team

Need more help? Check out our flashcards at:
http://MometrixFlashcards.com/MTTC

TABLE OF CONTENTS

Introduction

Thank you for purchasing this resource! You have made the choice to prepare yourself for a test that could have a huge impact on your future, and this guide is designed to help you be fully ready for test day. Obviously, it's important to have a solid understanding of the test material, but you also need to be prepared for the unique environment and stressors of the test, so that you can perform to the best of your abilities.

For this purpose, the first section that appears in this guide is the **Secret Keys**. We've devoted countless hours to meticulously researching what works and what doesn't, and we've boiled down our findings to the five most impactful steps you can take to improve your performance on the test. We start at the beginning with study planning and move through the preparation process, all the way to the testing strategies that will help you get the most out of what you know when you're finally sitting in front of the test.

We recommend that you start preparing for your test as far in advance as possible. However, if you've bought this guide as a last-minute study resource and only have a few days before your test, we recommend that you skip over the first two Secret Keys since they address a long-term study plan.

If you struggle with **test anxiety**, we strongly encourage you to check out our recommendations for how you can overcome it. Test anxiety is a formidable foe, but it can be beaten, and we want to make sure you have the tools you need to defeat it.

Secret Key #1 – Plan Big, Study Small

There's a lot riding on your performance. If you want to ace this test, you're going to need to keep your skills sharp and the material fresh in your mind. You need a plan that lets you review everything you need to know while still fitting in your schedule. We'll break this strategy down into three categories.

Information Organization

Start with the information you already have: the official test outline. From this, you can make a complete list of all the concepts you need to cover before the test. Organize these concepts into groups that can be studied together, and create a list of any related vocabulary you need to learn so you can brush up on any difficult terms. You'll want to keep this vocabulary list handy once you actually start studying since you may need to add to it along the way.

Time Management

Once you have your set of study concepts, decide how to spread them out over the time you have left before the test. Break your study plan into small, clear goals so you have a manageable task for each day and know exactly what you're doing. Then just focus on one small step at a time. When you manage your time this way, you don't need to spend hours at a time studying. Studying a small block of content for a short period each day helps you retain information better and avoid stressing over how much you have left to do. You can relax knowing that you have a plan to cover everything in time. In order for this strategy to be effective though, you have to start studying early and stick to your schedule. Avoid the exhaustion and futility that comes from last-minute cramming!

Study Environment

The environment you study in has a big impact on your learning. Studying in a coffee shop, while probably more enjoyable, is not likely to be as fruitful as studying in a quiet room. It's important to keep distractions to a minimum. You're only planning to study for a short block of time, so make the most of it. Don't pause to check your phone or get up to find a snack. It's also important to **avoid multitasking**. Research has consistently shown that multitasking will make your studying dramatically less effective. Your study area should also be comfortable and well-lit so you don't have the distraction of straining your eyes or sitting on an uncomfortable chair.

The time of day you study is also important. You want to be rested and alert. Don't wait until just before bedtime. Study when you'll be most likely to comprehend and remember. Even better, if you know what time of day your test will be, set that time aside for study. That way your brain will be used to working on that subject at that specific time and you'll have a better chance of recalling information.

Finally, it can be helpful to team up with others who are studying for the same test. Your actual studying should be done in as isolated an environment as possible, but the work of organizing the information and setting up the study plan can be divided up. In between study sessions, you can discuss with your teammates the concepts that you're all studying and quiz each other on the details. Just be sure that your teammates are as serious about the test as you are. If you find that your study time is being replaced with social time, you might need to find a new team.

Secret Key #2 – Make Your Studying Count

You're devoting a lot of time and effort to preparing for this test, so you want to be absolutely certain it will pay off. This means doing more than just reading the content and hoping you can remember it on test day. It's important to make every minute of study count. There are two main areas you can focus on to make your studying count:

Retention

It doesn't matter how much time you study if you can't remember the material. You need to make sure you are retaining the concepts. To check your retention of the information you're learning, try recalling it at later times with minimal prompting. Try carrying around flashcards and glance at one or two from time to time or ask a friend who's also studying for the test to quiz you.

To enhance your retention, look for ways to put the information into practice so that you can apply it rather than simply recalling it. If you're using the information in practical ways, it will be much easier to remember. Similarly, it helps to solidify a concept in your mind if you're not only reading it to yourself but also explaining it to someone else. Ask a friend to let you teach them about a concept you're a little shaky on (or speak aloud to an imaginary audience if necessary). As you try to summarize, define, give examples, and answer your friend's questions, you'll understand the concepts better and they will stay with you longer. Finally, step back for a big picture view and ask yourself how each piece of information fits with the whole subject. When you link the different concepts together and see them working together as a whole, it's easier to remember the individual components.

Finally, practice showing your work on any multi-step problems, even if you're just studying. Writing out each step you take to solve a problem will help solidify the process in your mind, and you'll be more likely to remember it during the test.

Modality

Modality simply refers to the means or method by which you study. Choosing a study modality that fits your own individual learning style is crucial. No two people learn best in exactly the same way, so it's important to know your strengths and use them to your advantage.

For example, if you learn best by visualization, focus on visualizing a concept in your mind and draw an image or a diagram. Try color-coding your notes, illustrating them, or creating symbols that will trigger your mind to recall a learned concept. If you learn best by hearing or discussing information, find a study partner who learns the same way or read aloud to yourself. Think about how to put the information in your own words. Imagine that you are giving a lecture on the topic and record yourself so you can listen to it later.

For any learning style, flashcards can be helpful. Organize the information so you can take advantage of spare moments to review. Underline key words or phrases. Use different colors for different categories. Mnemonic devices (such as creating a short list in which every item starts with the same letter) can also help with retention. Find what works best for you and use it to store the information in your mind most effectively and easily.

Secret Key #3 – Practice the Right Way

Your success on test day depends not only on how many hours you put into preparing, but also on whether you prepared the right way. It's good to check along the way to see if your studying is paying off. One of the most effective ways to do this is by taking practice tests to evaluate your progress. Practice tests are useful because they show exactly where you need to improve. Every time you take a practice test, pay special attention to these three groups of questions:

- The questions you got wrong
- The questions you had to guess on, even if you guessed right
- The questions you found difficult or slow to work through

This will show you exactly what your weak areas are, and where you need to devote more study time. Ask yourself why each of these questions gave you trouble. Was it because you didn't understand the material? Was it because you didn't remember the vocabulary? Do you need more repetitions on this type of question to build speed and confidence? Dig into those questions and figure out how you can strengthen your weak areas as you go back to review the material.

Additionally, many practice tests have a section explaining the answer choices. It can be tempting to read the explanation and think that you now have a good understanding of the concept. However, an explanation likely only covers part of the question's broader context. Even if the explanation makes sense, **go back and investigate** every concept related to the question until you're positive you have a thorough understanding.

As you go along, keep in mind that the practice test is just that: practice. Memorizing these questions and answers will not be very helpful on the actual test because it is unlikely to have any of the same exact questions. If you only know the right answers to the sample questions, you won't be prepared for the real thing. **Study the concepts** until you understand them fully, and then you'll be able to answer any question that shows up on the test.

It's important to wait on the practice tests until you're ready. If you take a test on your first day of study, you may be overwhelmed by the amount of material covered and how much you need to learn. Work up to it gradually.

On test day, you'll need to be prepared for answering questions, managing your time, and using the test-taking strategies you've learned. It's a lot to balance, like a mental marathon that will have a big impact on your future. Like training for a marathon, you'll need to start slowly and work your way up. When test day arrives, you'll be ready.

Start with the strategies you've read in the first two Secret Keys—plan your course and study in the way that works best for you. If you have time, consider using multiple study resources to get different approaches to the same concepts. It can be helpful to see difficult concepts from more than one angle. Then find a good source for practice tests. Many times, the test website will suggest potential study resources or provide sample tests.

Practice Test Strategy

If you're able to find at least three practice tests, we recommend this strategy:

UNTIMED AND OPEN-BOOK PRACTICE

Take the first test with no time constraints and with your notes and study guide handy. Take your time and focus on applying the strategies you've learned.

TIMED AND OPEN-BOOK PRACTICE

Take the second practice test open-book as well, but set a timer and practice pacing yourself to finish in time.

TIMED AND CLOSED-BOOK PRACTICE

Take any other practice tests as if it were test day. Set a timer and put away your study materials. Sit at a table or desk in a quiet room, imagine yourself at the testing center, and answer questions as quickly and accurately as possible.

Keep repeating timed and closed-book tests on a regular basis until you run out of practice tests or it's time for the actual test. Your mind will be ready for the schedule and stress of test day, and you'll be able to focus on recalling the material you've learned.

Secret Key #4 – Pace Yourself

Once you're fully prepared for the material on the test, your biggest challenge on test day will be managing your time. Just knowing that the clock is ticking can make you panic even if you have plenty of time left. Work on pacing yourself so you can build confidence against the time constraints of the exam. Pacing is a difficult skill to master, especially in a high-pressure environment, so **practice is vital**.

Set time expectations for your pace based on how much time is available. For example, if a section has 60 questions and the time limit is 30 minutes, you know you have to average 30 seconds or less per question in order to answer them all. Although 30 seconds is the hard limit, set 25 seconds per question as your goal, so you reserve extra time to spend on harder questions. When you budget extra time for the harder questions, you no longer have any reason to stress when those questions take longer to answer.

Don't let this time expectation distract you from working through the test at a calm, steady pace, but keep it in mind so you don't spend too much time on any one question. Recognize that taking extra time on one question you don't understand may keep you from answering two that you do understand later in the test. If your time limit for a question is up and you're still not sure of the answer, mark it and move on, and come back to it later if the time and the test format allow. If the testing format doesn't allow you to return to earlier questions, just make an educated guess; then put it out of your mind and move on.

On the easier questions, be careful not to rush. It may seem wise to hurry through them so you have more time for the challenging ones, but it's not worth missing one if you know the concept and just didn't take the time to read the question fully. Work efficiently but make sure you understand the question and have looked at all of the answer choices, since more than one may seem right at first.

Even if you're paying attention to the time, you may find yourself a little behind at some point. You should speed up to get back on track, but do so wisely. Don't panic; just take a few seconds less on each question until you're caught up. Don't guess without thinking, but do look through the answer choices and eliminate any you know are wrong. If you can get down to two choices, it is often worthwhile to guess from those. Once you've chosen an answer, move on and don't dwell on any that you skipped or had to hurry through. If a question was taking too long, chances are it was one of the harder ones, so you weren't as likely to get it right anyway.

On the other hand, if you find yourself getting ahead of schedule, it may be beneficial to slow down a little. The more quickly you work, the more likely you are to make a careless mistake that will affect your score. You've budgeted time for each question, so don't be afraid to spend that time. Practice an efficient but careful pace to get the most out of the time you have.

Secret Key #5 – Have a Plan for Guessing

When you're taking the test, you may find yourself stuck on a question. Some of the answer choices seem better than others, but you don't see the one answer choice that is obviously correct. What do you do?

The scenario described above is very common, yet most test takers have not effectively prepared for it. Developing and practicing a plan for guessing may be one of the single most effective uses of your time as you get ready for the exam.

In developing your plan for guessing, there are three questions to address:

- When should you start the guessing process?
- How should you narrow down the choices?
- Which answer should you choose?

When to Start the Guessing Process

Unless your plan for guessing is to select C every time (which, despite its merits, is not what we recommend), you need to leave yourself enough time to apply your answer elimination strategies. Since you have a limited amount of time for each question, that means that if you're going to give yourself the best shot at guessing correctly, you have to decide quickly whether or not you will guess.

Of course, the best-case scenario is that you don't have to guess at all, so first, see if you can answer the question based on your knowledge of the subject and basic reasoning skills. Focus on the key words in the question and try to jog your memory of related topics. Give yourself a chance to bring the knowledge to mind, but once you realize that you don't have (or you can't access) the knowledge you need to answer the question, it's time to start the guessing process.

It's almost always better to start the guessing process too early than too late. It only takes a few seconds to remember something and answer the question from knowledge. Carefully eliminating wrong answer choices takes longer. Plus, going through the process of eliminating answer choices can actually help jog your memory.

Summary: Start the guessing process as soon as you decide that you can't answer the question based on your knowledge.

How to Narrow Down the Choices

The next chapter in this book (**Test-Taking Strategies**) includes a wide range of strategies for how to approach questions and how to look for answer choices to eliminate. You will definitely want to read those carefully, practice them, and figure out which ones work best for you. Here though, we're going to address a mindset rather than a particular strategy.

Your chances of guessing an answer correctly depend on how many options you are choosing from.

How many choices you have	How likely you are to guess correctly
5	20%
4	25%
3	33%
2	50%
1	100%

You can see from this chart just how valuable it is to be able to eliminate incorrect answers and make an educated guess, but there are two things that many test takers do that cause them to miss out on the benefits of guessing:

- Accidentally eliminating the correct answer
- Selecting an answer based on an impression

We'll look at the first one here, and the second one in the next section.

To avoid accidentally eliminating the correct answer, we recommend a thought exercise called **the $5 challenge**. In this challenge, you only eliminate an answer choice from contention if you are willing to bet $5 on it being wrong. Why $5? Five dollars is a small but not insignificant amount of money. It's an amount you could afford to lose but wouldn't want to throw away. And while losing $5 once might not hurt too much, doing it twenty times will set you back $100. In the same way, each small decision you make—eliminating a choice here, guessing on a question there—won't by itself impact your score very much, but when you put them all together, they can make a big difference. By holding each answer choice elimination decision to a higher standard, you can reduce the risk of accidentally eliminating the correct answer.

The $5 challenge can also be applied in a positive sense: If you are willing to bet $5 that an answer choice *is* correct, go ahead and mark it as correct.

Summary: Only eliminate an answer choice if you are willing to bet $5 that it is wrong.

Which Answer to Choose

You're taking the test. You've run into a hard question and decided you'll have to guess. You've eliminated all the answer choices you're willing to bet $5 on. Now you have to pick an answer. Why do we even need to talk about this? Why can't you just pick whichever one you feel like when the time comes?

The answer to these questions is that if you don't come into the test with a plan, you'll rely on your impression to select an answer choice, and if you do that, you risk falling into a trap. The test writers know that everyone who takes their test will be guessing on some of the questions, so they intentionally write wrong answer choices to seem plausible. You still have to pick an answer though, and if the wrong answer choices are designed to look right, how can you ever be sure that you're not falling for their trap? The best solution we've found to this dilemma is to take the decision out of your hands entirely. Here is the process we recommend:

Once you've eliminated any choices that you are confident (willing to bet $5) are wrong, select the first remaining choice as your answer.

Whether you choose to select the first remaining choice, the second, or the last, the important thing is that you use some preselected standard. Using this approach guarantees that you will not be enticed into selecting an answer choice that looks right, because you are not basing your decision on how the answer choices look.

This is not meant to make you question your knowledge. Instead, it is to help you recognize the difference between your knowledge and your impressions. There's a huge difference between thinking an answer is right because of what you know, and thinking an answer is right because it looks or sounds like it should be right.

Summary: To ensure that your selection is appropriately random, make a predetermined selection from among all answer choices you have not eliminated.

Test-Taking Strategies

This section contains a list of test-taking strategies that you may find helpful as you work through the test. By taking what you know and applying logical thought, you can maximize your chances of answering any question correctly!

It is very important to realize that every question is different and every person is different: no single strategy will work on every question, and no single strategy will work for every person. That's why we've included all of them here, so you can try them out and determine which ones work best for different types of questions and which ones work best for you.

Question Strategies

READ CAREFULLY

Read the question and answer choices carefully. Don't miss the question because you misread the terms. You have plenty of time to read each question thoroughly and make sure you understand what is being asked. Yet a happy medium must be attained, so don't waste too much time. You must read carefully, but efficiently.

CONTEXTUAL CLUES

Look for contextual clues. If the question includes a word you are not familiar with, look at the immediate context for some indication of what the word might mean. Contextual clues can often give you all the information you need to decipher the meaning of an unfamiliar word. Even if you can't determine the meaning, you may be able to narrow down the possibilities enough to make a solid guess at the answer to the question.

PREFIXES

If you're having trouble with a word in the question or answer choices, try dissecting it. Take advantage of every clue that the word might include. Prefixes and suffixes can be a huge help. Usually they allow you to determine a basic meaning. Pre- means before, post- means after, pro - is positive, de- is negative. From prefixes and suffixes, you can get an idea of the general meaning of the word and try to put it into context.

HEDGE WORDS

Watch out for critical hedge words, such as *likely*, *may*, *can*, *sometimes*, *often*, *almost*, *mostly*, *usually*, *generally*, *rarely*, and *sometimes*. Question writers insert these hedge phrases to cover every possibility. Often an answer choice will be wrong simply because it leaves no room for exception. Be on guard for answer choices that have definitive words such as *exactly* and *always*.

SWITCHBACK WORDS

Stay alert for *switchbacks*. These are the words and phrases frequently used to alert you to shifts in thought. The most common switchback words are *but*, *although*, and *however*. Others include *nevertheless*, *on the other hand*, *even though*, *while*, *in spite of*, *despite*, *regardless of*. Switchback words are important to catch because they can change the direction of the question or an answer choice.

FACE VALUE

When in doubt, use common sense. Accept the situation in the problem at face value. Don't read too much into it. These problems will not require you to make wild assumptions. If you have to go beyond creativity and warp time or space in order to have an answer choice fit the question, then you should move on and consider the other answer choices. These are normal problems rooted in reality. The applicable relationship or explanation may not be readily apparent, but it is there for you to figure out. Use your common sense to interpret anything that isn't clear.

Answer Choice Strategies

ANSWER SELECTION

The most thorough way to pick an answer choice is to identify and eliminate wrong answers until only one is left, then confirm it is the correct answer. Sometimes an answer choice may immediately seem right, but be careful. The test writers will usually put more than one reasonable answer choice on each question, so take a second to read all of them and make sure that the other choices are not equally obvious. As long as you have time left, it is better to read every answer choice than to pick the first one that looks right without checking the others.

ANSWER CHOICE FAMILIES

An answer choice family consists of two (in rare cases, three) answer choices that are very similar in construction and cannot all be true at the same time. If you see two answer choices that are direct opposites or parallels, one of them is usually the correct answer. For instance, if one answer choice says that quantity x increases and another either says that quantity x decreases (opposite) or says that quantity y increases (parallel), then those answer choices would fall into the same family. An answer choice that doesn't match the construction of the answer choice family is more likely to be incorrect. Most questions will not have answer choice families, but when they do appear, you should be prepared to recognize them.

ELIMINATE ANSWERS

Eliminate answer choices as soon as you realize they are wrong, but make sure you consider all possibilities. If you are eliminating answer choices and realize that the last one you are left with is also wrong, don't panic. Start over and consider each choice again. There may be something you missed the first time that you will realize on the second pass.

AVOID FACT TRAPS

Don't be distracted by an answer choice that is factually true but doesn't answer the question. You are looking for the choice that answers the question. Stay focused on what the question is asking for so you don't accidentally pick an answer that is true but incorrect. Always go back to the question and make sure the answer choice you've selected actually answers the question and is not merely a true statement.

EXTREME STATEMENTS

In general, you should avoid answers that put forth extreme actions as standard practice or proclaim controversial ideas as established fact. An answer choice that states the "process should be used in certain situations, if…" is much more likely to be correct than one that states the "process should be discontinued completely." The first is a calm rational statement and doesn't even make a definitive, uncompromising stance, using a hedge word *if* to provide wiggle room, whereas the second choice is a radical idea and far more extreme.

BENCHMARK

As you read through the answer choices and you come across one that seems to answer the question well, mentally select that answer choice. This is not your final answer, but it's the one that will help you evaluate the other answer choices. The one that you selected is your benchmark or standard for judging each of the other answer choices. Every other answer choice must be compared to your benchmark. That choice is correct until proven otherwise by another answer choice beating it. If you find a better answer, then that one becomes your new benchmark. Once you've decided that no other choice answers the question as well as your benchmark, you have your final answer.

PREDICT THE ANSWER

Before you even start looking at the answer choices, it is often best to try to predict the answer. When you come up with the answer on your own, it is easier to avoid distractions and traps because you will know exactly what to look for. The right answer choice is unlikely to be word-for-word what you came up with, but it should be a close match. Even if you are confident that you have the right answer, you should still take the time to read each option before moving on.

General Strategies

TOUGH QUESTIONS

If you are stumped on a problem or it appears too hard or too difficult, don't waste time. Move on! Remember though, if you can quickly check for obviously incorrect answer choices, your chances of guessing correctly are greatly improved. Before you completely give up, at least try to knock out a couple of possible answers. Eliminate what you can and then guess at the remaining answer choices before moving on.

CHECK YOUR WORK

Since you will probably not know every term listed and the answer to every question, it is important that you get credit for the ones that you do know. Don't miss any questions through careless mistakes. If at all possible, try to take a second to look back over your answer selection and make sure you've selected the correct answer choice and haven't made a costly careless mistake (such as marking an answer choice that you didn't mean to mark). This quick double check should more than pay for itself in caught mistakes for the time it costs.

PACE YOURSELF

It's easy to be overwhelmed when you're looking at a page full of questions; your mind is confused and full of random thoughts, and the clock is ticking down faster than you would like. Calm down and maintain the pace that you have set for yourself. Especially as you get down to the last few minutes of the test, don't let the small numbers on the clock make you panic. As long as you are on track by monitoring your pace, you are guaranteed to have time for each question.

DON'T RUSH

It is very easy to make errors when you are in a hurry. Maintaining a fast pace in answering questions is pointless if it makes you miss questions that you would have gotten right otherwise. Test writers like to include distracting information and wrong answers that seem right. Taking a little extra time to avoid careless mistakes can make all the difference in your test score. Find a pace that allows you to be confident in the answers that you select.

KEEP MOVING

Panicking will not help you pass the test, so do your best to stay calm and keep moving. Taking deep breaths and going through the answer elimination steps you practiced can help to break through a stress barrier and keep your pace.

Final Notes

The combination of a solid foundation of content knowledge and the confidence that comes from practicing your plan for applying that knowledge is the key to maximizing your performance on test day. As your foundation of content knowledge is built up and strengthened, you'll find that the strategies included in this chapter become more and more effective in helping you quickly sift through the distractions and traps of the test to isolate the correct answer.

Now it's time to move on to the test content chapters of this book, but be sure to keep your goal in mind. As you read, think about how you will be able to apply this information on the test. If you've already seen sample questions for the test and you have an idea of the question format and style, try to come up with questions of your own that you can answer based on what you're reading. This will give you valuable practice applying your knowledge in the same ways you can expect to on test day.

Good luck and good studying!

English Language Arts and World Languages

Developmental Literacy and English Language Learning

LITERACY

Literacy is commonly understood to refer to the *ability to read and write*. UNESCO has further defined literacy as the "ability to identify, understand, interpret, create, communicate, compute, and use printed and written materials associated with varying contexts." Under the UNESCO definition, understanding cultural, political, and historical contexts of communities falls under the definition of literacy. While **reading literacy** may be gauged simply by the ability to read a newspaper, **writing literacy** includes spelling, grammar, and sentence structure. To be literate in a foreign language, one would also need to have the ability to understand a language by listening and to speak the language. Some argue that visual representation and numeracy should be included in the requirements one must meet to be considered literate. Computer literacy refers to one's ability to utilize the basic functions of computers and other technologies. Subsets of reading literacy include phonological awareness, decoding, comprehension, and vocabulary.

PHONOLOGICAL AWARENESS

A subskill of literacy, **phonological awareness** is the ability to perceive sound structures in a spoken word, such as syllables and the individual phonemes within syllables. **Phonemes** are the sounds represented by the letters in the alphabet. The ability to separate, blend, and manipulate sounds is critical to developing reading and spelling skills. Phonological awareness is concerned with not only syllables, but also **onset sounds** (the sounds at the beginning of words) and **rime** (the same thing as rhyme, but spelled differently to distinguish syllable rime from poetic rhyme). Phonological awareness is an auditory skill that does not necessarily involve print. It should be developed before the student has learned letter to sound correspondences. A student's phonological awareness is an indicator of future reading success.

ACTIVITIES THAT TEACH PHONOLOGICAL AWARENESS

Classroom activities that teach **phonological awareness** include language play and exposure to a variety of sounds and contexts of sounds. Activities that teach phonological awareness include:

- Clapping to the sounds of individual words, names, or all words in a sentence
- Practicing saying blended phonemes
- Singing songs that involve phoneme replacement (e.g., The Name Game)
- Reading poems, songs, and nursery rhymes out loud
- Reading patterned and predictable texts out loud
- Listening to environmental sounds or following verbal directions
- Playing games with rhyming chants or fingerplays
- Reading alliterative texts out loud
- Grouping objects by beginning sounds
- Reordering words in a well-known sentence or making silly phrases by deleting words from a well-known sentence (perhaps from a favorite storybook)

15

ALPHABETIC PRINCIPLE AND ALPHABET WRITING SYSTEMS

The **alphabetic principle** refers to the use of letters and combinations of letters to represent speech sounds. The way letters are combined and pronounced is guided by a system of rules that establishes relationships between written and spoken words and their letter symbols. Alphabet writing systems are common around the world. Some are **phonological** in that each letter stands for an individual sound and words are spelled just as they sound. However, there are other writing systems as well, such as the Chinese **logographic** system and the Japanese **syllabic** system.

DEVELOPMENT OF LANGUAGE SKILLS

Children learn language through interacting with others, by experiencing language in daily and relevant context, and through understanding that speaking and listening are necessary for effective communication. Teachers can promote **language development** by intensifying the opportunities a child has to experience and understand language.

Teachers can assist language development by:

- Modeling enriched vocabulary and teaching new words
- Using questions and examples to extend a child's descriptive language skills
- Providing ample response time to encourage children to practice speech
- Asking for clarification to provide students with the opportunity to develop communication skills
- Promoting conversations among children
- Providing feedback to let children know they have been heard and understood, and providing further explanation when needed

RELATIONSHIP BETWEEN ORAL AND WRITTEN LANGUAGE DEVELOPMENT

Oral and written language develops simultaneously. The acquisition of skills in one area supports the acquisition of skills in the other. However, oral language is not a prerequisite to written language. An immature form of oral language development is babbling, and an immature form of written language development is scribbling. **Oral language development** does not occur naturally, but does occur in a social context. This means it is best to include children in conversations rather than simply talk at them. **Written language development** can occur without direct instruction. In fact, reading and writing do not necessarily need to be taught through formal lessons if the child is exposed to a print-rich environment. A teacher can assist a child's language development by building on what the child already knows, discussing relevant and meaningful events and experiences, teaching vocabulary and literacy skills, and providing opportunities to acquire more complex language.

PRINT-RICH ENVIRONMENT

A teacher can provide a **print-rich environment** in the classroom in a number of ways. These include:

- **Displaying** the following in the classroom:
  - Children's names in print or cursive
  - Children's written work
  - Newspapers and magazines
  - Instructional charts
  - Written schedules
  - Signs and labels
  - Printed songs, poems, and rhymes

- Using **graphic organizers** such as KWL charts or story road maps to:
  - Remind students about what was read and discussed
  - Expand on the lesson topic or theme
  - Show the relationships among books, ideas, and words
- Using **big books** to:
  - Point out features of print, such as specific letters and punctuation
  - Track print from right to left
  - Emphasize the concept of words and the fact that they are used to communicate

BENEFITS OF PRINT AND BOOK AWARENESS

Print and book awareness helps a child understand:

- That there is a **connection** between print and messages contained on signs, labels, and other print forms in the child's environment
- That reading and writing are ways to obtain information and communicate ideas
- That **print** runs from left to right and from top to bottom
- That a book has **parts**, such as a title, a cover, a title page, and a table of contents
- That a book has an **author** and contains a **story**
- That **illustrations** can carry meaning
- That **letters and words** are different
- That **words and sentences** are separated by spaces and punctuation
- That different **text forms** are used for different functions
- That print represents **spoken language**
- How to **hold** a book.

FACTS CHILDREN SHOULD KNOW ABOUT LETTERS

To be appropriately prepared to learn to read and write, a child should learn:

- That each letter is **distinct** in appearance
- What **direction and shape** must be used to make each letter
- That each letter has a **name**, which can be associated with the shape of a letter
- That there are **26** letters in the English alphabet, and letters are grouped in a certain order
- That letters represent **sounds of speech**
- That **words** are composed of letters and have meaning
- That one must be able to **correspond** letters and sounds to read

DECODING

Decoding is the method or strategy used to make sense of printed words and figure out how to correctly pronounce them. In order to decode, a student needs to know the relationships between letters and sounds, including letter patterns; that words are constructed from phonemes and phoneme blends; and that a printed word represents a word that can be spoken. This knowledge will help the student recognize familiar words and make informed guesses about the pronunciation of unfamiliar words. Decoding is not the same as **comprehension**. It does not require an understanding of the meaning of a word, only a knowledge of how to recognize and pronounce it. Decoding can also refer to the skills a student uses to determine the meaning of a **sentence**. These skills include applying knowledge of vocabulary, sentence structure, and context.

TEACHING OF READING THROUGH PHONICS

Phonics is the process of learning to read by learning how spoken language is represented by letters. Students learn to read phonetically by sounding out the **phonemes** in words and then blending them together to produce the correct sounds in words. In other words, the student connects speech sounds with letters or groups of letters and blends the sounds together to determine the pronunciation of an unknown word. Phonics is a commonly used method to teach **decoding and reading**, but has been challenged by other methods, such as the whole language approach. Despite the complexity of pronunciation and combined sounds in the English language, research shows that phonics is a highly effective way to teach reading. Being able to read or pronounce a word does not mean the student comprehends the meaning of the word, but context aids comprehension. When phonics is used as a foundation for decoding, children eventually learn to recognize words automatically and advance to decoding multisyllable words with practice.

ROLE OF FLUENCY IN LITERACY DEVELOPMENT

Fluency is the goal of literacy development. It is the ability to read accurately and quickly. Evidence of fluency includes the ability to recognize words automatically and group words for comprehension. At this point, the student no longer needs to decode words except for complex, unfamiliar ones. He or she is able to move to the next level and understand the **meaning** of a text. The student should be able to self-check for comprehension and should feel comfortable expressing ideas in writing. Teachers can help students build fluency by continuing to provide: reading experiences and discussions about text, gradually increasing the level of difficulty; reading practice, both silently and out loud; word analysis practice; instruction on reading comprehension strategies; and opportunities to express responses to readings through writing.

ROLE OF VOCABULARY IN LITERACY DEVELOPMENT

When students do not know the meaning of words in a text, their comprehension is limited. As a result, the text becomes boring or confusing. The larger a student's **vocabulary** is, the better their reading comprehension will be. A larger vocabulary is also associated with an enhanced ability to **communicate** in speech and writing. It is the teacher's role to help students develop a good working vocabulary. Students learn most of the words they use and understand from listening to the world around them (adults, other students, media, etc.) They also learn from their reading experiences, which include being read to and reading independently. Carefully designed activities can also stimulate vocabulary growth, and should emphasize useful words that students see frequently, important words necessary for understanding text, and difficult words such as idioms or words with more than one meaning.

TEACHING TECHNIQUES PROMOTING VOCABULARY DEVELOPMENT

A student's **vocabulary** can be developed by:

- Calling upon a student's **prior knowledge** and making comparisons to that knowledge
- **Defining** a word and providing multiple examples of the use of the word in context
- Showing a student how to use **context clues** to discover the meaning of a word
- Providing instruction on **prefixes, roots, and suffixes** to help students break a word into its parts and decipher its meaning
- Showing students how to use a **dictionary and a thesaurus**
- Asking students to **practice** new vocabulary by using the words in their own writing
- Providing a **print-rich environment** with a word wall
- Studying a group of words related to a **single subject**, such as farm words, transportation words, etc. so that concept development is enhanced.

AFFIXES, PREFIXES, AND ROOT WORDS

Affixes are syllables attached to the beginning or end of a word to make a derivative or inflectional form of a word. Both prefixes and suffixes are affixes. A **prefix** is a syllable that appears at the beginning of a word that, in combination with the root or base word, creates a specific meaning. For example, the prefix "mis" means "wrong." When combined with the root word "spelling," the word "misspelling" is created, which means the "wrong spelling." A **root word** is the base of a word to which affixes can be added. For example, the prefix "in" or "pre" can be added to the root word "vent" to create "invent" or "prevent," respectively. The suffix "er" can be added to the root word "work" to create "worker," which means "one who works." The suffix "able," meaning "capable of," can be added to "work" to create "workable," which means "capable of working."

SUFFIXES

A suffix is a syllable that appears at the end of a word that, in combination with the root or base word, creates a specific meaning. There are three types of suffixes:

- **Noun suffixes** – There are two types of noun suffixes. One denotes the act of, state of, or quality of. For example, "-ment" added to "argue" becomes "argument," which is defined as "the act of arguing." The other denotes the doer, or one who acts. For example, "-eer" added to "auction" becomes "auctioneer," meaning "one who auctions." Other examples include "-hood," "-ness," "-tion," "-ship," and "-ism."
- **Verb suffixes** – These denote "to make" or "to perform the act of." For example, "-en" added to "soft" makes "soften," which means "to make soft." Other verb suffixes are "-ate" (perpetuate), "-fy" (dignify), and "-ize" (sterilize).
- **Adjectival suffixes** – These include suffixes such as "-ful," which means "full of." When added to "care," the word "careful" is formed, which means "full of care." Other examples are "-ish," "-less," and "-able."

STRATEGIES TO IMPROVE READING COMPREHENSION

Teachers can model in a read-aloud the strategies students can use on their own to better comprehend a text. First, the teacher should do a walk-through of the story **illustrations** and ask, "What's happening here?" Based on what they have seen, the teacher should then ask students to **predict** what the story will be about. As the book is read, the teacher should ask open-ended questions such as, "Why do you think the character did this?" and "How do you think the character feels?" The teacher should also ask students if they can **relate** to the story or have background knowledge of something similar. After the reading, the teacher should ask the students to **retell** the story in their own words to check for comprehension. This retelling can take the form of a puppet show or summarizing the story to a partner.

ROLE OF PRIOR KNOWLEDGE IN DETERMINING APPROPRIATE LITERACY EDUCATION

Even preschool children have some literacy skills, and the extent and type of these skills have implications for instructional approaches. Comprehension results from relating two or more pieces of information. One piece comes from the text, and another piece might come from **prior knowledge** (something from a student's long-term memory). For a child, that prior knowledge comes from being read to at home; taking part in other literacy experiences, such as playing computer or word games; being exposed to a print-rich environment at home; and observing examples of parents' reading habits. Children who have had **extensive literacy experience** are better prepared to further develop their literacy skills in school than children who have not been read to, have few books or magazines in their homes, are seldom exposed to high-level oral or written language activities, and seldom witness adults engaged in reading and writing. Children with a scant literacy background are at a disadvantage. The teacher must not make any

19

assumptions about their prior knowledge, and should use intense, targeted instruction. Otherwise, reading comprehension will be limited.

USING PUPPETRY IN THE CLASSROOM

Using puppets in the classroom puts students at ease and allows them to enjoy a learning experience as if it were play. The purpose of using puppetry is to generate ideas, encourage imagination, and foster language development. Using a puppet helps a child "become" the character and therefore experience a different **outlook**. **Language development** is enhanced through the student interpreting a story that has been read in class and practicing new words from that story in the puppet show. Children will also have the opportunity to practice using descriptive adjectives for the characters and the scene, which will help them learn the function of adjectives. **Descriptive adjectives and verbs** can also be learned by practicing facial expressions and movements with puppets. The teacher can model happy, sad, eating, sleeping, and similar words with a puppet, and then ask students to do the same with their puppets. This is an especially effective vocabulary activity for ESL children.

USING DRAMA OR STORY THEATER IN THE CLASSROOM

Drama activities are fun learning experiences that capture a child's attention, engage the imagination, and motivate vocabulary expansion. For example, after reading a story, the teacher could ask children to act it out as the teacher repeats the story. This activity, which works best with very young learners, will help children work on listening skills and their ability to pretend. The best stories to use for this passive improvisation are ones that have lots of simple actions that children will be able to understand and perform easily. Older children can create their own improvisational skits and possibly write scripts. **Visualization** also calls upon the imagination and encourages concentration and bodily awareness. Children can be given a prompt for the visualization and then asked to draw what they see in their mind's eye. **Charades** is another way to act out words and improve vocabulary skills. This activity can be especially helpful to encourage ESL students to express thoughts and ideas in English. These students should be given easier words to act out to promote confidence.

CLASSROOM PRACTICES BENEFITING SECOND LANGUAGE ACQUISITION

Since some students may have limited understanding of English, a teacher should employ the following practices to promote second language acquisition:

- Make all instruction as **understandable** as possible and use simple and repeated terms.
- Relate instruction to the **cultures** of ESL children.
- Increase **interactive activities** and use gestures or non-verbal actions when modeling.
- Provide language and literacy development instruction in **all curriculum areas**.
- Establish **consistent routines** that help children connect words and events.
- Use a **schedule** so children know what will happen next and will not feel lost.
- Integrate ESL children into **group activities** with non-ESL children.
- Appoint bilingual students to act as **student translators**.
- Explain actions as activities happen so that a **word to action relationship** is established.
- Initiate opportunities for ESL children to **experiment** with and practice new language.
- Employ multisensory learning.

THEORIES OF LANGUAGE DEVELOPMENT

Four theories of language development are:

- **Learning approach** – This theory assumes that language is first learned by imitating the speech of adults. It is then solidified in school through drills about the rules of language structures.
- **Linguistic approach** – Championed by Noam Chomsky in the 1950s, this theory proposes that the ability to use a language is innate. This is a biological approach rather than one based on cognition or social patterning.
- **Cognitive approach** – Developed in the 1970s and based on the work of Piaget, this theory states that children must develop appropriate cognitive skills before they can acquire language.
- **Sociocognitive approach** – In the 1970s, some researchers proposed that language development is a complex interaction of linguistic, social, and cognitive influences. This theory best explains the lack of language skills among children who are neglected, have uneducated parents, or lives in poverty.

TEACHING STRATEGIES TO PROMOTE LISTENING SKILLS OF ESL STUDENTS

Listening is a critical skill when learning a new language. Students spend a great deal more time listening than they do speaking, and far less time reading and writing than speaking. Two ways to encourage ESL students to listen are to:

- Talk about topics that are of **interest** to the ESL learner. Otherwise, students may tune out the speaker because they don't want to put in that much effort to learn about a topic they find boring.
- Talk about content or give examples that are **easy** to understand or are **related** to a topic that is familiar to ESL students. Culturally relevant materials will be more interesting to ESL students, will make them feel more comfortable, and will contain vocabulary that they may already be familiar with.

CONSIDERATIONS RELEVANT TO ESL STUDENTS RELATED TO LEARNING BY LISTENING

Listening is not a passive skill, but an **active** one. Therefore, a teacher needs to make the listening experience as rewarding as possible and provide as many auditory and visual clues as possible. Three ways that the teacher can make the listening experience rewarding for ESL students are:

- Avoid **colloquialisms** and **abbreviated or slang terms** that may be confusing to the ESL listener, unless there is enough time to define them and explain their use.
- Make the spoken English understandable by stopping to **clarify** points, **repeating** new or difficult words, and **defining** words that may not be known.
- Support the spoken word with as many **visuals** as possible. Pictures, diagrams, gestures, facial expressions, and body language can help the ESL learner correctly interpret the spoken language more easily and also leaves an image impression that helps them remember the words.

TOP-DOWN AND BOTTOM-UP PROCESSING

ESL students need to be given opportunities to practice both top-down and bottom-up processing. If they are old enough to understand these concepts, they should be made aware that these are two processes that affect their listening comprehension. In **top-down processing**, the listener refers to **background and global knowledge** to figure out the meaning of a message. For example, when asking an ESL student to perform a task, the steps of the task should be explained and accompanied by a review of the vocabulary terms the student already understands so that the student feels comfortable tackling new steps and new words. The teacher should also allow students to ask questions to verify comprehension. In **bottom-up processing**, the listener figures out the meaning of a message by using "**data**" obtained from what is said. This data includes sounds (stress, rhythm, and intonation), words, and grammatical relationships. All data can be used to make conclusions or interpretations. For example, the listener can develop bottom-up skills by learning how to detect differences in intonation between statements and questions.

LISTENING LESSONS

All students, but especially ESL students, can be taught **listening** through specific training. During listening lessons, the teacher should guide students through three steps:

- **Pre-listening activity** – This establishes the purpose of the lesson and engages students' background knowledge. This activity should ask students to think about and discuss something they already know about the topic. Alternatively, the teacher can provide background information.
- **The listening activity** – This requires the listener to obtain information and then immediately do something with that information. For example, the teacher can review the schedule for the day or the week. The students are being given information about a routine they already know, but need to be able to identify names, tasks, and times.
- **Post-listening activity** – This is an evaluation process that allows students to judge how well they did with the listening task. Other language skills can be included in the activity. For example, this activity could involve asking questions about who will do what according to the classroom schedule (Who is the lunch monitor today?) and could also involve asking students to produce whole sentence replies.

HELPING ESL STUDENTS UNDERSTAND SUBJECT MATTER
SPEAKING

To help ESL students better understand subject matter, the following teaching strategies using spoken English can be used:

- **Read aloud** from a textbook, and then ask ESL students to **verbally summarize** what was read. The teacher should assist by providing new words as needed to give students the opportunity to practice vocabulary and speaking skills. The teacher should then read the passage again to students to verify accuracy and details.
- The teacher could ask ESL students to explain why the subject matter is important to them and where they see it fitting into their lives. This verbalization gives them speaking practice and helps them relate to the subject.
- Whenever small group activities are being conducted, ESL students can be placed with **English-speaking students**. It is best to keep the groups to two or three students so that the ESL student will be motivated by the need to be involved. English-speaking students should be encouraged to include ESL students in the group work.

READING

There are supplemental printed materials that can be used to help ESL students understand subject matter. The following strategies can be used to help ESL students develop English reading skills.

- Make sure all ESL students have a **bilingual dictionary** to use. A thesaurus would also be helpful.
- Try to keep **content area books** written in the ESL students' native languages in the classroom. Students can use them side-by-side with English texts. Textbooks in other languages can be ordered from the school library or obtained from the classroom textbook publisher.
- If a student lacks confidence in his/her ability to read the textbook, the teacher can read a passage to the student and have him or her **verbally summarize** the passage. The teacher should take notes on what the student says and then read them back. These notes can be a substitute, short-form, in-their-own-words textbook that the student can understand.

GENERAL TEACHING STRATEGIES TO HELP ESL STUDENTS

Some strategies can help students develop more than one important skill. They may involve a combination of speaking, listening, and/or viewing. Others are mainly classroom management aids. General teaching strategies for ESL students include:

- **Partner** English-speaking students with ESL students as study buddies and ask the English-speaking students to share notes.
- Encourage ESL students to ask **questions** whenever they don't understand something. They should be aware that they don't have to be able to interpret every word of text to understand the concept.
- Dictate **key sentences** related to the content area being taught and ask ESL students to write them down. This gives them practice in listening and writing, and also helps them identify what is important.
- **Alternate** difficult and easy tasks so that ESL students can experience academic success.
- Ask ESL students to **label** objects associated with content areas, such as maps, diagrams, parts of a leaf, or parts of a sentence. This gives students writing and reading experience and helps them remember key vocabulary.

Poetry

MAJOR FORMS OF POETRY

From man's earliest days, he expressed himself with poetry. A large percentage of the surviving literature from ancient times is in epic poetry, utilized by Homer and other Greco-Roman poets. Epic poems typically recount heroic deeds and adventures, using stylized language and combining dramatic and lyrical conventions. Epistolary poems also developed in ancient times: poems that are written and read as letters. In the fourteenth and fifteenth centuries, the ballad became a popular convention. Ballads are often structured with rhyme and meter and focus on subjects such as love, death, and religious topics. From these early conventions, numerous other poetic forms developed, such as elegies, odes, and pastoral poems. Elegies are mourning poems written in three parts: lament, praise of the deceased, and solace for loss. Odes evolved from songs to the typical poem of the Romantic time period, expressing strong feelings and contemplative thoughts. Pastoral poems idealize nature and country living. Poetry can also be used to make short, pithy statements. Epigrams (memorable rhymes with one or two lines) and limericks (two lines of iambic dimeter

23

followed by two lines of iambic dimeter and another of iambic trimeter) are known for humor and wit.

HAIKU

Haiku was originally a Japanese poetry form. In the 13th century, haiku was the opening phrase of renga, a 100-stanza oral poem. By the 16th century, haiku diverged into a separate short poem. When Western writers discovered haiku, the form became popular in English, as well as other languages. A haiku has 17 syllables, traditionally distributed across three lines as 5/7/5, with a pause after the first or second line. Haiku are syllabic and unrhymed. Haiku philosophy and technique are that brevity's compression forces writers to express images concisely, depict a moment in time, and evoke illumination and enlightenment. An example is 17th-century haiku master Matsuo Basho's classic: "An old silent pond... / A frog jumps into the pond, / splash! Silence again." Modern American poet Ezra Pound revealed the influence of haiku in his two-line poem "In a Station of the Metro"—line 1 has 5+7 syllables, line 2 has 7, but it still preserves haiku's philosophy and imagistic technique: "The apparition of these faces in the crowd; / Petals on a wet, black bough."

SONNETS

The sonnet traditionally has 14 lines of iambic pentameter, tightly organized around a theme. The Petrarchan sonnet, named for 14th-century Italian poet Petrarch, has an eight-line stanza, the octave, and a six-line stanza, the sestet. There is a change or turn, known as the volta, between the eighth and ninth verses, setting up the sestet's answer or summary. The rhyme scheme is ABBA/ABBA/CDECDE or CDCDCD. The English or Shakespearean sonnet has three quatrains and one couplet, with the rhyme scheme ABAB/CDCD/EFEF/GG. This format better suits English, which has fewer rhymes than Italian. The final couplet often contrasts sharply with the preceding quatrains, as in Shakespeare's sonnets—for example, Sonnet 130, "My mistress' eyes are nothing like the sun...And yet, by heaven, I think my love as rare / As any she belied with false compare." Variations on the sonnet form include Edmund Spenser's Spenserian sonnet in the 16th century, John Milton's Miltonic sonnet in the 17th century, and sonnet sequences. Sonnet sequences are seen in works such as John Donne's *La Corona* and Elizabeth Barrett Browning's *Sonnets from the Portuguese*.

> **Review Video: Forms of Poetry**
> Visit mometrix.com/academy and enter code: 451705

Prose

MAJOR FORMS

Historical fiction is set in particular historical periods, including prehistoric and mythological. Examples include Walter Scott's *Rob Roy* and *Ivanhoe*; Leo Tolstoy's *War and Peace*; Robert Graves' *I, Claudius*; Mary Renault's *The King Must Die* and *The Bull from the Sea* (an historical novel using Greek mythology); Virginia Woolf's *Orlando* and *Between the Acts*; and John Dos Passos's *U.S.A* trilogy. Picaresque novels recount episodic adventures of a rogue protagonist or *pícaro,* like Miguel de Cervantes' *Don Quixote* or Henry Fielding's *Tom Jones.* Gothic novels originated as a reaction against 18th-century Enlightenment rationalism, featuring horror, mystery, superstition, madness, supernatural elements, and revenge. Early examples include Horace Walpole's *Castle of Otranto,* Matthew Gregory Lewis' *Monk*, Mary Shelley's *Frankenstein*, and Bram Stoker's *Dracula.* In America, Edgar Allan Poe wrote many Gothic works. Contemporary novelist Anne Rice has penned many Gothic novels under the pseudonym A. N. Roquelaure. Psychological novels, originating in 17th-

century France, explore characters' motivations. Examples include Abbé Prévost's *Manon Lescaut;* George Eliot's novels; Fyodor Dostoyevsky's *Crime and Punishment;* Tolstoy's *Anna Karenina;* Gustave Flaubert's *Madame Bovary;* and the novels of Henry James, James Joyce, and Vladimir Nabokov.

> **Review Video: Major Forms of Prose**
> Visit mometrix.com/academy and enter code: 565543

NOVEL OF MANNERS

Novels of manners are fictional stories that observe, explore, and analyze the social behaviors of a specific time and place. While deep psychological themes are more universal across different historical periods and countries, the manners of a particular society are shorter-lived and more varied; the novel of manners captures these societal details. Novels of manners can also be regarded as symbolically representing, in artistic form, certain established and secure social orders. Characteristics of novels of manners include descriptions of a society with defined behavioral codes; the use of standardized, impersonal formulas in their language; and inhibition of emotional expression, as contrasted with the strong emotions expressed in romantic or sentimental novels. Jane Austen's detailed descriptions of English society and characters struggling with the definitions and restrictions placed on them by society are excellent models of the novel of manners. In the 20th century, Evelyn Waugh's *Handful of Dust* is a novel of social manners, and his *Sword of Honour* trilogy is a novel of military manners. Another 20th-century example is *The Unbearable Bassington* by Saki (the pen name of writer H. H. Munro), focusing on Edwardian society.

WESTERN-WORLD SENTIMENTAL NOVELS

Sentimental love novels originated in the movement of Romanticism. Eighteenth-century examples of novels that depict emotional rather than only physical love include Samuel Richardson's *Pamela* (1740) and Jean-Jacques Rousseau's *Nouvelle Héloïse* (1761). Also in the 18th century, Laurence Sterne's novel *Tristram Shandy* (1760-1767) is an example of a novel with elements of sentimentality. The Victorian era's rejection of emotionalism caused the term "sentimental" to have undesirable connotations. Even non-sentimental novelists such as William Makepeace Thackeray and Charles Dickens incorporated sentimental elements in their writing. A 19th-century author of genuinely sentimental novels was Mrs. Henry Wood (e.g., *East Lynne,* 1861). In the 20th century, Erich Segal's sentimental novel *Love Story* (1970) was a popular bestseller.

EPISTOLARY NOVELS

Epistolary novels are told in the form of letters written by their characters rather than in narrative form. Samuel Richardson, the best-known author of epistolary novels like *Pamela* (1740) and *Clarissa* (1748), widely influenced early Romantic epistolary novels throughout Europe that freely expressed emotions. Richardson, a printer, published technical manuals on letter-writing for young gentlewomen; his epistolary novels were natural fictional extensions of those nonfictional instructional books. Nineteenth-century English author Wilkie Collins' *The Moonstone* (1868) was a mystery written in epistolary form. By the 20th century, the format of well-composed written letters came to be regarded as artificial and outmoded. A 20th-century evolution of letters was tape-recording transcripts in French playwright Samuel Beckett's drama *Krapp's Last Tape.* Though evoking modern alienation, Beckett still created a sense of fictional characters' direct communication without author intervention as Richardson had.

PASTORAL NOVELS

Pastoral novels lyrically idealize country life as idyllic and utopian, akin to the Garden of Eden. *Daphnis and Chloe,* written by Greek novelist Longus around the second or third century, influenced

25

Elizabethan pastoral romances like Thomas Lodge's *Rosalynde* (1590), which inspired Shakespeare's *As You Like It*, and Philip Sidney's *Arcadia* (1590). Jacques-Henri Bernardin de St. Pierre's French work *Paul et Virginie* (1787) demonstrated the early Romantic view of the innocence and goodness of nature. Though the style lost popularity by the 20th century, pastoral elements can still be seen in novels like *The Rainbow* (1915) and *Lady Chatterley's Lover* (1928), both by D. H. Lawrence. Growing realism transformed pastoral writing into less ideal and more dystopian, distasteful and ironic depictions of country life in George Eliot's and Thomas Hardy's novels. Saul Bellow's novel *Herzog* (1964) may demonstrate how urban ills highlight an alternative pastoral ideal. The pastoral style is commonly thought to be overly idealized and outdated today, as seen in Stella Gibbons' pastoral satire, Cold Comfort Farm (1932).

BILDUNGSROMAN

Bildungsroman is German for "education novel." This term is also used in English to describe "apprenticeship" novels focusing on coming-of-age stories, including youth's struggles and searches for things such as identity, spiritual understanding, or the meaning in life. Johann Wolfgang von Goethe's *Wilhelm Meisters Lehrjahre* (1796) is credited as the origin. Charles Dickens' two novels *David Copperfield* (1850) and *Great Expectations* (1861) also fit this form. H. G. Wells wrote *bildungsromans* about questing for apprenticeships to address modern life's complications in *Joan and Peter* (1918), and from a Utopian perspective in *The Dream* (1924). School *bildungsromans* include Thomas Hughes' *Tom Brown's School Days* (1857) and Alain-Fournier's *Le Grand Meaulnes* (1913). Many Hermann Hesse novels, including *Demian, Steppenwolf, Siddhartha, Magister Ludi,* and *Under the Wheel* are *bildungsromans* about struggling, searching youth. Samuel Butler's *The Way of All Flesh* (1903) and James Joyce's *A Portrait of the Artist as a Young Man* (1916) are two modern examples. Variations include J. D. Salinger's *The Catcher in the Rye* (1951), set both within and beyond school, and William Golding's *Lord of the Flies* (1955), a novel not set in a school but one that is a coming-of-age story nonetheless.

ROMAN À CLEF

Roman à clef, French for "novel with a key," refers to books that require a real-life frame of reference, or key, for full comprehension. In Geoffrey Chaucer's *Canterbury Tales,* the Nun's Priest's Tale contains details that confuse readers unaware of history about the Earl of Bolingbroke's involvement in an assassination plot. Other literary works fitting this form include John Dryden's political satirical poem "Absalom and Achitophel" (1681), Jonathan Swift's satire "A Tale of a Tub" (1704), and George Orwell's political allegory *Animal Farm* (1945), all of which cannot be understood completely without knowing their camouflaged historical contents. *Roman à clefs* disguise truths too dangerous for authors to state directly. Readers must know about the enemies of D. H. Lawrence and Aldous Huxley to appreciate their respective novels: Aaron's Rod (1922) and Point Counter Point (1928). Marcel Proust's *Remembrance of Things Past (À la recherché du temps perdu,* 1871-1922) is informed by his social context. James Joyce's *Finnegans Wake* is an enormous *roman à clef* containing multitudinous personal references.

REALISM

Realism is a literary form with the goal of representing reality as faithfully as possible. Its genesis in Western literature was a reaction against the sentimentality and extreme emotionalism of the works written in the literary movement of Romanticism, which championed feelings and their expression. Realists focused in great detail on immediacy of time and place, on specific actions of their characters, and the justifiable consequences of those actions. Some techniques of realism include writing in the vernacular (conversational language), using specific dialects and placing an emphasis on character rather than plot. Realistic literature often addresses ethical issues. Historically, realistic works have often concentrated on the middle classes of the authors' societies.

Realists eschew treatments that are too dramatic or sensationalistic as exaggerations of the reality that they strive to portray as closely as they are able. Influenced by his own bleak past, Fyodor Dostoevsky wrote several novels, such as *Crime and Punishment* (1866) that shunned romantic ideals and sought to portray a stark reality. Henry James was a prominent writer of realism in novels such as *Daisy Miller* (1879). Samuel Clemens (Mark Twain) skillfully represented the language and culture of lower-class Mississippi in his novel *Huckleberry Finn* (1885).

SATIRE

Satire uses sarcasm, irony, and/or humor as social criticism to lampoon human folly. Unlike realism, which intends to depict reality as it exists without exaggeration, satire often involves creating situations or ideas deliberately exaggerating reality to be ridiculous to illuminate flawed behaviors. Ancient Roman satirists included Horace and Juvenal. Alexander Pope's poem "The Rape of the Lock" satirized the values of fashionable members of the 18th-century upper-middle class, which Pope found shallow and trivial. The theft of a lock of hair from a young woman is blown out of proportion: the poem's characters regard it as seriously as they would a rape. Irishman Jonathan Swift satirized British society, politics, and religion in works like "A Tale of a Tub." In "A Modest Proposal," Swift used essay form and mock-serious tone, satirically "proposing" cannibalism of babies and children as a solution to poverty and overpopulation. He satirized petty political disputes in *Gulliver's Travels*.

Drama

EARLY DEVELOPMENT

English drama originally developed from religious ritual. Early Christians established traditions of presenting pageants or mystery plays, traveling on wagons and carts through the streets to depict biblical events. Medieval tradition assigned responsibility for performing specific plays to the different guilds. In Middle English, "mystery" meant both religious ritual/truth, and craft/trade. Historically, mystery plays were to be reproduced exactly the same every time like religious rituals. However, some performers introduced individual interpretations of roles and even improvised. Thus drama was born. Narrative detail and nuanced acting were evident in mystery cycles by the Middle Ages. As individualized performance evolved, plays on other subjects also developed. Middle English mystery plays extant include the York Cycle, Coventry Cycle, Chester Mystery Plays, N-Town Plays, and Towneley/Wakefield Plays. In recent times, these plays began to draw interest again, and several modern actors such as Dame Judi Dench began their careers with mystery plays.

> **Review Video: Dramas**
> Visit mometrix.com/academy and enter code: 216060

DEFINING CHARACTERISTICS

In the Middle Ages, plays were commonly composed in verse. By the time of the Renaissance, Shakespeare and other dramatists wrote plays that mixed prose, rhymed verse, and blank verse. The traditions of costumes and masks were seen in ancient Greek drama, medieval mystery plays, and Renaissance drama. Conventions like asides, in which actors make comments directly to the audience unheard by other characters, and soliloquies (dramatic monologues) were also common during Shakespeare's Elizabethan dramatic period. Monologues dated back to ancient Greek drama. Elizabethan dialogue tended to use colloquial prose for lower-class characters' speech and stylized verse for upper-class characters. Another Elizabethan convention was the play-within-a-play, as in *Hamlet*. As drama moved toward realism, dialogue became less poetic and more conversational, as in most modern English-language plays. Contemporary drama, both onstage and onscreen, includes a convention of breaking the fourth wall, as actors directly face and address audiences.

COMEDY

Today, most people equate the idea of comedy with something funny, and of tragedy with something sad. However, the ancient Greeks defined these differently. Comedy needed not be humorous or amusing: it needed only a happy ending. The classical definition of comedy, as included in Aristotle's works, is any work that tells the story of a sympathetic main character's rise in fortune. According to Aristotle, protagonists needed not be heroic or exemplary: he described them as not evil or worthless, but as ordinary people—"average to below average" morally. Comic figures who were sympathetic were usually of humble origins, proving their "natural nobility" through their actions as their characters were tested, rather than characters born into nobility—who were often satirized as self-important or pompous.

SHAKESPEAREAN COMEDY

William Shakespeare lived in England from 1564-1616. He was a poet and playwright of the Renaissance period in Western culture. He is generally considered the foremost dramatist in world literature and the greatest author to write in the English language. He wrote many poems, particularly sonnets, of which 154 survive today, and approximately 38 plays. Though his sonnets are greater in number and are very famous, he is best known for his plays, including comedies, tragedies, tragicomedies and historical plays. His play titles include: *All's Well That Ends Well, As You Like It, The Comedy of Errors, Love's Labour's Lost, Measure for Measure, The Merchant of Venice, The Merry Wives of Windsor, A Midsummer Night's Dream, Much Ado About Nothing, The Taming of the Shrew, The Tempest, Twelfth Night, The Two Gentlemen of Verona, The Winter's Tale, King John, Richard II, Henry IV, Henry V, Richard III, Romeo and Juliet, Coriolanus, Titus Andronicus, Julius Caesar, Macbeth, Hamlet, Troilus and Cressida, King Lear, Othello, Antony and Cleopatra,* and *Cymbeline*. Some scholars have suggested that Christopher Marlowe wrote several of Shakespeare's works. While most scholars reject this theory, Shakespeare did pay homage to his contemporary, alluding to several of his characters, themes, or verbiage, as well as borrowing themes from several of his plays: Marlowe's *Jew of Malta* influenced Shakespeare's *Merchant of Venice*, etc.

When Shakespeare was writing, during the Elizabethan period of the Renaissance, Aristotle's version of comedies was popular. While some of Shakespeare's comedies were humorous and others were not, all had happy endings. *A Comedy of Errors* is a farce. Based and expanding on a Classical Roman comedy, it is lighthearted and includes slapstick humor and mistaken identity. *Much Ado About Nothing* is a romantic comedy. It incorporates some more serious themes, including social mores; perceived infidelity; marriage's duality as both trap and ideal; and honor and its loss, public shame, and deception, but also much witty dialogue and a happy ending.

DRAMATIC COMEDY

Three types of dramas classified as comedy include the farce, the romantic comedy, and the satirical comedy.

FARCE

The farce is a zany, goofy type of comedy that includes pratfalls and other forms of slapstick humor. The characters appearing in a farce tend to be ridiculous or fantastical in nature. The plot also tends to contain highly improbable events, featuring complications and twists that continue throughout, and incredible coincidences that could never occur in reality. Mistaken identity, deceptions, and disguises are common devices used in farcical comedies. Shakespeare's play *The Comedy of Errors*, with its cases of accidental mistaken identity and slapstick, is an example of farce. Contemporary

examples of farce include the Marx Brothers' movies, the Three Stooges movies and TV episodes, and the *Pink Panther* movie series.

ROMANTIC COMEDY

Romantic comedies are probably the most popular of the types of comedy, in both live theater performances and movies. They include not only humor and a happy ending, but also love. In the typical plot of a romantic comedy, two people well suited to one another are either brought together for the first time, or reconciled after being separated. They are usually both sympathetic characters, and seem destined to be together yet separated by some intervening complication—such as ex-lovers, interfering parents or friends, or differences in social class. The happy ending is achieved through the lovers' overcoming all these obstacles. William Shakespeare's *Much Ado About Nothing;* Walt Disney's version of *Cinderella* (1950)*;* Broadway musical *Guys and Dolls* (1955); and movies *Princess Bride* (1987), directed by Rob Reiner; *Sleepless in Seattle* (1993) and *You've Got Mail* (1998), both directed by Nora Ephron and starring Tom Hanks and Meg Ryan; and *Forget Paris* (1995), co-written, produced, directed by and starring Billy Crystal, are examples of romantic comedies.

SATIRICAL COMEDY AND BLACK COMEDY

Satires generally mock and lampoon human foolishness and vices. Satirical comedies fit the classical definition of comedy by depicting a main character's rise in fortune, but they also fit the definition of satire by making that main character either a fool, morally corrupt, or cynical in attitude. All or most of the other characters in the satirical comedy display similar foibles. These include cuckolded spouses, dupes, and other gullible types; tricksters, con artists, and criminals; hypocrites; fortune seekers; and other deceptive types who prey on the latter, who are their willing and unwitting victims. Some classical examples of satirical comedies include *The Birds* by ancient Greek comedic playwright Aristophanes, and *Volpone* by 17th-century poet and playwright Ben Jonson, who made the comedy of humors popular. When satirical comedy is extended to extremes, it becomes black comedy, wherein the comedic occurrences are grotesque or terrible.

TRAGEDY

The opposite of comedy is tragedy, portraying a hero's fall in fortune. While by classical definitions, tragedies could be sad, Aristotle went further, requiring that they depict suffering and pain to cause "terror and pity" in audiences. Additionally, he decreed that tragic heroes be basically good, admirable, and/or noble, and that their downfalls be through personal action, choice, or error, not by bad luck or accident.

ARISTOTLE'S CRITERIA FOR TRAGEDY

In his *Poetics,* Aristotle defined five critical terms relative to tragedy. (1) *Anagnorisis:* Meaning tragic insight or recognition, this is a moment of realization by a tragic hero(ine) when s/he suddenly understands how s/he has enmeshed himself/herself in a "web of fate." (2) *Hamartia:* This is often called a "tragic flaw," but is better described as a tragic error. *Hamartia* is an archery term meaning a shot missing the bull's eye, used here as a metaphor for a mistake—often a simple one—which results in catastrophe. (3) *Hubris:* While often called "pride," this is actually translated as "violent transgression," and signifies an arrogant overstepping of moral or cultural bounds—the sin of the tragic hero who over-presumes or over-aspires. (4) *Nemesis:* translated as "retribution," this represents the cosmic punishment or payback that the tragic hero ultimately receives for committing hubristic acts. (5) *Peripateia:* Literally "turning," this is a plot reversal consisting of a tragic hero's pivotal action, which changes his/her status from safe to endangered.

HEGEL'S THEORY OF TRAGEDY

Georg Wilhelm Friedrich Hegel (1770-1831) proposed a different theory of tragedy than Aristotle (384-322 BCE), which was also very influential. Whereas Aristotle's criteria involved character and plot, Hegel defined tragedy as a dynamic conflict of opposite forces or rights. For example, if an individual believes in the moral philosophy of the conscientious objector, i.e., that fighting in wars is morally wrong, but is confronted with being drafted into military service, this conflict would fit Hegel's definition of a tragic plot premise. Hegel theorized that a tragedy must involve some circumstance in which two values, or two rights, are fatally at odds with one another and conflict directly. Hegel did not view this as good triumphing over evil, or evil winning out over good, but rather as one good fighting against another good unto death. He saw this conflict of two goods as truly tragic. In ancient Greek playwright Sophocles' tragedy *Antigone,* the main character experiences this tragic conflict between her public duties and her family and religious responsibilities.

REVENGE TRAGEDY

Along with Aristotelian definitions of comedy and tragedy, ancient Greece was the origin of the revenge tragedy. This genre became highly popular in Renaissance England, and is still popular today in contemporary movies. In a revenge tragedy, the protagonist has suffered a serious wrong, such as the assault and murder of a family member. However, the wrongdoer has not been punished. In contemporary plots, this often occurs when some legal technicality has interfered with the miscreant's conviction and sentencing, or when authorities are unable to locate and apprehend the criminal. The protagonist then faces the conflict of suffering this injustice, or exacting his or her own justice by seeking revenge. Greek revenge tragedies include *Agamemnon* and *Medea.* Playwright Thomas Kyd's *The Spanish Tragedy* (1582-1592) is credited with beginning the Elizabethan genre of revenge tragedies. Shakespearean revenge tragedies include *Hamlet* (1599-1602) and *Titus Andronicus* (1588-1593). A Jacobean example is Thomas Middleton's *The Revenger's Tragedy* (1606, 1607).

HAMLET'S "TRAGIC FLAW"

Despite virtually limitless interpretations, one way to view Hamlet's tragic error generally is as indecision: He suffers the classic revenge tragedy's conflict of whether to suffer with his knowledge of his mother's and uncle's assassination of his father, or to exact his own revenge and justice against Claudius, who has assumed the throne after his crime went unknown and unpunished. Hamlet's famous soliloquy, "To be or not to be" reflects this dilemma. Hamlet muses "Whether 'tis nobler in the mind to suffer the slings and arrows of outrageous fortune, / Or to take arms against a sea of troubles, / And by opposing end them?" Hamlet both longs for and fears death, as "the dread of something after death ... makes us rather bear those ills we have / Than fly to others that we know not ... Thus conscience does make cowards of us all." For most of the play, the protagonist struggles with his responsibility in avenging his father, who was killed by Hamlet's uncle Claudius. So Hamlet's tragic error at first might be considered a lack of action. But he then makes several attempts at revenge, each of which end in worse tragedy, until his efforts are ended by the final tragedy – Hamlet's own murder.

MAKING PREDICTIONS

When we read literature, making predictions about what will happen in the writing reinforces our purpose for reading and prepares us mentally. We can make predictions before we begin reading and during our reading. As we read on, we can test the accuracy of our predictions, revise them in light of additional reading, and confirm or refute our predictions. A reader can make predictions by observing the title and illustrations; noting the structure, characters, and subject; drawing on existing knowledge relative to the subject; and asking "why" and "who" questions. Connecting

reading to what we already know enables us to learn new information and construct meaning. For example, before third-graders read a book about Johnny Appleseed, they may start a KWL chart—a list of what they *Know*, what they *Want* to know or learn, and what they have *Learned* after reading. Activating existing background knowledge and thinking about the text before reading improves comprehension.

> **Review Video: <u>Predictions</u>**
> Visit mometrix.com/academy and enter code: 437248

DRAWING INFERENCES

Inferences about literary text are logical conclusions that readers make based on their observations and previous knowledge. By inferring, readers construct meanings from text relevant to them personally. By combining their own schemas or concepts and their background information pertinent to the text with what they read, readers interpret it according to both what the author has conveyed and their own unique perspectives. Authors do not always explicitly spell out every meaning in what they write; many meanings are implicit. Through inference, readers can comprehend implied meanings in the text, and also derive personal significance from it, making the text meaningful and memorable to them. Inference is a natural process in everyday life. When readers infer, they can draw conclusions about what the author is saying, predict what may reasonably follow, amend these predictions as they continue to read, interpret the import of themes, and analyze the characters' feelings and motivations through their actions.

> **Review Video: <u>Identifying Logical Conclusions</u>**
> Visit mometrix.com/academy and enter code: 281653

MAKING CONNECTIONS TO ENHANCE COMPREHENSION

Reading involves thinking. For good comprehension, readers make text-to-self, text-to-text, and text-to-world connections. Making connections helps readers understand text better and predict what might occur next based on what they already know, such as how characters in the story feel or what happened in another text. Text-to-self connections with the reader's life and experiences make literature more personally relevant and meaningful to readers. Readers can make connections before, during, and after reading—including whenever the text reminds them of something similar they have encountered in life or other texts. The genre, setting, characters, plot elements, literary structure and devices, and themes an author uses allow a reader to make connections to other works of literature or to people and events in their own lives. Venn diagrams and other graphic organizers help visualize connections. Readers can also make double-entry notes: key content, ideas, events, words, and quotations on one side, and the connections with these on the other.

SUMMARIZING LITERATURE TO SUPPORT COMPREHENSION

When reading literature, especially demanding works, summarizing helps readers identify important information and organize it in their minds. They can also identify themes, problems, and solutions, and can sequence the story. Readers can summarize before, during, and after they read. They should use their own words, as they do when describing a personal event or giving directions. Previewing a text's organization before reading by examining the book cover, table of contents, and illustrations also aids summarizing. So does making notes of key words and ideas in a graphic organizer while reading. Graphic organizers are another useful method: readers skim the text to determine main ideas and then narrow the list with the aid of the organizer. Unimportant details

should be omitted in summaries. Summaries can include description, problem-solution, comparison-contrast, sequence, main ideas, and cause-and-effect.

> **Review Video: Summarizing Text**
> Visit mometrix.com/academy and enter code: 172903

EVALUATION OF SUMMARIES

A summary of a literary passage is a condensation in the reader's own words of the passage's main points. Several guidelines can be used in evaluating a summary. The summary should be complete yet concise. It should be accurate, balanced, fair, neutral, and objective, excluding the reader's own opinions or reactions. It should reflect in similar proportion how much each point summarized was covered in the original passage. Summary writers should include tags of attribution, like "Macaulay argues that" to reference the original author whose ideas are represented in the summary. Summary writers should not overuse quotations: they should only quote central concepts or phrases they cannot precisely convey in words other than those of the original author. Another aspect in evaluating a summary is whether it can stand alone as a coherent, unified composition. In addition, evaluation of a summary should include whether its writer has cited the original source of the passage so that readers can find it.

TEXTUAL EVIDENCE TO ANALYZE LITERATURE

Knowing about the historical background and social context of a literary work, as well as the identity of that work's author, can help to inform the reader about the author's concerns and intended meanings. For example, George Orwell published his novel *1984* in the year 1949, soon after the end of World War II. At that time, following the defeat of the Nazis, the Cold War began between the Western Allied nations and the Eastern Soviet Communists. People were therefore concerned about the conflict between the freedoms afforded by Western democracies versus the oppression represented by Communism. Author Orwell had also previously fought in the Spanish Civil War against a Spanish regime that he and his fellows viewed as oppressive. From this information, readers can infer that Orwell was concerned about oppression by totalitarian governments. This informs *1984*'s story of Winston Smith's rebellion against the oppressive "Big Brother" government of the fictional dictatorial state of Oceania and his capture, torture, and ultimate conversion by that government.

TEXTUAL EVIDENCE TO EVALUATE PREDICTIONS

Textual evidence to evaluate reader predictions about literature includes specific synopses of the work, paraphrases of the work or parts of it, and direct quotations from it. The best literary analysis shows special insight into a theme, character trait, or change. The best textual evidence is strong, relevant, and accurate. Analysis that is not best, but enough, shows reasonable understanding of theme, character trait, or change; contains supporting textual evidence that is relevant and accurate, if not strong; and shows a specific and clear response. Analysis that partially meets criteria also shows reasonable understanding, but the textual evidence is generalized, incomplete, only partly relevant or accurate, or connected only weakly. Inadequate analysis is vague, too general, or incorrect; it may give irrelevant or incomplete textual evidence, or may simply summarize the plot rather than analyzing the work.

> **Review Video: Textual Evidence for Predictions**
> Visit mometrix.com/academy and enter code: 261070

Main Idea and Supporting Details

UNDERSTANDING A PASSAGE

One of the most important skills in reading comprehension is the identification of **topics** and **main ideas.** There is a subtle difference between these two features. The topic is the subject of a text (i.e., what the text is all about). The main idea, on the other hand, is the most important point being made by the author. The topic is usually expressed in a few words at the most while the main idea often needs a full sentence to be completely defined. As an example, a short passage might have the topic of penguins and the main idea could be written as *Penguins are different from other birds in many ways*. In most nonfiction writing, the topic and the main idea will be **stated directly** and often appear in a sentence at the very beginning or end of the text. When being tested on an understanding of the author's topic, you may be able to skim the passage for the general idea, by reading only the first sentence of each paragraph. A body paragraph's first sentence is often—but not always—the main **topic sentence** which gives you a summary of the content in the paragraph.

However, there are cases in which the reader must figure out an **unstated** topic or main idea. In these instances, you must read every sentence of the text and try to come up with an overarching idea that is supported by each of those sentences.

Note: The main idea should not be confused with the thesis statement. While the main idea gives a brief, general summary of a text, the thesis statement provides a specific perspective on an issue that the author supports with evidence.

> **Review Video: Topics and Main Ideas**
> Visit mometrix.com/academy and enter code: 407801

Supporting details provide evidence and backing for the main point. In order to show that a main idea is correct, or valid, authors add details that prove their point. All texts contain details, but they are only classified as supporting details when they serve to reinforce some larger point. Supporting details are most commonly found in informative and persuasive texts. In some cases, they will be clearly indicated with terms like *for example* or *for instance*, or they will be enumerated with terms like *first*, *second*, and *last*. However, you need to be prepared for texts that do not contain those indicators. As a reader, you should consider whether the author's supporting details really back up his or her main point. Supporting details can be factual and correct, yet they may not be **relevant** to the author's point. Conversely, supporting details can seem pertinent, but they can be ineffective because they are based on opinion or assertions that cannot be proven.

> **Review Video: Supporting Details**
> Visit mometrix.com/academy and enter code: 396297

An example of a main idea is: *Giraffes live in the Serengeti of Africa*. A supporting detail about giraffes could be: *A giraffe in this region benefits from a long neck by reaching twigs and leaves on tall trees.* The main idea gives the general idea that the text is about giraffes. The supporting detail gives a specific fact about how the giraffes eat.

EVALUATING A PASSAGE

When reading informational texts, there is importance in understanding the logical conclusion of the author's ideas. **Identifying a logical conclusion** can help you determine whether you agree with the writer or not. Coming to this conclusion is much like making an inference: the approach requires you to combine the information given by the text with what you already know in order to make a logical conclusion. If the author intended the reader to draw a certain conclusion, then you can expect the author's argumentation and detail to be leading in that direction.

One way to approach the task of drawing conclusions is to make brief **notes** of all the points made by the author. When the notes are arranged on paper, they may clarify the logical conclusion. Another way to approach conclusions is to consider whether the reasoning of the author raises any pertinent questions. Sometimes you will be able to draw several conclusions from a passage. On occasion these will be conclusions that were never imagined by the author. Therefore, be aware that these conclusions must be **supported directly by the text**.

> **Review Video: Identifying Logical Conclusions**
> Visit mometrix.com/academy and enter code: 281653.

MAKING LOGICAL CONCLUSIONS ABOUT A PASSAGE

A reader should always be drawing conclusions from the text. Sometimes conclusions are **implied** from written information, and other times the information is **stated directly** within the passage. One should always aim to draw conclusions from information stated within a passage, rather than to draw them from mere implications. At times an author may provide some information and then describe a counterargument. Readers should be alert for direct statements that are subsequently rejected or weakened by the author. Furthermore, you should always read through the entire passage before drawing conclusions. Many readers are trained to expect the author's conclusions at either the beginning or the end of the passage, but many texts do not adhere to this format.

Drawing conclusions from information implied within a passage requires confidence on the part of the reader. **Implications** are things that the author does not state directly, but readers can assume based on what the author does say. Consider the following passage: *I stepped outside and opened my umbrella. By the time I got to work, the cuffs of my pants were soaked.* The author never states that it is raining, but this fact is clearly implied. Conclusions based on implication must be well supported by the text. In order to draw a solid conclusion, readers should have **multiple pieces of evidence**. If readers have only one piece, they must be assured that there is no other possible explanation than their conclusion. A good reader will be able to draw many conclusions from information implied by the text, which will be a great help on the exam.

OUTLINING A PASSAGE

As an aid to drawing conclusions, **outlining** the information contained in the passage should be a familiar skill to readers. An effective outline will reveal the structure of the passage and will lead to solid conclusions. An effective outline will have a title that refers to the basic subject of the text though the title does not need not restate the main idea. In most outlines, the main idea will be the first major section. Each major idea of the passage will be established as the head of a category. For instance, the most common outline format calls for the main ideas of the passage to be indicated with Roman numerals. In an effective outline of this kind, each of the main ideas will be represented by a Roman numeral and none of the Roman numerals will designate minor details or secondary ideas. Moreover, all supporting ideas and details should be placed in the appropriate place on the outline. An outline does not need to include every detail listed in the text, but the outline should feature all of those that are central to the argument or message. Each of these details should be listed under the appropriate main idea.

USING GRAPHIC ORGANIZERS

Ideas from a text can also be organized using **graphic organizers**. A graphic organizer is a way to simplify information and take key points from the text. A graphic organizer such as a timeline may

have an event listed for a corresponding date on the timeline while an outline may have an event listed under a key point that occurs in the text. Each reader needs to create the type of graphic organizer that works the best for him or her in terms of being able to recall information from a story. Examples include a *spider-map,* which takes a main idea from the story and places it in a bubble with supporting points branching off the main idea. An *outline* is useful for diagramming the main and supporting points of the entire story, and a *Venn diagram* classifies information as separate or overlapping.

> **Review Video: Graphic Organizers**
> Visit mometrix.com/academy and enter code: 665513

SUMMARIZING

A helpful tool is the ability to **summarize** the information that you have read in a paragraph or passage format. This process is similar to creating an effective outline. First, a summary should accurately define the main idea of the passage though the summary does not need to explain this main idea in exhaustive detail. The summary should continue by laying out the most important supporting details or arguments from the passage. All of the significant supporting details should be included, and none of the details included should be irrelevant or insignificant. Also, the summary should accurately report all of these details. Too often, the desire for brevity in a summary leads to the sacrifice of clarity or accuracy. Summaries are often difficult to read because they omit all of the graceful language, digressions, and asides that distinguish great writing. However, an effective summary should contain much the same message as the original text.

PARAPHRASING

Paraphrasing is another method that the reader can use to aid in comprehension. When paraphrasing, one puts what they have read into their words by rephrasing what the author has written, or one "translates" all of what the author shared into their words by including as many details as they can.

Organization within a Passage

ORGANIZATION OF THE TEXT

The way a text is organized can help readers to understand the author's intent and his or her conclusions. There are various ways to organize a text, and each one has a purpose and use. Usually, authors will organize information logically in a passage so the reader can follow and locate the information within the text. However, since not all passages are written with the same logical structure, you need to be familiar with several different types of passage structure.

CHRONOLOGICAL

When using **chronological** order, the author presents information in the order that it happened. For example, biographies are typically written in chronological order. The subject's birth and childhood are presented first, followed by their adult life, and lastly the events leading up to the person's death.

CAUSE AND EFFECT

One of the most common text structures is **cause and effect**. A **cause** is an act or event that makes something happen, and an **effect** is the thing that happens as a result of the cause. A cause-and-effect relationship is not always explicit, but there are some terms in English that signal causes, such as *since, because,* and *due to.* Furthermore, terms that signal effects include *consequently,*

35

therefore, this leads to. As an example, consider the sentence *Because the sky was clear, Ron did not bring an umbrella.* The cause is the clear sky, and the effect is that Ron did not bring an umbrella. However, readers may find that sometimes the cause-and-effect relationship will not be clearly noted. For instance, the sentence *He was late and missed the meeting* does not contain any signaling words, but the sentence still contains a cause (he was late) and an effect (he missed the meeting).

MULTIPLE EFFECTS

Be aware of the possibility for a single cause to have **multiple effects** (e.g., *Single cause*: Because you left your homework on the table, your dog engulfs the assignment. *Multiple effects*: As a result, you receive a failing grade; your parents do not allow you to visit your friends; you miss out on the new movie and meeting a potential significant other).

MULTIPLE CAUSES

Also, the possibility of a single effect to have **multiple causes** (e.g., *Single effect*: Alan has a fever. *Multiple causes*: An unexpected cold front came through the area, and Alan forgot to take his multi-vitamin to avoid being sick.) Additionally, an effect can in turn be the cause of another effect, in what is known as a cause-and-effect chain. (e.g., As a result of her disdain for procrastination, Lynn prepared for her exam. This led to her passing her test with high marks. Hence, her resume was accepted and her application was approved.)

CAUSE AND EFFECT IN PERSUASIVE ESSAYS

Persuasive essays, in which an author tries to make a convincing argument and change the minds of readers, usually include cause-and-effect relationships. However, these relationships should not always be taken at face value. Frequently, an author will assume a cause or take an effect for granted. To read a persuasive essay effectively, readers need to judge the cause-and-effect relationships that the author is presenting. For instance, imagine an author wrote the following: *The parking deck has been unprofitable because people would prefer to ride their bikes.* The relationship is clear: the cause is that people prefer to ride their bikes, and the effect is that the parking deck has been unprofitable. However, readers should consider whether this argument is conclusive. Perhaps there are other reasons for the failure of the parking deck: a down economy, excessive fees, etc. Too often, authors present causal relationships as if they are fact rather than opinion. Readers should be on the alert for these dubious claims.

PROBLEM-SOLUTION

Some nonfiction texts are organized to **present a problem** followed by a solution. For this type of text, the problem is often explained before the solution is offered. In some cases, as when the problem is well known, the solution may be introduced briefly at the beginning. Other passages may focus on the solution, and the problem will be referenced only occasionally. Some texts will outline multiple solutions to a problem, leaving readers to choose among them. If the author has an interest or an allegiance to one solution, he or she may fail to mention or describe accurately some of the other solutions. Readers should be careful of the author's agenda when reading a problem-solution text. Only by understanding the author's perspective and interests can one develop a proper judgment of the proposed solution.

COMPARE AND CONTRAST

Many texts follow the **compare-and-contrast** model in which the similarities and differences between two ideas or things are explored. Analysis of the similarities between ideas is called comparison. In an ideal **comparison**, the author places ideas or things in an equivalent structure (i.e., the author presents the ideas in the same way). If an author wants to show the similarities between cricket and baseball, then he or she may do so by summarizing the equipment and rules for each game. Be mindful of the similarities as they appear in the passage and take note of any differences that are mentioned. Often, these small differences will only reinforce the more general similarity.

Thinking critically about ideas and conclusions can seem like a daunting task. One way to ease this task is to understand the basic elements of ideas and writing techniques. Looking at the way different ideas relate to each other can be a good way for readers to begin their analysis. For instance, sometimes authors will write about two ideas that are in opposition to each other. Or one author will provide his or her ideas on a topic, and another author may respond in opposition. The analysis of these opposing ideas is known as **contrast**. Contrast is often marred by the author's obvious partiality to one of the ideas. A discerning reader will be put off by an author who does not engage in a fair fight. In an analysis of opposing ideas, both ideas should be presented in clear and reasonable terms. If the author does prefer a side, you need to read carefully to determine the areas where the author shows or avoids this preference. In an analysis of opposing ideas, you should proceed through the passage by marking the major differences point by point with an eye that is looking for an explanation of each side's view. For instance, in an analysis of capitalism and communism, there is an importance in outlining each side's view on labor, markets, prices, personal responsibility, etc. Additionally, as you read through the passages, you should note whether the opposing views present each side in a similar manner.

SEQUENCE

Readers must be able to identify a text's **sequence**, or the order in which things happen. Often, when the sequence is very important to the author, the text is indicated with signal words like *first, then, next,* and *last*. However, a sequence can be merely implied and must be noted by the reader. Consider the sentence *He walked through the garden and gave water and fertilizer to the plants.* Clearly, the man did not walk through the garden before he collected water and fertilizer for the plants. So, the implied sequence is that he first collected water, then he collected fertilizer, next he walked through the garden, and last he gave water or fertilizer as necessary to the plants. Texts do not always proceed in an orderly sequence from first to last. Sometimes they begin at the end and start over at the beginning. As a reader, you can enhance your understanding of the passage by taking brief notes to clarify the sequence.

TRANSITIONS

Transitional words and phrases are devices that guide readers through a text. You are no doubt familiar with the common transitions, though you may never have considered how they operate. Some transitional phrases (*after, before, during, in the middle of*) give information about time. Some indicate that an example is about to be given (*for example, in fact, for instance*). Writers use them to compare (*also, likewise*) and contrast (*however, but, yet*). Transitional words and phrases can suggest addition (*and, also, furthermore, moreover*) and logical relationships (*if, then, therefore, as a result, since*). Finally, transitional words and phrases can separate the steps in a process (*first, second, last*).

POINT OF VIEW

Another element that impacts a text is the author's point of view. The **point of view** of a text is the perspective from which a passage is told. An author will always have a point of view about a story before he or she draws up a plot line. The author will know what events they want to take place, how they want the characters to interact, and how they want the story to resolve. An author will also have an opinion on the topic or series of events which is presented in the story that is based on their prior experience and beliefs.

The two main points of view that authors use, especially in a work of fiction, are first person and third person. If the narrator of the story is also the main character, or *protagonist*, the text is written in first-person point of view. In first person, the author writes from the perspective of *I*. Third-person point of view is probably the most common that authors use in their passages. Using third person, authors refer to each character by using *he* or *she*. In third-person omniscient, the narrator is not a character in the story and tells the story of all of the characters at the same time.

> **Review Video: Point of View**
> Visit mometrix.com/academy and enter code: 383336

PURPOSES FOR WRITING

In order to be an effective reader, one must pay attention to the author's **position** and purpose. Even those texts that seem objective and impartial, like textbooks, have a position and bias. Readers need to take these positions into account when considering the author's message. When an author uses emotional language or clearly favors one side of an argument, his or her position is clear. However, the author's position may be evident not only in what he or she writes, but also in what he or she doesn't write. In a normal setting, a reader would want to review some other texts on the same topic in order to develop a view of the author's position. If this was not possible, then you would want to acquire some background about the author. However, since you are in the middle of an exam and the only source of information is the text, you should look for language and argumentation that seems to indicate a particular stance on the subject.

> **Review Video: Author's Position**
> Visit mometrix.com/academy and enter code: 827954

Usually, identifying the **purpose** of an author is easier than identifying his or her position. In most cases, the author has no interest in hiding his or her purpose. A text that is meant to entertain, for instance, should be written to please the reader. Most narratives, or stories, are written to entertain, though they may also inform or persuade. Informative texts are easy to identify, while the most difficult purpose of a text to identify is persuasion because the author has an interest in making this purpose hard to detect. When a reader discovers that the author is trying to persuade, he or she should be skeptical of the argument. For this reason, persuasive texts often try to establish an entertaining tone and hope to amuse the reader into agreement. On the other hand, an informative tone may be implemented to create an appearance of authority and objectivity.

An author's purpose is evident often in the organization of the text (e.g., section headings in bold font points to an informative text). However, you may not have such organization available to you in your exam. Instead, if the author makes his or her main idea clear from the beginning, then the likely purpose of the text is to inform. If the author begins by making a claim and provides various arguments to support that claim, then the purpose is probably to persuade. If the author tells a story or seems to want the attention of the reader more than to push a particular point or deliver information, then his or her purpose is most likely to entertain. As a reader, you must judge authors

on how well they accomplish their purpose. In other words, you need to consider the type of passage (e.g., technical, persuasive, etc.) that the author has written and if the author has followed the requirements of the passage type.

EVALUATING AN ARGUMENT

Argumentative and persuasive passages take a stand on a debatable issue, seek to explore all sides of the issue, and find the best possible solution. Argumentative and persuasive passages should not be combative or abusive. The word *argument* may remind you of two or more people shouting at each other and walking away in anger. However, an argumentative or persuasive passage should be a calm and reasonable presentation of an author's ideas for others to consider. When an author writes reasonable arguments, his or her goal is not to win or have the last word. Instead, authors want to reveal current understanding of the question at hand and suggest a solution to a problem. The purpose of argument and persuasion in a free society is to reach the best solution.

EVIDENCE

The term **text evidence** refers to information that supports a main point or minor points and can help lead the reader to a conclusion. Information used as text evidence is precise, descriptive, and factual. A main point is often followed by supporting details that provide evidence to back up a claim. For example, a passage may include the claim that winter occurs during opposite months in the Northern and Southern hemispheres. Text evidence based on this claim may include countries where winter occurs in opposite months along with reasons that winter occurs at different times of the year in separate hemispheres (due to the tilt of the Earth as it rotates around the sun).

Evidence needs to be provided that supports the thesis and additional arguments. Most arguments must be supported by facts or statistics. Facts are something that is known with certainty and have been verified by several independent individuals. Examples and illustrations add an emotional component to arguments. With this component, you persuade readers in ways that facts and statistics cannot. The emotional component is effective when used with objective information that can be confirmed.

CREDIBILITY

The text used to support an argument can be the argument's downfall if the text is not credible. A text is **credible**, or believable, when the author is knowledgeable and objective, or unbiased. The author's motivations for writing the text play a critical role in determining the credibility of the text and must be evaluated when assessing that credibility. Reports written about the ozone layer by an environmental scientist and a hairdresser will have a different level of credibility.

APPEAL TO EMOTION

Sometimes, authors will appeal to the reader's emotion in an attempt to persuade or to distract the reader from the weakness of the argument. For instance, the author may try to inspire the pity of the reader by delivering a heart-rending story. An author also might use the bandwagon approach, in which he suggests that his opinion is correct because it is held by the majority. Some authors resort to name-calling, in which insults and harsh words are delivered to the opponent in an attempt to distract. In advertising, a common appeal is the celebrity testimonial, in which a famous person endorses a product. Of course, the fact that a famous person likes something should not really mean anything to the reader. These and other emotional appeals are usually evidence of poor reasoning and a weak argument.

COUNTER ARGUMENTS

When authors give both sides to the argument, they build trust with their readers. As a reader, you should start with an undecided or neutral position. If an author presents only his or her side to the argument, then you will need to be concerned at best.

Building common ground with neutral or opposed readers can be appealing to skeptical readers. Sharing values with undecided readers can allow people to switch positions without giving up what they feel is important. For people who may oppose a position, they need to feel that they can change their minds without betraying who they are as a person. This appeal to having an open mind can be a powerful tool in arguing a position without antagonizing other views. Objections can be countered on a point-by-point basis or in a summary paragraph. Be mindful of how an author points out flaws in counter arguments. If they are unfair to the other side of the argument, then you should lose trust with the author.

OPINIONS, FACTS, AND FALLACIES

Critical thinking skills are mastered through understanding various types of writing and the different purposes of authors in writing their passages. Every author writes for a purpose. When you understand their purpose and how they accomplish their goal, you will be able to analyze their writing and determine whether or not you agree with their conclusions.

Readers must always be conscious of the distinction between fact and opinion. A **fact** can be subjected to analysis and can be either proved or disproved. An **opinion**, on the other hand, is the author's personal thoughts or feelings which may not be alterable by research or evidence. If the author writes that the distance from New York City to Boston is about two hundred miles, then he or she is stating a fact. If the author writes that New York City is too crowded, then he or she is giving an opinion because there is no objective standard for "too crowded." Opinions are often supported by facts. For instance, the author might cite the population density of New York City as compared to that of other major American cities as evidence of an overcrowded population. An opinion supported by fact tends to be more convincing. On the other hand, when authors support their opinions with other opinions, readers should not be persuaded by the argument to any degree.

RELIABLE SOURCES

When you have an argumentative passage, you need to be sure that facts are presented to the reader from **reliable sources**. An opinion is what the author thinks about a given topic. An opinion is not common knowledge or proven by expert sources, instead the information is the personal beliefs and thoughts of the author. To distinguish between fact and opinion, a reader needs to consider the type of source that is presenting information, the information that backs-up a claim, and the author's motivation to have a certain point-of-view on a given topic. For example, if a panel of scientists has conducted multiple studies on the effectiveness of taking a certain vitamin, then the results are more likely to be factual than a company that is selling a vitamin and claims that taking the vitamin can produce positive effects. The company is motivated to sell their product, and the

scientists are using the scientific method to prove a theory. Remember: if you find sentences that contain phrases such as "I think...", then the statement is an opinion.

> **Review Video: Fact or Opinion**
> Visit mometrix.com/academy and enter code: 870899

BIASES

In their attempts to persuade, writers often make mistakes in their thinking patterns and writing choices. These patterns and choices are important to understand so you can make an informed decision. Every author has a point-of-view, but authors demonstrate a bias when they ignore reasonable counterarguments or distort opposing viewpoints. A **bias** is evident whenever the author is unfair or inaccurate in his or her presentation. Bias may be intentional or unintentional, and readers should be skeptical of the author's argument. Remember that a biased author may still be correct; however, the author will be correct in spite of his or her bias, not because of the bias.

A **stereotype** is a bias applied specifically to a group or place. Stereotyping is considered to be particularly abhorrent because the practice promotes negative generalizations about people. Readers should be very cautious of authors who stereotype in their writing. These faulty assumptions typically reveal the author's ignorance and lack of curiosity.

> **Review Video: Bias and Stereotype**
> Visit mometrix.com/academy and enter code: 644829

DENOTATIVE VS. CONNOTATIVE MEANING

The **denotative** meaning of a word is the literal meaning. The **connotative** meaning goes beyond the denotative meaning to include the emotional reaction that a word may invoke. The connotative meaning often takes the denotative meaning a step further due to associations which the reader makes with the denotative meaning. Readers can differentiate between the denotative and connotative meanings by first recognizing how authors use each meaning. Most non-fiction, for example, is fact-based and authors do not use flowery, figurative language. The reader can assume that the writer is using the denotative meaning of words. In fiction, the author may use the connotative meaning. Readers can determine whether the author is using the denotative or connotative meaning of a word by implementing context clues.

> **Review Video: Denotation and Connotation**
> Visit mometrix.com/academy and enter code: 310092

CONTEXT CLUES

Readers of all levels will encounter words that they have either never seen or encountered on a limited basis. The best way to define a word in **context** is to look for nearby words that can assist in learning the meaning of the word. For instance, unfamiliar nouns are often accompanied by examples that provide a definition. Consider the following sentence: *Dave arrived at the party in hilarious garb: a leopard-print shirt, buckskin trousers, and high heels.* If a reader was unfamiliar with the meaning of garb, he or she could read the examples (i.e., a leopard-print shirt, buckskin trousers, and high heels) and quickly determine that the word means *clothing*. Examples will not always be this obvious. Consider this sentence: *Parsley, lemon, and flowers were just a few of items he used as garnishes.* Here, the word *garnishes* is exemplified by parsley, lemon, and flowers. Readers who have eaten in a few restaurants will probably be able to identify a garnish as something used to decorate a plate.

USING CONTRAST IN CONTEXT CLUES

In addition to looking at the context of a passage, readers can use contrasts to define an unfamiliar word in context. In many sentences, the author will not describe the unfamiliar word directly; instead, he or she will describe the opposite of the unfamiliar word. Thus, you are provided with some information that will bring you closer to defining the word. Consider the following example: *Despite his intelligence, Hector's low brow and bad posture made him look obtuse.* The author writes that Hector's appearance does not convey intelligence. Therefore, *obtuse* must mean unintelligent. Here is another example: *Despite the horrible weather, we were beatific about our trip to Alaska.* The word *despite* indicates that the speaker's feelings were at odds with the weather. Since the weather is described as *horrible*, then *beatific* must mean something positive.

SUBSTITUTION TO FIND MEANING

In some cases, there will be very few contextual clues to help a reader define the meaning of an unfamiliar word. When this happens, one strategy that readers may employ is **substitution**. A good reader will brainstorm some possible synonyms for the given word, and he or she will substitute these words into the sentence. If the sentence and the surrounding passage continue to make sense, then the substitution has revealed at least some information about the unfamiliar word. Consider the sentence: *Frank's admonition rang in her ears as she climbed the mountain.* A reader unfamiliar with *admonition* might come up with some substitutions like *vow, promise, advice, complaint,* or *compliment*. All of these words make general sense of the sentence though their meanings are diverse. The process has suggested; however, that an admonition is some sort of message. The substitution strategy is rarely able to pinpoint a precise definition, but this process can be effective as a last resort.

Occasionally, you will be able to define an unfamiliar word by looking at the descriptive words in the context. Consider the following sentence: *Fred dragged the recalcitrant boy kicking and screaming up the stairs.* The words *dragged, kicking,* and *screaming* all suggest that the boy does not want to go up the stairs. The reader may assume that *recalcitrant* means something like unwilling or protesting. In this example, an unfamiliar adjective was identified.

Additionally, using description to define an unfamiliar noun is a common practice compared to unfamiliar adjectives, as in this sentence: *Don's wrinkled frown and constantly shaking fist identified him as a curmudgeon of the first order.* Don is described as having a *wrinkled frown and constantly shaking fist* suggesting that a *curmudgeon* must be a grumpy man. Contrasts do not always provide detailed information about the unfamiliar word, but they at least give the reader some clues.

WORDS WITH MULTIPLE MEANINGS

When a word has more than one meaning, readers can have difficulty with determining how the word is being used in a given sentence. For instance, the verb *cleave,* can mean either *join* or *separate*. When readers come upon this word, they will have to select the definition that makes the most sense. Consider the following sentence: *Hermione's knife cleaved the bread cleanly.* Since, a knife cannot join bread together, the word must indicate separation. A slightly more difficult example would be the sentence: *The birds cleaved to one another as they flew from the oak tree.* Immediately, the presence of the words *to one another* should suggest that in this sentence *cleave* is being used to mean *join*. Discovering the intent of a word with multiple meanings requires the same tricks as defining an unknown word: look for contextual clues and evaluate the substituted words.

SYNONYMS AND ANTONYMS

When you understand how words relate to each other, you will discover more in a passage. This is explained by understanding **synonyms** (e.g., words that mean the same thing) and **antonyms** (e.g., words that mean the opposite of one another). As an example, *dry* and *arid* are synonyms, and *dry* and *wet* are antonyms.

There are many pairs of words in English that can be considered synonyms, despite having slightly different definitions. For instance, the words *friendly* and *collegial* can both be used to describe a warm interpersonal relationship, and one would be correct to call them synonyms. However, *collegial* (kin to *colleague*) is often used in reference to professional or academic relationships, and *friendly* has no such connotation.

If the difference between the two words is too great, then they should not be called synonyms. *Hot* and *warm* are not synonyms because their meanings are too distinct. A good way to determine whether two words are synonyms is to substitute one word for the other word and verify that the meaning of the sentence has not changed. Substituting *warm* for *hot* in a sentence would convey a different meaning. Although warm and hot may seem close in meaning, warm generally means that the temperature is moderate, and hot generally means that the temperature is excessively high.

Antonyms are words with opposite meanings. *Light* and *dark*, *up* and *down*, *right* and *left*, *good* and *bad*: these are all sets of antonyms. Be careful to distinguish between antonyms and pairs of words that are simply different. *Black* and *gray*, for instance, are not antonyms because gray is not the opposite of black. *Black* and *white*, on the other hand, are antonyms.

Not every word has an antonym. For instance, many nouns do not: What would be the antonym of *chair*? During your exam, the questions related to antonyms are more likely to concern adjectives. You will recall that adjectives are words that describe a noun. Some common adjectives include *purple*, *fast*, *skinny*, and *sweet*. From those four adjectives, *purple* is the item that lacks a group of obvious antonyms.

> **Review Video: <u>Synonyms and Antonyms</u>**
> Visit mometrix.com/academy and enter code: 105612

Literary Analysis

SETTING AND TIME FRAME

A literary text has both a setting and time frame. A **setting** is the place in which the story as a whole is set. The **time frame** is the period in which the story is set. This may refer to the historical period the story takes place in or if the story takes place over a single day. Both setting and time frame are relevant to a text's meaning because they help the reader place the story in time and space. An author uses setting and time frame to anchor a text, create a mood, and enhance its meaning; helping a reader understand why a character acts the way he does, or why certain events in the story are important. The setting impacts the **plot** and character **motivations**, while the time frame helps place the story in **chronological context**.

<u>EXAMPLE</u>

Read the following excerpt from The Adventures of Huckleberry Finn by Mark Twain and analyze the relevance of setting to the text's meaning:

> We said there warn't no home like a raft, after all. Other places do seem so cramped up and smothery, but a raft don't. You feel mighty free and easy and comfortable on a raft.

This excerpt from *The Adventures of Huckleberry Finn* by Mark Twain reveals information about the **setting** of the book. By understanding that the main character, Huckleberry Finn, lives on a raft, the reader can place the story on a river, in this case, the Mississippi River in the South before the Civil War. The information about the setting also gives the reader clues about the **character** of Huck Finn: he clearly values independence and freedom and he likes the outdoors. The information about the setting in the quote helps the reader to better understand the rest of the text.

THEME

The theme of a passage is what the reader learns from the text or the passage. It is the lesson or **moral** contained in the passage. It also is a unifying idea that is used throughout the text; it can take the form of a common setting, idea, symbol, design, or recurring event. A passage can have two or more themes that convey its overall idea. The theme or themes of a passage are often based on **universal themes**. They can frequently be expressed using well-known sayings about life, society, or human nature, such as "Hard work pays off" or "Good triumphs over evil." Themes are not usually stated **explicitly**. The reader must figure them out by carefully reading the passage. Themes are often the reason why passages are written; they give a passage unity and meaning. Themes are created through **plot development**. The events of a story help shape the themes of a passage.

> **Review Video: <u>Theme</u>**
> Visit mometrix.com/academy and enter code: 732074

<u>EXAMPLE</u>

Explain why "Take care of what you care about" accurately describes the theme of the following excerpt.

> Luca collected baseball cards, but he wasn't very careful with them. He left them around the house. His dog liked to chew. Luca and his friend Bart were looking at his collection. Then they went outside. When Luca got home, he saw his dog chewing on his cards. They were ruined.

This excerpt tells the story of a boy who is careless with his baseball cards and leaves them lying around. His dog ends up chewing them and ruining them. The lesson is that if you care about something, you need to take care of it. This is the point of the story. The **theme** is the lesson that a story teaches. Some stories have more than one theme, but this is not really true of this excerpt. The reader needs to figure out the theme based on what happens in the story. Sometimes, as in the case of fables, the theme is stated directly in the text. However, this is not usually the case.

CONFLICT

Read the following paragraph and discuss the type of conflict present:

> Timothy was shocked out of sleep by the appearance of a bear just outside his tent. After panicking for a moment, he remembered some advice he had read in

preparation for this trip: he should make noise so the bear would not be startled. As Timothy started to hum and sing, the bear wandered away.

There are three main types of conflict in literature: **man versus man**, man versus nature, and **man versus self**. This paragraph is an example of man versus nature. Timothy is in conflict with the bear. Even though no physical conflict like an attack exists, Timothy is pitted against the bear. Timothy uses his knowledge to "defeat" the bear and keep himself safe. The solution to the conflict is that Timothy makes noise, the bear wanders away, and Timothy is safe.

> **Review Video: Conflict**
> Visit mometrix.com/academy and enter code: 559550

CONFLICT RESOLUTION

The way the conflict is **resolved** depends on the type of conflict. The plot of any book starts with the lead up to the conflict, then the conflict itself, and finally the solution, or **resolution**, to the conflict. In *man versus man* conflicts, the conflict is often resolved by two parties coming to some sort of agreement or by one party triumphing over the party. In *man versus nature* conflicts, the conflict is often resolved by man coming to some realization about some aspect of nature. In *man versus self* conflicts, the conflict is often resolved by the character growing or coming to an understanding about part of himself.

SYNTAX AND WORD CHOICE

Authors use words and **syntax**, or sentence structure, to make their texts unique, convey their own writing style, and sometimes to make a point or emphasis. They know that word choice and syntax contribute to the reader's understanding of the text as well as to the tone and mood of a text.

ALLUSION

An allusion is an uncited but recognizable reference to something else. Authors use language to make allusions to places, events, artwork, and other books in order to make their own text richer. For example, an author may allude to a very important text in order to make his own text seem more important. Martin Luther King, Jr. started his "I Have a Dream" speech by saying "Five score years ago..." This is a clear allusion to President Abraham Lincoln's "Gettysburg Address" and served to remind people of the significance of the event. An author may allude to a place to ground his text or make a cultural reference to make readers feel included. There are many reasons that authors make allusions.

COMIC RELIEF

Comic relief is the use of comedy by an author to break up a dramatic or tragic scene and infuse it with a bit of **lightheartedness**. In William Shakespeare's *Hamlet*, two gravediggers digging the grave for Ophelia share a joke while they work. The death and burial of Ophelia are tragic moments that directly follow each other. Shakespeare uses an instance of comedy to break up the tragedy and give his audience a bit of a break from the tragic drama. Authors sometimes use comic relief so that their work will be less depressing; other times they use it to create irony or contrast between the darkness of the situation and the lightness of the joke. Often, authors will use comedy to parallel what is happening in the tragic scenes.

CONFLICT

A conflict is a problem to be solved. Literary plots typically include one conflict or more. Characters' attempts to resolve conflicts drive the narrative's forward movement. Conflict resolution is often the protagonist's primary occupation. Physical conflicts like exploring, wars, and escapes tend to

45

make plots most suspenseful and exciting. Emotional, mental, or moral conflicts tend to make stories more personally gratifying or rewarding for many audiences. Conflicts can be external or internal. A major type of internal conflict is some inner personal battle, or "man against himself." Major types of external conflicts include "man against nature," "man against man," and "man against society." Readers can identify conflicts in literary plots by identifying the protagonist and antagonist and asking why they conflict, what events develop the conflict, where the climax occurs, and how they identify with the characters.

> **Review Video: Conflict**
> Visit mometrix.com/academy and enter code: 559550

MOOD AND TONE

Mood is a story's atmosphere, or the feelings the reader gets from reading it. The way authors set the mood in writing is comparable to the way filmmakers use music to set the mood in movies. Instead of music, though, writers judiciously select descriptive words to evoke certain moods. The mood of a work may convey joy, anger, bitterness, hope, gloom, fear, an ominous feeling, or any other emotion the author wants the reader to feel. In addition to vocabulary choices, authors also use figurative expressions, particular sentence structures, and choices of diction that project and reinforce the moods they want to create. Whereas mood is the reader's emotions evoked by reading what is written, tone is the emotions and attitudes of the writer that s/he expresses in the writing. Authors use the same literary techniques to establish tone as they do to establish mood. An author may use a humorous tone, an angry or sad tone, a sentimental or unsentimental tone, or something else entirely.

> **Review Video: Style, Tone, and Mood**
> Visit mometrix.com/academy and enter code: 416961

ANALYSIS OF CHARACTER DEVELOPMENT

To understand the meaning of a story, it is vital to understand the characters as the author describes them. We can look for contradictions in what a character thinks, says, and does. We can notice whether the author's observations about a character differ from what other characters in the story say about that character. A character may be dynamic (changing significantly during the story) or static (remaining the same from beginning to end). Characters may be two-dimensional, not fully developed, or may be well developed with characteristics that stand out vividly. Characters may also symbolize universal properties. Additionally, readers can compare and contrast characters to analyze how they were developed.

> **Review Video: Character Changes**
> Visit mometrix.com/academy and enter code: 408719

DIALOGUE

Effectively written dialogue serves at least one but usually several purposes. It advances the story and moves the plot. It develops the characters. It sheds light on the work's theme or meaning. It can, often subtly, account for the passage of time not otherwise indicated. It can alter the direction that the plot is taking, typically by introducing some new conflict or changing existing ones. Dialogue can establish a work's narrative voice and the characters' voices and set the tone of the story or of particular characters. When fictional characters display enlightenment or realization, dialogue can give readers an understanding of what those characters have discovered and how. Dialogue can illuminate the motivations and wishes of the story's characters. By using consistent thoughts and

syntax, dialogue can support character development. Skillfully created, it can also represent real-life speech rhythms in written form. Via conflicts and ensuing action, dialogue also provides drama.

DIALOGUE IN FICTION

In fictional works, effectively written dialogue should not only have the effect of breaking up or interrupting sections of narrative. While dialogue may supply exposition for readers, it must nonetheless be believable. Dialogue should be dynamic, not static, and it should not resemble regular prose. Authors should not use dialogue to write clever similes or metaphors, or to inject their own opinions. Nor should they use dialogue at all when narrative would be better; dialogue should not slow the plot movement. Dialogue must seem natural, which means careful construction of phrases rather than actually duplicating natural speech, which does not necessarily translate well to the written word. Finally, all dialogue must be pertinent to the story rather than just added conversation.

FIRST-PERSON NARRATION

First-person narratives let narrators express inner feelings and thoughts, especially when the narrator is the protagonist as Lemuel Gulliver is in Jonathan Swift's *Gulliver's Travels.* The narrator may be a close friend of the protagonist, like Dr. Watson in Arthur Conan Doyle's *Sherlock Holmes.* Or the narrator can be less involved with the main characters and plot, like Nick Carraway in F. Scott Fitzgerald's *The Great Gatsby.* When a narrator reports others' narratives secondhand or more, s/he is a "frame narrator," like the nameless narrator of Joseph Conrad's *Heart of Darkness* or Mr. Lockwood in Emily Brontë's *Wuthering Heights.* First-person plural is unusual but can be effective, as in Isaac Asimov's *I, Robot;* William Faulkner's *A Rose for Emily;* Maxim Gorky's *Twenty-Six Men and a Girl;* or Jeffrey Eugenides' *The Virgin Suicides.* Author Kurt Vonnegut is the first-person narrator in his semi-autobiographical novel *Timequake.* Also unusual but effective is a first-person omniscient (rather than the more common third-person omniscient) narrator, like Death in Markus Zusak's *The Book Thief* and the ghost in Alice Sebold's *The Lovely Bones.*

SECOND-PERSON NARRATION

While second-person address is very commonplace in popular song lyrics, it is the least used form of narrative voice in literary works. Popular serial books of the 1980s like *Fighting Fantasy* or *Choose Your Own Adventure* employed second-person narratives. In some cases, a narrative combines both second-person and first-person voices, speaking of "you" and "I." This can draw readers into the story, and it can also enable the authors to compare directly "your" and "my" feelings, thoughts, and actions. When the narrator is also a character in the story, as in Edgar Allan Poe's short story "The Tell-Tale Heart" or Jay McInerney's novel *Bright Lights, Big City,* the narrative is better defined as first-person despite its also addressing "you."

THIRD-PERSON NARRATION

Narration in the third person is the most prevalent type, as it allows authors the most flexibility. It is so common that readers simply assume without needing to be informed that the narrator is not a character in, or involved in the story. Third-person singular is used more frequently than third-person plural, though some authors have also effectively used plural. However, both singular and plural are most often included in stories according to which characters are being described. The third-person narrator may be either objective or subjective, and either omniscient or limited. Objective third-person narration does not include what the characters described are thinking or feeling, while subjective third-person narration does. The third-person omniscient narrator knows everything about all characters, including their thoughts and emotions, and all related places, times, and events, whereas the third-person limited narrator may know everything about a particular character of focus, but is limited to that character; in other words, the narrator cannot speak about anything that character does not know.

ALTERNATING-PERSON NARRATION

Although authors more commonly write stories from one point of view, there are also instances wherein they alternate the narrative voice within the same book. For example, they may sometimes use an omniscient third-person narrator and a more intimate first-person narrator at other times. In J. K. Rowling's series of *Harry Potter* novels, she often writes in a third-person limited narrative, but sometimes changes to narration by characters other than protagonist Harry Potter. George R. R. Martin's series *A Song of Ice and Fire* changes the point of view to coincide with divisions between chapters. The same technique is used by Erin Hunter (a pseudonym for several authors of the *Warriors, Seekers,* and *Survivors* book series). Authors using first-person narrative sometimes switch to third-person to describe significant action scenes, especially those where the narrator was absent or uninvolved, as Barbara Kingsolver does in her novel *The Poisonwood Bible.*

Theme and Plot

THEMES IN LITERATURE

When we read parables, their themes are the lessons they aim to teach. When we read fables, the moral of each story is its theme. When we read fictional works, the authors' perspectives regarding life and human behavior are their themes. Unlike in parables and fables, themes in literary fiction are not meant to preach or teach the readers a lesson. Hence themes in fiction are not as explicit as they are in parables or fables. Instead they are implicit, and the reader only infers them. By analyzing the fictional characters through thinking about their actions and behavior, and understanding the setting of the story and reflecting on how its plot develops, the reader comes to infer the main theme of the work. When writers succeed, they communicate with their readers such that common ground is established between author and audience. While a reader's individual experience may differ in its details from the author's written story, both may share universal underlying truths which allow author and audience to connect.

DETERMINING THEME

In well-crafted literature, theme, structure, and plot are interdependent and inextricable: each element informs and reflects the others. The structure of a work is how it is organized. The theme is the central idea or meaning found in it. The plot is what happens in the story. (Plots can be physical actions or mental processes—e.g., Marcel Proust.) Titles can also inform us of a work's theme. For instance, Edgar Allan Poe's title "The Tell-Tale Heart" informs us of its theme of guilt before we even read about the repeated heartbeat the protagonist begins hearing immediately before and constantly after committing and hiding a murder. Repetitive patterns of events or behaviors also give clues to themes. The same is true of symbols: in F. Scott Fitzgerald's *The Great Gatsby,* for Jay Gatsby the green light at the end of the dock symbolizes Daisy Buchanan and his own dreams for the future. More generally, it symbolizes the American Dream, and narrator Nick Carraway explicitly compares it to early settlers' sight of America rising from the ocean.

THEMATIC DEVELOPMENT
THEME IN THE GREAT GATSBY

In *The Great Gatsby*, F. Scott Fitzgerald portrayed 1920s America as greedy, cynical, and rife with moral decay. Jay Gatsby's lavish weekly parties symbolize the reckless excesses of the Jazz Age. The growth of bootlegging and organized crime in reaction to Prohibition is symbolized by the character of Meyer Wolfsheim and by Gatsby's own ill-gotten wealth. Fitzgerald symbolized social divisions using geography: the "old money" aristocrats like the Buchanans lived on East Egg, while the "new money" bourgeois like Gatsby lived on West Egg. Fitzgerald also used weather, as many authors have, to reinforce narrative and emotional tones in the novel. Just as in *Romeo and Juliet*, William Shakespeare set the confrontation of Tybalt and Mercutio and its deadly consequences on the hottest summer day under a burning sun, in *The Great Gatsby*, Fitzgerald did the same with Tom Wilson's deadly confrontation with Gatsby. Both works are ostensible love stories carrying socially critical themes about the destructiveness of pointless and misguided behaviors—family feuds in the former, pursuit of money in the latter.

Review Video: Thematic Development
Visit mometrix.com/academy and enter code: 576507

THEME IN LES MISÉRABLES

In Victor Hugo's novel *Les Misérables*, the overall metamorphosis of protagonist Jean Valjean from a cynical ex-convict into a noble benefactor demonstrates Hugo's theme of the importance of love and compassion for others. Hugo also reflects this in more specific plot events. For example, Valjean's love for Cosette sustains him through many difficult periods and trying events. Hugo illustrates how love and compassion for others beget the same in them: Bishop Myriel's kindness to Valjean eventually inspires him to become honest. Years later, Valjean, as M. Madeleine, has rescued Fauchelevent from under a fallen carriage, Fauchelevent returns the compassionate act by giving Valjean sanctuary in the convent. M. Myriel's kindness also ultimately enables Valjean to rescue Cosette from the Thénardiers. Receiving Valjean's father-like love enables Cosette to fall in love with and marry Marius. And the love between Cosette and Marius enables the couple to forgive Valjean for his past crimes when they are revealed.

THEME IN "THE TELL-TALE HEART"

In one of his shortest stories, "The Tell-Tale Heart," Poe used economy of language to emphasize the murderer-narrator's obsessive focus on bare details like the victim's cataract-milky eye, the sound of a heartbeat, and insistence he is sane. The narrator begins by denying he is crazy, even citing his extreme agitation as proof of sanity. Contradiction is then extended: the narrator loves the old man, yet kills him. His motives are irrational—not greed or revenge, but to relieve the victim of his "evil eye." Because "eye" and "I" are homonyms, readers may infer that eye/I symbolizes the old man's identity, contradicting the killer's delusion that he can separate them. The narrator distances himself from the old man by perceiving his eye as separate, and dismembering his dead body. This backfires in another body part when he imagines the victim's heartbeat, which is really his own. Guilty and paranoid, he gives himself away. Poe predated Freud in exploring the paradox of killing those we love and the concept of projecting our own processes onto others.

THEME IN THE WORKS OF WILLIAM FAULKNER AND CHARLES DICKENS

William Faulkner contrasts the traditions of the antebellum South with the rapid changes of post-Civil War industrialization in his short story "A Rose for Emily." Living inside the isolated world of her house, Emily Grierson denies the reality of modern progress. Contradictorily, she is both a testament to time-honored history and a mysterious, eccentric, unfathomable burden. Faulkner portrays her with deathlike imagery even in life, comparing her to a drowned woman and referring to her skeleton. Emily symbolizes the Old South; as her social status is degraded, so is the antebellum social order. Like Miss Havisham in Charles Dickens' *Great Expectations,* Emily preserves her bridal bedroom, denying change and time's passage. Emily tries to control death through denial, shown in her necrophilia with her father's corpse and her killing of Homer Barron to stop him from leaving her, then also denying his death. Faulkner uses the motif of dust

49

throughout to represent not only the decay of Emily, her house, and Old Southern traditions, but also how her secrets are obscured from others.

THEME IN MOBY-DICK

The great White Whale in *Moby-Dick* plays various roles to different characters. In Captain Ahab's obsessive, monomaniacal quest to kill it, the whale represents all evil, and Ahab believes it his duty and destiny to rid the world of it. Ishmael attempts through multiple scientific disciplines to understand the whale objectively, but fails—it is hidden underwater and mysterious to humans— reinforcing Melville's theme that humans can never know everything; here the whale represents the unknowable. Melville reverses white's usual connotation of purity in Ishmael's dread of white, associated with crashing waves, polar animals, albinos—all frightening and unnatural. White is often viewed as an absence of color, yet white light is the sum total of all colors in the spectrum. In the same way, white can signify both absence of meaning, and totality of meaning incomprehensible to humans. As a creature of nature, the whale also symbolizes how 19th-century white men's exploitative expansionistic actions were destroying the natural environment.

THEME IN THE OLD MAN AND THE SEA

Because of the old fisherman Santiago's struggle to capture a giant marlin, some people characterize Ernest Hemingway's *The Old Man and the Sea* as telling of man against nature. However, it can more properly be interpreted as telling of man's role as part of nature. Both man and fish are portrayed as brave, proud, and honorable. In Hemingway's world, all creatures, including humans, must either kill or be killed. Santiago reflects, "man can be destroyed but not defeated," following this principle in his life. As heroes are often created through their own deaths, Hemingway seems to believe that while being destroyed is inevitable, destruction enables living beings to transcend it by fighting bravely with honor and dignity. Hemingway echoes Romantic poet John Keats' contention that only immediately before death can we understand beauty as it is about to be destroyed. He also echoes ancient Greek and Roman myths and the Old Testament with the tragic flaw of overweening pride or overreaching. Like Icarus, Prometheus, and Adam and Eve, the old man "went out too far."

UNIVERSAL THEMES

The Old Testament book of Genesis, the Quran, and the Epic of Gilgamesh all contain flood stories. Versions differ somewhat: Genesis describes a worldwide flood, attributing it to God's decision that mankind, his creation, had become incontrovertibly wicked in spirit and must be destroyed for the world to start anew. The Quran describes the flood as regional, caused by Allah after sending Nuh (notice the similarity in name to Noah) as a messenger to his people to cease their evil. The Quran stipulates that Allah only destroys those who deny or ignore messages from his messengers. Marked similarities also exist: in the Gilgamesh poems Utnapishtim, like Noah, is instructed to build a ship to survive the flood. Both men send out birds afterward as tests, and both include doves and a raven, though with different outcomes. Historians and archeologists believe a Middle Eastern tidal wave was a real basis for these stories. However, their universal themes remain the same: the flood was seen as God's way of wiping out humans whose behavior had become ungodly.

THEME OF OVERREACHING

A popular theme throughout literature is the human trait of **reaching too far** or **presuming** too much. In Greek mythology, Daedalus constructed wings of feathers and wax that men might fly like birds. He permitted his son Icarus to try them, but cautioned the boy not to fly too close to the sun. The impetuous youth (in what psychologist David Elkind later named adolescence's myth of invincibility) ignored this, flying too close to the sun: the wax melted, the wings disintegrated, and Icarus fell into the sea and perished. In the Old Testament, God warned Adam and Eve not to eat `fruit from the tree of knowledge of good and evil. Because they ignored this command, they were banished from Eden's eternal perfection, condemning them to mortality and suffering. The Romans were themselves examples of overreaching in their conquest and assimilation of most of the then-known world and ultimate demise. In Christopher Marlowe's *Dr. Faustus* and Johann Wolfgang von Goethe's *Faust,* the protagonist sells his soul to the Devil for unlimited knowledge and success, ultimately leading to his own tragic end.

STORY VS. DISCOURSE

In terms of plot, "story" is the characters, places, and events originating in the author's mind, while "discourse" is how the author arranges and sequences events—which may be chronological or not. Story is imaginary; discourse is words on the page. Discourse allows story to be told in different ways. One element of plot structure is relating events differently from the order in which they occurred. This is easily done with cause-and-effect; for example, in the sentence, "He died following a long illness," we know the illness preceded the death, but the death precedes the illness in words. In Kate Chopin's short story "The Story of an Hour" (1894), she tells some of the events out of chronological order, which has the effect of amplifying the surprise of the ending for the reader. Another element of plot structure is selection. Chopin omits some details, such as Mr. Mallard's trip home; this allows readers to be as surprised at his arrival as Mrs. Mallard is.

PLOT AND MEANING

Novelist E. M. Forster has made the distinction between story as relating a series of events, such as a king dying and then his queen dying, versus plot as establishing motivations for actions and causes for events, such as a king dying and then his queen dying from grief over his death. Thus plot fulfills the function of helping readers understand cause-and-effect in events and underlying motivations in characters' actions, which in turn helps them understand life. This affects a work's meaning by supporting its ability to explain why things happen, why people do things, and ultimately the meaning of life. Some authors find that while story events convey meaning, they do not tell readers there is any one meaning in life or way of living, but rather are mental experiments with various meanings, enabling readers to explore. Hence stories may not necessarily be constructed to impose one definitive meaning, but rather to find some shape, direction, and meaning within otherwise random events.

CLASSIC ANALYSIS OF PLOT STRUCTURE

In *Poetics,* Aristotle defined plot as "the arrangement of the incidents." He meant not the story, but how it is structured for presentation. In tragedies, Aristotle found results driven by chains of cause-and-effect preferable to those driven by the protagonist's personality/character. He identified "unity of action" as necessary for a plot's wholeness; its events must be internally connected, not episodic or relying on *deus ex machina* or other external intervention. A plot must have a beginning, middle, and end. Gustav Freytag adapted Aristotle's ideas into his Triangle/Pyramid (1863). The beginning, today called the exposition/incentive/inciting moment, emphasizes causes and de-emphasizes effects. Aristotle called the ensuing cause-and-effect *desis*, or tying up, today called complications which occur during the rising action. These culminate in a crisis or climax, Aristotle's *peripateia*. This occurs at the plot's middle, where cause and effect are both emphasized. The falling action, which Aristotle called the *lusis* or unraveling, is today called the dénouement. The resolution comes at the catastrophe/outcome or end, when causes are emphasized and effects de-emphasized.

> **Review Video: Plot Line**
> Visit mometrix.com/academy and enter code: 944011

ANALYSIS OF PLOT STRUCTURES THROUGH RECURRING PATTERNS

Authors of fiction select characters, places, and events from their imaginations and arrange them in ways that will affect their readers. One way to analyze plot structure is to compare and contrast different events in a story. For example, in Kate Chopin's "The Story of an Hour," a very simple but key pattern of repetition is the husband's leaving and then returning. Such patterns fulfill the symmetrical aspect that Aristotle said was required of sound plot structure. In James Baldwin's short story, "Sonny's Blues," the narrator is Sonny's brother. In an encounter with one of Sonny's old friends early in the story, the brother initially disregards his communication. In a subsequent flashback, Baldwin informs us that this was the same way he had treated Sonny. In Nathaniel Hawthorne's "Young Goodman Brown," a pattern is created by the protagonist's recurrent efforts not to go farther into the wood; in Herman Melville's "Bartleby the Scrivener," by Bartleby's repeated refusals; and in William Faulkner's "Barn Burning," by the history of barn-burning episodes.

Drawing Inferences

MAKING INFERENCES

An **inference** is a conclusion that a reader can make based on the facts and other information in a passage or a story. An inference is based both on what is *found in a passage or a story* and what is *known from personal experience*. For instance, a story may say that a character is frightened and that he can hear the sounds of howling in the distance. Based on both what is in the text and personal knowledge, it might be a logical conclusion that the character is frightened because he hears the sound of wolves. A good inference is supported by the information in a passage. Inferences are different from **explicit information**, which is clearly stated in a passage. Inferences are not stated in a passage. A reader must put the information together to come up with a logical conclusion.

Read the excerpt and decide why Jana finally relaxed.

> Jana loved her job, but the work was very demanding. She had trouble relaxing. She called a friend, but she still thought about work. She ordered a pizza, but eating it did not help. Then her kitten jumped on her lap and began to purr. Jana leaned back and began to hum a little tune. She felt better.

You can draw the conclusion that Jana relaxes because her kitten jumped on her lap. The kitten purred, and Jana leaned back and hummed a tune. Then, she felt better. The excerpt does not explicitly say that this is the reason why she was able to relax. The text leaves the matter unclear, but the reader can infer or make a "best guess" that this is the reason she is relaxing. This is a logical conclusion based on the information in the passage. It is the best conclusion a reader can make based on the information he or she has read. Inferences are based on the information in a passage, but they are not directly stated in the passage.

Review Video: Inference
Visit mometrix.com/academy and enter code: 379203

Test-taking tip: While being tested on your ability to make correct inferences, you must look for **contextual clues**. An answer can be *true* but not *correct*. The contextual clues will help you find the answer that is the **best answer** out of the given choices. Be careful in your reading to understand the context in which a phrase is stated. When asked for the implied meaning of a statement made in the passage, you should immediately locate the statement and read the **context** in which the statement was made. Also, look for an answer choice that has a similar phrase to the statement in question.

MAKING PREDICTIONS

When reading a good passage, readers are moved to engage actively in the text. One part of being an active reader involves making predictions. A **prediction** is a guess about what will happen next. Readers constantly make predictions based on what they have read and what they already know. Consider the following sentence: *Staring at the computer screen in shock, Kim blindly reached over for the brimming glass of water on the shelf to her side.* The sentence suggests that Kim is agitated, and that she is not looking at the glass that she is going to pick up. So, a reader might predict that Kim is going to knock over the glass. Of course, not every prediction will be accurate: perhaps Kim will pick the glass up cleanly. Nevertheless, the author has certainly created the expectation that the water might be spilled. Predictions are always subject to revision as the reader acquires more information.

> **Review Video: Predictions**
> Visit mometrix.com/academy and enter code: 437248

Test-taking tip: To respond to questions requiring future predictions, your answers should be based on evidence of past or present behavior.

DRAWING CONCLUSIONS

A common type of inference that a reader has to make is **drawing a conclusion**. The reader makes this conclusion based on the information provided within a text. Certain facts are included to help a reader come to a specific conclusion. For example, a story may open with a man trudging through the snow on a cold winter day, dragging a sled behind him. The reader can logically **infer** from the setting of the story that the man is wearing heavy winter clothes in order to stay warm. Information is implied based on the setting of a story, which is why **setting** is an important element of the text. If the same man in the example was trudging down a beach on a hot summer day, dragging a surf board behind him, the reader would assume that the man is not wearing heavy clothes. The reader makes inferences based on their own experiences and the information presented to them in the story.

Test-taking tip: When asked for a *conclusion* that may be drawn, look for critical "hedge" phrases, such as *likely, may, can, will often*, among many others. When you are being tested on this knowledge, remember the question that writers insert into these hedge phrases to cover every possibility. Often an answer will be wrong simply because there is no room for exception. Extreme positive or negative answers (such as always or never) are usually not correct. The reader **should not** use any outside knowledge that is not gathered directly or reasonably inferred from the passage. Correct answers can be derived straight from the passage.

EXAMPLE

Read the following sentence and draw a conclusion based upon the information presented:

> "You know the reason Mother proposed not having any presents this Christmas was because it is going to be a hard winter for everyone; and she thinks we ought not to spend money for pleasure, when our men are suffering so in the army." (from *Little Women* by Louisa May Alcott)

Based on the information in the sentence, the reader can conclude, or **infer**, that the men are away at war while the women are still at home. The pronoun *our* gives a clue to the reader that the

character is speaking about men she knows. In addition, the reader can assume that the character is speaking to a brother or sister, since the term Mother is used by the character while speaking to another person. The reader can also come to the conclusion that the characters celebrate Christmas, since it is mentioned in the **context** of the sentence. In the sentence, the Mother is presented as an unselfish character who is opinionated and thinks about the wellbeing of other people.

COMPARING TWO STORIES

When presented with two different stories, there will be **similarities** and **differences** between the two. A reader needs to make a list or other graphic organizer of the points presented in each story. Once the reader has written down the main point and supporting points for each story, the two sets of ideas can be compared. The reader can then present each idea and show how it is the same or different in the other story. This is called **comparing and contrasting ideas**.

The reader can compare ideas by stating, for example: "In Story 1, the author believes that humankind will one day land on Mars, whereas in Story 2, the author believes that Mars is too far away for humans to ever step foot on." Note that the two viewpoints are different in each story that the reader is comparing. A reader may state that: "Both stories discussed the likelihood of humankind landing on Mars." This statement shows how the viewpoint presented in both stories is based on the same topic, rather than how each viewpoint is different. The reader will complete a comparison of two stories with a conclusion.

Literal and Figurative Language Use

LITERAL AND FIGURATIVE MEANING

When language is used literally, the words mean exactly what they say and nothing more. When language is used figuratively, the words mean something more and/or other than what they say. For example, "The weeping willow tree has long, trailing branches and leaves" is a literal description. But "The weeping willow tree looks as if it is bending over and crying" is a figurative description—specifically, a simile or stated comparison. Another figurative language form is metaphor, or an implied comparison. A good example is the metaphor of a city, state, or city-state as a ship, and its governance as sailing that ship. Ancient Greek lyrical poet Alcaeus is credited with first using this metaphor, and ancient Greek tragedian Aeschylus then used it in *Seven Against Thebes,* and then Plato used it in the *Republic.* Henry Wadsworth Longfellow later famously referred to it in his poem, "O Ship of State" (1850), which has an extended metaphor with numerous nautical references throughout.

FIGURATIVE LANGUAGE

Figurative language extends past the literal meanings of words. It offers readers new insight into the people, things, events, and subjects covered in a work of literature. Figurative language also enables readers to feel they are sharing the authors' experiences. It can stimulate the reader's senses, make comparisons that readers find intriguing or even startling, and enable readers to view the world in different ways. Seven specific types of figurative language include: alliteration, personification, imagery, similes, metaphors, onomatopoeia, and hyperbole.

Review Video: Figurative Language
Visit mometrix.com/academy and enter code: 584902

ALLITERATION, PERSONIFICATION, AND IMAGERY

Alliteration is using a series of words containing the same sounds—assonance with vowels, and consonance with consonants. Personification is describing a thing or animal as a person. Imagery is description using sensory terms that create mental images for the reader of how people, animals, or things look, sound, feel, taste, and/or smell. Alfred Tennyson's poem "The Eagle" uses all of these types of figurative language: "He clasps the crag with crooked hands." Tennyson used alliteration, repeating /k/ and /kr/ sounds. These hard-sounding consonants reinforce the imagery giving visual and tactile impressions of the eagle.

Tennyson also used personification, describing a bird as "he" and calling its talons "hands." In *Romeo and Juliet*, Shakespeare uses personification to describe the changing of the seasons: "When well-appareled April on the heel / Of limping winter treads...." Here "April" and "winter" are given the human characteristics of walking, dressing, and aging.

Review Video: Alliteration
Visit mometrix.com/academy and enter code: 462837

Review Video: Personification
Visit mometrix.com/academy and enter code: 260066

SIMILES

Similes are stated comparisons using "like" or "as." Similes can be used to stimulate readers' imaginations and appeal to their senses. By comparing fictional characters to well-known objects or experiences, the reader can better relate to them. William Wordsworth's poem about "Daffodils" begins, "I wandered lonely as a cloud." This simile compares his loneliness to that of a cloud. It is also personification, giving a cloud the human quality loneliness. In his novel *Lord Jim* (1900), Joseph Conrad writes in Chapter 33, "I would have given anything for the power to soothe her frail soul, tormenting itself in its invincible ignorance like a small bird beating about the cruel wires of a cage." Conrad uses the word "like" to compare the girl's soul to a small bird. His description of the bird beating at the cage shows the similar helplessness of the girl's soul to gain freedom.

Review Video: Simile
Visit mometrix.com/academy and enter code: 642949

METAPHORS AND ONOMATOPOEIA

Metaphor is an implied comparison that does not use "like" or "as" the way a simile does. Henry Wadsworth Longfellow echoes the ancient Greeks in "O Ship of State": the metaphor compares the state and its government to a nautical ship and its sailing. Onomatopoeia uses words imitating the sounds of things they name or describe. For example, in his poem "Come Down, O Maid," Alfred Tennyson writes of "The moan of doves in immemorial elms, / And murmuring of innumerable bees." The word "moan" sounds like some sounds doves make, "murmuring" represents the sounds of bees buzzing.

TED HUGHES' ANIMAL METAPHORS

Hughes frequently used animal metaphors in his poetry. In "The Thought Fox," a model of concise, structured beauty, Hughes characterizes the poet's creative process with succinct, striking imagery of an idea entering his head like a wild fox. Repeating "loneliness" in the first two stanzas emphasizes the poet's lonely work: "Something else is alive / Beside the clock's loneliness." He treats an idea's arrival as separate from himself. Three stanzas detail in vivid images a fox's approach from the outside winter forest at starless midnight —its nose, "Cold, delicately" touching twigs and leaves; "neat" paw prints in snow; "bold" body; brilliant green eyes; and self-contained, focused progress—"Till, with a sudden sharp hot stink of fox," he metaphorically depicts poetic inspiration as the fox's physical entry into "the dark hole of the head." Hughes ends by summarizing his vision of poet as an interior, passive idea recipient, with the outside world unchanged: "The window is starless still; the clock ticks, / The page is printed."

LITERARY EXAMPLES OF METAPHOR

A metaphor is an implied comparison, i.e. it compares something to something else without using "like", "as", or other comparative words. For example, in "The Tyger" (1794), William Blake writes, "Tyger Tyger, burning bright, / In the forests of the night." Blake compares the tiger to a flame not by saying it is like a fire, but by simply describing it as "burning." Henry Wadsworth Longfellow's poem "O Ship of State" (1850) uses an extended metaphor by referring consistently throughout the entire poem to the state, union, or republic as a seagoing vessel, referring to its keel, mast, sail, rope, anchors, and to its braving waves, rocks, gale, tempest, and "false lights on the shore". Within the extended metaphor, Wordsworth uses a specific metaphor: "the anchors of thy hope!"

> **Review Video: Metaphor**
> Visit mometrix.com/academy and enter code: 133295

HYPERBOLE

Hyperbole is excessive exaggeration used for humor or emphasis rather than for literal meaning. For example, in *To Kill a Mockingbird*, Harper Lee narrated, "People moved slowly then. There was no hurry, for there was nowhere to go, nothing to buy and no money to buy it with, nothing to see outside the boundaries of Maycomb County." This was not literally true; Lee exaggerates the scarcity of these things for emphasis. In "Old Times on the Mississippi," Mark Twain wrote, "I... could have hung my hat on my eyes, they stuck out so far." This is not literal, but makes his description vivid and funny. In his poem "As I Walked Out One Evening", W. H. Auden wrote, "I'll love you, dear, I'll love you / Till China and Africa meet, / And the river jumps over the mountain / And the salmon sing in the street." He used things not literally possible to emphasize the duration of his love.

> **Review Video: Hyperbole and Understatement**
> Visit mometrix.com/academy and enter code: 308470

LITERARY IRONY

In literature, irony demonstrates the opposite of what is said or done. Three types are verbal irony, situational irony, and dramatic irony. Verbal irony uses words opposite to the meaning. Sarcasm may use verbal irony. An everyday example is describing something confusing as "clear as mud." In his 1986 movie *Hannah and Her Sisters,* author/director/actor Woody Allen says to his character's date, "I had a great evening; it was like the Nuremburg Trials." Notice these employ similes. In situational irony, what happens contrasts with what was expected. In dramatic irony, narrative informs audiences of more than its characters know. O. Henry's short story *The Gift of the Magi* uses situational irony: a husband and wife each sacrifice their most prized possession to buy each other a Christmas present. The irony is that she sells her long hair to buy him a watch fob, while he sells his heirloom pocket-watch to buy her the jeweled combs for her hair she had long wanted; in the end, neither of them can use their gifts.

LITERARY TERMINOLOGY

In works of prose such as novels, a group of connected sentences covering one main topic is termed a paragraph. In works of poetry, a group of verses similarly connected is called a stanza. In drama, when early works used verse, these were also divided into stanzas or couplets. Drama evolved to use predominantly prose. Overall, whether prose or verse, the conversation in a play is called dialogue. Large sections of dialogue spoken by one actor are called soliloquies or monologues. Dialogue that informs audiences but is unheard by other characters is called an aside. Novels and plays share certain common elements, such as characters (the people in the story), plot (the action of the story), climax (when action and/or dramatic tension reaches its highest point), and denouement (the resolution following the climax). Sections dividing novels are called chapters, while sections of plays are called acts. Subsections of plays' acts are called scenes. Novel chapters are usually not subdivided, although some novels have larger sections divided into groups of chapters.

POETRY

Unlike prose, which traditionally (except in forms like stream of consciousness) consists of complete sentences connected into paragraphs, poetry is written in verses. These may form complete sentences, clauses, or phrases. Poetry may be written with or without rhyme. It can be metered, following a particular rhythmic pattern such as iambic, dactylic, spondaic, trochaic, or anapestic, or may be without regular meter. The terms iamb and trochee, among others, identify stressed and unstressed syllables in each verse. Meter is also described by the number of beats or stressed syllables per verse: dimeter (2), trimeter (3), tetrameter (4), pentameter (5), and so forth. Using the symbol ᴜ to denote unstressed and / to denote stressed syllables, iambic = ᴜ/; trochaic = /ᴜ; spondaic =//; dactylic =/ᴜᴜ; anapestic =ᴜᴜ/. Rhyme schemes identify which lines rhyme, such as ABAB, ABCA, AABA, and so on. Poetry with neither rhyme nor meter is called free verse. Poems may be in free verse, metered but unrhymed, rhymed but without meter, or using both rhyme and meter. In English, the most common meter is iambic pentameter. Unrhymed iambic pentameter is called blank verse.

LITERARY THEORIES AND CRITICISM AND INTERPRETATION

Literary theory gives a rationale for the literary subject matter of criticism, and also for the process of interpreting literature. For example, Aristotle's *Poetics'* requirement of unity underlies any discussion of unity in Sophocles' *Oedipus Rex.* Postcolonial theory, assuming historical racism and exploitation, informs Nigerian novelist and critic Chinua Achebe's contention that in *Heart of Darkness,* Joseph Conrad does not portray Africans with complete humanity. Gender and feminist theories support critics' interpretation of Edna Pontellier's drowning at the climax of Kate Chopin's novel *The Awakening* (1899) as suicide. Until the 19th century, critics largely believed literature referenced objective reality, holding "a mirror up to nature" as William Shakespeare wrote. Twentieth-century Structuralism and New Historicism were predated and influenced by non-traditional, historicized, cross-cultural comparative interpretations of biblical text in 19th-century German "higher criticism." Literary critic Charles Augustin Saint-Beuve maintained that biography could completely explain literature; contrarily, Marcel Proust demonstrated in narrative that art completely transformed biography. A profound 19th-century influence on literary theory was Friedrich Nietzsche's idea that facts must be interpreted to become facts.

World Literature

HISTORICAL BACKGROUND FOR ENGLISH LITERATURE

The ancient Greek Athenian elite were a highly educated society, developing philosophies and writing about principles for creating poetry and drama. During the Roman Empire, the Romans assimilated and adapted the culture of the Greeks they conquered into their own society. For example, the gods of Roman mythology were essentially the same as in Greek myth, only renamed in Latin. However, after the fall of the Roman Empire, the many European countries formerly united under Roman rule became fragmented. There followed a 1,000-year period of general public ignorance and illiteracy—called the Dark Ages as well as the Middle Ages. Only the Church remained a bastion of literacy: monks and priests laboriously copied manuscripts one at a time by hand. Johannes Gutenberg's 1450 invention of the movable-type printing press changed everything: multiple copies of books could be printed much faster. This enabled a public return to literacy, leading to the Renaissance, or "rebirth"—reviving access and interest for Greek and Roman classics, and generating a creative explosion in all arts.

MEDIEVAL POETRY

The medieval time period was heavily influenced by Greek and Latin Stoic philosophies. Medieval Christians appreciated Greek and Latin Stoic philosophies for their assigning more importance to spiritual virtues than material. Pagan stoic values were often adapted to Christian beliefs, and these were incorporated into early English literature.

GEOFFREY CHAUCER
THE CANTERBURY TALES

Medieval poet Geoffrey Chaucer (c. 1343-1400), called the "Father of English Literature," chiefly wrote long narrative poems, including *The Book of the Duchess, Anelida and Arcite, The House of Fame, The Parlement of Foules, The Legend of Good Women,* and *Troilus and Criseyde.* His most famous work is *The Canterbury Tales.* Its historical and cultural context is life during the Middle Ages, representing a cross-section of society—tradespeople, professionals, nobility, clergy, and housewives, among others—and religious pilgrimages, a common practice of the time. Its literary context is a frame-tale, a story within a story. Chaucer described a varied group of pilgrims on their way to Canterbury to visit the shrine of St. Thomas à Becket, taking turns telling stories to amuse the others. Tales encompass a broad range of subjects: bawdy comedy, chivalry, romance, and religion.

These include: *The Knight's Tale, The Miller's Tale, The Reeve's Tale, The Cook's Tale, The Man of Law's Tale, The Wife of Bath's Tale, The Friar's Tale, The Summoner's Tale, The Clerk's Tale, The Merchant's Tale, The Squire's Tale, The Franklin's Tale, The Physician's Tale, The Pardoner's Tale,* and *The Nun's Priest's Tale.*

THE PARLEMENT OF FOULES

In the brief preface to his poem "The Parlement of Foules," Chaucer refers to classic Roman author Cicero's "The Dream of Scipio," a dream-vision dialogue reflecting Stoic philosophy. Chaucer takes Cicero's broad scope of macrocosm (viewing the universe as a whole) and narrows it to a microcosm (individual focus) as he explores themes of order, disorder, and the role of humanity in nature. By using animals as characters, he is able to both parody and probe human nature for the reader.

SIR THOMAS BROWNE

Sir Thomas Browne (1605-1682) had an immeasurable influence on the development of English literature. Both his writing style and thought process were highly original. The Oxford English Dictionary credits Browne with coining over 100 new words (and quotes him in over 3,000 other

entries), such as approximate, literary, and ultimate. His creativity and vision have inspired other authors over the past four centuries and were instrumental in developing much of the vocabulary used in today's prose and poetry. In 1671 he was knighted by Charles II in recognition of his accomplishments, which continue to affect literature today.

METAPHYSICAL POETS

Dr. Samuel Johnson, a famous 18th-century figure, who wrote philosophy, poetry, and authoritative essays on literature, coined the term "Metaphysical Poets" to describe a number of mainly 17th-century lyric poets who shared certain elements of content and style in common. The poets included John Donne (considered the founder of the Metaphysical Poets), George Herbert, Andrew Marvell, Abraham Cowley, John Cleveland, Richard Crashaw, Thomas Traherne, and Henry Vaughan. These poets encouraged readers to see the world from new and unaccustomed perspectives by shocking and surprising them with paradox; contradictory imagery; original syntax; combinations of religious, philosophical, and artistic images; subtle argumentation; and extended metaphors called conceits. Unlike their contemporaries, they did not allude to classical mythology or nature imagery in their poetry, but to current geographical and scientific discoveries. Some, like Donne, showed Neo-Platonist influences—like the idea that a lover's beauty reflected Eternity's perfect beauty. They were called metaphysical for their transcendence—Donne in particular—of typical 17th-century rationalism's hierarchical organization through their adventurous exploration of religion, ideas, emotions, and language.

ROMANTICISM

The height of the Romantic movement occurred in the first half of the 19th century. It identified with and gained momentum from the French Revolution (1789) against the political and social standards of the aristocracy and its overthrowing of them. Romanticism was also part of the Counter-Enlightenment, a reaction of backlash against the Enlightenment's insistence on rationalism, scientific treatment of nature, and denial of emotionalism. Though expressed most overtly in the creative arts, Romanticism also affected politics, historiography, natural sciences, and education. Though often associated with radical, progressive, and liberal politics, it also included conservatism, especially in its influences on increased nationalism in many countries. The Romantics championed individual heroes, artists, and pioneers; freedom of expression; the exotic; and the power of the individual imagination. American authors Edgar Allan Poe and Nathaniel Hawthorne, Laurence Sterne in England, and Johann Wolfgang von Goethe in Germany were included among well-known Romantic authors. The six major English Romantic poets were William Blake, William Wordsworth, Samuel Taylor Coleridge, Lord Byron, Percy Bysshe Shelley, and John Keats.

WILLIAM BLAKE

William Blake (1757-1827) is considered one of the earliest and foremost English Romantic poets. He was also an artist and printmaker. In addition to his brilliant poetry, he produced paintings, drawings, and engravings, impressive for their technical expertise, artistic beauty, and spiritual subject matter. Because he held many idiosyncratic opinions, and moreover because he was subject to visions, reporting that he saw angels in the trees and other unusual claims, Blake was often thought crazy by others during his life. His work's creative, expressive character, and its mystical and philosophical elements, led people to consider him both precursor to and member of Romanticism, and a singular, original, unclassifiable artist at the same time. Blake illustrated most of his poetry with his own hand-colored, illuminated printing. His best-known poetry includes *Songs of Innocence and of Experience*, *The Book of Thel*, *The Marriage of Heaven and Hell*, and *Jerusalem*.

WILLIAM WORDSWORTH

William Wordsworth (1770-1850) was instrumental in establishing Romanticism when he and Samuel Taylor Coleridge collaboratively published *Lyrical Ballads* (1798). Wordsworth's "Preface to Lyrical Ballads" is considered a manifesto of English Romantic literary theory and criticism. In it, Wordsworth described the elements of a new kind of poetry, which he characterized as using "real language of men" rather than traditional 18th-century poetic style. In this Preface he also defined poetry as "the spontaneous overflow of powerful feelings [which] takes its origin from emotion recollected in tranquility." *Lyrical Ballads* included the famous works "The Rime of the Ancient Mariner" by Coleridge, and "Tintern Abbey" by Wordsworth. His semi-autobiographical poem, known during his life as "the poem to Coleridge," was published posthumously, entitled *The Prelude* and regarded as his major work. Wordsworth was England's Poet Laureate from 1843-1850. Among many others, his poems include "I Wandered Lonely as a Cloud" (often called "Daffodils"), "Ode: Intimations of Immortality," "Westminster Bridge," and "The World Is Too Much with Us."

SAMUEL TAYLOR COLERIDGE

Samuel Taylor Coleridge (1772-1834) was also a philosopher and literary critic and collaborated with William Wordsworth in launching the Romantic movement. He wrote very influential literary criticism, including the major two-volume autobiographical, meditative discourse *Biographia Literaria* (1817). Coleridge acquainted English-language intellectuals with German idealist philosophy. He also coined many now familiar philosophical and literary terms, like "the willing suspension of disbelief," meaning that readers would voluntarily withhold judgment of implausible stories if their authors could impart "human interest and a semblance of truth" to them. He strongly influenced the American Transcendentalists, including Ralph Waldo Emerson. Coleridge's poem *Love,* a ballad (written to Sara Hutchinson), inspired John Keats' poem "La Belle Dame Sans Merci." He is credited with the origin of "Conversational Poetry" and Wordsworth's adoption of it. Some of his best-known works include "The Rime of the Ancient Mariner," "Christabel," "Kubla Khan," "The Nightingale," "Dejection: An Ode," and "To William Wordsworth."

GEORGE GORDON, LORD BYRON

George Gordon Byron, commonly known as Lord Byron (1788-1824) is known for long narrative poems "Don Juan," "Childe Harold's Pilgrimage," and the shorter lyric poem "She Walks in Beauty." The aristocratic Byron travelled throughout Europe, living in Italy for seven years. He fought in the Greek War of Independence against the Ottoman Empire, making him a national hero in Greece, before dying a year later from a fever contracted there. He was the most notoriously profligate and flamboyant Romantic poet, with reckless behaviors including multiple bisexual love affairs, adultery, rumored incest, self-exile, and enormous debts. He became friends with fellow Romantic writers Percy Bysshe Shelley, the future Mary Shelley, and John Polidori. Their shared fantasy writing at a Swiss villa the summer of 1816 resulted in Mary Shelley's *Frankenstein*, Byron's *Fragment of a Novel*, and was the inspiration for Polidori's *The Vampyre*, establishing the romantic vampire genre. Byron also wrote linguistic volumes on American and Armenian grammars. His name is synonymous today with the mercurial Romantic.

PERCY BYSSHE SHELLEY

Percy Bysshe Shelley (1792-1822) was not famous during life but became so after death, particularly for his lyric poetry. His best-known works include "Ozymandias," "Ode to the West Wind," "To a Skylark," "Music," "When Soft Voices Die," "The Cloud," "The Masque of Anarchy"; longer poems "Queen Mab"/"The Daemon of the World" and "Adonaïs"; and the verse drama *Prometheus Unbound*. Shelley's second wife, Mary Shelley, was the daughter of his mentor William Godwin and the famous feminist Mary Wollstonecraft (*A Vindication of the Rights of Woman*), and became famous for her Gothic novel *Frankenstein*. Early in his career Shelley was influenced by

William Wordsworth's Romantic poetry, and wrote the long poem *Alastor, or the Spirit of Solitude.* Soon thereafter he met Lord Byron, and was inspired to write "Hymn to Intellectual Beauty". He composed "Mont Blanc," inspired by touring the French Alpine commune Chamonix-Mont-Blanc. Shelley also encouraged Byron to compose his epic poem *Don Juan.* Shelley inspired Henry David Thoreau, Mahatma Gandhi, and others to civil disobedience, nonviolent resistance, vegetarianism, and animal rights.

JOHN KEATS

John Keats (1795-1821), despite his short life, was a major English Romantic poet. He is known for his six Odes: "Ode on a Grecian Urn," "Ode on Indolence," "Ode on Melancholy," "Ode to a Nightingale," "Ode to Psyche," and "To Autumn." Other notable works include the sonnet "O Solitude," "Endymion," "La Belle Dame Sans Merci," "Hyperion," and the collection *Lamia, Isabella, The Eve of St. Agnes and Other Poems.* The intensity and maturity he achieved in only six years are often praised since his death, though during life he felt he accomplished nothing lasting. He wrote a year before dying, "I have left no immortal work behind me—nothing to make my friends proud of my memory—but I have lov'd the principle of beauty in all things, and if I had had time I would have made myself remember'd." He was proven wrong. His verse from "Ode on a Grecian Urn" is renowned: "'Beauty is truth, truth beauty'—that is all / Ye know on earth, and all ye need to know."

MODERNISM IN YEATS' POETRY

William Butler Yeats (1865-1939) was among the greatest influences in 20th-century English literature and was believed transitional from Romanticism to Modernism. His earlier verses were lyrical, but later became realistic, symbolic, and apocalyptic. He was fascinated with Irish legend, occult subjects, and historical cycles—"gyres." He incorporated Irish folklore, mythology, and legends in "The Stolen Child," "The Wanderings of Oisin," "The Death of Cuchulain," "Who Goes with Fergus?" and "The Song of Wandering Aengus." Early collections included *The Secret Rose* and *The Wind Among the Reeds.* His later, most significant poetry collections include *The Green Helmet, Responsibilities, The Tower,* and *The Winding Stair.* Yeats's visionary, apocalyptic poem "The Second Coming" (1920) reflects his belief that his times were the anarchic end of the Christian cycle/gyre: "what rough beast, its hour come round at last, / Slouches toward Bethlehem to be born?"

Poetic Themes and Devices

CARPE DIEM TRADITION IN POETRY

Carpe diem is Latin for "seize the day." A long poetic tradition, it advocates making the most of time because it passes swiftly and life is short. It is found in multiple languages, including Latin, Torquato Tasso's Italian, Pierre de Ronsard's French, and Edmund Spenser's English, and is often used in seduction to argue for indulging in earthly pleasures. Roman poet Horace's Ode 1.11 tells younger woman Leuconoe to enjoy the present, not worrying about inevitable aging. Two Renaissance Metaphysical Poets, Andrew Marvell and Robert Herrick, treated *carpe diem* more as a call to action. In "To His Coy Mistress," Marvell points out that time is fleeting, arguing for love, and concluding that because they cannot stop time, they may as well defy it, getting the most out of the short time they have. In "To the Virgins, to Make Much of Time," Herrick advises young women to take advantage of their good fortune in being young by getting married before they become too old to attract men and have babies.

"To His Coy Mistress" begins, "Had we but world enough, and time, / This coyness, lady, were no crime." Using imagery, Andrew Marvell describes leisure they could enjoy if time were unlimited. Arguing for seduction, he continues famously, "But at my back I always hear/Time's winged chariot hurrying near; / And yonder all before us lie / Deserts of vast eternity." He depicts time as turning beauty to death and decay. Contradictory images in "amorous birds of prey" and "tear our pleasures with rough strife / Through the iron gates of life" overshadow romance with impending death, linking present pleasure with mortality and spiritual values with moral considerations. Marvell's concluding couplet summarizes *carpe diem*: "Thus, though we cannot make our sun / Stand still, yet we will make him run." "To the Virgins, to Make Much of Time" begins with the famous "Gather ye rosebuds while ye may." Rather than seduction to live for the present, Robert Herrick's experienced persona advises young women's future planning: "Old time is still a-flying / And this same flower that smiles today, / Tomorrow will be dying."

COUPLETS AND METER TO ENHANCE MEANING IN POETRY

When a poet uses a couplet—a stanza of two lines, rhymed or unrhymed—it can function as the answer to a question asked earlier in the poem, or the solution to a problem or riddle. Couplets can also enhance the establishment of a poem's mood, or clarify the development of a poem's theme. Another device to enhance thematic development is irony, which also communicates the poet's tone and draws the reader's attention to a point the poet is making. The use of meter gives a poem a rhythmic context, contributes to the poem's flow, makes it more appealing to the reader, can represent natural speech rhythms, and produces specific effects. For example, in "The Song of Hiawatha," Henry Wadsworth Longfellow uses trochaic (/ ᴗ) tetrameter (four beats per line) to evoke for readers the rhythms of Native American chanting: "*By* the *shores* of *Gitch*e *Gum*ee, / *By* the *shin*ing *Big*-Sea-*Wat*er / *Stood* the *wig*wam *of* No*kom*is." (Italicized syllables are stressed; non-italicized syllables are unstressed.)

EFFECTS OF FIGURATIVE DEVICES ON MEANING IN POETRY

Through exaggeration, hyperbole communicates the strength of a poet's or persona's feelings and enhances the mood of the poem. Imagery appeals to the reader's senses, creating vivid mental pictures, evoking reader emotions and responses, and helping to develop themes. Irony also aids thematic development by drawing the reader's attention to the poet's point and communicating the poem's tone. Thematic development is additionally supported by the comparisons of metaphors and similes, which emphasize similarities, enhance imagery, and affect readers' perceptions. The use of mood communicates the atmosphere of a poem, can build a sense of tension, and evokes the reader's emotions. Onomatopoeia appeals to the reader's auditory sense and enhances sound imagery even when the poem is visual (read silently) rather than auditory (read aloud). Rhyme connects and unites verses, gives the rhyming words emphasis and makes poems more fluent. Symbolism communicates themes, develops imagery, and evokes readers' emotional and other responses.

POETIC STRUCTURE TO ENHANCE MEANING

The opening stanza of Romantic English poet, artist and printmaker William Blake's famous poem "The Tyger" demonstrates how a poet can create tension by using line length and punctuation independently of one another: "Tyger! Tyger! burning bright / In the forests of the night, / What immortal hand or eye / Could frame thy fearful symmetry?" The first three lines of this stanza are trochaic (/ᴗ), with "masculine" endings—that is, strongly stressed syllables at the ends of each of the lines. But Blake's punctuation contradicts this rhythmic regularity by not providing any divisions between the words "bright" and "In" or between "eye" and "Could." This irregular punctuation foreshadows how Blake disrupts the meter at the end of this first stanza by using a contrasting dactyl (/ᴗᴗ), with a "feminine" (unstressed) ending syllable in the last word, "symmetry." Thus Blake uses structural contrasts to heighten the intrigue of his work.

In enjambment, one sentence or clause in a poem does not end at the end of its line or verse, but runs over into the next line or verse. Clause endings coinciding with line endings give readers a feeling of completion, but enjambment influences readers to hurry to the next line to finish and understand the sentence. In his blank-verse epic religious poem "Paradise Lost," John Milton wrote: "Anon out of the earth a fabric huge / Rose like an exhalation, with the sound / Of dulcet symphonies and voices sweet, / Built like a temple, where pilasters round / Were set, and Doric pillars overlaid / With golden architrave." Only the third line is end-stopped. Milton, describing the palace of Pandemonium bursting from Hell up through the ground, reinforced this idea through phrases and clauses bursting through the boundaries of the lines. A caesura is a pause in mid-verse. Milton's commas in the third and fourth lines signal caesuras. They interrupt flow, making the narration jerky to imply that Satan's glorious-seeming palace has a shaky and unsound foundation.

REFLECTION OF CONTENT THROUGH STRUCTURE

Wallace Stevens' short yet profound poem "The Snow Man" is reductionist: the snow man is a figure without human biases or emotions. Stevens begins, "One must have a mind of winter," the criterion for realizing nature and life does not inherently possess subjective qualities; we only invest it with these. Things are not as we see them; they simply are. The entire poem is one long sentence of clauses connected by conjunctions and commas, and modified by relative clauses and phrases. The successive phrases lead readers continually to reconsider as they read. Stevens' construction of the poem mirrors the meaning he conveys. With a mind of winter, the snow man, Stevens concludes, "nothing himself, beholds nothing that is not there, and the nothing that is" (ultimate reductionism).

CONTRAST OF CONTENT AND STRUCTURE

Robert Frost's poem "Stopping by Woods on a Snowy Evening" (1923) is deceptively short and simple, with only four stanzas, each of only four lines, and short and simple words. Reinforcing this is Frost's use of regular rhyme and meter. The rhythm is iambic tetrameter throughout; the rhyme scheme is AABA in the first three stanzas and AAAA in the fourth. In an additional internal subtlety, B ending "here" in the first stanza is rhymed with A endings "queer," "near," and "year" of the second; B ending "lake" in the second is rhymed in A endings "shake", "mistake," and "flake" of the third. The final stanza's AAAA endings reinforce the ultimate darker theme. Though the first three stanzas seem to describe quietly watching snow fill the woods, the last stanza evokes the seductive pull of mysterious death: "The woods are lovely, dark and deep," countered by the obligations of living life: "But I have promises to keep, / And miles to go before I sleep, / And miles to go before I sleep." The last line's repetition strengthens Frost's message that despite death's temptation, life's course must precede it.

REPETITION TO ENHANCE MEANING

A villanelle is a nineteen-line poem composed of five tercets and one quatrain. The defining characteristic is the repetition: two lines appear repeatedly throughout the poem. In Theodore Roethke's "The Waking," the two repeated lines are "I wake to sleep, and take my waking slow," and "I learn by going where I have to go." At first these sound paradoxical, but the meaning is gradually revealed through the poem. The repetition also fits with the theme of cycle: the paradoxes of waking to sleep, learning by going, and thinking by feeling represent a constant cycle through life. They also symbolize abandoning conscious rationalism to embrace spiritual vision. We wake from the vision to "Great Nature," and "take the lively air." "This shaking keeps me steady"—another paradox—juxtaposes and balances fear of mortality with ecstasy in embracing experience. The transcendent vision of all life's interrelationship demonstrates, "What falls away is always. And is near." Readers experience the poem holistically, like music, through Roethke's integration of theme, motion, and sound.

Sylvia Plath's villanelle "Mad Girl's Love Song" narrows the scope from universal to personal but keeps the theme of cycle. The two repeated lines, "I shut my eyes and all the world drops dead" and

"(I think I made you up inside my head.)" reflect the existential viewpoint that nothing exists in any absolute reality outside of our own perceptions. In the first stanza, the middle line, "I lift my lids and all is born again," in its recreating the world, bridges between the repeated refrain statements—one of obliterating reality, the other of having constructed her lover's existence. Unlike other villanelles wherein key lines are subtly altered in their repetitions, Plath repeats these exactly each time. This reflects the young woman's love, constant throughout the poem as it neither fades nor progresses.

> **Review Video: Structural Elements of Poetry**
> Visit mometrix.com/academy and enter code: 265216

Informational Texts

LANGUAGE USE

LITERAL AND FIGURATIVE LANGUAGE

As in fictional literature, informational text also uses both **literal language**, which means just what it says, and **figurative language**, which imparts more than literal meaning. For example, an informational text author might use a simile or direct comparison, such as writing that a racehorse "ran like the wind." Informational text authors also use metaphors or implied comparisons, such as "the cloud of the Great Depression."

DENOTATIVE AND CONNOTATIVE MEANING

Similar to literal and figurative, **denotation** is the literal meaning or dictionary definition of a word whereas **connotation** is feelings or thoughts associated with a word not included in its literal definition. For example, "politician" and "statesman" have the same denotation, but in context, "politician" may have a negative connotation while "statesman" may have a positive connotation. Teachers can help students understand positive or negative connotations of words depending on their sentence contexts. For example, the word "challenge" has a positive connotation in this sentence: "Although I finished last, I still accomplished the challenge of running the race." Teachers can give students a multiple-choice game wherein they choose whether "challenge" here means (A) easy, (B) hard, (C) fun, or (D) taking work to overcome. The word "difficult" has a negative connotation in this sentence: "I finished last in the race because it was difficult." Students choose whether "difficult" here means (A) easy, (B) hard, (C) fun, or (D) lengthy. Positive and negative connotations for the same word can also be taught. Consider the following sentence: "When the teacher asked Johnny why he was in the restroom so long, he gave a *smart* answer." In this context, "smart" means disrespectful and carries a negative connotation. But in the sentence, "Johnny was *smart* to return to class from the restroom right away," the same word means wise and carries a positive connotation.

> **Review Video: Figurative Language**
> Visit mometrix.com/academy and enter code: 584902
>
> **Review Video: Denotation and Connotation**
> Visit mometrix.com/academy and enter code: 310092

EXPLICIT AND IMPLICIT INFORMATION

When informational text states something explicitly, the reader is told by the author exactly what is meant, which can include the author's interpretation or perspective of events. For example, a professor writes, "I have seen students go into an absolute panic just because they weren't able to finish administering the Peabody [Picture Vocabulary Test] in the time they were allotted." This

explicitly tells the reader that the students were afraid, and by using the words "just because," the writer indicates their fear was exaggerated out of proportion relative to what happened. However, another professor writes, "I have had students come to me, their faces drained of all color, saying 'We weren't able to finish the Peabody.'" This is an example of implicit meaning: the second writer did not state explicitly that the students were panicked. Instead, he wrote a description of their faces being "drained of all color." From this description, the reader can infer the students were so frightened that their faces paled.

Review Video: Explicit and Implicit Information
Visit mometrix.com/academy and enter code: 735771

TECHNICAL LANGUAGE

Technical language, found in scientific texts, is more impersonal than literary and vernacular language. Passive voice tone makes tone impersonal. For example, instead of writing, "We found this a central component of protein metabolism," scientists write, "This was found a central component of protein metabolism." While science professors traditionally instructed students to avoid active voice because it leads to first-person ("I" and "we") usage, science editors today find passive voice dull and weak. Many journal articles combine both. Tone in technical science writing should be detached, concise, and professional. While one writes in the vernacular, "This chemical has to be available for proteins to be digested," professionals write technically, "The presence of this chemical is required for the enzyme to break the covalent bonds of proteins."

MAKING INFERENCES ABOUT INFORMATIONAL TEXT

With informational text, reader comprehension depends not only on recalling important statements and details, but also on reader inferences based on examples and details. Readers add information from the text to what they already know to draw inferences about the text. These inferences help the readers to fill in the information that the text does not explicitly state, enabling them to understand the text better. When reading a nonfictional autobiography or biography, for example, the most appropriate inferences might concern the events in the book, the actions of the subject of the autobiography or biography, and the message the author means to convey. When reading a nonfictional expository (informational) text, the reader would best draw inferences about problems and their solutions, and causes and their effects. When reading a nonfictional persuasive text, the reader will want to infer ideas supporting the author's message and intent.

STANDARDS FOR CITING TEXTUAL EVIDENCE

Reading standards for informational texts expect sixth-graders to cite textual evidence to support their inferences and analyses. Seventh-graders are expected additionally to identify several specific pieces of textual evidence to defend each of their conclusions. Eighth-graders are expected to differentiate strong from weak textual evidence. Ninth- and 10th-graders are expected to be able to cite thorough evidence as well as strong evidence from text. Eleventh- and 12th-graders are expected, in combination with the previous grade-level standards, to determine which things are left unclear in a text. Students must be able to connect text to their background knowledge and make inferences to understand text, judge it critically, draw conclusions about it, and make their own interpretations of it. Therefore, they must be able to organize and differentiate between main ideas and details in a text to make inferences about them. They must also be able to locate evidence in the text.

PAIRED READING STRATEGY TO IDENTIFY MAIN IDEAS AND DETAILS

Students can support one another's comprehension of informational text by working in pairs. Each student silently reads a portion of text. One summarizes the text's main point, and then the other

must agree or disagree and explain why until they reach an agreement. Then each person takes a turn at identifying details in the text portion that support the main idea that they have identified. Finally, they repeat each step with their roles reversed. Each pair of students can keep track of the central ideas and supporting details by taking notes in two columns: one for main ideas and the other for the details that support those main ideas.

TEXT CODING

Some experts (cf. Harvey and Daniels, 2009) recommend text coding or text monitoring as an active reading strategy to support student comprehension of informational texts. As they read, students make text code notations on Post-it Notes or in the margins of the text. Teachers should model text coding for students one or two codes at a time until they have demonstrated all eight codes: A check mark means "I know this." An X means "This is not what I expected." An asterisk (*) means "This is important." A question mark means "I have a question about this." Two question marks mean "I am really confused about this." An exclamation point means "I am surprised at this." An L means "I have learned something new from this." And RR means "I need to reread this part."

STRUCTURES OR ORGANIZATIONAL PATTERNS IN INFORMATIONAL TEXTS

Informational text can be descriptive, invoking the five senses and answering the questions what, who, when, where, and why. Another structure of informational text is sequence and order: Chronological texts relate events in the sequence that they occurred, from start to finish, while how-to texts organize information into a series of instructions in the sequence in which the steps should be followed. Comparison-contrast structures of informational text describe various ideas to their readers by pointing out how things or ideas are similar and how they are different. Cause and effect structures of informational text describe events that occurred, and identify the causes or reasons that those events occurred. Problem and solution structures of informational text introduce and describe problems, and then offer one or more solutions for each problem described.

> **Review Video: <u>Organizational Methods to Structure Text</u>**
> Visit mometrix.com/academy and enter code: 606263

Media and Persuasion

CONNECTIONS AND DISTINCTIONS AMONG ELEMENTS IN TEXT

Students should be able to analyze how an informational text makes connections and distinctions among ideas, events, or individuals, such as by comparing them or contrasting them, making analogies between them, or dividing them into categories to show similarities and differences. For example, teachers can help eighth-graders analyze how to divide animals into categories of carnivores, which eat only meat; herbivores, which eat only plants; and omnivores, which eat both meat and plants. Teachers and students can identify the author's comparisons and contrasts of groups. Teachers can help students analyze these processes by supplying sentence frames. For example, "A _____ is a _____, so" and "A _____ is a _____ which means." The students fill these empty spaces in, such as, "A frog is a carnivore, so it eats only meat," and "A rabbit is an herbivore, which means it eats only plants."

TEXT FEATURES IN INFORMATIONAL TEXTS

The **title of a text** gives readers some idea of its content. The table of contents is a list near the beginning of a text, showing the book's sections and chapters and their coinciding page numbers. This gives readers an overview of the whole text, and helps them find specific chapters easily. An appendix, at the back of the book or document, adds important information not in the main text.

Also at the back, an index lists the book's important topics alphabetically with their page numbers to help students find them easily. Glossaries, usually found at the backs of books, list technical terms alphabetically with their definitions to aid vocabulary learning and comprehension. Boldface print is used to emphasize certain words, often identifying words included in the text's glossary where readers can look up their definitions. Headings separate sections of text and show the topic of each. Subheadings divide subject headings into smaller, more specific categories to help readers organize information. Footnotes, at the bottom of the page, give readers more information, such as citations or links. Bullet points list items separately, making facts and ideas easier to see and understand. A sidebar is a box of information to one side of the main text giving additional information, often on a more focused or in-depth example of a topic.

Illustrations and **photographs** are pictures visually emphasizing important points in text. The captions below the illustrations explain what those images show. Charts and tables are visual forms of information that make something easier and faster to understand. Diagrams are drawings that show relationships or explain a process. Graphs visually show relationships of multiple sets of information plotted along vertical and horizontal axes. Maps show geographical information visually to help students understand the relative locations of places covered in the text. Timelines are visual graphics showing historical events in chronological order to help readers see their sequence.

> **Review Video: Informative Text**
> Visit mometrix.com/academy and enter code: 924964

TECHNICAL MATERIAL FOR NON-TECHNICAL READERS

Writing about **technical subjects** for **non-technical readers** differs from writing for colleagues in that authors begin with a different goal: it may be more important to deliver a critical message than to impart the maximum technical content possible. Technical authors also must assume that non-technical audiences do not have the expertise to comprehend extremely scientific or technical messages, concepts, and terminology. They must resist the temptation to impress audiences with their scientific knowledge and expertise, and remember that their primary purpose is to communicate a message that non-technical readers will understand, feel, and respond to. Non-technical and technical styles include similarities: both should formally cite references when used and acknowledge other authors' work utilized. Both must follow intellectual property and copyright regulations. This includes the author's protecting his/her own rights, or a public domain statement, as s/he chooses.

NON-TECHNICAL AUDIENCES

Writers of technical or scientific material may need to write for many non-technical audiences. Some readers have no technical or scientific background, and those who do may not be in the same field as the authors. Government and corporate policymakers and budget managers need technical information they can understand for decision-making. Citizens affected by technology and/or science are another audience. Non-governmental organizations can encompass many of the preceding groups. Elementary and secondary school programs also need non-technical language for presenting technical subject matter. Additionally, technical authors will need to use non-technical language collecting consumer responses to surveys, presenting scientific or para-scientific material to the public, writing about the history of science, and writing about science and technology in developing countries.

USE OF EVERYDAY LANGUAGE

When authors of technical information must write about their subjects using non-technical language that readers outside their disciplinary fields can comprehend, they should not only use non-technical terms, they should also use normal, everyday language to accommodate non-native-language readers. For example, instead of writing that "eustatic changes" like "thermal expansion" causing "hazardous conditions" in the "littoral zone," an author would do better to write that a "rising sea level" is "threatening the coast." When technical terms cannot be avoided, authors should also define and/or explain them using non-technical language. Although authors must cite references and acknowledge others' work they use, they should avoid the kinds of references or citations that they would use in scientific journals—unless they reinforce author messages. They should not use endnotes, footnotes, or any other complicated referential techniques because non-technical journal publishers usually do not accept them. Including high-resolution illustrations, photos, maps, or satellite images and incorporating multimedia into digital publications will enhance public non-technical writing about technical subjects. Technical authors may publish using non-technical language in e-journals, trade journals, specialty newsletters, and daily newspapers.

EVALUATING ARGUMENTS MADE BY INFORMATIONAL TEXT WRITERS

When evaluating an informational text, the first step is to identify the argument's conclusion. Then identify the author's premises that support the conclusion. Try to paraphrase premises for clarification and make the conclusion and premises fit. List all premises first, sequentially numbered, then finish with the conclusion. Identify any premises or assumptions not stated by the author but required for the stated premises to support the conclusion. Read word assumptions sympathetically, as the author might. Evaluate whether premises reasonably support the conclusion: For inductive reasoning, the reader should ask if the premises are true, if the support the conclusion, and how strongly. For deductive reasoning, the reader should ask if the argument is valid or invalid. If all premises are true, the argument is valid unless the conclusion can be false. If it can, then the argument is invalid. Alter an invalid argument to become valid, adding any premises needed.

DETERMINING AN INFORMATIONAL AUTHOR'S PURPOSE

Informational authors' purposes are why they wrote texts. Readers must determine authors' motivations and goals. Readers gain greater insight into text by considering the author's motivation. This develops critical reading skills. Readers perceive writing as a person's voice, not simply printed words. Uncovering author motivations and purposes empowers readers to know what to expect from the text, read for relevant details, evaluate authors and their work critically, and respond effectively to the motivations and persuasions of the text. The main idea of a text is what the reader is supposed to understand from reading it; the purpose of the text is why the author has written it and what the author wants readers to do with its information. Authors state some purposes clearly, while others may be unstated but equally significant. When purposes stated contradict other parts of text, authors may have hidden agendas. Readers can better evaluate a text's effectiveness, whether they agree or disagree with it, and why they agree or disagree through identifying unstated author purposes.

> **Review Video: <u>Purpose of an Author</u>**
> Visit mometrix.com/academy and enter code: 497555

IDENTIFYING AUTHOR'S POINT OF VIEW OR PURPOSE

In some informational texts, readers find it easy to identify the author's point of view and/or purpose, as when the author explicitly states his or her position and/or reason for writing. But other texts are more difficult, either because of the content or because the authors give neutral or balanced viewpoints. This is particularly true in scientific texts, in which authors may state the purpose of their research in the report, but never state their point of view except by interpreting evidence or data.

To analyze text and identify point of view or purpose, readers should ask themselves the following four questions:

1. With what main point or idea does this author want to persuade readers to agree?
2. How do this author's choices of words affect the way that readers consider this subject?
3. How do this author's choices of examples and/or facts affect the way that readers consider this subject?
4. What is it that this author wants to accomplish by writing this text?

> **Review Video: <u>Author's Main Point or Purpose</u>**
> Visit mometrix.com/academy and enter code: 734339
>
> **Review Video: <u>Point of View</u>**
> Visit mometrix.com/academy and enter code: 383336

USE OF RHETORIC

There are many ways authors can support their claims, arguments, beliefs, ideas, and reasons for writing informational texts. For example, authors can appeal to readers' sense of logic by communicating their reasoning through a carefully sequenced series of logical steps to help "prove" the points made. Authors can appeal to readers' emotions by using descriptions and words that evoke feelings of sympathy, sadness, anger, righteous indignation, hope, happiness, or any other emotion to reinforce what they express and share with their audience. Authors may appeal to the moral or ethical values of readers by using words and descriptions that can convince readers that something is right or wrong. By relating personal anecdotes, authors can supply readers with more accessible, realistic examples of points they make, as well as appealing to their emotions. They can provide supporting evidence by reporting case studies. They can also illustrate their points by making analogies to which readers can better relate.

RHETORICAL DEVICES

- An **anecdote** is a brief story authors may relate, which can illustrate their points in a more real and relatable way.
- **Aphorisms** concisely state common beliefs and may rhyme. For example, Benjamin Franklin's "Early to bed and early to rise / Make a man healthy, wealthy, and wise" is an aphorism.
- **Allusions** refer to literary or historical figures to impart symbolism to a thing or person, and/or create reader resonance. In John Steinbeck's *Of Mice and Men,* protagonist George's last name is Milton, alluding to John Milton who wrote *Paradise Lost,* to symbolize George's eventual loss of his dream.
- **Satire** ridicules or pokes fun at human foibles or ideas, as in the works of Jonathan Swift and Mark Twain.
- A **parody** is a form of satire that imitates another work to ridicule its topic and/or style.
- A **paradox** is a statement that is true despite appearing contradictory.
- **Hyperbole** is overstatement using exaggerated language.
- An **oxymoron** combines seeming contradictions, such as "deafening silence."
- **Analogies** compare two things that share common elements.

- **Similes** (stated comparisons using the words "like" or "as") and **metaphors** (implied comparisons) are considered forms of analogy.
- When using logic to reason with audiences, **syllogism** refers either to deductive reasoning or a deceptive, very sophisticated, or subtle argument.
- **Deductive** reasoning moves from general to specific, inductive reasoning from specific to general.
- **Diction** is author word choice establishing tone and effect.
- **Understatement** achieves effects like contrast or irony by downplaying or describing something more subtly than warranted.
- **Chiasmus** uses parallel clauses, the second reversing the order of the first. Examples include T. S. Eliot's "Has the Church failed mankind, or has mankind failed the Church?" and John F. Kennedy's "Ask not what your country can do for you; ask what you can do for your country."
- **Anaphora** regularly repeats a word or phrase at the beginnings of consecutive clauses or phrases to add emphasis to an idea. A classic example of anaphora was Winston Churchill's emphasis of determination: "We shall fight in the trenches. We shall fight on the oceans. We shall fight in the sky."

EVALUATING MEDIA INFORMATION SOURCES

With the wealth of media in different formats available today, users are more likely to take media at face value. However, to understand the content of media, consumers must **critically evaluate each source**.

Users should ask themselves the following questions about media sources:

- Who is delivering this message, and why?
- What methods do a media source's publishers employ to gain and maintain users' attention?
- Which points of view is the media source representing?
- What are the various ways a message could be interpreted?
- And what information is missing from the message?
- Is the source scholarly, i.e., peer-reviewed?
- Does it include author names and their credentials pertinent to the information?
- Who publishes it, and why?
- Who is the target audience?
- Is the language technically specific or non-technical/public?
- Are sources cited, research claims documented, conclusions based on furnished evidence, and references provided?
- Is the publication current?

OTHER CONSIDERATIONS FOR THE VALIDITY OF SOURCES

For books, consider whether information is **up-to-date** and whether **historical perspectives** apply. Content is more likely to be **scholarly** if publishers are universities, government, or professional organizations. Book reviews can also provide useful information. For articles, identify the author, publisher, frequency of periodical publication, and what kind of advertising, if any, is included. Looking for book reviews also informs users. For articles, look for biographical author information; publisher name; frequency of periodical publication; and whether advertising is included and, if so, whether for certain occupations/disciplines. For web pages, check their domain names, identify publishers or sponsors (strip back URLs to uncover), look for author/publisher contact information, check dates of most recent page updates, and be alert to biases and verify information's validity. Quality and accuracy of web pages located through search engines rather than library databases ranges widely, requiring careful user inspection. Web page recommendations from reliable sources like university faculties can help indicate quality and accuracy. Citations of websites by credible or scholarly sources also show reliability. Authors' names, relevant credentials, affiliations, and contact information support their authority. Site functionality, such as ease of navigation, ability to search, site maps and/or indexes, are also criteria to consider.

PERSUASIVE MEDIA

Some media using **persuasion** are advertising, public relations, and advocacy. Advertisers use persuasion to sell goods and services. The public relations field uses persuasion to give good impressions of companies, governments, or organizations. Advocacy groups use persuasion to garner support or votes. Persuasion can come through commercials, public service announcements, speeches, websites, and newsletters, among others. Activists, lobbyists, government officials, and politicians use political rhetoric involving persuasive techniques. Basic techniques include using celebrity spokespersons, whom consumers admire or aspire to resemble; or, conversely, "everyday people" (albeit often portrayed by actors) with whom consumers identify. Using expert testimonials lends credibility. Explicit claims of content, effectiveness, quality, and reliability—which often cannot be proven or disproven—are used to persuade. While news and advocacy messages mostly eschew humor for credibility's sake (except in political satire), advertising often persuades via humor, which gets consumer attention and associates its pleasure with advertised products and services. "Weasel words," such as qualifiers, are often combined with exaggerated claims. Intensifiers—hyperbole, superlatives, and repetition—and sentimental appeals are also persuasive.

INTERMEDIATE TECHNIQUES

Dangerous propagandist Adolf Hitler said people suspect little lies more than big ones; hence the "Big Lie" is a persuasion method requiring consumers' keen critical thinking to identify. A related method is charisma, which can induce people to believe messages they would otherwise reject. Euphemism substitutes abstract, vague, or bland terms for more graphic, clear, and unpleasant ones. For example, the terms "layoffs" and "firing" are replaced by "downsizing," and "torture" is replaced with "intensive interrogation techniques." Extrapolation bases sweeping conclusions on small amounts of minor information to appeal to what consumers wish or hope. Flattery appeals to consumer self-esteem needs, such as L'Oreal's "You're worth it." Flattery is sometimes accomplished through contrast, like ads showing others' mistakes to make consumers feel superior and smarter. "Glittering generalities" are "virtue" concepts, such as beauty, love, health, democracy, freedom, and science. Persuaders hope these gain consumer acceptance without questioning what they mean. The opposite is name-calling to persuade consumers to reject someone or something.

American citizens love new ideas and technology. Persuaders exploit this by emphasizing the **newness** of products, services, and candidates. Conversely, they also use **nostalgia** to evoke consumers' happy memories, which they often remember more than unhappy ones. Citing "scientific evidence" is an intermediate version of the basic technique of expert testimonials. Consumers may accept this as proof, but some advertisers, politicians, and other persuaders may present inaccurate or misleading "evidence." Another intermediate technique is the "simple solution." Although the natures of people and life are complex, when consumers feel overwhelmed by complexity, persuaders exploit this by offering policies, products, or services they claim will solve complicated problems with simple means. Persuaders also use symbols—images, words, and names we associate with more general, emotional concepts like lifestyle, country, family, religion, and gender. While symbols have power, their significance also varies across individuals: for example, some consumers regard the Hummer SUV as a prestigious status symbol, while others regard it as environmentally harmful and irresponsible.

ADVANCED TECHNIQUES

Ad hominem, Latin for "against the man"—also called "shoot the messenger"—attacks someone delivering a message, not the message itself. It operates by association: problems with the messenger must indicate problems with the message. "Stacking the deck" misleads by presenting only selected information that supports one position. Denial evades responsibility, either directly or indirectly, for controversial or unpopular subjects: A politician saying, "I won't mention my opponent's tax evasion issues" manages to mention them while seeming less accusatory. Persuaders use majority belief, such as "Four out of five dentists recommend this brand" or the ubiquitous "[insert number] people can't be wrong." In an intensified version, persuaders exploit group dynamics at rallies, speeches, and other live-audience events where people are vulnerable to surrounding crowd influences. Scapegoating—blaming one person or group for complex problems, is a form of the intermediate "simple solution" technique, a practice common in politics. Timing also persuades, like advertising flowers and candy preceding Valentine's Day, ad campaigns preceding new technology rollouts, and politician speeches following big news events.

Foundations of Grammar

THE EIGHT PARTS OF SPEECH
NOUNS

When you talk about a person, place, thing, or idea, you are talking about **nouns**. The two main types of nouns are **common** and **proper** nouns. Also, nouns can be abstract (i.e., general) or concrete (i.e., specific).

Common nouns are the class or group of people, places, and things (Note: Do not capitalize common nouns). Examples of common nouns:

> *People*: boy, girl, worker, manager

> *Places*: school, bank, library, home

> *Things*: dog, cat, truck, car

Proper nouns are the names of a specific person, place, or thing (Note: Capitalize all proper nouns). Examples of proper nouns:

> *People*: Abraham Lincoln, George Washington, Martin Luther King, Jr.

> *Places*: Los Angeles, California / New York / Asia

> *Things*: Statue of Liberty, Earth*, Lincoln Memorial

> *Note: When you talk about the planet that we live on, you capitalize *Earth*. When you mean the dirt, rocks, or land, you lowercase *earth*.

General nouns are the names of conditions or ideas. **Specific nouns** name people, places, and things that are understood by using your senses.

General nouns:

Condition: beauty, strength

Idea: truth, peace

Specific nouns:

People: baby, friend, father

Places: town, park, city hall

Things: rainbow, cough, apple, silk, gasoline

Collective nouns are the names for a person, place, or thing that may act as a whole. The following are examples of collective nouns: *class, company, dozen, group, herd, team,* and *public.*

PRONOUNS

Pronouns are words that are used to stand in for a noun. A pronoun may be classified as personal, intensive, relative, interrogative, demonstrative, indefinite, and reciprocal.

Personal: *Nominative* is the case for nouns and pronouns that are the subject of a sentence. *Objective* is the case for nouns and pronouns that are an object in a sentence. *Possessive* is the case for nouns and pronouns that show possession or ownership.

SINGULAR

	Nominative	Objective	Possessive
First Person	I	me	my, mine
Second Person	you	you	your, yours
Third Person	he, she, it	him, her, it	his, her, hers, its

PLURAL

	Nominative	Objective	Possessive
First Person	we	us	our, ours
Second Person	you	you	your, yours
Third Person	they	them	their, theirs

Intensive: I myself, you yourself, he himself, she herself, the (thing) itself, we ourselves, you yourselves, they themselves

Relative: which, who, whom, whose

Interrogative: what, which, who, whom, whose

Demonstrative: this, that, these, those

Indefinite: all, any, each, everyone, either/neither, one, some, several

Reciprocal: each other, one another

Review Video: Nouns and Pronouns
Visit mometrix.com/academy and enter code: 312073

VERBS

If you want to write a sentence, then you need a verb in your sentence. Without a verb, you have no sentence. The verb of a sentence explains action or being. In other words, the verb shows the subject's movement or the movement that has been done to the subject.

TRANSITIVE AND INTRANSITIVE VERBS

A transitive verb is a verb whose action (e.g., drive, run, jump) points to a receiver (e.g., car, dog, kangaroo). Intransitive verbs do not point to a receiver of an action. In other words, the action of the verb does not point to a subject or object.

> **Transitive**: He plays the piano. | The piano was played by him.

> **Intransitive**: He plays. | John writes well.

A dictionary will let you know whether a verb is transitive or intransitive. Some verbs can be transitive and intransitive.

ACTION VERBS AND LINKING VERBS

An action verb is a verb that shows what the subject is doing in a sentence. In other words, an action verb shows action. A sentence can be complete with one word: an action verb. Linking verbs are intransitive verbs that show a condition (i.e., the subject is described but does no action).

Linking verbs link the subject of a sentence to a noun or pronoun, or they link a subject with an adjective. You always need a verb if you want a complete sentence. However, linking verbs are not able to complete a sentence.

Common linking verbs include *appear, be, become, feel, grow, look, seem, smell, sound,* and *taste.* However, any verb that shows a condition and has a noun, pronoun, or adjective that describes the subject of a sentence is a linking verb.

Action: He sings. | Run! | Go! | I talk with him every day. | She reads.

Linking:

> Incorrect: I am.

> Correct: I am John. | I smell roses. | I feel tired.

Note: Some verbs are followed by words that look like prepositions, but they are a part of the verb and a part of the verb's meaning. These are known as phrasal verbs and examples include *call off, look up,* and *drop off.*

VOICE

Transitive verbs come in active or passive voice. If the subject does an action or receives the action of the verb, then you will know whether a verb is active or passive. When the subject of the sentence is doing the action, the verb is **active voice**. When the subject receives the action, the verb is **passive voice**.

> **Active**: Jon drew the picture. (The subject *Jon* is doing the action of *drawing a picture.*)

> **Passive**: The picture is drawn by Jon. (The subject *picture* is receiving the action from Jon.)

74

VERB TENSES

A verb tense shows the different form of a verb to point to the time of an action. The present and past tense are shown by changing the verb's form. An action in the present *I talk* can change form for the past: *I talked*. However, for the other tenses, an auxiliary (i.e., helping) verb is needed to show the change in form. These helping verbs include *am, are, is | have, has, had | was, were, will* (or *shall*).

Present: I talk	Present perfect: I have talked
Past: I talked	Past perfect: I had talked
Future: I will talk	Future perfect: I will have talked

Present: The action happens at the current time.

> Example: He *walks* to the store every morning.

To show that something is happening right now, use the progressive present tense: I *am walking*.

Past: The action happened in the past.

> Example: He *walked* to the store an hour ago.

Future: The action is going to happen later.

> Example: I *will walk* to the store tomorrow.

Present perfect: The action started in the past and continues into the present.

> Example: I *have walked* to the store three times today.

Past perfect: The second action happened in the past. The first action came before the second.

> Example: Before I walked to the store (Action 2), I *had walked* to the library (Action 1).

Future perfect: An action that uses the past and the future. In other words, the action is complete before a future moment.

> Example: When she comes for the supplies (future moment), I *will have walked* to the store (action completed in the past).

CONJUGATING VERBS

When you need to change the form of a verb, you are **conjugating** a verb. The key parts of a verb are first person singular, present tense (dream); first person singular, past tense (dreamed); and the past participle (dreamed). Note: the past participle needs a helping verb to make a verb tense. For example, I *have dreamed* of this day. | I *am dreaming* of this day.

Present Tense: Active Voice

	Singular	**Plural**
First Person	I dream	We dream
Second Person	You dream	You dream
Third Person	He, she, it dreams	They dream

75

MOOD

There are three moods in English: the indicative, the imperative, and the subjunctive.

The **indicative mood** is used for facts, opinions, and questions.

> Fact: You can do this.

> Opinion: I think that you can do this.

> Question: Do you know that you can do this?

The **imperative** is used for orders or requests.

> Order: You are going to do this!

> Request: Will you do this for me?

The **subjunctive mood** is for wishes and statements that go against fact.

> Wish: I wish that I were going to do this.

> Statement against fact: If I were you, I would do this. (This goes against fact because I am not you. You have the chance to do this, and I do not have the chance.)

The mood that causes trouble for most people is the subjunctive mood. If you have trouble with any of the moods, then be sure to practice.

ADJECTIVES

An adjective is a word that is used to modify a noun or pronoun. An adjective answers a question: *Which one? What kind of?* or *How many?* Usually, adjectives come before the words that they modify, but they may also come after a linking verb.

> Which one? The *third* suit is my favorite.

> What kind? This suit is *navy blue*.

> How many? Can I look over the *four* neckties for the suit?

ARTICLES

Articles are adjectives that are used to mark nouns. There are only three: the **definite** (i.e., limited or fixed amount) article *the*, and the **indefinite** (i.e., no limit or fixed amount) articles *a* and *an*. Note: *An* comes before words that start with a vowel sound (i.e., vowels include *a, e, i, o, u,* and *y*). For example, "Are you going to get an **u**mbrella?"

> **Definite**: I lost *the* bottle that belongs to me.

> **Indefinite**: Does anyone have *a* bottle to share?

COMPARISON WITH ADJECTIVES

Some adjectives are relative and other adjectives are absolute. Adjectives that are **relative** can show the comparison between things. Adjectives that are **absolute** can show comparison. However, they show comparison in a different way. Let's say that you are reading two books. You think that one book is perfect, and the other book is not exactly perfect. It is not possible for the book to be more perfect than the other. Either you think that the book is perfect, or you think that the book is not perfect.

The adjectives that are relative will show the different **degrees** of something or someone to something else or someone else. The three degrees of adjectives include positive, comparative, and superlative.

The **positive** degree is the normal form of an adjective.

>   Example: This work is *difficult.* | She is *smart.*

The **comparative** degree compares one person or thing to another person or thing.

>   Example: This work is *more difficult* than your work. | She is *smarter* than me.

The **superlative** degree compares more than two people or things.

>   Example: This is the *most difficult* work of my life. | She is the *smartest* lady in school.

> **Review Video: <u>What is an Adjective?</u>**
> Visit mometrix.com/academy and enter code: 470154

ADVERBS

An adverb is a word that is used to **modify** a verb, adjective, or another adverb. Usually, adverbs answer one of these questions: *When?, Where?, How?,* and *Why?* . The negatives *not* and *never* are known as adverbs. Adverbs that modify adjectives or other adverbs **strengthen** or **weaken** the words that they modify.

Examples:

>   He walks quickly through the crowd.

>   The water flows smoothly on the rocks.

Note: While many adverbs end in *-ly,* you need to remember that not all adverbs end in *-ly.* Also, some words that end in *-ly* are adjectives, not adverbs. Some examples include: *early, friendly, holy, lonely, silly,* and *ugly.* To know if a word that ends in *-ly* is an adjective or adverb, you need to check your dictionary.

Examples:

>   He is *never* angry.

>   You talk *too* loudly.

COMPARISON WITH ADVERBS

The rules for comparing adverbs are the same as the rules for adjectives.

The **positive** degree is the standard form of an adverb.

>   Example: He arrives soon. | She speaks softly to her friends.

The **comparative** degree compares one person or thing to another person or thing.

Example: He arrives sooner than Sarah. | She speaks more softly than him.

The **superlative** degree compares more than two people or things.

Example: He arrives soonest of the group. | She speaks most softly of any of her friends.

PREPOSITIONS

A preposition is a word placed before a noun or pronoun that shows the relationship between an object and another word in the sentence.

Common prepositions:

about	before	during	on	under
after	beneath	for	over	until
against	between	from	past	up
among	beyond	in	through	with
around	by	of	to	within
at	down	off	toward	without

Examples:

The napkin is *in* the drawer.

The Earth rotates *around* the Sun.

The needle is *beneath* the haystack.

Can you find me *among* the words?

CONJUNCTIONS

Conjunctions join words, phrases, or clauses, and they show the connection between the joined pieces. **Coordinating** conjunctions connect equal parts of sentences. **Correlative** conjunctions show the connection between pairs. **Subordinating** conjunctions join subordinate (i.e., dependent) clauses with independent clauses.

COORDINATING CONJUNCTIONS

The coordinating conjunctions include: *and, but, yet, or, nor, for,* and *so*

Examples:

The rock was small, but it was heavy.

She drove in the night, and he drove in the day.

<u>CORRELATIVE CONJUNCTIONS</u>

The correlative conjunctions are: *either...or* | *neither...nor* | *not only...but also*

Examples:

Either you are coming *or* you are staying.

He ran *not only* three miles *but also* swam 200 yards.

<u>SUBORDINATING CONJUNCTIONS</u>

Common subordinating conjunctions include:

after	since	whenever
although	so that	where
because	unless	wherever
before	until	whether
in order that	when	while

Examples:

I am hungry *because* I did not eat breakfast.

He went home *when* everyone left.

INTERJECTIONS

An interjection is a word for **exclamation** (i.e., great amount of feeling) that is used alone or as a piece to a sentence. Often, they are used at the beginning of a sentence for an **introduction**. Sometimes, they can be used in the middle of a sentence to show a **change** in thought or attitude.

Common Interjections: Hey! | Oh, | Ouch! | Please! | Wow!

Agreement and Sentence Structure

SUBJECTS AND PREDICATES

SUBJECTS

Every sentence has two things: a subject and a verb. The **subject** of a sentence names who or what the sentence is all about. The subject may be directly stated in a sentence, or the subject may be the implied *you*.

The **complete subject** includes the simple subject and all of its modifiers. To find the complete subject, ask *Who* or *What* and insert the verb to complete the question. The answer is the complete subject. To find the **simple subject**, remove all of the modifiers (adjectives, prepositional phrases, etc.) in the complete subject. Being able to locate the subject of a sentence helps with many problems, such as those involving sentence fragments and subject-verb agreement.

Examples:

The small red car is the one that he wants for Christmas.

(The complete subject is *the small red car*.)

The young artist is coming over for dinner.

(The complete subject is *the young artist*.)

In **imperative** sentences, the verb's subject is understood (e.g., [You] Run to the store), but not actually present in the sentence. Normally, the subject comes before the verb. However, the subject comes after the verb in sentences that begin with *There are* or *There was*.

Direct:

John knows the way to the park.

(Who knows the way to the park? Answer: John)

The cookies need ten more minutes.

(What needs ten minutes? Answer: The cookies)

By five o' clock, Bill will need to leave.

(Who needs to leave? Answer: Bill)

Remember: The subject can come after the verb.

There are five letters on the table for him.

(What is on the table? Answer: Five letters)

There were coffee and doughnuts in the house.

(What was in the house? Answer: Coffee and doughnuts)

Implied:

Go to the post office for me.

(Who is going to the post office? Answer: You are.)

Come and sit with me, please?

(Who needs to come and sit? Answer: You do.)

PREDICATES

In a sentence, you always have a predicate and a subject. The subject tells what the sentence is about, and the **predicate** explains or describes the subject.

Think about the sentence: *He sings.* In this sentence, we have a subject (He) and a predicate (sings). This is all that is needed for a sentence to be complete. Would we like more information? Of course, we would like to know more. However, if this all the information that you are given, you have a complete sentence.

Now, let's look at another sentence:

John and Jane sing on Tuesday nights at the dance hall.

What is the subject of this sentence?

Answer: John and Jane.

What is the predicate of this sentence?

Answer: Everything else in the sentence (sing on Tuesday nights at the dance hall).

SUBJECT-VERB AGREEMENT

Verbs **agree** with their subjects in number. In other words, *singular* subjects need *singular* verbs. *Plural* subjects need *plural* verbs. Singular is for one person, place, or thing. Plural is for more than one person, place, or thing. Subjects and verbs must also agree in person: first, second, or third. The present tense ending *-s* is used on a verb if its subject is third person singular; otherwise, the verb takes no ending.

> **Review Video: <u>Subject Verb Agreement</u>**
> Visit mometrix.com/academy and enter code: 479190

NUMBER AGREEMENT EXAMPLES:

Single Subject and Verb: *Dan calls home.*

(Dan is one person. So, the singular verb *calls* is needed.)

Plural Subject and Verb: *Dan and Bob call home.*

(More than one person needs the plural verb *call.*)

PERSON AGREEMENT EXAMPLES:

First Person: I *am* walking.

Second Person: You *are* walking.

Third Person: He *is* walking.

COMPLICATIONS WITH SUBJECT-VERB AGREEMENT
WORDS BETWEEN SUBJECT AND VERB

Words that come between the simple subject and the verb may serve as an effective distraction, but they have no bearing on subject-verb agreement.

Examples:

> The joy of my life returns home tonight.
>
> (**Singular Subject**: joy. **Singular Verb**: returns)
>
> The phrase *of my life* does not influence the verb *returns*.
>
> The question that still remains unanswered is "Who are you?"
>
> (**Singular Subject**: question. **Singular Verb**: is)
>
> Don't let the phrase "*that still remains…*" trouble you. The subject *question* goes with *is*.

COMPOUND SUBJECTS

A compound subject is formed when two or more nouns joined by *and*, *or*, or *nor* jointly act as the subject of the sentence.

JOINED BY AND

When a compound subject is joined by *and*, it is treated as a plural subject and requires a plural verb.

Examples:

> You and Jon are invited to come to my house.
>
> (**Plural Subject**: You and Jon. **Plural Verb**: are)
>
> The pencil and paper belong to me.
>
> (**Plural Subject**: pencil and paper. **Plural Verb**: belong)

JOINED BY OR/NOR

For a compound subject joined by *or* or *nor*, the verb must agree in number with the part of the subject that is closest to the verb (italicized in the examples below).

Examples:

> Today or *tomorrow is* the day.
>
> (**Subject**: Today / tomorrow. **Verb**: is)
>
> Stan or *Phil wants* to read the book.
>
> (**Subject**: Stan / Phil. **Verb**: wants)
>
> Neither the books nor the *pen is* on the desk.
>
> (**Subject**: Books / Pen. **Verb**: is)

Either the blanket or *pillows arrive* this afternoon.

(**Subject**: Blanket / Pillows. **Verb**: arrive)

INDEFINITE PRONOUNS AS SUBJECT

An indefinite pronoun is a pronoun that does not refer to a specific noun. Indefinite pronouns may be only singular, be only plural, or change depending on how they are used.

ALWAYS SINGULAR

Pronouns such as *each*, *either*, *everybody*, *anybody*, *somebody*, and *nobody* are always singular.

Examples:

Each of the runners *has* a different bib number.

(**Singular Subject**: Each. **Singular Verb**: has)

Is either of you ready for the game?

(**Singular Subject**: Either. **Singular Verb**: is)

Note: The words *each* and *either* can also be used as adjectives (e.g., *each* person is unique). When one of these adjectives modifies the subject of a sentence, it is always a singular subject.

Everybody grows a day older every day.

(**Singular Subject**: Everybody. **Singular Verb**: grows)

Anybody is welcome to bring a tent.

(**Singular Subject**: Anybody. **Singular Verb**: is)

ALWAYS PLURAL

Pronouns such as *both*, *several*, and *many* are always plural.

Examples:

Both of the siblings *were* too tired to argue.

(**Plural Subject**: Both. **Plural Verb**: were)

Many have tried, but none have succeeded.

(**Plural Subject**: Many. **Plural Verb**: have tried)

DEPEND ON CONTEXT

Pronouns such as *some*, *any*, *all*, *none*, *more*, and *most* can be either singular or plural depending on what they are representing in the context of the sentence.

Examples:

> *All* of my dog's food *was* still there in his bowl

> (**Singular Subject**: All. **Singular Verb**: was)

> By the end of the night, *all* of my guests *were* already excited about coming to my next party.

> (**Plural Subject**: All. **Plural Verb**: were)

OTHER CASES INVOLVING PLURAL OR IRREGULAR FORM

Some nouns are **singular in meaning but plural in form**: news, mathematics, physics, and economics.

> The *news is* coming on now.

> *Mathematics is* my favorite class.

Some nouns are plural in form and meaning, and have **no singular equivalent**: scissors and pants.

> Do these *pants come* with a shirt?

> The *scissors are* for my project.

Mathematical operations are **irregular** in their construction, but are normally considered to be **singular in meaning**.

> *One plus one is* two.

> *Three times three is* nine.

Note: Look to your **dictionary** for help when you aren't sure whether a noun with a plural form has a singular or plural meaning.

COMPLEMENTS

A complement is a noun, pronoun, or adjective that is used to give more information about the subject or verb in the sentence.

DIRECT OBJECTS

A direct object is a noun or pronoun that takes or receives the **action** of a verb. (Remember: a complete sentence does not need a direct object, so not all sentences will have them. A sentence needs only a subject and a verb.) When you are looking for a direct object, find the verb and ask *who* or *what*.

Examples:

> I took the blanket. (Who or what did I take? *The blanket*)

> Jane read books. (Who or what does Jane read? *Books*)

INDIRECT OBJECTS

An indirect object is a word or group of words that show how an action had an **influence** on someone or something. If there is an indirect object in a sentence, then you always have a direct

object in the sentence. When you are looking for the indirect object, find the verb and ask *to/for whom or what*.

Examples:

> We taught the old dog a new trick.
>
> (To/For Whom or What was taught? *The old dog*)
>
> I gave them a math lesson.
>
> (To/For Whom or What was given? *Them*)

PREDICATE NOMINATIVES AND PREDICATE ADJECTIVES

As we looked at previously, verbs may be classified as either action verbs or linking verbs. A linking verb is so named because it links the subject to words in the predicate that describe or define the subject. These words are called predicate nominatives (if nouns or pronouns) or predicate adjectives (if adjectives).

Examples:

> My father is a *lawyer*.
>
> (Father is the **subject**. Lawyer is the **predicate nominative**.)
>
> Your mother is *patient*.
>
> (Mother is the **subject**. Patient is the **predicate adjective**.)

PRONOUN USAGE

The **antecedent** is the noun that has been replaced by a pronoun. A pronoun and its antecedent **agree** when they have the same number (singular or plural) and gender (male, female, or neuter).

Examples:

> **Singular agreement**: *John* came into town, and *he* played for us.
>
> (The word *he* replaces *John*.)
>
> **Plural agreement**: *John and Rick* came into town, and *they* played for us.
>
> (The word *they* replaces *John and Rick*.)

To determine which is the correct pronoun to use in a compound subject or object, try each pronoun **alone** in place of the compound in the sentence. Your knowledge of pronouns will tell you which one is correct.

Example:

> Bob and (I, me) will be going.
>
> Test: (1) *I will be going* or (2) *Me will be going*. The second choice cannot be correct because *me* cannot be used as the subject of a sentence. Instead, *me* is used as an object.

Answer: Bob and I will be going.

When a pronoun is used with a noun immediately following (as in "we boys"), try the sentence **without the added noun**.

Example:

(We/Us) boys played football last year.

Test: (1) *We played football last ye*ar or (2) *Us played football last year*. Again, the second choice cannot be correct because *us* cannot be used as a subject of a sentence. Instead, *us* is used as an object.

Answer: We boys played football last year.

> **Review Video: Pronoun Usage**
> Visit mometrix.com/academy and enter code: 666500

A pronoun should point clearly to the **antecedent**. Here is how a pronoun reference can be unhelpful if it is not directly stated or puzzling.

Unhelpful: Ron and Jim went to the store, and *he* bought soda.

(Who bought soda? Ron or Jim?)

Helpful: Jim went to the store, and *he* bought soda.

(The sentence is clear. Jim bought the soda.)

Some pronouns change their form by their placement in a sentence. A pronoun that is a subject in a sentence comes in the **subjective case**. Pronouns that serve as objects appear in the **objective case**. Finally, the pronouns that are used as possessives appear in the **possessive case**.

Examples:

Subjective case: *He* is coming to the show.

(The pronoun *He* is the subject of the sentence.)

Objective case: Josh drove *him* to the airport.

(The pronoun *him* is the object of the sentence.)

Possessive case: The flowers are *mine*.

(The pronoun *mine* shows ownership of the flowers.)

The word *who* is a subjective-case pronoun that can be used as a **subject**. The word *whom* is an objective-case pronoun that can be used as an **object**. The words *who* and *whom* are common in subordinate clauses or in questions.

Examples:

Subject: He knows who wants to come.

(*Who* is the subject of the verb *wants*.)

Object: He knows the man whom we want at the party.

(*Whom* is the object of *we want*.)

CLAUSES

A clause is a group of words that contains both a subject and a predicate (verb). There are two types of clauses: independent and dependent. An **independent clause** contains a complete thought, while a **dependent (or subordinate) clause** does not. A dependent clause includes a subject and a verb, and may also contain objects or complements, but it cannot stand as a complete thought without being joined to an independent clause. Dependent clauses function within sentences as adjectives, adverbs, or nouns.

Example:

Independent Clause: I am running

Dependent Clause: because I want to stay in shape

The clause *I am running* is an independent clause: it has a subject and a verb, and it gives a complete thought. The clause *because I want to stay in shape* is a dependent clause: it has a subject and a verb, but it does not express a complete thought. It adds detail to the independent clause to which it is attached.

Combined: I am running because I want to stay in shape.

> **Review Video: Clauses**
> Visit mometrix.com/academy and enter code: 940170

TYPES OF DEPENDENT CLAUSES

ADJECTIVE CLAUSES

An **adjective clause** is a dependent clause that modifies a noun or a pronoun. Adjective clauses begin with a relative pronoun (*who, whose, whom, which,* and *that*) or a relative adverb (*where, when,* and *why*).

Also, adjective clauses come after the noun that the clause needs to explain or rename. This is done to have a clear connection to the independent clause.

Examples:

I learned the reason *why I won the award.*

This is the place *where I started my first job.*

An adjective clause can be an essential or nonessential clause. An essential clause is very important to the sentence. **Essential clauses** explain or define a person or thing. **Nonessential clauses** give more information about a person or thing but are not necessary to define them. Nonessential clauses are set off with commas while essential clauses are not.

87

Examples:

> **Essential**: A person *who works hard at first* can often rest later in life.

> **Nonessential**: Neil Armstrong, *who walked on the moon*, is my hero.

ADVERB CLAUSES

An **adverb clause** is a dependent clause that modifies a verb, adjective, or adverb. In sentences with multiple dependent clauses, adverb clauses are usually placed immediately before or after the independent clause. An adverb clause is introduced with words such as *after, although, as, before, because, if, since, so, unless, when, where,* and *while*.

Examples:

> *When you walked outside*, I called the manager.

> I will go with you *unless you want to stay*.

NOUN CLAUSES

A **noun clause** is a dependent clause that can be used as a subject, object, or complement. Noun clauses begin with words such as *how, that, what, whether, which, who,* and *why*. These words can also come with an adjective clause. Unless the noun clause is being used as the subject of the sentence, it should come after the verb of the independent clause.

Examples:

> The real mystery is *how you avoided serious injury*.

> *What you learn from each other* depends on your honesty with others.

SUBORDINATION

When two related ideas are not of equal importance, the ideal way to combine them is to make the more important idea an independent clause, and the less important idea a dependent or subordinate clause. This is called **subordination**.

Example:

> **Separate ideas**: The team had a perfect regular season. The team lost the championship.

> **Subordinated**: Despite having a perfect regular season, *the team lost the championship*.

PHRASES

A phrase is a group of words that functions as a single part of speech, usually a noun, adjective, or adverb. A phrase is not a complete thought, but it adds **detail** or **explanation** to a sentence, or **renames** something within the sentence.

PREPOSITIONAL PHRASES

One of the most common types of phrases is the prepositional phrase. A **prepositional phrase** begins with a preposition and ends with a noun or pronoun that is the object of the preposition. Normally, the prepositional phrase functions as an **adjective** or an **adverb** within the sentence.

Examples:

The picnic is *on the blanket*.

I am sick *with a fever* today.

Among the many flowers, John found a four-leaf clover.

VERBAL PHRASES

A verbal is a word or phrase that is formed from a verb but does not function as a verb. Depending on its particular form, it may be used as a noun, adjective, or adverb. A verbal does **not** replace a verb in a sentence.

Examples:

Correct: *Walk* a mile daily.

(*Walk* is the verb of this sentence. The subject is the implied *you*.)

Incorrect: *To walk* a mile.

(*To walk* is a type of verbal. This is not a sentence since there is no functional verb)

There are three types of verbals: **participles**, **gerunds**, and **infinitives**. Each type of verbal has a corresponding **phrase** that consists of the verbal itself along with any complements or modifiers.

PARTICIPLES

A **participle** is a type of verbal that always functions as an adjective. The present participle always ends with -*ing*. Past participles end with -*d, -ed, -n,* or -*t.*

Examples: Verb: *dance* | Present Participle: *dancing* | Past Participle: *danced*

Participial phrases most often come right before or right after the noun or pronoun that they modify.

Examples:

Shipwrecked on an island, the boys started to fish for food.

Having been seated for five hours, we got out of the car to stretch our legs.

Praised for their work, the group accepted the first-place trophy.

GERUNDS

A **gerund** is a type of verbal that always functions as a noun. Like present participles, gerunds always end with -*ing*, but they can be easily distinguished from one another by the part of speech they represent (participles always function as adjectives). Since a gerund or gerund phrase always functions as a noun, it can be used as the subject of a sentence, the predicate nominative, or the object of a verb or preposition.

Examples:

> We want to be known for *teaching the poor*. (Object of preposition)
>
> *Coaching this team* is the best job of my life. (Subject)
>
> We like *practicing our songs* in the basement. (Object of verb)

<u>INFINITIVES</u>

An **infinitive** is a type of verbal that can function as a noun, an adjective, or an adverb. An infinitive is made of the word *to* + the basic form of the verb. As with all other types of verbal phrases, an infinitive phrase includes the verbal itself and all of its complements or modifiers.

Examples:

> *To join the team* is my goal in life. (Noun)
>
> The animals have enough food *to eat for the night*. (Adjective)
>
> People lift weights *to exercise their muscles*. (Adverb)

APPOSITIVE PHRASES

An **appositive** is a word or phrase that is used to explain or rename nouns or pronouns. Noun phrases, gerund phrases, and infinitive phrases can all be used as appositives.

Examples:

> Terriers, *hunters at heart*, have been dressed up to look like lap dogs.
>
> (The noun phrase *hunters at heart* renames the noun *terriers*.)
>
> His plan, *to save and invest his money*, was proven as a safe approach.
>
> (The infinitive phrase explains what the plan is.)

Appositive phrases can be **essential** or **nonessential**. An appositive phrase is essential if the person, place, or thing being described or renamed is too general for its meaning to be understood without the appositive.

Examples:

> **Essential**: Two Founding Fathers George Washington and Thomas Jefferson served as presidents.
>
> **Nonessential**: George Washington and Thomas Jefferson, two Founding Fathers, served as presidents.

ABSOLUTE PHRASES

An absolute phrase is a phrase that consists of **a noun followed by a participle**. An absolute phrase provides **context** to what is being described in the sentence, but it does not modify or explain any particular word; it is essentially independent.

Examples:

> *The alarm ringing*, he pushed the snooze button.

> *The music paused*, she continued to dance through the crowd.

Note: Absolute phrases can be confusing, so don't be discouraged if you have a difficult time with them.

PARALLELISM

When multiple items or ideas are presented in a sentence in series, such as in a list, the items or ideas must be stated in grammatically equivalent ways. In other words, if one idea is stated in gerund form, the second cannot be stated in infinitive form. For example, to write, *I enjoy <u>reading</u> and <u>to study</u>* would be incorrect. An infinitive and a gerund are not equivalent. Instead, you should write *I enjoy <u>reading</u> and <u>studying</u>*. In lists of more than two, it can be harder to keep straight, but all items in a list must be parallel.

Example:

> **Incorrect**: He stopped at the office, grocery store, and the pharmacy before heading home.

> The first and third items in the list of places include the article *the*, so the second item needs it as well.

> **Correct**: He stopped at the office, *the* grocery store, and the pharmacy before heading home.

Example:

> **Incorrect**: While vacationing in Europe, she went biking, skiing, and climbed mountains.

> The first and second items in the list are gerunds, so the third item must be as well.

> **Correct**: While vacationing in Europe, she went biking, skiing, and *mountain climbing*.

SENTENCE PURPOSE

There are four types of sentences: declarative, imperative, interrogative, and exclamatory.

A **declarative** sentence states a fact and ends with a period.

> Example: *The football game starts at seven o'clock.*

An **imperative** sentence tells someone to do something and generally ends with a period. (An urgent command might end with an exclamation point instead.)

> Example: *Don't forget to buy your ticket.*

An **interrogative** sentence asks a question and ends with a question mark.

> Example: *Are you going to the game on Friday?*

An **exclamatory** sentence shows strong emotion and ends with an exclamation point.

> Example: *I can't believe we won the game!*

SENTENCE STRUCTURE

Sentences are classified by structure based on the type and number of clauses present. The four classifications of sentence structure are the following:

Simple: A simple sentence has one independent clause with no dependent clauses. A simple sentence may have **compound elements** (i.e., compound subject or verb).

Examples:

> <u>Judy</u> *watered* the lawn. (single <u>subject</u>, single *verb*)
>
> <u>Judy and Alan</u> *watered* the lawn. (compound <u>subject</u>, single *verb*)
>
> <u>Judy</u> *watered* the lawn and *pulled* weeds. (single <u>subject</u>, compound *verb*)
>
> <u>Judy and Alan</u> *watered* the lawn and *pulled* weeds. (compound <u>subject</u>, compound *verb*)

Compound: A compound sentence has two or more <u>independent clauses</u> with no dependent clauses. Usually, the independent clauses are joined with a comma and a coordinating conjunction or with a semicolon.

Examples:

> <u>The time has come</u>, and <u>we are ready</u>.
>
> <u>I woke up at dawn</u>; <u>the sun was just coming up</u>.

Complex: A complex sentence has one <u>independent clause</u> and at least one *dependent clause*.

Examples:

> *Although he had the flu*, <u>Harry went to work</u>.
>
> <u>Marcia got married</u> *after she finished college*.

Compound-Complex: A compound-complex sentence has at least two <u>independent clauses</u> and at least one *dependent clause*.

Examples:

> <u>John is my friend</u> *who went to India*, and <u>he brought back souvenirs</u>.
>
> <u>You may not realize this</u>, but <u>we heard the music</u> *that you played last night*.

> **Review Video: <u>Sentence Structure</u>**
> Visit mometrix.com/academy and enter code: 700478

SENTENCE FRAGMENTS

Usually when the term *sentence fragment* comes up, it is because you have to decide whether or not a group of words is a complete sentence, and if it's not a complete sentence, you're about to have to fix it. Recall that a group of words must contain at least one **independent clause** in order to be considered a sentence. If it doesn't contain even one independent clause, it would be called a

sentence fragment. (If it contains two or more independent clauses that are not joined correctly, it would be called a run-on sentence.)

The process to use for **repairing** a sentence fragment depends on what type of fragment it is. If the fragment is a dependent clause, it can sometimes be as simple as removing a subordinating word (e.g., when, because, if) from the beginning of the fragment. Alternatively, a dependent clause can be incorporated into a closely related neighboring sentence. If the fragment is missing some required part, like a subject or a verb, the fix might be as simple as adding it in.

Examples:

Fragment: Because he wanted to sail the Mediterranean.

Removed subordinating word: He wanted to sail the Mediterranean.

Combined with another sentence: Because he wanted to sail the Mediterranean, he booked a Greek island cruise.

RUN-ON SENTENCES

Run-on sentences consist of multiple independent clauses that have not been joined together properly. Run-on sentences can be corrected in several different ways:

Join clauses properly: This can be done with a comma and coordinating conjunction, with a semicolon, or with a colon or dash if the second clause is explaining something in the first.

Example:

Incorrect: I went on the trip, we visited lots of castles.

Corrected: I went on the trip, and we visited lots of castles.

Split into separate sentences: This correction is most effective when the independent clauses are very long or when they are not closely related.

Example:

Incorrect: The drive to New York takes ten hours, my uncle lives in Boston.

Corrected: The drive to New York takes ten hours. My uncle lives in Boston.

Make one clause dependent: This is the easiest way to make the sentence correct and more interesting at the same time. It's often as simple as adding a subordinating word between the two clauses

Example:

Incorrect: I finally made it to the store and I bought some eggs.

Corrected: When I finally made it to the store, I bought some eggs.

Reduce to one clause with a compound verb: If both clauses have the same subject, remove the subject from the second clause, and you now have just one clause with a compound verb.

Example:

Incorrect: The drive to New York takes ten hours, it makes me very tired.

Corrected: The drive to New York takes ten hours and makes me very tired.

Note: While these are the simplest ways to correct a run-on sentence, often the best way is to completely reorganize the thoughts in the sentence and rewrite it.

> **Review Video: Fragments and Run-on Sentences**
> Visit mometrix.com/academy and enter code: 541989

DANGLING AND MISPLACED MODIFIERS

DANGLING MODIFIERS

A dangling modifier is a dependent clause or verbal phrase that does not have a **clear logical connection** to a word in the sentence.

Example:

Dangling: *Reading each magazine article*, the stories caught my attention.

The word *stories* cannot be modified by *Reading each magazine article*. People can read, but stories cannot read. Therefore, the subject of the sentence must be a person.

Corrected: Reading each magazine article, *I* was entertained by the stories.

Example:

Dangling: Ever since childhood, my grandparents have visited me for Christmas.

The speaker in this sentence can't have been visited by her grandparents when *they* were children, since she wouldn't have been born yet. Either the modifier should be **clarified** or the sentence should be **rearranged** to specify whose childhood is being referenced.

Clarified: Ever since I was a child, my grandparents have visited for Christmas.

Rearranged: Ever since childhood, I have enjoyed my grandparents visiting for Christmas.

MISPLACED MODIFIERS

Because modifiers are grammatically versatile, they can be put in many different places within the structure of a sentence. The danger of this versatility is that a modifier can accidentally be placed where it is modifying the wrong word or where it is not clear which word it is modifying.

Example:

Misplaced: She read the book to a crowd *that was filled with beautiful pictures.*

The book was filled with beautiful pictures, not the crowd.

Corrected: She read the book *that was filled with beautiful pictures* to a crowd.

Example:

> **Ambiguous**: Derek saw a bus nearly hit a man *on his way to work.*
>
> Was Derek on his way to work? Or was the other man?
>
> **Derek**: *On his way to work*, Derek saw a bus nearly hit a man.
>
> **The other man**: Derek saw a bus nearly hit a man *who was on his way to work.*

SPLIT INFINITIVES

A split infinitive occurs when a modifying word comes between the word *to* and the verb that pairs with *to*.

> Example: To *clearly* explain vs. *To explain* clearly | To *softly* sing vs. *To sing* softly

Though considered improper by some, split infinitives may provide better clarity and simplicity in some cases than the alternatives. As such, avoiding them should not be considered a universal rule.

DOUBLE NEGATIVES

Standard English allows **two negatives** only when a **positive** meaning is intended. For example, *The team was not displeased with their performance.* Double negatives to emphasize negation are not used in standard English.

> **Negative modifiers** (e.g., never, no, and not) should not be paired with other negative modifiers or negative words (e.g., none, nobody, nothing, or neither). The modifiers *hardly, barely*, and *scarcely* are considered negatives in standard English, so they should not be used with other negatives.

Punctuation

END PUNCTUATION

PERIODS

Use a period to end all sentences except direct questions, exclamations.

DECLARATIVE SENTENCE

A declarative sentence gives information or makes a statement.

> Examples: I can fly a kite. | The plane left two hours ago.

IMPERATIVE SENTENCE

An imperative sentence gives an order or command.

> Examples: You are coming with me. | Bring me that note.

PERIODS FOR ABBREVIATIONS

> Examples: 3 P.M. | 2 A.M. | Mr. Jones | Mrs. Stevens | Dr. Smith | Bill Jr. | Pennsylvania Ave.

Note: an abbreviation is a shortened form of a word or phrase.

QUESTION MARKS

Question marks should be used following a direct question. A polite request can be followed by a period instead of a question mark.

> **Direct Question**: What is for lunch today? | How are you? | Why is that the answer?

> **Polite Requests**: Can you please send me the item tomorrow. | Will you please walk with me on the track.

EXCLAMATION MARKS

Exclamation marks are used after a word group or sentence that shows much feeling or has special importance. Exclamation marks should not be overused. They are saved for proper **exclamatory interjections**.

> Example: We're going to the finals! | You have a beautiful car! | That's crazy!

COMMAS

The comma is a punctuation mark that can help you understand connections in a sentence. Not every sentence needs a comma. However, if a sentence needs a comma, you need to put it in the right place. A comma in the wrong place (or an absent comma) will make a sentence's meaning unclear. These are some of the rules for commas:

1. Use a comma **before a coordinating conjunction** joining independent clauses
   Example: Bob caught three fish, and I caught two fish.

2. Use a comma after an introductory phrase or an adverbial clause
   Examples:
   > *After the final out,* we went to a restaurant to celebrate.
   > *Studying the stars,* I was surprised at the beauty of the sky.

96

3. Use a comma between items in a series.

    Example: I will bring the turkey, the pie, and the coffee.

4. Use a comma **between coordinate adjectives** not joined with *and*

    Incorrect: The kind, brown dog followed me home.
    Correct: The *kind, loyal* dog followed me home.
    Not all adjectives are **coordinate** (i.e., equal or parallel). There are two simple ways to know if your adjectives are coordinate. One, you can join the adjectives with *and*: *The kind and loyal dog*. Two, you can change the order of the adjectives: *The loyal, kind dog.*

5. Use commas for **interjections** and **after *yes* and *no*** responses

    Examples:

    > **Interjection**: Oh, I had no idea. | Wow, you know how to play this game.
    > **Yes and No**: *Yes,* I heard you. | *No,* I cannot come tomorrow.

6. Use commas to separate nonessential modifiers and nonessential appositives

    Examples:

    > **Nonessential Modifier**: John Frank, who is coaching the team, was promoted today.
    > **Nonessential Appositive**: Thomas Edison, an American inventor, was born in Ohio.

7. Use commas to set off nouns of direct address, interrogative tags, and contrast

    Examples:

    > **Direct Address**: You, *John,* are my only hope in this moment.
    > **Interrogative Tag**: This is the last time, *correct*?
    > **Contrast**: You are my friend, *not my enemy.*

8. Use commas with dates, addresses, geographical names, and titles

    Examples:

    > **Date**: *July 4, 1776,* is an important date to remember.
    > **Address**: He is meeting me at *456 Delaware Avenue, Washington, D.C.,* tomorrow morning.
    > **Geographical Name**: *Paris, France,* is my favorite city.
    > **Title**: John Smith, *Ph. D.,* will be visiting your class today.

9. Use commas to **separate expressions like *he said* and *she said*** if they come between a sentence of a quote

    Examples:

    > "I want you to know," he began, "that I always wanted the best for you."
    > "You can start," Jane said, "with an apology."

> **Review Video: Commas**
> Visit mometrix.com/academy and enter code: 786797

SEMICOLONS

The semicolon is used to connect major sentence pieces of equal value. Some rules for semicolons include:

1. Use a semicolon **between closely connected independent clauses** that are not connected with a coordinating conjunction.

   Examples:

   > She is outside; we are inside.
   > You are right; we should go with your plan.

2. Use a semicolon **between independent clauses linked with a transitional word.**

   Examples:

   > I think that we can agree on this; *however,* I am not sure about my friends.
   > You are looking in the wrong places; *therefore,* you will not find what you need.

3. Use a semicolon **between items in a series that has internal punctuation.**

   Example: I have visited New York, New York; Augusta, Maine; and Baltimore, Maryland.

> **Review Video: <u>Semicolon Usage</u>**
> Visit mometrix.com/academy and enter code: 370605

COLONS

The colon is used to call attention to the words that follow it. A colon must come after a **complete independent clause**. The rules for colons are as follows:

1. Use a colon after an independent clause to **make a list**

   Example: I want to learn many languages: Spanish, German, and Italian.

2. Use a colon for **explanations** or to **give a quote**

   Examples:

   > **Quote**: He started with an idea: "We are able to do more than we imagine."
   > **Explanation**: There is one thing that stands out on your resume: responsibility.

3. Use a colon **after the greeting in a formal letter**, to **show hours and minutes**, and to **separate a title and subtitle**

   Examples:

   > **Greeting in a formal letter**: Dear Sir: | To Whom It May Concern:
   > **Time**: It is 3:14 P.M.
   > **Title**: The essay is titled "America: A Short Introduction to a Modern Country"

PARENTHESES

Parentheses are used for additional information. Also, they can be used to put labels for letters or numbers in a series. Parentheses should be not be used very often. If they are overused, parentheses can be a distraction instead of a help.

Examples:

> **Extra Information**: The rattlesnake (see Image 2) is a dangerous snake of North and South America.

> **Series**: Include in the email (1) your name, (2) your address, and (3) your question for the author.

QUOTATION MARKS

Use quotation marks to close off **direct quotations** of a person's spoken or written words. Do not use quotation marks around indirect quotations. An indirect quotation gives someone's message without using the person's exact words. Use **single quotation marks** to close off a quotation inside a quotation.

> **Direct Quote**: Nancy said, "I am waiting for Henry to arrive."

> **Indirect Quote**: Henry said that he is going to be late to the meeting.

> **Quote inside a Quote**: The teacher asked, "Has everyone read 'The Gift of the Magi'?"

Quotation marks should be used around the titles of **short works**: newspaper and magazine articles, poems, short stories, songs, television episodes, radio programs, and subdivisions of books or web sites.

Examples:

> "Rip van Winkle" (short story by Washington Irving)

> "O Captain! My Captain!" (poem by Walt Whitman)

Although it is not standard usage, quotation marks are sometimes used to highlight **irony**, or the use of words to mean something other than their dictionary definition. This type of usage should be employed sparingly, if at all.

Examples:

> The boss warned Frank that he was walking on "thin ice."

> (Frank is not walking on real ice. Instead, Frank is being warned to avoid mistakes.)

> The teacher thanked the young man for his "honesty."

> (In this example, the quotation marks around *honesty* show that the teacher does not believe the young man's explanation.)

Review Video: Quotation Marks
Visit mometrix.com/academy and enter code: 884918

Periods and commas are put **inside** quotation marks. Colons and semicolons are put **outside** the quotation marks. Question marks and exclamation points are placed inside quotation marks when they are part of a quote. When the question or exclamation mark goes with the whole sentence, the mark is left outside of the quotation marks.

Examples:

Period and comma: We read "The Gift of the Magi," "The Skylight Room," and "The Cactus."

Semicolon: They watched "The Nutcracker"; then, they went home.

Exclamation mark that is a part of a quote: The crowd cheered, "Victory!"

Question mark that goes with the whole sentence: Is your favorite short story "The Tell-Tale Heart"?

APOSTROPHES

An apostrophe is used to show **possession** or the **deletion of letters in contractions**. An apostrophe is not needed with the possessive pronouns *his, hers, its, ours, theirs, whose*, and *yours*.

Singular Nouns: David's car | a book's theme | my brother's board game

Plural Nouns with *-s*: the scissors' handle | boys' basketball

Plural Nouns without *-s*: Men's department | the people's adventure

> **Review Video: <u>Apostrophes</u>**
> Visit mometrix.com/academy and enter code: 213068
>
> **Review Video: <u>Punctuation Errors in Possessive Pronouns</u>**
> Visit mometrix.com/academy and enter code: 221438

HYPHENS

Hyphens are used to **separate compound words**. Use hyphens in the following cases:

1. **Compound numbers** between 21 and 99 when written out in words
   Example: This team needs *twenty-five* points to win the game.

2. **Written-out fractions** that are used as **adjectives**
   Correct: The recipe says that we need a *three-fourths* cup of butter.
   Incorrect: *One-fourth* of the road is under construction.

3. Compound words used as **adjectives that come before a noun**
   Correct: The *well-fed* dog took a nap.
   Incorrect: The dog was *well-fed* for his nap.

4. Compound words that would be **hard to read** or **easily confused with other words**
   Examples: Semi-irresponsible | Anti-itch | Re-sort

Note: This is not a complete set of the rules for hyphens. A dictionary is the best tool for knowing if a compound word needs a hyphen.

DASHES

Dashes are used to show a **break** or a **change in thought** in a sentence or to act as parentheses in a sentence. When typing, use two hyphens to make a dash. Do not put a space before or after the dash. The following are the rules for dashes:

1. To set off **parenthetical statements** or an **appositive with internal punctuation**

   Example: The three trees—oak, pine, and magnolia—are coming on a truck tomorrow.

2. To show a **break or change in tone or thought**

   Example: The first question—how silly of me—does not have a correct answer.

ELLIPSIS MARKS

The ellipsis mark has three periods (...) to show when **words have been removed** from a quotation. If a full sentence or more is removed from a quoted passage, you need to use four periods to show the removed text and the end punctuation mark. The ellipsis mark should not be used at the beginning of a quotation. The ellipsis mark should also not be used at the end of a quotation unless some words have been deleted from the end of the final sentence.

Example:

"Then he picked up the groceries...paid for them...later he went home."

BRACKETS

There are two main reasons to use brackets:

1. When **placing parentheses inside of parentheses**

   Example: The hero of this story, Paul Revere (a silversmith and industrialist [see Ch. 4]), rode through towns of Massachusetts to warn of advancing British troops.

2. When adding **clarification or detail** to a quotation that is **not part of the quotation**
   Example:

   The father explained, "My children are planning to attend my alma mater [State University]."

Common Errors

WORD CONFUSION

WHICH, THAT, AND WHO

Which is used for things only.

> Example: John's dog, *which was called Max,* is large and fierce.

That is used for people or things.

> Example: Is this the only book *that Louis L'Amour wrote?*

> Example: Is Louis L'Amour the author *that wrote Western novels?*

Who is used for people only.

> Example: Mozart was the composer *who wrote those operas.*

HOMOPHONES

Homophones are words that sound alike (or similar), but they have different **spellings** and **definitions**.

TO, TOO, AND TWO

To can be an adverb or a preposition for showing direction, purpose, and relationship. See your dictionary for the many other ways use *to* in a sentence.

> Examples: I went to the store. | I want to go with you.

Too is an adverb that means *also, as well, very, or more than enough.*

> Examples: I can walk a mile too. | You have eaten too much.

Two is the second number in the series of numbers (e.g., one (1), two, (2), three (3)…)

> Example: You have two minutes left.

THERE, THEIR, AND THEY'RE

There can be an adjective, adverb, or pronoun. Often, *there* is used to show a place or to start a sentence.

> Examples: I went there yesterday. | There is something in his pocket.

Their is a pronoun that is used to show ownership.

> Examples: He is their father. | This is their fourth apology this week.

They're is a contraction of *they are.*

> Example: Did you know that they're in town?

KNEW AND NEW

Knew is the past tense of *know*.

> Example: I knew the answer.

New is an adjective that means something is current, has not been used, or modern.

> Example: This is my new phone.

THEN AND THAN

Then is an adverb that indicates sequence or order:

> Example: I'm going to run to the library and then come home.

Than is special-purpose word used only for comparisons:

> Example: Susie likes chips better than candy.

ITS AND IT'S

Its is a pronoun that shows ownership.

> Example: The guitar is in its case.

It's is a contraction of *it is*.

> Example: It's an honor and a privilege to meet you.

Note: The *h* in honor is silent, so the sound of the vowel *o* must have the article *an*.

YOUR AND YOU'RE

Your is a pronoun that shows ownership.

> Example: This is your moment to shine.

You're is a contraction of *you are*.

> Example: Yes, you're correct.

AFFECT AND EFFECT

There are two main reasons that **affect** and **effect** are so often confused: 1) both words can be used as either a noun or a verb, and 2) unlike most homophones, their usage and meanings are closely related to each other. Here is a quick rundown of the four usage options:

Affect (n): feeling, emotion, or mood that is displayed

> Example: The patient had a flat *affect*. (i.e., his face showed little or no emotion)

Affect (v): to alter, to change, to influence

> Example: The sunshine *affects* the plant's growth.

Effect (n): a result, a consequence

> Example: What *effect* will this weather have on our schedule?

Effect (v): to bring about, to cause to be

Example: These new rules will *effect* order in the office.

The noun form of *affect* is rarely used outside of technical medical descriptions, so if a noun form is needed on the test, you can safely select *effect*. The verb form of *effect* is not as rare as the noun form of *affect*, but it's still not all that likely to show up on your test. If you need a verb and you can't decide which to use based on the definitions, choosing *affect* is your best bet.

HOMOGRAPHS

Homographs are words that share the same spelling, and they have multiple meanings. To figure out which meaning is being used, you should be looking for context clues. The context clues give hints to the meaning of the word. For example, the word *spot* has many meanings. It can mean "a place" or "a stain or blot." In the sentence "After my lunch, I saw a spot on my shirt," the word *spot* means "a stain or blot." The context clues of "After my lunch..." and "on my shirt" guide you to this decision.

BANK

(noun): an establishment where money is held for savings or lending

(verb): to collect or pile up

CONTENT

(noun): the topics that will be addressed within a book

(adjective): pleased or satisfied

FINE

(noun): an amount of money that acts a penalty for an offense

(adjective): very small or thin

INCENSE

(noun): a material that is burned in religious settings and makes a pleasant aroma

(verb): to frustrate or anger

LEAD

(noun): the first or highest position

(verb): to direct a person or group of followers

OBJECT

(noun): a lifeless item that can be held and observed

(verb): to disagree

PRODUCE

(noun): fruits and vegetables

(verb): to make or create something

REFUSE

> (noun): garbage or debris that has been thrown away

> (verb): to not allow

SUBJECT

> (noun): an area of study

> (verb): to force or subdue

TEAR

> (noun): a fluid secreted by the eyes

> (verb): to separate or pull apart

Modes of Writing

ESSAYS

The basic format of an essay can be said to have three major parts: the introduction, the body, and the conclusion. The body is further divided into the writer's main points. Short and simple essays may have three main points, while essays covering broader ranges and going into more depth can have almost any number of main points, depending on length.

An essay's introduction should answer three questions: (1) What is the subject of the essay? If a student writes an essay about a book, the answer would include the title and author of the book and any additional information needed—such as the subject or argument of the book. (2) How does the essay address the subject? To answer this, the writer identifies the essay's organization by briefly summarizing main points and/or evidence supporting them. (3) What will the essay prove? This is the thesis statement, usually the opening paragraph's last sentence, clearly stating the writer's message.

The body elaborates on all the main points related to the thesis and supporting evidence, introducing one main point at a time. Each body paragraph should state the point, explain its meaning, support it with quotations or other evidence, and then explain how this point and the evidence are related to the thesis. The writer should then repeat this procedure in a new paragraph for each additional main point. In addition to relating each point to the thesis, clearly restating the thesis in at least one sentence of each paragraph is also advisable.

The conclusion reiterates the content of the introduction, including the thesis, to review them for the reader. The essay writer may also summarize the highlights of the argument or description contained in the body of the essay, following the same sequence originally used in the body. For example, a conclusion might look like: Point 1 + Point 2 + Point 3 = Thesis, or Point 1 → Point 2 → Point 3 → Thesis Proof. Good organization makes essays easier for writers to compose and provides a guide for readers to follow. Well-organized essays hold attention better, and are more likely to get readers to accept their theses as valid.

Review Video: Reading Essays
Visit mometrix.com/academy and enter code: 169166

INFORMATIVE/EXPLANATORY VS. ARGUMENTATIVE WRITING

Informative/explanatory writing begins with the basis that something is true or factual, while argumentative writing strives to prove something that may or may not be true or factual. Whereas argument is intended to persuade readers to agree with the author's position, informative/explanatory text merely provides information and insight to readers. Informative/explanatory writing concentrates on informing readers about why or how something is as it is. This includes offering new information, explaining how a process works, and/or developing a concept for readers. In accomplishing these objectives, the writing may emphasize naming and differentiating various things within a category; providing definitions of things; providing details about the parts of something; explaining a particular function or behavior; and giving readers explanations for why a fact, object, event, or process exists or occurs.

Review Video: Argumentative Writing
Visit mometrix.com/academy and enter code: 561544

NECESSARY SKILLS FOR INFORMATIVE/EXPLANATORY WRITING

For students to write in informative/explanatory mode, they must be able to locate and select pertinent information from primary and secondary sources. They must also combine their own experiences and existing knowledge with this new information they find. They must not only select facts, details, and examples relevant to their topics, but also learn to incorporate this information into their writing. Students need at the same time to develop their skills in various writing techniques, such as comparing and contrasting, making transitions between topics/points, and citing scenarios and anecdotes related to their topics. In teaching explanatory/informative writing, teachers must "read like writers" to use mentor texts to consider author craft and technique. They can find mentor texts in blogs, websites, newspapers, novels, plays, picture books, and many more. Teachers should know the grade-level writing standards for informative/explanatory writing to select classroom-specific, appropriate mentor texts.

Review Video: Informative Text
Visit mometrix.com/academy and enter code: 924964

NARRATIVE WRITING

Put simply, narrative writing tells a story. The most common examples of literary narratives are novels. Non-fictional biographies, autobiographies, memoirs, and histories also use narrative. Narratives should tell stories in such a way that the readers learn something, or gain insight or understanding. Students can write more interesting narratives by relating events or experiences that were meaningful to them. Narratives should not begin with long descriptions or introductions, but start with the actions or events. Students should ensure that there is a point to each story by describing what they learned from the experience they narrate. To write effective description, students should include sensory details, asking themselves what they saw, heard, felt/touched, smelled, and tasted during the experiences they describe. In narrative writing, the details should be concrete rather than abstract. Using concrete details enables readers to imagine everything that the writer describes.

Review Video: Narratives
Visit mometrix.com/academy and enter code: 280100

SENSORY DETAILS

Students need vivid description to write descriptive essays. Narratives should also include description of characters, things, and events. Students should remember to describe not only the visual detail of what someone or something looks like, but details from other senses as well. For example, they can contrast the feelings of a sea breeze versus a mountain breeze, describe how they think something inedible would taste, and sounds they hear in the same location at different times of day and night. Readers have trouble visualizing images or imagining sensory impressions and feelings from abstract descriptions, so concrete descriptions make these more real.

CONCRETE VS. ABSTRACT DESCRIPTIONS IN NARRATIVE

Concrete language provides information that readers can grasp and may empathize with, while **abstract language**, which is more general, can leave readers feeling disconnected, empty, or even confused. "It was a lovely day" is abstract, but "The sun shone brightly, the sky was blue, the air felt warm, and a gentle breeze wafted across my skin" is concrete. "Ms. Couch was a good teacher" uses abstract language, giving only a general idea of the writer's opinion. But "Ms. Couch is excellent at helping us take our ideas and turn them into good essays and stories" uses concrete language, giving more specific examples of what makes Ms. Couch a good teacher. "I like writing poems but not essays" gives readers a general idea that the student prefers one genre over another, but not why. But by saying, "I like writing short poems with rhythm and rhyme, but I hate writing five-page essays that go on and on about the same ideas," readers understand that the student prefers the brevity, rhyme, and meter of short poetry over the length and redundancy of longer prose.

JOURNALS AND DIARIES

A **journal** is a personal account of events, experiences, feelings, and thoughts. Many people write journals to confide their feelings and thoughts or to help them process experiences they have had. Since journals are **private documents** not meant for sharing with others, writers may not be concerned with grammar, spelling, or other mechanics. However, authors may write journals that they expect or hope to publish someday; in this case, they not only express their thoughts and feelings and process their experiences, but they additionally attend to their craft in writing them. Some authors compose journals to document particular time periods or series of related events, such as a cancer diagnosis, treatment, surviving the disease, and how these experiences have changed/affected them; experiences in recovering from addiction; journeys of spiritual exploration and discovery; trips to or time spent in another country; or anything else someone wants to personally document. Journaling can also be therapeutic: some people use them to work through feelings of grief over loss or to wrestle with big decisions.

The Diary of a Young Girl by Dutch Jew Anne Frank (1947) contains her life-affirming, nonfictional diary entries from 1942-1944 while her family hid in an attic from World War II's genocidal Nazis. *Go Ask Alice* (1971) by Beatrice Sparks is a cautionary, fictional novel in the form of diary entries by an unhappy, rebellious teen who takes LSD, runs away from home and lives with hippies, and eventually returns home. Frank's writing reveals an intelligent, sensitive, insightful girl, raised by intellectual European parents—a girl who believes in the goodness of human nature despite surrounding atrocities. Character Alice, influenced by early 1970s counterculture, becomes less optimistic. However, similarities can be found: Frank dies in a Nazi concentration camp while the fictitious Alice dies in a drug overdose; both are unable to escape their surroundings. Additionally, adolescent searches for personal identity are evident in both books.

> **Review Video: Journals and Diaries, Letters, Blogs**
> Visit mometrix.com/academy and enter code: 432845

107

LETTERS

Letters are messages written to other people. In addition to letters written between individuals, some writers compose letters to the editors of newspapers, magazines, and other publications; some write "Open Letters" to be published and read by the general public. Open letters, while intended for everyone to read, may also identify a group of people or a single person whom the letter directly addresses. In everyday use, the most-used forms are business letters and personal or friendly letters. Both kinds share common elements: business or personal letterhead stationery; the writer's return address at the top; the addressee's address next; a salutation, such as "Dear [name]" or some similar opening greeting, followed by a colon in business letters or a comma in personal letters; the body of the letter, with paragraphs as indicated; and a closing, like "Sincerely/Cordially/Best regards/etc." or "Love," in intimate personal letters.

The Greek word for "letter" is *epistolē*, which became the English word "epistle." The earliest letters were called epistles, including the New Testament's Epistles from the Apostles to the Christians. In ancient Egypt, the writing curriculum in scribal schools included the epistolary genre. Epistolary novels frame a story in the form of letters. For example, 18th-century English novelist Samuel Richardson wrote the popular epistolary novels *Pamela* (1740) and *Clarissa* (1749). Henry Fielding's satire of *Pamela,* entitled *Shamela* (1741) mocked epistolary writing. French author Montesquieu wrote *Lettres persanes* (1721); Jean-Jacques Rousseau wrote *Julie, ou la nouvelle Héloïse* (1761); and Pierre Choderlos de Laclos penned *Les Liaisons dangereuses* (1782), which was adapted into a screenplay for the multiple Oscar-winning 1988 English-language movie *Dangerous Liaisons*. German author Johann Wolfgang von Goethe wrote *The Sorrows of Young Werther* in epistolary form. Frances Brooke also wrote the first North American novel, *The History of Emily Montague* (1769) using epistolary form. In the 19th century, epistolary novels included Honoré de Balzac's *Letters of Two Brides* (1842) and Mary Shelley's *Frankenstein* (1818).

BLOGS

The word "blog" is derived from "web log" and refers to writing done exclusively on the Internet. Readers of reputable newspapers expect quality content and layouts that enable easy reading. These expectations also apply to blogs. For example, readers can easily move visually from line to line when columns are narrow; overly wide columns cause readers to lose their places. Blogs must also be posted with layouts enabling online readers to follow them easily. However, because the way people read on computer, tablet, and smartphone screens differs from how they read print on paper, formatting and writing blog content is more complex than writing newspaper articles. Two major principles are the bases for blog-writing rules: (1) While readers of print articles skim to estimate their length, online they must scroll down to scan; therefore, blog layouts need more subheadings, graphics, and other indications of what information follows. (2) Onscreen reading is harder than reading printed paper, so legibility is crucial in blogs.

RULES AND RATIONALES FOR WRITING BLOGS

Expert web designer, copywriter, and blogger Annabel Cady (http://www.successfulblogging.com/) shares the following blog-posting rules: Format all posts for smooth page layout and easy scanning. Column width should be a maximum of 80 characters, including spaces, for easier reading. Headings and subheadings separate text visually, enable scanning or skimming, and encourage continued reading. Bullet-pointed or numbered lists enable quick information location and scanning. Punctuation is critical, so beginners should use shorter sentences until confident. Blog paragraphs should be far shorter—two to six sentences each—than paragraphs written on paper to enable "chunking" because reading onscreen is more difficult. Sans serif fonts are usually clearer than serif fonts, and larger font sizes are better. Highlight important material and draw attention with **boldface**, but avoid overuse. Avoid hard-to-read *italics* and ALL

CAPITALS. Include enough blank spaces: overly busy blogs tire eyes and brains. Images not only break up text, but also emphasize and enhance text, and can attract initial reader attention. Use background colors judiciously to avoid distracting the eye or making it difficult to read. Be consistent throughout posts, since people read them in different orders. Tell a story with a beginning, middle, and end.

Outlining and Organizing Ideas

MAIN IDEAS, SUPPORTING DETAILS, AND OUTLINING A TOPIC

A writer often begins the first paragraph of a paper by stating the **main idea** or point, also known as the **topic sentence**. The rest of the paragraph supplies particular details that develop and support the main point. One way to visualize the relationship between the main point and supporting information is as a table: the tabletop is the main point, and each of the table's legs is a supporting detail or group of details. Both professional authors and students can benefit from planning their writing by first making an outline of the topic. Outlines facilitate quick identification of the main point and supporting details without having to wade through the additional language that will exist in the fully developed essay, article, or paper. Outlining can also help readers to analyze a piece of existing writing for the same reason. The outline first summarizes the main idea in one sentence. Then, below that, it summarizes the supporting details in a numbered list. Writing the paper then consists of filling in the outline with detail, writing a paragraph for each supporting point and adding an introduction and conclusion.

SEQUENCE WORDS AND PHRASES

When a paragraph opens with the topic sentence, the second sentence may begin with a phrase like "First of all," introducing the first supporting detail/example. The writer may introduce the second supporting item with words or phrases like "Also," "In addition," and "Besides." The writer might introduce succeeding pieces of support with wording like, "Another thing," "Moreover" "Furthermore," or "Not only that, but." The writer may introduce the last piece of support with "Lastly," "Finally," or "Last but not least." Writers get off the point by presenting "off-target" items not supporting the main point. For example, a main point "My dog is not smart" is supported by the statement, "He's six years old and still doesn't answer to his name." But "He cries when I leave for school" is not supportive, as it does not indicate lack of intelligence. Writers stay on point by presenting only supportive statements that are directly relevant to and illustrative of their main point.

PARAGRAPHS

A **paragraph** is a group of sentences that forms a unit separate from (but connected to) other paragraphs. Typically, all of one paragraph's sentences relate to **one main idea or point**. Two major properties that make paragraphs effective or ineffective are focus and development, or lack thereof. Paragraphs with poor focus impede comprehension because the sentences seem unrelated. When writers attempt to include too many ideas in a paragraph rather than focusing on the most important idea, or fail to supply transitions between ideas, they produce unfocused paragraphs. Undeveloped or inadequately-developed paragraphs may use good writing, but are still not effective. When a writer misunderstands the audience, depends overly on generalization, and fails to offer specific details, paragraph development will be poor. S/he may omit key term definitions, supporting evidence, setting description, context for others' ideas, background, and other important details, falsely assuming that readers already know these things.

WRITING EFFECTIVE PARAGRAPHS

The first thing a writer should do for a good paragraph is to **focus on one main idea** as the subject. A writer may introduce a paragraph by stating this main idea in a topic sentence. However, the main idea may be so obvious that writers can imply it rather than state it overtly and readers can easily infer it. Second, a writer should use specific details to develop the main idea. **Details** should capture readers' attention and also explain the author's ideas. Insufficient detail makes a paragraph too abstract, which readers find boring or confusing. Excessive detail makes a paragraph unfocused, which readers find overwhelming and also confusing. Third, a writer should develop paragraphs using structural patterns.

> **Review Video: Writing Paragraphs, Structural Patterns**
> **(Narration, Compare and Contrast), and Coherence**
> Visit mometrix.com/academy and enter code: 682127

STRUCTURAL PATTERNS

Paragraphs have a nearly limitless range of structures, but certain patterns appear more often, including narration, description, definition, example and illustration, division and classification, comparison and contrast, analogy, cause and effect, and process.

NARRATION, DESCRIPTION, DEFINITION, EXAMPLE AND ILLUSTRATION, AND DIVISION AND CLASSIFICATION

In **narration**, a paragraph's main idea is developed with a story. Writers may use stories as anecdotal evidence to support the main point. In description, the writer constructs a clear image of a scene or event by including specific, sensory and other details that depict a person, thing, place, and/or time. Description shows readers instead of telling them. In definition, the writer provides a detailed explanation of a term that is central to the piece of writing. In example and illustration, the writer provides the readers with one or more examples that illustrate the point that the writer wants to make. Paragraphs using division divide a concept into its component parts—for example, body parts or experiment steps. Paragraphs using classification group separate things into categories by their similarities—such as mammals and insects, tragedies and comedies, and so on.

COMPARISON AND CONTRAST, ANALOGY, CAUSE AND EFFECT, AND PROCESS

Paragraphs that **compare** two or more things make note of their **similarities**. Paragraphs that **contrast** two or more things make note of **how they differ**. Another common paragraph technique is both comparing and contrasting two or more items within the same paragraph, showing both similarities and differences. Analogy compares two things in an unusual way, often things that belong to very different categories. This can afford new reader insight. Writers may use analogies to develop their ideas. Writers also develop their ideas in paragraphs through cause and effect, which either explains what caused some event or result, or shows the effects that something produced. Paragraphs may start with causes and proceed to effects, or begin with effects and then give causes. Process paragraphs describe and/or explain some process. They often sequence the stages, phases, or steps of the process using chronological order.

COHERENCE

When a paragraph is coherent, the details fit together so that readers can clearly understand the main point, and its parts flow well. Writers produce more coherent paragraphs when they select structural patterns appropriate to the conceptual content. There are several techniques writers can use to make paragraphs more coherent. Repetition connects sentences by repeating key words or phrases. This not only helps sentences flow together, but it also signals to readers the significance of the ideas these words and phrases communicate. Parallelism uses parallel structure, within or between sentences. Humorist Bill Maher once said, "We're feeding animals too sick to stand to

people too fat to walk." His parallelism emphasized and connected two issues: the practice of using downed cows as food and the obesity epidemic. Consistency keeps the viewpoint, tone, and linguistic register consistent within the paragraph or piece. Finally, transitions via connective words and phrases aid coherence immensely.

TRANSITIONS

Transitions between sentences and paragraphs guide readers from idea to idea. They also indicate relationships between sentences and paragraphs. Writers should be judicious in their use of transitions, inserting them sparingly. They should also be selected to fit the author's purpose—transitions can indicate time, comparison, and conclusion, among other purposes.

> **Review Video: Transitions in Writing**
> Visit mometrix.com/academy and enter code: 233246

TYPES OF TRANSITIONAL WORDS

Time	Afterward, immediately, earlier, meanwhile, recently, lately, now, since, soon, when, then, until, before, etc.
Sequence	too, first, second, further, moreover, also, again, and, next, still, too, besides, and finally
Comparison	similarly, in the same way, likewise, also, again, and once more
Contrasting	but, although, despite, however, instead, nevertheless, on the one hand... on the other hand, regardless, yet, and in contrast.
Cause and Effect	because, consequently, thus, therefore, then, to this end, since, so, as a result, if... then, and accordingly
Examples	for example, for instance, such as, to illustrate, indeed, in fact, and specifically
Place	near, far, here, there, to the left/right, next to, above, below, beyond, opposite, and beside
Concession	granted that, naturally, of course, it may appear, and although it is true that
Repetition, Summary, or Conclusion	as mentioned earlier, as noted, in other words, in short, on the whole, to summarize, therefore, as a result, to conclude, and in conclusion

> **Review Video: Transitional Words and Phrases**
> Visit mometrix.com/academy and enter code: 197796

INTRODUCTION

The purpose of the introduction is to capture the reader's attention and announce the essay's main idea. Normally, the introduction contains 50-80 words, or 3-5 sentences. An introduction can begin with an interesting quote, a question, or a strong opinion—something that will **engage** the reader's interest and prompt them to keep reading. If you are writing your essay to a specific prompt, your introduction should include a **restatement or summarization** of the prompt so that the reader will have some context for your essay. Finally, your introduction should briefly state your **thesis or main idea**: the primary thing you hope to communicate to the reader through your essay. Don't try to include all of the details and nuances of your thesis, or all of your reasons for it, in the introduction. That's what the rest of the essay is for!

> **Review Video: Introduction**
> Visit mometrix.com/academy and enter code: 961328

111

THESIS STATEMENT

The thesis is the main idea of the essay. A temporary thesis should be established early in the writing process because it will serve to keep the writer focused as ideas develop. This temporary thesis is subject to change as you continue to write.

The temporary thesis has two parts: a topic (i.e., the focus of your essay based on the prompt) and a comment. The comment makes an important point about the topic. A temporary thesis should be interesting and specific. Also, you need to limit the topic to a manageable scope. These three criteria are useful tools to measure the effectiveness of any temporary thesis:

- Does the focus of my essay have enough interest to hold an audience?
- Is the focus of my essay specific enough to generate interest?
- Is the focus of my essay manageable for the time limit? Too broad? Too narrow?

The thesis should be a generalization rather than a fact because the thesis prepares readers for facts and details that support the thesis. The process of bringing the thesis into sharp focus may help in outlining major sections of the work. Once the thesis and introduction are complete, you can address the body of the work.

> **Review Video: Thesis Statements**
> Visit mometrix.com/academy and enter code: 691033

SUPPORTING THE THESIS

Throughout your essay, the thesis should be **explained clearly and supported** adequately by additional arguments. The thesis sentence needs to contain a clear statement of the purpose of your essay and a comment about the thesis. With the thesis statement, you have an opportunity to state what is noteworthy of this particular treatment of the prompt. Each sentence and paragraph should build on and support the thesis.

When you respond to the prompt, use parts of the passage to support your argument or defend your position. With supporting evidence from the passage, you strengthen your argument because readers can see your attention to the entire passage and your response to the details and facts within the passage. You can use facts, details, statistics, and direct quotations from the passage to uphold your position. Be sure to point out which information comes from the original passage and base your argument around that evidence.

BODY

In an essay's introduction, the writer establishes the thesis and may indicate how the rest of the piece will be structured. In the body of the piece, the writer **elaborates** upon, **illustrates**, and **explains** the **thesis statement**. How writers sequence supporting details and their choices of paragraph types are development techniques. Writers may give examples of the concept introduced in the thesis statement. If the subject includes a cause-and-effect relationship, the author may explain its causality. A writer will explain and/or analyze the main idea of the piece throughout the body, often by presenting arguments for the veracity or credibility of the thesis statement. Writers may use development to define or clarify ambiguous terms. Paragraphs within the body may be organized with natural sequences, like space and time. Writers may employ inductive reasoning,

using multiple details to establish a generalization or causal relationship, or deductive reasoning, proving a generalized hypothesis or proposition through a specific example/case.

Review Video: Drafting Body Paragraphs
Visit mometrix.com/academy and enter code: 724590

PARAGRAPHS

After the introduction of a passage, a series of body paragraphs will carry a message through to the conclusion. A paragraph should be **unified around a main point**. Normally, a good topic sentence summarizes the paragraph's main point. A topic sentence is a general sentence that gives an introduction to the paragraph.

The sentences that follow are a support to the topic sentence. However, the topic sentence can come as the final sentence to the paragraph if the earlier sentences give a clear explanation of the topic sentence. Overall, the paragraphs need to stay true to the main point. This means that any unnecessary sentences that do not advance the main point should be removed.

The main point of a paragraph requires adequate development (i.e., a substantial paragraph that covers the main point). A paragraph of two or three sentences does not cover a main point. This is true when the main point of the paragraph gives strong support to the argument of the thesis. An occasional short paragraph is fine as a transitional device. However, a well-developed argument will have paragraphs with more than a few sentences.

METHODS OF DEVELOPING PARAGRAPHS

A common method of development with paragraphs can be done with **examples**. These examples are the supporting details to the main idea of a paragraph or a passage. When authors write about something that their audience may not understand, they can provide an example to show their point. When authors write about something that is not easily accepted, they can give examples to prove their point.

- **Illustrations** are extended examples that require several sentences. Well selected illustrations can be a great way for authors to develop a point that may not be familiar to their audience.
- **Analogies** make comparisons between items that appear to have nothing in common. Analogies are employed by writers to provoke fresh thoughts about a subject. These comparisons may be used to explain the unfamiliar, to clarify an abstract point, or to argue a point. Although analogies are effective literary devices, they should be used carefully in arguments. Two things may be alike in some respects but completely different in others.
- **Cause and effect** is an excellent device used when the cause and effect are accepted as true. One way that authors can use cause and effect is to state the effect in the topic sentence of a paragraph and add the causes in the body of the paragraph. With this method, an author's paragraphs can have structure which always strengthens writing.

TYPES OF PARAGRAPHS

A **paragraph of narration** tells a story or a part of a story. Normally, the sentences are arranged in chronological order (i.e., the order that the events happened). However, flashbacks (i.e., beginning the story at an earlier time) can be included.

A **descriptive paragraph** makes a verbal portrait of a person, place, or thing. When specific details are used that appeal to one or more of the senses (i.e., sight, sound, smell, taste, and touch), authors give readers a sense of being present in the moment.

A **process paragraph** is related to time order (i.e., First, you open the bottle. Second, you pour the liquid, etc.). Usually, this describes a process or teaches readers how to perform a process.

Comparing two things draws attention to their similarities and indicates a number of differences. When authors contrast, they focus only on differences. Both comparisons and contrasts may be used point-by-point or in following paragraphs.

Reasons for starting a new paragraph include:

1. To mark off the introduction and concluding paragraphs
2. To signal a shift to a new idea or topic
3. To indicate an important shift in time or place
4. To explain a point in additional detail
5. To highlight a comparison, contrast, or cause and effect relationship

PARAGRAPH LENGTH

Most readers find that their comfort level for a paragraph is between 100 and 200 words. Shorter paragraphs cause too much starting and stopping, and give a choppy effect. Paragraphs that are too long often test the attention span of readers. Two notable exceptions to this rule exist. In scientific or scholarly papers, longer paragraphs suggest seriousness and depth. In journalistic writing, constraints are placed on paragraph size by the narrow columns in a newspaper format.

The first and last paragraphs of a text will usually be the introduction and conclusion. These special-purpose paragraphs are likely to be shorter than paragraphs in the body of the work. Paragraphs in the body of the essay follow the subject's outline; one paragraph per point in short essays and a group of paragraphs per point in longer works. Some ideas require more development than others, so it is good for a writer to remain flexible. A paragraph of excessive length may be divided, and shorter ones may be combined.

COHERENT PARAGRAPHS

A smooth flow of sentences and paragraphs without gaps, shifts, or bumps will lead to paragraph coherence. Ties between old and new information can be smoothed by several methods:

- Linking ideas clearly, from the topic sentence to the body of the paragraph, is essential for a smooth transition. The topic sentence states the main point, and this should be followed by specific details, examples, and illustrations that support the topic sentence. The support may be direct or indirect. In indirect support, the illustrations and examples may support a sentence that in turn supports the topic directly.
- The repetition of key words adds coherence to a paragraph. To avoid dull language, variations of the key words may be used.
- Parallel structures are often used within sentences to emphasize the similarity of ideas and connect sentences giving similar information.
- Maintaining a consistent verb tense throughout the paragraph helps. Shifting tenses affects the smooth flow of words and can disrupt the coherence of the paragraph.

CONCLUSION

Two important principles to consider when writing a conclusion are strength and closure. A strong conclusion gives the reader a sense that the author's main points are meaningful and important, and that the supporting facts and arguments are convincing, solid, and well developed. When a conclusion achieves closure, it gives the impression that the writer has stated what needed stating and completed the work, rather than simply stopping after a specified length. Some things to avoid when writing concluding paragraphs include: introducing a completely new idea, beginning with obvious or unoriginal phrases like "In conclusion" or "To summarize," apologizing for one's opinions or writing, repeating the thesis word for word rather than rephrasing it, and believing that the conclusion must always summarize the piece.

> **Review Video: Drafting Conclusions**
> Visit mometrix.com/academy and enter code: 209408

Style and Form

WRITING STYLE AND LINGUISTIC FORM

Linguistic form encodes the literal meanings of words and sentences. It comes from the phonological, morphological, syntactic, and semantic parts of a language. **Writing style** consists of different ways of encoding the meaning and indicating figurative and stylistic meanings.

Writers' stylistic choices accomplish three basic effects on their audiences:

1. They **communicate meanings** beyond linguistically dictated meanings,
2. they communicate the **author's attitude**, such as persuasive/argumentative effects accomplished through style, and
3. they communicate or **express feelings**.

Within style, component areas include: narrative structure; viewpoint; focus; sound patterns; meter and rhythm; lexical and syntactic repetition and parallelism; writing genre; representational, realistic, and mimetic effects; representation of thought and speech; meta-representation (representing representation); irony; metaphor and other indirect meanings; representation and use of historical and dialectal variations; gender-specific and other group-specific speech styles, both real and fictitious; and analysis of the processes for inferring meaning from writing.

LEVEL OF FORMALITY

The relationship between writer and reader is important in choosing a **level of formality** as most writing requires some degree of formality. **Formal writing** is for addressing a superior in a school or work environment. Business letters, textbooks, and newspapers use a moderate to high level of formality. **Informal writing** is appropriate for private letters, personal e-mails, and business correspondence between close associates.

For your exam, you will want to be aware of informal and formal writing. One way that this can be accomplished is to watch for shifts in point of view in the essay. For example, unless writers are using a personal example, they will rarely refer to themselves (e.g., "*I* think that *my* point is very clear.") to avoid being informal when they need to be formal.

Also, be mindful of an author who addresses his or her audience **directly** in their writing (e.g., "Readers, *like you*, will understand this argument.") as this can be a sign of informal writing. Good writers understand the need to be consistent with their level of formality. Shifts in levels of formality or point of view can confuse readers and cause them to discount the message.

CLICHÉS

Clichés are phrases that have been **overused** to the point that the phrase has no importance or has lost the original meaning. The phrases have no originality and add very little to a passage. Therefore, most writers will avoid the use of clichés. Another option is to make changes to a cliché so that it is not predictable and empty of meaning.

Examples:

When life gives you lemons, make lemonade.

Every cloud has a silver lining.

JARGON

Jargon is a **specialized vocabulary** that is used among members of a trade or profession. Since jargon is understood by only a small audience, writers will use jargon in passages that will only be read by a specialized audience. For example, medical jargon should be used in a medical journal but not in a New York Times article. Jargon includes exaggerated language that tries to impress rather than inform. Sentences filled with jargon are not precise and difficult to understand.

Examples:

"He is going to *toenail* these frames for us." (Toenail is construction jargon for nailing at an angle.)

"They brought in a *kip* of material today." (Kip refers to 1000 pounds in architecture and engineering.)

SLANG

Slang is an **informal** and sometimes private language that is understood by some individuals. Slang has some usefulness, but the language can have a small audience. So, most formal writing will not include this kind of language.

Examples:

"Yes, the event was a blast!" (In this sentence, *blast* means that the event was a great experience.)

"That attempt was an epic fail." (By *epic fail*, the speaker means that his or her attempt was not a success.)

COLLOQUIALISM

A colloquialism is a word or phrase that is found in informal writing. Unlike slang, **colloquial language** will be familiar to a greater range of people. Colloquial language can include some slang, but these are limited to contractions for the most part.

Examples:

"Can *y'all* come back another time?" (Y'all is a contraction of "you all" which has become a colloquialism.)

"Will you stop him from building this *castle in the air*?" (A "castle in the air" is an improbable or unlikely event.)

TONE

Tone may be defined as the writer's **attitude** toward the topic, and to the audience. This attitude is reflected in the language used in the writing. The tone of a work should be **appropriate to the topic** and to the intended audience. Some texts should not contain slang or jargon, although these may be fine in a different piece. Tone can range from humorous to serious and all levels in between. It may be more or less formal, depending on the purpose of the writing and its intended audience. All these nuances in tone can flavor the entire writing and should be kept in mind as the work evolves.

WORD SELECTION

A writer's choice of words is a **signature** of their style. Careful thought about the use of words can improve a piece of writing. A passage can be an exciting piece to read when attention is given to the use of vivid or specific nouns rather than general ones. When using an active verb, one should be sure that the verb is used in the active voice instead of the passive voice. Verbs are in the active voice when the subject is the one doing the action. A verb is in the passive voice when the subject is the recipient of an action.

Example:

> General: His kindness will never be forgotten.

> Specific: His thoughtful gifts and bear hugs will never be forgotten.

Attention should also be given to the kind of verbs that are used in sentences. Active verbs (e.g., run, swim) should be about an action. Whenever possible, an **active verb should replace a linking verb** to provide clear examples for arguments and to strengthen a passage overall.

Example:

> Passive: The winners were called to the stage by the judges.

> Active: The judges called the winners to the stage.

Review Video: Word Usage
Visit mometrix.com/academy and enter code: 197863

CONCISENESS

Conciseness is writing what you need to get your message across in the fewest words possible. Planning is important in writing concise messages. If you have in mind what you need to write beforehand, it will be easier to make a message short and to the point. Do not state the obvious.

Revising is also important. After the message is written, make sure you have short sentences. When reviewing the information, imagine a conversation taking place, and concise writing will likely result.

TRANSITIONS

Transitions are bridges between what has been read and what is about to be read. Transitions smooth the reader's path between sentences and inform the reader of major connections to new

117

ideas forthcoming in the text. Transitional phrases should be used with care, selecting the appropriate phrase for a transition. Tone is another important consideration in using transitional phrases, varying the tone for different audiences. For example, in a scholarly essay, *in summary* would be preferable to the more informal *in short*.

When working with transitional words and phrases, writers usually find a natural flow that indicates when a transition is needed. In reading a draft of the text, it should become apparent where the flow is uneven or rough. At this point, the writer can add transitional elements during the revision process. Revising can also afford an opportunity to delete transitional devices that seem heavy handed or unnecessary.

TYPES OF TRANSITIONS

Appropriate transition words help clarify the relationships between sentences and paragraphs, and they create a much more cohesive essay. Below are listed several categories of transitions that you will need to be familiar with along with some associated transition words:

- **Logical Continuation**: therefore, as such, for this reason, thus, consequently, as a result
- **Extended Argument**: moreover, furthermore, also
- **Example or Illustration**: for instance, for example
- **Comparison**: similarly, likewise, in like manner
- **Contrast**: however, nevertheless, by contrast
- **Restatement or Clarification**: in other words, to put it another way
- **Generalization or General Application**: in broad terms, broadly speaking, in general

> **Review Video: Transitions**
> Visit mometrix.com/academy and enter code: 707563

Rhetorical Devices

RHETORICAL DEVICES

There are many types of language devices that authors use to convey their meaning in a descriptive way. Understanding these concepts will help you understand what you read. These types of devices are called **figurative language**—language that goes beyond the literal meaning of a word or phrase. **Descriptive language** specifically evokes imagery in the reader's mind to make a story come alive. **Exaggeration** is a type of figurative language in which an author carries an idea beyond the truth in order to emphasize something. A **simile** is a type of figurative language that compares two things that are not actually alike, using words such as *like* and *as*. A **metaphor** takes the comparison one step further by fully equating the two things rather than just saying they are similar.

A **figure-of-speech** is a word or phrase that departs from straightforward, literal language. Figures-of-speech are often used and crafted for emphasis, freshness of expression, or clarity. However, clarity of a passage may suffer from use of these devices. As an example of the figurative use of a word, consider the sentence: *I am going to crown you.* The author may mean:

- I am going to place a literal crown on your head.
- I am going to symbolically exalt you to the place of kingship.
- I am going to punch you in the head with my clenched fist.
- I am going to put a second checker piece on top of your checker piece to signify that it has become a king.

Review Video: Figure of Speech
Visit mometrix.com/academy and enter code: 111295

A **metaphor** is a type of figurative language in which the writer equates something with another thing that is not particularly similar. For instance, *the bird was an arrow arcing through the sky*. In this sentence, the arrow is serving as a metaphor for the bird. The point of a metaphor is to encourage the reader to consider the item being described in a *different way*. Let's continue with this metaphor for a bird: you are asked to envision the bird's flight as being similar to the arc of an arrow. So, you imagine the flight to be swift and bending. Metaphors are a way for the author to describe an item *without being direct and obvious*. This literary device is a lyrical and suggestive way of providing information. Note that the reference for a metaphor will not always be mentioned explicitly by the author. Consider the following description of a forest in winter: *Swaying skeletons reached for the sky and groaned as the wind blew through them.* In this example, the author is using *skeletons* as a metaphor for leafless trees. This metaphor creates a spooky tone while inspiring the reader's imagination.

Review Video: Metaphor
Visit mometrix.com/academy and enter code: 133295

A **simile** is a figurative expression that is similar to a metaphor, but the expression uses a distancing word: *like* or *as*. Examples include phrases such as *the sun was like an orange*, *eager as a beaver*, and *nimble as a mountain goat*. Because a simile includes *like* or *as,* the device creates more space between the description and the thing being described than does a metaphor. If an author says that *a house was like a shoebox*, then the tone is different than the author saying that the house *was* a shoebox. Authors will choose between a metaphor and a simile depending on their intended tone.

Review Video: Simile
Visit mometrix.com/academy and enter code: 642949

Another type of figurative language is **personification**. This is the description of a nonhuman thing as if the item were **human**. Literally, the word means the process of making something into a person. The general intent of personification is to describe things in a manner that will be comprehensible to readers. When an author states that a tree *groans* in the wind, he or she does not mean that the tree is emitting a low, pained sound from a mouth. Instead, the author means that the tree is making a noise similar to a human groan. Of course, this personification establishes a tone of sadness or suffering. A different tone would be established if the author said that the tree was *swaying* or *dancing*.

Review Video: Personification
Visit mometrix.com/academy and enter code: 260066

Target Audience

CONSIDERATIONS TO TEACH STUDENTS ABOUT OCCASIONS, PURPOSES, AND AUDIENCES

Teachers can explain to students that organizing their ideas, providing evidence to support the points they make in their writing, and correcting their grammar and mechanics are not simply for following writing rules or correctness for its own sake, but rather for ensuring that specific reader audiences understand what they intend to communicate. For example, upper-elementary-grade students writing for lower-elementary-grade students should write in print rather than script, use simpler vocabulary, and avoid writing in long, complex, compound, or complex-compound sentences. The purpose for writing guides word choice, such as encouraging readers to question opposing viewpoints or stimulate empathy and/or sympathy. It also influences narrative, descriptive, expository, or persuasive/argumentative format. For instance, business letters require different form and language than parent thank-you notes. Persuasive techniques, like words that evoke certain reader emotions, description that appeals to reader beliefs, and supporting information can all affect reader opinions.

> **Review Video: Purpose/Audience/Format for Writing**
> Visit mometrix.com/academy and enter code: 146627

QUESTIONS TO DETERMINE CONTENT AND FORMAT

When student writers have chosen a viewpoint or idea about which to write, teachers can help them select content to include and the writing format most appropriate to their subject. They should have students ask themselves what their readers need to know to enable them to agree with the viewpoint in the writing, or to believe what the writer is saying. Students can imagine another person hearing them say what they will write about, and responding, "Oh, yeah? Prove that!" Teachers should have students ask themselves what kinds of evidence they need to prove their positions/ideas to skeptical readers. They should have students consider what points might cause the reader to disagree. Students should consider what knowledge their reading audience shares in common with them. They should also consider what information they need to share with their readers. Teachers can have students adapt various writing formats, organizing techniques, and writing styles to different purposes and audiences to practice with choosing writing modes and language.

APPROPRIATE KINDS OF WRITING FOR DIFFERENT TASKS, PURPOSES, AND AUDIENCES

Students who are writing to persuade their parents to grant some additional privilege, such as permission for a more independent activity, should use more sophisticated vocabulary and diction that sounds more mature and serious to appeal to the parental audience. Students who are writing for younger children, however, should use simpler vocabulary and sentence structure, as well as choosing words that are more vivid and entertaining. They should treat their topics more lightly, and include humor as appropriate. Students who are writing for their classmates may use language that is more informal, as well as age-appropriate. Students wanting to convince others to agree with them should use persuasive/argumentative form. Those wanting to share an experience should use descriptive writing. Those wanting to relate a story and what can be learned from it should write narratives. Students can use speculative writing to invite others to join them in exploring ideas.

Vocabulary and Syntax

DIALECT

Dialect is the form of a language spoken by people according to their geographical region, social class, cultural group, or any other distinctive group. It includes pronunciation, grammar, and spelling. Literary authors often use dialect when writing dialogue to illustrate the social and geographical backgrounds of specific characters, which supports character development. For example, in *The Adventures of Huckleberry Finn* (1885), Mark Twain's novel is written in the dialect of the young and uneducated white Southern character, opening with this sentence: "You don't know about me without you have read a book by the name of The Adventures of Tom Sawyer, but that ain't no matter." Twain uses a different and exaggerated dialect to represent the speech of the

African-American slave Jim: "We's safe, Huck, we's safe! Jump up and crack yo' heels. Dat's de good ole Cairo at las', I jis knows it."

USE OF DIALECT IN MEDIA

In *To Kill a Mockingbird,* author Harper Lee used dialect in the characters' dialogue to portray an uneducated boy in the American South: "Reckon I have. Almost died the first year I come to school and et them pecans—folks say he pizened 'em." Lee also uses many Southern regional expressions, such as "right stove up," "What in the sam holy hill?", "sit a spell," "fess" (meaning "confess"), "jim-dandy," and "hush your fussing." These contribute to Lee's characterization of the people she describes, who live in a small town in Alabama circa the 1930s. In *Wuthering Heights* (1847), Emily Bronte reproduces Britain's 18th-19th-century Yorkshire dialect in the speech of servant Joseph: "Running after t'lads, as usuald!... If I war yah, maister, I'd just slam t'boards i' their faces all on 'em, gentle and simple! Never a day ut yah're off, but yon cat o' Linton comes sneaking hither; and Miss Nelly, shoo's a fine lass!"

In addition to using dialects to support character development in novels, plays, poems, and other literary works, authors also manipulate dialects to accomplish various purposes with their intended reading audiences. For example, in an English Language Arts lesson plan for eighth graders (Groome and Gibbs, 2008), teachers point out author Frances O'Roark Dowell set her novel *Dovey Coe* (2000) in the Western North Carolina mountains of 1928. Dowell writes protagonist Dovey's narration in the regional Appalachian Mountain dialect to remind readers of the significance of the novel's setting. This lesson plan further includes two poems by African-American author Paul Laurence Dunbar: "When Malindy Sings" and "We Wear the Mask." Students are asked why Dunbar wrote the former poem in Southern slave dialect and the latter in Standard English. Exercises include identifying dialect/Standard English features, rewriting dialect in Standard English, identifying audiences, and identifying how author choices of dialects or Standard English affect readers and accomplish author purposes.

DIALECT VS. DICTION

When written as characters' dialogue in literary works, dialect represents the particular pronunciation, grammar, and figurative expressions used by certain groups of people based on their geographic region, social class, and cultural background. For example, when a character says, "There's gold up in them thar hills," the author is using dialect to add to the characterization of that individual. Diction is more related to individual characters than to groups of people. The way in which a specific character speaks, including his or her choice of words, manner of expressing himself or herself, and use of grammar all represent individual types of diction. For example, two characters in the same novel might describe the same action or event using different diction: One says "I'm heading uptown for the evening," and the other says "I'm going out for a night on the town." These convey the same literal meaning, but due to their variations in diction they are expressed in different ways.

> **Review Video: Dialogue, Paradox, and Dialect**
> Visit mometrix.com/academy and enter code: 684341

SIMPLE SURVEY RESEARCH INTO LINGUISTIC DIALECTS

To learn about different dialects spoken in different geographic regions, social classes, and cultural groups, students can undertake simple surveys of small groups of informants. Students should first make a list of words they have heard used in certain dialects. Then they can ask their respondents to identify the words they know. Students can also ask respondents to identify words they have heard of but cannot define. Using their lists of dialect words, students can ask informants to identify which words they use in their day-to-day conversations. For a more multidimensional survey, a student can ask the sampled informants all three questions—words that they know, those that they have heard of but do not know the meanings, and those that they use in their speech.

INFLUENCES ON REGIONAL DIALECT

Linguistic researchers have identified regional variations in vocabulary choices, which have evolved because of differences in local climates and how they influence human behaviors. For example, in the Southern United States, the Linguistic Atlas of the Gulf States (LAGS) Project by Dr. Lee Pederson of Emory University discovered and documented that people living in the northern or Upland section of the Piedmont plateau region call the fungal infection commonly known as athlete's foot "toe itch," but people living in the southern or Lowland section call it "ground itch." The explanation for this difference is that in the north, temperatures are cooler and people accordingly wear shoes, so they associate the itching with the feet in their description, but in the south, temperatures are hotter and people traditionally went barefoot, so they associated the itching with the ground that presumably transmitted the infection.

AFFIXES

Affixes in the English language are morphemes that are added to words to create related but different words. Derivational affixes form new words based on and related to the original words. For example, the affix –ness added to the end of the adjective *happy* forms the noun *happiness.* Inflectional affixes form different grammatical versions of words. For example, the plural affix –s changes the singular noun *book* to the plural noun *books*, and the past tense affix –ed changes the present tense verb *look* to the past tense *looked.* Prefixes are affixes placed in front of words. For example, *heat* means to make hot; *preheat* means to heat in advance. Suffixes are affixes placed at the ends of words. The *happiness* example above contains the suffix –ness. Circumfixes add parts both before and after words, such as how *light* becomes *enlighten* with the prefix *en-* and the suffix –en. Interfixes create compound words via central affixes: *speed* and *meter* become *speedometer* via the interfix –o–.

> **Review Video: Affixes**
> Visit mometrix.com/academy and enter code: 782422

WORD ROOTS, PREFIXES, AND SUFFIXES TO HELP DETERMINE MEANINGS OF WORDS

Many English words were formed from combining multiple sources. For example, the Latin *habēre* means "to have," and the prefixes *in-* and *im-* mean a lack or prevention of something, as in *insufficient* and *imperfect*. Latin combined *in-* with *habēre* to form *inhibēre,* whose past participle was *inhibitus*. This is the origin of the English word *inhibit,* meaning to prevent from having. Hence by knowing the meanings of both the prefix and the root, one can decipher the word meaning. In Greek, the root *enkephalo-* refers to the brain. Many medical terms are based on this root, such as encephalitis and hydrocephalus. Understanding the prefix and suffix meanings (-*itis* means inflammation; *hydro-* means water) allows a person to deduce that encephalitis refers to brain inflammation and hydrocephalus refers to water (or other fluid) on the brain

> **Review Video: Determining Word Meanings**
> Visit mometrix.com/academy and enter code: 894894

PREFIXES

While knowing prefix meanings helps ESL and beginning readers learn new words, other readers take for granted the meanings of known words. However, prefix knowledge will also benefit them for determining meanings or definitions of unfamiliar words. For example, native English speakers and readers familiar with recipes know what *preheat* means. Knowing that *pre-* means in advance can also inform them that *presume* means to assume in advance, that *prejudice* means advance judgment, and that this understanding can be applied to many other words beginning with *pre-*. Knowing that the prefix *dis-* indicates opposition informs the meanings of words like *disbar, disagree, disestablish,* and many more. Knowing *dys-* means bad, impaired, abnormal, or difficult informs *dyslogistic, dysfunctional, dysphagia,* and *dysplasia.*

SUFFIXES

In English, certain suffixes generally indicate both that a word is a noun, and that the noun represents a state of being or quality. For example, *-ness* is commonly used to change an adjective into its noun form, as with *happy* and *happiness, nice* and *niceness,* and so on. The suffix *–tion* is commonly used to transform a verb into its noun form, as with *converse* and *conversation or move* and *motion.* Thus, if readers are unfamiliar with the second form of a word, knowing the meaning of the transforming suffix can help them determine meaning.

CONTEXT CLUES TO HELP DETERMINE MEANINGS OF WORDS

If readers simply bypass unknown words, they can reach unclear conclusions about what they read. However, if they look for the definition of every unfamiliar word in the dictionary, it can slow their reading progress. Moreover, the dictionary may list multiple definitions for a word, so readers must search the word's context for meaning. Hence context is important to new vocabulary regardless of reader methods. Four types of context clues are examples, definitions, descriptive words, and opposites. Authors may use a certain word, and then follow it with several different examples of what it describes. Sometimes authors actually supply a definition of a word they use, which is especially true in informational and technical texts. Authors may use descriptive words that elaborate upon a vocabulary word they just used. Authors may also use opposites with negation that help define meaning.

EXAMPLES AND DEFINITIONS

An author may use a word and then give examples that illustrate its meaning. Consider this text: "For students who are deaf or hard of hearing, teachers who do not know how to use sign language can help them understand certain instructions by using gestures instead, like pointing their fingers to indicate which direction to look or go; holding up a hand, palm outward, to indicate stopping; holding the hands flat, palms up, curling a finger toward oneself in a beckoning motion to indicate 'come here'; or curling all fingers toward oneself repeatedly to indicate 'come on', 'more', or 'continue.'" The author of this text has used the word "gestures" and then followed it with examples, so a reader unfamiliar with the word could deduce from the examples that "gestures" means "hand motions." Readers can find examples by looking for signal words "for example," "for instance," "like" "such as," and "e.g."

While readers sometimes have to look for definitions of unfamiliar words in a dictionary and/or do some work to determine a word's meaning from its surrounding context, at other times an author may make it easier for readers by defining certain words. For example, an author may write, "The company did not have sufficient capital, that is, available money, to continue operations." The author defined "capital" as "available money," and heralded the definition with the phrase "that is."

Another way that authors supply word definitions is with appositives. Rather than being introduced by a signal phrase like "that is," "namely," or "meaning," an appositive comes after the vocabulary word it defines and is enclosed within two commas. For example, an author may write, "The Indians introduced the Pilgrims to pemmican, cakes they made of lean meat dried and mixed with fat, which proved greatly beneficial to keep settlers from starving while trapping." In this example, the appositive phrase following "pemmican" and preceding "which" defines the word "pemmican."

DESCRIPTIONS

When readers encounter a word they do not recognize in a text, the author may expand on that word to illustrate it better. While the author may do this to make the prose more picturesque and vivid, the reader can also take advantage of this description to provide context clues to the meaning of the unfamiliar word. For example, an author may write, "The man sitting next to me on the airplane was obese. His shirt stretched across his vast expanse of flesh, strained almost to bursting." The descriptive second sentence elaborates on and helps to define the previous sentence's word "obese" to mean extremely fat. One author described someone who was obese simply, yet very descriptively, as "an epic in bloat." A reader unfamiliar with the word "repugnant" can decipher its meaning through an author's accompanying description: "The way the child grimaced and shuddered as he swallowed the medicine showed that its taste was particularly repugnant."

OPPOSITES

Text authors sometimes introduce a contrasting or opposing idea before or after a concept they present. They may do this to emphasize or heighten the idea they present by contrasting it with something that is the reverse. However, readers can also use these context clues to understand familiar words. For example, an author may write, "Our conversation was not cheery. We sat and talked very solemnly about his experience, and a number of similar events." The reader who is not familiar with the word "solemnly" can deduce by the author's preceding use of "not cheery" that "solemn" means the opposite of cheery or happy, so it must mean serious or sad. Or if someone writes, "Don't condemn his entire project because you couldn't find anything good to say about it," readers unfamiliar with "condemn" can understand from the sentence structure that it means the opposite of saying anything good, so it must mean reject, dismiss, or disapprove. "Entire" adds another context clue, meaning total or complete rejection.

SYNTAX TO DETERMINE PART OF SPEECH AND MEANINGS OF WORDS

Syntax refers to sentence structure and word order. Suppose that a reader encounters an unfamiliar word when reading a text. To illustrate, consider an invented word like "splunch." If this word is used in a sentence like "Please splunch that ball to me," the reader can assume from syntactic context that "splunch" is a verb. We would not use a noun, adjective, adverb, or preposition with the object "that ball," and the prepositional phrase "to me" further indicates "splunch" represents an action. However, in the sentence, "Please hand that splunch to me," the reader can assume that "splunch" is a noun. Demonstrative adjectives like "that" modify nouns. Also, we hand someone some*thing*—a thing being a noun; we do not hand someone a verb, adjective, or adverb. Some sentences contain further clues. For example, from the sentence, "The princess wore the glittering splunch on her head," the reader can deduce that it is a crown, tiara, or something similar from the syntactic context, without knowing the word.

SYNTAX TO INDICATE DIFFERENT MEANINGS OF SIMILAR SENTENCES

The syntax, or structure, of a sentence affords grammatical cues that aid readers in comprehending the meanings of words, phrases, and sentences in the texts that they read. Seemingly minor differences in how the words or phrases in a sentence are ordered can make major differences in meaning. For example, two sentences can use exactly the same words but have different meanings based on the word order: (1) "The man with a broken arm sat in a chair." (2) "The man sat in a chair with a broken arm." While both sentences indicate that a man sat in a chair, differing syntax indicates whether the man's or chair's arm was broken.

NUANCES OF WORD MEANING RELATIVE TO CONNOTATION, DENOTATION, DICTION, AND USAGE

A word's denotation is simply its objective dictionary definition. However, its connotation refers to the subjective associations, often emotional, that specific words evoke in listeners and readers. Two or more words can have the same dictionary meaning, but very different connotations. Writers use diction (a style element) to convey various nuances of thought and emotion by selecting synonyms for other words that best communicate the associations they want to trigger for readers. For example, a car engine is naturally greasy; in this sense, "greasy" is a neutral term. But when a person's smile, appearance, or clothing is described as "greasy," it has a negative connotation. Because of usages that have occurred in recent times, many words have gained additional and/or different meanings. The word "gay" originally meant happy or festive, as in the Christmas carol "Deck the Halls" lyrics, "Don we now our gay apparel," but in the 20th century, it also came to indicate a sexual preference.

> **Review Video: Denotation and Connotation**
> Visit mometrix.com/academy and enter code: 310092
>
> **Review Video: Word Usage**
> Visit mometrix.com/academy and enter code: 197863

FIGURES OF SPEECH

A figure of speech is a verbal expression whose meaning is figurative rather than literal. For example, the phrase "butterflies in the stomach" does not refer to actual butterflies in a person's stomach. It is a metaphor representing the fluttery feelings experienced when a person is nervous or excited—or when one "falls in love," which does not mean physically falling. "Hitting a sales target" does not mean physically hitting a target with arrows as in archery; it is a metaphor for meeting a sales quota. "Climbing the ladder of success" metaphorically likens advancing in one's career to ascending ladder rungs. Similes, such as "light as a feather" (meaning very light, not a feather's actual weight), and hyperbole, like "I'm starving/freezing/roasting," are also figures of speech.

> **Review Video: Figure of Speech**
> Visit mometrix.com/academy and enter code: 111295

Public Speaking

SPEECHES

Speeches are written to be delivered in spoken language in public, to various groups of people, at formal or informal events. Some generic types include welcome speeches, thank-you speeches, keynote addresses, position papers, commemorative and dedication speeches, and farewell speeches. Speeches are commonly written in present tense. Speeches begin with an introduction, greeting the audience. At official functions, specific audience members are named ("Chairperson [name]," "Principal [name], teachers, and students," etc.) and when audiences include a distinguished guest, s/he is often named as well. Then the speaker introduces him/herself by name, position, and department or organization as applicable. After the greeting, the speaker then introduces the topic and states the purpose of the speech. The body of the speech follows, similarly to the body of an essay, stating its main points, their elaboration, and supporting evidence. Finally, in the conclusion, the speaker states his/her hope for accomplishing the speech's purpose and thanks the audience for attending and listening to the speech.

EDUCATIONAL BENEFITS OF DIGITAL MEDIA

Digital media are powerful because they are flexible, versatile, and can be transformed, marked, and networked. For example, printed ink on paper and paint on canvas are permanent. However, digital images of these—while they sacrifice physical texture and some visual depth and tone—have the advantage that they can be displayed on anything from a giant public video screen, to a computer monitor, to a smartphone screen, around the world. Digital images can also be manipulated to sharpen, blur, darken/lighten, or alter portions. Images, text, and voice can be saved exactly and reliably over time periods, and also adapted or changed as needed for teaching. Digital media are not limited to text and pictures as books are: they also include video and audio, and can combine video and sound with text. Students can interact with multiple media at once, choose preferred formats, and adapt the media to help with learning difficulties.

Unlike hard copies, digitally-saved materials can be linked to each other. Embedded hyperlinks afford many learning supports to students, such as dictionaries, thesauruses, encyclopedias, reading comprehension prompts, supplementary materials to build student background knowledge, visual graphic organizers, and electronic notepads for keeping running notes. Students can rapidly navigate between words in a text and their dictionary definitions, images and their descriptions, videos and their captions, or passages of text and their audio recordings. Another advantage for teachers and students is that websites and pages are often constantly updated in real time. Educators and learners can access information and opinions contributed by a wide variety of peers, experts, and mentors—not just locally, but globally. Multimedia packages enable students to have multisensory experiences rather than simply reading print. Access is almost instantaneous. Networking affords teachers and students interconnected communication and information, plus formats and experiences that can be customized to the diversity of individual learners.

TRANSFORMING AND MARKING DIGITAL MEDIA

Students can use within-media transformations to change how website content is displayed by turning graphics or sound on or off, adjust volume, and change text and image appearance by using different browsers or adjusting browser settings. Cross-media transformations can use software to convert speech to text or text to speech, and can do so automatically by embedding into other software and browsers. This helps students with vision and hearing problems, auditory processing deficits, and reading or learning disabilities. HTML (Hypertext Markup Language) and XML (Extensible Markup Language), both used in web design, enable students to adjust font, etc., to accommodate different learning needs. For example, students can underline all summary sentences in detailed texts, and teachers can italicize all English words with Greek or Latin roots, or boldface all metaphors. Unlike highlightings on paper, digital markups can be hidden, displayed, expanded, deleted, and changed as needed.

INSTRUCTIONAL VIDEOS

Instructional videos have potential for excellent two-way communication because questions and feedback can be built in. Videos can be targeted to particular audiences, and they can be paused for discussion or replayed to reinforce concepts. Students can see processes, including "before," "during," and "after" phases. Videos are accessible, because most communities have at least one DVD player or computer. Moreover, video players and computers are continually becoming less expensive to buy and use. Disadvantages include the necessity of editing software and equipment in some cases, as well as support from other print materials. There is also danger of overuse if other

media or methods could be more appropriate, and higher up-front costs. Producers must account for the costs of script development and hiring local performers as needed.

DVDs and CDs

Interactive DVDs and CDs, such as games, give viewers the potential to participate, and are becoming increasingly popular. They are commonly used to target specific audiences, such as young people. Additionally, videos are considered to be a professional method of sharing information. Compared to many other media formats, discs are comparatively inexpensive to make, and are easy to transport due to their small size and weight. They are more resistant to damage and aging than older videotape technology, making them more durable. Some disadvantages include needing computer access to produce and play, and certain software programs to produce, especially if the producer wants to include video animation and audio commentary. Producers must also consider the time of paid staff and production and labeling expenses.

Media and Format Choices

Effective communication depends on choosing the correct method. Media and format choices are influenced by the target audience, the budget, and the needs of the audience.

> **Review Video: Media**
> Visit mometrix.com/academy and enter code: 785859

Television and Radio

Two media types are television and radio. Both are high-status mass media that reach many people. TV has the broadest reach: it can market to the general public or be customized for target audiences, while radio reaches specific target audiences. TV has the advantage of video plus audio, while audio only is one radio disadvantage. Both are useful for communicating simple slogans and messages, and both can generate awareness, interest, and excitement. However, television is more expensive than radio. Also, both TV and radio audiences can only interact directly during call-in programs. Programming times may be inconvenient, but tape, digital sound, and digital video recording (DVR) can remedy this.

Newspapers

Except for the occasional community columns, news releases, and letters to the editor, newspaper pages and features afford little opportunity for audience input or participation. However, they reach and appeal to the literate public, though the general public is unlikely to read them. Cost is an advantage: hiring a PR writer and paying for a news advertisement costs much less than a radio or TV spot. Additionally, newspaper features are high-status, and audiences can reread and review them as often as they like. However, newspaper ads may have difficulty affecting the reader as deeply without audio or video, and they require a literate audience. Their publication is also subject to editors' whims and biases. Newspaper pieces combining advertising and editorial—"advertorials"—afford inclusion of paid material, but are viewed as medium-status and cost more.

Internet Websites and Blogs, and Mobile Phones and Text Messaging

Computer literacy is required for online material, but participation potential is high via websites, e-networking, list-serves, and blogging. Mobile phones and text messaging have potential for enormous direct, public, two-way and one-on-one communication, with timely information and reminders. Web media need a literate public and can be tailored for specific audiences. They afford global information, are accessible by increasingly technology-literate populations, and are high-status. Web media disadvantages include the necessity of computers and people to design, manage, and supply content, as well as to provide technical support. Mobile and text media are globally popular, but appeal especially to certain demographics like teens and young adults. They are increasingly available, especially in rural regions, and are decreasing in cost. Mobile and text media disadvantages include required brevity in texts and provider messaging charges. List-serves can be inexpensive as well as reaching a broad audience through email. Links to related websites and pages within existing sites are also advantages.

PUBLIC PRESENTATIONS AND POWERPOINT

Public presentations have great potential for audience participation and can directly target various audiences. They can encourage the establishment of partnerships and groups, stimulate local ownership of issues and projects, and make information public. A drawback to public presentations is that they are limited to nights, weekends, or whenever audiences are available, and do not always attract the intended audience.

Another method of presentation is to use **PowerPoints**. These presentations are best for sophisticated audiences like professionals, civil servants, and service organizations. Well-designed PowerPoint presentations are good for stimulating audience interest, selling ideas, and marketing purposes. Also, they are accessible online as well as in-person so can reach a broader audience. PowerPoint disadvantages include the necessity of projectors and other equipment. Also, they are limited to communicating more general points, outlines, and summaries rather than conveying a multitude of information in more detail.

POSTERS AND BROCHURES

Both **posters** and **brochures** can target audiences of the general public and more specific public sectors. Posters are better for communicating simple slogans and messages, while brochures can include more detail and are better for printing instructional information. Both can be inexpensive to produce, especially if printed only as needed and in-house. Posters can often be printed in-house without using outside printing companies. However, it is difficult to get feedback on both posters and brochures—unless they have been broadly tested, or if their publication is accompanied by workshops and other participatory events. Disadvantages of posters include the simplicity required of their messages, and the requirement of literacy in written language and visual elements to understand them. Disadvantages of brochures include their limitations of distribution to specific groups or areas and, like posters, also requiring literacy.

FLYERS AND FACT SHEETS

Flyers and fact sheets have one-way communication potential because readers cannot give feedback. Their target audiences are general. Some advantages of using this form of media include flexibility: people can distribute them at meetings or events, put them on car windshields in parking lots, leave them in stores or on bulletin boards at community agencies and schools, hand them out from booths and other displays, or mail them. When printed in black and white, they can be very inexpensive. They afford recipients the convenience of being able to review them at their leisure. Organizations and individuals can produce flyers and fact sheets in-house, or even at home with desktop publishing software. Disadvantages include their limitation to single facts or tips and specific information on specified topics.

EVALUATING SPEECHES FOR CONCISE INFORMATION

To convince or persuade listeners and/or reinforce a message, speeches must be succinct. Audiences become confused by excessive anecdotes and details. If a speaker takes three minutes or more to get to the point, audience attention will flag, and will only worsen when details are off the subject. When answering a question, the asker and speaker may even forget the original question if the speaker takes too long. Speakers should practice not only rehearsing written speeches, but also developing skill for spontaneous question-and-answer sessions after speeches. Speakers should differentiate necessary from simply interesting information because brains will stop processing input beyond a certain limit, to prevent overload. Speakers should know what points they wish to make. They should not be afraid to pause before responding to questions, which indicates thoughtfulness and control rather than lack of knowledge. Restating questions increases comprehension and appropriate responses, and allows time to form answers mentally.

CLEARLY WRITTEN PROSE AND SPEECHES

To achieve **clarity**, a writer or speaker must first define his/her purpose carefully. The speech should be organized logically, so that sentences make sense and follow each other in an understandable order. Sentences must also be constructed well, with carefully chosen words and structure. Organizing a speech in advance using an outline provides the writer/speaker with a blueprint, directing and focusing the composition to meet its intended purpose. Organized speeches enable audiences to comprehend and retain the presented information more easily. Humans naturally seek to impose order on the world by seeking patterns. Hence, when ideas in a speech are well-organized and adhere to a consistent pattern, the speaker communicates better with listeners and is more convincing. Speechwriters can use chronological patterns to organize events, sequential patterns to organize processes by their steps, and spatial patterns to help audiences visualize geographical locations and movements or physical scenarios. Also, comparison-contrast patterns give audiences insight about similarities and differences between and among topics, especially when listeners are more familiar with one than the other.

ORGANIZATIONAL PATTERNS FOR SPEECHES

A speechwriter who uses an **advantages-disadvantages pattern of organization** presents the audience with the pros and cons of a topic. This aids writers in discussing two sides of an issue objectively without an argumentative position, enabling listeners to weigh both aspects. When a speechwriter uses a cause-and-effect pattern, it can help to persuade audiences to agree with an action or solution by showing significant relationships between factors. Writers may separate an outline into two main "cause" and "effect" sections, or separate it separate sections for each cause, including the effect for each. Persuasive writing also benefits from problem-solution patterns: by establishing the existence of a problem, writers induce audiences to realize a need for change. By supplying a solution and supporting its superiority above other solutions, the writer convinces audiences of the value of that solution. When none of these patterns—or chronological, sequential, spatial, or comparison-contrast patterns—applies, speechwriters often use topical patterns. These organize information by various subtopics and types within the main topic or category.

EFFECTIVE SPEECH DELIVERY

Speakers should deliver speeches in a natural, conversational manner rather than being rigidly formal or theatrical. Effective delivery is also supported by confidence. Speakers should be direct, building audience rapport through personal connection and vivid imagery. Speakers should be mindful of the occasion, subject, and audience of their speeches and take care to use appropriate language. Good speakers learn vocal control, including loudness, speed, pitch, use of pauses, tonal variety, correct pronunciation, and clear articulation. They can express enthusiasm and emphasize important points with their voices. Nonverbal behaviors, such as eye contact, facial expressions, gestures, good posture and body movements clarify communication, stress important ideas, and influence perceptions that the speaker is trustworthy, competent, and credible. Nonverbal communications should seem as spontaneous and natural as vocal or verbal ones. Speakers should know their speeches well and practice frequently, taking care to avoid nervous or irrelevant movements such as tapping or pacing.

English Language Arts Pedagogy

CLASSROOM MATERIALS THAT SUPPORT LITERACY ACROSS THE CURRICULUM

In a classroom that supports literacy, the teacher should provide **labels** combining words and pictures on all objects. This continually stimulates students to associate written language with the objects and concepts it represents. Especially to support disabled students, teachers should use their particular interests and needs as a guide for labeling things. Printed directions, signs, calendars, and schedules are materials that students should use regularly in the classroom. These help students realize how language is used in everyday life. When the class is studying a certain topic, theme, or book, the teacher and students can work together to redesign the classroom using printed/written materials that reflect that topic, theme, or book. This enables students to experience fully and "live" the lesson rather than just observing it. All of the materials must be adapted for any students' special needs. For instance, in a class including blind/visually impaired students, labels, signs and other print materials can incorporate Braille words and textured surfaces.

ADDRESSING DIVERSE STUDENT ABILITIES AND NEEDS

Teachers must consider the **diversity** among the skills and needs of their students as they design their classroom learning environments. The teachers should **individualize** the setting and their instruction so that these represent every student. Individualization and instructional differentiation should not only address disabled students' needs; they should also regularly provide suitable opportunities for these students to participate on an ongoing basis in activities that involve literacy and integrate it into all content areas. According to research, a salient need of students with diverse literacy backgrounds is that they often have trouble connecting new information to their existing knowledge. This ability is a critical component of learning. When teachers plan and organize their classrooms to offer literacy activities that are accessible to disabled students—and that immerse them in literacy experiences and give them opportunities to connect both new with old information, and spoken with printed language—these students can then access the general education curriculum.

ACTIVITIES FOR STUDENTS WITH DISABILITIES TO DEVELOP LITERACY SKILLS AND PARTICIPATE IN GENERAL CURRICULUM

To participate in the general curriculum, students with disabilities need to understand the **alphabetic principle**, i.e. that printed language represents spoken language; connect print with speech; and be able to relate new information to their prior knowledge. Teachers can support these developments by designing classrooms as literacy-rich settings, immersing special-needs and other students in **accessible literacy activities** across all content areas. For example, students can interact with alphabet-letter magnets, cookie-cutters, and stamps: concrete manipulatives allow students not developmentally ready for exclusively abstract thought to understand concepts using real objects. Discussing daily schedules requires students to read and comprehend printed language, and then use spoken language to demonstrate and apply their understanding. Playing letter/word games like Bingo, Pictionary, Boggle, and Scrabble gives practice with creating and manipulating language, enhancing recognition and cognitive flexibility. Providing photos of peers, teachers, staff, and classroom activities and having students label them helps students connect written language with familiar, meaningful images. Daily communication notebooks help students further integrate literacy into their school days.

IMPLICATIONS OF CULTURAL AND LINGUISTIC DIFFERENCES REGARDING LITERACY DEVELOPMENT

Educational research shows that the **cultural values** of families and/or communities influence children's literacy development, and also that culture is a significant factor to understanding children's home literacy environments. Researchers have also found that cultural purposes, perspectives, and contexts affect how students with disabilities in particular interact with the literacy environments they encounter. They say children's preparation levels entering formal education reflect their families'/communities' values and beliefs about literacy. Cultural attitudes about literacy then influence how schools deliver instruction and literacy experiences. Teachers must assess culturally diverse students' interactions with the environment, and design literacy-rich classrooms, with students' diverse backgrounds in mind. Students learning English (ELL/ESL) enter school either not knowing English or just learning it, lacking exposure to specific vocabulary and literature. Literacy-rich classrooms help them participate in regular curriculum. Teacher should read aloud often to these students; include print in their native language in classrooms; permit mistakes during student attempts to use English; encourage students to reread books repeatedly; and plan activities entailing language use.

DRAWBACKS OF WHOLE-CLASS AND SMALL-GROUP READING, AND FLEXIBLE GROUPING MODEL

A major disadvantage of **whole-class reading** is that students who read above the average class level go unchallenged and can become bored, while students reading below average level are lost. Yet the **small-group method** intended to remedy this also has the drawback that, as traditionally implemented, most time is used for skill instruction, leaving far too little time for students actually to read the text. One solution is a **flexible grouping model**, e.g., Grouping Without Tracking (Paratore, 1990). This model uses a "sandwich" structure: teachers give students shared-reading processes at the beginning and end of the lesson, but provide differentiated instruction to two groups in the middle as they read the text. Teachers give indirect guidance to students who can read more independently, and more direct support to struggling readers. Teachers reunite the groups to lead them in a final discussion. Students with reading difficulties gain reading proficiency and comprehension from direct teacher support, enabling them to contribute better to the whole-class discussion, so all share this experience equally.

JIGSAW APPROACH TO SHARED READING

Students reading below grade level may be able to access and comprehend some texts or portions of them, but have difficulty with harder parts/texts—for example, informational texts with more challenging subject matter and specialized vocabulary. When a text intended for the whole class contains such challenging material, one solution the teacher can use is a **jigsaw approach**. The teacher selects various portions of the text that are less difficult and assigns them to students reading below grade level. Whereas such texts overall might present struggles for these students, they find the easier portions more manageable when they tackle only these parts, as selected and assigned by the teacher, in small groups of students with comparable reading levels. The teacher makes each small student group responsible for comprehension of their assigned portion of text. Then the teacher brings the class back together, having each group report what they read, understood, and learned. The whole class then collaborates to help each other make connections among the learning each group reported.

USING THEMES TO CONNECT TEXTS

Any inclusive classroom will contain students who read at various age/grade levels. As a result, some books used as core texts are going to present difficulties for some of the students, who read below grade level and/or lack background knowledge and vocabulary of the subject. One way a teacher can facilitate all students' comprehension of such texts is to provide **supplementary texts** that allow readers at different levels easier access—texts on the same subject or theme as the more difficult core text. Teachers have students read these more accessible texts independently during small-group reading periods. This makes it easier for students with less reading proficiency to learn the core vocabulary and build their background knowledge. Thus, they are more prepared to tackle the more difficult core text during whole-class shared reading periods. With such preparation, less proficient readers are more likely to become engaged and active participants in the shared reading of a difficult text in the whole-group setting.

ASSIGNING STUDENTS TO SMALL GROUPS FOR GUIDED READING EXERCISES

Expert educators and researchers recommend that when teachers divide classes into small student groups for **guided reading**, they should not be overly concerned with assigning students to exact reading levels. Rather, though they will want to group students whose literacy development is similar and who read around a similar level, they should give more attention to organizing groups according to the students' *areas of need*. For example, a teacher might identify students who share in common a need for help with noticing changes in setting; other students who share difficulties with recognizing and differentiating characters; some students who demonstrate problems with following and/or reproducing events they read in a text in the correct chronological sequence; some students who have trouble identifying and/or articulating the main idea in a text portion, etc. The teacher can create a group of students sharing one of these challenges; announce to the class what this group's focus is; and then invite other students to join this group by choice if they experience the same need.

HELPING TEACHERS PROVIDE MORE EQUITABLE LEARNING OPPORTUNITIES USING WORD COUNTS

Books designed for lower reading levels typically contain fewer words, both per page and overall. Yet students who are reading below their grade levels require not fewer reading opportunities, but more, to practice and improve their reading skills. For example, within one class of second-grade students, the teacher might have one group using a text with over 80 words on just the first page, while another group uses a text with a total of 80 words in the entire book. This difference shows that the teacher will need to use several texts within certain groups to give them equal amounts of reading material and practice as readers of denser/longer texts during group reading times. Teachers can look at the backs of the books they assign during guided reading sessions, and maintain simple logs of their **word counts**. Comparing these word counts among groups can help teachers to equalize the numbers of words that each student group actually works with during small-group guided reading periods.

CONNECTING TEXT SETS FOR SMALL-GROUP GUIDED READING ACROSS DIFFERENT READING DIFFICULTY LEVELS

When teachers select textbooks to teach a unit/lesson on a certain topic, they often compile **text sets**—groups of books all related to the same topic/theme. Because classes usually include students reading at different levels, teachers also often gather books at different reading levels for text sets. When collecting books representing multiple reading levels, the teacher can also intentionally organize the text set so all books are connected. For example, the books might share similar content; similar language, style, and vocabulary words; or similar layouts. Selecting books sharing such a commonality at different reading levels makes it easier for students to draw useful connections between easier and harder texts. It also facilitates students' flexibility in working across multiple reading levels, which builds their skills and confidence for faster progress. Additionally, to prepare some students to read books that teachers felt would prove too difficult

132

otherwise, they can use easier texts with similar themes/language/formats to establish contexts for the harder ones.

ENHANCING STUDENTS' INDEPENDENT READING THROUGH THE READING MATERIAL PROVIDED

In addition to whole-class and small-group reading exercises, students need some time reading **texts of their own choice**, which they can easily read with little/no support, to attain comfort, fluency, and confidence. To ensure more opportunities for practice, with equal time for all students, teachers should provide text sets at multiple reading levels for each content area. Experts suggest 70% of books should be easily accessible; and, in addition to classroom libraries, using rolling carts lets book collections travel among classrooms. Multiple reading levels let more advanced readers peruse a harder text, while less advanced readers read several easier texts; this equalizes the time and words they have for practicing. Because critics find some leveled readers lack variety in gender/race/class/other sociocultural aspects of characters, teachers should build diverse book collections representing all students. Teachers can inform their selections via student interest surveys; and familiarity with students' individual identities, personalities, and special interests. Knowing individual students can help match them to texts as effectively as leveled book lists.

ENGAGING STUDENTS IN READING

Experts find excessive attention to **leveling** as a way of matching texts to students can be restrictive, undermining high-quality instruction that balances the needs of the reader with the demands of the text. Teachers must consider that assigning certain texts will cause students to disengage from reading and avoid it rather than engage in it. In the real world, people read many different kinds of materials. Therefore, a teacher has better chances of finding texts that engage students, and that motivate them to read and allow them to perceive themselves as readers, by mindfully selecting **varied text genres** with **varied difficulty**. In classrooms incorporating various student reading levels, this can be the best method to procure classroom acceptability of accessible texts. Teachers can also use **individualized instructional formats**, such as Readers Workshop (Atwell, 1998), which balance issues of difficulty, choice, and engagement; develop reader communities affording more reading experiences with authenticity, meaning, and enjoyment; and stronger positive teacher-student relationships via individualized consultations. Teachers should also incorporate **accessible alternative texts** for independent activities.

ALTERNATIVE READING AND WRITING FORMS TO HELP STUDENTS ATTAIN GREATER PROGRESS IN READING

When students read and write outside of school, they choose many alternative forms of reading and writing. To engage these students while they are in school, teachers should think about adding such **alternative materials** to their own instructional programs. For example, teachers might incorporate such media as graphic novels, magazines, newspapers, plays, anthologies of poetry, e-books and other digital/online content, and text that students have written themselves. Educational experts advise that just because it can be harder to determine the reading levels of such alternative text formats, teachers should not shy away from using them. Because they represent examples of text that people (including students) read in real life, they provide not only excellent practice for students' present and future reading of real-world materials, but also motivation to read and meaningful experiences in reading. Another boon of using these authentic, alternative texts is that they frequently incorporate multiple reading levels, so that nearly every student can read some portions of them.

VIEWING SKILLS

Viewing skills can be sharpened by having students look at a single image, such as a work of art or a cartoon, and simply asking students what they **see**. The teacher can ask what is happening in the image, and then elicit the details that clue the students in to what is happening. Of course, there may be more than one thing happening. The teacher should also question the students about the message of the image, its purpose, its point of view, and its intended audience. The teacher should ask for first impressions, and then provide some background or additional information to see if it changes the way students look at or interpret the image. The conclusion of the lesson should include questions about what students learned from the exercise about the topic, themselves, and others.

BENEFITS

Students are exposed to multiple **images** every day. It is important for them to be able to effectively **interpret** these images. They should be able to make sense of the images and the spoken and print language that often accompany them. Learning can be enhanced with images because they allow for quicker connections to prior knowledge than verbal information. Visuals in the classroom can also be motivational, can support verbal information, and can express main points, sometimes resulting in instant recognition.

Some of the common types of images that students see every day include: bulletin boards, computer graphics, diagrams, drawings, illustrations, maps, photographs, posters, book covers, advertisements, Internet sites, multimedia presentations, puppet shows, television, videos, print cartoons, models, paintings, animation, drama or dance performances, films, and online newscasts and magazines.

ACTIVITIES TO STRENGTHEN SKILLS

Activities at school that can be used to strengthen the **viewing skills** of students of varying ages include:

- **Picture book discussions** – Students can develop an appreciation of visual text and the language that goes with it through guided discussions of picture books that focus on the style and color of the images and other details that might capture a child's attention.
- **Gallery walks** – Students can walk around a room or hallway viewing the posted works of other students and hear presentations about the works. They can also view a display prepared by the teacher. Students are expected to take notes as they walk around, have discussions, and perhaps do a follow-up report.
- **Puppet theater and drama presentations** – Students can learn about plots, dialogue, situations, characters, and the craft of performance from viewing puppet or drama presentations, which also stimulate oral communication and strengthen listening skills. Discussions or written responses should follow performances to check for detail acquisition.

CLASSROOM VIEWING CENTER

A **classroom viewing center** should contain magazines, CD-ROMs, books, videos, and individual pictures (photographs or drawings). Students should have a **viewing guide** that explains expectations related to the viewing center (before, during, and after using the center). For younger

134

students, the teacher can ask questions that guide them through the viewing rather than expecting them to read the guidelines and write responses.

- **Before** viewing, students should think about what they already know about the subject and what they want to learn from the viewing.
- **During** the viewing, students should make notes about whatever interests them or is new to them.
- **After** viewing, students could discuss or individually write down what they found to be the most interesting idea or striking image and explain why it caught their attention.

TYPES OF QUESTIONS TO ASK IF VIEWING IS A NARRATIVE

A teacher should make students responsible for gaining information or insight from the **viewing**. Setting expectations increases student attention and critical thinking. As with any viewing, the students should consider what they already know about the topic and what they hope to gain by watching the narrative before viewing it. During the viewing, the students should take notes (perhaps to answer questions provided by the teacher).

After the viewing, students should be able to answer the following questions:

- What was the time period and setting of the story?
- Who were the main characters?
- How effective was the acting?
- What was the problem or goal in the story?
- How was the problem solved or the goal achieved?
- How would you summarize the story?
- What did you learn from the story?
- What did you like or dislike about the story or its presentation?
- Would you recommend this viewing to others?
- How would you rate it?

DIFFICULTIES RELATED TO LEARNING BY LISTENING

It is difficult to learn just by listening because the instruction is presented only in spoken form. Therefore, unless students take notes, there is nothing for them to review. However, an active listener will anticipate finding a **message** in an oral presentation and will listen for it, **interpreting** tone and gestures as the presentation progresses. In group discussions, students are often too busy figuring out what they will say when it is their turn to talk to concentrate on what others are saying. Therefore, they don't learn from others, but instead come away knowing only what they already knew. Students should be required to respond directly to the previous speaker before launching into their own comments. This practice will force students to listen to each other and learn that their own responses will be better because of what can be added by listening to others.

GRAPHIC ORGANIZERS

The purpose of **graphic organizers** is to help students classify ideas and communicate more efficiently and effectively. Graphic organizers are visual outlines or templates that help students grasp key concepts and master subject matter by simplifying them down to basic points. They also help guide students through processes related to any subject area or task. Examples of processes include brainstorming, problem solving, decision making, research and project planning, and studying. Examples of graphic organizers include:

- **Reading** – These can include beginning, middle, and end graphs or event maps.
- **Science** – These can include charts that show what animals need or how to classify living things.
- **Math** – These can include horizontal bar graphs or time lines.
- **Language arts** – These can include alphabet organizers or charts showing the components of the five-paragraph essay.
- **General** – These can include KWL charts or weekly planners.

SPEAKING SKILLS CHILDREN IN ELEMENTARY/INTERMEDIATE SCHOOL SHOULD HAVE

Children of elementary/intermediate school age should be able to:

- Speak at an appropriate volume, tone, and pace that is understandable and appropriate to the audience
- Pronounce most words accurately
- Use complete sentences
- Make eye contact
- Use appropriate gestures with speech
- Exhibit an awareness of audience and adjust content to fit the audience (adjust word choices and style to be appropriate for peers or adults)
- Ask relevant questions
- Respond appropriately when asked questions about information or an opinion, possibly also being able to provide reasons for opinions
- Speak in turn, not interrupt, and include others in conversations
- Provide a summary or report orally
- Participate in small and large group discussions and debates
- Read orally before an audience
- Conduct short interviews
- Provide directions and explanations orally, including explanations of class lessons

VIEWING SKILLS ELEMENTARY/INTERMEDIATE SCHOOL CHILDREN SHOULD HAVE

Children of elementary school age should be developing or have attained the ability to understand the importance of **media** in people's lives. They should understand that television, radio, films, and the Internet have a role in everyday life. They should also be able to use media themselves (printing out material from the Internet or making an audio or video tape, for example). They should also be aware that the purpose of advertising is to sell. Children of intermediate school age should be developing or have attained the ability to **obtain and compare information** from newspapers, television, and the Internet. They should also be able to judge its **reliability and accuracy** to some extent. Children of this age should be able to tell the difference between fictional and non-fictional materials in media. They should also be able to use a variety of media, visuals, and sounds to make a presentation.

LISTENING SKILLS CHILDREN SHOULD DEVELOP THROUGH THEIR ELEMENTARY/INTERMEDIATE SCHOOL YEARS

Through the elementary/intermediate school years, children should develop the following listening skills:

- Follow oral instructions consistently
- Actively listen to peers and teachers
- Avoid creating distracting behavior or being distracted by the behavior of others most of the time
- Respond to listening activities and exhibit the ability to discuss, illustrate, or write about the activity and show knowledge of the content and quality of the listening activity
- Respond to listening activities and exhibit the ability to identify themes, similarities/differences, ideas, forms, and styles of activities
- Respond to a persuasive speaker and exhibit the ability to analyze and evaluate the credibility of the speaker and form an opinion describing whether they agree or disagree with the point made
- Demonstrate appropriate social behavior while part of an audience

STAGES OF WRITING

The **three stages of writing** are drawing, dictating, and writing. During the **drawing stage**, young learners use scribbles or pictures to convey their message. When asked to "read" their drawing, children in the drawing stage will use their picture to tell a story, as if they were mimicking a book being read to them. In the **dictation stage**, learners will tell their thoughts to a literate person, who will in turn write the words for the child. During this stage, the student is aware that the written words on the page represent their thoughts and can sometimes recognize the beginning sounds of the words they are saying, including some sight words. In the third and final stage, the **writing stage**, students are able to write their own thoughts in a way that can be recognized by others. Both beginning and ending sounds are represented in the words, along with some vowels. Students in this stage also understand spacing between words and the idea of creating complete sentences.

NORM-REFERENCED AND CRITERION-REFERENCED ASSESSMENTS

Norm-referenced assessments are used to gauge a student success by comparing his or her score to a theoretical "average" score achieved by students of the same age or grade level. With a norm-referenced assessment, a student's achievement is decided based on how much better or worse that student scored in comparison to his or her peers. In contrast, **criterion-referenced assessments** are scored based on each student's individual ability to show mastery of specific learning standards. Students are deemed successful if they are able to achieve mastery of concepts that are appropriate for their age or grade level, regardless of how their peers perform.

IRI

The **Informal Reading Inventory (IRI)**, also known as the **Qualitative Reading Inventory (QRI)** is a survey used to assess the instructional needs of individual readers. The IRI is used to determine a reader's grade-level reading, fluency, comprehension, vocabulary, oral reading accuracy, word recognition, word meaning, and reading strategies. The IRI is an ongoing assessment that should be administered several times a year starting from first grade through twelfth grade. Teachers should use the outcomes of these assessments to determine appropriate reading material for individual students and to identify and implement specific needs and strategies for individual learners or groups of learners.

UNIVERSAL SCREENING ASSESSMENTS, DIAGNOSTIC ASSESSMENTS, AND PROGRESS MONITORING

Universal screening assessments are brief surveys given to all students at the beginning of each school year, which are used to determine the mastery of critical skills and concepts. These screenings should be repeated approximately three times a year to ensure that students are performing at age-appropriate levels. **Diagnostic assessments** are used to help educators make sense of universal screening assessment scores. Based on diagnostics, teachers can identify the specific educational gaps of individual students and use that information to modify and differentiate instruction. **Progress monitoring** is used to determine if the educational interventions and strategies put in place (based on the diagnostic testing) are actually working. Struggling students are often monitored more closely to ensure that educational gaps are being filled at an appropriate and sufficient rate.

FORMAL AND INFORMAL ASSESSMENTS

Formal assessments, which include norm-based assessments, criterion-based assessments, intelligence tests, and diagnostic assessments are data driven. These types of assessments are used to determine a student's overall achievement and can be used to compare each student's abilities to his or her peers. Formal assessments are often shared with students and stakeholders to determine whether or not a student is performing at an appropriate level for his or her age or grade level. **Informal assessments**, which include running records, cloze tests, reading inventories, portfolios, and so on are not data driven. Instead, informal assessments use performance-driven tasks to guide instruction and provide informal ratings about each student's individual progress. During these assessments, each student's performance is used to monitor his or her progress and guide future instruction, often in preparation for a formal assessment.

EVALUATING APPROPRIATENESS OF ASSESSMENT INSTRUMENT OR PRACTICE

The two main factors that must be considered when evaluating the appropriateness of assessment instruction and practices are curriculum alignment and cultural bias. **Curriculum alignment** is the act of teaching students the concepts that they will eventually be tested on. To reach proficiency on the standards outlined by state or district mandates, teachers must continuously teach and assess the standards. Avoiding **cultural bias** ensures that all students are given access to all relevant lessons, instruction, and materials. Furthermore, avoiding cultural bias ensures that all students are given a fair opportunity to succeed on any given assessment. This includes accommodating students of certain subgroups with assessment modifications, such as additional testing time, taking the test in his or her native language, and creating types of assessments that are accessible and achievable for students of all backgrounds.

EXAMPLE EVALUATION OF SCORING METHOD

A teacher is assessing a student's ability to identify the main idea of a text. The student correctly identifies the main idea but includes several spelling errors in her written response. The teacher lowers the student's grade, taking points off for misspellings. In this example, the teacher's scoring method is **inappropriate** for the concept being assessed. Although misspellings should be addressed and remedied, the question was designed to assess the student's ability to identify the main idea of the passage. It was not intended to assess the spelling abilities of the student. By lowering the student's score based on misspellings, the teacher is insinuating that the student is unable to correctly identify the main idea of a passage, which is not the case. When assessing a specific skill, it is important that teachers score students based on their ability to complete isolated skills for data to accurately drive future instruction.

PENMANSHIP

Penmanship is a word used to describe a person's *handwriting*. The three main characteristics of penmanship are letter formation, size, and spacing. When teaching penmanship, teachers should start by helping students to correctly form each letter, using arrows to dictate the order and direction in which parts of each letter should be written. Once students have mastered each letter, teachers should focus on letter size or proportion. For example, smaller letters (like c, e, and n) should be half the size of larger letters (such as k, l, or t). Finally, proper spacing should be taught, both between letters and words. Once spacing between words has been mastered, students should begin to work on including punctuation and appropriate spacing between sentences.

IMPORTANCE OF LISTENING AND SPEAKING STRATEGIES

Both listening and speaking strategies are important skills for students in all areas of education. To achieve the highest success, students should be taught how to effectively **speak** and exchange dialogue in large- and small-group settings. In addition, students should be encouraged to question, retell, or reenact the words of others. Equally important, students must learn to actively **listen** and visualize the words of others so that they are able to understand the purpose of what someone else is saying. To check for listening, students should be encouraged to summarize what they have heard and complete graphic organizers outlining important concepts or facts. When given ample opportunity to both speak and listen, students are more likely to excel across all content areas.

DEVELOPING LISTENING AND SPEAKING SKILLS WITH DRAMATIC PLAYS

Dramatic play is a type of play in which students are assigned specific roles and encouraged to act those roles out. In dramatic play, students are typically assigned a character but not a script. They are encouraged to take on the feelings and actions of the character they have been assigned and act as that character would act. Dramatic play is an excellent strategy for developing speaking skills as students must clearly identify and express the feelings of their characters. They must speak clearly and loud enough so that the other actors and audience can hear what they are saying. In addition, students must actively listen to what the other students in the play are saying to appropriately respond to the actions and words of the other characters in an effort to further develop the story line.

Social Studies

U.S. History

CONTRIBUTIONS OF EARLY FRENCH EXPLORERS

The **French** never succeeded in attracting settlers to their territories. Those who came were more interested in the fur and fish trades than in forming colonies. Eventually, the French ceded their southern possessions and New Orleans, founded in 1718, to Spain. However, the French made major contributions to the exploration of the new continent, including:

- **Giovanni da Verrazano** and **Jacques Cartier** explored the North American coast and the St. Lawrence Seaway for France.
- **Samuel de Champlain**, who founded Quebec and set up a fur empire on the St. Lawrence Seaway, also explored the coasts of Massachusetts and Rhode Island between 1604 and 1607.
- **Fr. Jacques Marquette**, a Jesuit missionary, and **Louis Joliet** were the first Europeans to travel down the Mississippi in 1673.
- **Rene-Robert de la Salle** explored the Great Lakes and the Illinois and Mississippi Rivers from 1679-1682, claiming all the land from the Great Lakes to the Gulf of Mexico and from the Appalachians to the Rockies for France.

EARLIEST SPANISH EXPLORERS

The **Spanish** claimed and explored huge portions of the United States after the voyages of Christopher Columbus. Among them were:

- **Juan Ponce de Leon** – In 1513, he became the first European in Florida; established the oldest European settlement in Puerto Rico; discovered the Gulf Stream; and searched for the fountain of youth.
- **Alonso Alvarez de Pineda** – He charted the Gulf Coast from Florida to Mexico in 1519. Probably the first European in Texas, he claimed it for Spain.
- **Panfilo de Narvaez** – He docked in Tampa Bay with Cabeza de Vaca in 1528, claimed Florida for Spain, and then sailed the Gulf Coast.
- **Alvar Nuñez Cabeza de Vaca** – He got lost on foot in Texas and New Mexico. Estevanico, or Esteban, a Moorish slave, was a companion who guided them to Mexico.
- **Francisco Vásquez de Coronado** – While searching for gold in 1540, he became the first European to explore Kansas, Oklahoma, Texas, New Mexico, and Arizona.
- **Hernando De Soto** – He was the first European to explore the southeastern United States from Tallahassee to Natchez.

COLONIZATION OF VIRGINIA AND THE VIRGINIA COMPANY

In 1585, **Sir Walter Raleigh** landed on Roanoke Island and sent Arthur Barlow to the mainland, which they named **Virginia**. Two attempts to establish settlements failed. The first permanent English colony was founded by Captain John Smith in **Jamestown** in 1607. The **Virginia Company** and the **Chesapeake Bay Company** successfully colonized other Virginia sites. By 1619, Virginia had a House of Burgesses. The crown was indifferent to the colony, so local government grew strong and tobacco created wealth. The First Families of Virginia dominated politics there for two centuries, and four of the first five United States presidents came from these families. The Virginia Company sent 24 Puritan families, known as **Pilgrims**, to Virginia on the **Mayflower**. In 1620, it landed at Plymouth, Massachusetts instead. The **Plymouth Plantation** was established and survived with the help of natives. This is where the first Thanksgiving is believed to have occurred.

COLONIZATION IN MASSACHUSETTS, MARYLAND, RHODE ISLAND, AND PENNSYLVANIA

In 1629, 400 Puritans arrived in **Salem**, which became an important port and was made famous by the witch trials in 1692. In 1628, the self-governed **Massachusetts Bay Company** was organized, and the Massachusetts Indians sold most of the land to the English. **Boston** was established in 1630 and **Harvard University** was established in 1636.

Maryland was established by Lord Baltimore in 1632 in the hopes of providing refuge for English Catholics. The Protestant majority, however, opposed this religious tolerance.

Roger Williams was banished from Massachusetts in 1636 because he called for separation of church and state. He established the **Rhode Island** colony in 1647 and had 800 settlers by 1650, including Anne Hutchinson and her "Antinomians," who attacked clerical authority.

In 1681, **William Penn** received a royal charter for the establishment of **Pennsylvania** as a colony for Quakers. However, religious tolerance allowed immigrants from a mixed group of denominations, who prospered from the beginning.

REASONS FOR AMERICAN REVOLUTION

The English colonies **rebelled** for the following reasons:

- England was remote yet **controlling**. By 1775, few Americans had ever been to England. They considered themselves Americans, not English.
- During the Seven Years' War (aka French and Indian War) from 1754-1763, Americans, including George Washington, served in the British army, but were treated as **inferiors**.
- It was feared that the Anglican Church might try to expand in the colonies and **inhibit religious freedom**.
- Heavy **taxation** such as the Sugar and Stamp Acts, which were created solely to create revenue for the crown, and business controls such as restricting trade of certain products to England only, were burdensome.
- The colonies had no official **representation** in the English Parliament and wanted to govern themselves.
- There were fears that Britain would block westward expansion and independent enterprise.
- **Local government**, established through elections by property holders, was already functioning.

IMPORTANT EVENTS AND GROUPS LEADING UP TO AMERICAN REVOLUTION

Over several years, various events and groups contributed to the rebellion that became a revolution:

- **Sons of Liberty** – This was the protest group headed by Samuel Adams that incited the Revolution.
- **Boston Massacre** – On March 5, 1770, soldiers fired on a crowd and killed five people.
- **Committees of Correspondence** – These were set up throughout the colonies to transmit revolutionary ideas and create a unified response.
- **The Boston Tea Party** – On December 6, 1773, the Sons of Liberty, dressed as Mohawks, dumped tea into the harbor from a British ship to protest the tea tax. The harsh British response further aggravated the situation.

- **First Continental Congress** – This was held in 1774 to list grievances and develop a response, including boycotts. It was attended by all the colonies with the exception of Georgia.
- **The Shot Heard Round the World** – In April, 1775, English soldiers on their way to confiscate arms in Concord passed through Lexington, Massachusetts and met the colonial militia called the Minutemen. A fight ensued. In Concord, a larger group of Minutemen forced the British to retreat.

> **Review Video: The First and Second Continental Congress**
> Visit mometrix.com/academy and enter code: 835211

ORIGINAL 13 COLONIES AND MAJOR TURNING POINTS OF THE REVOLUTION

The original **13 colonies** were: Connecticut, Delaware, Georgia, Maryland, Massachusetts, New Hampshire, New Jersey, New York, North Carolina, Pennsylvania, Rhode Island, South Carolina, and Virginia. Delaware was the first state to ratify the constitution.

The major turning points of the American Revolution were:

- The actions of the **Second Continental Congress** – This body established the Continental Army and chose George Washington as its commanding general. They allowed printing of money and created government offices.
- "**Common Sense**" – Published in 1776 by Thomas Paine, this pamphlet calling for independence was widely distributed.
- The **Declaration of Independence** – Written by Thomas Jefferson, it was ratified on July 4, 1776 by the Continental Congress assembled in Philadelphia.
- **Alliance with France** – Benjamin Franklin negotiated an agreement with France to fight with the Americans in 1778.
- **Treaty of Paris** – In 1782, it signaled the official end of the war, granted independence to the colonies, and gave them generous territorial rights.

> **Review Video: Declaration of Independence**
> Visit mometrix.com/academy and enter code: 256838
>
> **Review Video: Colonization of the Americas**
> Visit mometrix.com/academy and enter code: 438412

ARTICLES OF CONFEDERATION AND THE CONSTITUTION

The **Articles of Confederation**, designed to protect states' rights over those of the national government and sent to the colonies for ratification in 1777, had two major elements that proved unworkable. First, there was no centralized national government. Second, there was no centralized power to tax or regulate trade with other nations or between states. With no national tax, the Revolution was financed by printing more and more money, which caused inflation. In 1787, a convention was called to write a new **constitution**. This constitution created the three branches of government with checks and balances of power: **executive, legislative, and judicial**. It also created a **bicameral legislature** so that there would be equal representation for the states in the Senate and representation for the population in the House. Those who opposed the new constitution, the **Anti-Federalists**, wanted a bill of rights included. The **Federalist** platform was

explained in the "Federalist Papers," written by James Madison, John Jay, and Alexander Hamilton. The Constitution went into effect in 1789, and the **Bill of Rights** was added in 1791.

> **Review Video: Articles of Confederation**
> Visit mometrix.com/academy and enter code: 927401

LOUISIANA PURCHASE

The **Louisiana Purchase** in 1803 for $15 million may be considered **Thomas Jefferson's** greatest achievement as president. The reasons for the purchase were to gain the vital port of New Orleans, remove the threat of French interference with trade along the Mississippi River, and double the territory of the United States. The purchase both answered and raised new questions about the use of federal power, including the constitutionality of the president making such a purchase, Jefferson asking Congress for permission, and Jefferson taking the biggest federalist action up to that time, even though he was an anti-federalist. Jefferson sent **Meriwether Lewis and William Clark** to map the new territory and find a means of passage all the way to the Pacific Ocean. Although there was no river that flowed all the way west, their expedition and the richness of the land and game started the great western migration of settlers.

WAR OF 1812

A war between **France and Britain** caused blockades that hurt American trade and caused the British to attack American ships and impress sailors on them. An embargo against France and Britain was imposed by Jefferson, but rescinded by Madison with a renewed demand for respect for American sovereignty. However, Britain became more aggressive and war resulted. Native Americans under the leadership of **Tecumseh** sided with the British. The British captured Washington, D.C., and burned the White House, but Dolly Madison had enough forethought to save priceless American treasures, such as the Gilbert Stuart portrait of George Washington. Most battles, however, came to a draw. As a result, in 1815, when the British ended the war with France, they negotiated for peace with the United States as well under the **Treaty of Ghent**. A benefit of the war was that it motivated Americans to become more **self-sufficient** due to increased manufacturing and fewer imports.

MONROE DOCTRINE, MANIFEST DESTINY, AND MISSOURI COMPROMISE

Three important political actions in the 19th century were:

- The **Monroe Doctrine** – Conceived by President James Monroe in 1823, this foreign policy warned European powers to cease colonization of Central and South America or face military intervention by the United States. In return, the United States would not meddle in the political affairs or standing colonies of Europe.
- The **Missouri Compromise** – In 1820, there were 11 free states and 11 slave states. The fear of a power imbalance between slave and free states when Missouri petitioned to become a slave state brought about this agreement. Maine was brought in as a free state; the southern border of Missouri was set as the northernmost line of any slave territory; and the western states could come in as free states, while Arkansas and Florida could be slave states.
- **Manifest Destiny** – This was a popular belief during the 1840s that it was the right and duty of the United States to expand westward to the Pacific. The idea became a slogan for the flood of settlers and expansionist power grabs.

143

ANDREW JACKSON PRESIDENCY

A number of important milestones occurred in American history during the presidency of **Andrew Jackson**. They included:

- Jackson's election is considered the beginning of the modern political party system and the start of the **Democratic Party**.
- Jeffersonian Democracy, a system governed by middle and upper class educated property holders, was replaced by **Jacksonian Democracy**, a system that allowed universal white male suffrage.
- The **Indian Removal Act of 1830** took natives out of territories that whites wanted to settle, most notably the Trail of Tears that forcibly removed Cherokees from Georgia and relocated them to Oklahoma.
- The issue of **nullification**, the right of states to nullify any federal laws they thought unconstitutional, came to a head over tariffs. However, a strong majority vote in Congress supporting the Tariff Acts cemented the policy that states must comply with federal laws.

WHIG PARTY

The **Whig Party** existed from 1833 to 1856. It started in opposition to Jackson's **authoritarian policies** and was particularly concerned with defending the supremacy of Congress over the executive branch, states' rights, economic protectionism, and modernization. Notable members included: Daniel Webster, Henry Clay, Winfield Scott, and a young Abraham Lincoln. The Whigs had four presidents: William Henry Harrison, Zachary Taylor, John Tyler (expelled from the party), and Millard Fillmore. However, the Whigs won only two presidential elections. Harrison and Taylor were elected in 1840 and 1848, respectively. However, both died in office, so Tyler and Fillmore assumed the presidency. In 1852, the anti-slavery faction of the party kept Fillmore from getting the nomination. Instead, it went to Scott, who was soundly defeated. In 1856, the Whigs supported Fillmore and the National American Party, but lost badly. Thereafter, the **split over slavery** caused the party to dissolve.

IMPORTANT 19TH CENTURY AMERICAN WRITERS

In the 19th century, American literature became an entity of its own and provided a distinct voice for the American experience. **James Fenimore Cooper** was a great writer from this time period. He was the first to write about Native Americans, and was the author of the Leatherstocking series, which includes *The Last of the Mohicans* and *The Deerslayer*.

- **Ralph Waldo Emerson** – He was an essayist, philosopher, and poet, and also the leader of the Transcendentalist movement. His notable works include "Self-Reliance" and "The American Scholar."

- **Nathaniel Hawthorne** – This novelist and short story writer wrote *The Scarlet Letter*, *The House of Seven Gables*, "Young Goodman Brown," and "The Minister's Black Veil."
- **Herman Melville** – He was a novelist, essayist, short story writer, and poet who wrote *Moby Dick*, *Billy Budd*, and "Bartleby the Scrivener." **Edgar Allan Poe** – He was a poet, literary critic, and master of the short story, especially horror and detective stories. His notable works include "The Tell-Tale Heart," "The Pit and the Pendulum," "Annabel Lee," and "The Raven."
- **Harriet Beecher Stowe** – She was the author of *Uncle Tom's Cabin*.
- **Henry David Thoreau** – He was a poet, naturalist, and Transcendentalist who wrote *Walden* and *Civil Disobedience*.
- **Walt Whitman** – He was a poet, essayist, and journalist who wrote *Leaves of Grass* and "O Captain! My Captain!"

19ᴛʜ Century Social and Religious Leaders

Some of the important social and religious leaders from the 19th century were:

- **Susan B. Anthony** – A women's rights and abolition activist, she lectured across the nation for suffrage, property and wage rights, and labor organizations for women.
- **Dorothea Dix** – She created the first American asylums for the treatment of mental illness and served as the Superintendent of Army Nurses during the War Between the States.
- **Frederick Douglass** –An escaped slave who became an abolitionist leader, government official, and writer.
- **William Lloyd Garrison** –An abolitionist and the editor of the *Liberator*, the leading anti-slavery newspaper of the time.
- **Joseph Smith** – He founded the Latter-Day Saints (Mormonism) in 1829.
- **Horace Mann** – A leader of the common school movement that made public education a right of all Americans.
- **Elizabeth Cady Stanton** – With Lucretia Mott, she held the Seneca Falls Convention in 1848, demanding women's suffrage and other reforms.
- **Brigham Young** –The leader of the Mormons when they fled religious persecution, built Salt Lake City, and settled much of the West. He was the first governor of the Utah Territory.

Compromise of 1850, Fugitive Slave Law, Kansas-Nebraska Act, Bleeding Kansas, and Dred Scott Case

- The **Compromise of 1850**, calling upon the principle of popular sovereignty, allowed those who lived in the Mexican cession to decide for themselves whether to be a free or slave territory.
- The **Fugitive Slave Law of 1850** allowed slave owners to go into free states to retrieve their escaped slaves.
- The **Kansas-Nebraska Act of 1854** repealed the Missouri Compromise of 1820 to allow the lands from the Louisiana Purchase to settle the slavery issue by popular sovereignty. Outraged Northerners responded by defecting from the Whig Party and starting the Republican Party.
- **Bleeding Kansas** was the name applied to the state when a civil war broke out between pro- and anti-slavery advocates while Kansas was trying to formalize its statutes before being admitted as a state.
- The **Dred Scott vs. Sandford case** was decided by the Supreme Court in 1857. It was ruled that Congress had no authority to exclude slavery from the territories, which in effect meant that the Missouri Compromise had been unconstitutional.

STATES FORMING THE CONFEDERACY AND LEADERS OF THE WAR BETWEEN THE STATES

The states that **seceded** from the Union to form the **Confederacy** were: Georgia, Arkansas, South Carolina, North Carolina, Virginia, Florida, Mississippi, Alabama, Louisiana, Texas, and Tennessee. The slave-holding states that were kept in the Union were Delaware, Maryland, Kentucky, and Missouri.

- **Jefferson Davis** of Mississippi, a former U. S. senator and cabinet member, was the president of the Confederacy.
- **Abraham Lincoln** of Illinois was the President of the United States. His election triggered the secession of the south. He was assassinated shortly after winning a second term.
- **Robert E. Lee** of Virginia was offered the position of commanding general of the Union Army, but declined because of loyalty to his home state. He led the Army of Northern Virginia and the central Confederate force, and is still considered a military mastermind.
- **Ulysses S. Grant** of Ohio wasn't appointed to command the Union Army until 1864, after a series of other commanders were unsuccessful. He received Lee's surrender at the Appomattox Court House in Virginia in April, 1865, and went on to become President from 1869 to 1877.

RECONSTRUCTION AND 13TH, 14TH, AND 15TH AMENDMENTS

Reconstruction was the period from 1865 to 1877, during which the South was under strict control of the U.S. government. In March, 1867, all state governments of the former Confederacy were terminated, and **military occupation** began. Military commanders called for constitutional conventions to reconstruct the state governments, to which delegates were to be elected by universal male suffrage. After a state government was in operation and the state had **ratified the 14th Amendment**, its representatives were admitted to Congress. Three constitutional amendments from 1865 to 1870, which tried to rectify the problems caused by slavery, became part of the Reconstruction effort. The **13th Amendment** declared slavery illegal. The **14th Amendment** made all persons born or naturalized in the country U.S. citizens, and forbade any state to interfere with their fundamental civil rights.   The **15th Amendment** made it illegal to deny individuals the right to vote on the grounds of race. In his 1876 election campaign, President **Rutherford B. Hayes** promised to withdraw the troops, and did so in 1877.

MAJOR CHANGES IN INDUSTRY IN THE LATE 1800S

Important events during this time of enormous business growth and large-scale exploitation of natural resources were:

- **Industrialization** – Like the rest of the world, the United States' entry into the Industrial Age was marked by many new inventions and the mechanization of factories.
- **Railroad expansion** – The Transcontinental Railroad was built from 1865 to 1969. Railroad tracks stretched over 35,000 miles in 1865, but that distance reached 240,000 miles by 1910. The raw materials and manufactured goods needed for the railroads kept mines and factories very busy.
- **Gold and silver mining** – Mines brought many prospectors to the West from 1850 to about 1875, but mining corporations soon took over.
- **Cattle ranching** – This was a large-scale enterprise beginning in the late 1860s, but by the 1880s open ranges were being fenced and plowed for farming and pastures. Millions of farmers moved into the high plains, establishing the "Bread Basket," which was the major wheat growing area of the country.

GILDED AGE AND INFAMOUS ROBBER BARONS

The **Gilded Age**, from the 1870s to 1890, was so named because of the enormous wealth and grossly opulent lifestyle enjoyed by a handful of powerful families. This was the time when huge mansions were built as summer "cottages" in Newport, Rhode Island, and great lodges were built in mountain areas for the pleasure of families such as the Vanderbilts, Ascots, and Rockefellers. Control of the major industries was held largely by the following men, who were known as **Robber Barons** for their ruthless business practices and exploitation of workers: Jay Gould, railroads; Andrew Carnegie, steel; John D. Rockefeller, Sr., oil; Philip Danforth Armour, meatpacking; J. P. Morgan, banking; John Jacob Astor, fur pelts; and Cornelius Vanderbilt, steamboat shipping. Of course, all of these heads of industry diversified and became involved in multiple business ventures. To curb cutthroat competition, particularly among the railroads, and to prohibit restrained trade, Congress created the **Interstate Commerce Commission** and the **Sherman Anti-Trust Act**. Neither of these, however, was enforced.

> **Review Video: The Gilded Age: An Overview**
> Visit mometrix.com/academy and enter code: 684770
>
> **Review Video: The Gilded Age: Chinese Immigration**
> Visit mometrix.com/academy and enter code: 624166
>
> **Review Video: The Gilded Age: Labor Strikes**
> Visit mometrix.com/academy and enter code: 683116
>
> **Review Video: The Gilded Age: Labor Unions**
> Visit mometrix.com/academy and enter code: 749692

IMMIGRATION TRENDS IN LATE 1800s

The population of the United States doubled between 1860 and 1890, the period that saw 10 million **immigrants** arrive. Most lived in the north. Cities and their **slums** grew tremendously because of immigration and industrialization. While previous immigrants had come from Germany, Scandinavia, and Ireland, the 1880s saw a new wave of immigrants from Italy, Poland, Hungary, Bohemia, and Greece, as well as Jewish groups from central and eastern Europe, especially Russia. The Roman Catholic population grew from 1.6 million in 1850 to 12 million in 1900, a growth that ignited an anti-Catholic backlash from the anti-Catholic Know-Nothing Party of the 1880s and the Ku Klux Klan. Exploited immigrant workers started **labor protests** in the 1870s, and the **Knights of Labor** was formed in 1878, calling for sweeping social and economic reform. Its membership reached 700,000 by 1886. Eventually, this organization was replaced by the **American Federation of Labor**, headed by Samuel Gompers.

EFFECTS OF PROGRESSIVE MOVEMENT ON FOREIGN AFFAIRS

The **Progressive Era**, which was the time period from the 1890s to the 1920s, got its name from progressive, reform-minded political leaders who wanted to export a just and rational social order to the rest of the world while increasing trade with foreign markets. Consequently, the United States interfered in a dispute between Venezuela and Britain. America invoked the **Monroe Doctrine** and sided with Cuba in its independence struggle against Spain. The latter resulted in the **Spanish-American Wars** in 1898 that ended with Cuba, Puerto Rico, the Philippines, and Guam becoming American protectorates at the same time the United States annexed Hawaii. In 1900, America declared an **Open Door policy** with China to support its independence and open markets. In 1903, Theodore Roosevelt helped Panama become independent of Columbia, and then secured the right to build the **Panama Canal**. Roosevelt also negotiated the peace treaty to end the Russo-

Japanese War, which earned him the Nobel Peace prize. He then sent the American fleet on a world cruise to display his country's power.

DOMESTIC ACCOMPLISHMENTS OF PROGRESSIVE ERA

To the Progressives, promoting law and order meant cleaning up city governments to make them honest and efficient, bringing more democracy and humanity to state governments, and establishing a core of social workers to improve slum housing, health, and education. Also during the **Progressive Era**, the national government strengthened or created the following regulatory agencies, services, and acts to oversee business enterprise:

- Passed in 1906, the **Hepburn A**ct reinforced the Interstate Commerce Commission. In 1902, Roosevelt used the Justice Department and lawsuits to try to break monopolies and enforce the **Sherman Anti-Trust Act**. The **Clayton Anti-Trust Act** was added in 1914.
- From 1898 to 1910, the **Forest Service** guided lumber companies in the conservation and more efficient use of woodland resources under the direction of Gifford Pinchot.
- In 1906, the **Pure Food and Drug Act** was passed to protect consumers from fraudulent labeling and adulteration of products.
- In 1913, the **Federal Reserve System** was established to supervise banking and commerce. In 1914, the **Fair Trade Commission** was established to ensure fair competition.

US INVOLVEMENT IN WORLD WAR I

When World War I broke out in 1914, America declared **neutrality**. The huge demand for war goods by the Allies broke a seven-year industrial stagnation and gave American factories full-time work. The country's sympathies lay mostly with the Allies, and before long American business and banking were heavily invested in an Allied victory. In 1916, **Woodrow Wilson** campaigned on the slogan "He kept us out of war." However, when the British ship the *Lusitania* was torpedoed in 1915 by a German submarine and many Americans were killed, Wilson had already warned the Germans that the United States would enter the war if Germany interfered with neutral ships at sea. Eventually, when it was proven that Germany was trying to incite Mexico and Japan into attacking the United States, Wilson declared war in 1917, even though America was unprepared. Nonetheless, America quickly armed and transferred sufficient troops to Europe, bringing the **Allies** to victory in 1918.

DECADE OF OPTIMISM

After World War I, **Warren Harding** ran for President on the slogan "return to normalcy" and concentrated on domestic affairs. The public felt optimistic because life improved due to affordable automobiles from Henry Ford's mass production system, better roads, electric lights, airplanes, new communication systems, and voting rights for women (19th Amendment, 1920). Radio and movies helped develop a national culture. For the first time, the majority of Americans lived in **cities**. Young people shortened dresses and haircuts, and smoked and drank in public despite Prohibition (18th Amendment, 1919). Meantime, the **Russian Revolution** caused a **Red Scare** that strengthened the already strong Ku Klux Klan that controlled some states' politics. In 1925, the **Scopes trial** in Tennessee convicted a high school teacher for presenting Darwinian theories. The **Teapot Dome scandal** rocked the Harding administration. After Harding died in 1923, **Calvin Coolidge** became president. He was followed by **Herbert Hoover**, a strong proponent of capitalism under whom unregulated business led to the 1929 stock crash.

GREAT DEPRESSION AND DUST BOWL

In the 1920s, the rich got richer. After World War I, however, farmers were in a depression when foreign markets started growing their own crops again. Increased credit buying, bank war debts, a huge gap between rich and poor, and a belief that the stock market would always go up got the nation into financial trouble. The **Stock Market Crash** in October 1929 that destroyed fortunes dramatized the downward spiral of the whole economy. Banks failed, and customers lost all their money. By 1933, 14 million were unemployed, industrial production was down to one-third of its 1929 level, and national income had dropped by half. Adding to the misery of farmers, years of breaking sod on the prairies without adequate conservation techniques caused the topsoil to fly away in great **dust storms** that blackened skies for years, causing deaths from lung disease and failed crops.

US ROLE IN WORLD WAR II

World War II began in 1939. As with World War I, the United States tried to stay out of World War II, even though the **Lend-Lease program** transferred munitions to Great Britain. However, on December 7, 1941, Japan attacked **Pearl Harbor** in Hawaii. Since Japan was an ally of Germany, the United States declared war on all the Axis powers. Although there was fighting in both Europe and the Pacific, the decision was made to concentrate on defeating Hitler first. Since it did not have combat within its borders, the United States became the great manufacturer of goods and munitions for the war effort. Women went to work in the factories, while the men entered the military. All facets of American life were centered on the war effort, including rationing, metal collections, and buying war bonds. The benefit of this production was an **end to the economic depression**. The influx of American personnel and supplies eventually brought victory in Europe in April of 1945, and in Asia the following August.

> **Review Video: World War II**
> Visit mometrix.com/academy and enter code: 759402
>
> **Review Video: World War II: Germany**
> Visit mometrix.com/academy and enter code: 951452
>
> **Review Video: World War II: Japan**
> Visit mometrix.com/academy and enter code: 313104

MAJOR PROGRAMS AND EVENTS RESULTING FROM THE COLD WAR

After World War II, the Soviet Union kept control of Eastern Europe, including half of Germany. **Communism** spread around the world. Resulting fears led to:

- The **Truman Doctrine** (1947) – This was a policy designed to protect free peoples everywhere against oppression.
- The **Marshall Plan** (1948) – This devoted $12 billion to rebuild Western Europe and strengthen its defenses.
- The **Organization of American States** (1948) – This was established to bolster democratic relations in the Americas.
- The **Berlin Blockade** (1948-49) – The Soviets tried to starve out West Berlin, so the United States provided massive supply drops by air.
- The **North Atlantic Treaty Organization** (1949) – This was formed to militarily link the United States and western Europe so that an attack on one was an attack on both.
- The **Korean War** (1950-53) – This divided the country into the communist North and the democratic South.
- The **McCarthy era** (1950-54) – Senator Joseph McCarthy of Wisconsin held hearings on supposed Communist conspiracies that ruined innocent reputations and led to the blacklisting of suspected sympathizers in the government, Hollywood, and the media.

> **Review Video: The Cold War: The United States and Russia**
> Visit mometrix.com/academy and enter code: 981433

MAJOR EVENTS OF 1960S

The 1960s were a tumultuous time for the United States. Major events included:

- The **Cuban Missile Crisis** (1961) – This was a stand-off between the United States and the Soviet Union over a build-up of missiles in Cuba. Eventually, the Soviets stopped their shipments and a nuclear war was averted.
- The assassinations of President Kennedy (1963), Senator Robert Kennedy (1968), and Dr. Martin Luther King, Jr. (1968).
- The **Civil Rights Movement** – Protest marches held across the nation to draw attention to the plight of black citizens. From 1964 to 1968, race riots exploded in more than 100 cities.
- The **Vietnam War** (1964-73) – This resulted in a military draft. There was heavy involvement of American personnel and money. There were also protest demonstrations, particularly on college campuses. At Kent State, several students died after being shot by National Guardsmen.
- **Major legislation** – Legislation passed during this decade included the Civil Rights Act, the Clean Air Act, and the Water Quality Act. This decade also saw the creation of the Peace Corps, Medicare, and the War on Poverty, in which billions were appropriated for education, urban redevelopment, and public housing.

PRESIDENTS AND VICE PRESIDENTS FROM 1972 TO 1974

In a two-year time span, the United States had two presidents and two vice presidents. This situation resulted first from the resignation of Vice President **Spiro T. Agnew** in October of 1973 because of alleged kickbacks. President **Richard M. Nixon** then appointed House Minority Leader **Gerald R. Ford** to be vice president. This was accomplished through Senate ratification, a process that had been devised after Harry Truman succeeded to the presidency upon the death of Franklin Roosevelt and went through nearly four years of his presidency without a vice president. Nixon resigned the presidency in August of 1974 because some Republican party members broke into Democratic headquarters at the **Watergate** building in Washington, DC, and the president participated in covering up the crime. Ford succeeded Nixon, and had to appoint another vice president. He chose **Nelson Rockefeller**, former governor of New York.

Geography

IMPORTANT TERMS RELATED TO MAPS

The most important terms used when describing items on a map or globe are:

- **Latitude and longitude** – Latitude and longitude are the imaginary lines (horizontal and vertical, respectively) that divide the globe into a grid. Both are measured using the 360 degrees of a circle.
- **Coordinates** – These are the latitude and longitude measures for a place.
- **Absolute location** – This is the exact spot where coordinates meet. The grid system allows the location of every place on the planet to be identified.
- **Equator** – This is the line at 0° latitude that divides the earth into two equal halves called hemispheres.
- **Parallels** – This is another name for lines of latitude because they circle the earth in parallel lines that never meet.
- **Meridians** – This is another name for lines of longitude. The Prime Meridian is located at 0° longitude, and is the starting point for measuring distance (both east and west) around the globe. Meridians circle the earth and connect at the Poles.

> **Review Video: 5 Elements of any Map**
> Visit mometrix.com/academy and enter code: 437727

FOUR HEMISPHERES, NORTH AND SOUTH POLES, TROPICS OF CANCER AND CAPRICORN, AND ARCTIC AND ANTARCTIC CIRCLES

The definitions for these terms are as follows:

- **Northern Hemisphere** – This is the area above, or north, of the equator.
- **Southern Hemisphere** – This is the area below, or south, of the equator.
- **Western Hemisphere** – This is the area between the North and South Poles. It extends west from the Prime Meridian to the International Date Line.
- **Eastern Hemisphere** – This is the area between the North and South Poles. It extends east from the Prime Meridian to the International Date Line.
- **North and South Poles** – Latitude is measured in terms of the number of degrees north and south from the equator. The North Pole is located at 90°N latitude, while the South Pole is located at 90°S latitude.
- **Tropic of Cancer** – This is the parallel, or latitude, 23½° north of the equator.
- **Tropic of Capricorn** – This is the parallel, or latitude, 23½° south of the equator. The region between these two parallels is the tropics. The subtropics is the area located between 23½° and 40° north and south of the equator.
- **Arctic Circle** – This is the parallel, or latitude, 66½° north of the equator.
- **Antarctic Circle** – This is the parallel, or latitude, 66½° south of the equator.

> **Review Video: Geographical Features**
> Visit mometrix.com/academy and enter code: 773539

GPS

Global Positioning System (GPS) is a system of satellites that orbit the Earth and communicate with mobile devices to pinpoint the mobile device's position. This is accomplished by determining the distance between the mobile device and at least three satellites. A mobile device might calculate a distance of 400 miles between it and the first satellite. The possible locations that are 400 miles from the first satellite and the mobile device will fall along a circle. The possible locations on Earth relative to the other two satellites will fall somewhere along different circles. The point on Earth at which these three circles intersect is the location of the mobile device. The process of determining position based on distance measurements from three satellites is called **trilateration**.

> **Review Video: Cartography and Technology**
> Visit mometrix.com/academy and enter code: 642071

TYPES OF MAPS

- A **physical map** is one that shows natural features such as mountains, rivers, lakes, deserts, and plains. Color is used to designate the different features.
- A **topographic map** is a type of physical map that shows the relief and configuration of a landscape, such as hills, valleys, fields, forest, roads, and settlements. It includes natural and human-made features.
- A **topological map** is one on which lines are stretched or straightened for the sake of clarity, but retain their essential geometric relationship. This type of map is used, for example, to show the routes of a subway system.
- A **political map** uses lines for state, county, and country boundaries; points or dots for cities and towns; and various other symbols for features such as airports and roads.

PHYSICAL AND CULTURAL FEATURES OF GEOGRAPHIC LOCATIONS AND COUNTRIES

PHYSICAL FEATURES:

- **Vegetation zones, or biomes** – Forests, grasslands, deserts, and tundra are the four main types of vegetation zones.
- **Climate zones** – Tropical, dry, temperate, continental, and polar are the five different types of climate zones. Climate is the long-term average weather conditions of a place.

CULTURAL FEATURES:

- **Population density** – This is the number of people living in each square mile or kilometer of a place. It is calculated by dividing population by area.
- **Religion** – This is the identification of the dominant religions of a place, whether Christianity, Hinduism, Judaism, Buddhism, Islam, Shinto, Taoism, or Confucianism. All of these originated in Asia.
- **Languages** – This is the identification of the dominant or official language of a place. There are 12 major language families. The Indo-European family (which includes English, Russian, German, French, and Spanish) is spoken over the widest geographic area, but Mandarin Chinese is spoken by the most people.

> **Review Video: Physical vs. Cultural Geography**
> Visit mometrix.com/academy and enter code: 912136

CORAL REEFS

Coral reefs are formed from millions of tiny, tube-shaped **polyps**, an animal life form encased in tough limestone skeletons. Once anchored to a rocky surface, polyps eat plankton and miniscule shellfish caught with poisonous tentacles near the mouth. Polyps use calcium carbonate absorbed from chemicals given off by algae to harden their body armor and cement themselves together in fantastic shapes of many colors. Polyps reproduce through eggs and larvae, but the reef grows by branching out shoots of polyps. There are three types of coral reefs:

- **Fringing reefs** – These surround, or "fringe," an island.
- **Barrier reefs** – Over the centuries, a fringe reef grows so large that the island sinks down from the weight, and the reef becomes a barrier around the island. Water trapped between the island and the reef is called a lagoon.
- **Atolls** – Eventually, the sinking island goes under, leaving the coral reef around the lagoon.

FORMATION OF MOUNTAINS

Mountains are formed by the movement of geologic plates, which are rigid slabs of rocks beneath the earth's crust that float on a layer of partially molten rock in the earth's upper mantle. As the plates collide, they push up the crust to form mountains. This process is called **orogeny**. There are three basic forms of orogeny:

- If the collision of continental plates causes the crust to buckle and fold, a chain of **folded mountains**, such as the Appalachians, the Alps, or the Himalayas, is formed.
- If the collision of the plates causes a denser oceanic plate to go under a continental plate, a process called **subduction**; strong horizontal forces lift and fold the margin of the continent. A mountain range like the Andes is the result.
- If an oceanic plate is driven under another oceanic plate, **volcanic mountains** such as those in Japan and the Philippines are formed.

HARMFUL OR POTENTIALLY HARMFUL INTERACTION WITH ENVIRONMENT

Wherever humans have gone on the earth, they have made **changes** to their surroundings. Many are harmful or potentially harmful, depending on the extent of the alterations. Some of the changes and activities that can harm the **environment** include:

- Cutting into mountains by machine or blasting to build roads or construction sites
- Cutting down trees and clearing natural growth
- Building houses and cities
- Using grassland to graze herds
- Polluting water sources
- Polluting the ground with chemical and oil waste
- Wearing out fertile land and losing topsoil
- Placing communication lines cross country using poles and wires or underground cable
- Placing railway lines or paved roads cross country
- Building gas and oil pipelines cross country
- Draining wetlands
- Damming up or re-routing waterways
- Spraying fertilizers, pesticides, and defoliants
- Hunting animals to extinction or near extinction

ADAPTATION TO ENVIRONMENTAL CONDITIONS

The environment influences the way people live. People **adapt** to **environmental conditions** in ways as simple as putting on warm clothing in a cold environment; finding means to cool their surroundings in an environment with high temperatures; building shelters from wind, rain, and temperature variations; and digging water wells if surface water is unavailable. More complex adaptations result from the physical diversity of the earth in terms of soil, climate, vegetation, and topography. Humans take advantage of opportunities and avoid or minimize limitations. Examples of environmental limitations are that rocky soils offer few opportunities for agriculture and rough terrain limits accessibility. Sometimes, **technology** allows humans to live in areas that were once uninhabitable or undesirable. For example, air conditioning allows people to live comfortably in hot climates; modern heating systems permit habitation in areas with extremely low temperatures, as is the case with research facilities in Antarctica; and airplanes have brought people to previously inaccessible places to establish settlements or industries.

CARRYING CAPACITY AND NATURAL HAZARDS

Carrying capacity is the maximum, sustained level of use of an environment can incur without sustaining significant environmental deterioration that would eventually lead to environmental destruction. Environments vary in terms of their carrying capacity, a concept humans need to learn to measure and respect before harm is done. Proper **assessment of environmental conditions** enables responsible decision making with respect to how much and in what ways the resources of a particular environment should be consumed. **Energy and water conservation** as well as recycling can extend an area's carrying capacity. In addition to carrying capacity limitations, the physical environment can also have occasional extremes that are costly to humans. **Natural hazards** such as hurricanes, tornadoes, earthquakes, volcanoes, floods, tsunamis, and some forest fires and insect infestations are processes or events that are not caused by humans, but may have serious consequences for humans and the environment. These events are not preventable, and their precise timing, location, and magnitude are not predictable. However, some precautions can be taken to reduce the damage.

APPLYING GEOGRAPHY TO INTERPRETATION OF THE PAST

Space, environment, and chronology are three different points of view that can be used to study history. Events take place within **geographic contexts**. If the world is flat, then transportation choices are vastly different from those that would be made in a round world, for example. Invasions of Russia from the west have normally failed because of the harsh winter conditions, the vast distances that inhibit steady supply lines, and the number of rivers and marshes to be crossed, among other factors. Any invading or defending force anywhere must make choices based on consideration of space and environmental factors. For instance, lands may be too muddy or passages too narrow for certain equipment. Geography played a role in the building of the Panama Canal because the value of a shorter transportation route had to outweigh the costs of labor, disease, political negotiations, and equipment, not to mention a myriad of other effects from cutting a canal through an isthmus and changing a natural land structure as a result.

APPLYING GEOGRAPHY TO INTERPRETATION OF THE PRESENT AND PLANS FOR THE FUTURE

The decisions that individual people as well as nations make that may **affect the environment** have to be made with an understanding of spatial patterns and concepts, cultural and transportation connections, physical processes and patterns, ecosystems, and the impact, or "footprint," of people on the physical environment. Sample issues that fit into these considerations are recycling programs, loss of agricultural land to further urban expansion, air and water pollution, deforestation, and ease of transportation and communication. In each of these areas, present and future uses have to be balanced against possible harmful effects. For example, wind is a clean and readily available resource for electric power, but the access roads to and noise of wind turbines can make some areas unsuitable for livestock pasture. Voting citizens need to have an understanding of **geographical and environmental connections** to make responsible decisions.

SPATIAL ORGANIZATION

Spatial organization in geography refers to how things or people are grouped in a given space anywhere on earth. Spatial organization applies to the **placement of settlements**, whether hamlets, towns, or cities. These settlements are located to make the distribution of goods and services convenient. For example, in farm communities, people come to town to get groceries, to attend church and school, and to access medical services. It is more practical to provide these things to groups than to individuals. These settlements, historically, have been built close to water sources and agricultural areas. Lands that are topographically difficult, have few resources, or experience extreme temperatures do not have as many people as temperate zones and flat plains, where it is easier to live. Within settlements, a town or city will be organized into commercial and residential neighborhoods, with hospitals, fire stations, and shopping centers centrally located. All of these organizational considerations are spatial in nature.

THEMES OF GEOGRAPHY

The five themes of geography are:

- **Location** – This includes relative location (described in terms of surrounding geography such as a river, sea coast, or mountain) and absolute location (the specific point of latitude and longitude).
- **Place** – This includes physical characteristics (deserts, plains, mountains, and waterways) and human characteristics (features created by humans, such as architecture, roads, religion, industries, and food and folk practices).
- **Human-environmental interaction** – This includes human adaptation to the environment (using an umbrella when it rains), human modification of the environment (building terraces to prevent soil erosion), and human dependence on the environment for food, water, and natural resources.
- **Movement** –Interaction through trade, migration, communications, political boundaries, ideas, and fashions.
- **Regions** – This includes formal regions (a city, state, country, or other geographical organization as defined by political boundaries), functional regions (defined by a common function or connection, such as a school district), and vernacular regions (informal divisions determined by perceptions or one's mental image, such as the "Far East").

> **Review Video: Regional Geography**
> Visit mometrix.com/academy and enter code: 350378

GEOMORPHOLOGY

The study of landforms is call **geomorphology** or physiography, a science that considers the relationships between *geological structures* and *surface landscape features*. It is also concerned with the processes that change these features, such as erosion, deposition, and plate tectonics. Biological factors can also affect landforms. Examples are when corals build a coral reef or when plants contribute to the development of a salt marsh or a sand dune. Rivers, coastlines, rock types, slope formation, ice, erosion, and weathering are all part of geomorphology. A **landform** is a landscape feature or geomorphological unit. These include hills, plateaus, mountains, deserts, deltas, canyons, mesas, marshes, swamps, and valleys. These units are categorized according to elevation, slope, orientation, stratification, rock exposure, and soil type. Landform elements include pits, peaks, channels, ridges, passes, pools, and plains. The highest order landforms are continents and oceans. Elementary landforms such as segments, facets, and relief units are the smallest homogenous divisions of a land surface at a given scale or resolution.

OCEANS, SEAS, LAKES, RIVERS, AND CANALS

- **Oceans** are the largest bodies of water on earth and cover nearly 71% of the earth's surface. There are five major oceans: Atlantic, Pacific (largest and deepest), Indian, Arctic, and Southern (surrounds Antarctica).
- **Seas** are smaller than oceans and are somewhat surrounded by land like a lake, but lakes are fresh water and seas are salt water. Seas include the Mediterranean, Baltic, Caspian, Caribbean, and Coral.
- **Lakes** are bodies of water in a depression on the earth's surface. Examples of lakes are the Great Lakes and Lake Victoria.
- **Rivers** are a channeled flow of water that start out as a spring or stream formed by runoff from rain or snow. Rivers flow from higher to lower ground, and usually empty into a sea or ocean. Great rivers of the world include the Amazon, Nile, Rhine, Mississippi, Ganges, Mekong, and Yangtze.
- **Canals** are artificial waterways constructed by humans to connect two larger water bodies. Examples of canals are the Panama and the Suez.

MOUNTAINS, HILLS, FOOTHILLS, VALLEYS, PLATEAUS, AND MESAS

The definitions for these geographical features are as follows:

- **Mountains** are elevated landforms that rise fairly steeply from the earth's surface to a summit of at least 1,000-2,000 feet (definitions vary) above sea level.
- **Hills** are elevated landforms that rise 500-2,000 feet above sea level.
- **Foothills** are a low series of hills found between a plain and a mountain range.
- **Valleys** are a long depression located between hills or mountains. They are usually products of river erosion. Valleys can vary in terms of width and depth, ranging from a few feet to thousands of feet.
- **Plateaus** are elevated landforms that are fairly flat on top. They may be as high as 10,000 feet above sea level and are usually next to mountains.
- **Mesas** are flat areas of upland. Their name is derived from the Spanish word for table. They are smaller than plateaus and often found in arid or semi-arid areas.

PLAINS, DESERTS, DELTAS, AND BASINS

- **Plains** are extensive areas of low-lying, flat, or gently undulating land, and are usually lower than the landforms around them. Plains near the seacoast are called lowlands.
- **Deserts** are large, dry areas that receive less than 10 inches of rain per year. They are almost barren, containing only a few patches of vegetation.
- **Deltas** are accumulations of silt deposited at river mouths into the seabed. They are eventually converted into very fertile, stable ground by vegetation, becoming important crop-growing areas. Examples include the deltas of the Nile, Ganges, and Mississippi River.
- **Basins** come in various types. They may be low areas that catch water from rivers; large hollows that dip to a central point and are surrounded by higher ground, as in the Donets and Kuznetsk basins in Russia; or areas of inland drainage in a desert when the water can't reach the sea and flows into lakes or evaporates in salt flats as a result. An example is the Great Salt Lake in Utah.

MARSHES AND SWAMPS AND TUNDRA AND TAIGA

Marshes and swamps are both **wet lowlands**. The water can be fresh, brackish, or saline. Both host important ecological systems with unique wildlife. There are, however, some major differences. **Marshes** have no trees and are always wet because of frequent floods and poor drainage that

156

leaves shallow water. Plants are mostly grasses, rushes, reeds, typhas, sedges, and herbs. **Swamps** have trees and dry periods. The water is very slow-moving, and is usually associated with adjacent rivers or lakes.

Both taiga and tundra regions have many plants and animals, but they have few humans or crops because of their harsh climates. **Taiga** has colder winters and hotter summers than tundra because of its distance from the Arctic Ocean. **Tundra** is a Russian word describing marshy plain in an area that has a very cold climate but receives little snow. The ground is usually frozen, but is quite spongy when it is not. Taiga is the world's largest forest region, located just south of the tundra line. It contains huge mineral resources and fur-bearing animals.

HUMID CONTINENTAL, PRAIRIE, SUBTROPICAL, AND MARINE CLIMATES

- A **humid continental climate** is one that has four seasons, including a cold winter and a hot summer, and sufficient rainfall for raising crops. Such climates can be found in the United States, Canada, and Russia. The best farmlands and mining areas are found in these countries.
- **Prairie climates**, or steppe regions, are found in the interiors of Asia and North America where there are dry flatlands (prairies that receive 10-20 inches of rain per year). These dry flatlands can be grasslands or deserts.
- **Subtropical climates** are very humid areas in the tropical areas of Japan, China, Australia, Africa, South America, and the United States. The moisture, carried by winds traveling over warm ocean currents, produces long summers and mild winters. It is possible to produce a continuous cycle of a variety of crops.
- A **marine climate** is one near or surrounded by water. Warm ocean winds bring moisture, mild temperatures year-round, and plentiful rain. These climates are found in Western Europe and parts of the United States, Canada, Chile, New Zealand, and Australia.

PHYSICAL AND CULTURAL GEOGRAPHY AND PHYSICAL AND POLITICAL LOCATIONS

- **Physical geography** is the study of climate, water, and land and their relationships with each other and humans. Physical geography locates and identifies the earth's surface features and explores how humans thrive in various locations according to crop and goods production.
- **Cultural geography** is the study of the influence of the environment on human behaviors as well as the effect of human activities such as farming, building settlements, and grazing livestock on the environment. Cultural geography also identifies and compares the features of different cultures and how they influence interactions with other cultures and the earth.
- **Physical location** refers to the placement of the hemispheres and the continents.
- **Political location** refers to the divisions within continents that designate various countries. These divisions are made with borders, which are set according to boundary lines arrived at by legal agreements.

Both physical and political locations can be precisely determined by geographical surveys and by latitude and longitude.

NATURAL RESOURCES, RENEWABLE RESOURCES, NONRENEWABLE RESOURCES, AND COMMODITIES

Natural resources are things provided by nature that have commercial value to humans, such as minerals, energy, timber, fish, wildlife, and the landscape. **Renewable resources** are those that can be replenished, such as wind, solar radiation, tides, and water (with proper conservation and clean-up). Soil is renewable with proper conservation and management techniques, and timber can be replenished with replanting. Living resources such as fish and wildlife can replenish themselves if they are not over-harvested. **Nonrenewable resources** are those that cannot be replenished. These include fossil fuels such as oil and coal and metal ores. These cannot be replaced or reused once they have been burned, although some of their products can be recycled. **Commodities** are natural resources that have to be extracted and purified rather than created, such as mineral ores.

GEOGRAPHY

Geography involves learning about the world's primary **physical and cultural patterns** to help understand how the world functions as an interconnected and dynamic system. Combining information from different sources, geography teaches the basic patterns of climate, geology, vegetation, human settlement, migration, and commerce. Thus, geography is an **interdisciplinary** study of history, anthropology, and sociology. **History** incorporates geography in discussions of battle strategies, slavery (trade routes), ecological disasters (the Dust Bowl of the 1930s), and mass migrations. Geographic principles are useful when reading **literature** to help identify and visualize the setting, and also when studying **earth science**, **mathematics** (latitude, longitude, sun angle, and population statistics), and **fine arts** (song, art, and dance often reflect different cultures). Consequently, a good background in geography can help students succeed in other subjects as well.

AREAS COVERED BY GEOGRAPHY

Geography is connected to many issues and provides answers to many everyday questions. Some of the areas covered by geography include:

- Geography investigates global climates, landforms, economies, political systems, human cultures, and migration patterns.
- Geography answers questions not only about where something is located, but also why it is there, how it got there, and how it is related to other things around it.
- Geography explains why people move to certain regions (climate, availability of natural resources, arable land, etc.).
- Geography explains world trade routes and modes of transportation.
- Geography identifies where various animals live and where various crops and forests grow.
- Geography identifies and locates populations that follow certain religions.
- Geography provides statistics on population numbers and growth, which aids in economic and infrastructure planning for cities and countries.

GLOBE AND MAP PROJECTIONS

A **globe** is the only accurate representation of the earth's size, shape, distance, and direction since it, like the earth, is **spherical**. The flat surface of a map distorts these elements. To counter this problem, mapmakers use a variety of "**map projections**," a system for representing the earth's curvatures on a flat surface through the use of a grid that corresponds to lines of latitude and longitude. Some distortions are still inevitable, though, so mapmakers make choices based on the map scale, the size of the area to be mapped, and what they want the map to show. Some projections can represent a true shape or area, while others may be based on the equator and therefore become less accurate as they near the poles. In summary, all maps have some distortion in terms of the shape or size of features of the spherical earth.

TYPES OF MAP PROJECTIONS

There are three main types of map projections:

- **Conical** – This type of projection superimposes a cone over the sphere of the earth, with two reference parallels secant to the globe and intersecting it. There is no distortion along the standard parallels, but distortion increases further from the chosen parallels. A Bonne projection is an example of a conical projection, in which the areas are accurately represented but the meridians are not on a true scale.
- **Cylindrical** – This is any projection in which meridians are mapped using equally spaced vertical lines and circles of latitude (parallels) are mapped using horizontal lines. A Mercator's projection is a modified cylindrical projection that is helpful to navigators because it allows them to maintain a constant compass direction between two points. However, it exaggerates areas in high latitudes.
- **Azimuthal** – This is a stereographic projection onto a plane so centered at any given point that a straight line radiating from the center to any other point represents the shortest distance. This distance can be measured to scale.

PHYSICAL GEOGRAPHICAL FEATURES TO KNOW TO PERFORM WELL IN NATIONAL GEOGRAPHIC BEE

Organizing place names into categories of physical features helps students learn the type of information they need to know to compete in the **National Geographic Bee**. The physical features students need to be knowledgeable about are:

- The continents (Although everyone has been taught that there are seven continents, some geographers combine Europe and Asia into a single continent called Eurasia.)
- The five major oceans
- The highest and lowest points on each continent (Mt. Everest is the highest point in the world; the Dead Sea is the lowest point.)
- The 10 largest seas (The Coral Sea is the largest.)
- The 10 largest lakes (The Caspian Sea is actually the largest lake.)
- The 10 largest islands (Greenland is the largest island.)
- The longest rivers (The Nile is the longest river.)
- Major mountain ranges
- Earth's extremes such as the hottest (Ethiopia), the coldest (Antarctica), the wettest (India), and the driest (Atacama Desert) places; the highest waterfall (Angel Falls); the largest desert (Sahara); the largest canyon (Grand Canyon); the longest reef (Great Barrier Reef); and the highest tides.

U.S. Government

PRINCIPLES OF THE CONSTITUTION

The six basic principles of the Constitution are:

1. **Popular Sovereignty** – The people establish government and give power to it; the government can function only with the consent of the people.
2. **Limited Government** – The Constitution specifies limits on government authority, and no official or entity is above the law.
3. **Separation of Powers** – Power is divided among three government branches: the legislative (Congress), the executive (President), and the judicial (federal courts).

4. **Checks and Balances** – This is a system that enforces the separation of powers and ensures that each branch has the authority and ability to restrain the powers of the other two branches, thus preventing tyranny.
5. **Judicial Review** – Judges in the federal courts ensure that no act of government is in violation of the Constitution. If an act is unconstitutional, the judicial branch has the power to nullify it.
6. **Federalism** – This is the division of power between the central government and local governments, which limits the power of the federal government and allows states to deal with local problems.

CLASSIC FORMS OF GOVERNMENT

Forms of government that have appeared throughout history include:

- **Feudalism** – This is based on the rule of local lords who are loyal to the king and control the lives and production of those who work on their land.
- **Classical republic** – This form is a representative democracy. Small groups of elected leaders represent the interests of the electorate.
- **Absolute monarchy** – A king or queen has complete control of the military and government.
- **Authoritarianism** – An individual or group has unlimited authority. There is no system in place to restrain the power of the government.
- **Dictatorship** – Those in power are not held responsible to the people.
- **Autocracy** – This is rule by one person (despot), not necessarily a monarch, who uses power tyrannically.
- **Oligarchy** – A small, usually self-appointed elite rules a region.
- **Liberal democracy** – This is a government based on the consent of the people that protects individual rights and freedoms from any intolerance by the majority.
- **Totalitarianism** – All facets of the citizens' lives are controlled by the government.

INFLUENCES OF PHILOSOPHERS ON POLITICAL STUDY

Ancient Greek philosophers **Aristotle** and **Plato** believed political science would lead to order in political matters, and that this scientifically organized order would create stable, just societies.

Thomas Aquinas adapted the ideas of Aristotle to a Christian perspective. His ideas stated that individuals should have certain rights, but also certain duties, and that these rights and duties should determine the type and extent of government rule. In stating that laws should limit the role of government, he laid the groundwork for ideas that would eventually become modern constitutionalism. **Niccolò Machiavelli**, author of *The Prince*, was a proponent of politics based solely on power.

PARLIAMENTARY AND DEMOCRATIC SYSTEMS OF GOVERNMENT

In a **parliamentary system**, government involves a legislature and a variety of political parties. The head of government, usually a Prime Minister, is typically the head of the dominant party. A head of state can be elected, or this position can be taken by a monarch, such as in Great Britain's constitutional monarchy system.

In a **democratic system** of government, the people elect their government representatives. The term democracy is a Greek term that means "for the rule of the people." There are two forms of democracy—direct and indirect. In a direct democracy, each issue or election is decided by a vote where each individual is counted separately. An indirect democracy employs a legislature that

160

votes on issues that affect large number of people whom the legislative members represent. Democracy can exist as a Parliamentary system or a Presidential system. The US is a presidential, indirect democracy.

BILL OF RIGHTS

The **United States Bill of Rights** was based on principles established by the **Magna Carta** in 1215, the 1688 **English Bill of Rights**, and the 1776 **Virginia Bill of Rights**. In 1791, the federal government added 10 amendments to the United States Constitution that provided the following **protections**:

- Freedom of speech, religion, peaceful assembly, petition of the government, and petition of the press
- The right to keep and bear arms
- No quartering of soldiers on private property without the consent of the owner
- Regulations on government search and seizure
- Provisions concerning prosecution
- The right to a speedy, public trial and the calling of witnesses
- The right to trial by jury
- Freedom from excessive bail or cruel punishment
- These rights are not necessarily the only rights
- Powers not prohibited by the Constitution are reserved to the states.

> **Review Video: Bill of Rights**
> Visit mometrix.com/academy and enter code: 585149

MAKING A FORMAL AMENDMENT TO THE CONSTITUTION

So far, there have been only **27 amendments** to the federal Constitution. There are four different ways to change the wording of the constitution: two methods for proposal and two methods for ratification:

1. An amendment is proposed by a two-thirds vote in each house of Congress and ratified by three-fourths of the state legislatures.
2. An amendment is proposed by a two-thirds vote in each house of Congress and ratified by three-fourths of the states in special conventions called for that purpose.
3. An amendment is proposed by a national convention that is called by Congress at the request of two-thirds of the state legislatures and ratified by three-fourths of the state legislatures.
4. An amendment is proposed by a national convention that is called by Congress at the request of two-thirds of the state legislatures and ratified by three-fourths of the states in special conventions called for that purpose.

> **Review Video: Amending the Constitution**
> Visit mometrix.com/academy and enter code: 147023

DIVISION OF POWERS

The division of powers in the federal government system is as follows:

- **National** – This level can coin money, regulate interstate and foreign trade, raise and maintain armed forces, declare war, govern United States territories and admit new states, and conduct foreign relations.

- **Concurrent** – This level can levy and collect taxes, borrow money, establish courts, define crimes and set punishments, and claim private property for public use.
- **State** – This level can regulate trade and business within the state, establish public schools, pass license requirements for professionals, regulate alcoholic beverages, conduct elections, and establish local governments.

There are three types of delegated powers granted by the Constitution:

1. **Expressed or enumerated powers** – These are specifically spelled out in the Constitution.
2. **Implied** – These are not expressly stated, but are reasonably suggested by the expressed powers.
3. **Inherent** – These are powers not expressed by the Constitution but ones that national governments have historically possessed, such as granting diplomatic recognition.

Powers can also be classified or reserved or exclusive. **Reserved powers** are not granted to the national government, but not denied to the states. **Exclusive powers** are those reserved to the national government, including concurrent powers.

STAGES OF EXTENDING SUFFRAGE IN US

Originally, the Constitution of 1789 provided the right to vote only to white male property owners. Through the years, suffrage was extended through the following five stages.

1. In the early1800s, states began to eliminate **property ownership** and **tax payment qualifications**.
2. By 1810, there were no more **religious tests** for voting. In the late 1800s, the 15th Amendment protected citizens from being denied the right to vote because of **race or color**.
3. In 1920, the 19th Amendment prohibited the denial of the right to vote because of **gender**, and women were given the right to vote.
4. Passed in 1961 and ratified in 1964, the 23rd Amendment added the voters of the **District of Columbia** to the presidential electorate and eliminated the poll tax as a condition for voting in federal elections. The **Voting Rights Act of 1965** prohibited disenfranchisement through literacy tests and various other means of discrimination.
5. In 1971, the 26th Amendment set the minimum voting age at **18 years of age**.

MAJOR SUPREME COURT CASES

Out of the many Supreme Court rulings, several have had critical historical importance. These include:

- **Marbury v. Madison** (1803) – This ruling established judicial review as a power of the Supreme Court.
- **Dred Scott v. Sandford** (1857) – This decision upheld property rights over human rights in the case of a slave who had been transported to a free state by his master, but was still considered a slave.
- **Brown v. Board of Education** (1954) – The Court ruled that segregation was a violation of the Equal Protection Clause and that the "separate but equal" practice in education was unconstitutional. This decision overturned the 1896 Plessy v. Ferguson ruling that permitted segregation if facilities were equal.
- **Miranda v. Arizona** (1966) – This ruling made the reading of Miranda rights to those arrested for crimes the law. It ensured that confessions could not be illegally obtained and that citizen rights to fair trials and protection under the law would be upheld.

FAMOUS SPEECHES IN US HISTORY THAT DEFINED GOVERNMENT POLICY, FOREIGN RELATIONS, AND AMERICAN SPIRIT

Among the best-known speeches and famous lines known to modern Americans are the following:

- The **Gettysburg Address** – Made by Abraham Lincoln on November 19, 1863, it dedicated the battleground's cemetery.
- The **Fourteen Points** – Made by Woodrow Wilson on January 18, 1918, this outlined Wilson's plans for peace and the League of Nations.
- **Address to Congress** – Made by Franklin Roosevelt on December 8, 1941, it declared war on Japan and described the attack on Pearl Harbor as "a day which will live in infamy."
- **Inaugural Address** – Made by John F. Kennedy on January 20, 1961, it contained the famous line: "Ask not what your country can do for you, ask what you can do for your country."
- **Berlin Address** – Made by John F. Kennedy on June 26, 1963, it contained the famous line "Ich bin ein Berliner," which expressed empathy for West Berliners in their conflict with the Soviet Union.
- **"I Have a Dream"** and **"I See the Promised Land"** – Made by Martin Luther King, Jr. on August 28, 1963 and April 3, 1968, respectively, these speeches were hallmarks of the Civil Rights Movement.
- **Brandenburg Gate speech** – Made by Ronald Reagan on June 12, 1987, this speech was about the Berlin Wall and the end of the Cold War. It contained the famous line "Tear down this wall."

CLOSED AND OPEN PRIMARIES IN A DIRECT PRIMARY SYSTEM

The **direct primary system** is a means for members of a political party to participate in the selection of a candidate from their party to compete against the other party's candidate in a general election. A **closed primary** is a party nominating election in which only declared party members can vote. Party membership is usually established by registration. Currently, 26 states and the District of Columbia use this system. An **open primary** is a party nominating election in which any qualified voter can take part. The voter makes a public choice at the polling place about which primary to participate in, and the choice does not depend on any registration or previous choices. A **blanket primary**, which allowed voters to vote in the primaries of both parties, was used at various times by three states. The Supreme Court ruled against this practice in 2000.

IMPORTANT DOCUMENTS IN UNITED STATES HISTORY AND GOVERNMENT

The following are among the greatest **American documents** because of their impact on foreign and domestic policy:

- Declaration of Independence (1776)
- The Articles of Confederation (1777)
- The Constitution (1787) and the Bill of Rights (1791)
- The Northwest Ordinance (1787)
- The Federalist Papers (1787-88)
- George Washington's Inaugural Address (1789) and Farewell Address (1796)
- The Alien and Sedition Act (1798)
- The Louisiana Purchase Treaty (1803)

- The Monroe Doctrine (1823); The Missouri Compromise (1830)
- The Compromise of 1850
- The Kansas-Nebraska Act (1854)
- The Homestead Act (1862)
- The Emancipation Proclamation (1863)
- The agreement to purchase Alaska (1866)
- The Sherman Anti-Trust Act (1890)
- Theodore Roosevelt's Corollary to the Monroe Doctrine (1905)
- The Social Security Act (1935) and other acts of the New Deal in the 1930s; The Truman Doctrine (1947); The Marshall Plan (1948)
- The Civil Rights Act (1964)

FEDERAL TAXES

The four types of **federal taxes** are:

- **Income taxes on individuals** – This is a complex system because of demands for various exemptions and rates. Further, the schedule of rates can be lowered or raised according to economic conditions in order to stimulate or restrain economic activity. For example, a tax cut can provide an economic stimulus, while a tax increase can slow down the rate of inflation. Personal income tax generates about five times as much as corporate taxes. Rates are based on an individual's income, and range from 10 to 35 percent.
- **Income taxes on corporations** – The same complexity of exemptions and rates exists for corporations as individuals. Taxes can be raised or lowered according to the need to stimulate or restrain the economy.
- **Excise taxes** – These are taxes on specific goods such as tobacco, liquor, automobiles, gasoline, air travel, and luxury items, or on activities such as highway usage by trucks.
- **Customs duties** – These are taxes imposed on imported goods. They serve to regulate trade between the United States and other countries.

UNITED STATES CURRENCY SYSTEM

The Constitution of 1787 gave the United States Congress the central authority to **print or coin money** and to **regulate its value**. Before this time, states were permitted to maintain separate currencies. The currency system is based on a **modified gold standard**. There is an enormous store of gold to back up United States currency housed at Fort Knox, Kentucky. Paper money is actually **Federal Reserve notes** and coins. It is the job of the Bureau of Engraving and Printing in the Treasury Department to design plates, special types of paper, and other security measures for bills and bonds. This money is put into general circulation by the Treasury and Federal Reserve Banks, and is taken out of circulation when worn out. Coins are made at the Bureau of the Mint in Philadelphia, Denver, and San Francisco.

EMPLOYMENT ACT OF 1946

The **Employment Act of 1946** established the following entities to combat unemployment:

- The **Council of Economic Advisers** (CEA) – Composed of a chair and two other members appointed by the President and approved by the Senate, this council assists the President with the development and implementation of U.S. economic policy. The Council members and their staff, located in the Executive Office, are professionals in economics and statistics who forecast economic trends and provide analysis based on evidence-based research.

- The **Economic Report of the President** – This is presented every January by the President to Congress. Based on the work of the Council, the report recommends a program for maximizing employment, and may also recommend legislation.
- **Joint Economic Committee** (JEC) – This is a committee composed of 10 members of the House and 10 members of the Senate that makes a report early each year on its continuous study of the economy. Study is conducted through hearings and research, and the report is made in response to the president's recommendations.

QUALIFICATIONS OF A US CITIZEN

Anyone born in the US, born abroad to a US citizen, or who has gone through a process of **naturalization** to become a citizen, is considered a **citizen** of the United States. It is possible to lose US citizenship as a result of conviction of certain crimes such as treason. Citizenship may also be lost if a citizen pledges an oath to another country or serves in the military of a country engaged in hostilities with the US. A US citizen can also choose to hold dual citizenship, work as an expatriate in another country without losing US citizenship, or even renounce citizenship if he or she so chooses.

RIGHTS, DUTIES, AND RESPONSIBILITIES GRANTED TO OR EXPECTED FROM US CITIZENS

Citizens are granted certain rights under the US government. The most important of these are defined in the **Bill of Rights**, and include freedom of speech, religion, assembly, and a variety of other rights the government is not allowed to remove.

Duties of a US citizen include:

- Paying taxes
- Loyalty to the government, though the US does not prosecute those who criticize or seek to change the government
- Support and defend the Constitution
- Serve in the Armed Forces as required by law
- Obeying laws as set forth by the various levels of government.

Responsibilities of a US citizen include:

- Voting in elections
- Respecting one another's rights and not infringing upon them
- Staying informed about various political and national issues
- Respecting one another's beliefs

Civics and Citizenship

REPRESENTATIVE DEMOCRACY

In a system of government characterized as a representative democracy, voters elect **representatives** to act in their interests. Typically, a representative is elected by and responsible to a specific subset of the total population of eligible voters; this subset of the electorate is referred to as a representative's constituency. A **representative democracy** may foster a more powerful legislature than other forms of government systems; to compensate for a strong legislature, most constitutions stipulate that measures must be taken to balance the powers within government, such as the creation of a separate judicial branch. Representative democracy became popular in post-industrial nations where increasing numbers of people expressed an interest in politics, but where technology and census counts remained incompatible with systems of direct democracy. Today, the majority of the world's population resides in representative democracies, including constitutional monarchies that possess a strong representative branch.

DEMOCRACY

Democracy, or rule by the people, is a form of government in which power is vested in the people and in which policy decisions are made by the majority in a decision-making process such as an election that is open to all or most citizens. Definitions of democracy have become more generalized and include aspects of society and political culture in democratic societies that do not necessarily represent a form of government. What defines a democracy varies, but some of the characteristics of a democracy could include the presence of a middle class, the presence of a civil society, a free market, political pluralism, universal suffrage, and specific rights and freedoms. In practice however, democracies do have limits on specific freedoms, which are justified as being necessary to maintain democracy and ensure democratic freedoms. For example, freedom of association is limited in democracies for individuals and groups that pose a threat to government or to society.

PRESIDENTIAL/CONGRESSIONAL SYSTEM

In a **presidential system**, also referred to as a **congressional system**, the legislative branch and the executive branches are elected separately from one another. The features of a presidential system include a *president* who serves as both the head of state and the head of the government, who has no formal relationship with the legislative branch, who is not a voting member, who cannot introduce bills, and who has a fixed term of office. *Elections* are held at scheduled times. The president's *cabinet* carries out the policies of the executive branch and the legislative branch.

POLITICAL PARTIES

A **political party** is an organization that advocates a particular ideology and seeks to gain power within government. The tendency of members of political parties to support their party's policies and interests relative to those of other parties is referred to as partisanship. Often, a political party is comprised of members whose positions, interests and perspectives on policies vary, despite having shared interests in the general ideology of the party. As such, many political parties will have divisions within them that have differing opinions on policy. Political parties are often placed on a political spectrum, with one end of the spectrum representing conservative, traditional values and policies and the other end of the spectrum representing radical, progressive value and policies.

> **Review Video: Political Parties**
> Visit mometrix.com/academy and enter code: 640197

TYPES OF PARTY SYSTEMS

There is a variety of **party systems**, including single-party systems, dominant-party systems, and dual-party systems. In a **single-party system**, only one political party may hold power. In this type of system, minor parties may be permitted, but they must accept the leadership of the dominant party. **Dominant-party systems** allow for multiple parties in opposition of one another, however the dominant party is the only party considered to have power. A **two-party system**, such as in the United States, is one in which there are two dominant political parties. In such a system, it is very difficult for any other parties to win an election. In most two-party systems, there is typically one right wing party and one left wing party.

DEMOCRATIC PARTY

The **Democratic Party** was founded in 1792. In the United States, it is one of the two dominant political parties, along with the Republican Party. The Democratic Party is to the left of the

Republican Party. The Democratic Party began as a conservative party in the mid-1800s, shifting to the left during the 1900s. There are many factions within the Democratic Party in the United States. The **Democratic National Committee (DNC)** is the official organization of the Democratic Party, and it develops and promotes the party's platform and coordinates fundraising and election strategies. There are Democratic committees in every U.S. state and most U.S. counties. The official symbol of the Democratic Party is the donkey.

REPUBLICAN PARTY

The **Republican Party** is often referred to as the **GOP**, which stands for *Grand Old Party*. The Republican Party is considered socially conservative and economically neoliberal relative to the Democratic Party. Like the Democratic Party, there are factions within the Republic Party that agree with the party's overall ideology, but disagree with the party's positions on specific issues. The official symbol of the Republican Party is the elephant. The **Republican National Committee (RNC)** is the official organization of the Republican Party, and it develops and promotes the party's platform and coordinates fundraising and election strategies. There are Republican committees in every U.S. state and most U.S. counties.

POLITICAL CAMPAIGNS

A **political campaign** is an organized attempt to influence the decisions of a particular group of people . Examples of campaigns could include elections or efforts to influence policy changes. One of the first steps in a campaign is to develop a **campaign message**. The message must then be delivered to the individuals and groups that the campaign is trying to reach and influence through a campaign plan. There are various ways for a campaign to communicate its message to the intended audience, including public media; paid media such as television, radio and newspaper ads, billboards and the internet; public events such as protests and rallies; meetings with speakers; mailings; canvassing; fliers; and websites. Through these efforts, the campaign attempts to attract additional support and, ultimately, to reach the goal of the campaign.

> **Review Video: Political Campaigns**
> Visit mometrix.com/academy and enter code: 838608

VOTING

Voting is a method of decision making that allows people to express their opinion or preference for a candidate or for a proposed resolution of an issue. In a democratic system, voting typically takes place as part of an **election**. An individual participates in the voting process by casting a vote, or a **ballot**; ballots are produced by states A *secret ballot* can be used at polls to protect voters' privacy. Individuals can also vote via *absentee ballot*. In some states voters can write-in a name to cast a vote for a candidate that is not on the ballot. Some states also use *straight ticket voting*, allowing the voter to vote for one party for all the elected positions on the ballot.

US ELECTIONS

In the United States, **officials** are elected at the federal, state and local levels. The first two articles of the Constitution, as well as various amendments, establish how **federal elections** are to be held. The **President** is elected indirectly, by electors of an electoral college. Members of the electoral college nearly always vote along the lines of the popular vote of their respective states. Members of **Congress** are directly elected. At the state level, state law establishes most aspects of how elections are held. There are many elected offices at the state level, including a governor and state legislature. There are also elected offices at the local level.

VOTER ELIGIBILITY

The United States Constitution establishes that individual people are permitted to **vote** in elections if they are citizens of the United States and are at least eighteen years old. The **fifteenth** and **nineteenth amendments** of the United States Constitution stipulate that the right to vote cannot be denied to any United States citizen based on race or sex, respectively. States regulate voter eligibility beyond the minimum qualifications stipulated by the United States Constitution. Depending on the regulations of individual states, individuals may be denied the right to vote if they are convicted criminals.

> **Review Video: Voter Behavior**
> Visit mometrix.com/academy and enter code: 976272

ADVANTAGES AND DISADVANTAGES TO TWO-PARTY SYSTEM

Advocates of the **two-party system** argue that its advantages are that they are stable because they enable policies and government to change slowly rather than rapidly due to the relative lack of influence from small parties representing unconventional ideologies. In addition, they seem to drive voters toward a middle ground and are less susceptible to revolutions, coups, or civil wars. Among the critiques of the two-party system is the claim that stability in and of itself is not necessarily desirable, as it often comes at the expense of democracy. Critics also argue that the two-party system promotes negative political campaigns, in which candidates and their respective parties only take positions on issues that will differentiate themselves from their opponents, rather than focusing on policy issues that are of significance to citizens. Another concern is that if one of the two major parties becomes weak, a dominant-party system may develop.

CAMPAIGN MESSAGE

Political campaigns consist of three main elements, which are the campaign message, the money that is necessary to run the campaign and "machine," or the capital that is necessary run the campaign. A campaign message is a succinct statement expressing why voters should support the campaign and the individual or policy associated with that campaign. The message is one of the most significant aspects of a political campaign, and a considerable amount of time, money and effort is invested in devising a successful campaign message, as it will be repeated throughout the campaign and will be one of the most identifying factors of the campaign.

MODERN ELECTION CAMPAIGNS IN US

Political campaigns in the U.S. have changed and continue to change as advances in technology permit varied campaign methods. Campaigns represent a civic practice, and today they are a high profit industry. The U.S. has an abundance of professional political consultants that employ highly sophisticated campaign management strategies and tools. The election process varies widely between the federal, state and local levels. Campaigns are typically controlled by individual candidates, rather than by the parties that they are associated with. Larger campaigns utilize a vast array of media to reach their targeted audiences, while smaller campaigns are typically limited to direct contact with voters, direct mailings and other forms of low-cost advertising to reach their audiences. In addition to fundraising and spending done by individual candidates, party committees and political action committees also raise money and spend it in ways that will advance the cause of the particular campaign they are associated with.

VOTER REGISTRATION

Individuals have the responsibility of **registering to vote**. Every state except North Dakota requires citizens to register to vote. In an effort to increase voter turnout, Congress passed the

National Voter Registration Act in 1993. The Act is also known as "Motor Voter," because it required states to make the voter registration process easier by providing registration services through drivers' license registration centers, as well as through disability centers, schools, libraries, and mail-in registration. Some states are exempt because they permit same-day voter registration, which enables voters to register to vote on the day of the election.

PRESIDENTIAL ELECTIONS

The President of the United States is elected **indirectly**, by members of an **electoral college**. Members of the electoral college nearly always vote along the lines of the popular vote of their respective states. The winner of a presidential election is the candidate with at least 270 electoral college votes. It is possible for a candidate to win the electoral vote, and lose the popular vote. Incumbent Presidents and challengers typically prefer a balanced ticket, where the President and Vice President are elected together and generally balance one another with regard to geography, ideology, or experience working in government. The nominated Vice Presidential candidate is referred to as the President's *running mate*.

ELECTORAL COLLEGE

Electoral college votes are cast by state by a group of electors; each elector casts one electoral college vote. State law regulates how states cast their electoral college votes. In all states except Maine and Nebraska, the candidate winning the most votes receives all the state's electoral college votes. In Maine and Nebraska two electoral votes are awarded based on the winner of the statewide election, and the rest go to the highest vote-winner in each of the state's congressional districts. Critics of the electoral college argue that it is undemocratic because the President is elected indirectly as opposed to directly, and that it creates inequality between voters in different states because candidates focus attention on voters in swing states who could influence election results. Critics argue that the electoral college provides more representation for voters in small states than large states, where more voters are represented by a single electoral than in small states and discriminates against candidates that do not have support concentrated in a given state.

CONGRESSIONAL ELECTIONS

Congressional elections are every two years. Members of the **House of Representatives** are elected for a two year term and elections occur every two years on the first Tuesday after November 1st in even years. A Representative is elected from each of 435 House districts in the U.S. House elections usually occur in the same year as Presidential elections. Members of the **Senate** are elected to six year terms; one-third of the Senate is elected every two years. Per the Seventeenth Amendment to the Constitution, which was passed in 1913, Senators are elected by the electorate of states. The country is divided into **Congressional districts**, and critics argue that this division eliminates voter choice, sometimes creating areas in which Congressional races are uncontested. Every ten years **redistricting** of Congressional districts occurs. However, redistricting is often partisan and therefore reduces the number of competitive districts. The division of voting districts resulting in an unfair advantage to one party in elections is known as gerrymandering. Gerrymandering has been criticized as being undemocratic.

STATE AND LOCAL ELECTIONS

State elections are regulated by state laws and constitutions. In keeping with the ideal of separation of powers, the legislature and the executive are elected separately at the state level, as they are at the federal level. In each state, a **Governor** and a **Lieutenant Governor** are elected. In some states, the Governor and Lieutenant Governor are elected on a joint ticket, while in other states they are elected separately from one another. In some states, executive positions such as Attorney General and Secretary of State are also elected offices. All members of state legislatures are elected, including state senators and state representatives. Depending on the state, members of the state supreme court and other members of the state judiciary may be chosen in elections. Local government can include the governments of counties and cities. At this level, nearly all government offices are filled through an election process. Elected local offices may include sheriffs, county school boards, and city mayors.

CAMPAIGN FINANCE AND INDEPENDENT EXPENDITURES

An individual or group is legally permitted to make unlimited **independent expenditures** in association with federal elections. An independent expenditure is an expenditure that is made to pay for a form of communication that supports the election or defeat of a candidate; the expenditure must be made independently from the candidate's own campaign. To be considered independent, the communication may not be made with the cooperation or consultation with, or at the request or suggestion of, any candidate, any committees or political party associated with the candidate, or any agent that acts on behalf of the candidate. There are no restrictions on the amount that anyone may spend on an independent expenditure, however, any individual making an independent expenditure must report it and disclose the source of the funds they used.

CAMPAIGN FINANCE AND ACTIVITIES OF POLITICAL PARTIES

Political parties participate in federal elections at the local, state and national levels. Most **party committees** must register with the **Federal Election Committee** and file reports disclosing federal campaign activities. While party committees may contribute funds directly to federal candidates, the amounts that they contribute are restricted by the campaign finance contribution limits. National and state party committees are permitted to make additional **coordinated expenditures**, within limits, to assist their nominees in general elections. However, national party committees are not permitted to make unlimited **independent expenditures** to support or oppose federal candidates using soft money. State and local party committees are also not permitted to use soft money for the purpose of supporting or opposing federal candidates, but they are allowed to spend soft money, up to a limit of $10,000 per source, on voter registration and on efforts aimed at increasing voter participation. All party committees are required to register themselves and file disclosure reports with the Federal Election Committee once their federal election activities exceed specified monetary limits.

PUBLIC OPINION

Public opinion represents the collective attitudes of individual members of the adult population in the United States of America. There are many varied forces that may influence public opinion. These forces include *public relations efforts* on the part of political campaigns and political parties. Another force affecting political opinion is the *political media* and the *mass media*. Public opinion is very important during elections, particularly Presidential elections, as it is an indicator of how candidates are perceived by the public and of how well candidates are doing during their election campaigns. Public opinion is often measured and evaluated using survey sampling.

MASS MEDIA AND PUBLIC OPINION

The **mass media** is critical in developing public opinion. In the short term people generally evaluate information they receive relative to their own beliefs; in the long term the media may have a considerable impact on people's beliefs. Due to the impact of the media on an individual's beliefs, some experts consider the effects of the media on an individual's independence and autonomy to be negative. Others view the impact of the media on individuals as a positive one, because the media provides information that expands worldviews and enriches life, and fosters the development of opinions that are informed by many sources of information. A critical aspect of the relationship between the media and public opinion is who is in control of the knowledge and information that is

170

disseminated through the media. Whoever controls the media can propagate their own agenda. The extent to which an individual interprets and evaluates information received through the media can influence behaviors such as voting patterns or consumer behavior, as well as social attitudes.

Economics

EFFECTS ECONOMY CAN HAVE ON PURCHASING DECISIONS OF CONSUMERS

The **economy** plays an important role in how careful consumers are when using their resources and what they perceive as needs as opposed to what they perceive as wants. When the economy is doing well, unemployment figures are low, which means that people can easily attain their basic necessities. As a result, consumers are typically more willing to spend their financial resources. Consumers will also be more willing to spend their resources on products and services that are not necessary to their survival, but are instead products and services that consumers enjoy having and believe increase their quality of life. On the other hand, when the economy is in a slump, consumers are much more likely to cut back on their spending because they perceive a significantly higher risk of being unable to acquire basic necessities due to a lack of financial resources.

SUPPLY AND DEMAND, SCARCITY AND CHOICE, AND MONEY AND RESOURCES

Supply is the amount of a product or service available to consumers. **Demand** is how much consumers are willing to pay for the product or service. These two facets of the market determine the price of goods and services. The higher the demand, the higher the price the supplier will charge; the lower the demand, the lower the price.

Scarcity is a measure of supply in that demand is high when there is a scarcity, or low supply, of an item. **Choice** is related to scarcity and demand in that when an item in demand is scarce, consumers have to make difficult choices. They can pay more for an item, go without it, or go elsewhere for the item.

Money is the cash or currency available for payment. **Resources** are the items one can barter in exchange for goods. Money is also the cash reserves of a nation, while resources are the minerals, labor force, armaments, and other raw materials or assets a nation has available for trade.

EFFECTS OF ECONOMIC DOWNTURN OR RECESSION

When a **recession** happens, people at all levels of society feel the economic effects. For example:

- High **unemployment** results because businesses have to cut back to keep costs low, and may no longer have the work for the labor force they once did.
- **Mortgage rates** go up on variable-rate loans as banks try to increase their revenues, but the higher rates cause some people who cannot afford increased housing costs to sell or suffer foreclosure.
- **Credit** becomes less available as banks try to lessen their risk. This decreased lending affects business operations, home and auto loans, etc.
- **Stock market prices** drop, and the lower dividends paid to stockholders reduce their income. This is especially hard on retired people who rely on stock dividends.
- **Psychological depression and trauma** may occur in those who suffer bankruptcy, unemployment, or foreclosure during a depression.

POSITIVE AND NEGATIVE ECONOMIC EFFECTS OF ABUNDANT NATURAL RESOURCES

The **positive economic aspects** of abundant natural resources are an increase in **revenue and new jobs** where those resources have not been previously accessed. For example, the growing demand for oil, gas, and minerals has led companies to venture into new regions.

The **negative economic aspects** of abundant natural resources are:

- **Environmental degradation**, if sufficient regulations are not in place to counter strip mining, deforestation, and contamination.
- **Corruption**, if sufficient regulations are not in place to counter bribery, political favoritism, and exploitation of workers as greedy companies try to maximize their profits.
- **Social tension**, if the resources are privately owned such that the rich become richer and the poor do not reap the benefits of their national resources. Class divisions become wider, resulting in social unrest.
- **Dependence**, if the income from the natural resources is not used to develop other industries as well. In this situation, the economy becomes dependent on one source, and faces potential crises if natural disasters or depletion take away that income source.

ECONOMICS AND KINDS OF ECONOMIES

Economics is the study of the buying choices that people make, the production of goods and services, and how our market system works. The two kinds of economies are command and market. In a **command economy**, the government controls what and how much is produced, the methods used for production, and the distribution of goods and services. In a market economy, producers make decisions about methods and distribution on their own. These choices are based on what will sell and bring a profit in the marketplace. In a **market economy**, consumers ultimately affect these decisions by choosing whether or not to buy certain goods and services. The United States has a market economy.

MARKET ECONOMY

The five characteristics of a **market economy** are:

- **Economic freedom** – There is freedom of choice with respect to jobs, salaries, production, and price.
- **Economic incentives** – A positive incentive is to make a profit. However, if the producer tries to make too high a profit, the consequences might be that no one will purchase the item at that price. A negative incentive would be a drop in profits, causing the producer to decrease or discontinue production. A boycott, which might cause the producer to change business practices or policies, is also a negative economic incentive.
- **Competition** – There is more than one producer for any given product. Consumers thereby have choices about what to buy, which are usually made based on quality and price. Competition is an incentive for a producer to make the best product at the best price. Otherwise, producers will lose business to the competition.
- **Private ownership** – Production and profits belong to an individual or to a private company, not to the government.
- **Limited government** – Government plays no role in the economic decisions of its individual citizens.

FACTORS OF PRODUCTION AND TYPES OF MARKETS THAT CREATE ECONOMIC FLOW

The factors of **production** are:

- **Land** – This includes not only actual land, but also forests, minerals, water, etc.
- **Labor** – This is the work force required to produce goods and services, including factors such as talent, skills, and physical labor.
- **Capital** – This is the cash and material equipment needed to produce goods and services, including buildings, property, tools, office equipment, roads, etc.
- **Entrepreneurship** – Persons with initiative can capitalize on the free market system by producing goods and services.

The two types of markets are factor and product markets. The **factor market** consists of the people who exchange their services for wages. The people are sellers and companies are buyers. The **product market** is the selling of products to the people who want to buy them. The people are the buyers and the companies are the sellers. This exchange creates a circular economic flow in which money goes from the producers to workers as wages, and then flows back to producers in the form of payment for products.

ECONOMIC IMPACT OF TECHNOLOGY

At the start of the 21st century, the role of **information and communications technologies** (ICT) grew rapidly as the economy shifted to a knowledge-based one. Output is increasing in areas where ICT is used intensively, which are service areas and knowledge-intensive industries such as finance; insurance; real estate; business services, health care, and environmental goods and services; and community, social, and personal services. Meanwhile, the economic share for manufacturers is declining in medium- and low-technology industries such as chemicals, food products, textiles, gas, water, electricity, construction, and transport and communication services. Industries that have traditionally been high-tech, such as aerospace, computers, electronics, and pharmaceuticals are remaining steady in terms of their economic share. Technology has become the strongest factor in determining **per capita income** for many countries. The ease of technology investments as compared to industries that involve factories and large labor forces has resulted in more foreign investments in countries that do not have natural resources to call upon.

Social Studies Skills and Pedagogy

ESSENTIAL QUESTIONS USED IN LEARNING PROCESS

Essential questions for learning include those that:

1. Ask for **evaluation, synthesis, and analysis** – the highest levels of Bloom's Taxonomy
2. Seek **information** that is important to know
3. Are worth the student's **awareness**
4. Will result in enduring **understanding**
5. Tend to focus on the questions "**why**?" or "**how** do we know this information?"
6. Are more open-ended and reflective in nature
7. Often address **interrelationships** or lend themselves to multi-disciplinary investigations
8. Spark **curiosity** and a sense of wonder, and invite investigation and activity
9. Can be asked **over and over** and in a variety of instances
10. Encourage related questions
11. Have answers that may be **extended** over time

12. Seek to identify key understandings
13. Engage students in **real-life**, applied problem solving
14. May not be answerable without a **lifetime of investigation**, and maybe not even then

VARIOUS DISCIPLINES OF SOCIAL STUDIES

- **Anthropology and sociology** provide an understanding of how the world's many cultures have developed and what these cultures and their values have to contribute to society.
- **Sociology, economics, and political science** provide an understanding of the institutions in society and each person's role within social groups. These topics teach the use of charts, graphs, and statistics.
- **Political science, civics, and government** teach how to see another person's point of view, accept responsibility, and deal with conflict. They also provide students with an understanding of democratic norms and values, such as justice and equality. Students learn how to apply these norms and values in their community, school, and family.
- **Economics** teaches concepts such as work, exchange (buying, selling, and other trade transactions), production of goods and services, the origins of materials and products, and consumption.
- **Geography** teaches students how to use maps, globes, and locational and directional terms. It also provides them with an understanding of spatial environments, landforms, climate, world trade and transportation, ecological systems, and world cultures.

CONSTRUCTIVIST LEARNING THEORY AND INFORMATION SEEKING BEHAVIOR THEORY

The **Constructivist Learning Theory** supports a view of inquiry-based learning as an opportunity for students to experience learning through inquiry and problem solving. This process is characterized by exploration and risk taking, curiosity and motivation, engagement in critical and creative thinking, and connections with real-life situations and real audiences. The **Information Seeking Behavior Theory** purports that students progress through levels of question specificity, from vague notions of the information needed to clearly defined needs or questions. According to this theory, students are more successful in the search process if they have a realistic understanding of the information system and problem. They should understand that the inquiry process is not linear or confined to certain steps, but is a flexible, individual process that leads back to the original question.

STUDY OF CULTURES AND COMMUNITY RELATIONS

An important part of social studies, whether anthropology, sociology, history, geography, or political science, is the study of **local and world cultures**, as well as individual community dynamics. Students should be able to:

- Identify **values** held by their own culture and community
- Identify **values** held by other cultures and communities
- Recognize the **influences** of other cultures on their own culture
- Identify major **social institutions** and their roles in the students' communities
- Understand how individuals and groups **interact** to obtain food, clothing, and shelter
- Understand the role of language, literature, the arts, and traditions in a culture
- Recognize the role of **media and technology** in cultures, particularly in the students' own cultures
- Recognize the influence of various types of **government, economics, the environment, and technology** on social systems and cultures

- Evaluate the effectiveness of **social institutions** in solving problems in a community or culture
- Examine changes in **population, climate, and production**, and evaluate their effects on the community or culture

TYPES OF MAPS AND SCALE

There are three basic types of maps:

- **Base maps** – Created from aerial and field surveys, base maps serve as the starting point for topographic and thematic maps.
- **Topographic maps** – These show the natural and human-made surface features of the earth, including mountain elevations, river courses, roads, names of lakes and towns, and county and state lines.
- **Thematic maps** – These use a base or topographic map as the foundation for showing data based on a theme, such as population density, wildlife distribution, hill-slope stability, economic trends, etc.

Scale is the size of a map expressed as a ratio of the actual size of the land (for example, 1 inch on a map represents 1 mile on land). In other words, it is the proportion between a distance on the map and its corresponding distance on earth. The scale determines the level of detail on a map. **Small-scale maps** depict larger areas, but include fewer details. **Large-scale maps** depict smaller areas, but include more details.

TIME ZONES

Time is linked to **longitude** in that a complete rotation of the Earth, or 360° of longitude, occurs every 24 hours. Each hour of time is therefore equivalent to 15° of longitude, or 4 minutes for each 1° turn. By the agreement of 27 nations at the 1884 International Meridian Conference, the time zone system consists of **24 time zones** corresponding to the 24 hours in a day. Although high noon technically occurs when the sun is directly above a meridian, calculating time that way would result in 360 different times for the 360 meridians. Using the 24-hour system, the time is the same for all locations in a 15° zone. The 1884 conference established the meridian passing through Greenwich, England, as the zero point, or **prime meridian**. The halfway point is found at the 180th meridian, a half day from Greenwich. It is called the **International Date Line**, and serves as the place where each day begins and ends on earth.

CARTOGRAPHY

Cartography is the art and science of **mapmaking**. Maps of local areas were drawn by the Egyptians as early as 1300 BC, and the Greeks began making maps of the known world in the 6th century BC. Cartography eventually grew into the field of geography. The first step in modern mapmaking is a **survey**. This involves designating a few key sites of known elevation as benchmarks to allow for measurement of other sites. **Aerial photography** is then used to chart the area by taking photos in sequence. Overlapping photos show the same area from different positions along the flight line. When paired and examined through a stereoscope, the cartographer gets a three-dimensional view that can be made into a **topographical map**. In addition, a field survey (on the ground) is made to determine municipal borders and place names. The second step is to compile the information and **computer-draft** a map based on the collected data. The map is then reproduced or printed.

SKILLS AND MATERIALS NEEDED TO BE SUCCESSFUL IN SOCIAL STUDIES COURSE

For classes in history, geography, civics/government, anthropology, sociology, and economics, the goal is for students to explore issues and learn key concepts. **Social studies** help improve communication skills in reading and writing, but students need sufficient **literacy skills** to be able to understand specialized vocabulary, identify key points in text, differentiate between fact and opinion, relate information across texts, connect prior knowledge and new information, and synthesize information into meaningful knowledge. These literacy skills will be enhanced in the process, and will extend into higher order thinking skills that enable students to compare and contrast, hypothesize, draw inferences, explain, analyze, predict, construct, and interpret. Social studies classes also depend on a number of different types of **materials beyond the textbook**, such as nonfiction books, biographies, journals, maps, newspapers (paper or online), photographs, and primary documents.

BENEFITS OF SOCIAL STUDIES FOR STUDENTS

Social studies cover the political, economic, cultural, and environmental aspects of societies not only in the past, as in the study of history, but also in the present and future. Students gain an understanding of **current conditions** and learn how to prepare for the **future** and cope with **change** through studying geography, economics, anthropology, government, and sociology. Social studies classes teach assessment, problem solving, evaluation, and decision making skills in the context of good citizenship. Students learn about scope and sequence, designing investigations, and following up with research to collect, organize, and present information and data. In the process, students learn how to search for patterns and their meanings in society and in their own lives. Social studies build a **positive self-concept** within the context of understanding the similarities and differences of people. Students begin to understand that they are unique, but also share many feelings and concerns with others. As students learn that each individual can contribute to society, their self-awareness builds self-esteem.

INQUIRY-BASED LEARNING

Facilitated by the teacher who models, guides, and poses a starter question, **inquiry-based learning** is a process in which students are involved in their learning. This process involves formulating questions, investigating widely, and building new understanding and meaning. This combination of steps asks students to think independently, and enables them to answer their questions with new knowledge, develop solutions, or support a position or point of view. In inquiry-based learning activities, teachers engage students, ask for authentic assessments, require research using a variety of resources (books, interviews, Internet information, etc.), and involve students in cooperative interaction. All of these require the **application of processes and skills**. Consequently, new knowledge is usually shared with others, and may result in some type of action. Inquiry-based learning focuses on finding a solution to a question or a problem, whether it is a matter of curiosity, a puzzle, a challenge, or a disturbing confusion.

CREDIBILITY OF RESEARCH SOURCES

Some sources are not reliable, so the student must have a means to evaluate the **credibility** of a source when doing research, particularly on the Internet. The value of a source depends on its intended use and whether it fits the subject. For example, students researching election campaigns in the 19th century would need to go to historical documents, but students researching current election practices could use candidate brochures, television advertisements, and web sites. A checklist for examining sources might include:

- Check the **authority and reputation** of the author, sponsoring group, or publication
- Examine the language and illustrations for **bias**

- Look for a clear, logical **arrangement** of information
- If online, check out the associated links, archives, contact ability, and the date of last update

COMMON RESEARCH METHODS IN SOCIAL SCIENCES

Social science research relies heavily on **empirical research**, which is original data gathering and analysis through direct observation or experiment. It also involves using the library and Internet to obtain raw data, locate information, or review expert opinion. Because social science projects are often interdisciplinary, students may need assistance from the librarian to find related search terms. While arguments still exist about the superiority of quantitative versus qualitative research, most social scientists understand that research is an eclectic mix of the two methods. **Quantitative research** involves using techniques to gather data, which is information dealing with numbers and measurable values. Statistics, tables, and graphs are often the products. **Qualitative research** involves non-measurable factors, and looks for meaning in the numbers produced by quantitative research. Qualitative research takes data from observations and analyzes it to find underlying meanings and patterns of relationships.

PBA

The acronym **PBA** stands for **performance-based assessment**. A PBA is an alternative assessment, defined as a multistep task or project aligned to meet the specific state standards of any given subject. In social sciences, PBAs are used to assess a student's ability to use the concepts learned in a unit and apply those concepts to complete tasks that require higher-order thinking skills. The goal of most PBAs is to create a product or complete a process in which students connect what they have learned to their own experience or environment. These assessments are typically graded using a rubric, which focuses on both the final product and the process followed throughout the project.

ASSESSMENT OF SOCIAL SCIENCES

Assessment **social sciences** should be assessed before, during, and after instruction. The data from these assessments should be used to guide, monitor, and revise instruction at both the whole-class and individual levels. Before instruction, assessments should be used to plan for an upcoming unit, whereas assessments that occur during instruction should be used to identify students who may need modified instruction or provide for an expansion of the current curriculum for accelerated learners. Assessments occurring after instruction should be used to gauge whether or not students have mastered the intended standards, at which point reteaching may need to occur.

Visual and Performing Arts

Visual Arts

CREATIVE EXPRESSION

Being **creative** means the ability to produce or bring into existence a work of art (music, painting, sculpture, comedy, drama, and literature) that is original and imaginative. To express something is to convey an idea, an emotion or an opinion, or to depict a direct or indirect representation of an idea, an emotion or an opinion. The idea, emotion or opinion can be shown in words, pictures, gestures, signs and symbols. A person with **creative expression** has the burning need to bring forth a unique manifestation of his or her understanding and interpretation of mankind's primal desires. A soaring music score by Beethoven, a memorable scene by Grandma Moses, a gentle poem by Emily Dickinson, a moving performance by Sir Laurence Olivier are all examples of individual creative expression by artists of uncompromising vision.

ELEMENTS OF ART

There are five basic **elements of art**: line, shape, space, texture and color. Each has a specific function; each must be understood to truly appreciate the objet d'art being studied. The following definitions are composed from the *American Heritage College Dictionary*:

- **Line** is a continuous path made by a moving pen, pencil or brush that makes a real or imaginary mark in relation to a point of reference.
- **Shape** is the characteristic outline or contour of an object that is distinguished from its surroundings by its distinctive form.
- **Space** is a three-dimensional empty area with a specific outline that is reserved for a particular purpose.
- **Texture** is a surface of elements woven together that has distinctive or identifying characteristics.
- **Color** is the appearance of objects caused by different qualities of reflected light that involves hue, lightness, darkness, value and purity.

USE OF LIGHT AND DARK IN TWO AND THREE DIMENSIONAL ART FORMS

In western culture, the reaction to light and dark arouses strong, primitive emotions. **Light** suggests goodness, intelligence and wholeness. **Dark** expresses mystery, ignorance and evil. Contrasting these opposites in a work of art helps convey feelings and has a powerful psychological impact. Light and dark can also depict space and enhance form in two and three dimensional art. On a two dimensional surface, the effects of light and shadow can be very dramatic. When light is blocked by different parts of a form and casts a shadow, the figures in a painting seem to come alive. This technique is called chiaroscuro. Light and shadow on sculpture and architecture define the form of the piece. As the contour fades away, the light grows dimmer causing changes in contrast and tonal value on the surface, which makes the object seem to swell and recede while enhancing the drama of its structural composition.

PRINCIPLES OF ART

In art, there are five basic **principles**: balance and harmony, proportion and unity and variety. Each has a unique function and needs to be understood to appreciate the artist's vision whether it is shown in a painting, sculpture or a piece of architecture. The following definitions are composed from the *American Heritage College Dictionary*:

- **Balance and Harmony** is a state of equilibrium between parts that creates a pleasant arrangement in the whole and depicts a difference in dimension between opposing forces or influences.
- **Proportion** is the pleasing symmetry between objects or their parts with respect to comparative size, quantity or degree.
- **Unity** is the state of being in accord and having a continuity of purpose or action. Its partner is **Variety**, which is diversity in a collection that has specific characteristics.

TERMS ASSOCIATED WITH COLOR

- **Hue** — any specific color
- **Shade** — a color made by adding black to a hue
- **Tone** — a color made by adding grey to a hue
- **Value** — the degree of light or darkness
- **Achromatic** — black, white and grays; artwork executed without color
- **Black** — the complete absence of light
- **Chroma** — the intensity, strength or purity of a color
- **Complementary Colors** — colors which appear opposite one another on a color wheel
- **Secondary colors** — orange, violet, green; each is midway between the Primaries from which it can be mixed
- **Shade** — using a mixture of black mixed with a color to make it darker; the opposite of shade is tint
- **Spectrum** — colors that are the result of a beam of white light that is broken by a form of prism into its hues
- **Tint** — the opposite of shade; combining white with a color to make it lighter
- **Value** — shadows, darkness, contrasts and light

TERMS RELATED TO POSITIONING OF SUBJECT MATTER WITHIN A PAINTING

- **Background** — the part of the scene intended to be the most distant from the perspective of the viewer
- **Foreground** — the part of the scene intended to be nearest the viewer
- **Horizon** — the line where sky and earth meet; also referred to as "ground line"
- **Landscape** — a view of a section of country – applicable to outdoor scenes only
- **Middle ground** — the area between the foreground and the most distant part of a scene
- **Vertical lines** — lines that are painted straight up and down
- **Horizontal lines** — lines that are painted across the picture (90 degrees from straight up and down)
- **Point-of-view** — the angle from which the viewer is observing the work
- **Negative space** — the space behind and around an object; in two-dimensional art it is often synonymous with background
- **Overlapping** — occurs when one object partially covers another; usually done for compositional purposes
- **Design** — the arrangement of the elements of a picture

APPRECIATION OF VISUAL ART

The act of **appreciating visual art** is, in its simplest form, one of simply deriving satisfaction or pleasure from observing the beauty given to it by its creator. Research has shown that a capacity for appreciating (or, alternatively, creating) aesthetically pleasing art appears to be present within every individual although it does seem to vary in terms of degrees. For most people, innate abilities remain untrained or underdeveloped – not so much in terms of the possession of individual tastes and opinions or in terms of an ability to find something beautiful, but rather in an ability to recognize artistic mastery with respect to technique or style. Education can reconcile such a deficiency. Therefore, anyone can truly appreciate art, but true "art appreciation" requires some understanding of the creative process involved in production, or perhaps, some particular insight into the thoughts and feelings of the creator. Ideally, art is best appreciated when one considers both dimensions.

WOOD CARVING AND ENGRAVING

Wood carving is an ancient art which has changed very little in its history. The process is relatively straightforward. After selecting a suitable wood, most carving is done with a limited set of tools to create works which don't typically exhibit an abundance of fine detail. Engraving is a more refined version of carving and is sometimes a preliminary step in other artistic activities such as printmaking where fine detail and exacting shapes are desired. Several varieties of wood can be used successfully by the engraver although boxwood is a preferred type for its favorable characteristics. The wood is sawn cross-grain which results in a block with both a tighter grain and better shape-holding ability. Due to its exacting nature, **engraving** often requires tools similar to those used by copper and steel workers. The tools are arranged into groups such as gravers, tint tools, scorpers, spit stickers, and small chisels. A typical beginning set includes flat, round, burin and lozenge, as well as both large and small U and V cutters.

PASTELS

Pastels are chemically pure pigments gently bound by gum or resin and are much softer than their harder chalk crayon cousins. Due to the nature of the pigment cohesion, durability is a primary concern when using them. The ability to correct mistakes is also severely limited. For this reason, pre-planning a work is crucial. A fairly recent addition to the arts, pastel work was pioneered mostly by French artists in the 18th century. Notable pastel artists of the era included Quentin de la Tour, Jean-Baptiste Perroneau and Jean-Baptiste Chardin. More recent artists include Odilon Redon and Mary Cassatt. Having never gained the popularity of other forms such as oils and watercolor, pastels remain one the less regarded mediums within the artistic community.

PEN AND INK

Pen and ink is one of the least demanding art forms in terms of equipment requirements. Pen and ink artists simply need the addition of virtually any kind of paper to produce their work. Historically, medieval monks employed pen and ink on prepared animal skins such as goat, sheep, calf, lamb or kid using the quills of goose feathers. Pen use continued during the Renaissance and along with mixed media such as white highlighting, crayon and watercolors it flourished as an art form. It gained even more widespread use during the Post-Renaissance era by such artists as Rubens and Van Dyck. Hogarth is considered an exemplary penman of the 18th century while the advent of magazines and the mass production of books in the 19th century provided an outlet for notables such as Charles Keene and George du Maurier. By the 20th century, pen and ink luminaries included Matisse, Pascin and Picasso.

ELEMENTS OF SCULPTURE DESIGN

- **Mass** — he most influential element in sculpture that can have a dramatic effect upon interpretation, light reflectivity and symmetry.
- **Space** — Space in a multi-piece sculpture is an element that can be manipulated to effect interpretation by yielding clues with respect to the relationship between individual pieces.

- **Plane** — An element with two dimensions – length and width; plane thickness is typically minimized to provide the most dramatic differentiation between plane and volume
- **Line** — Line lends an element of space to a sculpture; vertical lines belie support and strength lending a monumental quality while horizontal lines have a somewhat less dramatic effect. Convex lines can create tension while concave lines often indicate either real or implied forces.
- **Movement** — generally an implied effect; often a function of reflected light that can be altered through the manipulation of the sculpture's mass. Some sculptors, such as Alexander Calder, employ actual movement in their work through mobiles or similar effects.
- **Scale** — the relative size of the work; often a product of the manipulation of other elements such as mass
- **Texture** — the surface quality of the work; primarily manipulated to either enhance or diminish light reflectivity and shadowing
- **Color** — achieved through a variety of effects; can often add a sense of realism or a particular quality, such as age, to a work

PERSPECTIVE

Perspective is a system of creating the illusion of three dimensions on a two-dimensional surface. There are two basic categories of perspective – aerial and linear. **Aerial perspective** refers to atmospheric effects on objects in space and can be seen as diminishing tones for objects which are receding from view. Put simply, **linear perspective** describes a process of seeing lines on objects from various angles converge and diverge. The position from which an object is seen and drawn is called the **station point** or **point of sight**. The **horizon** is represented by the eye level or horizon line. **Ground plane** refers to the horizontal plane where the artist is standing. The **center of vision** is the point on the horizon immediately opposite the eye. **Vanishing points** occur where parallel lines converge.

SHAPE, FORM, AND PROPORTION

Shape is an aspect of form which constitutes the individual masses, groupings or aesthetics that the artist uses to render the overall work. It is form, combined with content, which constitutes the basis of the art work itself. **Proportion** refers to the symmetrical three-dimensionality or solidity of a work. In representational art, the intent is to create an illusion of reality by rendering a work which is convincing in form. The mathematical concept known as the "**Golden Mean**" is often employed, either purposefully or incidentally, when rendering proportion. Put simply, it is the precept that the proportion of the smaller part to the larger part of a whole is equal to that of the larger to the whole. Perhaps the most well-known demonstration of the "Golden Mean" is the 1509 Leonardo da Vinci work titled "Divine Proportion."

PROTECTIVE APPAREL

Protective apparel such as gloves, long sleeves, long pants and boots or shoes rather than sandals help prevent contact of chemicals with the skin. The garments should be dedicated for use in the studio or work area and washed frequently in a separate load from other laundry. If skin contact does occur, flush immediately with soapy water or other suitable cleaners. Avoid the use of solvents or bleach to clean the skin as these will often absorb and enter the blood stream where they can accumulate in internal organs. If splashes or flying debris are concerns, goggles should be worn in the work area. Ear protection is generally advised when working with noisy equipment for extended periods. Wear a properly fitted respirator or dust mask if vapors or dust are present. Refrain from wearing jewelry when working and tie long hair back to prevent it from being caught in tools and equipment. Do not work when fatigued and always wash hands before drinking, eating or smoking.

MATERIALS TO AVOID WHEN CHILDREN ARE PARTICIPATING IN ART PROJECTS

Numerous materials specially designed for **children** are available commercially. Adult supervision is also advisable when children are working with art materials. All adult materials should be avoided as these may contain toxic chemicals, including solvents, thinners, shellacs, acids, alkalis, bleaches, rubber cement and permanent markers. Materials which must be sprayed such as paints, fixatives, adhesives and airbrush paints should be avoided as well as pottery glazes, copper enamels, stained glass and pastels. Also, any materials requiring solvents for clean-up such as oil paint or oil-based printmaking inks should be substituted for water-based alternatives when available. It is often best to limit the amount or quantity of material given to very young children to reduce the risk should ingestion occur. Children should also be taught to wash their hands thoroughly after working with the materials.

LOCAL ART AND ARCHITECTURE

The architecture of **home construction** is one obvious place. Although many newer areas around cities lack compelling diversity and creativity, there are almost always exceptions. This is particularly true of older areas with established traditions. **Churches** are another excellent place to discover art. The relationship between religion and art is as old as most religions themselves. Christianity is certainly no exception. Modern churches frequently have collections of paintings and sculpture consistent with the beliefs of their own individual congregations. For those fortunate enough live in Europe or in the Eastern United States, numerous older churches are accessible. Many of these are exemplary works of art in themselves. A number of **businesses**, particularly large corporations, have substantial art collections in their common areas, many of which are accessible to visitors. Shopping centers, banks government buildings (particularly with respect to sculpture) are often rich resources for art seekers.

ART FORMS

The following definitions are taken from *The American Heritage College Dictionary*:

- A **painting** is a picture or design created in oil or water-based paint.
- **Literature** is a body of creative writing that helps define a language, period or culture.
- **Music** is sounds arranged to produce a unified composition that has melody, rhythm and timber.
- A **sculpture** is an object created by chiseling marble, molding clay or casting in metal into a real or abstract figure.
- **Theater** is dramatic or comedic literature or other such material performed by actors impersonating characters through dialogue and action.
- **Drama** is verbal literature composed of serious subject matter written specifically to be performed by actors in the theater or on television, radio or film.
- **Comedy** is humorous or satirical verbal literature depicting funny themes, situations or characters that is written to be performed by actors in the theater or on television, radio or film.

ART TERMS

These definitions are from the *New York City Public Library Desk Reference*, Second Edition:

- **Carving** means to cut hard material such as stone, wood or marble to create a form.
- In **Casting**, the sculptor pours plaster or molten metal into a mold and lets the substance harden into the desired form.
- A **Collage** is made of separate pieces of various materials and other objects glued to a surface.
- **Drypoint** is an engraving technique that uses a sharp steel needle to create a rough edge, which produces soft, velvety lines.
- **Engraving** is the art of carving, cutting or etching a design on a wood or metal surface then adding ink so the design can be printed.
- **Etching** is the art of cutting into a metal or glass surface then bathing the surface in acid, adding ink to the plate, and printing the design.
- In architecture, a **frieze** is a horizontal band of painted or sculpted decoration usually found at the top of a wall between the molding and the cornice.
- **Lithography** is a printing process in which a stone or metal plate has been treated with an oily substance so that the desired design retains ink while the rest of the surface is treated to repel ink.
- When a sculptor uses clay or wax to build up a form, it is called **modeling**. Using color and light to create the illusion of a three-dimensional plane in drawing and painting is also known as modeling.
- A **polyptych** is multiple scenes hinged together. A **diptych** has two panels; a triptych has three panels.
- In architecture when a form sticks out from the background, depending on how far it protrudes, it is known as **high relief** or **low relief** (bas-relief). In painting or drawing, if an object appears to project out from the flat surface suggesting three dimensions, it is called relief.
- **Stenciling** is the technique of applying paint or ink to forms cut out of cardboard, metal, plastic or other flat materials to create letters, numbers and other images and designs.
- A **still life** is a study of ordinary objects in an every day setting in a painting, drawing or photograph. A still life can also be created on a tabletop or in a bookcase or a shadow box.
- **Woodcutting** is the art of carving an image on a wood block then using ink or paint to print the design.

Performing Arts

TERMS RELATING TO DRAMATIC PERFORMANCES

- **Acting process**—refers to the methods and materials from which an actor draws his or her ability to perform; actors should be able to verbalize the tools they use in their acting processes.
- **Affective memory**—a technique in which an actor reactivates a past experience to gain the emotional and psychological feelings associated with those events and then transferring them to a performance; used when the actor believes the character they are portraying is undergoing an event that emotionally parallels that which the actor experienced in real life.
- **Atmospheres**—defined by Michael Chekhov as the inherent energy within a specific place; actors may imagine they are in a specific location while performing in order to depict the corresponding emotions and actions that would best suit that environment thus creating an atmosphere.

- **Character acting**—occurs when an actor must make a change to their physical person in order to perform a role; may include the use of dialect or accents that are not part of the actor's real persona or using stage makeup to create a specific facial disfigurement.

TERMS USED IN THEATRE

- **Articulation**—the ability to clearly pronounce words while acting or performing.
- **Blocking**—developing the movements of actors on stage in relation to other actors, scenery, and props.
- **Catharsis**—the purging of an emotion, such as fear or grief, while performing on stage.
- **Concentration**—the ability of an actor to be in character through use of dialogue, attitude, voice, costume, expressions, and mannerisms.
- **Cold reading**—occurs when actors read a script for the first time.
- **Context**—the conditions or climate in which a play was written or meant to be performed.
- **Cue**—a signal that serves as an indicator of another action that is about to occur.

EXTERNALS

The elements that an actor can use in his or her environment to aid in creating specific characters are known as **externals**. An external can be a costume, a vocal change, makeup, or a set of mannerisms. For many actors, externals are the primary tool they use to create a character. By dressing or speaking in the way a character would, the actor can begin to relate to the feelings that the character would experience. Using externals to create a character is a method called **outside-in**. This means that the actor uses outside elements to cause internal changes. In order to be a character actor, one must be able to shed the restrictions of his or her everyday persona. In essence, her or she must be able to create a blank slate upon which the new character can be created.

CONSIDERATIONS FOR COSTUME DESIGNERS

The **costume designer's** role is very important in helping to achieve the director's vision because the costumes used should contribute to the tone and style of a production. It is important for costume designers to consult with the director in order to ensure that the costume designs will be consistent with the *theme* of the production. A costume designer must consider the *time period* in which the play is set. They must also consider the many facets of a character's *personality* and *lifestyle*, including his or her job and social status. The costumes also serve to *differentiate* and *unify* certain characters. For example, a play in which the characters are divided between servants and aristocracy should involve two distinct costuming groups. Costumes must also be practical for the actors and should allow them to move freely and change quickly.

TOOLS USED BY SOUND TECHNICIANS

In the early days of theatre, **sound** was created by any means available. For example, the sound of thunder was simulated by rolling a cannonball down a narrow trench carved into the roof of a theatre. Now, the sound of thunder can be created through the use of **digital sound equipment**. Technicians have the ability to reproduce sounds made by such things as door bells and telephones. Technicians can also reinforce these sounds through the use of amplification. The variety of technologies available in modern theatre allows for technicians to reproduce nearly any sound that might be needed for a performance. Background music and actors' voices can all be controlled through use of speakers, microphones, and sound boards. **Sound quality** is a crucial part of any theatre experience, and a successful performance allows the audience to both see and hear the performance without distraction.

LIGHTING

Lighting in theatre can be used in several ways. The most basic purpose of theatre lighting is to allow the audience to see what is happening on stage. Lighting is also useful for providing depth to the stage and actors. The use of highlights and shadows, called modeling, create a three-dimensional effect. Lighting can serve an overall compositional purpose by helping to create a series of connected imagery that brings the director's *interpretation* to life. It can be used to give information about the *setting* of a play: time of day, season, and location. Light can also be used to focus the audience's attention on a particular *element* in the production. Lighting can be used to create a *mood* for a play. The proper lighting can reflect the *emotional content* of a performance, which leads to a cohesive and balanced production.

GOALS FOR 9TH-12TH GRADE UNIT ON THEATRICAL PRESENTATION

Theatrical presentation involves familiarizing students with a broad range of activities that can be considered theatrical forms. Such forms include music, dance, performance, and visual arts. Students should examine the structure of each kind of dramatic form in order to determine how that particular form relates to the structure of all arts. Students should be given the opportunity to integrate their knowledge of various forms of theatre into an original performance they create themselves. Lessons should provide a means for students to study both traditional and non-traditional methods of artistic production. Lessons should also provide students with knowledge of and hands-on experience in emerging technology in theatrical productions including film, video, and computer applications.

APPLYING LESSONS FROM THEATRE CLASS TO OTHER SUBJECT AREAS OR LIFE SKILLS

In **first grade**, students can learn to cooperate in *group activities*. They also begin to understand the concept that all things in life have a beginning, a middle, and an end, just like they see in stories. In **second grade**, students learn *problem-solving skills*, which can be carried into other courses. In **third grade**, students are taught to question events and gain information through applying the *5 Ws* (who, what, when, where and why). In **fourth grade**, students learn to use acting as a tool for *understanding local history*. They also learn to work with a *team* to accomplish a specific goal. In **fifth grade**, students learn about the various *career options* available to professional actors and theatrical technicians. In **sixth grade**, students learn how theatrical skills are used in the *social sciences*, such as advertising and marketing. In **seventh grade**, students learn how the voice can be used to project *confidence* during oral presentations. In **eighth grade**, students begin to understand the various *jobs* available in theatre, and they are encouraged to research the educational requirements necessary for those jobs.

COMPREHENDING DANCE PERFORMANCE BY GENRE

Every form of dance has signature **characteristics** that identify and define it—and that make it beautiful and distinct from all other forms. An audience member can look for these when watching particular styles of dance, and can then discern whether those characteristics are present and strongly represented. For example, **tap** exemplifies rhythm and improvisation. If choreography ignores or contradicts the rhythm in an unpleasant way, or simply repeats time steps without ever choosing to improvise movements during the breaks, it could be considered an unsuccessful representation of its form. The same methods can be applied to evaluate modern dance's expressiveness and inquiry into creative movement types, ballet's fluidity and weightlessness, and flamenco's rhythm, passion, and footwork. It should be noted, however, that working contrary to form does not necessarily make a dance "bad." Looking at form is simply a place to start when considering the elements and effects of a dance.

Eliciting Particular Feelings or Reactions

Some dances are created to elicit an **emotional response** from audiences. They may represent characters, settings, or situations about which people already have strong feelings. For example, mythological stories have always been a favorite theme across many forms of dance, as the characters are strong, their defeats disheartening, and their triumphs inspiring. Dances with a **dramatic** or **comedic** objective often borrow methods from theater, such as staging, costumes, props, and sets. These methods help set the tone for bringing forth certain feelings. In these dances, dancers often portray more emotion than usual through facial expression, gestures, and the particular kind of energy in their movements. Whereas **formalistic dances** ask audiences to focus on the "what" and "how" of a dance, **dramatic pieces** draw the viewer into the humanity of the situation. They focus on the "why" or—in **comedic pieces** portraying the absurd behavior of a character—the "who."

Importance of Audience Member's Experience and Perspective

The performance of any **dynamic** (moving) work of art involves three essential parties: the choreographer, who creates; the dancers, who perform; and the audience member, who receives and interprets. It is important for audience members to understand that their own perspectives will color their responses to a dance every bit as much as anything the choreographer or dancers do. **Choreographers** contribute intention, knowledge, and craft. **Dancers** supply their training, focus, interpretation, and energy. **Viewers** bring their own influential elements to a dance: past experiences; a sociopolitical orientation; aesthetic preferences; and a certain degree—or lack—of knowledge about dance in general and the specific choreographer, company, or presenting institution behind the dance. As the saying goes, "We can only see what we can see." Differing combinations of the viewer characteristics mentioned above create a different version of the dance for every viewer, shaping perception more strongly than any choreographic intention.

Design Elements in Formalistic Dance Pieces

A **choreographer** may create a dance to explore the relationship between floor patterns and the directions dancers face, or to explore patterns in time created by combining long delays and short bursts of movement. The choreographer might even include "what happens if" scenarios that are based on chance. In these dances, the **space** is quite visible in varying shapes made by bodies and the movements themselves, as well as levels, planes, facings, directions, and floor patterns in which the dancers move. **Time** can also be measured in the speed, duration, rhythms, arrangement, and sequencing of the movements. Choreographers can also explore **dynamics** by varying the weight put into the movements and the energy and timing with which the dancers approach, maintain, and release movements. Although **abstract dances** do not specifically aim to evoke viewers' emotions, they may still do so—and will certainly create impressions and elicit reactions of some kind.

Questions to Gain Greater Insight into a Dance

Many viewers leave a dance performance asking one main **question**: "What was that all about?" However, there are other questions audience members can ask and answer for themselves or other spectators that are slightly smaller in scope and more likely to conjure up bits of understanding. These include: Did a clear message come through in the dance? What was that message? Did the dance tell a story, express feelings, solve a puzzle, comment on a situation, or just look pretty? Were there repeated movements or series that were easy to identify? Did specific images catch your attention? What images caught your attention, and what were they likely meant to express? What might the choreographer's intentions have been? What was the choreographer trying to say? Did the dance say it clearly? How did you feel after the dance? Can you distill the description of that feeling down to one sentence? Can you express that feeling using a single word?

CULTURAL CONTEXT OF BODY OF WORK OR PARTICULAR DANCE

Cultural context—the time, place, cultural climate, and artistic influences surrounding artists and their work—can provide a strong set of clues to a viewer trying to analyze a dance or canon of work, and can be understood by using several methods. Comparing and contrasting a dance with other dances from the **same time period**—whether works made by the choreographer in question or several different choreographers—can give a clear "snapshot" of a certain era, especially if it is or was defined by particular historical or political events. Comparing and contrasting a dance with other forms of art from the same time period can provide an even clearer picture of the cultural climate of the time. Comparing and contrasting a dance with **earlier works** by the same choreographer can illustrate the development of the artist's canon throughout his or her career.

USING IMAGERY TO IMPROVE TECHNIQUE

Imagery connects the unfamiliar with the familiar, allowing a dancer to understand and feel the movement being performed. Following are some examples of imagery that could be used to improve technique, and their desired effects:

- **To improve balance**: The image of sand slowly falling and accumulating (as in an hourglass) to fill up a standing leg
- **To prolong lift in a leap**: The image of a gazelle leaping and remaining suspended for a second before landing
- **To achieve deeper abdominal contraction**: The image of a snail curling deep into its spiraling shell
- **To sharpen angular movement and shapes**: The image of skyscrapers that are full of hard lines and acute angles
- **To soften tension in port de bras**: The image of a soft blanket gently gliding over the skin, or of gentle waves washing the arms
- **To accelerate attack in an assemblé**: The image of stepping on a dollar bill before someone else gets it
- To better employ plié in preparation for jumps: The image of a floor made out of springs

CLASSICAL BALLET

Classical ballet technique revolves around a dancer's lifted, contracted torso. To provide stability, strength in the core muscles of the body is needed. The limbs are elevated from the core. Arms are typically extended away from the body in "airy" postures. The legs perform movements in a position rotated or "turned out" from the hips, requiring flexibility in the muscles of the hips and legs. Balances are often held upon the tips of the toes, known as "en pointe." The majority of movement is done in **upright positions**—balanced, locomoting upon, or jumping/leaping and landing upon the feet. This requires both flexibility and strength in the legs and feet. Movement is largely directed away from the floor, as the ballet dancer continually strives to create the illusion of weightlessness and effortlessness. The ultimate visual goal is elevation and elongation of the "lines" of the body, and of movement.

MODERN DANCE

Although **modern dance** shares some features with ballet, it was largely a response to—and rebellion against—ballet. It took shape under a banner of individual exploration into natural, instinctive, expressive movement styles, and has developed ever since into its own always-evolving entity that encompasses as many styles of movement as there are dancers. Movement philosophies prevalent in modern dance are: an emphasis on coordinating movement with the breath; a focus on shifting the weight freely across the feet, hands, shoulders, pelvis, spine, or any other body part that touches the floor; the use of an articulated spine and the limbs; a focus on working with the floor and the force of gravity; and an intention to explore or express a personal, intellectual, emotional, design, philosophical, or other concept through movement.

TERMINOLOGY AND FORM IN MODERN DANCE

Modern dance emphasizes the finding of an **individual, personally authentic movement style** over the codification of form and structure. Individual styles are often informed by the specific focus of a dancer's creative exploration and the needs of the physical body. Modern dance has **no standardized terminology**, so even though it uses many standard terms from its predecessor, ballet (plié, tendu, and battement, for example), these are augmented by countless other movement words that range from basic commands (bend, contract, and swing, for instance) to terms specific to one teacher's movement philosophy. Modern dance classes do not share a universally codified structure or sequence, although, like ballet classes, they begin with warm-up movements. Instead of being performed at a barre, however, they are usually performed at center, sometimes beginning from a supine position on the floor. From warm-ups, classes then progress through a series of increasingly demanding movements before finishing with the learning and performing of a choreographic combination.

FLOOR WORK

Because of modern dance's emphasis on **groundedness**, a connection to the floor, and a working cooperation with gravity—as well as its openness to experimentation—the modern form of dance involves more **floor work** than other forms of dance, such as ballet or tap. In these forms, dancers usually stand on their feet. Floor work can be done while kneeling, crouching, on hands and knees, sitting, or lying on the floor. Combinations of these positions can also be used. Movements can include crawling, rolling, scooting, dragging, slithering, etc. Often, movements at this level can express ideas of earth, gravity, weight, debasement, filth, ugliness, evil, disadvantage, poverty, sadness, or dejection, among others. Floor work also supports the modern ethos by affording opportunities to use **unconventional body parts** for balance, locomotion, and pivoting (as in shoulder stands, dragging the prone body forward with the elbows, or spinning on one sitz bone), as well as to invert the body in unfamiliar orientations.

SOCIAL DANCE AND OTHER TRADITIONAL DANCE THROUGHOUT THE WORLD

"**Folk dance**" is a catch-all term for any traditional dance participated in communally by non-professionals. Worldwide, these dances can be placed into two main categories: religious dance and social dance. Both are an effective way of transmitting culture and reinforcing a people's communal values and experiences.

Religious dances reflect a people's spiritual beliefs. They include storytelling dances to transfer knowledge, medicine dances for healing or protection, imitation dances (mimicking important animals or events), commemorative dances demarcating annual events (solstices, harvests, animal migrations, etc.) or personal landmarks in individuals' lives (birth, initiation, marriage, death, etc.), and dances to achieve a spiritual connection with deities.

Social dances are primarily for recreation and community. They include work dances (mimicking movements of a particular kind of labor); courtship dances (less prevalent in cultures that impose strict limitations on contact between the sexes); war dances to prepare, motivate, or intimidate before battle; and communal dances to enhance cooperation.

Social dance is, by definition, communal dance. It is created for the purpose of affirming a community's shared knowledge, culture, and experiences. The dance steps, as well as the music, costumes, and other accompanying traditions, are handed down from one generation to the next through observation and participation, rather than via a rigid scholastic format.

To best facilitate this informal learning, traditional dance steps are usually simple and somewhat natural. In many cases, steps are based on movements used in the work and daily lives of the people and their ancestors, and so are already familiar to the people learning them. Possible examples of familiar movements are fishermen pulling nets and farmers planting seeds.

Often, steps are rhythmic and feature set foot patterns, as rhythm and patterns are both easy devices for categorizing and recalling information. Most importantly, dances are taught in a fun, social environment, which motivates dancers to learn the dance steps, remember them, and look forward to performing them.

Music

EMERGENCE OF MUSIC

Music as an artistic expression became documented during the Middle Ages. Prior to that time, music was used as an equally contributing part of worship, poetry, dance and served society by uniting a community to complete necessary labors, soothe mourners, express different emotions, and offer homage to a higher power. The older or ancient forms of musical expression set the foundation for the more disciplined arts of music since there was no musical notation for sharing these ideas until the Middle Ages. The Greeks with their love of the lyre established that musical foundation as surely as they did modern theories regarding culture and philosophy. Greek musical theory introduced intervals, or relationships between pitches, using a tightened string to show how the shortening of the string 3:2 or 4:3 could change the tone when plucked.

STYLE OF MUSIC AND CHRONOLOGICAL CLASSIFICATIONS OF MUSIC

The **style** of music showcases not only the time and political or spiritual mood of the period, but also the composers and the mindset of the people. Music is meant to be listened to and, as such, can be repeated, expounded upon through different media, appreciated in different ways at different times, accepted as an individualistic part of the hearer, respected as a demonstration of a culture or belief system, and touted as a societal bragging right. Music offers these different abstract feelings, but its primary purpose and people's eternal fascination falls back on the fact that music is created for people's enjoyment. The styles of music are usually classified into chronological sections and referred to as Renaissance, Baroque, Classical, Romantic, and Twentieth Century.

QUALITY OF MUSIC

Music is difficult to label as good and bad since the biggest deciding factor of the quality of music is the **listener**. Defining any **greatness** in art by comparing the positive and negative aspects limits the artistic voice of the creator and the imagination of the audience. Critics have been in the business of defining the quality of art for centuries and have often made poor calls because of their inability to accept a new style or the enduring aspect of the composer and the audience reception of that style. For any musician to become accepted, he or she must master a particular style or technique and perform or compose with a kind of genius that inspires others. To be considered great, music must be able to stand the test of time as being an indispensable example of a kind of work for the period, country, or composer.

SYMPHONY

As a work for an orchestra with multiple movements or multiple parts in one movement, the **symphony** contained three movements of fast-slow-fast and was named for the Italian opera

Sinfonia. Performed with strings and winds, these musical pieces were enjoyed at private gatherings in palaces, monasteries, and residences, as well as civic functions and public concerts. The foundation for the symphony genre comes from Sammartini whose works used the three-part movement with both strings and winds. As the Classical Period developed, the symphonic format increased to four parts or movements with an even greater transition in the third movement. After being expertly worked by Haydn, the symphony became a more celebrated style of music that allowed for great freedom in composition and features.

BAROQUE STYLE AND CLASSICAL STYLE

While the stylistic choices for music differ between Baroque and Classical, the integrity and depth of composition evident in both. Music requires a certain kind of simplicity for comprehension, and the simpler styles of the **Classical Period** did not take away that complexity. While Bach may create incredible musical feats on his polyphonic style, he incorporated a lucid design in his work. The surface sounds of works by Haydn and Mozart may appear simple but are in actuality incredibly organized and conceived, using a great amount of material and genius in that simplicity. The **Baroque** composers sought to express magnificence and grandeur in their music, while the Classical composers adopted an unpretentious format of hiding deep feelings. Baroque gave us the motet and opera, but from the Classical Period came the symphony, string quartet, and sonata.

INTERVALS

As the basis for any discussion of melodic or harmonic relationships, the **interval** refers to the measurement from pitch to pitch. The half step or **semitone** is the smallest movement and is the distance from one key to the next in the chromatic scale, such as C to C#. The whole step or **tone** refers to a full movement in which the notes are 2 keys apart, such as from C to D. The half step and whole step act as the basis of measurement for intervallic discussions. These intervals are defined by quantity and quality. The **quantity**, or numeric value assigned to the note, is established by the musical arrangement, such as C D E F G A B. Any interval created with C and G will always be a fifth, regardless of any sharps or flats.

SCALES

A **musical scale** is the sequenced arrangement of notes or pitches that are located within the octave. Both major and minor scales have seven different notes or scale degrees, and each scale degree is indicated by the Arabic number showing the position of the note as it appears in the scale. Each major scale has two similar units of four notes, or tetrachords, that are separated by a whole step where each tetrachord has two whole steps and one half step. **Minor scales** are classified as natural, harmonic, and melodic and all start with the same minor tetrachord of 1-2- b3-4 with variations occurring on degrees 6 and 7 in the upper tetrachord.

DYNAMICS

Dynamics is the degree of loudness or softness of a musical piece. Certain terms can indicate this degree, as well as specific abbreviations and symbols used within the music and at specific places. Dynamic marks can also indicate a change in volume or sound quality and usually suggest the character of the piece to be observed during its performance. Usually written in Italian, dynamic marks are often abbreviated and range from very soft pianissimo (pp) to mezzo piano (mp) to mezzo forte (mf) to fortissimo (ff) which is very loud. Gradual changes in volume can be represented by a < or the word **crescendo** for increasing in volume and by a > or the words diminuendo or decrescendo for decreasing in volume. These marks for the changing of volume can be several measures long or just a span of a few notes.

190

TEMPO

The **tempo** or speed of the piece of music can be designated by specific tempo marks as well as certain Italian words that describe the speed and also the character of the piece. The words used include *grave* for very slow and serious, *largo* for broad, *lento* for slow, *adagio* for slow and with ease, *andante* for steadily moving, *moderato* for moderate, *allegretto* for fast, *allegro* for fast and cheerful, *vivace* for lively, *presto* for very fast, and *prestissimo* for as fast as possible. Other relative changes in tempo can be described with the words *ritardando*, or rit., for slowing, as well as *accelerando* for quickening and *più mosso* for faster. The tempo marking are a guide for the performance and can be interpreted differently by different conductors.

RHYTHM

As the pattern of movement in a particular time, **rhythm** has referred to both the flow of a piece and the ability of the piece to maintain or uphold the pulse. Rhythm can be generally assigned to cover any aspect of music that is not related to pitch, although it has also been used as another factor for consideration with melody and harmony. As an equal partner to meter and tempo, rhythm can describe a pattern of *stresses* and *retreats* that are defined by a particular tempo or meter and are composed of hazy pitches or subtle harmonies as well as percussive bursts. For rhythm to sustain, the stresses and retreats should be frequent enough to maintain the melodic or harmonic thought and have defined articulation.

ACOUSTICS

Acoustics refers to the study of the production and perception of sound within a particular room or area. By producing musical sound, musicians create mechanical vibrations from the stretching of strings or membranes, movement of wooden parts, and the oscillatory movement of air columns. This sound action affects the air, which carries the energy of the vibrations from the musician to the audience member. The sound is transmitted through to the brain where it is deciphered and interpreted. The perceived sound is referred to as a pure tone and has a frequency of full oscillations occurring each second. The human ear can perceive 20 to 20,000 cycles per second, or cps, and the corresponding frequency of the pure tone determines the pitch.

MUSIC EDUCATOR'S ROLE

Any **educator** of children is in a position to exert remarkable control and **influence** over these young lives. As such, educators are responsible in making that influence a positive one, so that the child can reach his or her fullest potential. All teachers should seek out ways to prepare for curriculum planning and designing instructions that are appropriate for the child's particular educational level. Music combines with all developmental, cognitive, language, physical, emotional, and social arenas of education and makes the music educator one of the most fundamental of teachers. Training is necessary for any teacher dealing with children; it is especially important for teachers dealing with children who are still young enough to be easily influenced. Music educators should be able to guide children in their musical experiences and encourage their progress as it occurs.

SINGING AND CHANTING WITH YOUNG CHILDREN

Young children explore their world with a different perspective than adults do, and the sense of **touch** is especially important when learning new things. Percussion and other simple instruments allow children to see and feel how an accented beat corresponds to music and the words in songs. Rhythmic songs and chants are important for children to understand the combination of sounds and beats and apply that process to their own sensory perceptions. When music educators participate in the singing or chanting, they can interact with the children, and show them how much fun moving to music and creating music can be for all ages. Through this type of exercise, children can learn how words work together and how they should sound by following the example of the music educator.

TEACHING SONGS TO YOUNG CHILDREN

Music educators must determine the best way to teach young children the **words** of songs, especially when those children cannot read and must learn songs by rote. The music educator can sing the same song repeatedly or incorporate different methods of participation for the children . Folk songs and nursery rhymes are easy to teach to children, since they are usually written in the limited vocal range of children and are composed of small segments. Parents may also be able to sing these songs with their children. Folk songs are usually specific to a culture or area and would probably be shared across generations. Music educators can also sing to children in order to teach them a new song that may be too complex for their abilities as yet or to show them how much fun music is.

CREATIVE AND SYNCHRONIZED MOVEMENT

Movements that are associated with music and performed as dance or exercise by young children are classified as either creative movement or synchronized movement. **Creative movement** gives children a freer avenue for expression and allows them to improvise and enjoy the physical act itself. **Synchronized movement** follows an established routine and is choreographed to the rhythm and beat of the selected music. Synchronized movement helps children work as a group and realize the importance of teamwork, while creative movement allows them to freely express themselves to song. Both types of movement allow children to develop their listening skills and focus on what they are hearing. Focused listening is also considered perceptive or active listening.

CREATIVE MOVEMENT

Creative movement involves a child's interpretation of the song without paying attention to the beat. Before a child can be expected to move freely, he or she must have a repertoire of movements already learned, and must feel comfortable choosing from that list. Before being allowed to move creatively, children should be familiar with walking, marching, running, galloping, dancing, clapping, hopping, sliding, and jumping to music. Music educators can help children expand their basis even more by suggesting **imagery exercises**, such as asking children to show how an ice cube melts or how a wind-up doll moves. Young children can also watch how older children and adults move and then attempt to duplicate those movements.

BENEFITS OF MUSIC EDUCATION

Combining music education with other facets of education improves the overall educational experience for children in many ways. One benefit is allowing them to learn about the use of symbols in different formats. Music education allows students to see the application of math in different subjects, learn the fulfillment of self-expression while developing a personal creativeness, and discover the fundamentals of self-image and self-discipline through music practice. Students of music education find their problem-solving skills becoming more advanced, as well as experiencing the intellectual satisfaction of sharing in the work required for a performance and of completing the challenge. Students do not suffer from music education and often broaden their own experiences with activities that are uplifting and wholesome.

INCLUDING MUSIC IN CURRICULUM

Music should be included in the **basic curriculum** for several reasons. As a topic and area of expression, music is worth learning about since it tells a lot about people and culture. Every person has the potential for musical abilities, as is evidenced in the elementary classrooms, and school is the perfect place for a child to explore that possibility. By learning about music and how different voices depend on each other, students can view the interdependence of people of various backgrounds and cultures. The study of music improves other studies, especially for students who may have difficulty in some subjects. The hearing and creating of music inspires the listeners and the performers.

INCREASING FOCUS ON MUSIC AND THE ARTS

Music currently stands as a **sideline** to the major focus of science, math, and language regardless of the studies that show how music education can improve students' whole educational experience. An increased focus on music and the arts could motivate students to learn more in other areas, and all educational encouragement avenues should be considered for the changing student body. More researchers and educators are beginning to recognize music as a form of intellectual development along the same lines as Howard Gardner's multiple intelligence theory that encompasses linguistic, spatial, intra-personal, bodily-kinesthetic, logical-mathematical, inter-personal, naturalistic, musical, and possibly existential intelligences. These theoretical systems support the inclusion of music in the basic curriculum and argue that teaching music is only the first step to teaching all other subjects students must learn. Any learning that occurs can be fortified in other areas.

GOALS OF MUSIC EDUCATION

Music educators, parents, other teachers, and other adults have witnessed an **improvement** in children who participate in instrumental and choral music education and practice, not only in their musical abilities, but also in their social skills and teamwork. These children learn about *self-discipline* while improving their *self-esteem* and enhancing their *self-expression* and *creativity*. The basic foundations of learning an instrument and then mastering that instrument to play a beginner piece and eventually an advanced piece serve to instill within the child a sense of accomplishment that correlates to improved self-image and a greater confidence in an ability to complete other tasks and to persevere even when those tasks appear daunting. The goal, then, of music education should be to foster a sense of purpose and self-worth in the student.

INSTRUCTING YOUNG CHILDREN TO RECOGNIZE RHYTHM OF FAMILIAR SONGS

Once young children have grasped the concept of reading the rhythm and are comfortable with the musical notation, the music educator should lead them in the **clapping of the beats** for songs that are familiar, such as "Twinkle, Twinkle Little Star." This exercise will allow children to associate their lesson on rhythm with music they know. Music educators can also clap a measure or phrase and have the children clap the same pattern back. This will involve the children in the motor skills exercise of clapping with the perceptive listening of the rhythm and the particular emphasis as it is placed on the first note or another accented note within the phrase.

CHANGES TECHNOLOGY HAS MADE IN MUSIC

With different inventions and increases in technology, the music of the twentieth century and modern music can be **shared** on a grander scale and in more different formats than at any time before 1900. Whereas the music of the previous centuries was expressed from one person or ensemble to another person or audience, the twentieth century saw music disseminated to larger groups of people through radio and television broadcasts, as well as through pre-recorded sessions on other media. There has also been developments in the field of electronically-produced music.

RISE AND FALL OF DIFFERENT TYPES OF MUSIC WITHIN PAST 100 YEARS

America has seen different **styles of musical expression** rise and fall within 100 years. The African-American styles of ragtime, blues, and jazz appealed to listeners, just as the folk and classical traditions of music entertained audiences years before. Western popular culture and Rock 'n' Roll have permeated musical preferences worldwide. While composers of earlier periods had to please their audience to continue creating music, the Modern composers could alienate audience members since some will listen to music because of a popular trend. The composers from non-Western countries have also affected Western composers, so that Modern music may hearken to a traditional mode but incorporate the more rhythmic pulses of monophonic Indian music. With a larger choice for musical style, modern musicians have become better able to play many different styles and have improved their own techniques and performances. This expansion has allowed for more prominent composers than any other musical period.

INSTRUCTING YOUNG CHILDREN TO READ MEASURES

Music is written in **measures** within the staff. To introduce young children to the concept of the measure, the music educator should have the children count the measures or sections separated by bar lines. Much of today's sheet music provides a count for the measure so that professional musicians can follow along when they are not playing or so that the conductor can call attention to a particular part of the music. Music educators can ask children to count the measures and to locate a specific measure of the music. Once children are comfortable with the basic format for musical notation, they can be instructed more effectively on how to interpret other musical notations, such as the time signature or the rhythm.

INSTRUCTING YOUNG CHILDREN TO READ TIME SIGNATURES

Music educators can show children how each measure contains a specific number of beats and how that is indicated at the beginning of the first measure with the **time signature**. Music educators can show students that the top note of the time signature tells how many beats occur in the measure and the bottom note shows which note gets one beat. The music educator can explain how a 4/4 time signature shows that there are four beats in each measure, counted as 1, 2, 3, 4. Contrasting that with a 3/4 time signature, the music educator can show that there are only three beats in each measure, and can then ask students what other time signatures would show. Eventually, music educators can show students the mathematical relationship between quarter notes and half notes, whole notes, and sixteenth notes.

INSTRUCTING YOUNG CHILDREN TO READ RHYTHM

The bottom number of the **time signature** becomes important when music educators try to teach children how to read rhythm. The bottom number shows which note gets one beat. In the 4/4 time signature, the quarter note gets one beat and is counted as 1, 2, 3, 4 within the measure. A mathematical explanation of how the bottom number relates to other notes can be incorporated into the lesson, and children can see how two half notes are counted as 1, 3 while eight eighth notes are counted as 1 &, 2 &, 3&, 4&. This exercise combines a study of math with the basic fundamentals of music, and music educators can lead the children toward reading combinations of the notes and playing or clapping those rhythms.

NATIONAL MUSIC EDUCATION STANDARDS FOR INSTRUCTING CHILDREN IN GRADES K-4

The **National Music Education Standards** as outlined for music educators instructing students in grades K-4 as they read and notate music involve the following abilities:

- Ability of each child to **read** whole, half, dotted half, quarter, and eighth notes and rests in time signatures of 2/4, 3/4, 4/4, and others
- Ability of each child to incorporate the use of a system to determine basic **pitch notation** within the treble clef as it relates to major keys

- Ability of each child to identify traditional **terms and symbols** and differentiate their meanings in regards to articulation, dynamics, and tempo while correctly interpreting these symbols during Visual and Performing Arts
- Ability of each child to incorporate the use of standard **symbols** to indicate meter, pitch, rhythm, and dynamics in easy phrases as presented by the music educator

ASSISTING CHILDREN IN ABILITY TO IMPROVE MOTOR SKILLS WHILE IMPROVISING OR SINGING NEW SONGS

As children get older, there is an increase in their vocabulary and in their ability to add experiences and movements to their personal repertoire. Music educators can assist children in their ability to improve their motor skills while improvising or singing new songs. Children between five and nine enjoy games that involve rhythm and rhyme, so jump rope rhymes or chants are a great way to show children that music can be fun and entertaining. The music educator can show children a simple or even age-specific complex rhyme or chant, and the children can add clapping or stomping as they become more familiar with the rhyme and feel comfortable enough to improvise. Such rhymes include "Teddy Bear, Teddy Bear" and "The Lady with the Alligator Purse."

ENCOURAGING CHILDREN'S MUSIC EDUCATION AT HOME

To continue a child's musical education outside of school, music educators should encourage parents to involve their children in **music outings**, such as free concerts or performances in outdoor theaters where children can listen to the music as well as to the sounds of the outdoors and the audience members. Parents can even plan to attend with other families, so that the children can enjoy the outing socially as well as musically. Music educators can also help parents locate musical instructors who would be willing to provide lessons for the children. As a limited option, music educators could create a marching band take-home box for parents that includes books on the music of marching bands or even composers like John Philip Sousa, CDs of marching band songs, index cards describing how to make small instruments, and party hats to remind the parents and children that music is fun.

INSTRUCTING CHILDREN THE CONCEPT OF RESTS

Music is an important skill for music educators and parents to teach, and different children will be focused on certain sounds or the volume of those sounds. **Silences** or **rests** within the music can be the most difficult to teach young children who are interested in playing or singing continuously. Based on the same concept as the whole, half, quarter and eighth note beats, rests are set up with a corresponding count and also adhere to the restrictions put in place by the time signature. Children should be introduced to the **symbols** used to indicate rests and instructed how to count each rest. When interspersing beats with rests, some music educators find that clapping the beat and then turning the palms out for the rest is an easy way to show children how the rests function in relation to the beat.

ATTITUDE OF MUSIC EDUCATOR

Music educators should always approach any musical assignment or practice with children with the right **attitude** of patience and exploration in order for the children to get the most out of their musical experience. The best equipment and the most up-to-date books will not guarantee that children have a good experience with musical instruments and music appreciation in general, so the attitude of the music educator is paramount to the children's success. Children learn best in a classroom and musical environment that includes structure even while fostering an individualized, creative movement format of learning. Music educators should adopt a philosophy of how to introduce children to music successfully that is based on core values and life experiences.

ACCOMMODATING CHILDREN WHO ARE SELF-CONSCIOUS

Not all children between six and nine are comfortable dancing and moving in front of other children or the music educator unless they have been doing so since they were much younger. One of the easiest ways to foster an environment of acceptability is to sing and dance **alongside** the children, so that they can see others behaving in a particular way without being ostracized or ridiculed. Music educators could also provide areas for creative movement that have higher walls or are separated and somewhat shielded from the rest of the room. The music center can include headphones so that children do not feel they are encroaching on others' quiet time for homework. Room dividers combined with rugs and drapes can also provide some basic soundproofing.

MUSIC CLASSROOMS
EQUIPMENT

Music classrooms for children of all ages include different types of materials that are appropriate for the development of the children. Besides large **instruments** such as pianos and large or small keyboards, the music classroom will also include rhythm instruments, percussion instruments, string instruments, Orff instruments, Montessori sound cylinders and bells, guitar, and autoharp. Optional **hardware** includes tape recorders, headphones, tapes, CDs, players, and a karaoke machine. Some music educators like to provide specific furniture for the classroom, such as containers or shelving systems for storage, tables, tents, and rocking chairs. **Music boxes** are a nice addition to smaller sections, and computer **software** may be more appropriate for older children. Music-related **pictures** can be hung around the room as well as unbreakable **mirrors** for children to watch their own movements.

MATERIALS

Music educators may have to create simple **instruments** or may find the children are creative enough to benefit from a more hands-on experience so as to appreciate this part of the work. The **construction materials** used in a music classroom may include paper, glue, and paint, as well as rubber bands, shoe boxes, and milk cartons of different sizes. Regular **household items** such as paper or disposable plastic plates, cans with lids, plastic bottles, toilet paper tubes, mailing tubes, and wrapping paper tubes act as containers and can be filled with such items as rocks, rice, beans, sand, or seeds. The containers can be further enhanced with guitar strings, bells, or brass pipes in different lengths. Scarves and ribbons can help with movement visualization, and drum heads and sandpaper samples can introduce different textures. As always, music educators can employ whatever materials imaginable to teach children about sound.

SINGING

The **voice** can be used as a musical instrument through singing or humming. With a strong link to community relations predating recorded history, **singing** has been a task of the priest, healer, actor, poet, and entertainer. Greatly popular during the Middle Ages and the Renaissance, singing became less popular with the progression of instrumental music. Vocalists were encouraged to pursue musical instruction in how to use the voice as a musical instrument and not in the folk traditions enjoyed by previous audience members. As a result, music was composed to show off the vocal ranges of singers, and it was expected that vocalists would ornament their vocal pieces the same way instrumentalists would ornament theirs. Popular music and jazz have allowed singers to develop their voices more independently than the composers of the Romantic period did.

Mathematics

Mathematics Pedagogy

REPRESENTATIONS

Representations are the tools of symbols and materials. They are used to help students understand mathematics by giving them visual guides in their thinking. For example, the conventional symbols that indicate addition, subtraction, equality, and so on (into the higher realms of symbols used in geometry, algebra, and calculus) tell students, at a glance, the process that is being calculated. Materials that are used as representations are called **manipulatives**. These can be small plastic objects or pictures for the students to count, line up, or otherwise use to solve a problem. Representations make abstract concepts become concrete. They put mathematics into the students,' hands as well as heads, and the result is improved learning. Using familiar manipulatives with new problems helps the student to make connections and feel more confident and capable of expanding their skills.

CONCEPTS TAUGHT IN KINDERGARTEN BEFORE INTRODUCING NUMBERS

In kindergarten, children can be prepared for the study of mathematics by practicing certain concepts such as:

- **position** – top, middle, bottom, above, below, before, after, between, under, inside, outside, left, and right
- **visual attributes** – same and different colors, shapes, and sizes; identifying items that are out-of-place or don't belong
- **sorting** – by size, color, type, or shape; identifying an equal number, more, or fewer of a given item
- **graphing** – the use of picture graphs and using data from graphs
- **patterns** – identifying, copying, extending, and making patterns; finding patterns that are different or alike, making predictions from patterns
- **measurements** – longer and shorter; how much they weigh, heavier and lighter; how much an item can hold

PROBLEM-SOLVING STRATEGIES FOR MATHEMATICS AND STEPS FOR SOLVING WORD PROBLEMS

For any problem, the following **strategies** can be used according to their appropriateness to the type of problem or calculation: i) Use manipulatives or act out the problem, ii) draw a picture, iii) look for a pattern, iv) guess and check, v) use logical reasoning, vi) make an organized list, vii) make a table, viii) solve a simpler problem, and ix) work backward.

In order to solve a word problem, the following steps can be used:

- Achieve an understanding of the problem by reading it carefully, finding and separating the information needed to solve the problem, and discerning the ultimate question in the problem.
- Make a plan as to what needs to be done to solve the problem.
- Solve the problem using the plan from step 2.
- Review the word problem to make sure that the answer is the correct solution to the problem and makes sense.

BUILDING NUMBER SENSE AMONG STUDENTS

It is important to think **flexibly** to develop number sense. Therefore, it is imperative to impress upon students that there is more than one right way to solve a problem. Otherwise, students will try to learn only one method of computation, rather than think about what makes sense or contemplate the possibility of an easier way. Some strategies for helping students develop number sense include the following:

- Frequently asking students to make their calculations mentally and rely on their reasoning ability. Answers can be checked manually afterwards, if needed.
- Having a class discussion about solutions the students found using their minds only and comparing the different approaches to solving the problem. Have the students explain their reasoning in their own words.
- Modeling the different ideas by tracking them on the board as the discussion progresses.
- Presenting problems to the students that can have more than one answer.

USING MANIPULATIVE MATERIALS IN MATHEMATICS CLASSROOMS

As with all classroom supplies, the students must understand that there are rules for their use, including how to store the materials when they are not in use. In addition:

- the teacher should discuss with the students the purpose of the manipulatives and how they will help the students to learn,
- the students should understand that the manipulatives are intended for use with specific problems and activities; however, time for free exploration should be made available so students are less tempted to play when assigned specific tasks,
- a chart posted in the classroom of the manipulatives with their names will help the students to gain familiarity with them and develop mathematical literacy skills, and
- loans of manipulatives for home use with a letter of explanation to the parents about the purpose and value of the manipulatives will encourage similar strategies with homework.

IMPLICATIONS OF MATHEMATICS TODAY

Today, mathematics is used throughout the world in many **fields**, including natural science, engineering, medicine, and the social sciences, such as economics. **Applied mathematics**, the application of mathematics to such fields, inspires and makes use of new mathematical discoveries and sometimes leads to the development of entirely new disciplines. Mathematicians also engage in **pure mathematics**, or mathematics for its own sake, without having any application in mind, although applications for what began as pure mathematics are often discovered later.

CONNECTING MATH AND SCIENCE TO REAL LIFE FOR GIFTED STUDENTS

Since math and science are so often heavy in calculations and facts, students are usually not taught how these subjects relate to the real world. All students, especially gifted students, need to find meaning in an academic subject and understand how it **applies** in life. We may not appreciate enough that math and science are not like people whose opinions we can disagree with; they provide hard, objective, unchangeable facts. Teachers can show students the consequences of ignoring facts with examples like these: mathematicians and engineers advised not launching the Challenger space shuttle, but management overruled them, thereby leading to the deadly explosion. Pop singer Aaliyah died in a plane crash after pilot and crew ignored the mathematics indicating airplane overload and flew regardless. A mathematician proved racial bias in jury selection by calculating that the mathematical probability of fair selection was approximately 1 in 1,000,000,000,000,000.

ANALYZING THE USE OF APPROPRIATE MATHEMATICAL CONCEPTS, PROCEDURES, AND VOCABULARY WHEN EVALUATING STUDENT SOLUTIONS

When evaluating student solutions, it is important to analyze the use of appropriate mathematical concepts, procedures, and vocabulary for a variety of reasons. First and foremost, we must be sure that we have provided adequate practice and instruction of **important concepts** before assessing them. Once we have established that instruction is sufficient, we must ensure that students are following the appropriate **procedures** when faced with various tasks and that those procedures are executed correctly. Finally, we must hold students accountable for using high-level **vocabulary** to ensure that students are able to read, understand, and communicate their mathematics thoughts at age- and grade-appropriate levels.

CORRECTING STUDENT ERRORS

A student is asked to find the area of a rectangle measuring 8 feet by 4 feet. The student is able to break the rectangle into 32 squares but states that the area is 24 square feet. The student calculated the perimeter of the rectangle rather than the area. The perimeter of a rectangle is the sum of its sides. Here, the rectangle's sides measure 8 feet, 8 feet, 4 feet, and 4 feet, which total to 24 feet. To calculate area, the student must multiply the length by the width (8×4), which equals 32 square feet. To help the student correct his or her error, the teacher can explain that the student was on the right track when he or she broke the rectangle into 32 squares. Because area is the amount of unit squares that can be contained in a two-dimensional figure, the student could have also opted to simply count the unit squares he or she created, which would have also led him or her to the correct answer of 32 square feet.

EXPLORING PROBLEM STRUCTURES WITH UNKNOWNS IN ALL POSITIONS

It is important to provide students with the opportunity to explore and find solutions for **problem structures** to develop their higher-level thinking skills and problem-solving strategies. By exposing students to problems with unknowns in all positions, students are forced to not only memorize procedures but also to analyze the framework of a problem, make connections for relationships within the problem, and develop strategies for solving problems that may not follow specific rules or procedures. Problems that include put-together/take-apart scenarios are excellent problem structures for teachers to use in an effort to develop higher-level thinking skills. In addition, providing students the opportunity to use arrays to model their solutions provides teachers with a glimpse into the thought processes of each student's solution.

UNKNOWN ADDENDS

A teacher tells her students that she has five pieces of fruit in her refrigerator. Two are apples, and the rest are oranges. She asks the students how many oranges are in her refrigerator. In this type of problem, there is an **unknown addend**. When dealing with unknown addends and numbers up to 20 (typically in the elementary classroom), this type of problem is known as a put-together/take apart problem. Ideally, the teacher's goal is for the students to visualize this the scenario as $2+? = 5$. Depending on the students' approach (drawing a picture, subtracting, number facts, modeling, etc.), they may choose to put together or take apart the problem in a variety of ways. To analyze the students' process, the teacher should check that each student has developed a strategy that will result in correctly identifying the missing addend in a way that could be applied to other problems similar in nature, continually resulting in the correct answer.

EVALUATING VALIDITY OF MATHEMATICAL MODEL OR ARGUMENT WHEN ANALYZING A SOLUTION

When assessing a student's **proficiency**, simply arriving at the correct answer does not validate true mastery of a mathematical concept. To determine that a student has truly mastered a skill or concept, that student must be able to explain or defend his or her **process** as well as the solution. By requiring a model or compelling students to defend their answers, teachers can truly assess the validity of each solution and determine whether or not each student has a true grasp of the concept being assessed. A teacher can be confident that a student has truly mastered a concept when that student can describe his or her process, explain the meaning behind his or her solution, and defend why that solution is logical and appropriate.

ANALYZING VALIDITY OF STUDENT'S MATHEMATICAL PROCESS

A teacher is assessing a student's ability to multiply two-digit numbers. A student in the class arrives at the correct answer without using the traditional algorithm. In mathematics, there is often more than one way to arrive at the correct answer. The focus of the teacher should be to analyze the **validity** of the student's mathematical process to determine if it is a process that could be applied to other multiplication problems, which would result in the correct answer. If the student has modeled his or her thought process, or can argue that the inventive strategy is applicable across all multiplication problems, then that student should be considered to have mastered the skill of multiplication. However, if the student's argument or model is not applicable to other multiplication problems, that student should be provided with more instruction and opportunity for improvement.

USING INDIVIDUAL STUDENT MATHEMATICS ASSESSMENT DATA TO GUIDE INSTRUCTIONAL DECISIONS AND DIFFERENTIATE INSTRUCTION

Teachers should constantly **assess** student learning. These assessments should be quick in nature and offer immediate feedback to both the teacher and student. Assessments such as quick "exit tickets" at the end of each lesson can tell a teacher whether or not students achieved the objective of the day. If the majority of the class achieved mastery, the teacher should look to modify and reteach that lesson to the students who did not achieve mastery. On the other hand, if the majority of the class did not achieve mastery, the teacher should reflect on the way in which the lesson was presented and try another whole-class approach before moving on. By monitoring student learning on a constant basis, teachers are able to improve their teaching skills as well as identify and differentiate for struggling learners more quickly and effectively.

CREATING STRUCTURED EXPERIENCES FOR GROUPS ACCORDING TO COGNITIVE COMPLEXITY OF TASKS

Depending on the complexity of the task, teachers should modify the **delivery** of instruction. For less complex tasks, the teacher may opt for **whole-group instruction**, in which the entire class is introduced to a new concept together. Whole-group instruction usually includes a connection to prior knowledge, direct instruction, and some form of media. For more complex tasks, the teacher may choose **small-group instruction**, where students are grouped based on ability levels. The more accelerated learners are given a quicker, more direct form of instruction, whereas the struggling learners work independently at a math center or station activity. After a rotation, the struggling learners are given a modified form of instruction by the teacher, which has been differentiated and allows for more gradual release based on individual needs and abilities.

DISTANCE FORMULA

A car is traveling at a speed of 40 miles per hour for 2.5 hours. How far, in miles, has the car traveled? The **distance formula** is $d = rt$, where d represents the distance, r represents the rate of speed, and t represents the time elapsed. The distance formula tells us that by multiplying the rate of speed by the time elapsed, we can determine the distance traveled. Here, when we substitute our rate, 40, for r and 2.5 for our time, t, we have the expression $d = 40(2.5)$. The product of 40 and 2.5 is 100, which simplifies our expression to $d = 100$. We can now conclude that the car has traveled a distance of 100 miles in 2.5 hours at a rate of 40 miles per hour.

EXAMPLE PROBLEMS

PROBLEM 1

The area of a closet is $25\frac{1}{4}$ square feet. New carpet (including labor and materials) costs \$8.00 per square foot to install. What will it cost to re-carpet the entire closet?

To find the total cost to re-carpet the closet, we must multiply the area of the closet, $25\frac{1}{4}$, by the cost of the carpet, \$8.00 per square foot. To multiply these values, we must convert both of them to improper fractions, creating the expression $\frac{101}{4} \times \frac{\$8}{1}$. We can use cross-cancellation to simplify our expression by dividing both 4 and 8 by 4, which changes our expression to $\frac{101}{1} \times \frac{\$2}{1}$. When we multiply across, we arrive at our product, \$202.00. Without cross-cancellation, our product would be $\frac{808}{4}$, which still reduces to \$202.00. It will cost \$202.00 to re-carpet the closet.

Problem 2

A fish tank measures 5 feet long, 3 feet wide, and 3 feet tall. Each cubic foot of the tank holds 7.48 gallons of water. The fish tank is filled with water, leaving 6 inches of empty space at the top of the tank. How much water, in cubic feet, is in the fish tank?

To calculate the **volume of a rectangular prism** we would typically multiply the length, width, and height of the prism. However, the prompt tells us that 6 inches (or half a foot) of the tank is left empty. Given this information, we must use a measurement of 2.5 in place of 3 feet for the height of our tank. To calculate the volume of the portion of the tank filled with water we must multiply $5 \times 3 \times 2.5$, which equals 37.5 cubic feet. If each cubic foot holds 7.48 gallons of water, we can multiply 37.5 by 7.48 to determine the number of gallons of water contained in the tank. The product of 37.5 and 7.48 is 280.5. There are 280.5 gallons of water in the fish tank.

Numbers and Operations

CLASSIFICATIONS OF NUMBERS

Numbers are the basic building blocks of mathematics. Specific features of numbers are identified by the following terms:

Integer – any positive or negative whole number, including zero. Integers do not include fractions $\left(\frac{1}{3}\right)$, decimals (0.56), or mixed numbers $\left(7\frac{3}{4}\right)$.

Prime number – any whole number greater than 1 that has only two factors, itself and 1; that is, a number that can be divided evenly only by 1 and itself.

Composite number – any whole number greater than 1 that has more than two different factors; in other words, any whole number that is not a prime number. For example: The composite number 8 has the factors of 1, 2, 4, and 8.

Even number – any integer that can be divided by 2 without leaving a remainder. For example: 2, 4, 6, 8, and so on.

Odd number – any integer that cannot be divided evenly by 2. For example: 3, 5, 7, 9, and so on.

Decimal number – any number that uses a decimal point to show the part of the number that is less than one. Example: 1.234.

Decimal point – a symbol used to separate the ones place from the tenths place in decimals or dollars from cents in currency.

Decimal place – the position of a number to the right of the decimal point. In the decimal 0.123, the 1 is in the first place to the right of the decimal point, indicating tenths; the 2 is in the second place, indicating hundredths; and the 3 is in the third place, indicating thousandths.

The **decimal**, or base 10, system is a number system that uses ten different digits (0, 1, 2, 3, 4, 5, 6, 7, 8, 9). An example of a number system that uses something other than ten digits is the **binary**, or base 2, number system, used by computers, which uses only the numbers 0 and 1. It is thought that the decimal system originated because people had only their 10 fingers for counting.

Rational numbers include all integers, decimals, and fractions. Any terminating or repeating decimal number is a rational number.

Irrational numbers cannot be written as fractions or decimals because the number of decimal places is infinite and there is no recurring pattern of digits within the number. For example, pi (π) begins with 3.141592 and continues without terminating or repeating, so pi is an irrational number.

Real numbers are the set of all rational and irrational numbers.

> **Review Video: <u>Numbers and Their Classifications</u>**
> Visit mometrix.com/academy and enter code: 461071
>
> **Review Video: <u>Rational and Irrational Numbers</u>**
> Visit mometrix.com/academy and enter code: 280645

THE NUMBER LINE

A number line is a graph to see the distance between numbers. Basically, this graph shows the relationship between numbers. So, a number line may have a point for zero and may show negative numbers on the left side of the line. Also, any positive numbers are placed on the right side of the line. For example, consider the points labeled on the following number line:

We can use the dashed lines on the number line to identify each point. Each dashed line between two whole numbers is $\frac{1}{4}$. The line halfway between two numbers is $\frac{1}{2}$.

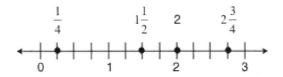

NUMBERS IN WORD FORM AND PLACE VALUE

When writing numbers out in word form or translating word form to numbers, it is essential to understand how a place value system works. In the decimal or base-10 system, each digit of a number represents how many of the corresponding place value – a specific factor of 10 – are contained in the number being represented. To make reading numbers easier, every three digits to the left of the decimal place is preceded by a comma. The following table demonstrates some of the place values:

Power of 10	10^3	10^2	10^1	10^0	10^{-1}	10^{-2}	10^{-3}
Value	1,000	100	10	1	0.1	0.01	0.001
Place	thousands	hundreds	tens	ones	tenths	hundredths	thousandths

For example, consider the number 4,546.09, which can be separated into each place value like this:

4: thousands
5: hundreds
4: tens
6: ones
0: tenths
9: hundredths

This number in word form would be *four thousand five hundred forty-six and nine hundredths*.

ABSOLUTE VALUE

A precursor to working with negative numbers is understanding what **absolute values** are. A number's absolute value is simply the distance away from zero a number is on the number line. The absolute value of a number is always positive and is written $|x|$. For example, the absolute value of 3, written as $|3|$, is 3 because the distance between 0 and 3 on a number line is three units. Likewise, the absolute value of –3, written as $|-3|$, is 3 because the distance between 0 and –3 on a number line is three units. So, $|3| = |-3|$.

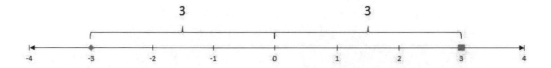

OPERATIONS

Mathematical expressions consist of a combination of values and operations. An **operation** is simply a mathematical process that takes some value(s) as input(s) and produces an output. Elementary operations are often written in the following form: *value operation value*. For instance, in the expression $1 + 2$ the values are 1 and 2 and the operation is addition. Performing the operation gives the output of 3. In this way we can say that $1 + 2$ and 3 are equal, or $1 + 2 = 3$.

ADDITION

Addition increases the value of one quantity by the value of another quantity (both called **addends**). For example, $2 + 4 = 6$; $8 + 9 = 17$. The result is called the **sum**. With addition, the order does not matter, $4 + 2 = 2 + 4$.

When adding signed numbers, if the signs are the same simply add the absolute values of the addends and apply the original sign to the sum. For example, $(+4) + (+8) = +12$ and $(-4) + (-8) = -12$. When the original signs are different, take the absolute values of the addends and subtract the smaller value from the larger value, then apply the original sign of the larger value to the difference. For instance, $(+4) + (-8) = -4$ and $(-4) + (+8) = +4$.

SUBTRACTION

Subtraction is the opposite operation to addition; it decreases the value of one quantity (the **minuend**) by the value of another quantity (the **subtrahend**). For example, $6 - 4 = 2$; $17 - 8 = 9$. The result is called the **difference**. Note that with subtraction, the order does matter, $6 - 4 \neq 4 - 6$.

For subtracting signed numbers, change the sign of the subtrahend and then follow the same rules used for addition. For example, $(+4) - (+8) = (+4) + (-8) = -4$.

MULTIPLICATION

Multiplication can be thought of as repeated addition. One number (the **multiplier**) indicates how many times to add the other number (the **multiplicand**) to itself. For example, 3×2 (three times two) $= 2 + 2 + 2 = 6$. With multiplication, the order does not matter: $2 \times 3 = 3 \times 2$ or $3 + 3 = 2 + 2 + 2$, either way the result (the **product**) is the same.

If the signs are the same the product is positive when multiplying signed numbers. For example, $(+4) \times (+8) = +32$ and $(-4) \times (-8) = +32$. If the signs are opposite, the product is negative. For example, $(+4) \times (-8) = -32$ and $(-4) \times (+8) = -32$. When more than two factors are multiplied together, the sign of the product is determined by how many negative factors are present. If there are an odd number of negative factors then the product is negative, whereas an even number of negative factors indicates a positive product. For instance, $(+4) \times (-8) \times (-2) = +64$ and $(-4) \times (-8) \times (-2) = -64$.

DIVISION

Division is the opposite operation to multiplication; one number (the **divisor**) tells us how many parts to divide the other number (the **dividend**) into. The result of division is called the **quotient**. For example, $20 \div 4 = 5$; if 20 is split into 4 equal parts, each part is 5. With division, the order of the numbers does matter, $20 \div 4 \neq 4 \div 20$.

The rules for dividing signed numbers are similar to multiplying signed numbers. If the dividend and divisor have the same sign, the quotient is positive. If the dividend and divisor have opposite signs, the quotient is negative. For example, $(-4) \div (+8) = -0.5$.

> **Review Video: Multiplication and Division**
> Visit mometrix.com/academy and enter code: 643326

PARENTHESES

Parentheses are used to designate which operations should be done first when there are multiple operations. Example: $4 - (2 + 1) = 1$; the parentheses tell us that we must add 2 and 1, and then subtract the sum from 4, rather than subtracting 2 from 4 and then adding 1 (this would give us an answer of 3).

> **Review Video: Mathematical Parentheses**
> Visit mometrix.com/academy and enter code: 978600

EXPONENTS

An **exponent** is a superscript number placed next to another number at the top right. It indicates how many times the base number is to be multiplied by itself. Exponents provide a shorthand way to write what would be a longer mathematical expression, for example: $2^4 = 2 \times 2 \times 2 \times 2$. A number with an exponent of 2 is said to be "squared," while a number with an exponent of 3 is said to be "cubed." The value of a number raised to an exponent is called its power. So, 8^4 is read as "8 to the 4th power," or "8 raised to the power of 4."

The properties of exponents are as follows:

Property	Description
$a^1 = a$	Any number to the power of 1 is equal to itself
$1^n = 1$	The number 1 raised to any power is equal to 1
$a^0 = 1$	Any number raised to the power of 0 is equal to 1
$a^n \times a^m = a^{n+m}$	Add exponents to multiply powers of the same base number
$a^n \div a^m = a^{n-m}$	Subtract exponents to divide powers of the same base number
$(a^n)^m = a^{n \times m}$	When a power is raised to a power, the exponents are multiplied
$(a \times b)^n = a^n \times b^n$ $(a \div b)^n = a^n \div b^n$	Multiplication and division operations inside parentheses can be raised to a power. This is the same as each term being raised to that power.
$a^{-n} = \dfrac{1}{a^n}$	A negative exponent is the same as the reciprocal of a positive exponent

Note that exponents do not have to be integers. Fractional or decimal exponents follow all the rules above as well. Example: $5^{\frac{1}{4}} \times 5^{\frac{3}{4}} = 5^{\frac{1}{4}+\frac{3}{4}} = 5^1 = 5$.

> **Review Video: Exponents**
> Visit mometrix.com/academy and enter code: 600998

ROOTS

A **root**, such as a square root, is another way of writing a fractional exponent. Instead of using a superscript, roots use the radical symbol ($\sqrt{}$) to indicate the operation. A radical will have a number underneath the bar, and may sometimes have a number in the upper left: $\sqrt[n]{a}$, read as "the nth root of a." The relationship between radical notation and exponent notation can be described by this equation: $\sqrt[n]{a} = a^{\frac{1}{n}}$. The two special cases of $n = 2$ and $n = 3$ are called square roots and cube roots. If there is no number to the upper left, it is understood to be a square root ($n = 2$). Nearly all of the roots you encounter will be square roots. A square root is the same as a number raised to the one-half power. When we say that a is the square root of b ($a = \sqrt{b}$), we mean that a multiplied by itself equals b: ($a \times a = b$).

A **perfect square** is a number that has an integer for its square root. There are 10 perfect squares from 1 to 100: 1, 4, 9, 16, 25, 36, 49, 64, 81, 100 (the squares of integers 1 through 10).

ORDER OF OPERATIONS

Order of operations is a set of rules that dictates the order in which we must perform each operation in an expression so that we will evaluate it accurately. If we have an expression that includes multiple different operations, order of operations tells us which operations to do first. The most common mnemonic for order of operations is **PEMDAS**, or "Please Excuse My Dear Aunt Sally." PEMDAS stands for parentheses, exponents, multiplication, division, addition, and subtraction. It is important to understand that multiplication and division have equal precedence, as do addition and subtraction, so those pairs of operations are simply worked from left to right in order.

For example, evaluating the expression $5 + 20 \div 4 \times (2 + 3) - 6$ using the correct order of operations would be done like this:

- **P:** Perform the operations inside the parentheses: $(2 + 3) = 5$
- **E:** Simplify the exponents.
  - The equation now looks like this: $5 + 20 \div 4 \times 5 - 6$
- **MD:** Perform multiplication and division from left to right: $20 \div 4 = 5$; then $5 \times 5 = 25$
  - The equation now looks like this: $5 + 25 - 6$
- **AS:** Perform addition and subtraction from left to right: $5 + 25 = 30$; then $30 - 6 = 24$

SUBTRACTION WITH REGROUPING

A great way to make use of some of the features built into the decimal system would be regrouping when attempting longform subtraction operations. When subtracting within a place value, sometimes the minuend is smaller than the subtrahend, **regrouping** enables you to 'borrow' a unit from a place value to the left in order to get a positive difference. For example, consider subtracting 189 from 525 with regrouping.

First, set up the subtraction problem in vertical form:

```
    525
  − 189
```

Notice that the numbers in the ones and tens columns of 525 are smaller than the numbers in the ones and tens columns of 189. This means you will need to use regrouping to perform subtraction:

```
    5   2   5
  − 1   8   9
```

To subtract 9 from 5 in the ones column you will need to borrow from the 2 in the tens columns:

```
    5   1   15
  − 1   8    9
                6
```

Next, to subtract 8 from 1 in the tens column you will need to borrow from the 5 in the hundreds column:

```
    4   11   15
  − 1    8    9
            3    6
```

Last, subtract the 1 from the 4 in the hundreds column:

```
    4   11   15
  − 1    8    9
    3    3    6
```

FACTORS AND GREATEST COMMON FACTOR

Factors are numbers that are multiplied together to obtain a **product**. For example, in the equation $2 \times 3 = 6$, the numbers 2 and 3 are factors. A **prime number** has only two factors (1 and itself), but other numbers can have many factors.

A **common factor** is a number that divides exactly into two or more other numbers. For example, the factors of 12 are 1, 2, 3, 4, 6, and 12, while the factors of 15 are 1, 3, 5, and 15. The common factors of 12 and 15 are 1 and 3.

A **prime factor** is also a prime number. Therefore, the prime factors of 12 are 2 and 3. For 15, the prime factors are 3 and 5.

The **greatest common factor (GCF)** is the largest number that is a factor of two or more numbers. For example, the factors of 15 are 1, 3, 5, and 15; the factors of 35 are 1, 5, 7, and 35. Therefore, the greatest common factor of 15 and 35 is 5.

> **Review Video: <u>Factors</u>**
> Visit mometrix.com/academy and enter code: 920086

MULTIPLES AND LEAST COMMON MULTIPLE

Often listed out in multiplication tables, **multiples** are integer increments of a given factor. In other words, dividing a multiple by the factor number will result in an integer. For example, the multiples of 7 include: $1 \times 7 = 7$, $2 \times 7 = 14$, $3 \times 7 = 21$, $4 \times 7 = 28$, $5 \times 7 = 35$. Dividing 7, 14, 21, 28, or 35 by 7 will result in the integers 1, 2, 3, 4, and 5, respectively.

The least common multiple (**LCM**) is the smallest number that is a multiple of two or more numbers. For example, the multiples of 3 include 3, 6, 9, 12, 15, etc.; the multiples of 5 include 5, 10, 15, 20, etc. Therefore, the least common multiple of 3 and 5 is 15.

PRACTICE

P1. Write the place value of each digit in 14,059.826

P2. Write out each of the following in words:

    (a) 29
    (b) 478
    (c) 98,542
    (d) 0.06
    (e) 13.113

P3. Write each of the following in numbers:

    (a) nine thousand four hundred thirty-five
    (b) three hundred two thousand eight hundred seventy-six
    (c) nine hundred one thousandths
    (d) nineteen thousandths
    (e) seven thousand one hundred forty-two and eighty-five hundredths

P4. Demonstrate how to subtract 477 from 620 using regrouping.

P5. Simplify the following expressions with exponents:

    (a) 37^0
    (b) 1^{30}
    (c) $2^3 \times 2^4 \times 2^x$
    (d) $(3^x)^3$
    (e) $(12 \div 3)^2$

Practice Solutions

P1. The place value for each digit would be as follows:

Digit	Place Value
1	ten-thousands
4	thousands
0	hundreds
5	tens
9	ones
8	tenths
2	hundredths
6	thousandths

P2. Each written out in words would be:

  (a) twenty-nine
  (b) four hundred seventy-eight
  (c) ninety-eight thousand five hundred forty-two
  (d) six hundredths
  (e) thirteen and one hundred thirteen thousandths

P3. Each in numeric form would be:

  (a) 9,435
  (b) 302, 876
  (c) 0.901
  (d) 0.019
  (e) 7,142.85

P4. First, set up the subtraction problem in vertical form:

```
    6   2   0
 -  4   7   7
_____
```

To subtract 7 from 0 in the ones column you will need to borrow from the 2 in the tens column:

```
    6   1  10
 -  4   7   7
_____
            3
```

Next, to subtract 7 from the 1 that's still in the tens column you will need to borrow from the 6 in the hundreds column:

```
    5  11  10
 -  4   7   7
_____
        4   3
```

Lastly, subtract 4 from the 5 remaining in the hundreds column:

```
    5  11  10
 -  4   7   7
_____
    1   4   3
```

P5. Using the properties of exponents and the proper order of operations:

(a) Any number raised to the power of 0 is equal to 1: $37^0 = 1$
(b) The number 1 raised to any power is equal to 1: $1^{30} = 1$
(c) Add exponents to multiply powers of the same base: $2^3 \times 2^4 \times 2^x = 2^{(3+4+x)} = 2^{(7+x)}$
(d) When a power is raised to a power, the exponents are multiplied: $(3^x)^3 = 3^{3x}$
(e) Perform the operation inside the parentheses first: $(12 \div 3)^2 = 4^2 = 16$

Rational Numbers

FRACTIONS

A **fraction** is a number that is expressed as one integer written above another integer, with a dividing line between them $\left(\frac{x}{y}\right)$. It represents the **quotient** of the two numbers "x divided by y." It can also be thought of as x out of y equal parts.

The top number of a fraction is called the **numerator**, and it represents the number of parts under consideration. The 1 in $\frac{1}{4}$ means that 1 part out of the whole is being considered in the calculation. The bottom number of a fraction is called the **denominator**, and it represents the total number of equal parts. The 4 in $\frac{1}{4}$ means that the whole consists of 4 equal parts. A fraction cannot have a denominator of zero; this is referred to as "*undefined.*"

Fractions can be manipulated, without changing the value of the fraction, by multiplying or dividing (but not adding or subtracting) both the numerator and denominator by the same number. If you divide both numbers by a common factor, you are **reducing** or simplifying the fraction. Two fractions that have the same value but are expressed differently are known as **equivalent fractions**. For example, $\frac{2}{10}, \frac{3}{15}, \frac{4}{20}$, and $\frac{5}{25}$ are all equivalent fractions. They can also all be reduced or simplified to $\frac{1}{5}$.

When two fractions are manipulated so that they have the same denominator, this is known as finding a **common denominator**. The number chosen to be that common denominator should be the least common multiple of the two original denominators. Example: $\frac{3}{4}$ and $\frac{5}{6}$; the least common multiple of 4 and 6 is 12. Manipulating to achieve the common denominator: $\frac{3}{4} = \frac{9}{12}; \frac{5}{6} = \frac{10}{12}$.

PROPER FRACTIONS AND MIXED NUMBERS

A fraction whose denominator is greater than its numerator is known as a **proper fraction**, while a fraction whose numerator is greater than its denominator is known as an **improper fraction**. Proper fractions have values *less than one* and improper fractions have values *greater than one*.

A **mixed number** is a number that contains both an integer and a fraction. Any improper fraction can be rewritten as a mixed number. Example: $\frac{8}{3} = \frac{6}{3} + \frac{2}{3} = 2 + \frac{2}{3} = 2\frac{2}{3}$. Similarly, any mixed number can be rewritten as an improper fraction. Example: $1\frac{3}{5} = 1 + \frac{3}{5} = \frac{5}{5} + \frac{3}{5} = \frac{8}{5}$.

> ### Review Video: Proper and Improper Fractions and Mixed Numbers
> Visit mometrix.com/academy and enter code: 211077
>
> ### Review Video: Fractions
> Visit mometrix.com/academy and enter code: 262335

OPERATIONS WITH FRACTIONS

ADDING AND SUBTRACTING FRACTIONS

If two fractions have a common denominator, they can be added or subtracted simply by adding or subtracting the two numerators and retaining the same denominator. Example: $\frac{1}{2} + \frac{1}{4} = \frac{2}{4} + \frac{1}{4} = \frac{3}{4}$. If the two fractions do not already have the same denominator, one or both of them must be manipulated to achieve a common denominator before they can be added or subtracted.

> ### Review Video: Adding and Subtracting Fractions
> Visit mometrix.com/academy and enter code: 378080

MULTIPLYING FRACTIONS

Two fractions can be multiplied by multiplying the two numerators to find the new numerator and the two denominators to find the new denominator. Example: $\frac{1}{3} \times \frac{2}{3} = \frac{1 \times 2}{3 \times 3} = \frac{2}{9}$.

> ### Review Video: Multiplying Fractions
> Visit mometrix.com/academy and enter code: 638849

DIVIDING FRACTIONS

Two fractions can be divided by flipping the numerator and denominator of the second fraction and then proceeding as though it were a multiplication. Example: $\frac{2}{3} \div \frac{3}{4} = \frac{2}{3} \times \frac{4}{3} = \frac{8}{9}$.

> ### Review Video: Dividing Fractions
> Visit mometrix.com/academy and enter code: 300874

DECIMALS

Decimals are one way to represent parts of a whole. Using the place value system, each digit to the right of a decimal point denotes the number of units of a corresponding *negative* power of ten. For example, consider the decimal 0.24. We can use a model to represent the decimal. Since a dime is worth one-tenth of a dollar and a penny is worth one-hundredth of a dollar, one possible model to represent this fraction is to have 2 dimes representing the 2 in the tenths place and 4 pennies representing the 4 in the hundredths place:

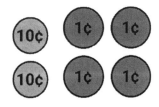

211

To write the decimal as a fraction, put the decimal in the numerator with 1 in the denominator. Multiply the numerator and denominator by tens until there are no more decimal places. Then simplify the fraction to lowest terms. For example, converting 0.24 to a fraction:

$$0.24 = \frac{0.24}{1} = \frac{0.24 \times 100}{1 \times 100} = \frac{24}{100} = \frac{6}{25}$$

Review Video: Decimals
Visit mometrix.com/academy and enter code: 837268

OPERATIONS WITH DECIMALS

ADDING AND SUBTRACTING DECIMALS

When adding and subtracting decimals, the decimal points must always be aligned. Adding decimals is just like adding regular whole numbers. Example: $4.5 + 2 = 6.5$.

If the problem-solver does not properly align the decimal points, an incorrect answer of 4.7 may result. An easy way to add decimals is to align all of the decimal points in a vertical column visually. This will allow one to see exactly where the decimal should be placed in the final answer. Begin adding from right to left. Add each column in turn, making sure to carry the number to the left if a column adds up to more than 9. The same rules apply to the subtraction of decimals.

Review Video: Adding and Subtracting Decimals
Visit mometrix.com/academy and enter code: 381101

MULTIPLYING DECIMALS

A simple multiplication problem has two components: a **multiplicand** and a **multiplier**. When multiplying decimals, work as though the numbers were whole rather than decimals. Once the final product is calculated, count the number of places to the right of the decimal in both the multiplicand and the multiplier. Then, count that number of places from the right of the product and place the decimal in that position.

For example, 12.3×2.56 has a total of three places to the right of the respective decimals. Multiply 123×256 to get 31488. Now, beginning on the right, count three places to the left and insert the decimal. The final product will be 31.488.

Review Video: Multiplying Decimals
Visit mometrix.com/academy and enter code: 731574

DIVIDING DECIMALS

Every division problem has a **divisor** and a **dividend**. The dividend is the number that is being divided. In the problem $14 \div 7$, 14 is the dividend and 7 is the divisor. In a division problem with decimals, the divisor must be converted into a whole number. Begin by moving the decimal in the divisor to the right until a whole number is created. Next, move the decimal in the dividend the same number of spaces to the right. For example, 4.9 into 24.5 would become 49 into 245. The decimal was moved one space to the right to create a whole number in the divisor, and then the same was done for the dividend. Once the whole numbers are created, the problem is carried out normally: $245 \div 49 = 5$.

Review Video: Dividing Decimals
Visit mometrix.com/academy and enter code: 560690

PERCENTAGES

Percentages can be thought of as fractions that are based on a whole of 100; that is, one whole is equal to 100%. The word **percent** means "per hundred." Percentage problems are often presented in three main ways:

- Find what percentage of some number another number is.
  - Example: What percentage of 40 is 8?
- Find what number is some percentage of a given number.
  - Example: What number is 20% of 40?
- Find what number another number is a given percentage of.
  - Example: What number is 8 20% of?

There are three components in each of these cases: a **whole** (W), a **part** (P), and a **percentage** (%). These are related by the equation: $P = W \times \%$. This can easily be rearranged into other forms that may suit different questions better: $\% = \frac{P}{W}$ and $W = \frac{P}{\%}$. Percentage problems are often also word problems. As such, a large part of solving them is figuring out which quantities are what. For example, consider the following word problem:

In a school cafeteria, 7 students choose pizza, 9 choose hamburgers, and 4 choose tacos. What percentage of student choose tacos?

To find the whole, you must first add all of the parts: $7 + 9 + 4 = 20$. The percentage can then be found by dividing the part by the whole ($\% = \frac{P}{W}$): $\frac{4}{20} = \frac{20}{100} = 20\%$.

> **Review Video: Percentages**
> Visit mometrix.com/academy and enter code: 141911
>
> **Review Video: Finding Percentage of Number Given Whole**
> Visit mometrix.com/academy and enter code: 932623

CONVERTING BETWEEN PERCENTAGES, FRACTIONS, AND DECIMALS

Converting decimals to percentages and percentages to decimals is as simple as moving the decimal point. To *convert from a decimal to a percentage*, move the decimal point **two places to the right**. To *convert from a percentage to a decimal*, move it **two places to the left**. It may be helpful to remember that the percentage number will always be larger than the equivalent decimal number. For example:

$$0.23 = 23\% \quad 5.34 = 534\% \quad 0.007 = 0.7\%$$
$$700\% = 7.00 \quad 86\% = 0.86 \quad 0.15\% = 0.0015$$

To convert a fraction to a decimal, simply divide the numerator by the denominator in the fraction. To convert a decimal to a fraction, put the decimal in the numerator with 1 in the denominator.

Multiply the numerator and denominator by tens until there are no more decimal places. Then simplify the fraction to lowest terms. For example, converting 0.24 to a fraction:

$$0.24 = \frac{0.24}{1} = \frac{0.24 \times 100}{1 \times 100} = \frac{24}{100} = \frac{6}{25}$$

Fractions can be converted to a percentage by finding equivalent fractions with a denominator of 100. For example,

$$\frac{7}{10} = \frac{70}{100} = 70\% \quad \frac{1}{4} = \frac{25}{100} = 25\%$$

To convert a percentage to a fraction, divide the percentage number by 100 and reduce the fraction to its simplest possible terms. For example,

$$60\% = \frac{60}{100} = \frac{3}{5} \quad 96\% = \frac{96}{100} = \frac{24}{25}$$

Review Video: <u>Converting Decimals to Fractions and Percentages</u>
Visit mometrix.com/academy and enter code: 986765

Review Video: <u>Converting Fractions to Percentages and Decimals</u>
Visit mometrix.com/academy and enter code: 306233

Review Video: <u>Converting Percentages to Decimals and Fractions</u>
Visit mometrix.com/academy and enter code: 287297

RATIONAL NUMBERS

The term **rational** means that the number can be expressed as a ratio or fraction. That is, a number, r, is rational if and only if it can be represented by a fraction $\frac{a}{b}$ where a and b are integers and b does not equal 0. The set of rational numbers includes integers and decimals. If there is no finite way to represent a value with a fraction of integers, then the number is **irrational**. Common examples of irrational numbers include: $\sqrt{5}, \left(1 + \sqrt{2}\right),$ and π.

Review Video: <u>Rational Numbers</u>
Visit mometrix.com/academy and enter code: 280645

PRACTICE

P1. What is 30% of 120?

P2. What is 150% of 20?

P3. What is 14.5% of 96?

P4. Simplify the following expressions:

(a) $\left(\frac{2}{5}\right)/\left(\frac{4}{7}\right)$

(b) $\frac{7}{8} - \frac{8}{16}$

(c) $\frac{1}{2} + \left(3\left(\frac{3}{4}\right) - 2\right) + 4$

(d) $0.22 + 0.5 - (5.5 + 3.3 \div 3)$

(e) $\frac{3}{2} + (4(0.5) - 0.75) + 2$

P5. Convert the following to a fraction and to a decimal: **(a)** 15%; **(b)** 24.36%

P6. Convert the following to a decimal and to a percentage. **(a)** 4/5; **(b)** $3\frac{2}{5}$

P7. A woman's age is thirteen more than half of 60. How old is the woman?

P8. A patient was given pain medicine at a dosage of 0.22 grams. The patient's dosage was then increased to 0.80 grams. By how much was the patient's dosage increased?

P9. At a hotel, $\frac{3}{4}$ of the 100 rooms are occupied today. Yesterday, $\frac{4}{5}$ of the 100 rooms were occupied. On which day were more of the rooms occupied and by how much more?

P10. At a school, 40% of the teachers teach English. If 20 teachers teach English, how many teachers work at the school?

P11. A patient was given blood pressure medicine at a dosage of 2 grams. The patient's dosage was then decreased to 0.45 grams. By how much was the patient's dosage decreased?

P12. Two weeks ago, $\frac{2}{3}$ of the 60 customers at a skate shop were male. Last week, $\frac{3}{6}$ of the 80 customers were male. During which week were there more male customers?

P13. Jane ate lunch at a local restaurant. She ordered a $4.99 appetizer, a $12.50 entrée, and a $1.25 soda. If she wants to tip her server 20%, how much money will she spend in all?

P14. According to a survey, about 82% of engineers were highly satisfied with their job. If 145 engineers were surveyed, how many reported that they were highly satisfied?

P15. A patient was given 40 mg of a certain medicine. Later, the patient's dosage was increased to 45 mg. What was the percent increase in his medication?

P16. Order the following rational numbers from least to greatest: 0.55, 17%, $\sqrt{25}$, $\frac{64}{4}$, $\frac{25}{50}$, 3.

P17. Order the following rational numbers from greatest to least: 0.3, 27%, $\sqrt{100}$, $\frac{72}{9}$, $\frac{1}{9}$, 4.5

PRACTICE SOLUTIONS

P1. The word *of* indicates multiplication, so 30% of 120 is found by multiplying 120 by 30%. Change 30% to a decimal, then multiply: $120 \times 0.3 = 36$

P2. The word *of* indicates multiplication, so 150% of 20 is found by multiplying 20 by 150%. Change 150% to a decimal, then multiply: $20 \times 1.5 = 30$

P3. Change 14.5% to a decimal before multiplying. $0.145 \times 96 = 13.92$.

P4. Follow the order of operations and utilize properties of fractions to solve each:

(a) Rewrite the problem as a multiplication problem: $\frac{2}{5} \times \frac{7}{4} = \frac{2\times7}{5\times4} = \frac{14}{20}$. Make sure the fraction is reduced to lowest terms. Both 14 and 20 can be divided by 2.

$$\frac{14}{20} = \frac{14 \div 2}{20 \div 2} = \frac{7}{10}$$

(b) The denominators of $\frac{7}{8}$ and $\frac{8}{16}$ are 8 and 16, respectively. The lowest common denominator of 8 and 16 is 16 because 16 is the least common multiple of 8 and 16. Convert the first fraction to its equivalent with the newly found common denominator of 16: $\frac{7 \times 2}{8 \times 2} = \frac{14}{16}$. Now that the fractions have the same denominator, you can subtract them.

$$\frac{14}{16} - \frac{8}{16} = \frac{6}{16} = \frac{3}{8}$$

(c) When simplifying expressions, first perform operations within groups. Within the set of parentheses are multiplication and subtraction operations. Perform the multiplication first to get $\frac{1}{2} + \left(\frac{9}{4} - 2\right) + 4$. Then, subtract two to obtain $\frac{1}{2} + \frac{1}{4} + 4$. Finally, perform addition from left to right:

$$\frac{1}{2} + \frac{1}{4} + 4 = \frac{2}{4} + \frac{1}{4} + \frac{16}{4} = \frac{19}{4} = 4\frac{3}{4}$$

(d) First, evaluate the terms in the parentheses $(5.5 + 3.3 \div 3)$ using order of operations. $3.3 \div 3 = 1.1$, and $5.5 + 1.1 = 6.6$. Next, rewrite the problem: $0.22 + 0.5 - 6.6$. Finally, add and subtract from left to right: $0.22 + 0.5 = 0.72$; $0.72 - 6.6 = -5.88$. The answer is -5.88.

(e) First, simplify within the parentheses, then change the fraction to a decimal and perform addition from left to right:

$$\frac{3}{2} + (2 - 0.75) + 2 =$$
$$\frac{3}{2} + 1.25 + 2 =$$
$$1.5 + 1.25 + 2 = 4.75$$

P5. (a) 15% can be written as $\frac{15}{100}$. Both 15 and 100 can be divided by 5: $\frac{15 \div 5}{100 \div 5} = \frac{3}{20}$

When converting from a percentage to a decimal, drop the percent sign and move the decimal point two places to the left: $15\% = 0.15$

(b) 24.36% written as a fraction is $\frac{24.36}{100}$, or $\frac{2436}{10,000}$, which reduces to $\frac{609}{2500}$. 24.36% written as a decimal is 0.2436. Recall that dividing by 100 moves the decimal two places to the left.

P6. (a) Recall that in the decimal system the first decimal place is one tenth: $\frac{4 \times 2}{5 \times 2} = \frac{8}{10} = 0.8$

Percent means "per hundred." $\frac{4 \times 20}{5 \times 20} = \frac{80}{100} = 80\%$

(b) The mixed number $3\frac{2}{5}$ has a whole number and a fractional part. The fractional part $\frac{2}{5}$ can be written as a decimal by dividing 5 into 2, which gives 0.4. Adding the whole to the part gives 3.4.

To find the equivalent percentage, multiply the decimal by 100. $3.4(100) = 340\%$. Notice that this percentage is greater than 100%. This makes sense because the original mixed number $3\frac{2}{5}$ is greater than 1.

P7. "More than" indicates addition, and "of" indicates multiplication. The expression can be written as $\frac{1}{2}(60) + 13$. So, the woman's age is equal to $\frac{1}{2}(60) + 13 = 30 + 13 = 43$. The woman is 43 years old.

P8. The first step is to determine what operation (addition, subtraction, multiplication, or division) the problem requires. Notice the keywords and phrases "by how much" and "increased." "Increased" means that you go from a smaller amount to a larger amount. This change can be found by subtracting the smaller amount from the larger amount: 0.80 grams– 0.22 grams = 0.58 grams.

Remember to line up the decimal when subtracting:

$$
\begin{array}{r}
0.80 \\
-\ 0.22 \\
\hline
0.58
\end{array}
$$

P9. First, find the number of rooms occupied each day. To do so, multiply the fraction of rooms occupied by the number of rooms available:

$$\text{Number occupied} = \text{Fraction occupied} \times \text{Total number}$$
$$\text{Number of rooms occupied today} = \frac{3}{4} \times 100 = 75$$
$$\text{Number of rooms occupied} = \frac{4}{5} \times 100 = 80$$

The difference in the number of rooms occupied is: $80 - 75 = 5$ rooms

P10. To answer this problem, first think about the number of teachers that work at the school. Will it be more or less than the number of teachers who work in a specific department such as English? More teachers work at the school, so the number you find to answer this question will be greater than 20.

40% of the teachers are English teachers. "Of" indicates multiplication, and words like "is" and "are" indicate equivalence. Translating the problem into a mathematical sentence gives $40\% \times t = 20$, where t represents the total number of teachers. Solving for t gives $t = \frac{20}{40\%} = \frac{20}{0.40} = 50$. Fifty teachers work at the school.

P11. The decrease is represented by the difference between the two amounts:

$$2 \text{ grams} - 0.45 \text{ grams} = 1.55 \text{ grams}.$$

Remember to line up the decimal point before subtracting.

$$\begin{array}{r} 2.00 \\ -\ 0.45 \\ \hline 1.55 \end{array}$$

P12. First, you need to find the number of male customers that were in the skate shop each week. You are given this amount in terms of fractions. To find the actual number of male customers, multiply the fraction of male customers by the number of customers in the store.

$$\text{Actual number of male customers} = \text{fraction of male customers} \times \text{total customers}$$
$$\text{Number of male customers two weeks ago} = \frac{2}{3} \times 60 = \frac{120}{3} = 40$$
$$\text{Number of male customers last week} = \frac{3}{6} \times 80 = \frac{1}{2} \times 80 = \frac{80}{2} = 40$$

The number of male customers was the same both weeks.

P13. To find total amount, first find the sum of the items she ordered from the menu and then add 20% of this sum to the total.

$$\$4.99 + \$12.50 + \$1.25 = \$18.74$$

$$\$18.74 \times 20\% = (0.20)(\$18.74) = \$3.748 \approx \$3.75$$

$$\text{Total} = \$18.74 + \$3.75 = \$22.49$$

P14. 82% of 145 is $0.82 \times 145 = 118.9$. Because you can't have 0.9 of a person, we must round up to say that 119 engineers reported that they were highly satisfied with their jobs.

P15. To find the percent increase, first compare the original and increased amounts. The original amount was 40 mg, and the increased amount is 45 mg, so the dosage of medication was increased by 5 mg $(45-40 = 5)$. Note, however, that the question asks not by how much the dosage increased but by what percentage it increased.

$$\text{Percent increase} = \frac{\text{new amount} - \text{original amount}}{\text{original amount}} \times 100\%$$
$$= \frac{45 \text{ mg} - 40 \text{ mg}}{40 \text{ mg}} \times 100\% = \frac{5}{40} \times 100\% = 0.125 \times 100\% = 12.5\%$$

P16. Recall that the term rational simply means that the number can be expressed as a ratio or fraction. Notice that each of the numbers in the problem can be written as a decimal or integer:

$$17\% = 0.1717$$
$$\sqrt{25} = 5$$
$$\frac{64}{4} = 16$$
$$\frac{25}{50} = \frac{1}{2} = 0.5$$

So, the answer is $17\%, \frac{25}{50}, 0.55, 3, \sqrt{25}, \frac{64}{4}$.

P17. Converting all the numbers to integers and decimals makes it easier to compare the values:

$$27\% = 0.27$$
$$\sqrt{100} = 10$$
$$\frac{72}{9} = 8$$
$$\frac{1}{9} \approx 0.11$$

So, the answer is $\sqrt{100}, \frac{72}{9}, 4.5, 0.3, 27\%, \frac{1}{9}$.

> **Review Video: Ordering Rational Numbers**
> Visit mometrix.com/academy and enter code: 419578

Proportions and Ratios

PROPORTIONS

A proportion is a relationship between two quantities that dictates how one changes when the other changes. A **direct proportion** describes a relationship in which a quantity increases by a set amount for every increase in the other quantity, or decreases by that same amount for every decrease in the other quantity. Example: Assuming a constant driving speed, the time required for a car trip increases as the distance of the trip increases. The distance to be traveled and the time required to travel are directly proportional.

Inverse proportion is a relationship in which an increase in one quantity is accompanied by a decrease in the other, or vice versa. Example: the time required for a car trip decreases as the speed increases, and increases as the speed decreases, so the time required is inversely proportional to the speed of the car.

> **Review Video: Proportions**
> Visit mometrix.com/academy and enter code: 505355

RATIOS

A **ratio** is a comparison of two quantities in a particular order. Example: If there are 14 computers in a lab, and the class has 20 students, there is a student to computer ratio of 20 to 14, commonly written as 20:14. Ratios are normally reduced to their smallest whole number representation, so 20:14 would be reduced to 10:7 by dividing both sides by 2.

CONSTANT OF PROPORTIONALITY

When two quantities have a proportional relationship, there exists a **constant of proportionality** between the quantities; the product of this constant and one of the quantities is equal to the other quantity. For example, if one lemon costs $0.25, two lemons cost $0.50, and three lemons cost $0.75, there is a proportional relationship between the total cost of lemons and the number of lemons purchased. The constant of proportionality is the **unit price**, namely $0.25/lemon. Notice that the total price of lemons, t, can be found by multiplying the unit price of lemons, p, and the number of lemons, n: $t = pn$.

WORK/UNIT RATE

Unit rate expresses a quantity of one thing in terms of one unit of another. For example, if you travel 30 miles every two hours, a unit rate expresses this comparison in terms of one hour: in one hour you travel 15 miles, so your unit rate is 15 miles per hour. Other examples are how much one ounce of food costs (price per ounce) or figuring out how much one egg costs out of the dozen (price per 1 egg, instead of price per 12 eggs). The denominator of a unit rate is always 1. Unit rates are used to compare different situations to solve problems. For example, to make sure you get the best deal when deciding which kind of soda to buy, you can find the unit rate of each. If soda #1 costs $1.50 for a 1-liter bottle, and soda #2 costs $2.75 for a 2-liter bottle, it would be a better deal to buy soda #2, because its unit rate is only $1.375 per 1-liter, which is cheaper than soda #1. Unit rates can also help determine the length of time a given event will take. For example, if you can paint 2 rooms in 4.5 hours, you can determine how long it will take you to paint 5 rooms by solving for the unit rate per room and then multiplying that by 5.

SLOPE

On a graph with two points, (x_1, y_1) and (x_2, y_2), the **slope** is found with the formula $m = \frac{y_2 - y_1}{x_2 - x_1}$; where $x_1 \neq x_2$ and m stands for slope. If the value of the slope is **positive**, the line has an *upward direction* from left to right. If the value of the slope is **negative**, the line has a *downward direction* from left to right. Consider the following example:

A new book goes on sale in bookstores and online stores. In the first month, 5,000 copies of the book are sold. Over time, the book continues to grow in popularity. The data for the number of copies sold is in the table below.

# of Months on Sale	1	2	3	4	5
# of Copies Sold (In Thousands)	5	10	15	20	25

So, the number of copies that are sold and the time that the book is on sale is a proportional relationship. In this example, an equation can be used to show the data: $y = 5x$, where x is the number of months that the book is on sale. Also, y is the number of copies sold. So, the slope of the corresponding line is $\frac{rise}{run} = \frac{5}{1} = 5$.

FINDING AN UNKNOWN IN EQUIVALENT EXPRESSIONS

It is often necessary to apply information given about a rate or proportion to a new scenario. For example, if you know that Jedha can run a marathon (26 miles) in 3 hours, how long would it take her to run 10 miles at the same pace? Start by setting up equivalent expressions:

$$\frac{26 \text{ mi}}{3 \text{ hr}} = \frac{10 \text{ mi}}{x \text{ hr}}$$

Now, cross multiply and, solve for x:

$$26x = 30$$
$$x = \frac{30}{26} = \frac{15}{13}$$
$$x \cong 1.15 \text{ hrs } or \text{ 1 hr 9 min}$$

So, at this pace, Jedha could run 10 miles in about 1.15 hours or about 1 hour and 9 minutes.

PRACTICE

P1. Solve the following for x.

(a) $\frac{45}{12} = \frac{15}{x}$

(b) $\frac{0.50}{2} = \frac{1.50}{x}$

(c) $\frac{40}{8} = \frac{x}{24}$

P2. At a school, for every 20 female students there are 15 male students. This same student ratio happens to exist at another school. If there are 100 female students at the second school, how many male students are there?

P3. In a hospital emergency room, there are 4 nurses for every 12 patients. What is the ratio of nurses to patients? If the nurse-to-patient ratio remains constant, how many nurses must be present to care for 24 patients?

P4. In a bank, the banker-to-customer ratio is 1:2. If seven bankers are on duty, how many customers are currently in the bank?

P5. Janice made $40 during the first 5 hours she spent babysitting. She will continue to earn money at this rate until she finishes babysitting in 3 more hours. Find how much money Janice earns per hour and the total she earned babysitting.

P6. The McDonalds are taking a family road trip, driving 300 miles to their cabin. It took them 2 hours to drive the first 120 miles. They will drive at the same speed all the way to their cabin. Find the speed at which the McDonalds are driving and how much longer it will take them to get to their cabin.

P7. It takes Andy 10 minutes to read 6 pages of his book. He has already read 150 pages in his book that is 210 pages long. Find how long it takes Andy to read 1 page and also find how long it will take him to finish his book if he continues to read at the same speed.

PRACTICE SOLUTIONS

P1. First, cross multiply; then, solve for x:

(a) $45x = 12 \times 15$
$45x = 180$
$x = \frac{180}{45} = 4$

(b) $0.5x = 1.5 \times 2$
$0.5x = 3$
$x = \frac{3}{0.5} = 6$

(c) $8x = 40 \times 24$
$8x = 960$
$x = \frac{960}{8} = 120$

P2. One way to find the number of male students is to set up and solve a proportion.

$$\frac{\text{number of female students}}{\text{number of male students}} = \frac{20}{15} = \frac{100}{\text{number of male students}}$$

Represent the unknown number of male students as the variable x: $\frac{20}{15} = \frac{100}{x}$

Cross multiply and then solve for x:

$$20x = 15 \times 100$$
$$x = \frac{1500}{20}$$
$$x = 75$$

P3. The ratio of nurses to patients can be written as 4 to 12, 4:12, or $\frac{4}{12}$. Because four and twelve have a common factor of four, the ratio should be reduced to 1:3, which means that there is one nurse present for every three patients. If this ratio remains constant, there must be eight nurses present to care for 24 patients.

P4. Use proportional reasoning or set up a proportion to solve. Because there are twice as many customers as bankers, there must be fourteen customers when seven bankers are on duty. Setting up and solving a proportion gives the same result:

$$\frac{\text{number of bankers}}{\text{number of customers}} = \frac{1}{2} = \frac{7}{\text{number of customers}}$$

Represent the unknown number of patients as the variable x: $\frac{1}{2} = \frac{7}{x}$.

To solve for x, cross multiply: $1 \times x = 7 \times 2$, so $x = 14$.

P5. Janice earns \$8 per hour. This can be found by taking her initial amount earned, \$40, and dividing it by the number of hours worked, 5. Since $\frac{40}{5} = 8$, Janice makes \$8 in one hour. This can also be found by finding the unit rate, money earned per hour: $\frac{40}{5} = \frac{x}{1}$. Since cross multiplying yields $5x = 40$, and division by 5 shows that $x = 8$, Janice earns \$8 per hour.

Janice will earn \$64 babysitting in her 8 total hours (adding the first 5 hours to the remaining 3 gives the 8 hour total). Since Janice earns \$8 per hour and she worked 8 hours, $\frac{\$8}{\text{hr}} \times 8 \text{ hrs} = \$64$. This can also be found by setting up a proportion comparing money earned to babysitting hours. Since she earns \$40 for 5 hours and since the rate is constant, she will earn a proportional amount in 8 hours: $\frac{40}{5} = \frac{x}{8}$. Cross multiplying will yield $5x = 320$, and division by 5 shows that $x = 64$.

P6. The McDonalds are driving 60 miles per hour. This can be found by setting up a proportion to find the unit rate, the number of miles they drive per one hour: $\frac{120}{2} = \frac{x}{1}$. Cross multiplying yields $2x = 120$ and division by 2 shows that $x = 60$.

Since the McDonalds will drive this same speed, it will take them another 3 hours to get to their cabin. This can be found by first finding how many miles the McDonalds have left to drive, which is $300 - 120 = 180$. The McDonalds are driving at 60 miles per hour, so a proportion can be set up to determine how many hours it will take them to drive 180 miles: $\frac{180}{x} = \frac{60}{1}$. Cross multiplying yields $60x = 180$, and division by 60 shows that $x = 3$. This can also be found by using the formula $D = r \times t$ (or distance = rate × time), where $180 = 60 \times t$, and division by 60 shows that $t = 3$.

P7. It takes Andy 10 minutes to read 6 pages, $\frac{10}{6} = 1\frac{2}{3}$ minutes, which is 1 minute and 40 seconds.

Next, determine how many pages Andy has left to read, $210 - 150 = 60$. Since it is now known that it takes him $1\frac{2}{3}$ minutes to read each page, then that rate must be multiplied by however many pages he has left to read (60) to find the time he'll need: $60 \times 1\frac{2}{3} = 100$, so it will take him 100 minutes, or 1 hour and 40 minutes, to read the rest of his book.

> **Review Video: Proportions in the Real World**
> Visit mometrix.com/academy and enter code: 221143

Expressions, Equations and Inequalities

LINEAR EQUATIONS

Equations that can be written as $ax + b = 0$, where $a \neq 0$ are referred to as **one variable linear equations**. A solution to such an equation is called a **root**. In the case where we have the equation $5x + 10 = 0$, if we solve for x we get a solution of $x = -2$. In other words, the root of the equation is -2. This is found by first subtracting 10 from both sides, which gives $5x = -10$. Next, simply divide both sides by the coefficient of the variable, in this case 5, to get $x = -2$. This can be checked by plugging -2 back into the original equation $(5)(-2) + 10 = -10 + 10 = 0$.

The **solution set** is the set of all solutions of an equation. In our example, the solution set would simply be -2. If there were more solutions (there usually are in multivariable equations) then they would also be included in the solution set. When an equation has no true solutions, this is referred to as an **empty set**. Equations with identical solution sets are **equivalent equations**. An **identity** is a term whose value or determinant is equal to 1.

Linear equations can be written many ways. Below is a list of some forms linear equations can take:

- **Standard Form**: $Ax + By = C$; the slope is $\frac{-A}{B}$ and the y-intercept is $\frac{C}{B}$
- **Slope Intercept Form**: $y = mx + b$, where m is the slope and b is the y-intercept
- **Point-Slope Form**: $y - y_1 = m(x - x_1)$, where m is the slope and (x_1, y_1) is a point on the line
- **Two-Point Form**: $\frac{y-y_1}{x-x_1} = \frac{y_2-y_1}{x_2-x_1}$, where (x_1, y_1) and (x_2, y_2) are two points on the given line
- **Intercept Form**: $\frac{x}{x_1} + \frac{y}{y_1} = 1$, where $(x_1, 0)$ is the point at which a line intersects the x-axis, and $(0, y_1)$ is the point at which the same line intersects the y-axis

> **Review Video: Slope-Intercept and Point-Slope Forms**
> Visit mometrix.com/academy and enter code: 113216

SOLVING ONE-VARIABLE LINEAR EQUATIONS

Multiply all terms by the lowest common denominator to eliminate any fractions. Look for addition or subtraction to undo so you can isolate the variable on one side of the equal sign. Divide both sides by the coefficient of the variable. When you have a value for the variable, substitute this value into the original equation to make sure you have a true equation. Consider the following example:

Kim's savings is represented by the table below. Represent her savings, using an equation.

X (Months)	Y (Total Savings)
2	$1300
5	$2050
9	$3050
11	$3550
16	$4800

The table shows a function with a constant rate of change, or slope, or 250. Given the points on the table, the slopes can be calculated as $(2050 - 1300)/(5 - 2)$, $(3050 - 2050)/(9 - 5)$, $(3550 - 3050)/(11 - 9)$, and $(4800 - 3550)/(16 - 11)$, each of which equals 250. Thus, the table shows a constant rate of change, indicating a linear function. The slope-intercept form of a linear equation is written as $y = mx + b$, where m represents the slope and b represents the y-intercept. Substituting the slope into this form gives $y = 250x + b$. Substituting corresponding x- and y-values from any point into this equation will give the y-intercept, or b. Using the point, $(2, 1300)$, gives $1300 = 250(2) + b$, which simplifies as b = 800. Thus, her savings may be represented by the equation, $y = 250x + 800$.

RULES FOR MANIPULATING EQUATIONS

LIKE TERMS

Like terms are terms in an equation that have the same variable, regardless of whether or not they also have the same coefficient. This includes terms that *lack* a variable; all constants (i.e. numbers

224

without variables) are considered like terms. If the equation involves terms with a variable raised to different powers, the like terms are those that have the variable raised to the same power.

For example, consider the equation $x^2 + 3x + 2 = 2x^2 + x - 7 + 2x$. In this equation, 2 and –7 are like terms; they are both constants. $3x$, x, and $2x$ are like terms: they all include the variable x raised to the first power. x^2 and $2x^2$ are like terms; they both include the variable x, raised to the second power. $2x$ and $2x^2$ are not like terms; although they both involve the variable x, the variable is not raised to the same power in both terms. The fact that they have the same coefficient, 2, is not relevant.

CARRYING OUT THE SAME OPERATION ON BOTH SIDES OF AN EQUATION

When solving an equation, the general procedure is to carry out a series of operations on both sides of an equation, choosing operations that will tend to simplify the equation when doing so. The reason why the same operation must be carried out on both sides of the equation is because that leaves the meaning of the equation unchanged, and yields a result that is equivalent to the original equation. This would not be the case if we carried out an operation on one side of an equation and not the other. Consider what an equation means: it is a statement that two values or expressions are equal. If we carry out the same operation on both sides of the equation—add 3 to both sides, for example—then the two sides of the equation are changed in the same way, and so remain equal. If we do that to only one side of the equation—add 3 to one side but not the other—then that wouldn't be true; if we change one side of the equation but not the other then the two sides are no longer equal.

ADVANTAGE OF COMBINING LIKE TERMS

Combining like terms refers to adding or subtracting like terms—terms with the same variable—and therefore reducing sets of like terms to a single term. The main advantage of doing this is that it simplifies the equation. Often combining like terms can be done as the first step in solving an equation, though it can also be done later, such as after distributing terms in a product.

For example, consider the equation $2(x + 3) + 3(2 + x + 3) = -4$. The 2 and the 3 in the second set of parentheses are like terms, and we can combine them, yielding $2(x + 3) + 3(x + 5) = -4$. Now we can carry out the multiplications implied by the parentheses, distributing outer 2 and 3 accordingly: $2x + 6 + 3x + 15 = -4$. The $2x$ and the $3x$ are like terms, and we can add them together: $5x + 6 + 15 = -4$. Now, the constants 6, 15, and –4 are also like terms, and we can combine them as well: subtracting 6 and 15 from both sides of the equation, we get $5x = -4 - 6 - 15$, or $5x = -25$, which simplifies further to $x = -5$.

CANCELING TERMS ON OPPOSITE SIDES OF AN EQUATION

Two terms on opposite sides of an equation can be canceled if and only if they *exactly* match each other. They must have the same variable raised to the same power and the same coefficient. For example, in the equation $3x + 2x^2 + 6 = 2x^2 - 6$, $2x^2$ appears on both sides of the equation, and can be canceled, leaving $3x + 6 = -6$. The 6 on each side of the equation cannot be canceled, because it is added on one side of the equation and subtracted on the other. While they cannot be canceled, however, the 6 and –6 are like terms and can be combined, yielding $3x = -12$, which simplifies further to $x = -4$.

It's also important to note that the terms to be canceled must be independent terms and cannot be part of a larger term. For example, consider the equation $2(x + 6) = 3(x + 4) + 1$. We cannot cancel the xs, because even though they match each other they are part of the larger terms $2(x + 6)$ and $3(x + 4)$. We must first distribute the 2 and 3, yielding $2x + 12 = 3x + 12 + 1$. Now we see that the terms with the x's do not match, but the 12's do, and can be canceled, leaving $2x = 3x + 1$, which simplifies to $x = -1$.

PROCESS FOR MANIPULATING EQUATIONS

ISOLATING VARIABLES

To **isolate a variable** means to manipulate the equation so that the variable appears by itself on one side of the equation, and does not appear at all on the other side. Generally, an equation or inequality is considered to be solved once the variable is isolated and the other side of the equation or inequality is simplified as much as possible. In the case of a two-variable equation or inequality, only one variable need be isolated; it will not usually be possible to simultaneously isolate both variables.

For a linear equation—an equation in which the variable only appears raised to the first power—isolating a variable can be done by first moving all the terms with the variable to one side of the equation and all other terms to the other side. (*Moving* a term really means adding the inverse of the term to both sides; when a term is *moved* to the other side of the equation its sign is flipped.) Then combine like terms on each side. Finally, divide both sides by the coefficient of the variable, if applicable. The steps need not necessarily be done in this order, but this order will always work.

EQUATIONS WITH MORE THAN ONE SOLUTION

Some types of non-linear equation, such as equations involving squares of variables, may have more than one solution. For example, the equation $x^2 = 4$ has two solutions: 2 and –2. Equations with absolute values can also have multiple solutions: $|x| = 1$ has the solutions $x = 1$ and $x = -1$.

It is also possible for a linear equation to have more than one solution, but only if the equation is true regardless of the value of the variable. In this case, the equation is considered to have infinitely many solutions, because any possible value of the variable is a solution. We know a linear equation has infinitely many solutions if when we combine like terms the variables cancel, leaving a true statement. For example, consider the equation $2(3x + 5) = x + 5(x + 2)$. Distributing, we get $6x + 10 = x + 5x + 10$; combining like terms gives $6x + 10 = 6x + 10$, and the $6x$ terms cancel to leave $10 = 10$. This is clearly true, so the original equation is true for any value of x. We could also have canceled the 10s leaving $0 = 0$, but again this is clearly true—in general if both sides of the equation match exactly, it has infinitely many solutions.

EQUATIONS WITH NO SOLUTION

Some types of non-linear equation, such as equations involving squares of variables, may have no solution. For example, the equation $x^2 = -2$ has no solutions in the real numbers, because the square of any real number must be positive. Similarly, $|x| = -1$ has no solution, because the absolute value of a number is always positive.

It is also possible for an equation to have no solution even if does not involve any powers greater than one or absolute values or other special functions. For example, the equation $2(x + 3) + x = 3x$ has no solution. We can see that if we try to solve it: first we distribute, leaving $2x + 6 + x = 3x$. But now if we try to combine all the terms with the variable, we find that they cancel: we have $3x$ on the left and $3x$ on the right, canceling to leave us with $6 = 0$. This is clearly false. In general, whenever the variable terms in an equation cancel leaving different constants on both sides, it means that the equation has no solution. (If we are left with the *same* constant on both sides, the equation has infinitely many solutions instead.)

FEATURES OF EQUATIONS THAT REQUIRE SPECIAL TREATMENT

LINEAR EQUATIONS

A linear equation is an equation in which variables only appear by themselves: not multiplied together, not with exponents other than one, and not inside absolute value signs or any other functions. For example, the equation $x + 1 - 3x = 5 - x$ is a linear equation: while x appears multiple times, it never appears with an exponent other than one, or inside any function. The two-variable equation $2x - 3y = 5 + 2x$ is also a linear equation. In contrast, the equation $x^2 - 5 = 3x$ is *not* a linear equation, because it involves the term x^2. $\sqrt{x} = 5$ is not a linear equation, because it involves a square root. $(x - 1)^2 = 4$ is not a linear equation because even though there's no exponent on the x directly, it appears as part of an expression that is squared. The two-variable equation $x + xy - y = 5$ is not a linear equation because it includes the term xy, where two variables are multiplied together.

Linear equations can always be solved (or shown to have no solution) by combining like terms and performing simple operations on both sides of the equation. Some non-linear equations can also be solved by similar methods, but others may require more advanced methods of solution, if they can be solved analytically at all.

SOLVING EQUATIONS INVOLVING ROOTS

In an equation involving roots, the first step is to isolate the term with the root, if possible, and then raise both sides of the equation to the appropriate power to eliminate it. Consider an example equation, $2\sqrt{x + 1} - 1 = 3$. In this case, begin by adding 1 to both sides, yielding $2\sqrt{x + 1} = 4$, and then dividing both sides by 2, yielding $\sqrt{x + 1} = 2$. Now square both sides, yielding $x + 1 = 4$. Finally, subtracting 1 from both sides yields $x = 3$.

Squaring both sides of an equation may, however, yield a spurious solution—a solution to the squared equation that is *not* a solution of the original equation. It's therefore necessary to plug the solution back into the original equation to make sure it works. In this case, it does: $2\sqrt{3 + 1} - 1 = 2\sqrt{4} - 1 = 2(2) - 1 = 4 - 1 = 3$.

The same procedure applies for roots other than square roots. For example, given the equation $3 + \sqrt[3]{2x} = 5$, we can first subtract 3 from both sides, yielding $\sqrt[3]{2x} = 2$ and isolating the root. Raising both sides to the third power yields $2x = 2^3$, i.e. $2x = 8$. We can now divide both sides by 2 to get $x = 4$.

SOLVING EQUATIONS WITH EXPONENTS

To solve an equation involving an exponent, the first step is to isolate the variable with the exponent. We can then take the appropriate root of both sides to eliminate the exponent. For instance, for the equation $2x^3 + 17 = 5x^3 - 7$, we can subtract $5x^3$ from both sides to get $-3x^3 + 17 = -7$, and then subtract 17 from both sides to get $-3x^3 = -24$. Finally, we can divide both sides by –3 to get $x^3 = 8$. Finally, we can take the cube root of both sides to get $x = \sqrt[3]{8} = 2$.

One important but often overlooked point is that equations with an exponent greater than 1 may have more than one answer. The solution to $x^2 = 9$ isn't simply $x = 3$; it's $x = \pm 3$: that is, $x = 3$ or $x = -3$. For a slightly more complicated example, consider the equation $(x - 1)^2 - 1 = 3$. Adding one to both sides yields $(x - 1)^2 = 4$; taking the square root of both sides yields $x - 1 = 2$. We can then add 1 to both sides to get $x = 3$. However, there's a second solution: we also have the possibility that $x - 1 = -2$, in which case $x = -1$. Both $x = 3$ and $x = -1$ are valid solutions, as can be verified by substituting them both into the original equation.

SOLVING EQUATIONS WITH ABSOLUTE VALUES

When solving an equation with an absolute value, the first step is to isolate the absolute value term. We then consider the two possibilities: when the expression inside the absolute value is positive or when it is negative. In the former case, the expression in the absolute value equals the expression on the other side of the equation; in the latter, it equals the additive inverse of that expression—the expression times negative one. We consider each case separately, and finally check for spurious solutions.

For instance, consider solving $|2x - 1| + x = 5$ for x. We can first isolate the absolute value by moving the x to the other side: $|2x - 1| = -x + 5$. Now, we have two possibilities. First, that $2x - 1$ is positive, and hence $2x - 1 = -x + 5$. Rearranging and combining like terms yields $3x = 6$, and hence $x = 2$. The other possibility is that $2x - 1$ is negative, and hence $2x - 1 = -(-x + 5) = x - 5$. In this case, rearranging and combining like terms yields $x = -4$. Substituting $x = 2$ and $x = -4$ back into the original equation, we see that they are both valid solutions.

Note that the absolute value of a sum or difference applies to the sum or difference as a whole, not to the individual terms: in general, $|2x - 1|$ is not equal to $|2x + 1|$ or to $|2x| - 1$.

SPURIOUS SOLUTIONS

A **spurious solution** may arise when we square both sides of an equation as a step in solving it, or under certain other operations on the equation. It is a solution to the squared or otherwise modified equation that is *not* a solution of the original equation. To identify a spurious solution, it's useful when you solve an equation involving roots or absolute values to plug the solution back into the original equation to make sure it's valid.

CHOOSING WHICH VARIABLE TO ISOLATE IN TWO-VARIABLE EQUATIONS

Similar to methods for a one-variable equation, solving a two-variable equation involves isolating a variable: manipulating the equation so that a variable appears by itself on one side of the equation, and not at all on the other side. However, in a two-variable equation, you will usually only be able to isolate one of the variables; the other variable may appear on the other side along with constant terms, or with exponents or other functions.

Often one variable will be much more easily isolated than the other, and therefore that's the variable you should choose. If one variable appears with various exponents, and other only raised to the first power, the latter variable is the one to isolate: given the equation $a^2 + 2b = a^3 + b + 3$, the b only appears to the first power, whereas a appears squared and cubed, so b is the variable that can be solved for: combining like terms and isolating the b on the left side of the equation, we get $b = a^3 - a^2 + 3$. If both variables are equally easy to isolate, then it's best to isolate the independent variable, if one is defined; if the two variables are x and y, the convention is that y is the independent variable.

WORKING WITH INEQUALITIES

Commonly in algebra and other upper-level fields of math you find yourself working with mathematical expressions that do not equal each other. The statement comparing such expressions with symbols such as < (less than) or > (greater than) is called an *inequality*. An example of an inequality is $7x > 5$. To solve for x, simply divide both sides by 7 and the solution is shown to

228

be $x > \frac{5}{7}$. Graphs of the solution set of inequalities are represented on a number line. Open circles are used to show that an expression approaches a number but is never quite equal to that number.

Review Video: Inequalities
Visit mometrix.com/academy and enter code: 347842

Conditional inequalities are those with certain values for the variable that will make the condition true and other values for the variable where the condition will be false. **Absolute inequalities** can have any real number as the value for the variable to make the condition true, while there is no real number value for the variable that will make the condition false. Solving inequalities is done by following the same rules as for solving equations with the exception that when multiplying or dividing by a negative number the direction of the inequality sign must be flipped or reversed. **double inequalities** are situations where two inequality statements apply to the same variable expression. An example of this is $-c < ax + b < c$.

DETERMINING SOLUTIONS TO INEQUALITIES

To determine whether a coordinate is a solution of an inequality, you can substitute the values of the coordinate into the inequality, simplify, and check whether the resulting statement holds true. For instance, to determine whether $(-2, 4)$ is a solution of the inequality $y \geq -2x + 3$, substitute the values into the inequality, $4 \geq -2(-2) + 3$. Simplify the right side of the inequality and the result is $4 \geq 7$, which is a false statement. Therefore, the coordinate is not a solution of the inequality. You can also use this method to determine which part of the graph of an inequality is shaded. The graph of $y \geq -2x + 3$ includes the solid line $y = -2x + 3$ and, since it excludes the point $(-2, 4)$ to the left of the line, it is shaded to the right of the line.

FLIPPING INEQUALITY SIGNS

When given an inequality, we can always turn the entire inequality around, swapping the two sides of the inequality and changing the inequality sign. For instance, $x + 2 > 2x - 3$ is equivalent to $2x - 3 < x + 2$. Aside from that, normally the inequality does not change if we carry out the same operation on both sides of the inequality. There is, however, one principal exception: if we *multiply* or *divide* both sides of the inequality by a *negative number*, the inequality is flipped. For example, if we take the inequality $-2x < 6$ and divide both sides by -2, the inequality flips and we are left with $x > -3$. This *only* applies to multiplication and division, and only with negative numbers. Multiplying or dividing both sides by a positive number, or adding or subtracting any number regardless of sign, does not flip the inequality.

COMPOUND INEQUALITIES

A **compound inequality** is an equality that consists of two inequalities combined with *and* or *or*. The two components of a proper compound inequality must be of opposite type: that is, one must be greater than (or greater than or equal to), the other less than (or less than or equal to). For instance, "$x + 1 < 2$ or $x + 1 > 3$" is a compound inequality, as is "$2x \geq 4$ and $2x \leq 6$." An *and* inequality can be written more compactly by having one inequality on each side of the common part: "$2x \geq 1$ and $2x \leq 6$," can also be written as $1 \leq 2x \leq 6$.

In order for the compound inequality to be meaningful, the two parts of an *and* inequality must overlap; otherwise no numbers satisfy the inequality. On the other hand, if the two parts of an *or* inequality overlap, then *all* numbers satisfy the inequality and as such is usually not meaningful.

Solving a compound inequality requires solving each part separately. For example, given the compound inequality "$x + 1 < 2$ or $x + 1 > 3$," the first inequality, $x + 1 < 2$, reduces to $x < 1$, and

229

the second part, $x + 1 > 3$, reduces to $x > 2$, so the whole compound inequality can be written as "$x < 1$ or $x > 2$." Similarly, $1 \leq 2x \leq 6$ can be solved by dividing each term by 2, yielding $\frac{1}{2} \leq x \leq 3$.

SOLVING INEQUALITIES INVOLVING ABSOLUTE VALUES

To solve an inequality involving an absolute value, first isolate the term with the absolute value. Then proceed to treat the two cases separately as with an absolute value equation, but flipping the inequality in the case where the expression in the absolute value is negative (since that essentially involves multiplying both sides by -1.) The two cases are then combined into a compound inequality; if the absolute value is on the greater side of the inequality, then it is an *or* compound inequality, if on the lesser side, then it's an *and*.

Consider the inequality $2 + |x - 1| \geq 3$. We can isolate the absolute value term by subtracting 2 from both sides: $|x - 1| \geq 1$. Now, we're left with the two cases $x - 1 \geq 1$ or $x - 1 \leq -1$: note that in the latter, negative case, the inequality is flipped. $x - 1 \geq 1$ reduces to $x \geq 2$, and $x - 1 \leq -1$ reduces to $x \leq 0$. Since in the inequality $|x - 1| \geq 1$ the absolute value is on the greater side, the two cases combine into an *or* compound inequality, so the final, solved inequality is "$x \leq 0$ or $x \geq 2$."

SOLVING INEQUALITIES INVOLVING SQUARE ROOTS

Solving an inequality with a square root involves two parts. First, we solve the inequality as if it were an equation, isolating the square root and then squaring both sides of the equation. Second, we restrict the solution to the set of values of x for which the value inside the square root sign is non-negative.

For example, in the inequality, $\sqrt{x - 2} + 1 < 5$, we can isolate the square root by subtracting 1 from both sides, yielding $\sqrt{x - 2} < 4$. Squaring both sides of the inequality yields $x - 2 < 16$, so $x < 18$. Since we can't take the square root of a negative number, we also require the part inside the square root to be non-negative. In this case, that means $x - 2 \geq 0$. Adding 2 to both sides of the inequality yields $x \geq 2$. Our final answer is a compound inequality combining the two simple inequalities: $x \geq 2$ and $x < 18$, or $2 \leq x < 18$.

Note that we only get a compound inequality if the two simple inequalities are in opposite directions; otherwise we take the one that is more restrictive.

The same technique can be used for other even roots, such as fourth roots. It is *not*, however, used for cube roots or other odd roots—negative numbers *do* have cube roots, so the condition that the quantity inside the root sign cannot be negative does not apply.

SPECIAL CIRCUMSTANCES

Sometimes an inequality involving an absolute value or an even exponent is true for all values of x, and we don't need to do any further work to solve it. This is true if the inequality, once the absolute value or exponent term is isolated, says that term is greater than a negative number (or greater than or equal to zero). Since an absolute value or a number raised to an even exponent is *always* non-negative, this inequality is always true.

GRAPHICAL SOLUTIONS TO EQUATIONS AND INEQUALITIES

When equations are shown graphically, they are usually shown on a **Cartesian coordinate plane**. The Cartesian coordinate plane consists of two number lines placed perpendicular to each other, and intersecting at the zero point, also known as the origin. The horizontal number line is known as the x-axis, with positive values to the right of the origin, and negative values to the left of the origin.

The vertical number line is known as the *y*-axis, with positive values above the origin, and negative values below the origin. Any point on the plane can be identified by an ordered pair in the form (x, y), called coordinates. The *x*-value of the coordinate is called the abscissa, and the *y*-value of the coordinate is called the ordinate. The two number lines divide the plane into **four quadrants**: I, II, III, and IV.

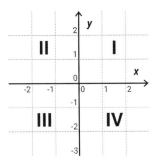

Note that in quadrant I $x > 0$ and $y > 0$, in quadrant II $x < 0$ and $y > 0$, in quadrant III $x < 0$ and $y < 0$, and in quadrant IV $x > 0$ and $y < 0$.

Recall that if the value of the slope of a line is positive, the line slopes upward from left to right. If the value of the slope is negative, the line slopes downward from left to right. If the *y*-coordinates are the same for two points on a line, the slope is 0 and the line is a **horizontal line**. If the *x*-coordinates are the same for two points on a line, there is no slope and the line is a **vertical line**. Two or more lines that have equivalent slopes are **parallel lines**. **Perpendicular lines** have slopes that are negative reciprocals of each other, such as $\frac{a}{b}$ and $\frac{-b}{a}$.

GRAPHING SIMPLE INEQUALITIES

To graph a simple inequality, we first mark on the number line the value that signifies the end point of the inequality. If the inequality is strict (involves a less than or greater than), we use a hollow circle; if it is not strict (less than or equal to or greater than or equal to), we use a solid circle. We then fill in the part of the number line that satisfies the inequality: to the left of the marked point for less than (or less than or equal to), to the right for greater than (or greater than or equal to).

For example, we would graph the inequality $x < 5$ by putting a hollow circle at 5 and filling in the part of the line to the left:

GRAPHING COMPOUND INEQUALITIES

To graph a compound inequality, we fill in both parts of the inequality for an *or* inequality, or the overlap between them for an *and* inequality. More specifically, we start by plotting the endpoints of each inequality on the number line. For an *or* inequality, we then fill in the appropriate side of the line for each inequality. Typically, the two component inequalities do not overlap, that means the shaded part is *outside* the two points. For an *and* inequality, we instead fill in the part of the line that meets both inequalities.

For the inequality "$x \leq -3$ or $x > 4$," we first put a solid circle at -3 and a hollow circle at 4. We then fill the parts of the line *outside* these circles:

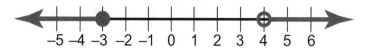

GRAPHING INEQUALITIES INCLUDING ABSOLUTE VALUES

An inequality with an absolute value can be converted to a compound inequality. To graph the inequality, first convert it to a compound inequality, and then graph that normally. If the absolute value is on the greater side of the inequality, we end up with an *or* inequality; we plot the endpoints of the inequality on the number line and fill in the part of the line *outside* those points. If the absolute value is on the smaller side of the inequality, we end up with an *and* inequality; we plot the endpoints of the inequality on the number line and fill in the part of the line *between* those points.

For example, the inequality $|x + 1| \geq 4$ can be rewritten as $x \geq 3$ or $x \leq -5$. We place solid circles at the points 3 and -5 and fill in the part of the line *outside* them:

GRAPHING EQUATIONS IN TWO VARIABLES

One way of graphing an equation in two variables is to plot enough points to get an idea for its shape, and then draw the appropriate curve through those points. A point can be plotted by substituting in a value for one variable and solving for the other. If the equation is linear, we only need two points, and can then draw a straight line between them.

For example, consider the equation $y = 2x - 1$. This is a linear equation—both variables only appear raised to the first power—so we only need two points. When $x = 0$, $y = 2(0) - 1 = -1$. When $x = 2$, $y = 2(2) - 1 = 3$. We can therefore choose the points $(0, -1)$ and $(2, 3)$, and draw a line between them:

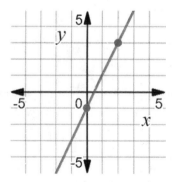

GRAPHING INEQUALITIES IN TWO VARIABLES

To graph an inequality in two variables, we first graph the border of the inequality. This means graphing the equation that we get if we replace the inequality sign with an equals sign. If the inequality is strict (> or <), we graph the border with a dashed or dotted line; if it is not strict (≥ or ≤), we use a solid line. We can then test any point not on the border to see if it satisfies the inequality. If it does, we shade in that side of the border; if not, we shade in the other side. As an example, consider $y > 2x + 2$. To graph this inequality, we first graph the border, $y = 2x + 2$. Since it is a strict inequality, we use a dashed line. Then, we choose a test point. This can be any point not on the border; in this case, we will choose the origin, $(0, 0)$. (This makes the calculation easy and is generally a good choice unless the border passes through the origin.) Putting this into the original inequality, we get $0 > 2(0) + 2$, i.e. $0 > 2$. This is *not* true, so we shade in the side of the border that does *not* include the point $(0, 0)$:

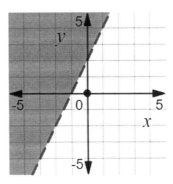

GRAPHING COMPOUND INEQUALITIES IN TWO VARIABLES

One way to graph a compound inequality in two variables is to first graph each of the component inequalities. For an *and* inequality, we then shade in only the parts where the two graphs overlap; for an *or* inequality, we shade in any region that pertains to either of the individual inequalities.

Consider the graph of "$y \geq x - 1$ *and* $y \leq -x$":

We first shade in the individual inequalities:

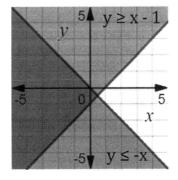

Now, since the compound inequality has an *and*, we only leave shaded the overlap—the part that pertains to *both* inequalities:

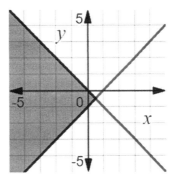

If instead the inequality had been "$y \geq x - 1$ *or* $y \leq -x$," our final graph would involve the *total* shaded area:

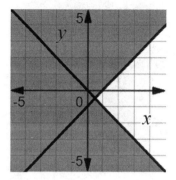

SOLVING SYSTEMS OF EQUATIONS

Systems of equations are a set of simultaneous equations that all use the same variables. A solution to a system of equations must be true for each equation in the system. **Consistent systems** are those with at least one solution. **Inconsistent systems** are systems of equations that have no solution.

> **Review Video: Systems of Equations**
> Visit mometrix.com/academy and enter code: 658153

SUBSTITUTION

To solve a system of linear equations by **substitution**, start with the easier equation and solve for one of the variables. Express this variable in terms of the other variable. Substitute this expression in the other equation, and solve for the other variable. The solution should be expressed in the form (x, y). Substitute the values into both of the original equations to check your answer. Consider the following system of equations:

$$x + 6y = 15$$
$$3x - 12y = 18$$

Solving the first equation for x: $x = 15 - 6y$

Substitute this value in place of x in the second equation, and solve for y:

$$3(15 - 6y) - 12y = 18$$
$$45 - 18y - 12y = 18$$
$$30y = 27$$
$$y = \frac{27}{30} = \frac{9}{10} = 0.9$$

Plug this value for y back into the first equation to solve for x:

$$x = 15 - 6(0.9) = 15 - 5.4 = 9.6$$

Check both equations if you have time:

$$9.6 + 6(0.9) = 15 \qquad 3(9.6) - 12(0.9) = 18$$
$$9.6 + 5.4 = 15 \qquad 28.8 - 10.8 = 18$$
$$15 = 15 \qquad 18 = 18$$

Therefore, the solution is (9.6, 0.9).

ELIMINATION

To solve a system of equations using **elimination**, begin by rewriting both equations in standard form $Ax + By = C$. Check to see if the coefficients of one pair of like variables add to zero. If not, multiply one or both of the equations by a non-zero number to make one set of like variables add to zero. Add the two equations to solve for one of the variables. Substitute this value into one of the original equations to solve for the other variable. Check your work by substituting into the other equation. Now consider let's look at solving the following system using the elimination method:

$$5x + 6y = 4$$
$$x + 2y = 4$$

If we multiply the first equation by -3, we can eliminate the y terms:

$$5x + 6y = 4$$
$$-3x - 6y = -12$$

Add the equations together and solve for x:

$$2x = -8$$
$$x = \frac{-8}{2} = -4$$

Plug the value for x back in to either of the original equations and solve for y:

$$-4 + 2y = 4$$
$$y = \frac{4 + 4}{2} = 4$$

Check both equations if you have time:

$$5(-4) + 6(4) = 4 \qquad -4 + 2(4) = 4$$
$$-20 + 24 = 4 \qquad -4 + 8 = 4$$
$$4 = 4 \qquad 4 = 4$$

Therefore, the solution is (-4, 4).

> **Review Video: Substitution and Elimination for Solving Linear Systems**
> Visit mometrix.com/academy and enter code: 958611

GRAPHICALLY

To solve a system of linear equations **graphically**, plot both equations on the same graph. The solution of the equations is the point where both lines cross. If the lines do not cross (are parallel), then there is **no solution**.

For example, consider the following system of equations:

$$y = 2x + 7$$
$$y = -x + 1$$

Since these equations are given in slope-intercept form, they are easy to graph; the y intercepts of the lines are $(0, 7)$ and $(0, 1)$. The respective slopes are 2 and –1, thus the graphs look like this:

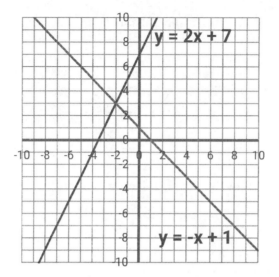

The two lines intersect at the point $(-2, 3)$, thus this is the solution to the system of equations.

Solving a system graphically is generally only practical if both coordinates of the solution are integers; otherwise the intersection will lie between gridlines on the graph and the coordinates will be difficult or impossible to determine exactly. It also helps if, as in this example, the equations are in slope-intercept form or some other form that makes them easy to graph. Otherwise, another method of solution (by substitution or elimination) is likely to be more useful.

SOLVING SYSTEMS OF EQUATIONS USING THE TRACE FEATURE

Using the **trace feature** on a calculator requires that you rewrite each equation, isolating the y-variable on one side of the equal sign. Enter both equations in the graphing calculator and plot the graphs simultaneously. Use the trace cursor to find where the two lines cross. Use the zoom feature if necessary to obtain more accurate results. Always check your answer by substituting into the original equations. The trace method is likely to be less accurate than other methods due to the resolution of graphing calculators, but is a useful tool to provide an approximate answer.

CALCULATIONS USING POINTS

Sometimes you need to perform calculations using only points on a graph as input data. Using points, you can determine what the **midpoint** and **distance** are. If you know the equation for a line you can calculate the distance between the line and the point.

To find the **midpoint** of two points (x_1, y_1) and (x_2, y_2), average the x-coordinates to get the x-coordinate of the midpoint, and average the y-coordinates to get the y-coordinate of the midpoint. The formula is: $\left(\frac{x_1+x_2}{2}, \frac{y_1+y_2}{2}\right)$.

The **distance** between two points is the same as the length of the hypotenuse of a right triangle with the two given points as endpoints, and the two sides of the right triangle parallel to the x-axis and y-axis, respectively. The length of the segment parallel to the x-axis is the difference between the x-coordinates of the two points. The length of the segment parallel to the y-axis is the difference between the y-coordinates of the two points. Use the Pythagorean theorem $a^2 + b^2 = c^2$ or $c = \sqrt{a^2 + b^2}$ to find the distance. The formula is $d = \sqrt{(x_2 - x_1)^2 + (y_2 - y_1)^2}$.

When a line is in the format $Ax + By + C = 0$, where A, B, and C are coefficients, you can use a point (x_1, y_1) not on the line and apply the formula $d = \frac{|Ax_1 + By_1 + C|}{\sqrt{A^2 + B^2}}$ to find the distance between the line and the point (x_1, y_1).

PRACTICE

P1. Seeing the equation $2x + 4 = 4x + 7$, a student divides the first terms on each side by 2, yielding $x + 4 = 2x + 7$, and then combines like terms to get $x = -3$. However, this is incorrect, as can be seen by substituting –3 into the original equation. Explain what is wrong with the student's reasoning.

P2. Describe the steps necessary to solve the equation $2x + 1 - x = 4 + 3x + 7$.

P3. Describe the steps necessary to solve the equation $2(x + 5) = 7(4 - x)$.

P4. Find all real solutions to the equation $1 - \sqrt{x} = 2$.

P5. Find all real solutions to the equation $|x + 1| = 2x + 5$.

P6. Solve for x: $-x + 2\sqrt{x + 5} + 1 = 3$.

P7. Ray earns $10 an hour at his job. Write an equation for his earnings as a function of time spent working. Determine how long Ray has to work in order to earn $360.

P8. Simplify the following: $3x + 2 + 2y = 5y - 7 + |2x - 1|$

P9. Analyze the following inequalities:

    (a) $2 - |x + 1| < 3$
    (b) $2(x - 1)^2 + 7 \leq 1$

P10. Graph the following on a number line:

    (a) $x \geq 3$
    (b) $-2 \leq x \leq 6$
    (c) $|x| < 2$

P11. Graph $y = x^2 - 3x + 2$.

P12. Solve the following systems of equations:

    (a) $3x + 4y = 9$
        $-12x + 7y = 10$

    (b) $-3x + 2y = -1$
        $4x - 5y = 6$

P13. Find the distance and midpoint between points (2, 4) and (8,6).

PRACTICE SOLUTIONS

P1. As stated, it's easy to verify that the student's solution is incorrect: $2(-3) + 4 = -2$ and $4(-3) + 7 = -5$; clearly $-2 \neq -5$. The mistake was in the first step, which illustrates a common type of error in solving equations. The student tried to simplify the two variable terms by dividing them by 2. However, it's not valid to multiply or divide only one term on each side of an equation by a number; when multiplying or dividing, the operation must be applied to *every* term in the equation. So, dividing by 2 would yield not $x + 4 = 2x + 7$, but $x + 2 = 2x + \frac{7}{2}$. While this is now valid, that fraction is inconvenient to work with, so this may not be the best first step in solving the equation. Rather, it may have been better to first combine like terms: subtracting $4x$ from both sides yields $-2x + 4 = 7$; subtracting 4 from both sides yields $-2x = 3$; and *now* we can divide both sides by –2 to get $x = -\frac{3}{2}$.

P2. Our ultimate goal is to isolate the variable, x. To that end we first move all the terms containing x to the left side of the equation, and all the constant terms to the right side. Note that when we move a term to the other side of the equation its sign changes. We are therefore now left with $2x - x - 3x = 4 + 7 - 1$.

Next, we combine the like terms on each side of the equation, adding and subtracting the terms as appropriate. This leaves us with $-2x = 10$.

At this point, we're almost done; all that remains is to divide both sides by -2 to leave the x by itself. We now have our solution, $x = -5$. We can verify that this is a correct solution by substituting it back into the original equation.

P3. Generally, in equations that have a sum or difference of terms multiplied by another value or expression, the first step is to multiply those terms, distributing as necessary: $2(x + 5) = 2(x) + 2(5) = 2x + 10$, and $7(4 - x) = 7(4) - 7(x) = 28 - 7x$. So, the equation becomes $2x + 10 = 28 - 7x$. We can now add $7x$ to both sides to eliminate the variable from the right-hand side: $9x + 10 = 28$. Similarly, we can subtract 10 from both sides to move all the constants to the right: $9x = 18$. Finally, we can divide both sides by 9, yielding the final answer, $x = 2$.

P4. It's not hard to isolate the root: subtract one from both sides, yielding $-\sqrt{x} = 1$. Finally, multiply both sides by -1, yielding $\sqrt{x} = -1$. Squaring both sides of the equation yields $x = 1$. However, if we plug this back into the original equation, we get $1 - \sqrt{1} = 2$, which is false. Therefore $x = 1$ is a spurious solution, and the equation has no real solutions.

P5. This equation has two possibilities: $x + 1 = 2x + 5$, which simplifies to $x = -4$; or $x + 1 = -(2x + 5) = -2x - 5$, which simplifies to $x = -2$. However, if we try substituting both values back into the original equation, we see that only $x = -2$ yields a true statement. $x = -4$ is a spurious solution; $x = -2$ is the only valid solution to the equation.

P6. Start by isolating the term with the root. We can do that by moving the $-x$ and the 1 to the other side, yielding $2\sqrt{x + 5} = 3 + x - 1$, or $2\sqrt{x + 5} = x + 2$. Dividing both sides of the equation by 2 would give us a fractional term that could be messy to deal with, so we won't do that for now. Instead, we square both sides of the equation; note that on the left-hand side the 2 is outside the square root sign, so we have to square it. As a result, we get $4(x + 5) = (x + 2)^2$. Expanding both sides gives us $4x + 20 = x^2 + 4x + 4$. In this case, we see that we have $4x$ on both sides, so we can cancel the $4x$ (which is what allows us to solve this equation despite the different powers of x). We now have $20 = x^2 + 4$, or $x^2 = 16$. Since the variable is raised to an even power, we need to take the positive and negative roots, so $x = \pm 4$: that is, $x = 4$ or $x = -4$. Substituting both values into the original equation, we see that $x = 4$ satisfies the equation but $x = -4$ does not; hence $x = -4$ is a spurious solution, and the only solution to the equation is $x = 4$.

P7. The number of dollars that Ray earns is dependent on the number of hours he works, so earnings will be represented by the dependent variable y and hours worked will be represented by the independent variable x. He earns 10 dollars per hour worked, so his earning can be calculated as $y = 10x$. To calculate the number of hours Ray must work in order to earn \$360, plug in 360 for y and solve for x:

$$360 = 10x$$
$$x = \frac{360}{10} = 36$$

P8. To simplify this equation, we must isolate one of its variables on one side of the equation. In this case, the x appears under an absolute value sign, which makes it difficult to isolate. The y, on the other hand, only appears without an exponent—the equation is linear in y. We will therefore choose to isolate the y. The first step, then, is to move all the terms with y to the left side of the equation, which we can do by subtracting $5y$ from both sides:

$$3x + 2 - 3y = -7 + |2x - 1|$$

We can then move all the terms that do *not* include y to the right side of the equation, by subtracting $3x$ and 2 from both sides of the equation:

$$-3y = -3x - 9 + |2x - 1|$$

Finally, we can isolate the y by dividing both sides by –3.

$$y = x + 3 - \frac{1}{3}|2x - 1|$$

This is as far as we can simplify the equation; we cannot combine the terms inside and outside the absolute value sign. We can therefore consider the equation to be solved.

P9. (a) Subtracting 2 from both sides yields $-|x + 1| < 1$; multiplying by -1—and flipping the inequality, since we're multiplying by a negative number—yields $|x + 1| > -1$. But since the absolute value cannot be negative, it's *always* greater than –1, so this inequality is true for all values of x.

(b) Subtracting 7 from both sides yields $2(x - 1)^2 \leq -6$; dividing by 2 yields $(x - 1)^2 \leq -3$. But $(x - 1)^2$ must be nonnegative, and hence cannot be less than or equal to -3; this inequality has no solution.

P10. (a) We would graph the inequality $x \geq 3$ by putting a solid circle at 3 and filling in the part of the line to the right:

(b) The inequality $-2 \leq x \leq 6$ is equivalent to "$x \geq -2$ and $x \leq 6$." To plot this compound inequality, we first put solid circles at –2 and 6, and then fill in the part of the line *between* these circles:

(c) The inequality $|x| < 2$ can be rewritten as "$x > -2$ and $x < 2$." We place hollow circles at the points –2 and 2 and fill in the part of the line between them:

P11. The equation $y = x^2 - 3x + 2$ is not linear, so we may need more points to get an idea of its shape. By substituting in different values of x, we find the points $(0, 2)$, $(1, 0)$, $(2, 0)$, and $(3, 2)$. That may be enough to give us an idea of the shape, though we can find more points if we're still not sure:

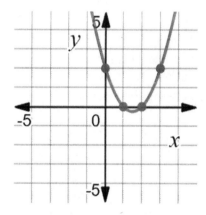

P12. (a) If we multiply the first equation by 4, we can eliminate the x terms:

$$12x + 16y = 36$$
$$-12x + 7y = 10$$

Add the equations together and solve for y:

$$23y = 46$$
$$y = 2$$

Plug the value for y back in to either of the original equations and solve for x:

$$3x + 4(2) = 10$$
$$x = \frac{10 - 8}{3} = \frac{2}{3}$$

The solution is $\left(\frac{2}{3}, 2\right)$

(b) Solving the first equation for y:

$$-3x + 2y = -1$$
$$2y = 3x - 1$$
$$y = \frac{3x - 1}{2}$$

240

Substitute this expression in place of y in the second equation, and solve for x:

$$4x - 5\left(\frac{3x - 1}{2}\right) = 6$$
$$4x - \frac{15x}{2} + \frac{5}{2} = 6$$
$$8x - 15x + 5 = 12$$
$$-7x = 7$$
$$x = -1$$

Plug the value for x back in to either of the original equations and solve for y:

$$-3(-1) + 2y = -1$$
$$3 + 2y = -1$$
$$2y = -4$$
$$y = -2$$

The solution is $(-1, -2)$

P13. Use the formulas for distance and midpoint:

$$\text{Distance} = \sqrt{(x_2 - x_1)^2 + (y_2 - y_1)^2}$$
$$= \sqrt{(8 - 2)^2 + (6 - 4)^2}$$
$$= \sqrt{(6)^2 + (2)^2}$$
$$= \sqrt{36 + 4}$$
$$= \sqrt{40} \text{ or } 2\sqrt{10}$$

$$\text{Midpoint} = \left(\frac{x_1 + x_2}{2}, \frac{y_1 + y_2}{2}\right)$$
$$= \left(\frac{2 + 8}{2}, \frac{4 + 6}{2}\right)$$
$$= \left(\frac{10}{2}, \frac{10}{2}\right)$$
$$= (5,5)$$

Polynomial Algebra

POLYNOMIALS

Equations are made up of monomials and polynomials. A **monomial** is a single variable or product of constants and variables, such as x, $2x$, or $\frac{2}{x}$. There will never be addition or subtraction symbols in a monomial. Like monomials have like variables, but they may have different coefficients. **Polynomials** are algebraic expressions which use addition and subtraction to combine two or more monomials. Two terms make a **binomial**, three terms make a **trinomial**, etc. The **degree of a monomial** is the sum of the exponents of the variables. The **degree of a polynomial** is the highest degree of any individual term.

> **Review Video: Polynomials**
> Visit mometrix.com/academy and enter code: 305005

SIMPLIFYING POLYNOMIALS

Simplifying polynomials requires combining like terms. The like terms in a polynomial expression are those that have the same variable raised to the same power. It is often helpful to connect the like terms with arrows or lines in order to separate them from the other monomials. Once you have determined the like terms, you can rearrange the polynomial by placing them together. Remember to include the sign that is in front of each term. Once the like terms are placed together, you can apply each operation and simplify. When adding and subtracting polynomials, only add and subtract the **coefficient**, or the number part; the variable and exponent stay the same.

THE FOIL METHOD

In general, multiplying polynomials is done by multiplying each term in one polynomial by each term in the other and adding the results. In the specific case for multiplying binomials, there is useful acronym, FOIL, that can help you make sure to cover each combination of terms. The **FOIL method** for $(Ax + By)(Cx + Dy)$ would be:

F	Multiply the *first* terms of each binomial	$(\overset{first}{\overbrace{Ax}} + By)(\overset{first}{\overbrace{Cx}} + Dy)$	ACx^2
O	Multiply the *outer* terms	$(\overset{outer}{\overbrace{Ax}} + By)(Cx + \overset{outer}{\overbrace{Dy}})$	$ADxy$
I	Multiply the *inner* terms	$(Ax + \overset{inner}{\overbrace{By}})(\overset{inner}{\overbrace{Cx}} + Dy)$	$BCxy$
L	Multiply the *last* terms of each binomial	$(Ax + \overset{last}{\overbrace{By}})(Cx + \overset{last}{\overbrace{Dy}})$	BDy^2

Then add up the result of each and combine like terms: $ACx^2 + (AD + BC)xy + BDy^2$.

For example, using the FOIL method on binomials $(x + 2)$ and $(x - 3)$:

$$\begin{aligned}
\text{First:} \quad & (\boxed{x} + 2)(\boxed{x} + (-3)) \ \rightarrow \ (x)(x) \ = x^2 \\
\text{Outer:} \quad & (\boxed{x} + 2)(x + \boxed{(-3)}) \ \rightarrow \ (x)(-3) \ = -3x \\
\text{Inner:} \quad & (x + \boxed{2})(\boxed{x} + (-3)) \ \rightarrow \ (2)(x) \ = 2x \\
\text{Last:} \quad & (x + \boxed{2})(x + \boxed{(-3)}) \ \rightarrow \ (2)(-3) \ = -6
\end{aligned}$$

This results in: $(x^2) + (-3x) + (2x) + (-6)$

Combine like terms: $x^2 + (-3 + 2)x + (-6) = x^2 - x - 6$

Review Video: Multiplying Terms Using the FOIL Method
Visit mometrix.com/academy and enter code: 854792

DIVIDING POLYNOMIALS

To divide polynomials, set up a long division problem, dividing a polynomial by either a monomial or another polynomial of equal or lesser degree.

When **dividing by a monomial**, divide each term of the polynomial by the monomial.

When **dividing by a polynomial**, begin by arranging the terms of each polynomial in order of one variable. You may arrange in ascending or descending order, but be consistent with both polynomials. To get the first term of the quotient, divide the first term of the dividend by the first term of the divisor. Multiply the first term of the quotient by the entire divisor and subtract that product from the dividend. Repeat for the second and successive terms until you either get a remainder of zero or a remainder whose degree is less than the degree of the divisor. If the quotient has a remainder, write the answer as a mixed expression in the form:

$$\text{quotient} + \frac{\text{remainder}}{\text{divisor}}$$

For example, we can evaluate the following expression in the same way as long division:

$$\frac{x^3 - 3x^2 - 2x + 5}{x - 5}$$

$$
\begin{array}{r}
x^2 + 2x + 8 \\
x - 5 \overline{\smash{\big)}\ x^3 - 3x^2 - 2x + 5} \\
\underline{x^3 - 5x^2} \\
2x^2 - 2x \\
\underline{2x^2 - 10x} \\
8x + 5 \\
\underline{8x + 40} \\
45
\end{array}
$$

$$\frac{x^3 - 3x^2 - 2x + 5}{x - 5} = x^2 + 2x + 8 + \frac{45}{x - 5}$$

When **factoring** a polynomial, first check for a common monomial factor, that is look to see if each coefficient has a common factor or if each term has an x in it. If the factor is a trinomial but not a perfect trinomial square, look for a factorable form, such as one of these:

$$x^2 + (a + b)x + ab = (x + a)(x + b)$$
$$(ac)x^2 + (ad + bc)x + bd = (ax + b)(cx + d)$$

For factors with four terms, look for groups to factor. Once you have found the factors, write the original polynomial as the product of all the factors. Make sure all of the polynomial factors are prime. Monomial factors may be *prime* or *composite*. Check your work by multiplying the factors to make sure you get the original polynomial.

Below are patterns of some special products to remember to help make factoring easier:

- Perfect trinomial squares: $x^2 + 2xy + y^2 = (x + y)^2$ or $x^2 - 2xy + y^2 = (x - y)^2$
- Difference between two squares: $x^2 - y^2 = (x + y)(x - y)$
- Sum of two cubes: $x^3 + y^3 = (x + y)(x^2 - xy + y^2)$
    - Note: the second factor is *not* the same as a perfect trinomial square, so do not try to factor it further.
- Difference between two cubes: $x^3 - y^3 = (x - y)(x^2 + xy + y^2)$
    - Again, the second factor is *not* the same as a perfect trinomial square.
- Perfect cubes: $x^3 + 3x^2y + 3xy^2 + y^3 = (x + y)^3$ and $x^3 - 3x^2y + 3xy^2 - y^3 = (x - y)^3$

RATIONAL EXPRESSIONS

Rational expressions are fractions with polynomials in both the numerator and the denominator; the value of the polynomial in the denominator cannot be equal to zero. Be sure to keep track of values that make the denominator of the original expression zero as the final result inherits the same restrictions. For example, a denominator of $x - 3$ indicates that the expression is not defined when $x = 3$ and as such, regardless of any operations done to the expression, it remains undefined there.

To **add or subtract** rational expressions, first find the common denominator, then rewrite each fraction as an equivalent fraction with the common denominator. Finally, add or subtract the numerators to get the numerator of the answer, and keep the common denominator as the denominator of the answer.

When **multiplying** rational expressions factor each polynomial and cancel like factors (a factor which appears in both the numerator and the denominator). Then, multiply all remaining factors in the numerator to get the numerator of the product, and multiply the remaining factors in the denominator to get the denominator of the product. Remember: cancel entire factors, not individual terms.

To **divide** rational expressions, take the reciprocal of the divisor (the rational expression you are dividing by) and multiply by the dividend.

SIMPLIFYING RATIONAL EXPRESSIONS

To simplify a rational expression, factor the numerator and denominator completely. Factors that are the same and appear in the numerator and denominator have a ratio of 1. For example, look at the following expression:

$$\frac{x-1}{1-x^2}$$

The denominator, $(1-x^2)$, is a difference of squares. It can be factored as $(1-x)(1+x)$. The factor $1-x$ and the numerator $x-1$ are opposites and have a ratio of –1. Rewrite the numerator as $-1(1-x)$. So, the rational expression can be simplified as follows:

$$\frac{x-1}{1-x^2} = \frac{-1(1-x)}{(1-x)(1+x)} = \frac{-1}{1+x}$$

Note that since the original expression is only defined for $x \neq \{-1,1\}$, the simplified expression has the same restrictions.

SOLVING QUADRATIC EQUATIONS

Quadratic equations are a special set of trinomials of the form $y = ax^2 + bx + c$ that occur commonly in math and real world applications. The **roots** of a quadratic equation are the solutions that satisfy the equation when $y = 0$; in other words, where the graph touches the x-axis. There are several ways to determine these solutions including using the quadratic formula, factoring, completing the square, and graphing the function.

QUADRATIC FORMULA

The **quadratic formula** is used to solve quadratic equations when other methods are more difficult. To use the quadratic formula to solve a quadratic equation, begin by rewriting the equation in standard form $ax^2 + bx + c = 0$, where a, b, and c are coefficients. Once you have identified the values of the coefficients, substitute those values into the quadratic formula

$$x = \frac{-b \pm \sqrt{b^2 - 4ac}}{2a}$$

Evaluate the equation and simplify the expression. Again, check each root by substituting into the original equation. In the quadratic formula, the portion of the formula under the radical ($b^2 - 4ac$) is called the **discriminant**. If the discriminant is zero, there is only one root: $-\frac{b}{2a}$. If the discriminant is positive, there are two different real roots. If the discriminant is negative, there are no real roots, you will instead find complex roots. Often these solutions don't make sense in context and are ignored.

> **Review Video: Using the Quadratic Formula**
> Visit mometrix.com/academy and enter code: 163102

FACTORING

To solve a quadratic equation by factoring, begin by rewriting the equation in standard form, $x^2 + bx + c = 0$. Remember that the goal of factoring is to find numbers f and g such that $(x + f)(x + g) = x^2 + (f + g)x + fg$, in other words $(f + g) = b$ and $fg = c$ or . This can be a really useful method when b and c are integers. Determine the factors of c and look for pairs that could sum to b.

For example, consider finding the roots of $x^2 + 6x - 16 = 0$. The factors of -16 include, -4 and 4, -8 and 2, -2 and 8, -1 and 16, and 1 and -16. The factors that sum to 6 are -2 and 8. Write these factors as the product of two binomials, $0 = (x - 2)(x + 8)$. Finally, since these binomials multiply together to equal zero, set them each equal to zero and solve each for x. This results in $x - 2 = 0$, which simplifies to $x = 2$ and $x + 8 = 0$, which simplifies to $x = -8$. Therefore, the roots of the equation are 2 and -8.

> **Review Video: Factoring Quadratic Equations**
> Visit mometrix.com/academy and enter code: 336566

COMPLETING THE SQUARE

One way to find the roots of a quadratic equation is to find a way to manipulate it such that it follows the form of a perfect square ($x^2 + 2px + p^2$) by adding and subtracting a constant. This process is called **completing the square**. In other words, if are given a quadratic that is not a perfect square, $x^2 + bx + c = 0$, you can find a constant d that could be added in to make it a perfect square:

$$x^2 + bx + c + (d - d) = 0; \ \{\text{Let } b = 2p \text{ and } c + d = p^2\}$$
$$\text{then: } x^2 + 2px + p^2 - d = 0 \text{ and } d = \frac{b^2}{4} - c$$

Once you have completed the square you can find the roots of the resulting equation:

$$x^2 + 2px + p^2 - d = 0$$
$$(x + p)^2 = d$$
$$x + p = \pm\sqrt{d}$$
$$x = -p \pm \sqrt{d}$$

It is worth noting that substituting the original expressions into this solution gives the same result as the quadratic formula where $a = 1$:

$$x = -p \pm \sqrt{d} = -\frac{b}{2} \pm \sqrt{\frac{b^2}{4} - c} = -\frac{b}{2} \pm \frac{\sqrt{b^2 - 4c}}{2} = \frac{-b \pm \sqrt{b^2 - 4c}}{2}$$

Completing the square can be seen as arranging block representations of each of the terms to be as close to a square as possible and then filling in the gaps. For example, consider the quadratic expression $x^2 + 6x + 2$:

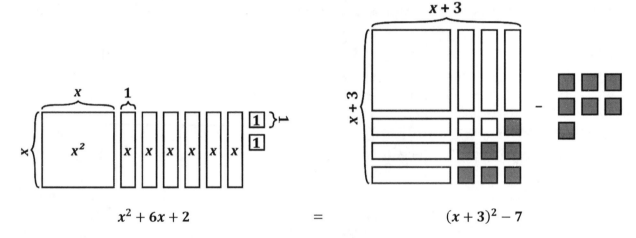

$$x^2 + 6x + 2 \qquad = \qquad (x + 3)^2 - 7$$

USING GIVEN ROOTS TO FIND QUADRATIC EQUATION

One way to find the roots of a quadratic equation is to factor the equation and use the **zero product property**, setting each factor of the equation equal to zero to find the corresponding root. We can use this technique in reverse to find an equation given its roots. Each root corresponds to a linear equation which in turn corresponds to a factor of the quadratic equation.

For example, we can find a quadratic equation whose roots are $x = 2$ and $x = -1$. The root $x = 2$ corresponds to the equation $x - 2 = 0$, and the root $x = -1$ corresponds to the equation $x + 1 = 0$.

These two equations correspond to the factors $(x - 2)$ and $(x + 1)$, from which we can derive the equation $(x - 2)(x + 1) = 0$, or $x^2 - x - 2 = 0$.

Any integer multiple of this entire equation will also yield the same roots, as the integer will simply cancel out when the equation is factored. For example, $2x^2 - 2x - 4 = 0$ factors as $2(x - 2)(x + 1) = 0$.

SOLVING A SYSTEM OF EQUATIONS CONSISTING OF A LINEAR EQUATION AND A QUADRATIC EQUATION

ALGEBRAICALLY

Generally, the simplest way to solve a system of equations consisting of a linear equation and a quadratic equation algebraically is through the method of substitution. One possible strategy is to solve the linear equation for y and then substitute that expression into the quadratic equation. After expansion and combining like terms, this will result in a new quadratic equation for x which, like all quadratic equations, may have zero, one, or two solutions. Plugging each solution for x back into one of the original equations will then produce the corresponding value of y.

For example, consider the following system of equations:

$$x + y = 1$$
$$y = (x + 3)^2 - 2$$

We can solve the linear equation for y to yield $y = -x + 1$. Substituting this expression into the quadratic equation produces $-x + 1 = (x + 3)^2 - 2$. We can simplify this equation:

$$-x + 1 = (x + 3)^2 - 2$$
$$-x + 1 = x^2 + 6x + 9 - 2$$
$$-x + 1 = x^2 + 6x + 7$$
$$0 = x^2 + 7x + 6$$

This quadratic equation can be factored as $(x + 1)(x + 6) = 0$. It therefore has two solutions: $x_1 = -1$ and $x_2 = -6$. Plugging each of these back into the original linear equation yields $y_1 = -x_1 + 1 = -(-1) + 1 = 2$ and $y_2 = -x_2 + 1 = -(-6) + 1 = 7$. Thus, this system of equations has two solutions, $(-1, 2)$ and $(-6, 7)$.

It may help to check your work by putting each x and y value back into the original equations and verifying that they do provide a solution.

GRAPHICALLY

To solve a system of equations consisting of a linear equation and a quadratic equation graphically, plot both equations on the same graph. The linear equation will of course produce a straight line, while the quadratic equation will produce a parabola. These two graphs will intersect at zero, one, or two points; each point of intersection is a solution of the system.

For example, consider the following system of equations:

$$y = -2x + 2$$
$$y = -2x^2 + 4x + 2$$

The linear equation describes a line with a y-intercept of $(0, 2)$ and a slope of -2.

To graph the quadratic equation, we can first find the vertex of the parabola: the x-coordinate of the vertex is $h = -\frac{b}{2a} = -\frac{4}{2(-2)} = 1$, and the y coordinate is $k = -2(1)^2 + 4(1) + 2 = 4$. Thus, the vertex lies at $(1, 4)$. To get a feel for the rest of the parabola, we can plug in a few more values of x to find more points; by putting in $x = 2$ and $x = 3$ in the quadratic equation, we find that the points

$(2, 2)$ and $(3, -4)$ lie on the parabola; by symmetry thus do $(0, 2)$ and $(-1, -4)$. We can now plot both equations:

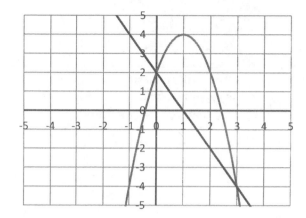

These two curves intersect at the points $(0, 2)$ and $(3, -4)$, thus these are the solutions of the equation.

PRACTICE

P1. Expand the following polynomials:

    (a) $(x + 3)(x - 7)(2x)$

    (b) $(x + 2)^2(x - 2)^2$

    (c) $(x^2 + 5x + 5)(3x - 1)$

P2. Find the roots of $y = 2x^2 + 8x + 4$.

P3. Find a quadratic equation with roots $x = 4$ and $x = -6$.

P4. Evaluate the following rational expressions:

    (a) $\dfrac{x^3 - 2x^2 - 5x + 6}{3x + 6}$

    (b) $\dfrac{x^2 + 4x + 4}{4 - x^2}$

PRACTICE SOLUTIONS

P1. (a) Apply the FOIL method and the distributive property of multiplication:

$$(x + 3)(x - 7)(2x) = (x^2 - 7x + 3x - 21)(2x)$$
$$= (x^2 - 4x - 21)(2x)$$
$$= 2x^3 - 8x - 42x$$

    (b) Note the difference of squares form:

$$(x + 2)^2(x - 2)^2 = (x + 2)(x + 2)(x - 2)(x - 2)$$
$$= [(x + 2)(x - 2)][(x + 2)(x - 2)]$$
$$= (x^2 - 4)(x^2 - 4)$$
$$= x^4 - 8x^2 + 16$$

(c) Multiply each pair of monomials and combine like terms:

$$(x^2 + 5x + 5)(3x - 1) = 3x^3 + 15x^2 + 15x - x^2 - 5x - 5$$
$$= 3x^3 + 14x^2 + 10x - 5$$

P2. First, substitute 0 in for y in the quadratic equation: $0 = 2x^2 + 8x + 4$

Next, try to factor the quadratic equation. Since $a \neq 1$, list the factors of ac, or 8:

$$(1, 8), (-1, -8), (2, 4), (-2, -4)$$

Look for the factors of ac that add up to b, or 8. Since none do, the equation cannot be factored with whole numbers. Substitute the values of a, b, and c into the quadratic formula, $x = \frac{-b \pm \sqrt{b^2 - 4ac}}{2a}$:

$$x = \frac{-8 \pm \sqrt{8^2 - 4(2)(4)}}{2(2)}$$

Use the order of operations to simplify:

$$x = \frac{-8 \pm \sqrt{64 - 32}}{4}$$
$$x = \frac{-8 \pm \sqrt{32}}{4}$$

Reduce and simplify:

$$x = \frac{-8 \pm \sqrt{(16)(2)}}{4}$$
$$x = \frac{-8 \pm 4\sqrt{2}}{4}$$
$$x = -2 \pm \sqrt{2}$$
$$x = \left(-2 + \sqrt{2}\right) \text{ and } \left(-2 - \sqrt{2}\right)$$

P3. The root $x = 4$ corresponds to the equation $x - 4 = 0$, and the root $x = -6$ corresponds to the equation $x + 6 = 0$. These two equations correspond to the factors $(x - 4)$ and $(x + 6)$, from which we can derive the equation $(x - 4)(x + 6) = 0$, or $x^2 - 10x - 24 = 0$.

P4. (a) Rather than trying to factor the fourth-degree polynomial, we can use long division:

$$\frac{x^3 - 2x^2 - 5x + 6}{3x + 6} = \frac{x^3 - 2x^2 - 5x + 6}{3(x + 2)}$$

$$
\begin{array}{r}
x^2 - 4x + 3 \\
x + 2 \overline{)\ x^3 - 2x^2 - 5x + 6} \\
\underline{x^3 + 2x^2} \\
-4x^2 - 5x \\
\underline{-4x^2 - 8x} \\
3x + 6 \\
\underline{3x + 6} \\
0
\end{array}
$$

$$\frac{x^3 - 2x^2 - 5x + 6}{3(x + 2)} = \frac{x^2 - 4x + 3}{3}$$

Note that since the original expression is only defined for $x \neq \{-2\}$, the simplified expression has the same restrictions.

(b) The denominator, $(4 - x^2)$, is a difference of squares. It can be factored as $(2 - x)(2 + x)$. The numerator, $(x^2 + 4x + 4)$, is a perfect square. It can be factored as $(x + 2)(x + 2)$. So, the rational expression can be simplified as follows:

$$\frac{x^2 + 4x + 4}{4 - x^2} = \frac{(x + 2)(x + 2)}{(2 - x)(2 + x)} = \frac{(x + 2)}{(2 - x)}$$

Note that since the original expression is only defined for $x \neq \{-2, 2\}$, the simplified expression has the same restrictions.

Functions

FUNCTION AND RELATION

When expressing functional relationships, the **variables** x and y are typically used. These values are often written as the **coordinates** (x, y). The x-value is the independent variable and the y-value is the dependent variable. A **relation** is a set of data in which there is not a unique y-value for each x-value in the dataset. This means that there can be two of the same x-values assigned to different y-values. A relation is simply a relationship between the x and y-values in each coordinate but does not apply to the relationship between the values of x and y in the data set. A **function** is a relation where one quantity depends on the other. For example, the amount of money that you make depends on the number of hours that you work. In a function, each x-value in the data set has one unique y-value because the y-value depends on the x-value.

> **Review Video: Definition of a Function**
> Visit mometrix.com/academy and enter code: 784611

FUNCTIONS

A function has exactly one value of **output variable** (dependent variable) for each value of the **input variable** (independent variable). The set of all values for the input variable (here assumed to be x) is the domain of the function, and the set of all corresponding values of output variable (here assumed to be y) is the range of the function. When looking at a graph of an equation, the easiest way to determine if the equation is a function or not is to conduct the vertical line test. If a vertical line drawn through any value of x crosses the graph in more than one place, the equation is not a function.

DETERMINING A FUNCTION

You can determine whether an equation is a **function** by substituting different values into the equation for x. These values are called input values. All possible input values are referred to as the **domain**. The result of substituting these values into the equation is called the output, or **range**. You can display and organize these numbers in a data table. A **data table** contains the values for x and y, which you can also list as coordinates. In order for a function to exist, the table cannot contain any repeating x-values that correspond with different y-values. If each x-coordinate has a unique y-coordinate, the table contains a function. However, there can be repeating y-values that correspond with different x-values. An example of this is when the function contains an exponent. For example, if $x^2 = y$, $2^2 = 4$, and $(-2)^2 = 4$.

> **Review Video: Basics of Functions**
> Visit mometrix.com/academy and enter code: 822500

WRITING A FUNCTION RULE USING A TABLE

If given a set of data, place the corresponding x and y-values into a table and analyze the relationship between them. Consider what you can do to each x-value to obtain the corresponding y-value. Try adding or subtracting different numbers to and from x and then try multiplying or dividing different numbers to and from x. If none of these **operations** give you the y-value, try combining the operations. Once you find a rule that works for one pair, make sure to try it with each additional set of ordered pairs in the table. If the same operation or combination of operations satisfies each set of coordinates, then the table contains a function. The rule is then used to write the equation of the function in "$y =$" form.

DIRECT AND INVERSE VARIATIONS OF VARIABLES

Variables that vary directly are those that either both increase at the same rate or both decrease at the same rate. For example, in the functions $y = kx$ or $y = kx^n$, where k and n are positive, the value of y increases as the value of x increases and decreases as the value of x decreases.

Variables that vary inversely are those where one increases while the other decreases. For example, in the functions $y = \frac{k}{x}$ or $y = \frac{k}{x^n}$ where k and n are positive, the value of y increases as the value of x decreases, and decreases as the value of x increases.

In both cases, k is the constant of variation.

PROPERTIES OF FUNCTIONS

There are many different ways to classify functions based on their structure or behavior. Important features of functions include:

- **End behavior**: the behavior of the function at extreme values ($f(x)$ as $x \to \pm\infty$)
- **y-intercept**: the value of function at $f(0)$
- **Roots**: the values of x where the function equals zero ($f(x) = 0$)
- **Extrema**: minimum or maximum values of the function or where the function changes direction ($f(x) \geq k$ or $f(x) \leq k$)

251

CLASSIFICATION OF FUNCTIONS

An **invertible function** is defined as a function, $f(x)$, for which there is another function, $f^{-1}(x)$, such that $f^{-1}(f(x)) = x$. For example, if $f(x) = 3x - 2$ the inverse function, $f^{-1}(x)$, can be found:

$$x = 3(f^{-1}(x)) - 2$$
$$\frac{x+2}{3} = f^{-1}(x)$$

$$f^{-1}(f(x)) = \frac{3x - 2 + 2}{3}$$
$$= \frac{3x}{3}$$
$$= x$$

Note that $f^{-1}(x)$ is a valid function over all values of x.

In a **one-to-one function**, each value of x has exactly one value for y on the coordinate plane (this is the definition of a function) and each value of y has exactly one value for x. While the vertical line test will determine if a graph is that of a function, the horizontal line test will determine if a function is a one-to-one function. If a horizontal line drawn at any value of y intersects the graph in more than one place, the graph is not that of a one-to-one function. Do not make the mistake of using the horizontal line test exclusively in determining if a graph is that of a one-to-one function. A one-to-one function must pass both the vertical line test and the horizontal line test. As such, one-to-one functions are invertible functions.

A **many-to-one function** is a function whereby the relation is a function, but the inverse of the function is not a function. In other words, each element in the domain is mapped to one and only one element in the range. However, one or more elements in the range may be mapped to the same element in the domain. A graph of a many-to-one function would pass the vertical line test, but not the horizontal line test. One result of this is the fact that many-to-one functions are not invertible.

A **monotone function** is a function whose graph either constantly increases or constantly decreases. Examples include the functions $f(x) = x$, $f(x) = -x$, or $f(x) = x^3$.

An **even function** has a graph that is symmetric with respect to the y-axis and satisfies the equation $f(x) = f(-x)$. Examples include the functions $f(x) = x^2$ and $f(x) = ax^n$, where a is any real number and n is a positive even integer.

An **odd function** has a graph that is symmetric with respect to the origin and satisfies the equation $f(x) = -f(-x)$. Examples include the functions $f(x) = x^3$ and $f(x) = ax^n$, where a is any real number and n is a positive odd integer.

Algebraic functions are those that exclusively use polynomials and roots. These would include polynomial functions, rational functions, square root functions, and all combinations of these functions, such as polynomials as the radicand. These combinations may be joined by addition, subtraction, multiplication, or division, but may not include variables as exponents.

Transcendental functions are all functions that are non-algebraic. Any function that includes logarithms, trigonometric functions, variables as exponents, or any combination that includes any of these is not algebraic in nature, even if the function includes polynomials or roots.

Constant functions are given by the equation $f(x) = b$, where b is a real number. There is no independent variable present in the equation, so the function has a constant value for all x. The graph of a constant function is a horizontal line of slope 0 that is positioned b units from the x-axis. If b is positive, the line is above the x-axis; if b is negative, the line is below the x-axis.

Identity functions are identified by the equation $f(x) = x$, where every value of the function is equal to its corresponding value of x. The only zero is the point $(0, 0)$. The graph is a line with slope of 1.

In **linear functions**, the value of the function changes in direct proportion to x. The rate of change, represented by the slope on its graph, is constant throughout. The standard form of a linear equation is $ax + cy = d$, where a, c, and d are real numbers. As a function, this equation is commonly in the form $y = mx + d$ or $f(x) = mx + d$ where $m = -\frac{a}{c}$ and $b = \frac{d}{c}$. This is known as the slope-intercept form, because the coefficients give the slope of the graphed function (m) and its y-intercept (b). Solve the equation $mx + b = 0$ for x to get $x = -\frac{b}{m}$, which is the only zero of the function. The domain and range are both the set of all real numbers.

QUADRATIC FUNCTIONS

A **quadratic function** is a function in the form $y = ax^2 + bx + c$, where a does not equal 0. While a linear function forms a line, a quadratic function forms a **parabola**, which is a u-shaped figure that either opens upward or downward. A parabola that opens upward is said to be a **positive quadratic function** and a parabola that opens downward is said to be a **negative quadratic function**. The shape of a parabola can differ, depending on the values of a, b, and c. All parabolas contain a **vertex**, which is the highest possible point, the **maximum**, or the lowest possible point, the **minimum**. This is the point where the graph begins moving in the opposite direction. A quadratic function can have zero, one, or two solutions, and therefore, zero, one, or two x-intercepts. Recall that the x-intercepts are referred to as the zeros, or roots, of a function. A quadratic function will have only one y-intercept. Understanding the basic components of a quadratic function can give you an idea of the shape of its graph.

Example graph of a positive quadratic function, $x^2 + 2x - 3$:

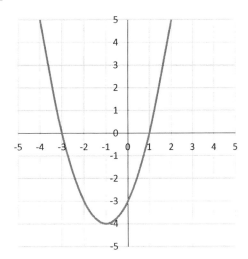

POLYNOMIAL FUNCTIONS

A **polynomial function** is a function with multiple terms and multiple powers of x, such as:

$$f(x) = a_n x^n + a_{n-1} x^{n-1} + a_{n-2} x^{n-2} + \cdots + a_1 x + a_0$$

where n is a non-negative integer that is the highest exponent in the polynomial, and $a_n \neq 0$. The domain of a polynomial function is the set of all real numbers. If the greatest exponent in the polynomial is even, the polynomial is said to be of even degree and the range is the set of real numbers that satisfy the function. If the greatest exponent in the polynomial is odd, the polynomial is said to be odd and the range, like the domain, is the set of all real numbers.

RATIONAL FUNCTIONS

A **rational function** is a function that can be constructed as a ratio of two polynomial expressions: $f(x) = \frac{p(x)}{q(x)}$, where $p(x)$ and $q(x)$ are both polynomial expressions and $q(x) \neq 0$. The domain is the set of all real numbers, except any values for which $q(x) = 0$. The range is the set of real numbers that satisfies the function when the domain is applied. When you graph a rational function, you will have vertical asymptotes wherever $q(x) = 0$. If the polynomial in the numerator is of lesser degree than the polynomial in the denominator, the x-axis will also be a horizontal asymptote. If the numerator and denominator have equal degrees, there will be a horizontal asymptote not on the x-axis. If the degree of the numerator is exactly one greater than the degree of the denominator, the graph will have an oblique, or diagonal, asymptote. The asymptote will be along the line $y = \frac{p_n}{q_{n-1}} x + \frac{p_{n-1}}{q_{n-1}}$, where p_n and q_{n-1} are the coefficients of the highest degree terms in their respective polynomials.

SQUARE ROOT FUNCTIONS

A **square root function** is a function that contains a radical and is in the format $f(x) = \sqrt{ax + b}$. The domain is the set of all real numbers that yields a positive radicand or a radicand equal to zero. Because square root values are assumed to be positive unless otherwise identified, the range is all real numbers from zero to infinity. To find the zero of a square root function, set the radicand equal to zero and solve for x. The graph of a square root function is always to the right of the zero and always above the x-axis.

Example graph of a square root function, $f(x) = \sqrt{2x + 1}$:

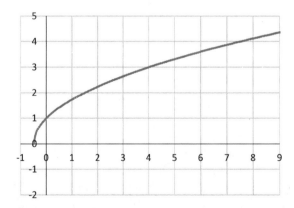

ABSOLUTE VALUE FUNCTIONS

An **absolute value function** is in the format $f(x) = |ax + b|$. Like other functions, the domain is the set of all real numbers. However, because absolute value indicates positive numbers, the range is limited to positive real numbers. To find the zero of an absolute value function, set the portion inside the absolute value sign equal to zero and solve for x.

An absolute value function is also known as a piecewise function because it must be solved in pieces – one for if the value inside the absolute value sign is positive, and one for if the value is negative. The function can be expressed as

$$f(x) = \begin{cases} ax + b \text{ if } ax + b \geq 0 \\ -(ax + b) \text{ if } ax + b < 0 \end{cases}$$

This will allow for an accurate statement of the range. The graph of an example absolute value function, $f(x) = |2x - 1|$, is below:

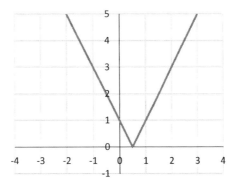

EXPONENTIAL FUNCTIONS

Exponential functions are equations that have the format $y = b^x$, where base $b > 0$ and $b \neq 1$. The exponential function can also be written $f(x) = b^x$. Recall the properties of exponents, like the product of terms with the same base is equal to the base raised to the sum of the exponents: $a^x \times a^y = a^{x+y}$ and a term with an exponent that is raised to an exponent is equal to the base of the original term raised to the product of the exponents: $(a^x)^y = a^{xy}$. The graph of an example exponential function, $f(x) = 2^x$, is below:

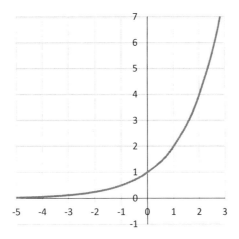

Note in the graph that the y value approaches zero to the left and infinity to the right. One of the key features of an exponential function is that there will be one end that goes off to infinity and another that asymptotically approaches a lower bound. Common forms of exponential functions include:

Geometric sequences: $a_n = a_1 \times r^{n-1}$, where a_n is the value of the nth term, a_1 is the initial value, r is the common ratio, and n is the number of terms. Note that $a_1 \times r^{1-1} = a_1 \times r^0 = a_1 \times 1 = a_1$.

Population growth: $f(t) = ae^{rt}$, where $f(t)$ is the population at time $t \geq 0$, a is the initial population, and r is the growth rate.

255

Compound interest: $f(t) = P\left(1 + \frac{r}{n}\right)^{nt}$, where $f(t)$ is the account value at a certain number time periods $t \geq 0$, P is the initial principle balance, r is the interest rate, and n is the number of times the interest is applied per time period.

General exponential growth or decay: $f(t) = a(1 + r)^t$, where $f(t)$ is the future count, a is the current or initial count, r is the growth or decay rate, and t is the time.

For example, suppose the initial population of a town was 1,200 people. The population growth is 5%. The current population is 2,400. To find out how much time has passed since the town was founded, we can use the following function:

$$2400 = 1200e^{0.05t}.$$

The general form for population growth may be represented as $f(t) = ae^{rt}$, where $f(t)$ represents the current population, a represents the initial population, r represents the growth rate, and t represents the time. Thus, substituting the initial population, current population, and rate into this form gives the equation above.

The number of years that have passed were found by first dividing both sides of the equation by 1,200. Doing so gives $2 = e^{0.05t}$. Taking the natural logarithm of both sides gives $\ln(2) = ln(e^{0.05t})$. Applying the power property of logarithms, the equation may be rewritten as $\ln(2) = 0.05t \times \ln(e)$, which simplifies as $\ln(2) = 0.05t$. Dividing both sides of this equation by 0.05 gives $t \approx 13.86$. Thus, approximately 13.86 years passed.

LOGARITHMIC FUNCTIONS

Logarithmic functions are equations that have the format $y = \log_b x$ or $f(x) = \log_b x$. The base b may be any number except one; however, the most common bases for logarithms are base 10 and base e. The log base e is known the natural logarithm, or ln, expressed by the function $f(x) = \ln x$.

Any logarithm that does not have an assigned value of b is assumed to be base 10: $\log x = \log_{10} x$. Exponential functions and logarithmic functions are related in that one is the inverse of the other. If $f(x) = b^x$, then $f^{-1}(x) = \log_b x$. This can perhaps be expressed more clearly by the two equations: $y = b^x$ and $x = \log_b y$.

The following properties apply to logarithmic expressions:

Property	Description
$\log_b 1 = 0$	The log of 1 is equal to 0 for any base
$\log_b b = 1$	The log of the base is equal to 1
$\log_b b^p = p$	The log of the base raised to a power is equal to that power
$\log_b MN = \log_b M + \log_b N$	The log of a product is the sum of the log of each factor
$\log_b \frac{M}{N} = \log_b M - \log_b N$	The log of a quotient is equal to the log of the dividend minus the log of the divisor
$\log_b M^p = p \log_b M$	The log of a value raised to a power is equal to the power times the log of the value

The graph of an example logarithmic function, $f(x) = \log_2(x + 2)$, is below:

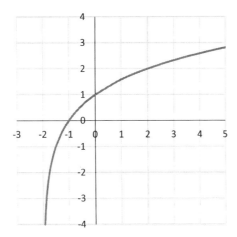

MANIPULATION OF FUNCTIONS

Translation occurs when values are added to or subtracted from the x or y values. If a constant is added to the y portion of each point, the graph shifts up. If a constant is subtracted from the y portion of each point, the graph shifts down. This is represented by the expression $f(x) \pm k$, where k is a constant. If a constant is added to the x portion of each point, the graph shifts left. If a constant is subtracted from the x portion of each point, the graph shifts right. This is represented by the expression $f(x \pm k)$, where k is a constant.

Stretching, compression, and reflection occur when different parts of a function are multiplied by different groups of constants. If the function as a whole is multiplied by a real number constant greater than 1, $(k \times f(x))$, the graph is stretched vertically. If k in the previous equation is greater than zero but less than 1, the graph is compressed vertically. If k is less than zero, the graph is reflected about the x-axis, in addition to being either stretched or compressed vertically if k is less than or greater than -1, respectively. If instead, just the x-term is multiplied by a constant greater than 1 $(f(k \times x))$, the graph is compressed horizontally. If k in the previous equation is greater than zero but less than 1, the graph is stretched horizontally. If k is less than zero, the graph is reflected about the y-axis, in addition to being either stretched or compressed horizontally if k is greater than or less than -1, respectively.

ALGEBRAIC THEOREMS

According to the **fundamental theorem of algebra**, every non-constant, single variable polynomial has exactly as many roots as the polynomial's highest exponent. For example, if x^4 is the largest exponent of a term, the polynomial will have exactly 4 roots. However, some of these roots may have multiplicity or be non-real numbers. For instance, in the polynomial function $f(x) = x^4 - 4x + 3$, the only real roots are 1 and -1. The root 1 has multiplicity of 2 and there is one non-real root $(-1 - \sqrt{2}i)$.

The **remainder theorem** is useful for determining the remainder when a polynomial is divided by a binomial. The remainder theorem states that if a polynomial function $f(x)$ is divided by a binomial $x - a$, where a is a real number, the remainder of the division will be the value of $f(a)$. If $f(a) = 0$, then a is a root of the polynomial.

The **factor theorem** is related to the remainder theorem and states that if $f(a) = 0$ then $(x - a)$ is a factor of the function.

According to the **rational root theorem,** any rational root of a polynomial function $f(x) = a_n x^n + a_{n-1} x^{n-1} + \cdots + a_1 x + a_0$ with integer coefficients will, when reduced to its lowest terms, be a positive or negative fraction such that the numerator is a factor of a_0 and the denominator is a factor of a_n. For instance, if the polynomial function $f(x) = x^3 + 3x^2 - 4$ has any rational roots, the numerators of those roots can only be factors of 4 (1, 2, 4), and the denominators can only be factors of 1 (1). The function in this example has roots of 1 $\left(\text{or } \frac{1}{1} \right)$ and -2 $\left(\text{or } -\frac{2}{1} \right)$.

APPLYING THE BASIC OPERATIONS TO FUNCTIONS

For each of the basic operations, we will use these functions as examples: $f(x) = x^2$ and $g(x) = x$.

To find the sum of two functions f and g, assuming the domains are compatible, simply add the two functions together: $(f + g)(x) = f(x) + g(x) = x^2 + x$

To find the difference of two functions f and g, assuming the domains are compatible, simply subtract the second function from the first: $(f - g)(x) = f(x) - g(x) = x^2 - x$.

To find the product of two functions f and g, assuming the domains are compatible, multiply the two functions together: $(f \times g)(x) = f(x) \times g(x) = x^2 \times x = x^3$.

To find the quotient of two functions f and g, assuming the domains are compatible, divide the first function by the second: $\frac{f}{g}(x) = \frac{f(x)}{g(x)} = \frac{x^2}{x} = x \, ; x \neq 0$.

The example given in each case is fairly simple, but on a given problem, if you are looking only for the value of the sum, difference, product or quotient of two functions at a particular x-value, it may be simpler to solve the functions individually and then perform the given operation using those values.

The composite of two functions f and g, written as $(f \circ g)(x)$ simply means that the output of the second function is used as the input of the first. This can also be written as $f\big(g(x)\big)$. In general, this can be solved by substituting $g(x)$ for all instances of x in $f(x)$ and simplifying. Using the example functions $f(x) = x^2 - x + 2$ and $g(x) = x + 1$, we can find that $(f \circ g)(x)$ or $f\big(g(x)\big)$ is equal to $f(x + 1) = (x + 1)^2 - (x + 1) + 2$, which simplifies to $x^2 + x + 2$.

It is important to note that $(f \circ g)(x)$ is not necessarily the same as $(g \circ f)(x)$. The process is not always commutative like addition or multiplication expressions. It *can* be commutative, but most often this is not the case.

PRACTICE

P1. A professor wishes to invest $20,000 in a CD that compounds annually. The interest rate at his bank is 1.9%. How many years will it take for his account to reach $50,000?

P2. Suppose a new bacteria, after x days, shows a growth rate of 10%. The current count for the new bacteria strain is 100. How many days will pass before the count reaches 1 million bacteria?

P3. Each of the following functions cross the x- and y-axes at the same points. Identify the most likely function type of each graph

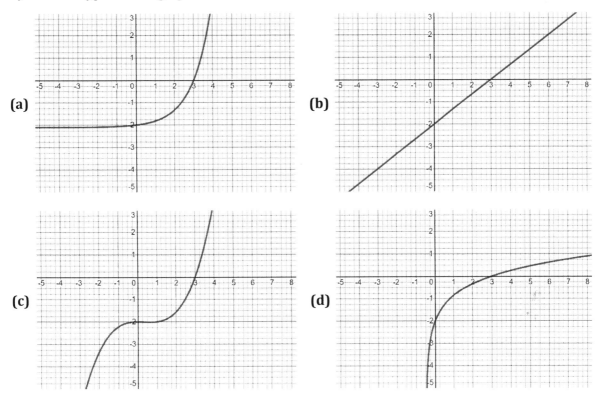

(a)

(b)

(c)

(d)

P4. Given the functions $f(x) = -3x + 3$, $g(x) = e^x + 3$, and $h(x) = x^2 - 2x + 1$, perform the following operations and write out the resulting function:

(a) Shift $g(x)$ 4 units to the left and 1 unit up, then compress the new function by a factor of 1/2

(b) $\frac{f(x)}{h(x)}$

(c) $h(g(x))$

(d) $\frac{f(x)+h(x)}{x-1}$

P5. Martin needs a 20% medicine solution. The pharmacy has a 5% solution and a 30% solution. He needs 50 mL of the solution. If the pharmacist must mix the two solutions, how many milliliters of 5% solution and 30% solution should be used?

P6. Describe two different strategies for solving the following problem:

Kevin can mow the yard in 4 hours. Mandy can mow the same yard in 5 hours. If they work together, how long will it take them to mow the yard?

P7. A car, traveling at 65 miles per hour, leaves Flagstaff and heads east on I-40. Another car, traveling at 75 miles per hour, leaves Flagstaff 2 hours later, from the same starting point and also heads east on I-40. Determine how many hours it will take the second car catch the first car by:

(a) Using a table.

(b) Using algebra.

PRACTICE SOLUTIONS

P1. In order to solve, the compound interest formula should be evaluated for a future value of $50,000, principal of $20,000, rate of 0.019, and number of years of t. The exponential equation may then be solved by taking the logarithm of both sides. The process is shown below:

$$50,000 = 20,000 \left(1 + \frac{0.019}{1}\right)^t$$

Dividing both sides of the equation by 20,000 gives $2.5 = 1.019^t$. Taking the logarithm of both sides gives $\log(2.5) = t \log(1.019)$. Dividing both sides of this equation by $\log(1.019)$ gives $t \approx 48.68$. Thus, after approximately 49 years, the professor's account will reach $50,000.

P2. The problem may be solved by writing and solving an exponential growth function, in the form, $f(x) = a(1 + r)^x$, where $f(x)$ represents the future count, a represents the current count, r represents the growth rate, and x represents the time. Once the function is evaluated for a future count of 1,000,000, a current count of 100, and a growth rate of 0.10, the exponential equation may be solved by taking the logarithm of both sides.

The problem may be modeled with the equation, $1,000,000 = 100 \times (1.10)^x$. Dividing both sides of the equation by 100 gives $10,000 = 1.10^x$. Taking the logarithm of both sides gives $\log(10,000) = x \log(1.10)$. Dividing both sides of this equation by $\log(1.10)$ gives $x \approx 96.6$. Thus, after approximately 97 days, the bacteria count will reach 1 million.

P3. (a) Exponential function – positive, increasing slope

(b) Linear function – positive, continuous slope.

(c) Polynomial function (odd degree) – positive, changing slope. Note that the graph goes off to infinity in opposite quadrants I and III, thus it is an odd degree.

(d) Logarithmic function – positive, decreasing slope

P4. (a) Shifting $g(x)$ to the left 4 units is the same as $g(x + 4)$ and shifting the function up one unit is $g(x) + 1$. Combining these and multiplying by ½ results in the following:

$$\frac{1}{2}(g(x + 4) + 1) = \frac{1}{2}\left((e^{x+4} + 3) + 1\right)$$
$$= \frac{e^{x+4}}{2} + 2$$

(b) Factor $h(x)$, noting that it is a perfect square, and be sure to note the constraint on x due to the original denominator of the rational expression:

$$\frac{f(x)}{h(x)} = \frac{-3x + 3}{x^2 - 2x + 1} = \frac{-3(x - 1)}{(x - 1)(x - 1)} = \frac{-3}{(x - 1)}; x \neq 1$$

(c) Evaluate the composition as follows:

$$\begin{aligned} h(g(x)) &= (e^x + 3)^2 - 2(e^x + 3) + 1 \\ &= (e^x)^2 + 6e^x + 9 - 2e^x - 6 + 1 \\ &= e^{2x} + 4e^x + 4 \\ &= (e^x + 2)^2 \end{aligned}$$

(d) Note the constraint on x due to the original denominator of the rational expression:

$$\begin{aligned} \frac{f(x) + h(x)}{x - 1} &= \frac{(-3x + 3) + (x^2 - 2x + 1)}{x - 1} \\ &= \frac{-3(x - 1) + (x - 1)(x - 1)}{x - 1} \\ &= -3 + (x - 1) \\ &= x - 4; x \neq 1 \end{aligned}$$

P5. To solve this problem, a table may be created to represent the variables, percentages, and total amount of solution. Such a table is shown below:

	mL solution	% medicine	Total mL medicine
5% solution	x	0.05	$0.05x$
30% solution	y	0.30	$0.30y$
Mixture	$x + y = 50$	0.20	$(0.20)(50) = 10$

The variable, x, may be rewritten as $50 - y$, so the equation, $0.05(50 - y) + 0.30y = 10$, may be written and solved for y. Doing so gives $y = 30$. So, 30 mL of 30% solution are needed. Evaluating the expression, $50 - y$ for an x-value of 20, shows that 20 mL of 5% solution are needed.

P6. Two possible strategies both involve the use of rational equations to solve. The first strategy involves representing the fractional part of the yard mowed by each person in one hour and setting this sum equal to the ratio of 1 to the total time needed. The appropriate equation is $1/4 + 1/5 = 1/t$, which simplifies as $9/20 = 1/t$, and finally as $t = 20/9$. So, the time it will take them to mow the yard, when working together, is a little more than 2.2 hours.

A second strategy involves representing the time needed for each person as two fractions and setting the sum equal to 1 (representing 1 yard). The appropriate equation is $t/4 + t/5 = 1$, which simplifies as $9t/20 = 1$, and finally as $t = 20/9$. This strategy also shows the total time to be a little more than 2.2 hours.

P7. (a) One strategy might involve creating a table of values for the number of hours and distances for each car. The table may be examined to find the same distance traveled and the corresponding number of hours taken. Such a table is shown below:

Car A		Car B	
x (hours)	y (distance)	x (hours)	y (distance)
0	0	0	
1	65	1	
2	130	2	0
3	195	3	75
4	260	4	150
5	325	5	225
6	390	6	300
7	455	7	375
8	520	8	450
9	585	9	525
10	650	10	600
11	715	11	675
12	780	12	750
13	845	13	825
14	910	14	900
15	975	15	975

The table shows that after 15 hours, the distance traveled is the same. Thus, the second car catches up with the first car after a distance of 975 miles and 15 hours.

(b) A second strategy might involve setting up and solving an algebraic equation. This situation may be modeled as $65x = 75(x - 2)$. This equation sets the distances traveled by each car equal to one another. Solving for x gives $x = 15$. Thus, once again, the second car will catch up with the first car after 15 hours.

Measurement

PRECISION, ACCURACY, AND ERROR

Precision: How reliable and repeatable a measurement is. The more consistent the data is with repeated testing, the more precise it is. For example, hitting a target consistently in the same spot, which may or may not be the center of the target, is precision.

Accuracy: How close the data is to the correct data. For example, hitting a target consistently in the center area of the target, whether or not the hits are all in the same spot, is accuracy.

Note: it is possible for data to be precise without being accurate. If a scale is off balance, the data will be precise, but will not be accurate. For data to have precision and accuracy, it must be repeatable and correct.

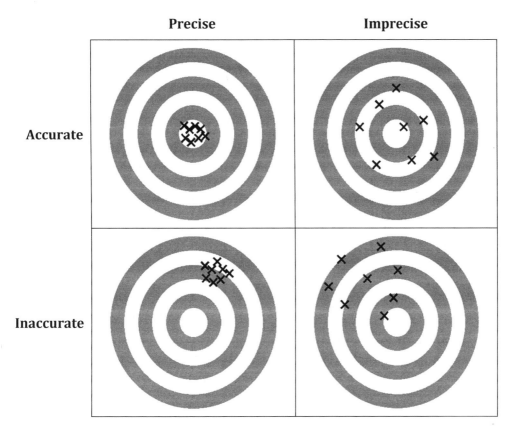

Approximate error: The amount of error in a physical measurement. Approximate error is often reported as the measurement, followed by the ± symbol and the amount of the approximate error.

Maximum possible error: Half the magnitude of the smallest unit used in the measurement. For example, if the unit of measurement is 1 centimeter, the maximum possible error is $\frac{1}{2}$ cm, written as ± 0.5 cm following the measurement. It is important to apply significant figures in reporting maximum possible error. Do not make the answer appear more accurate than the least accurate of your measurements.

ROUNDING AND ESTIMATION

Rounding is reducing the digits in a number while still trying to keep the value similar. The result will be less accurate, but will be in a simpler form, and will be easier to use. Whole numbers can be rounded to the nearest ten, hundred or thousand.

When you are asked to estimate the solution a problem, you will need to provide only an approximate figure or **estimation** for your answer. In this situation, you will need to round each number in the calculation to the level indicated (nearest hundred, nearest thousand, etc.) or to a level that makes sense for the numbers involved. When estimating a sum **all numbers must be**

rounded to the same level. You cannot round one number to the nearest thousand while rounding another to the nearest hundred.

SCIENTIFIC NOTATION

Scientific notation is a way of writing large numbers in a shorter form. The form $a \times 10^n$ is used in scientific notation, where a is greater than or equal to 1, but less than 10, and n is the number of places the decimal must move to get from the original number to a. Example: The number 230,400,000 is cumbersome to write. To write the value in scientific notation, place a decimal point between the first and second numbers, and include all digits through the last non-zero digit ($a = 2.304$). To find the appropriate power of 10, count the number of places the decimal point had to move ($n = 8$). The number is positive if the decimal moved to the left, and negative if it moved to the right. We can then write 230,400,000 as 2.304×10^8. If we look instead at the number 0.00002304, we have the same value for a, but this time the decimal moved 5 places to the right ($n = -5$). Thus, 0.00002304 can be written as 2.304×10^{-5}. Using this notation makes it simple to compare very large or very small numbers. By comparing exponents, it is easy to see that 3.28×10^4 is smaller than 1.51×10^5, because 4 is less than 5.

METRIC MEASUREMENT PREFIXES

Giga-: one billion (1 *giga*watt is one billion watts)
Mega-: one million (1 *mega*hertz is one million hertz)
Kilo-: one thousand (1 *kilo*gram is one thousand grams)
Deci-: one tenth (1 *deci*meter is one tenth of a meter)
Centi-: one hundredth (1 *centi*meter is one hundredth of a meter)
Milli-: one thousandth (1 *milli*liter is one thousandth of a liter)
Micro-: one millionth (1 *micro*gram is one millionth of a gram)

MEASUREMENT CONVERSION

When converting between units, the goal is to maintain the same meaning but change the way it is displayed. In order to go from a larger unit to a smaller unit, multiply the number of the known amount by the equivalent amount. When going from a smaller unit to a larger unit, divide the number of the known amount by the equivalent amount.

For complicated conversions, it may be helpful to set up conversion fractions. In these fractions, one fraction is the **conversion factor**. The other fraction has the unknown amount in the numerator. So, the known value is placed in the denominator. Sometimes the second fraction has the known value from the problem in the numerator, and the unknown in the denominator. Multiply the two fractions to get the converted measurement. Note that since the numerator and the denominator of the factor are equivalent, the value of the fraction is 1. That is why we can say that the result in the new units is equal to the result in the old units even though they have different numbers.

It can often be necessary to chain known conversion factors together. As an example, consider converting 512 square inches to square meters. We know that there are 2.54 centimeters in an inch, 100 centimeters in a meter, and that squaring each of these

$$\frac{512 \text{ in}^2}{1} \times \left(\frac{2.54 \text{ cm}}{1 \text{ in}}\right)^2 \times \left(\frac{1 \text{ m}}{100 \text{ cm}}\right)^2 = \frac{512 \text{ in}^2}{1} \times \left(\frac{6.4516 \text{ cm}^2}{1 \text{ in}^2}\right) \times \left(\frac{1 \text{ m}^2}{10000 \text{ cm}^2}\right) = 0.330 \text{ m}^2$$

COMMON UNITS AND EQUIVALENTS

METRIC EQUIVALENTS

1000 µg (microgram)	1 mg
1000 mg (milligram)	1 g
1000 g (gram)	1 kg
1000 kg (kilogram)	1 metric ton
1000 mL (milliliter)	1 L
1000 µm (micrometer)	1 mm
1000 mm (millimeter)	1 m
100 cm (centimeter)	1 m
1000 m (meter)	1 km

DISTANCE AND AREA MEASUREMENT

Unit	Abbreviation	U.S. equivalent	Metric equivalent
Inch	in	1 inch	2.54 centimeters
Foot	ft	12 inches	0.305 meters
Yard	yd	3 feet	0.914 meters
Mile	mi	5280 feet	1.609 kilometers
Acre	ac	4840 square yards	0.405 hectares
Square Mile	mi^2	640 acres	2.590 square kilometers

CAPACITY MEASUREMENTS

Unit	Abbreviation	U.S. equivalent	Metric equivalent
Fluid Ounce	fl oz	8 fluid drams	29.573 milliliters
Cup	cp	8 fluid ounces	0.237 liter
Pint	pt	16 fluid ounces	0.473 liter
Quart	qt	2 pints	0.946 liter
Gallon	gal	4 quarts	3.785 liters
Teaspoon	t or tsp	1 fluid dram	5 milliliters
Tablespoon	T or tbsp	4 fluid drams	15 or 16 milliliters
Cubic Centimeter	cc or cm^3	0.271 drams	1 milliliter

WEIGHT MEASUREMENTS

Unit	Abbreviation	U.S. equivalent	Metric equivalent
Ounce	oz	16 drams	28.35 grams
Pound	lb	16 ounces	453.6 grams
Ton	t	2,000 pounds	907.2 kilograms

VOLUME AND WEIGHT MEASUREMENT CLARIFICATIONS

Always be careful when using ounces and fluid ounces. They are not equivalent.

1 pint = 16 fluid ounces   1 fluid ounce ≠ 1 ounce
1 pound = 16 ounces   1 pint ≠ 1 pound

265

Having one pint of something does not mean you have one pound of it. In the same way, just because something weighs one pound does not mean that its volume is one pint.

In the United States, the word "ton" by itself refers to a short ton or a net ton. Do not confuse this with a long ton (also called a gross ton) or a metric ton (also spelled *tonne*), which have different measurement equivalents.

$$1 \text{ U.S. ton} = 2000 \text{ pounds} \quad \neq \quad 1 \text{ metric ton} = 1000 \text{ kilograms}$$

PRACTICE

P1. Round each number to the indicated degree:

   (a) Round to the nearest ten: 11; 47; 118

   (b) Round to the nearest hundred: 78; 980; 248

   (c) Round each number to the nearest thousand: 302; 1274; 3756

P2. Estimate the solution to 345,932 + 96,369 by rounding each number to the nearest ten thousand.

P3. A runner's heart beats 422 times over the course of six minutes. About how many times did the runner's heart beat during each minute?

P4. Perform the following conversions:

   (a) 1.4 meters to centimeters

   (b) 218 centimeters to meters

   (c) 42 inches to feet

   (d) 15 kilograms to pounds

   (e) 80 ounces to pounds

   (f) 2 miles to kilometers

   (g) 5 feet to centimeters

   (h) 15.14 liters to gallons

   (i) 8 quarts to liters

   (j) 13.2 pounds to grams

PRACTICE SOLUTIONS

P1. (a) When rounding to the nearest ten, anything ending in 5 or greater rounds up. So, 11 rounds to 10, 47 rounds to 50, and 118 rounds to 120.

   (b) When rounding to the nearest hundred, anything ending in 50 or greater rounds up. So, 78 rounds to 100, 980 rounds to 1000, and 248 rounds to 200.

(c) When rounding to the nearest thousand, anything ending in 500 or greater rounds up. So, 302 rounds to 0, 1274 rounds to 1000, and 3756 rounds to 4000.

P2. Start by rounding each number to the nearest ten thousand: 345,932 becomes 350,000, and 96,369 becomes 100,000. Then, add the rounded numbers: 350,000 + 100,000 = 450,000. So, the answer is approximately 450,000. The exact answer would be 345,932 + 96,369 = 442,301. So, the estimate of 450,000 is a similar value to the exact answer.

P3. "About how many" indicates that you need to estimate the solution. In this case, look at the numbers you are given. 422 can be rounded down to 420, which is easily divisible by 6. A good estimate is 420 ÷ 6 = 70 beats per minute. More accurately, the patient's heart rate was just over 70 beats per minute since his heart actually beat a little more than 420 times in six minutes.

P4. (a) $\frac{100 \text{ cm}}{1 \text{ m}} = \frac{x \text{ cm}}{1.4 \text{ m}}$ Cross multiply to get $x = 140$

(b) $\frac{100 \text{ cm}}{1 \text{ m}} = \frac{218 \text{ cm}}{x \text{ m}}$ Cross multiply to get $100x = 218$, or $x = 2.18$

(c) $\frac{12 \text{ in}}{1 \text{ ft}} = \frac{42 \text{ in}}{x \text{ ft}}$ Cross multiply to get $12x = 42$, or $x = 3.5$

(d) 15 kilograms $\times \frac{2.2 \text{ pounds}}{1 \text{ kilogram}} = 33$ pounds

(e) 80 ounces $\times \frac{1 \text{ pound}}{16 \text{ ounces}} = 5$ pounds

(f) 2 miles $\times \frac{1.609 \text{ kilometers}}{1 \text{ mile}} = 3.218$ kilometers

(g) 5 feet $\times \frac{12 \text{ inches}}{1 \text{ foot}} \times \frac{2.54 \text{ centimeters}}{1 \text{ inch}} = 152.4$ centimeters

(h) 15.14 liters $\times \frac{1 \text{ gallon}}{3.785 \text{ liters}} = 4$ gallons

(i) 8 quarts $\times \frac{1 \text{ gallon}}{4 \text{ quarts}} \times \frac{3.785 \text{ liters}}{1 \text{ gallon}} = 7.57$ liters

(j) 13.2 pounds $\times \frac{1 \text{ kilogram}}{2.2 \text{ pounds}} \times \frac{1000 \text{ grams}}{1 \text{ kilogram}} = 6000$ grams

Geometry

LINES AND PLANES

A **point** is a fixed location in space; has no size or dimensions; commonly represented by a dot. A **line** is a set of points that extends infinitely in two opposite directions. It has length, but no width or depth. A line can be defined by any two distinct points that it contains. A **line segment** is a portion of a line that has definite endpoints. A **ray** is a portion of a line that extends from a single point on that line in one direction along the line. It has a definite beginning, but no ending.

Intersecting lines are lines that have exactly one point in common. **Concurrent lines** are multiple lines that intersect at a single point. **Perpendicular lines** are lines that intersect at right angles.

267

They are represented by the symbol ⊥. The shortest distance from a line to a point not on the line is a perpendicular segment from the point to the line. **Parallel lines** are lines in the same plane that have no points in common and never meet. It is possible for lines to be in different planes, have no points in common, and never meet, but they are not parallel because they are in different planes.

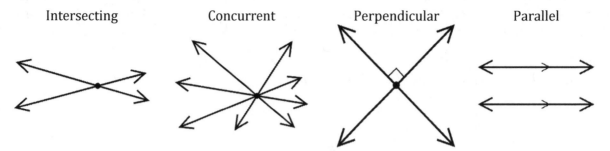

Intersecting   Concurrent   Perpendicular   Parallel

A **transversal** is a line that intersects at least two other lines, which may or may not be parallel to one another. A transversal that intersects parallel lines is a common occurrence in geometry. A **bisector** is a line or line segment that divides another line segment into two equal lengths. A **perpendicular bisector** of a line segment is composed of points that are equidistant from the endpoints of the segment it is dividing.

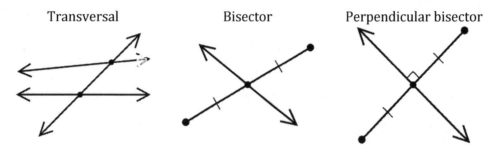

Transversal   Bisector   Perpendicular bisector

The **projection of a point on a line** is the point at which a perpendicular line drawn from the given point to the given line intersects the line. This is also the shortest distance from the given point to the line. The **projection of a segment on a line** is a segment whose endpoints are the points formed when perpendicular lines are drawn from the endpoints of the given segment to the given line. This is similar to the length a diagonal line appears to be when viewed from above.

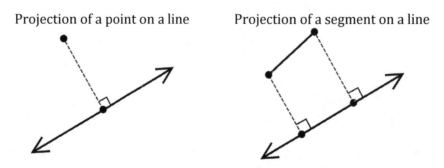

Projection of a point on a line   Projection of a segment on a line

A **plane** is a two-dimensional flat surface defined by three non-collinear points. A plane extends an infinite distance in all directions in those two dimensions. It contains an infinite number of points, parallel lines and segments, intersecting lines and segments, as well as parallel or intersecting rays. A plane will never contain a three-dimensional figure or skew lines. Two given planes are either parallel or they intersect at a line. A plane may intersect a circular conic surface to form **conic sections**, such as a parabola, hyperbola, circle or ellipse.

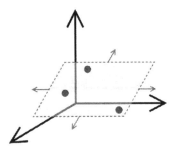

ANGLES

An **angle** is formed when two lines or line segments meet at a common point. It may be a common starting point for a pair of segments or rays, or it may be the intersection of lines. Angles are represented by the symbol ∠.

The **vertex** is the point at which two segments or rays meet to form an angle. If the angle is formed by intersecting rays, lines, and/or line segments, the vertex is the point at which four angles are formed. The pairs of angles opposite one another are called vertical angles, and their measures are equal.

- An **acute** angle is an angle with a degree measure less than 90°.
- A **right** angle is an angle with a degree measure of exactly 90°.
- An **obtuse** angle is an angle with a degree measure greater than 90° but less than 180°.
- A **straight angle** is an angle with a degree measure of exactly 180°. This is also a semicircle.
- A **reflex angle** is an angle with a degree measure greater than 180° but less than 360°.
- A **full angle** is an angle with a degree measure of exactly 360°.

Review Video: Geometric Symbols: Angles
Visit mometrix.com/academy and enter code: 452738

Two angles whose sum is exactly 90° are said to be **complementary**. The two angles may or may not be adjacent. In a right triangle, the two acute angles are complementary.

Two angles whose sum is exactly 180° are said to be **supplementary**. The two angles may or may not be adjacent. Two intersecting lines always form two pairs of supplementary angles. Adjacent supplementary angles will always form a straight line.

Two angles that have the same vertex and share a side are said to be **adjacent**. Vertical angles are not adjacent because they share a vertex but no common side.

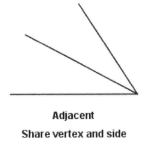

Adjacent
Share vertex and side

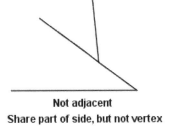

Not adjacent
Share part of side, but not vertex

269

When two parallel lines are cut by a transversal, the angles that are between the two parallel lines are **interior angles**. In the diagram below, angles 3, 4, 5, and 6 are interior angles.

When two parallel lines are cut by a transversal, the angles that are outside the parallel lines are **exterior angles**. In the diagram below, angles 1, 2, 7, and 8 are exterior angles.

When two parallel lines are cut by a transversal, the angles that are in the same position relative to the transversal and a parallel line are **corresponding angles**. The diagram below has four pairs of corresponding angles: angles 1 and 5; angles 2 and 6; angles 3 and 7; and angles 4 and 8. Corresponding angles formed by parallel lines are congruent.

When two parallel lines are cut by a transversal, the two interior angles that are on opposite sides of the transversal are called **alternate interior angles**. In the diagram below, there are two pairs of alternate interior angles: angles 3 and 6, and angles 4 and 5. Alternate interior angles formed by parallel lines are congruent.

When two parallel lines are cut by a transversal, the two exterior angles that are on opposite sides of the transversal are called **alternate exterior angles**.

In the diagram below, there are two pairs of alternate exterior angles: angles 1 and 8, and angles 2 and 7. Alternate exterior angles formed by parallel lines are congruent.

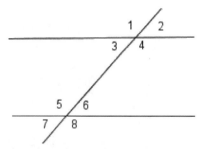

When two lines intersect, four angles are formed. The non-adjacent angles at this vertex are called vertical angles. Vertical angles are congruent. In the diagram, $\angle ABD \cong \angle CBE$ and $\angle ABC \cong \angle DBE$.

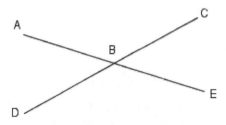

TRANSFORMATIONS

A **rotation** is a transformation that turns a figure around a point called the **center of rotation**, which can lie anywhere in the plane. If a line is drawn from a point on a figure to the center of rotation, and another line is drawn from the center to the rotated image of that point, the angle between the two lines is the **angle of rotation**. The vertex of the angle of rotation is the center of rotation.

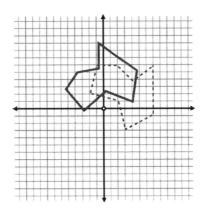

A **translation** is a transformation which slides a figure from one position in the plane to another position in the plane. The original figure and the translated figure have the same size, shape, and orientation. A **dilation** is a transformation which proportionally stretches or shrinks a figure by a **scale factor**. The dilated image is the same shape and orientation as the original image but a different size. A polygon and its dilated image are similar.

Translation

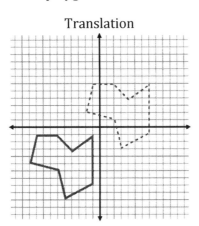

Dilation

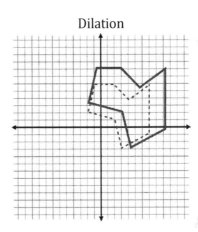

A **reflection of a figure over a line** (a "flip") creates a congruent image that is the same distance from the line as the original figure but on the opposite side. The **line of reflection** is the perpendicular bisector of any line segment drawn from a point on the original figure to its reflected image (unless the point and its reflected image happen to be the same point, which happens when a figure is reflected over one of its own sides). A **reflection of a figure over a point** (an inversion) in two dimensions is the same as the rotation of the figure 180° about that point. The image of the figure is congruent to the original figure. The **point of reflection** is the midpoint of a line segment which connects a point in the figure to its image (unless the point and its reflected image happen to be the same point, which happens when a figure is reflected in one of its own points).

Reflection of a figure over a line

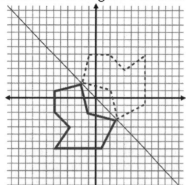

Reflection of a figure over a point

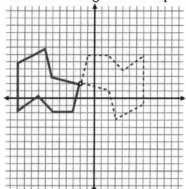

Review Video: **Rotation**
Visit mometrix.com/academy and enter code: 602600
Review Video: **Translation**
Visit mometrix.com/academy and enter code: 718628
Review Video: **Dilation**
Visit mometrix.com/academy and enter code: 471630
Review Video: **Reflection**
Visit mometrix.com/academy and enter code: 955068

POLYGONS

A **polygon** is a closed, two-dimensional figure with three or more straight line segments called **sides**. The point at which two sides of a polygon intersect is called the **vertex**. In a polygon, the number of sides is always equal to the number of vertices. A polygon with all sides congruent and all angles equal is called a **regular polygon**. Common polygons are:

Triangle = 3 sides
Quadrilateral = 4 sides
Pentagon = 5 sides
Hexagon = 6 sides
Heptagon = 7 sides
Octagon = 8 sides
Nonagon = 9 sides
Decagon = 10 sides
Dodecagon = 12 sides

More generally, an *n*-gon is a polygon that has *n* angles and *n* sides.

The sum of the interior angles of an *n*-sided polygon is $(n - 2) \times 180°$. For example, in a triangle $n = 3$. So, the sum of the interior angles is $(3 - 2) \times 180° = 180°$. In a quadrilateral, $n = 4$, and the sum of the angles is $(4 - 2) \times 180° = 360°$.

A line segment from the center of a polygon that is perpendicular to a side of the polygon is called the **apothem**. A line segment from the center of a polygon to a vertex of the polygon is called a

272

radius. In a regular polygon, the apothem can be used to find the area of the polygon using the formula $A = \frac{1}{2}ap$, where a is the apothem, and p is the perimeter.

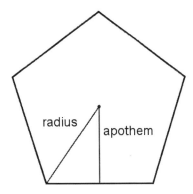

A **diagonal** is a line segment that joins two non-adjacent vertices of a polygon. The number of diagonals a polygon has can be found by using the formula:

$$\text{number of diagonals} = \frac{n(n-3)}{2}$$

Note that n is the number of sides in the polygon. This formula works for all polygons, not just regular polygons.

A **convex polygon** is a polygon whose diagonals all lie within the interior of the polygon. A **concave polygon** is a polygon with a least one diagonal that is outside the polygon. In the diagram below, quadrilateral *ABCD* is concave because diagonal $\overline{AC}$ lies outside the polygon and quadrilateral *EFGH* is concave because both diagonals lie inside the polygon

Concave   Convex

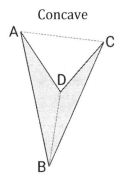 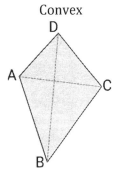

Congruent figures are geometric figures that have the same size and shape. All corresponding angles are equal, and all corresponding sides are equal. It is indicated by the symbol ≅.

Congruent polygons

Similar figures are geometric figures that have the same shape, but do not necessarily have the same size. All corresponding angles are equal, and all corresponding sides are proportional, but they do not have to be equal. It is indicated by the symbol ~.

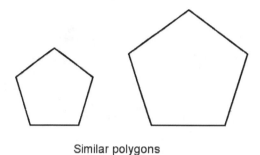

Similar polygons

Note that all congruent figures are also similar, but not all similar figures are congruent.

Review Video: Polygons, Similarity, and Congruence
Visit mometrix.com/academy and enter code: 686174

Review Video: Polygons
Visit mometrix.com/academy and enter code: 271869

LINE OF SYMMETRY

A line that divides a figure or object into congruent parts is called a **line of symmetry**. An object may have no lines of symmetry, one line of symmetry, or multiple (i.e., more than one) lines of symmetry.

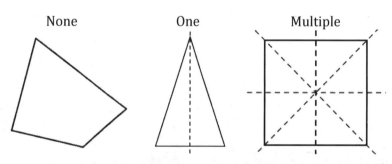

Review Video: Symmetry
Visit mometrix.com/academy and enter code: 528106

QUADRILATERALS

A **quadrilateral** is a closed two-dimensional geometric figure that has four straight sides. The sum of the interior angles of any quadrilateral is 360°.

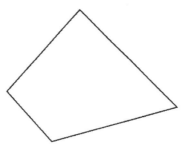

A **kite** is a quadrilateral with two pairs of adjacent sides that are congruent. A result of this is perpendicular diagonals. A kite can be concave or convex and has one line of symmetry.

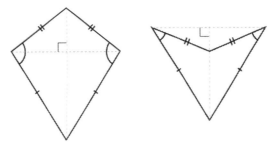

Trapezoid: A trapezoid is defined as a quadrilateral that has at least one pair of parallel sides. There are no rules for the second pair of sides. So, there are no rules for the diagonals and no lines of symmetry for a trapezoid.

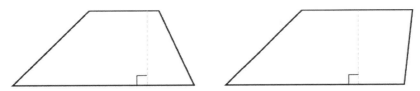

The **area of a trapezoid** is found by the formula $A = \frac{1}{2}h(b_1 + b_2)$, where h is the height (segment joining and perpendicular to the parallel bases), and b_1 and b_2 are the two parallel sides (bases). Do not use one of the other two sides as the height unless that side is also perpendicular to the parallel bases.

The **perimeter of a trapezoid** is found by the formula $P = a + b_1 + c + b_2$, where a, b_1, c, and b_2 are the four sides of the trapezoid.

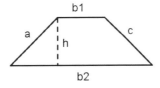

Review Video: Area and Perimeter of a Trapezoid
Visit mometrix.com/academy and enter code: 587523

Parallelogram: A quadrilateral that has two pairs of opposite parallel sides. As such it is a special type of trapezoid. The sides that are parallel are also congruent. The opposite interior angles are always congruent, and the consecutive interior angles are supplementary. The diagonals of a parallelogram divide each other. Each diagonal divides the parallelogram into two congruent triangles. A parallelogram has no line of symmetry, but does have 180-degree rotational symmetry about the midpoint.

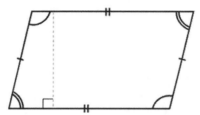

The **area of a parallelogram** is found by the formula $A = bh$, where b is the length of the base, and h is the height. Note that the base and height correspond to the length and width in a rectangle, so this formula would apply to rectangles as well. Do not confuse the height of a parallelogram with the length of the second side. The two are only the same measure in the case of a rectangle.

The **perimeter of a parallelogram** is found by the formula $P = 2a + 2b$ or $P = 2(a + b)$, where a and b are the lengths of the two sides.

> **Review Video: <u>Parallelogram</u>**
> Visit mometrix.com/academy and enter code: 129981
>
> **Review Video: <u>Area and Perimeter of a Parallelogram</u>**
> Visit mometrix.com/academy and enter code: 718313

Isosceles trapezoid: A trapezoid with equal base angles. This gives rise to other properties including: the two nonparallel sides have the same length, the two non-base angles are also equal, and there is one line of symmetry through the midpoints of the parallel sides.

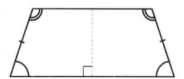

Rectangle: A quadrilateral with four right angles. All rectangles are parallelograms and trapezoids, but not all parallelograms or trapezoids are rectangles. The diagonals of a rectangle are congruent. Rectangles have 2 lines of symmetry (through each pair of opposing midpoints) and 180-degree rotational symmetry about the midpoint.

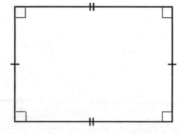

The **area of a rectangle** is found by the formula $A = lw$, where A is the area of the rectangle, l is the length (usually considered to be the longer side) and w is the width (usually considered to be the shorter side). The numbers for l and w are interchangeable.

The **perimeter of a rectangle** is found by the formula $P = 2l + 2w$ or $P = 2(l + w)$, where l is the length, and w is the width. It may be easier to add the length and width first and then double the result, as in the second formula.

Rhombus: A quadrilateral with four congruent sides. All rhombuses are parallelograms and kites; thus, they inherit all the properties of both types of quadrilaterals. The diagonals of a rhombus are perpendicular to each other. Rhombi have 2 lines of symmetry (along each of the diagonals) and 180-degree rotational symmetry. The **area of a rhombus** is half the product of the diagonals: $A = \frac{d_1 d_2}{2}$ and the perimeter of a rhombus is: $P = 2\sqrt{(d_1)^2 + (d_2)^2}$

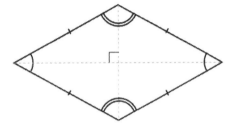

Square: A quadrilateral with four right angles and four congruent sides. Squares satisfy the criteria of all other types of quadrilaterals. The diagonals of a square are congruent and perpendicular to each other. Squares have 4 lines of symmetry (through each pair of opposing midpoints and along each of the diagonals) as well as 90-degree rotational symmetry about the midpoint.

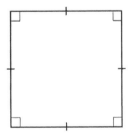

The **area of a square** is found by using the formula $A = s^2$, where and s is the length of one side. The **perimeter of a square** is found by using the formula $P = 4s$, where s is the length of one side. Because all four sides are equal in a square, it is faster to multiply the length of one side by 4 than to add the same number four times. You could use the formulas for rectangles and get the same answer.

The hierarchy of quadrilaterals can be shown as follows:

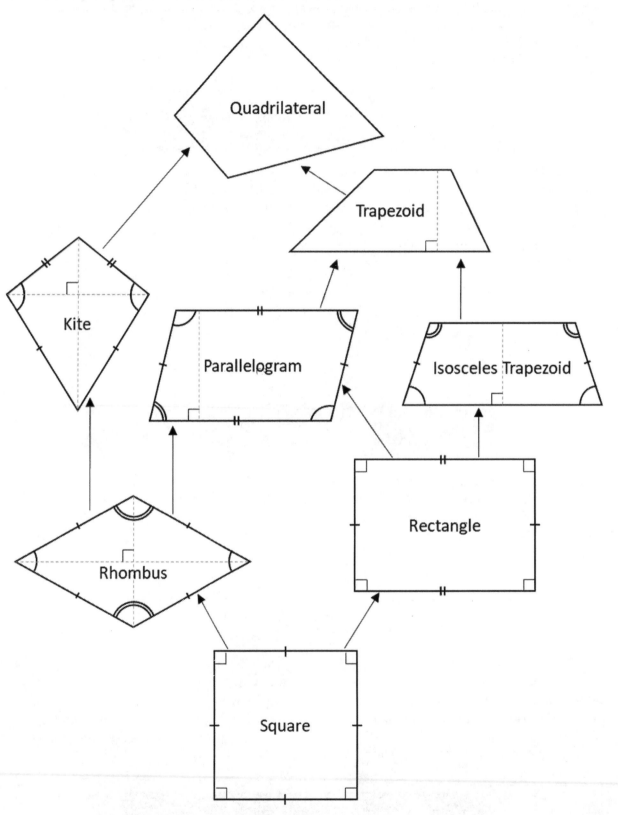

SOLIDS

The **surface area of a solid object** is the area of all sides or exterior surfaces. For objects such as prisms and pyramids, a further distinction is made between base surface area (B) and lateral surface area (LA). For a prism, the total surface area (SA) is $SA = LA + 2B$. For a pyramid or cone, the total surface area is $SA = LA + B$.

The **surface area of a sphere** can be found by the formula $A = 4\pi r^2$, where r is the radius. The volume is given by the formula $V = \frac{4}{3}\pi r^3$, where r is the radius. Both quantities are generally given in terms of π.

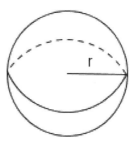

The **volume of any prism** is found by the formula $V = Bh$, where B is the area of the base, and h is the height (perpendicular distance between the bases). The surface area of any prism is the sum of the areas of both bases and all sides. It can be calculated as $SA = 2B + Ph$, where P is the perimeter of the base.

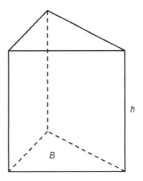

For a **rectangular prism**, the volume can be found by the formula $V = lwh$, where V is the volume, l is the length, w is the width, and h is the height. The surface area can be calculated as $SA = 2lw + 2hl + 2wh$ or $SA = 2(lw + hl + wh)$.

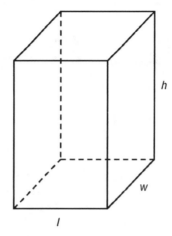

The **volume of a cube** can be found by the formula $V = s^3$, where s is the length of a side. The surface area of a cube is calculated as $SA = 6s^2$, where SA is the total surface area and s is the length of a side. These formulas are the same as the ones used for the volume and surface area of a rectangular prism, but simplified since all three quantities (length, width, and height) are the same.

> **Review Video: Volume and Surface Area of a Cube**
> Visit mometrix.com/academy and enter code: 664455

The **volume of a cylinder** can be calculated by the formula $V = \pi r^2 h$, where r is the radius, and h is the height. The surface area of a cylinder can be found by the formula $SA = 2\pi r^2 + 2\pi rh$. The first term is the base area multiplied by two, and the second term is the perimeter of the base multiplied by the height.

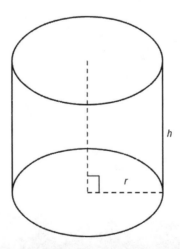

> **Review Video: Volume and Surface Area of a Right Circular Cylinder**
> Visit mometrix.com/academy and enter code: 226463

The **volume of a pyramid** is found by the formula $V = \frac{1}{3}Bh$, where B is the area of the base, and h is the height (perpendicular distance from the vertex to the base). Notice this formula is the same as $\frac{1}{3}$ times the volume of a prism. Like a prism, the base of a pyramid can be any shape.

Finding the **surface area of a pyramid** is not as simple as the other shapes we've looked at thus far. If the pyramid is a right pyramid, meaning the base is a regular polygon and the vertex is directly over the center of that polygon, the surface area can be calculated as $SA = B + \frac{1}{2}Ph_s$, where P is the perimeter of the base, and h_s is the slant height (distance from the vertex to the midpoint of one side of the base). If the pyramid is irregular, the area of each triangle side must be calculated individually and then summed, along with the base.

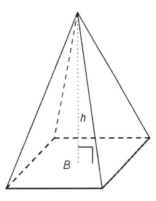

The **volume of a cone** is found by the formula $V = \frac{1}{3}\pi r^2 h$, where r is the radius, and h is the height. Notice this is the same as $\frac{1}{3}$ times the volume of a cylinder. The surface area can be calculated as $SA = \pi r^2 + \pi rs$, where s is the slant height. The slant height can be calculated using the pythagorean thereom to be $\sqrt{r^2 + h^2}$, so the surface area formula can also be written as $SA = \pi r^2 + \pi r\sqrt{r^2 + h^2}$.

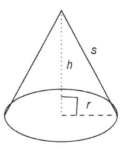

PRACTICE

P1. Find the measure of angles **(a)**, **(b)**, and **(c)** based on the figure with two parallel lines, two perpendicular lines and one transversal:

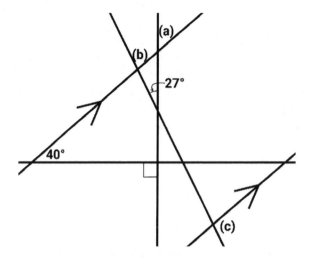

P2. Use the coordinate plane to reflect the figure below across the *y*-axis.

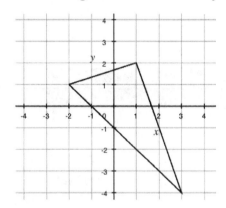

P3. Use the coordinate plane to enlarge the figure below by a factor of 2.

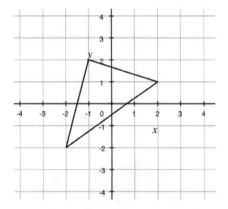

P4. Find the area and perimeter of the following quadrilaterals:

(a) A square with side length 2.5 cm.

(b) A parallelogram with height 3 m, base 4 m, and other side 6 m.

(c) A rhombus with diagonals 15 in and 20 in.

P5. Find the surface area and volume of the following solids:

(a) A cylinder with radius 5 m and height 0.5 m.

(b) A trapezoidal prism with base area of 254 mm^2, base perimeter 74 mm, and height 10 mm.

(c) A half sphere (radius 5 yds) on the base of an inverted cone with the same radius and a height of 7 yds.

PRACTICE SOLUTIONS

P1. (a) The vertical angle paired with (a) is part of a right triangle with the 40° angle. Thus the measure can be found:

$$90° = 40° + a$$
$$a = 50°$$

(b) The triangle formed by the supplementary angle to (b) is part of a triangle with the vertical angle paired with (a) and the given angle of 27°. Since $a = 50°$:

$$180° = (180° - b) + 50° + 27°$$
$$103° = 180° - b$$
$$-77° = -b$$
$$77° = b$$

(c) As they are part of a transversal crossing parallel lines, angles (b) and (c) are supplementary. Thus $c = 103°$

P2. To reflect the image across the y-axis, replace each x-coordinate of the points that are the vertex of the triangle, x, with its negative, $-x$.

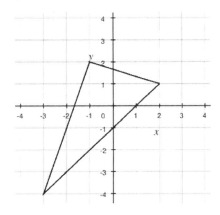

P3. An enlargement can be found by multiplying each coordinate of the coordinate pairs located at the triangle's vertices by 2. The original coordinates were $(-1, 2), (2, 1), (-2, -2)$, so the new coordinates are $(-2, 4), (4, 2), (-4, -4)$:

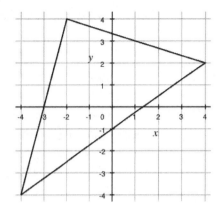

P4. (a) $A = s^2 = (2.5 \text{ cm})^2 = 6.25 \text{ cm}^2; P = 4s = 4 \times 2.5 \text{ cm} = 10 \text{ cm}$

(b) $A = bh = (3 \text{ m})(4 \text{ m}) = 12 \text{ m}^2; P = 2a + 2b = 2 \times 6 \text{ m} + 2 \times 4 \text{ m} = 20 \text{ m}$

(c) $A = \frac{d_1 d_2}{2} = \frac{(15 \text{ in})(20 \text{ in})}{2} = 150 \text{ in}^2;$
$P = 2\sqrt{(d_1)^2 + (d_2)^2} = 2\sqrt{(15 \text{ in})^2 + (20 \text{ in})^2} = 2\sqrt{625 \text{ in}^2} = 50 \text{ in}$

P5. (a) $SA = 2\pi r^2 + 2\pi rh = 2\pi(5 \text{ m})^2 + 2\pi(5 \text{ m})(0.5 \text{ m}) = 55\pi \text{ m}^2 \cong 172.79 \text{ m}^2;$
$V = \pi r^2 h = \pi(5 \text{ m})^2(0.5 \text{ m}) = 12.5\pi \text{ m}^3 \cong 39.27 \text{ m}^3$

(b) $SA = 2B + Ph = 2(254 \text{ mm}^2) + (74 \text{ mm})(10 \text{ mm}) = 1248 \text{ mm}^2;$
$V = Bh = (254 \text{ mm}^2)(10 \text{ mm}) = 2540 \text{ mm}^3$

(c) We can find s, the slant height using Pythagoras' theorem, and since this solid is made of parts of simple solids, we can combine the formulas to find surface area and volume:
$$s = \sqrt{r^2 + h^2} = \sqrt{(5 \text{ yd})^2 + (7 \text{ yd})^2} = \sqrt{74} \text{ yd}$$
$$SA = \frac{4\pi r^2}{2} + \pi rs = \frac{4\pi(5 \text{ yd})^2}{2} + \pi(5 \text{ yd})(\sqrt{74} \text{ yd}) = \left(5\pi + 5\pi\sqrt{74}\right) \text{ yd}^2 \cong 150.83 \text{ yd}^2$$
$$V = \frac{1}{3}\pi r^2 h = \frac{1}{3}\pi(5 \text{ yd})^2(7 \text{ yd}) = \frac{35\pi}{3} \text{ yd}^3 \cong 36.65 \text{ yd}^3$$

Triangles

A **scalene triangle** is a triangle with no congruent sides. A scalene triangle will also have three angles of different measures. The angle with the largest measure is opposite the longest side, and the angle with the smallest measure is opposite the shortest side. An **acute triangle** is a triangle whose three angles are all less than 90°. If two of the angles are equal, the acute triangle is also an **isosceles triangle**. An isosceles triangle will also have two congruent angles opposite the two congruent sides.If the three angles are all equal, the acute triangle is also an **equilateral triangle**. An equilateral triangle will also have three congruent angles, each 60°. All equilateral triangles are also acute triangles. An **obtuse triangle** is a triangle with exactly one angle greater than 90°. The other two angles may or may not be equal. If the two remaining angles are equal, the obtuse triangle is also an isosceles triangle. A **right triangle** is a triangle with exactly one angle equal to

90°. All right triangles follow the Pythagorean theorem. A right triangle can never be acute or obtuse.

The table below illustrates how each descriptor places a different restriction on the triangle:

Angles / Sides	Acute: All angles < 90°	Obtuse: One angle > 90°	Right: One angle = 90°
Scalene: No equal side lengths	$90° > \angle a > \angle b > \angle c$ $x > y > z$	$\angle a > 90° > \angle b > \angle c$ $x > y > z$	$90° = \angle a > \angle b > \angle c$ $x > y > z$
Isosceles: Two equal side lengths	$90° > \angle a, \angle b, or \angle c$ $\angle b = \angle c, \quad y = z$	$\angle a > 90° > \angle b = \angle c$ $x > y = z$	$\angle a = 90°, \angle b = \angle c = 45°$ $x > y = z$
Equilateral: Three equal side lengths	$60° = \angle a = \angle b = \angle c$ $x = y = z$		

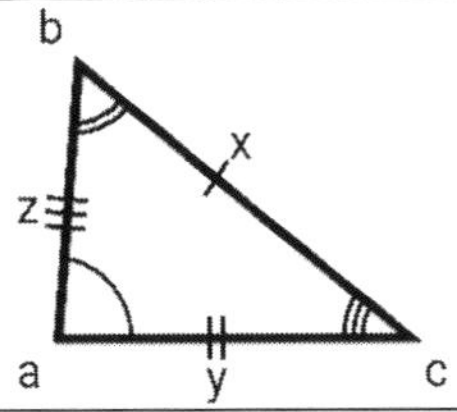

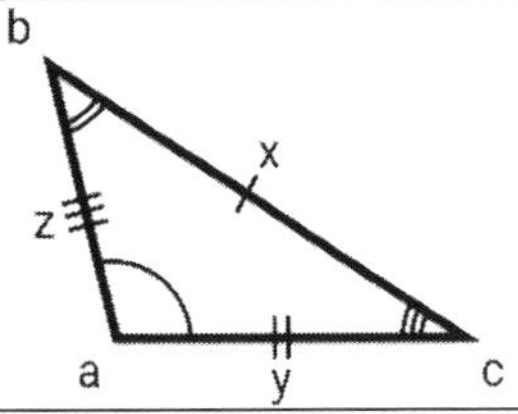

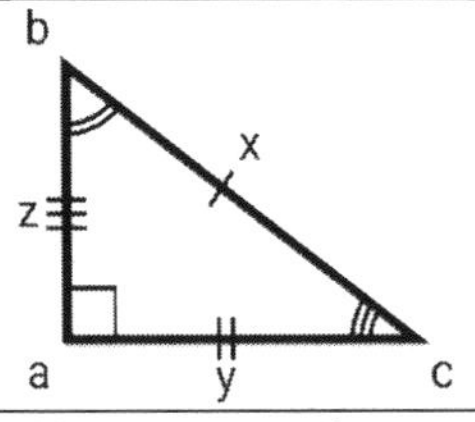

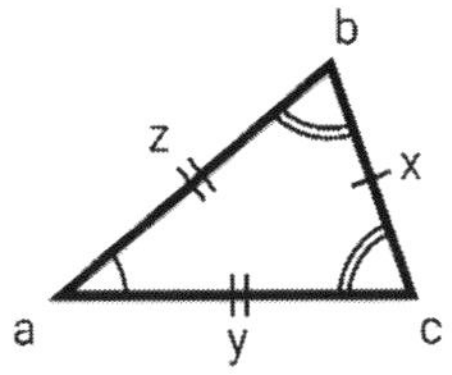

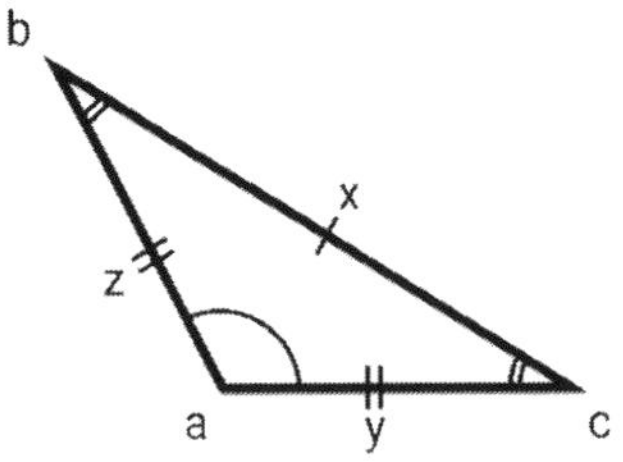

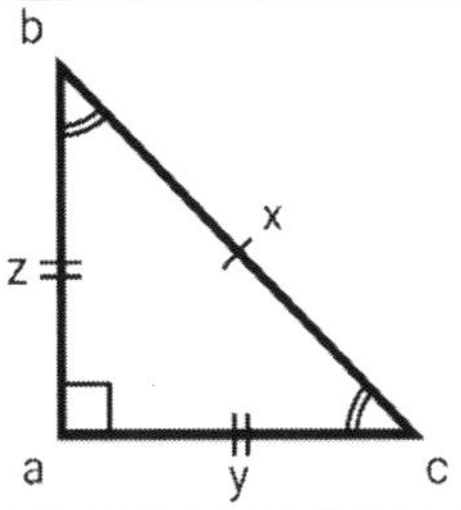

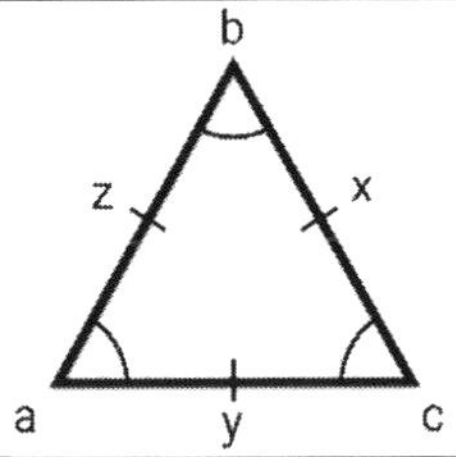

Review Video: Introduction to Types of Triangles
Visit mometrix.com/academy and enter code: 511711

PARTS OF A TRIANGLE

An **altitude** of a triangle is a line segment drawn from one vertex perpendicular to the opposite side. In the diagram below, $\overline{BE}, \overline{AD}$, and $\overline{CF}$ are altitudes. The length of an altitude is also called the height of the triangle. The three altitudes in a triangle are always concurrent. The point of concurrency of the altitudes of a triangle, O, is called the **orthocenter**. Note that in an obtuse triangle, the orthocenter will be outside the triangle, and in a right triangle, the orthocenter is the vertex of the right angle.

A **median** of a triangle is a line segment drawn from one vertex to the midpoint of the opposite side. In the diagram below, $\overline{BH}, \overline{AG}$, and $\overline{CI}$ are medians. This is not the same as the altitude, except the altitude to the base of an isosceles triangle and all three altitudes of an equilateral triangle. The point of concurrency of the medians of a triangle, T, is called the **centroid**. This is the same point as the orthocenter only in an equilateral triangle. Unlike the orthocenter, the centroid is always inside the triangle. The centroid can also be considered the exact center of the triangle. Any shape triangle can be perfectly balanced on a tip placed at the centroid. The centroid is also the point that is two-thirds the distance from the vertex to the opposite side.

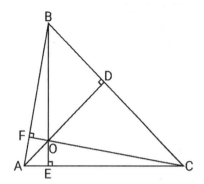 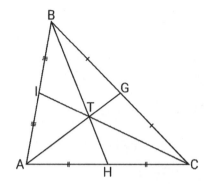

AREA AND PERIMETER OF A TRIANGLE

The **perimeter of any triangle** is found by summing the three side lengths; $P = a + b + c$. For an equilateral triangle, this is the same as $P = 3a$, where a is any side length, since all three sides are the same length.

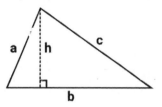

The **area of any triangle** can be found by taking half the product of one side length referred to as the base often given the variable b and the perpendicular distance from that side to the opposite vertex called the altitude or height and given the variable h. In equation form that is $A = \frac{1}{2}bh$. Another formula that works for any triangle is $A = \sqrt{s(s-a)(s-b)(s-c)}$, where s is the semiperimeter: $\frac{a+b+c}{2}$, and a, b, and c are the lengths of the three sides. Special cases include isosceles triangles: $A = \frac{1}{2}b\sqrt{a^2 - \frac{b^2}{4}}$, where b is the the unique side and a is the length of one of the two congruent sides, and equilateral triangles: $A = \frac{\sqrt{3}}{4}a^2$, where a is the length of a side.

Review Video: <u>Area and Perimeter of a Triangle</u>
Visit mometrix.com/academy and enter code: 853779

SIMILARITY AND CONGRUENCE RULES

Similar triangles are triangles whose corresponding angles are equal and whose corresponding sides are proportional. Represented by AAA. Similar triangles whose corresponding sides are congruent are also congruent triangles.

The triangles can be shown to be **congruent** in 5 ways:

- **SSS**: Three sides of one triangle are congruent to the three corresponding sides of the second triangle.
- **SAS**: Two sides and the included angle (the angle formed by those two sides) of one triangle are congruent to the corresponding two sides and included angle of the second triangle.
- **ASA**: Two angles and the included side (the side that joins the two angles) of one triangle are congruent to the corresponding two angles and included side of the second triangle.
- **AAS**: Two angles and a non-included side of one triangle are congruent to the corresponding two angles and non-included side of the second triangle.
- **HL**: The hypotenuse and leg of one right triangle are congruent to the corresponding hypotenuse and leg of the second right triangle.

> **Review Video: Similar Triangles**
> Visit mometrix.com/academy and enter code: 398538

GENERAL RULES FOR TRIANGLES

The **triangle inequality theorem** states that the sum of the measures of any two sides of a triangle is always greater than the measure of the third side. If the sum of the measures of two sides were equal to the third side, a triangle would be impossible because the two sides would lie flat across the third side and there would be no vertex. If the sum of the measures of two of the sides was less than the third side, a closed figure would be impossible because the two shortest sides would never meet. In other words, for a triangle with sides lengths A, B, and C: $A + B > C$, $B + C > A$, and $A + C > B$

The sum of the measures of the interior angles of a triangle is always $180°$. Therefore, a triangle can never have more than one angle greater than or equal to $90°$.

In any triangle, the angles opposite congruent sides are congruent, and the sides opposite congruent angles are congruent. The largest angle is always opposite the longest side, and the smallest angle is always opposite the shortest side.

The line segment that joins the midpoints of any two sides of a triangle is always parallel to the third side and exactly half the length of the third side.

PYTHAGOREAN THEOREM

The side of a triangle opposite the right angle is called the **hypotenuse**. The other two sides are called the legs. The pythagorean theorem states a relationship among the legs and hypotenuse of a right triangle: $a^2 + b^2 = c^2$, where a and b are the lengths of the legs of a right triangle, and c is the length of the hypotenuse. Note that this formula will only work with right triangles.

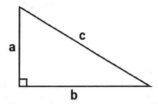

TRIGONOMETRIC FORMULAS

In the diagram below, angle C is the right angle, and side c is the hypotenuse. Side a is the side opposite to angle A and side b is the side opposite to angle B. Using ratios of side lengths as a means to calculate the sine, cosine, and tangent of an acute angle only works for right triangles.

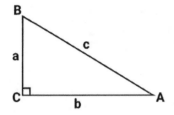

$$\sin A = \frac{\text{opposite side}}{\text{hypotenuse}} = \frac{a}{c} \qquad \csc A = \frac{1}{\sin A} = \frac{\text{hypotenuse}}{\text{opposite side}} = \frac{c}{a}$$

$$\cos A = \frac{\text{adjacent side}}{\text{hypotenuse}} = \frac{b}{c} \qquad \sec A = \frac{1}{\cos A} = \frac{\text{hypotenuse}}{\text{adjacent side}} = \frac{c}{b}$$

$$\tan A = \frac{\text{opposite side}}{\text{adjacent side}} = \frac{a}{b} \qquad \cot A = \frac{1}{\tan A} = \frac{\text{adjacent side}}{\text{opposite side}} = \frac{b}{a}$$

LAWS OF SINES AND COSINES

The **law of sines** states that $\frac{\sin A}{a} = \frac{\sin B}{b} = \frac{\sin C}{c}$, where A, B, and C are the angles of a triangle, and a, b, and c are the sides opposite their respective angles. This formula will work with all triangles, not just right triangles.

The **law of cosines** is given by the formula $c^2 = a^2 + b^2 - 2ab(\cos C)$, where a, b, and c are the sides of a triangle, and C is the angle opposite side c. This is a generalized form of the pythagorean theorem that can be used on any triangle.

PRACTICE

P1. Given the following pairs of triangles, determine whether they are similar, congruent, or neither (note that the figures are not drawn to scale):

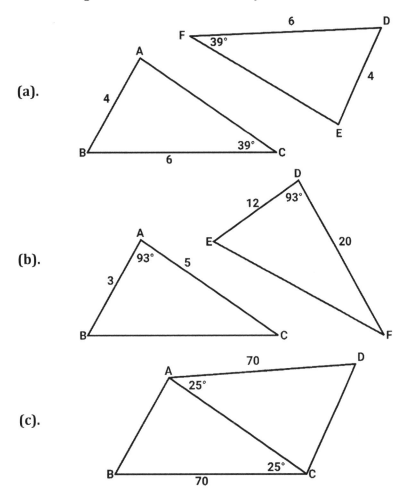

(a).

(b).

(c).

P2. Calculate the area of a triangle with side lengths of 7 ft, 8 ft, and 9 ft.

P3. Calculate the following values based on triangle MNO:

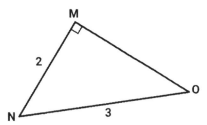

    (a) length of $\overline{MO}$

    (b) $\sin(\angle NOM)$

    (c) area of the triangle, if the units of the measurements are in miles

PRACTICE SOLUTIONS

P1. (a). Neither: We are given that two sides lengths and an angle are equal, however, the angle given is not between the given side lengths. That means there are two possible triangles that could satisfy the given measurements. Thus, we cannot be certain of congruence:

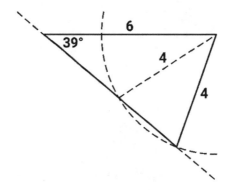

(b) Similar: Since we are given a side-angle-side of each triangle and the side lengths given are scaled evenly $\left(\frac{3}{5} \times \frac{4}{4} = \frac{12}{20}\right)$ and the angles are equal. Thus, $\Delta ABC \sim \Delta DEF$. If the side lengths were equal, then they would be congruent.

(c) Congruent: Even though we aren't given a measurement for the shared side of the figure, since it is shared it is equal. So, this is a case of SAS. Thus, $\Delta ABC \cong \Delta CDA$

P2. Given only side lengths, we can use the semi perimeter to the find the area based on the formula, $A = \sqrt{s(s-a)(s-b)(s-c)}$, where s is the semiperimeter, $\frac{a+b+c}{2} = \frac{7+8+9}{2} = 12$ ft:

$$A = \sqrt{12(12-7)(12-8)(12-9)}$$
$$= \sqrt{(12)(5)(4)(3)}$$
$$= 12\sqrt{5} \text{ ft}^2$$

P3. (a) Since triangle MNO is a right triangle, we can use the simple form of Pythagoras theorem to find the missing side length:

$$\left(\overline{MO}\right)^2 + 2^2 = 3^2$$
$$\left(\overline{MO}\right)^2 = 9 - 4$$
$$\overline{MO} = \sqrt{5}$$

(b) Recall that sine of an angle in a right triangle is the ratio of the opposite side to the hypotenuse. So, $\sin(\angle NOM) = 2/3$

(c) Since triangle MNO is a right triangle, we can use either of the legs as the height and the other as the base in the simple formula for area of a triangle:

$$A = \frac{bh}{2}$$
$$= \frac{(2 \text{ mi})(\sqrt{5} \text{ mi})}{2}$$
$$= \sqrt{5} \text{ mi}^2$$

Circles and Conic Sections

CIRCLES

The **center** of a circle is the single point from which every point on the circle is **equidistant**. The **radius** is a line segment that joins the center of the circle and any one point on the circle. All radii of a circle are equal. Circles that have the same center, but not the same length of radii are **concentric**. The **diameter** is a line segment that passes through the center of the circle and has both endpoints on the circle. The length of the diameter is exactly twice the length of the radius. Point O in the diagram below is the center of the circle, segments $\overline{OX}$, $\overline{OY}$, and $\overline{OZ}$ are radii, and segment $\overline{XZ}$ is a diamter.

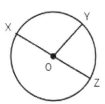

> **Review Video: Points of a Circle**
> Visit mometrix.com/academy and enter code: 420746
>
> **Review Video: The Diameter, Radius, and Circumference of Circles**
> Visit mometrix.com/academy and enter code: 448988

The **area of a circle** is found by the formula $A = \pi r^2$, where r is the length of the radius. If the diameter of the circle is given, remember to divide it in half to get the length of the radius before proceeding.

The **circumference** of a circle is found by the formula $C = 2\pi r$, where r is the radius. Again, remember to convert the diameter if you are given that measure rather than the radius.

> **Review Video: Area and Circumference of a Circle**
> Visit mometrix.com/academy and enter code: 243015

An **arc** is a portion of a circle. Specifically, an arc is the set of points between and including two points on a circle. An arc does not contain any points inside the circle. When a segment is drawn from the endpoints of an arc to the center of the circle, a sector is formed. A **minor arc** is an arc that has a measure less than 180°. A **major arc** is an arc having a measure of at least 180°. Every minor arc has a corresponding major arc that can be found by subtracting the measure of the minor arc from 360°. A **semicircle** is an arc whose endpoints are the endpoints of the diameter of a circle. A semicircle is exactly half of a circle.

A **central angle** is an angle whose vertex is the center of a circle and whose legs intercept an arc of the circle. The measure of a central angle is equal to the measure of the minor arc it intercepts.

An **inscribed angle** is an angle whose vertex lies on a circle and whose legs contain chords of that circle. The portion of the circle intercepted by the legs of the angle is called the intercepted arc. The measure of the intercepted arc is exactly twice the measure of the inscribed angle. In the following diagram, angle ABC is an inscribed angle. $\widehat{AC} = 2(m\angle ABC)$

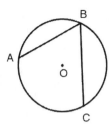

Any angle inscribed in a semicircle is a right angle. The intercepted arc is 180°, making the inscribed angle half that, or 90°. In the diagram below, angle ABC is inscribed in semicircle ABC, making angle ABC equal to 90°.

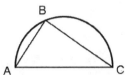

A **secant** is a line that intersects a circle in two points. The segment of a secant line that is contained within the circle is called a **chord**. Two secants may intersect inside the circle, on the circle, or outside the circle. When the two secants intersect on the circle, an inscribed angle is formed. When two secants intersect inside a circle, the measure of each of two vertical angles is equal to half the sum of the two intercepted arcs. Consider the following diagram where $m\angle AEB = \frac{1}{2}(\widehat{AB} + \widehat{CD})$ and $m\angle BEC = \frac{1}{2}(\widehat{BC} + \widehat{AD})$.

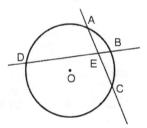

When two secants intersect outside a circle, the measure of the angle formed is equal to half the difference of the two arcs that lie between the two secants. In the diagram below, $m\angle AEB = \frac{1}{2}(\widehat{AB} - \widehat{CD})$.

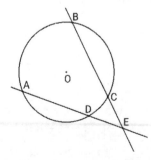

A **tangent** is a line in the same plane as a circle that touches the circle in exactly one point. The point at which a tangent touches a circle is called the **point of tangency**. While a line segment can be tangent to a circle as part of a line that is tangent, it is improper to say a tangent can be simply a line segment that touches the circle in exactly one point.

In the diagram below, $\overleftrightarrow{EB}$ is a secant and contains chord $\overline{EB}$ and $\overleftrightarrow{CD}$ is tangent to circle A. Notice that $\overline{FB}$ is not tangent to the circle. $\overline{FB}$ is a line segment that touches the circle in exactly one point, but if the segment were extended, it would touch the circle in a second point. In the diagram below, point B is the point of tangency.

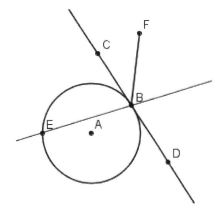

The **arc length** is the length of that portion of the circumference between two points on the circle. The formula for arc length is $s = \frac{\pi r \theta}{180°}$ where s is the arc length, r is the length of the radius, and θ is the angular measure of the arc in degrees, or $s = r\theta$, where θ is the angular measure of the arc in radians (2π radians = 360 degrees).

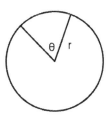

A **sector** is the portion of a circle formed by two radii and their intercepted arc. While the arc length is exclusively the points that are also on the circumference of the circle, the sector is the entire area bounded by the arc and the two radii.

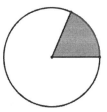

The **area of a sector** of a circle is found by the formula, $A = \frac{\theta r^2}{2}$, where A is the area, θ is the measure of the central angle in radians, and r is the radius. To find the area with the central angle in degrees, use the formula, $A = \frac{\theta \pi r^2}{360}$, where θ is the measure of the central angle and r is the radius.

INSCRIBED AND CIRCUMSCRIBED FIGURES

These terms can be both used to describe a given arrangement of figures, depending on perspective. If each of the vertices of figure A lie on figure B, then it can be said that figure A is **inscribed** in figure B, but it can also be said that figure B is **circumscribed** about figure A. The following table and examples help to illustrate the concept. Note that the figures cannot both be circles, as they would be completely overlapping and neither would be inscribed or circumscribed.

Given	Description	Equivalent Description	Figures
Each of the sides of a pentagon is tangent to a circle	The circle is inscribed in the pentagon	The pentagon is circumscribed about the circle	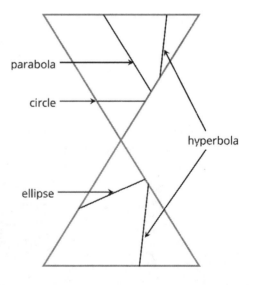
Each of the vertices of a pentagon lie on a circle	The pentagon is inscribed in the circle	The circle is circumscribed about the pentagon	

CONIC SECTIONS

Conic sections are a family of shapes that can be thought of as cross sections of a pair of infinite, right cones stacked vertex to vertex. This is easiest to see with a visual representation:

A three-dimensional look at representative conic sections. (Note that a hyperbola intersects both cones.)

A side-on look at representative conic sections. (Note that the parabola is parallel to the slant of the cones.)

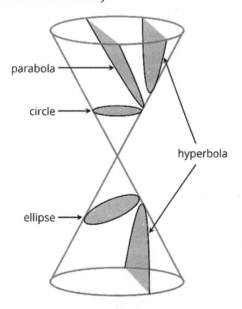

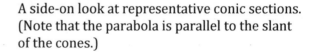

In short, a circle is a horizontal cross section, a parabola is a cross section parallel to the slant of the cone, an ellipse is a cross section at an angle *less than* the slant of the cone, and a hyperbola is a cross section at an angle *greater than* the slant of the cone.

ELLIPSE

An **ellipse** is the set of all points in a plane, whose total distance from two fixed points called the **foci** (singular: focus) is constant, and whose center is the midpoint between the foci.

The standard equation of an ellipse that is taller than it is wide is $\frac{(x-h)^2}{a^2} + \frac{(y-k)^2}{b^2} = 1$, where a and b are coefficients. The center is the point (h, k) and the foci are the points $(h, k + c)$ and $(h, k - c)$, where $c^2 = a^2 - b^2$ and $a^2 > b^2$.

The major axis has length $2a$, and the minor axis has length $2b$.

Eccentricity (e) is a measure of how elongated an ellipse is, and is the ratio of the distance between the foci to the length of the major axis. Eccentricity will have a value between 0 and 1. The closer to 1 the eccentricity is, the closer the ellipse is to being a circle. The formula for eccentricity is $= \frac{c}{a}$.

PARABOLA

A **parabola** is the set of all points in a plane that are equidistant from a fixed line, called the **directrix**, and a fixed point not on the line, called the **focus**. The **axis** is the line perpendicular to the directrix that passes through the focus.

For parabolas that open up or down, the standard equation is $(x - h)^2 = 4c(y - k)$, where h, c, and k are coefficients. If c is positive, the parabola opens up. If c is negative, the parabola opens down. The vertex is the point (h, k). The directrix is the line having the equation $y = -c + k$, and the focus is the point $(h, c + k)$.

For parabolas that open left or right, the standard equation is $(y - k)^2 = 4c(x - h)$, where k, c, and h are coefficients. If c is positive, the parabola opens to the right. If c is negative, the parabola opens to the left. The vertex is the point (h, k). The directrix is the line having the equation $x = -c + h$, and the focus is the point $(c + h, k)$.

HYPERBOLA

A **hyperbola** is the set of all points in a plane, whose distance from two fixed points, called foci, has a constant difference.

The standard equation of a horizontal hyperbola is $\frac{(x-h)^2}{a^2} - \frac{(y-k)^2}{b^2} = 1$, where a, b, h, and k are real numbers. The center is the point (h, k), the vertices are the points $(h + a, k)$ and $(h - a, k)$, and the foci are the points that every point on one of the parabolic curves is equidistant from and are found using the formulas $(h + c, k)$ and $(h - c, k)$, where $c^2 = a^2 + b^2$. The asymptotes are two lines the graph of the hyperbola approaches but never reaches, and are given by the equations $y = \left(\frac{b}{a}\right)(x - h) + k$ and $y = -\left(\frac{b}{a}\right)(x - h) + k$.

The standard equation of a vertical hyperbola is $\frac{(y-k)^2}{a^2} - \frac{(x-h)^2}{b^2} = 1$, where a, b, k, and h are real numbers. The center is the point (h, k), the vertices are the points $(h, k + a)$ and $(h, k - a)$, and the foci are the points that every point on one of the hyperbolic curves is equidistant from and are found using the formulas $(h, k + c)$ and $(h, k - c)$, where $c^2 = a^2 + b^2$. The asymptotes are two lines the graph of the hyperbola approaches but never reach, and are given by the equations $y = \left(\frac{a}{b}\right)(x - h) + k$ and $y = -\left(\frac{a}{b}\right)(x - h) + k$.

PRACTICE

P1. Given that $\angle DEB = 80°$ and $\widehat{BC} = 90°$, determine the following values abased on the figure:

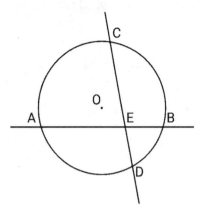

(a) $\widehat{AD}$

(b) $\widehat{DB} + \widehat{CA}$

P2. Given that $\angle OCB = 50°$, $\overleftrightarrow{EF}$ is tangent to the circle at B, and $\overline{CB} = 6$ km, determine the following values abased on the figure:

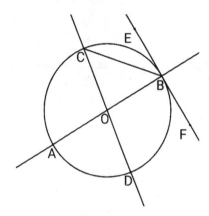

(a) The angle made between $\overleftrightarrow{CD}$ and a line tangent to the circle at A.

(b) The area of the sector of the circle between C and B.

P3. Square ABCD is inscribed in a circle with radius 20 m. What is the area of the part of the circle outside of the square?

PRACTICE SOLUTIONS

P1. (a). Recall that when two secants intersect inside of a circle, the measure of each of two vertical angles is equal to half the sum of the two intercepted arcs. Also, since $\angle DEB$ and $\angle CEB$ are supplementary, the measure of $\angle CEB = 180° - 80° = 100°$ In other words:

$$\angle CEB = \frac{1}{2}\left(\widehat{BC} + \widehat{AD}\right)$$
$$100° = \frac{1}{2}\left(90° + \widehat{AD}\right)$$
$$200° = 90° + \widehat{AD}$$
$$110° = \widehat{AD}$$

(b) Note that the whole circle is divided into four arcs. Thus,

$$\widehat{AD} + \widehat{DB} + \widehat{BC} + \widehat{CA} = 360°$$
$$110° + \widehat{DB} + 90° + \widehat{CA} = 360°$$
$$\widehat{DB} + \widehat{CA} = 160°$$

P2. (a) A line tangent to the circle at A creates a right triangle with one vertex at O, one at A, and the final vertex where $\overleftrightarrow{CD}$ intersects the tangent line, let us call that point G.

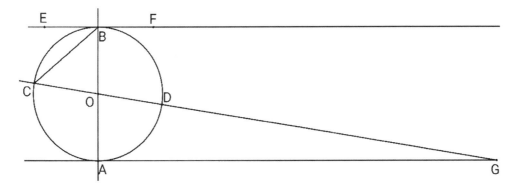

Since AB is a diameter, the line tangent at A is perpendicular to AB, so $\angle OAG = 90°$. The triangle COB has two legs that are the radius of the circle and so must be isosceles. So, $50° \times 2 + \angle COB = 180°$, which means that $\angle COB$ and the vertical angle $\angle GOA$ both equal $80°$. Knowing this we can find $\angle AGO$:

$$80° + 90° + \angle AGO = 180°$$
$$\angle AGO = 10°$$

(b) We know $\angle OCB = 50°$ that triangle COB is isosceles with two legs equal to the radius, so a perpendicular bisector of the triangle as shown will create a right triangle:

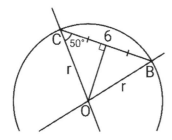

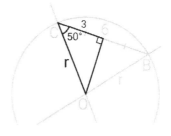

Recall that cosine of an angle in a right triangle is the ratio of the adjacent side to the hypotenuse. Thus, we can find r:

$$\cos 50° = \frac{3}{r}$$

$$r = \frac{3}{\cos 50°}$$

As noted in part (a), $\angle COB = 80°$ so, the area of the sector is:

$$A = \frac{\theta \pi r^2}{360°}$$

$$= \frac{80°\pi \left(\frac{3}{\cos 50°}\right)^2}{360°}$$

$$= \frac{2\pi \left(\frac{9}{\cos^2 50°}\right)}{9}$$

$$= \frac{2\pi}{\cos^2 50°} \cong 15.2 \text{ km}^2$$

P3. Begin by drawing a diagram of the situation, where we want to find the shaded area:

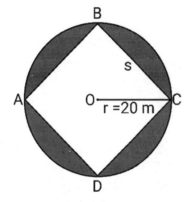
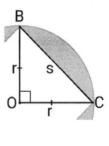

The area of the square is s^2, so the area we want to find is: $\pi r^2 - s^2$. Since the inscribed figure is a square, the triangle BCO is a 45-45-90 right triangle. Now, we can find $s^2 = r^2 + r^2 = 2r^2$. So, the shaded area is:

$$A = \pi r^2 - s^2$$
$$= \pi r^2 - 2r^2$$
$$= (\pi - 2)r^2$$
$$= (\pi - 2) \times 400$$
$$\cong 456.6 \text{ m}^2$$

Probability

Probability is the likelihood of a certain outcome occurring for a given event. An **event** is a situation that produces a result; that could be something as simple as flipping a coin or as complex as launching a rocket. Determining the probability of an outcome for an event can be equally simple or complex. As such there are specific terms used in the study of probability that need to be understood:

- **Compound event** – event that involves two or more independent events (rolling a pair of dice and taking the sum)
- **Desired outcome** (or success) – an outcome that meets a particular set of criteria (a roll of 1 or 2 if we are looking for numbers less than 3)
- **Independent events** – two or more events whose outcomes do not affect one another (two coins tossed at the same time)
- **Dependent events** – two or more events whose outcomes affect one another (two cards drawn consecutively from the same deck)
- **Certain outcome** – probability of outcome is 100% or 1
- **Impossible outcome** – probability of outcome is 0% or 0
- **Mutually exclusive outcomes** – two or more outcomes whose criteria cannot all be satisfied in a single event (a coin coming up heads and tails on the same toss)
- **Random variable** – refers to all possible outcomes of a single event which may be discrete or continuous.

> **Review Video: Intro to Probability**
> Visit mometrix.com/academy and enter code: 212374

THEORETICAL AND EXPERIMENTAL PROBABILITY

Theoretical probability can usually be determined without actually performing the event. The likelihood of a outcome occurring, or the probability of an outcome occurring, is given by the formula:

$$P(A) = \frac{\text{Number of acceptable outcomes}}{\text{Number of possible outcomes}}$$

Note that $P(A)$ is the probability of an outcome A occurring, and each outcome is just as likely to occur as any other outcome. If each outcome has the same probability of occurring as every other possible outcome, the outcomes are said to be equally likely to occur. The total number of acceptable outcomes must be less than or equal to the total number of possible outcomes. If the two are equal, then the outcome is certain to occur and the probability is 1. If the number of acceptable outcomes is zero, then the outcome is impossible and the probability is 0. For example, if there are 20 marbles in a bag and 5 are red, then the theoretical probability of randomly selecting a red marble is 5 out of 20, ($\frac{5}{20} = \frac{1}{4}$, 0.25, or 25%).

If the theoretical probability is unknown or too complicated to calculate, it can be estimated by an experimental probability. **Experimental probability**, also called empirical probability, is an estimate of the likelihood of a certain outcome based on repeated experiments or collected data. In other words, while theoretical probability is based on what *should* happen, experimental probability is based on what *has* happened. Experimental probability is calculated in the same way as theoretical, except that actual outcomes are used instead of possible outcomes. The more experiments performed or datapoints gathered, the better the estimate should be.

Theoretical and experimental probability do not always line up with one another. Theoretical probability says that out of 20 coin-tosses, 10 should be heads. However, if we were actually to toss 20 coins, we might record just 5 heads. This doesn't mean that our theoretical probability is incorrect; it just means that this particular experiment had results that were different from what was predicted. A practical application of empirical probability is the insurance industry. There are no set functions that define lifespan, health, or safety. Insurance companies look at factors from hundreds of thousands of individuals to find patterns that they then use to set the formulas for insurance premiums.

OBJECTIVE AND SUBJECTIVE PROBABILITY

Objective probability is based on mathematical formulas and documented evidence. Examples of objective probability include raffles or lottery drawings where there is a pre-determined number of possible outcomes and a predetermined number of outcomes that correspond to an event. Other cases of objective probability include probabilities of rolling dice, flipping coins, or drawing cards. Most gambling games are based on objective probability.

In contrast, **subjective probability** is based on personal or professional feelings and judgments. Often, there is a lot of guesswork following extensive research. Areas where subjective probability is applicable include sales trends and business expenses. Attractions set admission prices based on subjective probabilities of attendance based on varying admission rates in an effort to maximize their profit.

SAMPLE SPACE

The total set of all possible results of a test or experiment is called a **sample space**, or sometimes a universal sample space. The sample space, represented by one of the variables S, Ω, or U (for universal sample space) has individual elements called outcomes. Other terms for outcome that may be used interchangeably include elementary outcome, simple event, or sample point. The number of outcomes in a given sample space could be infinite or finite, and some tests may yield multiple unique sample sets. For example, tests conducted by drawing playing cards from a standard deck would have one sample space of the card values, another sample space of the card suits, and a third sample space of suit-denomination combinations. For most tests, the sample spaces considered will be finite.

An **event**, represented by the variable E, is a portion of a sample space. It may be one outcome or a group of outcomes from the same sample space. If an event occurs, then the test or experiment will generate an outcome that satisfies the requirement of that event. For example, given a standard deck of 52 playing cards as the sample space, and defining the event as the collection of face cards, then the event will occur if the card drawn is a J, Q, or K. If any other card is drawn, the event is said to have not occurred.

For every sample space, each possible outcome has a specific likelihood, or probability, that it will occur. The probability measure, also called the **distribution**, is a function that assigns a real number probability, from zero to one, to each outcome. For a probability measure to be accurate, every outcome must have a real number probability measure that is greater than or equal to zero and less than or equal to one. Also, the probability measure of the sample space must equal one, and the probability measure of the union of multiple outcomes must equal the sum of the individual probability measures.

Probabilities of events are expressed as real numbers from zero to one. They give a numerical value to the chance that a particular event will occur. The probability of an event occurring is the sum of the probabilities of the individual elements of that event. For example, in a standard deck of 52 playing cards as the sample space and the collection of face cards as the event, the probability of drawing a specific face card is $\frac{1}{52} = 0.019$, but the probability of drawing any one of the twelve face cards is $12(0.019) = 0.228$. Note that rounding of numbers can generate different results. If you multiplied 12 by the fraction $\frac{1}{52}$ before converting to a decimal, you would get the answer $\frac{12}{52} = 0.231$.

TREE DIAGRAM

For a simple sample space, possible outcomes may be determined by using a **tree diagram** or an organized chart. In either case, you can easily draw or list out the possible outcomes. For example, to determine all the possible ways three objects can be ordered, you can draw a tree diagram:

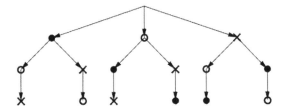

You can also make a chart to list all the possibilities:

First object	Second object	Third object
●	X	O
●	O	X
O	●	X
O	X	●
X	●	O
X	O	●

Either way, you can easily see there are six possible ways the three objects can be ordered.

If two events have no outcomes in common, they are said to be **mutually exclusive**. For example, in a standard deck of 52 playing cards, the event of all card suits is mutually exclusive to the event of all card values. If two events have no bearing on each other so that one event occurring has no influence on the probability of another event occurring, the two events are said to be independent. For example, rolling a standard six-sided die multiple times does not change that probability that a particular number will be rolled from one roll to the next. If the outcome of one event does affect the probability of the second event, the two events are said to be dependent. For example, if cards are drawn from a deck, the probability of drawing an ace after an ace has been drawn is different than the probability of drawing an ace if no ace (or no other card, for that matter) has been drawn.

In probability, the **odds in favor of an event** are the number of times the event will occur compared to the number of times the event will not occur. To calculate the odds in favor of an event, use the formula $\frac{P(A)}{1-P(A)}$, where $P(A)$ is the probability that the event will occur. Many times, odds in favor is given as a ratio in the form $\frac{a}{b}$ or $a{:}b$, where a is the probability of the event occurring and b is the complement of the event, the probability of the event not occurring. If the odds in favor are given as 2:5, that means that you can expect the event to occur two times for every 5 times that it does not occur. In other words, the probability that the event will occur is $\frac{2}{2+5} = \frac{2}{7}$.

In probability, the **odds against an event** are the number of times the event will not occur compared to the number of times the event will occur. To calculate the odds against an event, use the formula $\frac{1-P(A)}{P(A)}$, where $P(A)$ is the probability that the event will occur. Many times, odds against is given as a ratio in the form $\frac{b}{a}$ or $b{:}a$, where b is the probability the event will not occur (the complement of the event) and a is the probability the event will occur. If the odds against an event are given as 3:1, that means that you can expect the event to not occur 3 times for every one time it does occur. In other words, 3 out of every 4 trials will fail.

PERMUTATIONS AND COMBINATIONS

When trying to calculate the probability of an event using the $\frac{\text{desired outcomes}}{\text{total outcomes}}$ formula, you may frequently find that there are too many outcomes to individually count them. **Permutation** and **combination formulas** offer a shortcut to counting outcomes. A permutation is an arrangement of a specific number of a set of objects in a specific order. The number of **permutations** of r items given a set of n items can be calculated as $_nP_r = \frac{n!}{(n-r)!}$. Combinations are similar to permutations, except there are no restrictions regarding the order of the elements. While ABC is considered a different permutation than BCA, ABC and BCA are considered the same combination. The number of **combinations** of r items given a set of n items can be calculated as $_nC_r = \frac{n!}{r!(n-r)!}$ or $_nC_r = \frac{_nP_r}{r!}$.

Suppose you want to calculate how many different 5-card hands can be drawn from a deck of 52 cards. This is a combination since the order of the cards in a hand does not matter. There are 52 cards available, and 5 to be selected. Thus, the number of different hands is $_{52}C_5 = \frac{52!}{5! \times 47!} =$ 2,598,960.

COMPLEMENT OF AN EVENT

Sometimes it may be easier to calculate the possibility of something not happening, or the **complement of an event**. Represented by the symbol $\bar{A}$, the complement of A is the probability that event A does not happen. When you know the probability of event A occurring, you can use the formula $P(\bar{A}) = 1 - P(A)$, where $P(\bar{A})$ is the probability of event A not occurring, and $P(A)$ is the probability of event A occurring.

ADDITION RULE

The **addition rule** for probability is used for finding the probability of a compound event. Use the formula $P(A \text{ or } B) = P(A) + P(B) - P(A \text{ and } B)$, where $P(A \text{ and } B)$ is the probability of both events occurring to find the probability of a compound event. The probability of both events occurring at the same time must be subtracted to eliminate any overlap in the first two probabilities.

CONDITIONAL PROBABILITY

Conditional probability is the probability of an event occurring once another event has already occurred. Given event A and dependent event B, the probability of event B occurring when event A has already occurred is represented by the notation $P(A|B)$. To find the probability of event B occurring, take into account the fact that event A has already occurred and adjust the total number of possible outcomes. For example, suppose you have ten balls numbered 1–10 and you want ball number 7 to be pulled in two pulls. On the first pull, the probability of getting the 7 is $\frac{1}{10}$ because there is one ball with a 7 on it and 10 balls to choose from. Assuming the first pull did not yield a 7, the probability of pulling a 7 on the second pull is now $\frac{1}{9}$ because there are only 9 balls remaining for the second pull.

302

MULTIPLICATION RULE

The **multiplication rule** can be used to find the probability of two independent events occurring using the formula $P(A \text{ and } B) = P(A) \times P(B)$, where $P(A \text{ and } B)$ is the probability of two independent events occurring, $P(A)$ is the probability of the first event occurring, and $P(B)$ is the probability of the second event occurring.

The multiplication rule can also be used to find the probability of two dependent events occurring using the formula $P(A \text{ and } B) = P(A) \times P(B|A)$, where $P(A \text{ and } B)$ is the probability of two dependent events occurring and $P(B|A)$ is the probability of the second event occurring after the first event has already occurred. Before using the multiplication rule, you MUST first determine whether the two events are *dependent* or *independent*.

Use a **combination of the multiplication** rule and the rule of complements to find the probability that at least one outcome of the element will occur. This given by the general formula $P(\text{at least one event occurring}) = 1 - P(\text{no outcomes occurring})$. For example, to find the probability that at least one even number will show when a pair of dice is rolled, find the probability that two odd numbers will be rolled (no even numbers) and subtract from one. You can always use a tree diagram or make a chart to list the possible outcomes when the sample space is small, such as in the dice-rolling example, but in most cases it will be much faster to use the multiplication and complement formulas.

EXPECTED VALUE

Expected value is a method of determining expected outcome in a random situation. It is really a sum of the weighted probabilities of the possible outcomes. Multiply the probability of an event occurring by the weight assigned to that probability (such as the amount of money won or lost). A practical application of the expected value is to determine whether a game of chance is really fair. If the sum of the weighted probabilities is equal to zero, the game is generally considered fair because the player has a fair chance to at least to break even. If the expected value is less than zero, then players lose more than they win. For example, a lottery drawing might allow the player to choose any three-digit number, 000–999. The probability of choosing the winning number is 1:1000. If it costs \$1 to play, and a winning number receives \$500, the expected value is $\left(-\$1 \times \frac{999}{1,000}\right) + \left(\$499 \times \frac{1}{1,000}\right) = -\$0.50$. You can expect to lose on average 50 cents for every dollar you spend.

> **Review Video: Expected Value**
> Visit mometrix.com/academy and enter code: 643554

EXPECTED VALUE AND SIMULATORS

A die roll simulator will show the results of n rolls of a die. The result of each die roll may be recorded. For example, suppose a die is rolled 100 times. All results may be recorded. The numbers of 1s, 2s, 3s, 4s, 5s, and 6s, may be counted. The experimental probability of rolling each number will equal the ratio of the frequency of the rolled number to the total number of rolls. As the number of rolls increases, or approaches infinity, the experimental probability will approach the theoretical probability of 1/6. Thus, the expected value for the roll of a die is shown to be $(1 \times 1/6) + (2 \times 1/6) + (3 \times 1/6) + (4 \times 1/6) + (5 \times 1/6) + (6 \times 1/6)$, or 3.5.

PRACTICE

P1. Determine the theoretical probability of the following events:

(a) Rolling an even number on a regular 6-sided die.

(b) Not getting a red ball when selecting one from a bag of 3 red balls, 4 black balls, and 2 green balls.

(c) Rolling a standard die and then selecting a card from a standard deck that is less than the value rolled.

P2. There is a game of chance involving a standard deck of cards that has been shuffled and then laid on a table. The player wins $10 if they can turn over 2 cards of matching color (black or red), $50 for 2 cards with matching value (A-K), and $100 for 2 cards with both matching color and value. What is the expected value of playing this game?

PRACTICE SOLUTIONS

P1. (a). The values on the faces of a regular die are 1, 2, 3, 4, 5, and 6. Since three of these are even numbers (2, 4, 6), The probability of rolling an even number is $\frac{3}{6} = \frac{1}{2} = 0.5 = 50\%$.

(b) The bag contains a total of 9 balls, 6 of which are not red, so the probability of selecting one non-red ball would be $\frac{6}{9} = \frac{2}{3} \cong 0.667 \cong 66.7\%$.

(c) In this scenario, we need to determine the how many cards could satisfy the condition for each possible value of the die roll. If a one is rolled, there is no way to achieve the desired outcome, since no cards in a standard deck are less than 1. If a two is rolled, then any of the four aces would achieve the desired result. If a three is rolled, then either an ace or a two would satisfy the condition, and so on. Note that any value on the die is equally likely to occur, meaning that the probability of each roll is $\frac{1}{6}$. Putting all this in a table can help:

Roll	Cards < Roll	Probability of Card	Probability of Event
1	-	$\frac{0}{52} = 0$	$\frac{1}{6} \times 0 = 0$
2	1	$\frac{4}{52} = \frac{1}{13}$	$\frac{1}{6} \times \frac{1}{13} = \frac{1}{78}$
3	1,2	$\frac{8}{52} = \frac{2}{13}$	$\frac{1}{6} \times \frac{2}{13} = \frac{2}{78}$
4	1,2,3	$\frac{12}{52} = \frac{3}{13}$	$\frac{1}{6} \times \frac{3}{13} = \frac{3}{78}$
5	1,2,3,4	$\frac{16}{52} = \frac{4}{13}$	$\frac{1}{6} \times \frac{4}{13} = \frac{4}{78}$
6	1,2,3,4,5	$\frac{20}{52} = \frac{5}{13}$	$\frac{1}{6} \times \frac{5}{13} = \frac{5}{78}$

Assuming that each value of the die is equally likely, then the probability is the sum of the probabilities of each way to achieve the desired outcome: $\frac{0+1+2+3+4+5}{78} = \frac{15}{78} = \frac{5}{26} \cong 0.192 \cong 19.2\%$.

P2. First, determine the probability of each way of winning each way. In each case, the fist card simply determines which of the remaining 51 cards in the deck correspond to a win. For the color of the cards to match, there are 25 cards of remaining in the deck that match the color of the first, but one of the 25 also matches the value, so only 24 are left in this category. For the value of the cards to match, there are 3 cards of remaining in the deck that match the value of the first, but one of the three also matches the color, so only 2 are left in this category. For the cards to match both color and value, there is only one card in the deck that will work. Finally, there are 24 cards left that don't match at all.

Now we can find the expected value of playing the game, where we multiply the value of each event by the probability it will occur and sum over all of them:

$$\$10 \times \frac{24}{51} = \$4.71$$
$$\$50 \times \frac{2}{51} = \$1.96$$
$$\$100 \times \frac{1}{51} = \$1.96$$
$$\$0 \times \frac{24}{51} = \$0$$

$$\$4.71 + \$1.96 + \$1.96 = \$8.63$$

This game therefore has an expected value of $8.63 each time you play, which means if the cost to play is less than $8.63 then you would, on average, *gain* money. However, if the cost to play is more than $8.63, then you would, on average, *lose* money.

Statistics

Statistics is the branch of mathematics that deals with collecting, recording, interpreting, illustrating, and analyzing large amounts of **data**. The following terms are often used in the discussion of data and **statistics**:

- **Data** – the collective name for pieces of information (singular is datum).
- **Quantitative data** – measurements (such as length, mass, and speed) that provide information about quantities in numbers
- **Qualitative data** – information (such as colors, scents, tastes, and shapes) that cannot be measured using numbers
- **Discrete data** – information that can be expressed only by a specific value, such as whole or half numbers. For example, since people can be counted only in whole numbers, a population count would be discrete data.
- **Continuous data** – information (such as time and temperature) that can be expressed by any value within a given range
- **Primary data** – information that has been collected directly from a survey, investigation, or experiment, such as a questionnaire or the recording of daily temperatures. Primary data that has not yet been organized or analyzed is called **raw data**.
- **Secondary data** – information that has been collected, sorted, and processed by the researcher
- **Ordinal data** – information that can be placed in numerical order, such as age or weight
- **Nominal data** – information that *cannot* be placed in numerical order, such as names or places.

DATA COLLECTION

POPULATION

In statistics, the **population** is the entire collection of people, plants, etc., that data can be collected from. For example, a study to determine how well students in the area schools perform on a standardized test would have a population of all the students enrolled in those schools, although a study may include just a small sample of students from each school. A **parameter** is a numerical value that gives information about the population, such as the mean, median, mode, or standard deviation. Remember that the symbol for the mean of a population is μ and the symbol for the standard deviation of a population is σ.

SAMPLE

A **sample** is a portion of the entire population. Whereas a parameter helped describe the population, a **statistic** is a numerical value that gives information about the sample, such as mean, median, mode, or standard deviation. Keep in mind that the symbols for mean and standard deviation are different when they are referring to a sample rather than the entire population. For a sample, the symbol for mean is $\bar{x}$ and the symbol for standard deviation is s. The mean and standard deviation of a sample may or may not be identical to that of the entire population due to a sample only being a subset of the population. However, if the sample is random and large enough, statistically significant values can be attained. Samples are generally used when the population is too large to justify including every element or when acquiring data for the entire population is impossible.

INFERENTIAL STATISTICS

Inferential statistics is the branch of statistics that uses samples to make predictions about an entire population. This type of statistics is often seen in political polls, where a sample of the population is questioned about a particular topic or politician to gain an understanding about the attitudes of the entire population of the country. Often, exit polls are conducted on election days using this method. Inferential statistics can have a large margin of error if you do not have a valid sample.

SAMPLING DISTRIBUTION

Statistical values calculated from various samples of the same size make up the **sampling distribution**. For example, if several samples of identical size are randomly selected from a large population and then the mean of each sample is calculated, the distribution of values of the means would be a sampling distribution.

The **sampling distribution of the mean** is the distribution of the sample mean, $\bar{x}$, derived from random samples of a given size. It has three important characteristics. First, the mean of the sampling distribution of the mean is equal to the mean of the population that was sampled. Second, assuming the standard deviation is non-zero, the standard deviation of the sampling distribution of the mean equals the standard deviation of the sampled population divided by the square root of the sample size. This is sometimes called the standard error. Finally, as the sample size gets larger, the sampling distribution of the mean gets closer to a normal distribution via the central limit theorem.

SURVEY STUDY

A **survey study** is a method of gathering information from a small group in an attempt to gain enough information to make accurate general assumptions about the population. Once a survey study is completed, the results are then put into a summary report.

Survey studies are generally in the format of surveys, interviews, or questionnaires as part of an effort to find opinions of a particular group or to find facts about a group.

It is important to note that the findings from a survey study are only as accurate as the sample chosen from the population.

CORRELATIONAL STUDIES

Correlational studies seek to determine how much one variable is affected by changes in a second variable. For example, correlational studies may look for a relationship between the amount of time a student spends studying for a test and the grade that student earned on the test or between student scores on college admissions tests and student grades in college.

It is important to note that correlational studies cannot show a cause and effect, but rather can show only that two variables are or are not potentially correlated.

EXPERIMENTAL STUDIES

Experimental studies take correlational studies one step farther, in that they attempt to prove or disprove a cause-and-effect relationship. These studies are performed by conducting a series of experiments to test the hypothesis. For a study to be scientifically accurate, it must have both an experimental group that receives the specified treatment and a control group that does not get the treatment. This is the type of study pharmaceutical companies do as part of drug trials for new medications. Experimental studies are only valid when proper scientific method has been followed. In other words, the experiment must be well-planned and executed without bias in the testing process, all subjects must be selected at random, and the process of determining which subject is in which of the two groups must also be completely random.

OBSERVATIONAL STUDIES

Observational studies are the opposite of experimental studies. In observational studies, the tester cannot change or in any way control all of the variables in the test. For example, a study to determine which gender does better in math classes in school is strictly observational. You cannot change a person's gender, and you cannot change the subject being studied. The big downfall of observational studies is that you have no way of proving a cause-and-effect relationship because you cannot control outside influences. Events outside of school can influence a student's performance in school, and observational studies cannot take that into consideration.

RANDOM SAMPLES

For most studies, a **random sample** is necessary to produce valid results. Random samples should not have any particular influence to cause sampled subjects to behave one way or another. The goal is for the random sample to be a **representative sample**, or a sample whose characteristics give an accurate picture of the characteristics of the entire population. To accomplish this, you must make sure you have a proper **sample size**, or an appropriate number of elements in the sample.

BIASES

In statistical studies, biases must be avoided. **Bias** is an error that causes the study to favor one set of results over another. For example, if a survey to determine how the country views the president's job performance only speaks to registered voters in the president's party, the results will be skewed because a disproportionately large number of responders would tend to show approval, while a disproportionately large number of people in the opposite party would tend to express disapproval. **Extraneous variables** are, as the name implies, outside influences that can affect the outcome of a study. They are not always avoidable, but could trigger bias in the result.

MEASURES OF CENTRAL TENDENCY

A **measure of central tendency** is a statistical value that gives a reasonable estimate for the center of a group of data. There are several different ways of describing the measure of central tendency. Each one has a unique way it is calculated, and each one gives a slightly different perspective on the data set. Whenever you give a measure of central tendency, always make sure the units are the same. If the data has different units, such as hours, minutes, and seconds, convert all the data to the same unit, and use the same unit in the measure of central tendency. If no units are given in the data, do not give units for the measure of central tendency.

MEAN

The **statistical mean** of a group of data is the same as the arithmetic average of that group. To find the mean of a set of data, first convert each value to the same units, if necessary. Then find the sum of all the values, and count the total number of data values, making sure you take into consideration each individual value. If a value appears more than once, count it more than once. Divide the sum of the values by the total number of values and apply the units, if any. Note that the mean does not have to be one of the data values in the set, and may not divide evenly.

$$\text{mean} = \frac{\text{sum of the data values}}{\text{quantity of data values}}$$

For instance, the mean of the data set {88, 72, 61, 90, 97, 68, 88, 79, 86, 93, 97, 71, 80, 84, 89} would be the sum of the fifteen numbers divided by 15:

$$\frac{88 + 72 + 61 + 90 + 97 + 68 + 88 + 79 + 86 + 93 + 97 + 71 + 80 + 84 + 88}{15} = \frac{1242}{15}$$
$$= 82.8$$

While the mean is relatively easy to calculate and averages are understood by most people, the mean can be very misleading if used as the sole measure of central tendency. If the data set has outliers (data values that are unusually high or unusually low compared to the rest of the data values), the mean can be very distorted, especially if the data set has a small number of values. If unusually high values are countered with unusually low values, the mean is not affected as much. For example, if five of twenty students in a class get a 100 on a test, but the other 15 students have an average of 60 on the same test, the class average would appear as 70. Whenever the mean is skewed by outliers, it is always a good idea to include the median as an alternate measure of central tendency.

A **weighted mean**, or weighted average, is a mean that uses "weighted" values. The formula is weighted mean $= \frac{w_1 x_1 + w_2 x_2 + w_3 x_3 \ldots + w_n x_n}{w_1 + w_2 + w_3 + \cdots + w_n}$. Weighted values, such as $w_1, w_2, w_3, \ldots w_n$ are assigned to each member of the set $x_1, x_2, x_3, \ldots x_n$. If calculating weighted mean, make sure a weight value for each member of the set is used.

MEDIAN

The **statistical median** is the value in the middle of the set of data. To find the median, list all data values in order from smallest to largest or from largest to smallest. Any value that is repeated in the set must be listed the number of times it appears. If there are an odd number of data values, the median is the value in the middle of the list. If there is an even number of data values, the median is the arithmetic mean of the two middle values.

308

For example, the median of the data set {88, 72, 61, 90, 97, 68, 88, 79, 86, 93, 97, 71, 80, 84, 88} is 86 since the ordered set is {61, 68, 71, 72, 79, 80, 84, **86**, 88, 88, 88, 90, 93, 97, 97}.

The big disadvantage of using the median as a measure of central tendency is that is relies solely on a value's relative size as compared to the other values in the set. When the individual values in a set of data are evenly dispersed, the median can be an accurate tool. However, if there is a group of rather large values or a group of rather small values that are not offset by a different group of values, the information that can be inferred from the median may not be accurate because the distribution of values is skewed.

MODE

The **statistical mode** is the data value that occurs the most number of times in the data set. It is possible to have exactly one mode, more than one mode, or no mode. To find the mode of a set of data, arrange the data like you do to find the median (all values in order, listing all multiples of data values). Count the number of times each value appears in the data set. If all values appear an equal number of times, there is no mode. If one value appears more than any other value, that value is the mode. If two or more values appear the same number of times, but there are other values that appear fewer times and no values that appear more times, all of those values are the modes.

For example, the mode of the data set {**88**, 72, 61, 90, 97, 68, **88**, 79, 86, 93, 97, 71, 80, 84, **88**} is 88.

The main disadvantage of the mode is that the values of the other data in the set have no bearing on the mode. The mode may be the largest value, the smallest value, or a value anywhere in between in the set. The mode only tells which value or values, if any, occurred the most number of times. It does not give any suggestions about the remaining values in the set.

> **Review Video: Mean, Median, and Mode**
> Visit mometrix.com/academy and enter code: 286207

DISPERSION

The **measure of dispersion** is a single value that helps to "interpret" the measure of central tendency by providing more information about how the data values in the set are distributed about the measure of central tendency. The measure of dispersion helps to eliminate or reduce the disadvantages of using the mean, median, or mode as a single measure of central tendency, and give a more accurate picture of the dataset as a whole. To have a measure of dispersion, you must know or calculate the range, standard deviation, or variance of the data set.

RANGE

The **range** of a set of data is the difference between the greatest and lowest values of the data in the set. To calculate the range, you must first make sure the units for all data values are the same, and then identify the greatest and lowest values. If there are multiple data values that are equal for the highest or lowest, just use one of the values in the formula. Write the answer with the same units as the data values you used to do the calculations.

STANDARD DEVIATION

Standard deviation is a measure of dispersion that compares all the data values in the set to the mean of the set to give a more accurate picture. To find the standard deviation of a sample, use the formula

$$s = \sqrt{\frac{\sum_{i=1}^{n}(x_i - \bar{x})^2}{n-1}}$$

Note that s is the standard deviation of a sample, x represents the individual values in the data set, $\bar{x}$ is the mean of the data values in the set, and n is the number of data values in the set. The higher the value of the standard deviation is, the greater the variance of the data values from the mean. The units associated with the standard deviation are the same as the units of the data values.

VARIANCE

The **variance** of a sample, or just variance, is the square of the standard deviation of that sample. While the mean of a set of data gives the average of the set and gives information about where a specific data value lies in relation to the average, the variance of the sample gives information about the degree to which the data values are spread out and tell you how close an individual value is to the average compared to the other values. The units associated with variance are the same as the units of the data values squared.

PERCENTILE

Percentiles and quartiles are other methods of describing data within a set. **Percentiles** tell what percentage of the data in the set fall below a specific point. For example, achievement test scores are often given in percentiles. A score at the 80th percentile is one which is equal to or higher than 80 percent of the scores in the set. In other words, 80 percent of the scores were lower than that score.

Quartiles are percentile groups that make up quarter sections of the data set. The first quartile is the 25th percentile. The second quartile is the 50th percentile; this is also the median of the dataset. The third quartile is the 75th percentile.

SKEWNESS

Skewness is a way to describe the symmetry or asymmetry of the distribution of values in a dataset. If the distribution of values is symmetrical, there is no skew. In general the closer the mean of a data set is to the median of the data set, the less skew there is. Generally, if the mean is to the right of the median, the data set is *positively skewed*, or right-skewed, and if the mean is to the left of the median, the data set is *negatively skewed*, or left-skewed. However, this rule of thumb is not infallible. When the data values are graphed on a curve, a set with no skew will be a perfect bell curve.

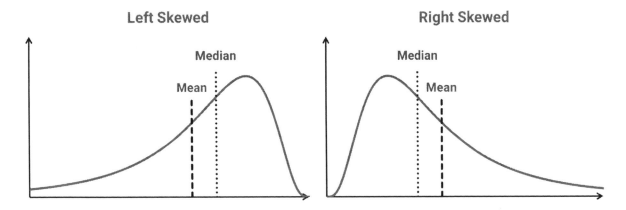

| Left Skewed | Right Skewed |

To estimate skew, use the formula:

$$\text{skew} = \frac{\sqrt{n(n-1)}}{n-2} \left(\frac{\frac{1}{n}\sum_{i=1}^{n}(x_i - \bar{x})^3}{\left(\frac{1}{n}\sum_{i=1}^{n}(x_i - \bar{x})^2\right)^{\frac{3}{2}}} \right)$$

Note that n is the datapoints in the set, x_i is the ith value in the set, and $\bar{x}$ is the mean of the set.

UNIMODAL VS. BIMODAL

If a distribution has a single peak, it would be considered **unimodal**. If it has two discernible peaks it would be considered **bimodal**. Bimodal distributions may be an indication that the set of data being considered is actually the combination of two sets of data with significant differences. A **uniform distribution** is a distribution in which there is *no distinct peak or variation* in the data. No values or ranges are particularly more common than any other values or ranges.

OUTLIER

An outlier is an extremely high or extremely low value in the data set. It may be the result of measurement error, in which case, the outlier is not a valid member of the data set. However, it may also be a valid member of the distribution. Unless a measurement error is identified, the experimenter cannot know for certain if an outlier is or is not a member of the distribution. There are arbitrary methods that can be employed to designate an extreme value as an outlier. One method designates an outlier (or possible outlier) to be any value less than $Q_1 - 1.5(IQR)$ or any value greater than $Q_3 + 1.5(IQR)$.

DATA ANALYSIS

SIMPLE REGRESSION

In statistics, **simple regression** is using an equation to represent a relation between an independent and dependent variables. The independent variable is also referred to as the explanatory variable or the predictor, and is generally represented by the variable x in the equation. The dependent variable, usually represented by the variable y, is also referred to as the response variable. The equation may be any type of function – linear, quadratic, exponential, etc. The best way to handle this task is to use the regression feature of your graphing calculator. This will easily give you the curve of best fit and provide you with the coefficients and other information you need to derive an equation.

LINE OF BEST FIT

In a scatter plot, the **line of best fit** is the line that best shows the trends of the data. The line of best fit is given by the equation $\hat{y} = ax + b$, where a and b are the regression coefficients. The regression coefficient a is also the slope of the line of best fit, and b is also the y-coordinate of the point at which the line of best fit crosses the y-axis. Not every point on the scatter plot will be on the line of best fit. The differences between the y-values of the points in the scatter plot and the corresponding y-values according to the equation of the line of best fit are the residuals. The line of best fit is also called the least-squares regression line because it is also the line that has the lowest sum of the squares of the residuals.

CORRELATION COEFFICIENT

The **correlation coefficient** is the numerical value that indicates how strong the relationship is between the two variables of a linear regression equation. A correlation coefficient of –1 is a perfect negative correlation. A correlation coefficient of +1 is a perfect positive correlation. Correlation coefficients close to –1 or +1 are very strong correlations. A correlation coefficient equal to zero indicates there is no correlation between the two variables. This test is a good indicator of whether or not the equation for the line of best fit is accurate. The formula for the correlation coefficient is

$$r = \frac{\sum_{i=1}^{n}(x_i - \bar{x})(y_i - \bar{y})}{\sqrt{\sum_{i=1}^{n}(x_i - \bar{x})^2}\sqrt{\sum_{i=1}^{n}(y_i - \bar{y})^2}}$$

where r is the correlation coefficient, n is the number of data values in the set, (x_i, y_i) is a point in the set, and $\bar{x}$ and $\bar{y}$ are the means.

Z-SCORE

A **z-score** is an indication of how many standard deviations a given value falls from the mean. To calculate a z-score, use the formula $\frac{x-\mu}{\sigma}$, where x is the data value, μ is the mean of the data set, and σ is the standard deviation of the population. If the z-score is positive, the data value lies above the mean. If the z-score is negative, the data value falls below the mean. These scores are useful in interpreting data such as standardized test scores, where every piece of data in the set has been counted, rather than just a small random sample. In cases where standard deviations are calculated from a random sample of the set, the z-scores will not be as accurate.

AREA UNDER A NORMAL CURVE

The area under a normal curve can be represented using one or two z-scores or a mean and a z-score. A z-score represents the number of standard deviations a score falls above, or below, the mean. A normal distribution table (z-table) shows the mean to z area, small portion area, and larger portion area, for any z-score from 0 to 4. The area between a mean and z-score is simply equal to the mean to z area. The area under the normal curve, between two z-scores, may be calculated by adding or subtracting the mean to z areas. An area above, or below, a z-score is equal to the smaller or larger portion area. The area may also be calculated by subtracting the mean to z area from 0.5, when looking at the smaller area, or adding the mean to z area to 0.5, when looking at the larger area.

CENTRAL LIMIT THEOREM

According to the **central limit theorem**, regardless of what the original distribution of a sample is, the distribution of the means tends to get closer and closer to a normal distribution as the sample size gets larger and larger (this is necessary because the sample is becoming more all-encompassing of the elements of the population). As the sample size gets larger, the distribution of the sample mean will approach a normal distribution with a mean of the population mean and a variance of the population variance divided by the sample size.

DISPLAYING INFORMATION

FREQUENCY TABLES

Frequency tables show how frequently each unique value appears in the set. A **relative frequency table** is one that shows the proportions of each unique value compared to the entire set. Relative frequencies are given as percents; however, the total percent for a relative frequency table will not necessarily equal 100 percent due to rounding. An example of a frequency table with relative frequencies is below.

Favorite Color	Frequency	Relative Frequency
Blue	4	13%
Red	7	22%
Green		9%
Purple	6	19%
Cyan	12	38%

A **two-way frequency table** quickly shows intersections and total frequencies. These values would have to be calculated from a manual list. The conditional probability, $P(B|A)$, read as "The probability of B, given A," is equal to $P(B \cap A)/A$. A two-way frequency table can quickly show these frequencies. Consider the table below:

	Cat	Dog	Bird	Total
Male	24	16	26	66
Female	32	12	20	64
Total	56	28	46	130

Find $P(Cat|Female)$. The two-way frequency table shows $C \cap F$ to be 32, while the total for female is 64. Thus, $P(Cat \mid Female) = 32/64 = 1/2$.

PICTOGRAPHS

A **pictograph** is a graph, generally in the horizontal orientation, that uses pictures or symbols to represent the data. Each pictograph must have a key that defines the picture or symbol and gives the quantity each picture or symbol represents. Pictures or symbols on a pictograph are not always shown as whole elements. In this case, the fraction of the picture or symbol shown represents the same fraction of the quantity a whole picture or symbol stands for. For example, a row with $3\frac{1}{2}$ ears of corn, where each ear of corn represents 100 stalks of corn in a field, would equal $3\frac{1}{2} \times 100 = 350$ stalks of corn in the field.

CIRCLE GRAPHS

Circle graphs, also known as *pie charts*, provide a visual depiction of the relationship of each type of data compared to the whole set of data. The circle graph is divided into sections by drawing radii to create central angles whose percentage of the circle is equal to the individual data's percentage of the whole set. Each 1% of data is equal to 3.6° in the circle graph. Therefore, data represented by a 90° section of the circle graph makes up 25% of the whole. When complete, a circle graph often looks like a pie cut into uneven wedges. The pie chart below shows the data from the frequency table referenced earlier where people were asked their favorite color.

Favorite Color

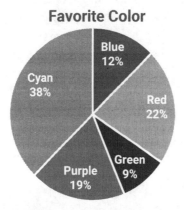

LINE GRAPHS

Line graphs have one or more lines of varying styles (solid or broken) to show the different values for a set of data. The individual data are represented as ordered pairs, much like on a Cartesian plane. In this case, the x- and y-axes are defined in terms of their units, such as dollars or time. The individual plotted points are joined by line segments to show whether the value of the data is increasing (line sloping upward), decreasing (line sloping downward) or staying the same (horizontal line). Multiple sets of data can be graphed on the same line graph to give an easy visual comparison. An example of this would be graphing achievement test scores for different groups of students over the same time period to see which group had the greatest increase or decrease in performance from year-to-year (as shown below).

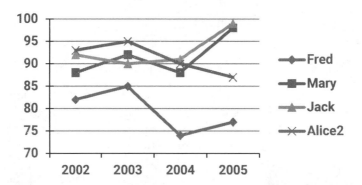

LINE PLOTS

A **line plot**, also known as a *dot plot*, has plotted points that are not connected by line segments. In this graph, the horizontal axis lists the different possible values for the data, and the vertical axis lists the number of times the individual value occurs. A single dot is graphed for each value to show the number of times it occurs. This graph is more closely related to a bar graph than a line graph. Do not connect the dots in a line plot or it will misrepresent the data.

> **Review Video: Line Plot**
> Visit mometrix.com/academy and enter code: 754610

STEM AND LEAF PLOTS

A **stem and leaf plot** is useful for depicting groups of data that fall into a range of values. Each piece of data is separated into two parts: the first, or left, part is called the stem; the second, or right, part is called the leaf. Each stem is listed in a column from smallest to largest. Each leaf that has the common stem is listed in that stem's row from smallest to largest. For example, in a set of two-digit numbers, the digit in the tens place is the stem, and the digit in the ones place is the leaf. With a stem and leaf plot, you can easily see which subset of numbers (10s, 20s, 30s, etc.) is the largest. This information is also readily available by looking at a histogram, but a stem and leaf plot also allows you to look closer and see exactly which values fall in that range. Using all of the test scores from above, we can assemble a stem and leaf plot like the one below.

Test Scores

7	4 8
8	2 5 7 8 8
9	0 0 1 2 2 3 5 8 9

BAR GRAPHS

A **bar graph** is one of the few graphs that can be drawn correctly in two different configurations – both horizontally and vertically. A bar graph is similar to a line plot in the way the data is organized on the graph. Both axes must have their categories defined for the graph to be useful. Rather than placing a single dot to mark the point of the data's value, a bar, or thick line, is drawn from zero to the exact value of the data, whether it is a number, percentage, or other numerical value. Longer bar lengths correspond to greater data values. To read a bar graph, read the labels for the axes to find the units being reported. Then look where the bars end in relation to the scale given on the corresponding axis and determine the associated value.

The bar chart below represents the responses from our favorite color survey.

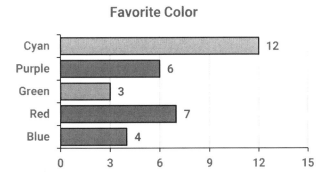

315

HISTOGRAMS

At first glance, a **histogram** looks like a vertical bar graph. The difference is that a bar graph has a separate bar for each piece of data and a histogram has one continuous bar for each *range* of data. For example, a histogram may have one bar for the range 0–9, one bar for 10–19, etc. While a bar graph has numerical values on one axis, a histogram has numerical values on both axes. Each range is of equal size, and they are ordered left to right from lowest to highest. The height of each column on a histogram represents the number of data values within that range. Like a stem and leaf plot, a histogram makes it easy to glance at the graph and quickly determine which range has the greatest quantity of values. A simple example of a histogram is below.

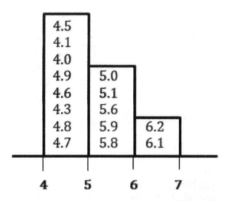

BIVARIATE DATA

Bivariate data is simply data from two different variables. (The prefix *bi-* means *two*.) In a *scatter plot*, each value in the set of data is plotted on a grid similar to a Cartesian plane, where each axis represents one of the two variables. By looking at the pattern formed by the points on the grid, you can often determine whether or not there is a relationship between the two variables, and what that relationship is, if it exists. The variables may be directly proportionate, inversely proportionate, or show no proportion at all. It may also be possible to determine if the data is linear, and if so, to find an equation to relate the two variables. The following scatter plot shows the relationship between preference for brand "A" and the age of the consumers surveyed.

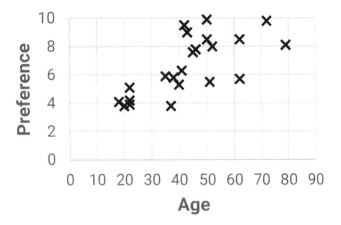

SCATTER PLOTS

Scatter plots are also useful in determining the type of function represented by the data and finding the simple regression. Linear scatter plots may be positive or negative. Nonlinear scatter plots are generally exponential or quadratic. Below are some common types of scatter plots:

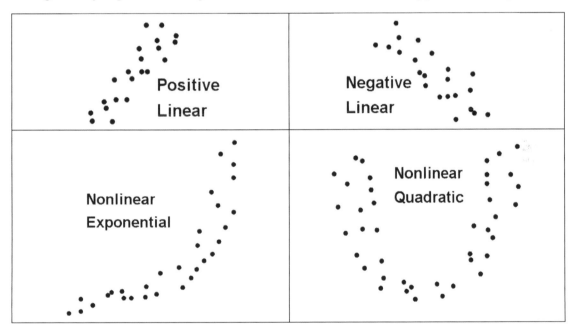

Review Video: Scatter Plot
Visit mometrix.com/academy and enter code: 596526

5-NUMBER SUMMARY

The **5-number summary** of a set of data gives a very informative picture of the set. The five numbers in the summary include the minimum value, maximum value, and the three quartiles. This information gives the reader the range and median of the set, as well as an indication of how the data is spread about the median.

BOX AND WHISKER PLOTS

A **box-and-whisker plot** is a graphical representation of the 5-number summary. To draw a box-and-whiskers plot, plot the points of the 5-number summary on a number line. Draw a box whose ends are through the points for the first and third quartiles. Draw a vertical line in the box through the median to divide the box in half. Draw a line segment from the first quartile point to the minimum value, and from the third quartile point to the maximum value.

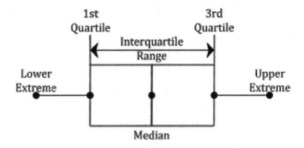

68-95-99.7 RULE

The **68–95–99.7 rule** describes how a normal distribution of data should appear when compared to the mean. This is also a description of a normal bell curve. According to this rule, 68 percent of the data values in a normally distributed set should fall within one standard deviation of the mean (34 percent above and 34 percent below the mean), 95 percent of the data values should fall within two standard deviations of the mean (47.5 percent above and 47.5 percent below the mean), and 99.7 percent of the data values should fall within three standard deviations of the mean, again, equally distributed on either side of the mean. This means that only 0.3 percent of all data values should fall more than three standard deviations from the mean. On the graph below, the normal curve is centered on the y-axis. The x-axis labels are how many standard deviations away from the center you are. Therefore, it is easy to see how the 68-95-99.7 rule can apply.

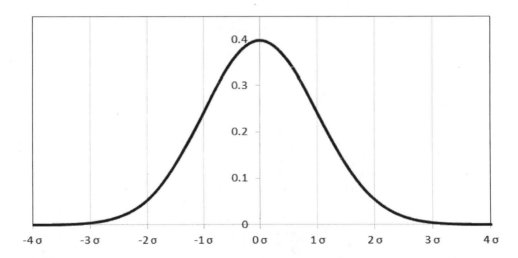

PRACTICE

P1. Determine of the following statements are TRUE or FALSE:

(a) Just because a sample is random, does not guarantee that it is representative.

(b) Qualitative data cannot be statistically analyzed, since the data is non-numeric.

(c) Sample statistics are a useful tool to estimate population parameters.

P2. Suppose the class average on a final exam is 87, with a standard deviation of 2 points. Find the z-score of a student that got an 82.

P3. Given the following graph, determine the range of patient ages:

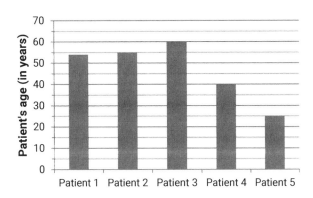

P4. Calculate the sample standard deviation for the dataset $\{10, 13, 11, 5, 8, 18\}$

P5. Today, there were two food options for lunch at a local college cafeteria. Given the following survey data, what is the probability that a junior selected at random from the sample had a sandwich?

	Freshman	Sophomore	Junior	Senior
Salad	15	12	27	36
Sandwich	24	40	43	35
Nothing	42	23	23	30

PRACTICE SOLUTIONS

P1. (a). TRUE: A good representative sample will also be a random sample, but sampling 10 random people from a city of 4 million will not be a representative sample.

(b) FALSE: Even though qualitative data is often non-numeric, there are special methods designed specifically tally and analyze qualitative data.

(c) TRUE: The entire field of statistics is built upon this, since it is almost always beyond the scope of researchers to survey or collect data on an entire population.

P2. Using the formula for z-score: $z = \frac{82-87}{2} = -2.5$

P3. Patient 1 is 54 years old; Patient 2 is 55 years old; Patient 3 is 60 years old; Patient 4 is 40 years old; and Patient 5 is 25 years old. The range of patient ages is the age of the oldest patient minus the age of the youngest patient. In other words, $60 - 25 = 35$. The range of ages is 35 years.

P4. To find the standard deviation, first find the mean:

$$\frac{10 + 13 + 12 + 5 + 8 + 18}{6} = \frac{66}{6} = 11$$

Now, apply the formula for sample standard deviation:

$$s = \sqrt{\frac{\sum_{i=1}^{n}(x_i - \bar{x})^2}{n - 1}} = \sqrt{\frac{\sum_{i=1}^{6}(x_i - 11)^2}{6 - 1}}$$

$$= \frac{\sqrt{(10 - 11)^2 + (13 - 11)^2 + (12 - 11)^2 + (5 - 11)^2 + (8 - 11)^2 + (18 - 11)^2}}{5}$$

$$= \frac{\sqrt{(-1)^2 + 2^2 + 1^2 + (-6)^2 + (-3)^2 + 7^2}}{5}$$

$$= \frac{\sqrt{1 + 4 + 1 + 36 + 9 + 49}}{5}$$

$$= \frac{\sqrt{100}}{5} = \frac{10}{5} = 2$$

P5. With two-way tables it is often most helpful to start by totaling the rows and columns:

	Freshman	Sophomore	Junior	Senior	Total
Salad	15	12	27	36	90
Sandwich	24	40	43	35	142
Nothing	42	23	23	30	118
Total	81	75	93	101	350

Since the question is focused on juniors, we can focus on that column. There was a total of 93 juniors surveyed and 43 of them had a sandwich for lunch. Thus, the probability that a junior selected at random had a sandwich would be $\frac{43}{93} \cong 0.462 \cong 46.2\%$.

Science

Scientific Inquiry and Lab Safety

COMPONENTS OF SCIENTIFIC EXPERIMENTATION

- A **hypothesis** is a tentative supposition about a phenomenon (or a fact or set of facts) made in order to examine and test its logical or empirical consequences through investigation or methodological experimentation.
- A **theory** is a scientifically proven, general principle offered to explain phenomena. A theory is derived from a hypothesis and verified by experimentation and research.
- A **scientific law** is a generally accepted conclusion about a body of observations to which no exceptions have been found. Scientific laws explain things, but do not describe them.
- A **control** is a normal, unchanged situation used for comparison against experimental data.
- **Constants** are factors in an experiment that remain the same.
- **Independent variables** are factors, traits, or conditions that are changed in an experiment. A good experiment has only one independent variable so that the scientist can track one thing at a time. The independent variable changes from experiment to experiment.
- **Dependent variables** are changes that result from variations in the independent variable.

> **Review Video: Experimental Science**
> Visit mometrix.com/academy and enter code: 283092
>
> **Review Video: Experimental Science Project**
> Visit mometrix.com/academy and enter code: 584444

SCIENCE AS A SERIES OF PROCESSES

Science is not just the steps of experimentation. While the process of posing a question, forming a hypothesis, testing the hypothesis, recording data, and drawing a conclusion is at the heart of **scientific inquiry**, there are other processes that are important as well. Once the scientist has completed the testing of a hypothesis and possibly come up with a theory, the scientist should then go through the process of getting feedback from colleagues, publishing an article about the work in a peer-reviewed journal, or otherwise reporting the results to the scientific community, replicating the experiment for verification of results (by the original scientist or others), and developing new questions. Science is not just a means of satisfying curiosity, but is also a process for developing technology, addressing social issues, building knowledge, and solving everyday problems.

> **Review Video: Scientific Hypothesis and Theories**
> Visit mometrix.com/academy and enter code: 918083

DRAWING CONCLUSIONS AFTER EXPERIMENTS

Conclusions are based on data analysis and background research. The scientist has to take a hard look at the results of an experiment and check the accuracy of the data to draw preliminary conclusions. These should be compared to the background research to find out if the preliminary conclusion can be supported by previous research experiments. If the results do not support the hypothesis, or if they are contrary to what the background research predicted, then further research is needed. The focus should be on finding a reason for the different results. Finally, the scientist provides a discussion of findings that includes a summary of the results of the experiment, a statement as to whether the hypothesis was proven or disproven, a statement of the relationship

321

between the independent and dependent variable, a summary and evaluation of the procedures of the experiment (including comments about successes and effectiveness), and suggestions for changes/modifications in procedures for further studies.

STEPS OF THE SCIENTIFIC METHOD

The steps of the **scientific method** are as follows:

1. The scientific method begins with, and absolutely depends upon, the **observation** of objective, unbiased data. Any prejudice or bias in the observed data nullifies its validity. Thus the basic input from the observations must be rigorously screened to ensure objectivity.
2. The development of a **theory or hypotheses** based on objective data is the next step in the scientific method. These theories or hypotheses pose logical expectations that the experiment may yield.
3. Construction of a rigorous and valid **experimental method** designed to test the theories is the next phase of the scientific method. This experimental method must be carefully constructed to give objective, unbiased conclusions based on the hypotheses posited.
4. Careful and statistically correct **analysis and evaluation** of the experimental results make up the next stage.
5. **Modification and replication** of the experiment must then follow to provide a statistically accurate demonstration of the validity of the hypotheses. Equivalent results must be shown from a number of repetitions of the experiment.

> **Review Video: The Scientific Method**
> Visit mometrix.com/academy and enter code: 191386

STEPS OF THE SCIENTIFIC INQUIRY

Scientific inquiry is the impetus and catalyst for all scientific research and experimentation. It grows from questions about the observed world and gives us a template with which to apply the scientific method. Steps in scientific inquiry include the following principles:

- Determination and scope of the questions to be investigated are the first step. These may range from simple to extremely complex questions to be explored by scientists.
- The design, strategy, and method of the inquiry are then carefully considered, and a model for the inquiry is constructed.
- The formulation of theories and models based on the careful observation of objective, unbiased data then follows. This formulation is derived from the scope of the scientific inquiry and the questions to be investigated.
- Analysis of possible alternative conclusions drawn from the models and results of experimentation follows.
- Postulating a theory or constructing a scientific statement based on conclusions is the next logical step.
- Defending the scientific statement against alternative hypotheses is a critical function of scientific inquiry.
- Defense of the theory or conclusion against critical analysis is the final step in the process.

SCIENCE

Science is a method of acquiring and obtaining knowledge. It is the process of gaining reliable information about the real world, including the explanation of phenomena. It is the development of a body of knowledge about observable phenomena, using the best capabilities humans have at their disposal. The process of organizing and classifying knowledge, through objective observation and evaluation, is a major goal of science. Science can be considered *reliable*, but it is not *infallible*. The limits of human knowledge are constantly growing, often making yesterday's science obsolete and simplistic. Science is thus never fixed; it is always subject to change as new information is gained and synthesized with existing knowledge. Ultimately, science is the sum total of knowledge in any period of time, based on the current abilities of man to understand the world of phenomena, verifiable by observable data.

LIMITATIONS OF SCIENCE

There are clear **limits** on what science can explain. The demand for objectivity both strengthens knowledge we gain from scientific experiments and limits what we can explore. Beyond the realm of scientific inquiry are such questions as "Why does anything exist?" or "What is the meaning of life?" These are subjective questions that do not lend themselves easily to scientific inquiry. These questions, and others like them, come from within, and their conclusions, not validated by science, shape the very fabric of a society. They attempt to give meaning to what may be viewed as chaos.

Periodically, science will impact these **subjective conclusions** with new evidence. For example, the theory of evolution is regarded as blasphemy by many religious fundamentalists. These conflicts may cause great upheavals in society, leaving many to wonder how science and religious belief can be reconciled. Ultimately, observation of the external world must stand as the true test of science.

HYPOTHETICO-DEDUCTIVE PROCESS

The **hypothetico-deductive process** states that to have an idea and then formulate a hypothesis are essentially creative processes, driven by eons of human experience. Statements about reality are the logical conclusions of observed experience. Such creative propositions are the basis for scientific inquiry. Empirical evidence must then validate these hypotheses. Creative inspiration and scientific validation are interdependent aspects of scientific inquiry. New observations often are the catalyst for creative new theories. Science thus proceeds through creative thinking and scientific validation. There are criticisms of the hypothetico-deductive process: The problem of deduction points out that the original hypothesis may be proved wrong in the future, thus invalidating all subsequent conclusions. The problem of induction, building a theory from generalizations, is that any generalization may be proved wrong by future objective observations. This hypothetico-deductive process, and its problems, is a fascinating subject to philosophers of science.

HYPOTHESIS

It is important to form a **hypothesis** in order to make a tentative explanation that accounts for an unbiased observation. To be scientific, the hypothesis must be testable through experimentation. Careful construction of the experiment provides that predictions derived from the hypothesis are valid. The hypothesis must be formulated in a manner designed to provide a framework for evaluating the results of an experiment. In many scientific experiments, a hypothesis is posited in negative terms because scientists may accept logically plausible ideas until they are proven false. It is more difficult to prove that a hypothesis is true because its validity must be proven in all possible situations under endless variable conditions. Scientists tend to construct hypotheses for testing by creating experiments that might prove them false. If they succeed, the hypothesis must be modified or discarded.

BASIC SCIENCE AND APPLIED SCIENCE

Basic science and applied science share many attributes but are generally motivated by different influences:

- **Basic science** is spurred on by scientific inquiry, the human need to explain the observed physical world. It may have no specific goal, but is man's response to questions that arise from human curiosity and interest. It is usually an attempt to explain the laws of nature by using the scientific method.
- **Applied science** has a specific practical goal or application: It is designed to solve a problem. Industry and government are institutions that use applied science regularly.

Thus, basic and applied science share many qualities, including scientific inquiry and the scientific method. The goals of each can be very different. It should be pointed out that basic science very often provides results that have uses in applied science.

BENEFITS OF BASIC SCIENCE

Although **basic science** may have no stated goal or target, it provides many benefits to society:

- Basic science contributes greatly to human understanding and culture, enriching society in many ways.
- Basic science has been responsible for major breakthroughs that have great social and economic impact.
- Basic science provides derivative solutions that can be used in applied science. For example, basic science was critical to the development of the space program, from which countless valuable applications have been derived.
- Basic science contributes to education and research across the broad spectrum of society.

MEASURING, ORGANIZING, AND CLASSIFYING DATA

Measuring data is a crucial part of the scientific process. Measurements are most useful if they are quantified—expressed in numbers. Measuring is the process of determining variables such as time, space, and temperature of objects and processes in precise numbers. The metric system is the universal standard of measurement in science. Data must be **organized** in a practical, useful manner to be valuable. Scientists use graphs, charts, tables, and other organizational tools to make data more useful. Data must then be **classified**—grouped into organizational schemes for easy access and use. These schemes attempt to organize the maximum amount of useful data in a format

that scientists can use. Although these steps may be less glamorous than other areas of science, they are essential.

SCIENTIFIC LAWS

Scientific principles must meet a high standard to be classified as laws; scientific laws are identified as follows:

- **Scientific laws** must be true, not just probable. A highly probable principle may still be proven false.
- Laws are statements of patterns found in nature.
- Laws may have a universal form but be stated conditionally. For example, the statement "All living human beings breathe," may be restated "If a thing is a living human being it must breathe."
- Laws refer to a general, not a particular, class.
- Laws have purely qualitative predicates.
- Laws must have a formal language of expression to be fully understood. Such a language does not exist now.
- Laws may be probabilistic. For example, a law may state "Eight percent of all dogs are terriers."

COMMON CRITICISMS OF DEDUCTIVE MODEL

The **deductive model** of the scientific method has the following criticisms:

- The deductive model fails to make logical distinctions among explanations, predictions, and descriptions of things to be explained.
- The deductive model is restrictive: It excludes most scientific examples.
- The deductive model is too inclusive: It admits data that cannot be explained.
- The deductive model requires an account of cause, law, and probability, which are basically unsound.
- The deductive model leaves out the elements of context, judgment, and understanding.

PREDICTION

These are the two widely accepted definitions of **scientific prediction**:

1. In the language of science, prediction is stating in advance the outcome from testing a theory or hypothesis in a controlled experiment. Based on objective observation of data, scientists move from observation of facts to a general explanation, or hypothesis, which must be confirmed by testing through experimentation.

2.   Another definition of prediction favored by scientific philosophers is the ability of a hypothesis to lead to deductions of scientific statements that could not be anticipated when the hypothesis was posited. In this sense, prediction means what the scientist can verify from what he or she has deduced from the hypothesis.

LABORATORY SAFETY

The following basic rules should be supplemented by standards appropriate to individual laboratories:

- Hazardous areas must be identified and warnings posted regarding risks.
- A hazard containment plan must be in effect and readily available.
- Safe control of airflow must be maintained at all times.
- Safe work practices must be taught to all who work in the lab.
- Proper maintenance of laboratory equipment must be enforced.
- Safe storage of hazardous material must be implemented.
- Procedures for safe disposal of hazardous wastes must be followed at all times.
- An updated emergency procedure manual must be available.
- A complete emergency first aid kit should be accessible at all times.
- Regular education on the basics of lab safety should be implemented.

VERIFICATION AND CONFIRMATION OF DATA IN VALID SCIENCE

A critical distinction should be made between confirmation and verification of scientific data. **Verification** establishes once and for all the truth of the statement. **Confirmation** is the testing of claims to see how true they are. For a claim to be testable, an experiment must be devised to ensure the validity of the results. A claim can only be confirmed when we know the conditions for verification. A claim confirmation is always relative to the testing procedures. Test results must always be objective and observable. Actually, no factual claim can ever be verified because there is always the possibility of new evidence appearing that proves the claim false. A scientific law must also be confirmed by making predictions based on unbiased, observable data.

SCIENTIFIC MEASUREMENT AND UNIT SYSTEMS

The basis of quantitative measurement is the **unit system**. In order to properly describe how large, how heavy, or how hot something is, it is necessary to have some reference unit. The most commonly used unit system in the world is the **SI**, short for the Systeme International d'Unites, although the English system is still in popular use in the United States. In SI, there are base units and derived units. Derived units may be stated as some combination of the base units. The SI base units for length, mass, time, temperature, and electric current are meter (m), kilogram (kg), second (s), kelvin (K), and ampere (A), respectively. Some common derived units are newtons ($kg\text{-}m/s^2$) and pascals ($kg/m\text{-}s^2$). Most SI units can be scaled up or down by adding a prefix. To alter a unit by 10^3, 10^6, or 10^9, add a prefix of kilo (k), mega (M), or giga (G). For instance, a kilometer (km) is 10^3 meters. To change the unit by a factor of 10^{-3}, 10^{-6}, or 10^{-9}, add a prefix of milli (m), micro (μ), or nano (n). For instance, a microsecond (μs) is 10^{-6} seconds. It is important to note that the SI base unit kilogram has already employed a prefix to scale up the smaller unit, gram (g). *Order of magnitude* is a concept that deals with comparison between two values. If one value differs from the other by a factor of 10^n, it may be said that it differs by n orders of magnitude. Other SI base units include the mole and the candela. Some lesser used prefixes include: hecto (h), 10^2; deca (da), 10^1; deci (d), 10^{-1}; and centi (c), 10^{-2}.

DATA COLLECTION AND ANALYSIS

In order to take **data measurements** from their experimental setups, scientists will often use measurement devices wired to a computer running data-acquisition software. This allows them to take numerous readings per second if necessary. Once the data is collected, it will often be organized using a spreadsheet, such as Microsoft Excel. This multipurpose program contains several options for displaying the data in graphs or charts, as well as tools for performing statistical analyses or linear regressions. Linear regression is a technique used to determine whether gathered data fits a particular trend or equation. It attempts to fit a common line or curve equation to the data set. A very important concept to understand when taking data is that of **significant figures**. Significant figures, or significant digits, indicate how precisely a quantity is known. Each non-zero digit is always significant. A zero is significant if either: 1) it is to the right of both a non-zero digit and the decimal point; or 2) it is between two other significant digits. For instance, 1.0230 has five significant figures while 0.0230 has only three because the trailing zero is the only zero to the right of both a non-zero and the decimal. When multiplying (or dividing), the product (quotient) has as many significant figures as the factor (dividend or divisor) with the fewest. When adding (or subtracting), the sum (difference) should be rounded to the highest final decimal place of the involved terms.

(3.4 + 56.78 = 60.18 --> 60.2, three significant figures)

INTERPRETATION AND DRAWING OF CONCLUSIONS FROM DATA PRESENTED IN TABLES, CHARTS, AND GRAPHS

One of the reasons data are so often plotted on graphs is that this format makes it much easier to see **trends** and draw **conclusions**. For instance, on a simple position vs. time graph, the slope of the curve indicates the object's velocity at each point in time. If the curve becomes level, this means the object is not moving. In a simple velocity vs. time graph, the slope of the curve indicates the object's acceleration at each point in time. Additionally, the area contained under the curve indicates the total distance traveled. For instance, if the object is traveling at a constant 5 m/s for 10 s, the velocity vs. time graph will be a straight line at y = 5 between x = 0 and x = 10. The area under this curve is (5 m/s)(10 s) = 50 m. Thus, the object traveled 50 meters. Nearly any type of quantity may be graphed, so it is important to always check the axis labels to ensure that you know what the graph represents and what units are being used.

DATA ERRORS AND ERROR ANALYSIS

No measurements are ever 100% accurate. There is always some amount of **error** regardless of how careful the observer or how good his equipment. The important thing for the scientist to know is how much error is present in a given measurement. Two commonly misunderstood terms regarding error are accuracy and precision. **Accuracy** is a measure of how close a measurement is to the true value. **Precision** is a measure of how close repeated measurements are to one another. Error is usually quantified using a confidence interval and an uncertainty value. For instance, if the quantity is measured as 100 ± 2 on a 95% confidence interval, this means that there is a 95% chance that the actual value falls between 98 and 102. When looking for the uncertainty in a derived quantity such as density, the errors in the constituent quantities, mass and volume in this case, are propagated to the derived quantity. The percent uncertainty in the density, U_ρ/ρ, can be found by the equation:

$$U_\rho/\rho = \text{sqrt}((U_m/m)^2 + (U_V/V)^2).$$

Science, Technology, and Society

DEBATE OVER SCIENCE AND ETHICS

Debates over issues paramount to **science and ethics** are rarely resolved unambiguously. Ethical conclusions should be based on reason, logic, and accepted principles that represent a consensus of current thinking on a question. Education and debate are important in clarifying issues and allowing intelligent participation in a democratic process. Deciding issues of science and society usually requires an examination of individual cases. Generalizations in these areas tend to lead to extreme positions that exclude mainstream opinions. Both intrinsic and consequential arguments for or against any question may be advanced. There are no blanket solutions to most problems involving science, technology, and societal ethics.

MAJOR EFFECTS OF IMPROVEMENTS IN SCIENTIFIC AND TECHNOLOGICAL KNOWLEDGE ON HUMAN AND OTHER LIFE

Since the Industrial Revolution, **technological improvements** to agricultural production have made agriculture productive on an industrial scale, while advances in medical knowledge have brought about the cures for many diseases. People in many parts of the world live longer and enjoy a higher standard of living than ever before. However, this progress does not come without a price. The effects on the **environment** of industrialization are almost exclusively negative. Monoculture farming practices resulting from industrialization mean that farming no longer exists as a closed ecosystem; the chemical fertilizers that create record crop yields have changed the nutrient environment, and the waste products of industrial agriculture pollute the water rather than fertilizing the soil. Increased travel creates dangerous carbon dioxide emissions and depletes the earth's limited store of fossil fuels. Water pollution means limited access to potable water, and deforestation has begun to change the makeup of ecosystems and cause the extinction of many species. Through the increased contact made available by improved technology, however, humans are also collaborating on solutions to these new problems.

MAJOR ENERGY ISSUES

Since the Industrial Revolution, **energy** for industrialized human needs has come from fossil fuels, particularly coal and petroleum, but increased use means that this source of fuel is quickly being depleted, in addition to causing pollution. The search for **alternative, safe sources** of energy for an increasingly industrialized world population is therefore increasingly important to scientists. An ideal source of energy would be efficient, renewable, and sustainable. Various sources of alternative energy have been proposed, including wind, water, solar, nuclear, geothermal, and biomass, but thus far none have been made practically available on a large scale. Some, such as wind and water, blight the landscape, while the conversion methods for other sources, such as solar and biomass, are still relatively inefficient. The scientific community is still unclear on the best way to harness the power of photosynthesis and biomass for energy needs in a way that would allow a large-scale energy industry to use it. Scientists remain at work studying the long-term solutions to an increasingly urgent problem for humanity.

CONTROVERSIES SURROUNDING USE OF NUCLEAR POWER

Nuclear fission power, while sustainable, has a host of attendant controversial problems. Among them is the incredibly dangerous transportation and long-term storage of its radioactive waste products, for which there is still no safe long-term solution. Its effects on those environments and creatures that come in contact with nuclear waste are still largely unknown. In addition, nuclear materials can be used in weaponry, and accidents at nuclear power plants like the one at Chernobyl can be devastating for thousands of years. Scientists continue their study of the process of **nuclear**

fusion, hoping that if humans can learn to harness the energy produced by smashing atoms rather than splitting them, the attendant problems of nuclear waste storage will be minimized.

> **Review Video: Nuclear Fusion**
> Visit mometrix.com/academy and enter code: 381782

EFFECTS OF INCREASED PRODUCTION OF CONSUMER GOODS AFTER INDUSTRIAL REVOLUTION

Electric-based, industrial production of **manufactured goods** has led to an increase in the standard of living for many, especially those in the industrialized world. Consumer goods are produced more cheaply than ever before, since the means of production is not as dependent on the physical abilities of human beings. Scientific advancements have led to a huge number of new synthetic materials from which goods can be made, including plastics and nylon. However, this increased production damages the **environment**. Waste products are now created of which humans can make no use, a new phenomenon. Trash created from these new products is buried in landfills, where it has no access to the air, water, and sunlight that are a necessary part of biodegradation; trash made from some synthetic materials does not biodegrade at all. While some waste products can be recycled, many byproducts of industrial manufacturing are hazardous, with no safe way to dispose of them. The long-term sustainability of the environment as a result of massively increased consumer production is an issue of increasing urgency for scientists.

ISSUES CONCERNING MANAGEMENT OF RENEWABLE RESOURCES

Natural resources can be divided into two types, renewable and non-renewable. **Renewable resources** include plants and animals, along with water, air, and soil. A pre-industrial earth was a self-sustaining system, maintaining a natural balance among plants, animals, and non-living elements in which waste products from one natural process were the fuel for another. Modern humans have intervened in this process in a way that upsets the natural balance of life. Humans have introduced non-native species from one part of the world to another, resulting in the devastation of local populations. Industrial-scale buildings can create disasters for local ecosystems, ruining habitats for animal populations. Humans remove an increasing amount of the world's resources for industrial use, too quickly for nature to recover from easily. Renewable resources must be carefully managed to maintain a balanced ecosystem; over-harvesting of forests or over-hunting of animal populations can be devastating. Pollution of the air and water with chemical pollutants has far-reaching effects on the ecosystems of the earth, including the depletion of the ozone layer that protects earth life from ultraviolet rays, as does the removal of forests that produce the earth's oxygen.

ISSUES CONCERNING MANAGEMENT OF NON-RENEWABLE RESOURCES

Non-renewable resources include minerals, which are created naturally over millions of years. The industrialized world extracts minerals for fuel as well as for use in electronic equipment and medicine. Increased human extraction of non-renewable resources has endangered their availability, and over-mining has created other ecological problems, including runoff and water pollution. The use of fossil fuels for energy and transportation causes air pollution and is unsustainable. Fossil fuels cannot be replaced once depleted, and they are being depleted at an increasing rate. The need to find a sustainable alternative to the use of non-renewable fossil fuels is imperative.

RECENT APPLICATIONS OF SCIENCE AND TECHNOLOGY TO HEALTH CARE, THE ENVIRONMENT, AGRICULTURE, AND INFORMATION TECHNOLOGY

Scientific and technological developments have led to the widespread availability of **technologies** heretofore unheard of, including cellular phones, satellite-based applications, and a worldwide network of connected computers. Some of the notable recent applications include:

- **Health care**: Antibiotics, genetic screening for diseases, the sequencing of the human genome. Issues include problems with health care distribution on an increasingly industrialized planet.
- **The environment**: Computerized models of climate change and pollution monitoring. Issues include increased pollution of the water, air, and soil, and the over-harvesting of natural resources with mechanized equipment.
- **Agriculture**: Genetic improvements in agricultural practices, including increased output on the same amount of arable land. Issues include unknown environmental effects of hybrid species, cross-pollination with organic species, and pollution caused by synthetic chemical fertilizers.
- **Information technology**: New Internet-based industries, increased worldwide collaboration, and access to information. Issues include the depletion of natural resources for electronics production.

SOCIAL IMPACTS OF RECENT DEVELOPMENTS IN SCIENCE AND TECHNOLOGY

Recent **developments in science and technology** have had both positive and negative effects on human society. The issue of sustainable growth is an increasingly important one, as humans realize that the resources they use are not unlimited. Genetic research into diseases, stem cell research, and cloning technology have created great controversies as they have been introduced, and an increasing number of people reject the morality of scientific practices like animal testing in the pursuit of scientific advancement. In addition, an increasingly technology-based world has produced a new social inequality based on access to computers and Internet technology. These issues are beginning to be debated at all levels of human government, from city councils to the United Nations. Does science provide the authoritative answer to all human problems, or do ethics carry weight in scientific debates as well? Ultimately, humans must weigh the competing needs of facilitating scientific pursuits and maintaining an ethical society as they face new technological questions.

HUMAN IMPACTS ON ECOSYSTEMS

Human impacts on ecosystems take many forms and have many causes. They include widespread disruptions and specific niche disturbances. Humans practice many forms of environmental manipulation that affect plants and animals in many biomes and ecosystems. Many human practices involve the consumption of natural resources for food and energy production, the changing of the environment to produce food and energy, and the intrusion on ecosystems to provide shelter. These general behaviors include a multitude of specific behaviors, including the use and overuse of pesticides, the encroachment upon habitat, over hunting and over fishing, the introduction of plant and animal species into non-native ecosystems, not recycling, and the introduction of hazardous wastes and chemical byproducts into the environment. These behaviors have led to a number of consequences, such as acid rain, ozone depletion, deforestation, urbanization, accelerated species loss, genetic abnormalities, endocrine disruption in populations, and harm to individual animals.

GREENHOUSE EFFECT

The **greenhouse effect** refers to a naturally occurring and necessary process. **Greenhouse gasses**, which are ozone, carbon dioxide, water vapor, and methane, trap infrared radiation that is reflected toward the atmosphere. This is actually beneficial in that warm air is trapped. Without the greenhouse effect, it is estimated that the temperature on Earth would be 30 degrees less on average. The problem occurs because human activity generates more greenhouse gases than necessary. The practices that increase the amount of greenhouse gases are the burning of natural gas and oil, farming practices that result in the release of methane and nitrous oxide, factory operations that produce gases, and deforestation practices that decrease the amount of oxygen available to offset greenhouse gases. Population growth also increases the volume of gases released. Excess greenhouse gases cause more infrared radiation to become trapped, which increases the temperature at the Earth's surface.

IMPACT

Rising temperatures may lead to an increase in sea levels as polar ice melts, lower amounts of available fresh water as coastal areas flood, species extinction because of changes in habitat, increases in certain diseases, and a decreased standard of living for humans. Less fresh water and losses of habitat for humans and other species can also lead to decreased agricultural production and food supply shortages. Increased desertification leads to habitat loss for humans and certain other species. Decreases in animal populations from losses of habitat and increased hunting by other species can lead to extinction. Increases in severe weather, such as huge sustained snowstorms, may also occur at unlikely latitudes. Even though global warming results in weather that is drier and warmer overall, it still gets cold enough to snow. There may be more moisture in the atmosphere due to evaporation. **Global warming** may cause the permanent loss of glaciers and permafrost. There might also be increases in air pollution and acid rain.

IMPACT OF SCIENCE AND TECHNOLOGY ON ENVIRONMENT AND HUMAN AFFAIRS

Since the industrial revolution, science and technology have had a profound impact on **human affairs**. There has been a rapid increase in the number of discoveries in many fields. Many major and minor discoveries have led to a great improvement in the quality of life of many people. This includes longer life spans because of better nutrition, access to medical care, and a decrease in workplace health hazards. Not all of these problems have been solved, and many still exist in one form or another. For example, even though there are means to recycle, not every business does so because of economic factors. These advances, while improving the lives of many humans, have also taken their toll on the environment. A possible solution may arise when the carrying capacity for humans on Earth is reached. The population will decline, and solutions will have to be found. Otherwise, an immediate halt or decrease in the human behaviors that are causing environmental damage will need to happen.

PURPOSE OF STUDYING INTERACTIONS AMONG HUMANS, NATURAL HAZARDS, AND THE ENVIRONMENT

In science class, students will learn that the **human population** on earth can be affected by various factors from both their natural environments and from the technologies they use in their daily lives. These factors can be positive or negative, so students need to learn how to prepare for, respond to, and evaluate the consequences of environmental occurrences over a long period of time. Natural disasters are a negative experience, but so are human-made disasters such as pollution and deforestation. Students need to understand that science is involved in the interactions between the human population, natural hazards, and the environment. They should know that the aim of science is to make these interactions **balanced and positive**. Science is a discipline that can help find ways to increase safety during and remediate after natural disasters, advance technology and transportation in an environmentally safe manner, prevent and cure diseases, and remediate the environmental damage that has already been done.

SUBJECTS COVERED IN PERSONAL HEALTH PORTION OF SCIENCE CLASS

Among the personal and social perspectives of science are the issues of **personal and public health care**. In this area, students learn such things as:

- The importance of regular **exercise** to the maintenance and improvement of health
- The need for **risk assessment** and educated decisions to prevent injuries and illnesses because of the potential for accidents and the existence of hazards
- The risk of illness and the social and psychological factors associated with the use of **tobacco products**
- The dangers of abusing **alcohol and other drug substances**, including addiction and damage to body functions
- The energy and nutrition values of various **foods**, their role in growth and development, and the requirements of the body according to variable factors
- The complexities of **human sexuality** and the dangers of sexually transmitted diseases
- The relationship between **environmental and human health**, and the need to monitor soil, water, and air standards

RISK AND BENEFIT ANALYSIS AS STUDIED IN PERSONAL AND SOCIAL PERSPECTIVES OF SCIENCE

Risk analysis considers the type of hazard and estimates the number of people who might be exposed and the number likely to suffer consequences. The results are used to determine options for reducing or eliminating risks. For example, the Center for Disease Control must analyze the risk of a certain new virus strain causing a pandemic, how many people and what age groups need to be vaccinated first, and what precautions can be taken to guard against the spread of the disease. **Risk and benefit analysis** involves having students consider the dangers of natural (major storms), chemical (pollution), biological (pollen and bacteria), social (occupational safety and transportation), and personal (smoking, dieting, and drugs) hazards. Students then use a systematic approach to think critically about these hazards, apply probability estimates to the risks, and compare them to estimated and perceived personal and social benefits.

INTERACTIONS OF SCIENCE AND TECHNOLOGY WITH SOCIETY

The interactions of science and technology with society include:

- **Scientific knowledge** and the procedures used by scientists influence the way many people think about themselves, others, and the environment.
- **Technology** influences society through its products and processes. It influences quality of life and the ways people act and interact. Technological changes are often accompanied by social, political, and economic changes. Science and technology contribute enormously to economic growth and productivity. The introduction of the cell phone into society is a perfect example of technology influencing society, quality of life, human interaction, and the economy.
- **Societal challenges** often inspire questions for scientific research, and social priorities often influence research priorities through the availability of research funding.

Science and technology have been advanced through the contributions of many different people in a variety of cultures during different time periods in history. Scientists and engineers work in colleges, businesses and industries, research institutes, and government agencies, touching many lives in a variety of settings.

Biology

SUBFIELDS OF BIOLOGY

There are a number of subfields of biology:

- **Zoology** – The study of animals
- **Botany** – The study of plants
- **Biophysics** – The application of the laws of physics to the processes of organisms and the application of the facts about living things to human processes and inventions
- **Biochemistry** – The study of the chemistry of living organisms, including diseases and the pharmaceutical drugs used to cure them
- **Cytology** – The study of cells
- **Histology** – The study of the tissues of plants and animals
- **Organology** – The study of tissues organized into organs
- **Physiology** – The study of the way organisms function, including metabolism, the exchange of matter and energy in nutrition, the senses, reproduction and development, and the work of the nervous system and brain
- **Genetics** – The study of heredity as it relates to the transmission of genes
- **Ethology** – The study of animal behavior
- **Ecology** – The study of the relationship of living organisms to their environments

CLASSIFICATION OF LIFE FORMS

All living creatures can be classified into one of three domains and then into one of six kingdoms:

- Domain Bacteria
  - **Kingdom Eubacteria**—single celled prokaryotes with little internal complexity, contains peptidoglycan. Members have just one chromosome, reproduce asexually, may have flagella, and are very simple in form.

- Domain Archaea
  - **Kingdom Archaebacteria**—single celled prokaryotes with little internal complexity, does not contain peptidoglycan. Members have just one chromosome, reproduce asexually, may have flagella, and are very simple in form.

- Domain Eukarya
  - **Kingdom Protista**—single celled eukaryotes with greater internal complexity than Bacteria or Archaea. They have a true nucleus surrounded by a membrane that separates it from the cytoplasm. Most are one-celled and have no complex tissues like plants.
  - **Kingdom Fungi**—single celled or multicellular with considerable variation and complexity. Members have no chlorophyll, so they don't make their own food like plants. They reproduce using spores. Fungi are made up of filaments called hyphae that, in larger fungi, can interlace to form a tissue called mycelium.

- o **Kingdom Plantae**—multicellular with great variation and complexity, rigid cell walls. This group consists of organisms that have chlorophyll and make their own food. Plants have differentiated tissues and reproduce either sexually or asexually.
- o **Kingdom Animalia**—multicellular with much variation and complexity, cell membrane. This group consists of organisms that move around and have to feed on existing organic material.

Review Video: Kingdom Animalia
Visit mometrix.com/academy and enter code: 558413

Review Video: Kingdom Fungi
Visit mometrix.com/academy and enter code: 315081

Review Video: Kingdom Plantae
Visit mometrix.com/academy and enter code: 710084

CHARACTERISTICS OF INVERTEBRATES

Invertebrates are animals with no internal skeletons. They can be divided into three groups:

1. **Marine Invertebrates** – Members of this group live in oceans and seas. Marine invertebrates include sponges, corals, jellyfish, snails, clams, octopuses, squids, and crustaceans, none of which live on the surface.
2. **Freshwater Invertebrates** – Members of this group live in lakes and rivers. Freshwater invertebrates include worms on the bottom, microscopic crustaceans, and terrestrial insect larvae that live in the water column, but only where there is no strong current. Some live on the surface of the water.
3. **Terrestrial Invertebrates** – Members of this group live on dry ground. Terrestrial invertebrates include insects, mollusks (snails, slugs), arachnids, and myriapods (centipedes and millipedes). Terrestrial invertebrates breathe through a series of tubes that penetrate into the body (trachea) and deliver oxygen into tissues. Underground terrestrial invertebrates are generally light-colored with atrophied eyes and no cuticle to protect them from desiccation. They include worms that live underground and in caves and rock crevices. This group also includes insects such as ants that create colonies underground.

CHARACTERISTICS OF VERTEBRATE GROUPS

The **vertebrates**, animals with an internal skeleton, are divided into four groups:

1. **Fish** – This group is the most primitive, but is also the group from which all other groups evolved. Fish live in water, breathe with gills, are cold-blooded, have fins and scales, and are typically oviparous. Fish typically have either cartilaginous skeletons (such as rays and sharks) or bony skeletons.
2. **Amphibians** – The skin of animals in this group is delicate and permeable, so they need water to keep it moist. Amphibians are oviparous. The young start out in water with gills, but the adults use lungs.
3. **Reptiles and birds** – The skin of animals in this group has very hard, horn-like scales. Birds have exchanged scales for feathers. Reptiles and birds are oviparous, although birds care for their eggs and reptiles do not. Members have a cloaca, an excretory and reproductive cavity that opens to the outside. Reptiles are cold-blooded, but birds are warm-blooded.

4. **Mammals** – These are the most highly evolved vertebrates. Mammals have bodies covered with fur; are warm-blooded; are viviparous, meaning they give birth to live young which are fed with milk from female mammary glands; and are tetrapods (four-legged). Most live on the ground (except whales and dolphins) and a few fly (bats).

HUNTERS AND PREY ANIMALS

The interaction between **predators** and their **prey** is important to controlling the balance of an ecosystem. **Hunters** are **carnivorous** animals at the top of the ecological pyramid that eat other animals. Hunters tend to be territorial, leaving signs to warn others to stay out or risk a fight. Hunters are equipped to capture with claws, curved beaks, spurs, fangs, etc. They try to use a minimum amount of energy for each capture, so they prey upon the more vulnerable (the old, ill, or very young) when given a choice. Predators never kill more than they can eat. Some hunters have great speed, some stalk, and some hunt in groups. **Prey** animals are those that are captured by predators for food. They are usually **herbivores** further down the ecological pyramid. Prey animals have special characteristics to help them flee from predators. They may hide in nests or caves, become totally immobile to escape detection, have protective coloration or camouflage, have warning coloration to indicate being poisonous, or have shells or quills for protection.

LIFE PROCESSES THAT ALL LIVING THINGS HAVE IN COMMON

Living things share many **processes** that are necessary to survival, but the ways these processes and interactions occur is highly diverse. Processes include those related to:

- **Nutrition** – the process of obtaining, ingesting, and digesting foods; excreting unused or excess substances; and extracting energy from the foods to maintain structure.
- **Transport** (circulation) – the process of circulating essential materials such as nutrients, cells, hormones, and gases (oxygen and hydrogen) to the places they are needed by moving them through veins, arteries, and capillaries. Needed materials do not travel alone, but are "piggybacked" on transporting molecules.
- **Respiration** – the process of breathing, which is exchanging gases between the interior and exterior using gills, trachea (insects), or lungs.
- **Regulation** – the process of coordinating life activities through the nervous and endocrine systems.
- **Reproduction and growth** – the process of producing more of one's own kind and growing from birth to adulthood. The more highly evolved an animal is, the longer its growth time is.
- **Locomotion** (in animals) – the process of moving from place to place in the environment by using legs, flight, or body motions.

ORGANISMS THAT INTERFERE WITH CELL ACTIVITY

Viruses, bacteria, fungi, and other parasites may infect plants and animals and interfere with normal life functions, create imbalances, or disrupt the operations of cells.

- **Viruses** – These enter the body by inhalation (airborne) or through contact with contaminated food, water, or infected tissues. They affect the body by taking over the cell's protein synthesis mechanism to make more viruses. They kill the host cell and impact tissue and organ operations. Examples of viruses include measles, rabies, pneumonia, and AIDS.
- **Bacteria** – These enter the body through breaks in the skin or contaminated food or water, or by inhalation. They reproduce rapidly and produce toxins that kill healthy host tissues. Examples include diphtheria, bubonic plague, tuberculosis, and syphilis.

- **Fungi** – These feed on healthy tissues of the body by sending rootlike tendrils into the tissues to digest them extracellularly. Examples include athlete's foot and ringworm.
- **Parasites** – These enter the body through the skin, via insect bites, or through contaminated food or water. Examples include tapeworms, malaria, or typhus.

HYDROCARBONS AND CARBOHYDRATES

Carbon is an element found in all living things. Two types of carbon molecules that are essential to life are hydrocarbons and carbohydrates. **Hydrocarbons**, composed only of hydrogen and carbon, are the simplest organic molecules. The simplest of these is methane, which has one carbon atom and four hydrogen atoms. Methane is produced by the decomposition of animal or vegetable matter, and is part of petroleum and natural gas. **Carbohydrates** are compounds made of hydrogen, carbon, and oxygen. There are three types of these macromolecules (large molecules):

1. **Sugars** are soluble in water and, although they have less energy than fats, provide energy more quickly.
2. **Starches**, insoluble in water, are long chains of glucose that act as reserve substances. Potatoes and cereals are valuable foods because they are rich in starch. Animals retain glucose in their cells as glucogen, a special type of starch.
3. **Cellulose**, composed of glucose chains, makes up the cells and tissues of plants. It is one of the most common organic materials.

> **Review Video: Basics of Hydrocarbons**
> Visit mometrix.com/academy and enter code: 824749

LIPIDS, PROTEINS, AND NUCLEIC ACIDS

Besides hydrocarbons and carbohydrates, there are three other types of carbon molecules that are essential to life: lipids, proteins, and nucleic acids. **Lipids** are compounds that are insoluble or only partially soluble in water. There are three main types: fats, which act as an energy reserve for organisms; phospholipids, which are one of the essential components of cell membranes; and steroids such as cholesterol and estrogen, which are very important to metabolism. **Proteins** are complex substances that make up almost half the dry weight of animal bodies. These molecules contain hydrogen, carbon, oxygen, and other elements, chiefly nitrogen and sulfur. Proteins make up muscle fibers and, as enzymes, act as catalysts. **Nucleic acids** are large molecules (polymers) composed of a large number of simpler molecules (nucleotides). Each one has a sugar containing five carbons (pentose), a phosphorous compound (phosphate group), and a nitrogen compound (nitrogenated base). Nucleic acids facilitate perpetuation of the species because they carry genetic information as DNA and RNA.

CELL

The **cell** is the basic organizational unit of all living things. Each piece within a cell has a function that helps organisms grow and survive. There are many different types of cells, but cells are unique to each type of organism. The one thing that all cells have in common is a **membrane**, which is comparable to a semi-permeable plastic bag. The membrane is composed of phospholipids. There are also some **transport holes**, which are proteins that help certain molecules and ions move in and out of the cell. The cell is filled with a fluid called **cytoplasm** or cytosol. Within the cell are a variety of **organelles**, groups of complex molecules that help a cell survive, each with its own

unique membrane that has a different chemical makeup from the cell membrane. The larger the cell, the more organelles it will need to live.

NUCLEUS AND MITOCHONDRIA IN EUKARYOTIC CELLS

Eukaryotic cells have a nucleus, a big dark spot floating somewhere in the center that acts like the brain of the cell by controlling eating, movement, and reproduction. A **nuclear envelope** surrounds the nucleus and its contents, but allows RNA and proteins to pass through. **Chromatin**, made up of DNA, RNA, and nuclear proteins, is present in the nucleus. The nucleus also contains a nucleolus made of RNA and protein. **Mitochondria** are very small organelles that take in nutrients, break them down, and create energy for the cell through a process called cellular respiration. There might be thousands of mitochondria depending on the cell's purpose. A muscle cell needs more energy for movement than a cell that transmits nerve impulses, for example. Mitochondria have two membranes: a **cover** and the **inner cristae** that folds over many times to increase the surface work area. The fluid inside the mitochondria, the matrix, is filled with water and enzymes that take food molecules and combine them with oxygen so they can be digested.

CHLOROPLASTS OF PLANT CELLS

Chloroplasts, which make plants green, are the food producers of a plant cell. They differ from an animal cell's mitochondria, which break down sugars and nutrients. **Photosynthesis** occurs when the energy from the sun hits a chloroplast and the chlorophyll uses that energy to combine carbon dioxide and water to make sugars and oxygen. The nutrition and oxygen obtained from plants makes them the basis of all life on earth. A chloroplast has two membranes to contain and protect the inner parts. The **stroma** is an area inside the chloroplast where reactions occur and starches are created. A **thylakoid** has chlorophyll molecules on its surface, and a stack of thylakoids is called a granum. The stacks of sacs are connected by **stromal lamellae**, which act like the skeleton of the chloroplast, keeping all the sacs a safe distance from each other and maximizing the efficiency of the organelle.

PASSIVE AND ACTIVE TRANSPORT

Passive transport within a cell does not require energy and work. For example, when there is a large concentration difference between the outside and the inside of a cell, the pressure of the greater concentration, not energy, will move molecules across the lipid bilayer into the cell. Another example of passive transport is osmosis, which is the movement of water across a membrane. Too much water in a cell can cause it to burst, so the cell moves ions in and out to help equalize the amount of water. **Active transport** is when a cell uses energy to move individual molecules across the cell membrane to maintain a proper balance. **Proteins** embedded in the lipid bilayer do most of the transport work. There are hundreds of different types of proteins because they are specific. For instance, a protein that moves glucose will not move calcium. The activity of these proteins can be stopped by inhibitors or poisons, which can destroy or plug up a protein.

MITOTIC CELL REPLICATION

Mitosis is the duplication of a cell and all its parts, including the DNA, into two identical daughter cells. There are five phases in the life cycle of a cell:

1. **Prophase** – This is the process of duplicating everything in preparation for division.
2. **Metaphase** – The cell's different pieces align themselves for the split. The DNA lines up along a central axis and the centrioles send out specialized tubules that connect to the centromere. The centromere has two strands of a chromosome (condensed DNA) attached to it.
3. **Anaphase** – Half of the chromosomes go one way and half go another.
4. **Telophase** – When the chromosomes get to the side of the cell, the cell membrane closes in and splits the cell into two pieces. This results in two separate cells, each with half of the original DNA.
5. **Interphase** – This is the normal state of the cell, or the resting stage between divisions. During this stage, the cell duplicates nucleic acids in preparation for the next division.

MICROBES

Microbes are the smallest, simplest, and most abundant organisms on earth. Their numbers are incalculable, and a microscope is required to see them. There is a huge variety of microbes, including bacteria, fungi, some algae, and protozoa. Microbes can be harmful or helpful.

Microbes can be **heterotrophic** (eat other things) or **autotrophic** (make food for themselves). They can be solitary or colonial, sexual or asexual. Examples include mold, a multi-cellular type of fungus, and yeasts, which are single-celled (but may live in colonies). A **mushroom** is a fungus that lives as a group of strands underground called hyphae that decompose leaves or bark on the ground. When it reproduces, it develops a mushroom whose cap contains spores. **Mold** is a type of zygote fungi that reproduces with a stalk, but releases zygospores. **Good bacteria** can be those that help plants absorb the nitrogen needed for growth or help grazing animals break down the cellulose in plants. Some **bad bacteria** are killed by the penicillin developed from a fungus.

ROOTS, STEMS, AND LEAVES

Roots are structures designed to pull water and minerals from soil or water. In large plants such as trees, the roots usually go deep into the ground to not only reach the water, but also to support and stabilize the tree. There are some plant species that have roots above ground, and there are also plants called epiphytes that live in trees with their roots clinging to the branches. Some roots, like carrots and turnips, serve as food. Roots are classified as **primary** and **lateral** (like a trunk and branches). The **apical meristem** is the tip of a root or shoot that helps the plant increase in length. **Root hairs** are fuzzy root extensions that help with the absorption of water and nutrients. The majority of the plant above ground is made up of the stems (trunk and branches) and leaves. **Stems** transport food and water and act as support structures. **Leaves** are the site for photosynthesis, and are connected to the rest of the plant by a vascular system.

GYMNOSPERMS, CYCADS, AND CONIFERS

Gymnosperms are plants with vascular systems and seeds but no flowers (flowers are an evolutionary advancement). The function of the seed is to ensure offspring can be produced by the plant by providing a protective coating that lets the plant survive for long periods until it germinates. It also stores food for the new plant to use until it can make its own. Seeds can be spread over a wide area. **Cycads** are sturdy plants with big, waxy fronds that make them look like ferns or palms. They can survive in harsh conditions if there is warm weather. For reproduction, they have big cones located in the center of the plant. The female plant grows a fruit in the middle of

338

the stem. **Conifers** are trees that thrive in northern latitudes and have cones. Examples of conifers are pine, cedar, redwood, and spruce. Conifers are evergreens because they have needles that take full advantage of the sun year-round. They are also very tall and strong because of the chemical substance xylem in their systems.

ANGIOSPERMS

Angiosperms are plants that have flowers. This is advantageous because the plant's seeds and pollen can be spread not only by gravity and wind, but also by insects and animals. Flowers are able to attract organisms that can help pollinate the plant and distribute seeds. Some flowering plants also produce fruit. When an animal eats the fruit, the plant seeds within will be spread far and wide in the animal's excrement. There are two kinds of angiosperm seeds: monocotyledons (monocots) and dicotyledons (dicots). A **cotyledon** is the seed leaf or food package for the developing plant. **Monocots** are the simple flowering plants such as grasses, corn, palm trees, and lilies. They always have three petals on their flowers, and their leaves are long strands (like a palm frond). A **dicot** has seeds with two cotyledons, or two seed leaves of food. Most everyday flowers are dicots with four or five petals and extremely complex leaves with veins. Examples include roses, sunflowers, cacti, and cherry trees.

ARTHROPODS

Arthropods have a number of unique characteristics:

- They have an **exoskeleton** (outside instead of inside).
- They **molt**. As the arthropod grows, it must shed its old shell and grow a new one.
- They have several **legs**, which are jointed.
- Their advanced **nervous systems** allow for hunting, moving around, finding a mate, and learning new behaviors for adaptation.
- They develop through **metamorphosis**. As arthropods develop, they change body shape. There are two types of metamorphosis:
- *Complete* – The entire body shape changes. An example is butterflies, which change from worm-like larvae to insects with wings.
- *Gradual* – The arthropod starts off small with no wings, and then molts and grows wings. Example: Grasshoppers.

Arthropods include spiders, crustaceans, and the enormous insect species (26 orders) called uniramians. Ranging from fleas to mosquitoes, beetles, dragonflies, aphids, bees, flies, and many more, uniramians have exoskeletons made of chitin, compound eyes, complex digestive systems, and usually six legs. This group is extremely diverse. Some can fly, some have toxins or antennae, and some can make wax, silk, or honey.

> **Review Video: Arthropoda**
> Visit mometrix.com/academy and enter code: 523466

REPTILES

One group of vertebrates is the **reptile**. This group includes:

- **Crocodilia** – This is a group of reptiles that can grow quite large, and includes alligators and crocodiles. Normally found near the water in warmer climates, Crocodilia might be more closely related to birds than other reptiles.

- **Squamata** – This is the order of reptiles that includes snakes and lizards. Snakes are special because they have no legs and no ears. They feel vibrations, smell with their tongues, have specialized scales, and can unhinge their jaws to swallow prey that is larger than they are. Like snakes, lizards have scales, but they differ in that they have legs, can dig, can climb trees, and can grab things.
- **Chelonia** – This is the order of reptiles that includes turtles and tortoises. It is a special group because its members have shells. Different varieties live in forests, water, and deserts, or anywhere the climate is warm enough. They also live a long time, even hundreds of years. Turtles are typically found near water and tortoises on land, even dry areas.

REPRODUCTION IN MAMMALS

When classified according to how they reproduce, there are three types of mammals:

1. **Monotremes** are rare mammals that lay eggs. These were the first mammals, and are more closely related to reptiles than other mammals. Examples include the duck-billed platypus and the spiny anteater.
2. **Marsupials** are special mammals. They give birth to live young, but the babies mature in pouches, where they are carried and can feed on milk. Many are found in Australia. The isolation of this island continent prevented placental mammals from taking hold. Examples of marsupials include kangaroos, possums, and koalas.
3. **Placental mammals** give birth from the females' placenta to live young. The young may be able to walk immediately, or they may need to be carried. They are still dependent on parental care for at least a short time. Placental mammals are the dominant form of mammals. Members of this group include cetaceans such as whales and dolphins, which are mammals that evolved but returned to the ocean.

RESPIRATORY SYSTEM

The **respiratory system** exchanges gases with the environment. Amphibians exchange gases through their moist skin and fish use gills, but mammals, birds, and reptiles have lungs. The human respiratory system is made up of the nose, mouth, pharynx, trachea, and two lungs. The purpose of the respiratory system is to bring oxygen into the body and expel carbon dioxide. The respiratory system can inhale viruses, bacteria, and dangerous chemicals, so it is vulnerable to toxins and diseases such as pneumonia, which causes the lungs to fill with fluid until they cannot take in enough oxygen to support the body. **Emphysema**, often caused by smoking tobacco, destroys the tissues in the lungs, which cannot be regenerated. The respiratory system interacts with the **digestive system** in that the mouth and pharynx are used to swallow food and drink, as well as to breathe. It interacts with the circulatory system in that it provides fresh oxygen through blood vessels that pass through the lungs. This oxygen is then carried by the circulatory system throughout the body.

Review Video: Respiratory System
Visit mometrix.com/academy and enter code: 783075

SKELETAL SYSTEM

The human body has an **endoskeleton**, meaning it is inside the body. It is made up of bones instead of the hard plate of exoskeletons or fluids in tubes, which comprise the hydrostatic system of the starfish. The purpose of the skeleton is to support the body, provide a framework to which the muscles and organs can connect, and protect the inner organs. The skull protects the all-important brain and the ribs protect the internal organs from impact. The skeletal system interacts with the muscular system to help the body move, and softer cartilage works with the calcified bone to allow

smooth movement of the body. The skeletal system also interacts with the circulatory system in that the marrow inside the bones helps produce both white and red blood cells.

NERVOUS SYSTEM

The **nervous system** is divided into two parts: the **central nervous system** (brain and spinal cord) and the **peripheral nervous system** (a network of billions of neurons of different types throughout the entire body). The neurons are connected end to end, and transmit electrical impulses to each other. **Efferent neurons** send impulses from the central system to the limbs and organs. **Afferent neurons** receive sensory information and transmit it back to the central system. The nervous system is concerned with **senses and action**. In other words, it senses something and then acts upon it. An example is a predator sensing prey and attacking it. The nervous system also automatically senses activity inside the body and reacts to stimuli. For example, the first bite of a meal sets the whole digestive system into motion. The nervous system **interacts** with every other system in the body because all the tissues and organs need instruction, even when individuals are not aware of any activity occurring. For instance, the endocrine system is constantly working to produce hormones or adrenalin as needed.

GENETICS, GENES, AND CHROMOSOMES

Genetics is the science devoted to the study of how characteristics are transmitted from one generation to another. In the 1800s, Gregor Mendel discovered the three laws of heredity that explain how genetics works. Genes are the hereditary units of material that are transmitted from one generation to the next. They are capable of undergoing mutations, can be recombined with other genes, and can determine the nature of an organism, including its color, shape, and size. **Genotype** is the genetic makeup of an individual based on one or more characteristics, while phenotype is the external manifestation of the genotype. For example, genotype can determine hair color, and phenotype is the actual color of the hair. **Chromosomes** are the structures inside the nucleus of a cell made up primarily of deoxyribonucleic acid (DNA) and proteins. The chromosomes carry the genes. The numbers vary according to the species, but they are always the same for each species. For example, the human has 46 chromosomes, and the water lily has 112.

MENDEL'S CONTRIBUTIONS TO GENETICS

Johann Gregor Mendel is known as the father of **genetics**. Mendel was an Austrian monk who performed thousands of experiments involving the breeding of the common pea plant in the monastery garden. Mendel kept detailed records including seed color, pod color, seed type, flower color, and plant height for eight years and published his work in 1865. Unfortunately, his work was largely ignored until the early 1900s. Mendel's work showed that genes come in pairs and that dominant and recessive traits are inherited independently of each other. His work established the law of segregation, the law of independent assortment, and the law of dominance.

DARWIN'S CONTRIBUTIONS TO THE THEORY OF EVOLUTION

Charles Darwin's theory of evolution is the unifying concept in biology today. From 1831 to 1836, Darwin traveled as a naturalist on a five-year voyage on the *H.M.S. Beagle* around the tip of South America and to the Galápagos Islands. He studied finches, took copious amounts of meticulous notes, and collected thousands of plant and animal specimens. He collected 13 species of finches each with a unique bill for a distinct food source, which led him to believe that due to similarities between the finches, that the finches shared a common ancestor. The similarities and differences of fossils of extinct rodents and modern mammal fossils led him to believe that the mammals had changed over time. Darwin believed that these changes were the result of random genetic changes called mutations. He believed that mutations could be beneficial and eventually result in a different organism over time. In 1859, in his first book, *On the Origin of Species*, Darwin proposed that natural selection was the means by which adaptations would arise over time. He coined the term "natural selection" and said that natural selection is the mechanism of evolution. Because variety exists among individuals of a species, he stated that those individuals must compete for the same limited resources. Some would die, and others would survive. According to Darwin, evolution is a slow, gradual process. In 1871, Darwin published his second book, *Descent of Man, and Selection in Relation to Sex*, in which he discussed the evolution of man.

> **Review Video: Darwin's Contributions to Theory of Evolution**
> Visit mometrix.com/academy and enter code: 898980

CONTRIBUTION TO GENETICS MADE BY ALFRED HERSHEY AND MARTHA CHASE

Alfred Hershey and Martha Chase did a series of experiments in 1952 known as the **Hershey-Chase experiments**. These experiments showed that deoxyribonucleic acid (DNA), not protein, is the genetic material that transfers information for inheritance. The Hershey-Chase experiments used a bacteriophage, a virus that infects bacteria, to infect the bacteria *Escherichia coli*. The bacteriophage T2 is basically a small piece of DNA enclosed in a protein coating. The DNA contains phosphorus, and the protein coating contains sulfur. In the first set of experiments, the T2 was marked with radioactive phosphorus-32. In the second set of experiments, the T2 was marked with radioactive sulfur-35. For both sets of experiments, after the *E. coli* was infected by the T2, the *E. coli* was isolated using a centrifuge. In the first set of experiments, the radioactive isotope (P-32) was found in the *E. coli*, showing that the genetic information was transferred by the DNA. In the second set of experiments, the radioactive isotope (S-35) was not found in the *E. coli*, showing that the genetic information was not transferred by the protein as was previously thought. Hershey and Chase conducted further experiments allowing the bacteria from the first set of experiments to reproduce, and the offspring was also found to contain the radioactive isotope (P-32) further confirming that the DNA transferred the genetic material.

Ecology

AUTOTROPHS, PRODUCERS, HERBIVORES, CARNIVORES, OMNIVORES, AND DECOMPOSERS

Energy flows in one direction: from the sun, through photosynthetic organisms such as green plants (producers) and algae (autotrophs), and then to herbivores, carnivores, and decomposers. **Autotrophs** are organisms capable of producing their own food. The organic molecules they produce are food for all other organisms (heterotrophs). **Producers** are green plants that manufacture food by photosynthesis. **Herbivores** are animals that eat only plants (deer, rabbits, etc.). Since they are the first animals to receive the energy captured by producers, herbivores are called primary consumers. **Carnivores**, or secondary consumers, are animals that eat the bodies of other animals for food. Predators (wolves, lions, etc.) kill other animals, while scavengers consume animals that are already dead from predation or natural causes (buzzards). **Omnivores** are animals that eat both plants and other animals (humans). **Decomposers** include saprophytic fungi and bacteria that break down the complex structures of the bodies of living things into simpler forms that can be used by other living things. This recycling process releases energy from organic molecules.

ABIOTIC FACTORS AND BIOTIC FACTORS

Abiotic factors are the physical and chemical factors in the environment that are nonliving, but upon which the growth and survival of living organisms depends. These factors can determine the types of plants and animals that will establish themselves and thrive in a particular area. Abiotic factors include:

- Light intensity available for photosynthesis
- Temperature range
- Available moisture
- Type of rock substratum
- Type of minerals
- Type of atmospheric gases
- Relative acidity (pH) of the system

Biotic factors are the living components of the environment that affect, directly or indirectly, the ecology of an area, possibly limiting the type and number of resident species. The relationships of predator/prey, producer/consumer, and parasite/host can define a community. Biotic factors include:

- Population levels of each species
- The food requirements of each species
- The interactions between species
- The wastes produced

HOW PLANTS MANUFACTURE FOOD

Plants are the only organisms capable of transforming **inorganic material** from the environment into **organic matter** by using water and solar energy. This transformation is made possible by chloroplasts, flat structures inside plant cells. **Chloroplasts**, located primarily in the leaves, contain chlorophyll (the pigment capable of absorbing light and storing it in chemical compounds), DNA, ribosomes, and numerous enzymes. Chloroplasts are surrounded by a membrane. The leaves of plants are the main producers of oxygen, which helps purify the air. The **chlorophyll** in chloroplasts is responsible for the light, or luminous, phase of photosynthesis. The energy it absorbs breaks down water absorbed through the roots into hydrogen and oxygen to form ATP molecules that store energy. In the dark phase, when the plant has no light, the energy molecules are used to attach carbon dioxide to water and form glucose, a sugar.

PRODUCERS, CONSUMERS, AND DECOMPOSERS

The **food chain**, or food web, is a series of events that happens when one organism consumes another to survive. Every organism is involved in dozens of connections with others, so what happens to one affects the environment of the others. In the food chain, there are three main categories:

- **Producers** – Plants and vegetables are at the beginning of the food chain because they take energy from the sun and make food for themselves through photosynthesis. They are food sources for other organisms.
- **Consumers** – There are three levels of consumers: the organisms that eat plants (primary consumers, or herbivores); the organisms that eat the primary consumers (secondary consumers, or carnivores); and, in some ecosystems, the organisms that eat both plants and animals (tertiary consumers, or omnivores).
- **Decomposers** – These are the organisms that eat dead things or waste matter and return the nutrients to the soil, thus returning essential molecules to the producers and completing the cycle.

SYSTEM OF CLASSIFICATION FOR LIVING ORGANISMS

The main characteristic by which living organisms are classified is the degree to which they are **related**, not the degree to which they resemble each other. The science of classification is called **taxonomy**. This classification is challenging since the division lines between groups is not always clear. Some animals have characteristics of two separate groups. The current system of taxonomy involves placing an organism into a **domain** (Bacteria, Archaea, and Eukarya), and then into a **kingdom** (Eubacteria, Archaeabacteria, Protista, Fungi, Plantae, and Animalia). The kingdoms are divided into phyla, then classes, then orders, then families, and finally genuses and species. For example, the family cat is in the domain of eukaryotes, the kingdom of animals, the phylum of chordates, the class of mammals, the order of carnivores, the family of felidae, and the genus of felis. All species of living beings can be identified with Latin scientific names that are assigned by the worldwide binomial system. The genus name comes first, and is followed by the name of the species. The family cat is *felis domesticus*.

PROPERTIES THAT CONTRIBUTE TO EARTH'S LIFE-SUSTAINING SYSTEM

Life on earth is dependent on:

- All three states of **water** – gas (water vapor), liquid, and solid (ice)
- A variety of forms of **carbon**, the basis of life (carbon-based units)
- In the atmosphere, carbon dioxide in the forms of methane and black carbon soot produce the **greenhouse effect** that provides a habitable atmosphere.
- The earth's **atmosphere and electromagnetic field**, which shield the surface from harmful radiation and allow useful radiation to go through
- The **earth's relationship to the sun and the moon**, which creates the four seasons and the cycles of plant and animal life
- The combination of **water, carbon, and nutrients**, which provides sustenance for life and regulates the climate system in a habitable temperature range with non-toxic air.

Geology

EARTH SYSTEM SCIENCE

The complex and interconnected dynamics of the continents, atmosphere, oceans, ice, and life forms are the subject of **earth system science**. These interconnected dynamics require an interdisciplinary approach that includes chemistry, physics, biology, mathematics, and applied sciences in order to study the Earth as an integrated system and determine (while considering human impact and interaction) the past, present, and future states of the earth. Scientific inquiry in this field includes exploration of:

- Extreme weather events as they pertain to a changing climate
- Earthquakes and volcanic eruptions as they pertain to tectonic shifts
- Losses in biodiversity in relation to the changes in the earth's ecosystems
- Causes and effects in the environment
- The sun's solar variability in relation to the earth's climate
- The atmosphere's increasing concentrations of carbon dioxide and aerosols
- Trends in the earth's systems in terms of changes and their consequences

TRADITIONAL EARTH SCIENCE DISCIPLINES

Modern science is approaching the study of the earth in an integrated fashion that sees the earth as an interconnected system that is impacted by humankind and, therefore, must include social dimensions. Traditionally, though, the following were the earth science disciplines:

- **Geology** – This is the study of the origin and structure of the earth and of the changes it has undergone and is in the process of undergoing. Geologists work from the crust inward.
- **Meteorology** – This is the study of the atmosphere, including atmospheric pressure, temperature, clouds, winds, precipitation, etc. It is also concerned with describing and explaining weather.
- **Oceanography** – This is the study of the oceans, which includes studying their extent and depth, the physics and chemistry of ocean waters, and the exploitation of their resources.
- **Ecology** – This is the study of living organisms in relation to their environment and to other living things. It is the study of the interrelations between the different components of the ecosystem.

GEOLOGICAL ERAS

Geologists divide the history of the earth into units of time called **eons**, which are divided into **eras**, then into **periods**, then into **epochs** and finally into **ages**. Dates are approximate of course, and there may be variations of a few million years. (Million years ago is abbreviated as Ma.) Some of the most commonly known periods are:

- **Hadean Period** – About 4.5 to 3.8 billion years ago
- **Archaean Period** – 3.8 to 2.5 billion years ago
- **Proterozoic Period** – 2.5 billion to 542 Ma
- **Cambrian Period** – 542 to 488 Ma
- Ordovician Period – 488 to 443 Ma
- **Silurian Period** – 443 to 416 Ma
- **Devonian Period** – 416 to 359 Ma
- Carboniferous Period – 359 to 290 Ma
- **Permian Period** – 290 to 248 Ma
- **Triassic Period** – 251 to 200 Ma
- **Jurassic Period** – 200 to 150 Ma
- Cretaceous Period – 150 to 65 Ma
- Paleogene Period – 65 to 28 Ma
- Neogene Period – 28 to 2 Ma
- **Quaternary Period** – about 2 Ma to the present

DEVELOPMENT OF LIFE ON EARTH ACCORDING TO TIME PERIODS

The **evolution** of life on earth is believed to have occurred as follows:

- Igneous rocks formed. (Hadean)
- The continents formed. (Archaean Eon)
- The first multi-cellular creatures such as hydras, jellyfish, and sponges appeared about 600 Ma.
- Flatworms, roundworms, and segmented worms appeared about 550 Ma.
- Moss, arthropods, octopus, and eels appeared. (Cambrian Period)
- Mushrooms, fungi, and other primitive plants appeared; sea animals began to use calcium to build bones and shells. (Ordovician Period)
- Fish with jaws appeared. (Silurian Period)
- Fish developed lungs and legs (frogs) and went on land; ferns appeared. (Devonian period)
- Reptiles developed the ability to lay eggs on land and pine trees appeared. (Carboniferous Period)
- Dinosaurs dominated the land during the Triassic and Jurassic Periods.
- Flying insects, birds, and the first flowering plants appeared; dinosaurs died out. (Cretaceous Period)
- Mammals evolved and dominated; grasses became widespread. (50 Ma)
- Hominids appeared more than 2 Ma.

HYDROSPHERE AND HYDROLOGIC CYCLE

The **hydrosphere** is anything on earth that is related to water, whether it is in the air, on land, or in a plant or animal system. A water molecule consists of only two atoms of hydrogen and one of oxygen, yet it is what makes life possible. Unlike the other planets, earth is able to sustain life because its temperature allows water to be in its liquid state most of the time. Water vapor and ice are of no use to living organisms. The **hydrologic cycle** is the journey water takes as it assumes different forms. Liquid surface water evaporates to form the gaseous state of a cloud, and then becomes liquid again in the form of rain. This process takes about 10 days if water becomes a cloud. Water at the bottom of the ocean or in a glacier is not likely to change form, even over periods of thousands of years.

> **Review Video: Hydrologic Cycle**
> Visit mometrix.com/academy and enter code: 426578

AQUIFERS

An **aquifer** is an underground water reservoir formed from groundwater that has infiltrated from the surface by passing through the soil and permeable rock layers (the zone of aeration) to a zone of saturation where the rocks are impermeable. There are two types of aquifers. In one, the water is under pressure (**confined**) as the supply builds up between layers of impermeable rocks and has to move back towards the surface, resulting in a spring or artesian well. The second type of aquifer is called "**unconfined**" because it has room to expand and contract, and the water has to be pumped out. The highest level of the aquifer is called the water table. If water is pumped out of the aquifer such that the water table dips in a specific area, that area is called a cone of depression.

BIOSPHERE

Biosphere is the term used by physical geographers to describe the living world of trees, bugs, and animals. It refers to any place where life exists on earth, and is the intersection of the hydrosphere, the atmosphere, the land, and the energy that comes from space. The biosphere includes the upper areas of the atmosphere where birds and insects can travel, areas deep inside caves, and hydrothermal vents at the bottom of the ocean.

Factors that affect the biosphere include:

- The **distance and tilt** between the earth and the sun – This produces temperatures that are conducive to life and causes the seasons.
- **Climate, daily weather, and erosion** – These change the land and the organisms on and in it.
- Earthquakes, tornadoes, volcanoes, tsunamis, and other **natural phenomena** – These all change the land.
- **Chemical erosion** – This changes the composition of rocks and organic materials, as well as how bacteria and single-celled organisms break down organic and inorganic materials.

ECOLOGICAL SYSTEM AND BIOME

An **ecological system**, or ecosystem, is the community of all the living organisms in a specific area interacting with non-living factors such as temperature, sunlight, atmospheric pressure, weather patterns, wind, types of nutrients, etc. An ecosystem's development depends on the energy that passes in and out of it. The boundaries of an ecosystem depend on the use of the term, whether it refers to an ecosystem under a rock or in a valley, pond, or ocean.

A **biome** is a general ecosystem type defined by the plants and animals that live there and the local climate patterns. Examples include tropical rainforests or savannas, deserts, grasslands, deciduous forests, tundra, woodlands, and ice caps. There can be more than one type of biome within a larger climate zone. The transition area between two biomes is an ecotone, which may have characteristics of both biomes.

EROSION

Erosion is the process that breaks down matter, whether it is a rock that is broken into pebbles or mountains that are rained on until they become hills. Erosion always happens in a downhill direction. The erosion of land by weather or breaking waves is called **denudation**. **Mass wasting** is the movement of masses of dirt and rock from one place to another. This can occur in two ways: **mechanical** (such as breaking a rock with a hammer) or **chemical** (such as pouring acid on a rock to dissolve it). If the material changes color, it indicates that a break down was chemical in nature. Whatever is broken down must go somewhere, so erosion eventually builds something up. For example, an eroded mountain ends up in a river that carries the sediment towards the ocean, where it builds up and creates a wetland or delta at the mouth of the river.

CLIMATES
Scientists have determined the following different types of **climates**:

- Polar (ice caps)
- Polar (tundra)
- Subtropical (dry summer)
- Subtropical (dry winter)
- Subtropical (humid)
- Subtropical (marine west coast)
- Subtropical (Mediterranean)
- Subtropical (wet)
- Tropical (monsoon)

- Tropical (savannah/grasslands)
- Tropical (wet)

Several factors make up and affect climates. These include:

- Temperature
- Atmospheric pressure
- The number of clouds and the amount of dust or smog
- Humidity
- Winds

The moistest and warmest of all the climates is that of the tropical rainforest. It has daily convection thunderstorms caused by the surface daytime heat and the high humidity, which combine to form thunderclouds.

> **Review Video: Climates**
> Visit mometrix.com/academy and enter code: 991320

LAYERS OF THE EARTH

The earth has several distinct **layers**, each with its own properties:

- **Crust** – This is the outermost layer of the earth that is comprised of the continents and the ocean basins. It has a variable thickness (35-70 km in the continents and 5-10 km in the ocean basins) and is composed mostly of alumino-silicates.
- **Mantle** – This is about 2900 km thick, and is made up mostly of ferro-magnesium silicates. It is divided into an upper and lower mantle. Most of the internal heat of the earth is located in the mantle. Large convective cells circulate heat, and may cause plate tectonic movement.
- **Core** – This is separated into the liquid outer core and the solid inner core. The outer core is 2300 km thick (composed mostly of nickel-iron alloy), and the inner core (almost entirely iron) is 12 km thick. The earth's magnetic field is thought to be controlled by the liquid outer core.

COMPOSITION OF EARTH'S ATMOSPHERE

The earth's **atmosphere** is 79% nitrogen, 20% oxygen, and 1% other gases. The oxygen was originally produced almost entirely by algae-type plants. The atmosphere has four layers:

- **Troposphere** – This is the layer closest to the earth where all weather takes place. It is the region that contains rising and falling packets of air. Air pressure at sea level is 0.1 atmospheres, but the top of the troposphere is about 10% of that amount.
- **Stratosphere** – In this layer, air flow is mainly horizontal. The upper portion has a thin layer of concentrated ozone (a reactive form of oxygen) that is largely responsible for absorbing the sun's ultraviolet rays.
- **Mesosphere** – This is the coldest layer. Temperatures drop to -100°C at the top.
- **Thermosphere** – This is divided into the lower ionosphere and the higher exosphere. This layer is very thin and has many ionized atoms with a net electrical charge. The aurora and Van Allen Belts are here. This layer also absorbs the most energetic photons from the sun and reflects radio waves, enabling long distance radio communication.

PALEONTOLOGY

Paleontology is the study of prehistoric plant and animal life through the analysis of **fossil remains**. These fossils reveal the ecologies of the past and the path of evolution for both extinct and living organisms. A historical science, paleontology seeks information about the identity, origin, environment, and evolution of past organisms and what they can reveal about the past of the earth as a whole. Paleontology explains causes as opposed to conducting experiments to observe effects. It is related to the fields of biology, geology, and archaeology, and is divided into several sub-disciplines concerned with the types of fossils studied, the process of fossilization, and the ecology and climate of the past. Paleontologists also help identify the composition of the earth's rock layers by the fossils that are found, thus identifying potential sites for oil, mineral, and water extraction.

DETERMINING THE ORDER IN WHICH GEOLOGIC EVENTS OCCURRED USING THE ROCK RECORD

The **Law of Superposition** logically assumes that the bottom layer of a series of sedimentary layers is the oldest, unless it has been overturned or older rock has been pushed over it. In addition, since **igneous intrusions** can cut through or flow above other rocks, these other rocks are older. For example, molten rock (lava) flows out over already present, older rocks. Another guideline for the rock record is that **rock layers** are older than the folds and faults in them because the rocks must exist before they can be folded or faulted. If a rock contains **atomic nuclei**, reference tables of the half-lives of commonly used radio isotopes can be used to match the decay rate of known substances to the nuclei in a rock, and thereby determine its age. Ages of rocks can also be determined from **contact metamorphism**, the re-crystallization of pre-existing rocks due to changes in physical and chemical conditions, such as heat, pressure, and chemically active fluids that might be present in lava or polluted waters.

MATCHING ROCKS AND GEOLOGIC EVENTS IN ONE PLACE WITH THOSE OF ANOTHER

Geologists physically follow rock layers from one location to another by a process called "walking the outcrop." Geologists walk along the outcropping to see where it goes and what the differences and similarities of the neighboring locations they cross are. Similar rock **types** or **patterns** of rock layers that are similar in terms of thickness, color, composition, and fossil remains tell geologists that two locations have a similar geologic history. Fossils are found all over the earth, but are from a relatively **small time period** in earth's history. Therefore, fossil evidence helps date a rock layer, regardless of where it occurs. **Volcanic ash** is a good time indicator since ash is deposited quickly over a widespread area. Matching the date of an eruption to the ash allows for a precise identification of time. Similarly, the **meteor impact** at the intersection of the Cretaceous and Tertiary Periods left a time marker. Wherever the meteor's iridium content is found, geologists are able to date rock layers.

SEQUENCING THE EARTH'S GEOLOGIC HISTORY FROM THE FOSSIL AND ROCK RECORD

Reference tables are used to match specimens and time periods. For example, the fossil record has been divided into time units of the earth's history. Rocks can therefore be dated by the fossils found with them. There are also reference tables for dating plate motions and mountain building events in geologic history. Since humans have been around for a relatively short period of time, **fossilized human remains** help to affix a date to a location. Some areas have missing **geologic layers** because of erosion or other factors, but reference tables specific to a region will list what is complete or missing. The theory of **uniformitarianism** assumes that geologic processes have been the same throughout history. Therefore, the way erosion or volcanic eruptions happen today is the same as the way these events happened millions of years ago because there is no reason for them to have changed. Therefore, knowledge about current events can be applied to the past to make judgments about events in the rock record.

Revealing Changes in Earth's History by the Fossil and Rock Records

Fossils can show how animal and plant life have changed or remained the same over time. For example, fossils have provided evidence of the existence of dinosaurs even though they no longer roam the earth, and have also been used to prove that certain insects have been around forever. Fossils have been used to identify four basic eras: **Proterozoic**, the age of primitive life; **Paleozoic**, the age of fishes; **Mesozoic**, the age of dinosaurs; and **Cenozoic**, the age of mammals. Most ancient forms of life have disappeared, and there are reference tables that list when this occurred. Fossil records also show the evolution of certain life forms, such as the horse from the eohippus. However, the majority of changes do not involve evolution from simple to complex forms, but rather an increase in the variety of forms.

Mountains

A **mountain** is a portion of the earth that has been raised above its surroundings by volcanic action or tectonic plate movement. Mountains are made up of igneous, metamorphic, and sedimentary rocks, and most lie along active plate boundaries. There are two major mountain systems. The **Circum-Pacific** encircles the entire Pacific Ocean, from New Guinea up across Japan and the Aleutians and down to southern South America. The **Alpine-Himalaya** stretches from northern Africa across the Alps and to the Himalayas and Indonesia. **Orogeny** is the term for the process of natural mountain formation. Therefore, physical mountains are orogens. **Folded mountains** are created through the folding of rock layers when two crustal plates come together. The Alps and Himalayas are folded mountains. The latter was formed by the collision of India with Asia. **Fault-block mountains** are created from the tension forces of plate movements. These produce faults that vertically displace one section to form a mountain. **Dome mountains** are created from magma pushing up through the earth's crust.

Volcanoes and Volcanic Mountains

Volcanoes are classified according to their activity level. An **active** volcano is in the process of erupting or building to an eruption; a dormant volcano has erupted before and may erupt again someday, but is not currently active; and an **extinct** volcano has died out volcanically and will not erupt ever again. Active volcanoes endanger plant and animal life, but lava and ash add enriching minerals to the soil. There are three types of volcanic mountains:

- **Shield volcanoes** are the largest volcanic mountains because of a repeated, viscous lava flow from small eruptions over a long period of time that cause the mountain to grow.
- **Cinder cone volcanoes**, or linear volcanoes, are small in size, but have massive explosions through linear shafts that spread cinders and ash around the vent. This results in a cone-shaped hill.
- **Composite volcanoes** get their name from the mix of lava and ash layers that build the mountain.

SUBDIVISIONS OF ROCK

The three major subdivisions of rock are:

- **Igneous** (magmatites) – This type is formed from the cooling of liquid magma. In the process, minerals crystallize and amalgamate. If solidification occurs deep in the earth (plutonic rock), the cooling process is slow. This allows for the formation of large crystals, giving rock a coarse-grained texture (granite). Quickly cooled magma has a glassy texture (obsidian).
- **Metamorphic** – Under conditions of high temperature and pressure within the earth's crust, rock material melts and changes structure, transitioning or metamorphosing into a new type of rock with different minerals. If the minerals appear in bands, the rock is foliated. Examples include marble (unfoliated) and slate (foliated).
- **Sedimentary** – This is the most common type of rock on earth. It is formed by sedimentation, compaction, and then cementation of many small particles of mineral, animal, or plant material. There are three types of sedimentary rocks: clastic, clay, and sand that came from disintegrated rocks; chemical (rock salt and gypsum), formed by evaporation of aqueous solutions; and biogenic (coal), formed from animal or plant remnants.

> **Review Video: Igneous, Sedimentary, and Metamorphic Rocks**
> Visit mometrix.com/academy and enter code: 689294

GLACIERS

Glaciers start high in the mountains, where snow and ice accumulate inside a cirque (a small semicircular depression). The snow becomes firmly packed into masses of coarse-grained ice that are slowly pulled down a slope by gravity. Glaciers grow with large amounts of snowfall and retreat (diminish) if warm weather melts more ice than can be replaced. Glaciers once covered large areas of both the northern and southern hemispheres with mile-thick ice that carved out valleys, fjords, and other land formations. They also moved plants, animals, and rocks from one area to another. There were two types of glaciers: **valley**, which produced U-shaped erosion and sharp-peaked mountains; and **continental**, which moved over and rounded mountain tops and ridges. These glaciers existed during the ice ages, the last of which occurred from 2.5 million years ago to 12,000 years ago.

Earth Science and Weather

LAYERS ABOVE SURFACE OF EARTH OTHER THAN FIVE MAIN LAYERS

The **ozone layer**, although contained within the stratosphere, is determined by ozone (O_3) concentrations. It absorbs the majority of ultraviolet light from the Sun. The ionosphere is part of both the exosphere and the thermosphere. It is characterized by the fact that it is a plasma, a partially ionized gas in which free electrons and positive ions are attracted to each other, but are too energetic to remain fixed as a molecule. It starts at about 50 km above Earth's surface and goes to 1,000 km. It affects radio wave transmission and auroras. The ionosphere pushes against the inner edge of the Earth's magnetosphere, which is the highly magnetized, non-spherical region around the Earth. The homosphere encompasses the troposphere, stratosphere, and mesosphere. Gases in the homosphere are considered well mixed. In the heterosphere, the distance that particles can move without colliding is large. As a result, gases are stratified according to their molecular weights. Heavier gases such as oxygen and nitrogen occur near the bottom of the heterosphere, while hydrogen, the lightest element, is found at the top.

TROPOSPHERIC CIRCULATION

Most weather takes place in the **troposphere**. Air circulates in the atmosphere by convection and in various types of "cells." Air near the equator is warmed by the Sun and rises. Cool air rushes under it, and the higher, warmer air flows toward Earth's poles. At the poles, it cools and descends to the surface. It is now under the hot air, and flows back to the equator. Air currents coupled with ocean currents move heat around the planet, creating winds, weather, and climate. Winds can change direction with the seasons. For example, in Southeast Asia and India, summer monsoons are caused by air being heated by the Sun. This air rises, draws moisture from the ocean, and causes daily rains. In winter, the air cools, sinks, pushes the moist air away, and creates dry weather.

COMMON WEATHER PHENOMENA AND EQUIPMENT TO MEASURE THEM

Common **atmospheric conditions** that are frequently measured are temperature, precipitation, wind, and humidity. These weather conditions are often measured at permanently fixed **weather stations** so weather data can be collected and compared over time and by region. Measurements may also be taken by ships, buoys, and underwater instruments. Measurements may also be taken under special circumstances. The measurements taken include temperature, barometric pressure, humidity, wind speed, wind direction, and precipitation. Usually, the following instruments are used: A *thermometer* is used for measuring temperature; a *barometer* is used for measuring barometric/air pressure; a *hygrometer* is used for measuring humidity; an *anemometer* is used for measuring wind speed; a *weather vane* is used for measuring wind direction; and a *rain gauge* is used for measuring precipitation.

WEATHER, CLIMATE, AND METEOROLOGY

Meteorology is the study of the atmosphere, particularly as it pertains to forecasting the weather and understanding its processes. **Weather** is the condition of the atmosphere at any given moment. Most weather occurs in the troposphere. Weather includes changing events such as clouds, storms, and temperature, as well as more extreme events such as tornadoes, hurricanes, and blizzards. **Climate** refers to the average weather for a particular area over time, typically at least 30 years. Latitude is an indicator of climate. Changes in climate occur over long time periods.

> **Review Video: Weather vs. Climate**
> Visit mometrix.com/academy and enter code: 237380

WINDS AND GLOBAL WIND BELTS

Winds are the result of air moving by convection. Masses of warm air rise, and cold air sweeps into their place. The warm air also moves, cools, and sinks. The term "prevailing wind" refers to the wind that usually blows in an area in a single direction. *Dominant winds* are the winds with the highest speeds. Belts or bands that run latitudinally and blow in a specific direction are associated with *convection cells*. *Hadley cells* are formed directly north and south of the equator. The *Farrell cells* occur at about 30° to 60°. The jet stream runs between the Farrell cells and the polar cells. At the higher and lower latitudes, the direction is easterly. At mid latitudes, the direction is westerly. From the North Pole to the south, the surface winds are Polar High Easterlies, Subpolar Low Westerlies, Subtropical High or Horse Latitudes, North-East Trade winds, Equatorial Low or Doldrums, South-East Trades, Subtropical High or Horse Latitudes, Subpolar Low Easterlies, and Polar High.

RELATIVE HUMIDITY, ABSOLUTE HUMIDITY, AND DEW POINT TEMPERATURE

Humidity refers to water vapor contained in the air. The amount of moisture contained in air depends upon its temperature. The higher the air temperature, the more moisture it can hold.

These higher levels of moisture are associated with higher humidity. **Absolute humidity** refers to the total amount of moisture air is capable of holding at a certain temperature. **Relative humidity** is the ratio of water vapor in the air compared to the amount the air is capable of holding at its current temperature. As temperature decreases, absolute humidity stays the same and relative humidity increases. A hygrometer is a device used to measure humidity. The **dew point** is the temperature at which water vapor condenses into water at a particular humidity.

PRECIPITATION

After clouds reach the dew point, **precipitation** occurs. Precipitation can take the form of a liquid or a solid. It is known by many names, including rain, snow, ice, dew, and frost. **Liquid** forms of precipitation include rain and drizzle. Rain or drizzle that freezes on contact is known as freezing rain or freezing drizzle. **Solid or frozen** forms of precipitation include snow, ice needles or diamond dust, sleet or ice pellets, hail, and graupel or snow pellets. Virga is a form of precipitation that evaporates before reaching the ground. It usually looks like sheets or shafts falling from a cloud. The amount of rainfall is measured with a rain gauge. Intensity can be measured according to how fast precipitation is falling or by how severely it limits visibility. Precipitation plays a major role in the water cycle since it is responsible for depositing much of the Earth's fresh water.

CLOUDS

Clouds form when air cools and warm air is forced to give up some of its water vapor because it can no longer hold it. This vapor condenses and forms tiny droplets of water or ice crystals called clouds. Particles, or aerosols, are needed for water vapor to form water droplets. These are called **condensation nuclei**. Clouds are created by surface heating, mountains and terrain, rising air masses, and weather fronts. Clouds precipitate, returning the water they contain to Earth. Clouds can also create atmospheric optics. They can scatter light, creating colorful phenomena such as rainbows, colorful sunsets, and the green flash phenomenon.

> **Review Video: Clouds**
> Visit mometrix.com/academy and enter code: 803166

HIGH, MIDDLE, AND LOW CLOUD TYPES

Most clouds can be classified according to the altitude of their base above Earth's surface. **High clouds** occur at altitudes between 5,000 and 13,000 meters. **Middle clouds** occur at altitudes between 2,000 and 7,000 meters. **Low clouds** occur from the Earth's surface to altitudes of 2,000 meters. Types of high clouds include cirrus (Ci), thin wispy mare's tails that consist of ice; cirrocumulus (Cc), small, pillow-like puffs that often appear in rows; and cirrostratus (Cs), thin, sheet-like clouds that often cover the entire sky. Types of middle clouds include altocumulus (Ac), gray-white clouds that consist of liquid water; and altostratus (As), grayish or blue-gray clouds that span the sky. Types of low clouds include stratus (St), gray and fog-like clouds consisting of water droplets that take up the whole sky; stratocumulus (Sc), low-lying, lumpy gray clouds; and nimbostratus (Ns), dark gray clouds with uneven bases that indicate rain or snow. Two types of clouds, cumulus (Cu) and cumulonimbus (Cb), are capable of great vertical growth. They can start at a wide range of altitudes, from the Earth's surface to altitudes of 13,000 meters.

AIR MASSES

Air masses are large volumes of air in the troposphere of the Earth. They are categorized by their temperature and by the amount of water vapor they contain. *Arctic* and *Antarctic* air masses are cold, polar air masses are cool, and tropical and equatorial air masses are hot. Other types of air masses include *maritime* and *monsoon*, both of which are moist and unstable. There are also *continental* and *superior* air masses, which are dry. A **weather front** separates two masses of air of different densities. It is the principal cause of meteorological phenomena. Air masses are quickly and easily affected by the land they are above. They can have certain characteristics, and then develop new ones when they get blown over a different area.

WEATHER FRONTS AND WEATHER MAPS

A **weather front** is the area between two differing masses of air that affects weather. Frontal movements are influenced by the jet stream and other high winds. Movements are determined by the type of front. Cold fronts move up to twice as fast as warm ones. It is in the turbulent frontal area that commonplace and dramatic weather events take place. This area also creates temperature changes. Weather phenomena include rain, thunderstorms, high winds, tornadoes, cloudiness, clear skies, and hurricanes. Different fronts can be plotted on weather maps using a set of designated symbols. Surface weather maps can also include symbols representing clouds, rain, temperature, air pressure, and fair weather.

Space Science

ASTRONOMY

Astronomy is the scientific study of celestial objects and their positions, movements, and structures. *Celestial* does not refer to the Earth in particular, but does include its motions as it moves through space. Other objects include the Sun, the Moon, planets, satellites, asteroids, meteors, comets, stars, galaxies, the universe, and other space phenomena. The term astronomy has its roots in the Greek words "astro" and "nomos," which means "laws of the stars."

> **Review Video: Astronomy**
> Visit mometrix.com/academy and enter code: 640556

UNIVERSE

ORIGIN

The **universe** can be said to consist of everything and nothing. The universe is the source of everything we know about space, matter, energy, and time. There are likely still phenomena that have yet to be discovered. The universe can also be thought of as nothing, since a vast portion of the known universe is empty space. It is believed that the universe is expanding. The *Big Bang theory*, which is widely accepted among astronomers, was developed to explain the origin of the universe. There are other theories regarding the origin of the universe, such as the *Steady-State theory* and the *Creationist theory*. The Big Bang theory states that all the matter in the universe was once in one place. This matter underwent a huge explosion that spread the matter into space. Galaxies formed from this material and the universe is still expanding.

STRUCTURE

What can be seen of the universe is believed to be at least 93 billion light years across. To put this into perspective, the Milky Way galaxy is about 100,000 light years across. Our view of matter in the universe is that it forms into clumps. Matter is organized into stars, galaxies, clusters of galaxies, superclusters, and the Great Wall of galaxies. **Galaxies** consist of stars, some with planetary systems. Some estimates state that the universe is about 13 billion years old. It is not considered dense, and is believed to consist of 73 percent dark energy, 23 percent cold dark matter, and 4 percent regular matter. Cosmology is the study of the universe. Interstellar medium (ISM) is the gas and dust in the interstellar space between a galaxy's stars.

GALAXIES

Galaxies consist of stars, stellar remnants, and dark matter. **Dwarf galaxies** contain as few as 10 million stars, while giant galaxies contain as many as 1 trillion stars. Galaxies are gravitationally bound, meaning the stars, star systems, other gases, and dust orbits the galaxy's center. The Earth exists in the **Milky Way galaxy** and the nearest galaxy to ours is the **Andromeda galaxy**. Galaxies can be classified by their visual shape into elliptical, spiral, irregular, and starburst galaxies. It is estimated that there are more than 100 billion galaxies in the universe ranging from 1,000 to 100,000 parsecs in diameter. Galaxies can be megaparsecs apart. Intergalactic space consists of a gas with an average density of less than one atom per cubic meter. Galaxies are organized into clusters which form superclusters. Dark matter may account for up to 90% of the mass of galaxies. Dark matter is still not well understood.

> **Review Video: Galaxies**
> Visit mometrix.com/academy and enter code: 226539

PLANETS

In order of their distance from the sun (closest to furthest away), the **planets** are: Mercury, Venus, Earth, Mars, Jupiter, Saturn, Uranus, and Neptune (Pluto is now considered to be a dwarf planet). All the planets revolve around the sun, which is an average-sized star in the spiral Milky Way galaxy. They revolve in the same direction in nearly circular orbits. If the planets were viewed by looking down from the sun, they would rotate in a counter-clockwise direction. All the planets are in or near the same plane, called the ecliptic, and the axis of rotation is nearly perpendicular to the ecliptic. The only exception is Uranus, which is tipped on its side.

TERRESTRIAL PLANETS, JOVIAN PLANETS, AND MASS OF PLANETS

The **Terrestrial Planets** are: Mercury, Venus, Earth, and Mars. These are the four planets closest to the sun. They are called terrestrial because they all have a compact, rocky surface similar to the Earth's. Venus, Earth, and Mars have significant atmospheres, but Mercury has almost no atmosphere.

The **Jovian Planets** are: Jupiter (the largest planet), Saturn, Uranus, and Neptune. They are called Jovian (Jupiter-like) because of their huge sizes in relation to that of the Earth, and because they all have a gaseous nature like Jupiter. Although gas giants, some or all of the Jovian Planets may have small, solid cores.

Pluto does not have the characteristics necessary to fit into either the Terrestrial or the Jovian group, and is no longer considered to be a planet. The sun represents 99.85% of all the matter in our solar system. Combined, the planets make up only 0.135% of the mass of the solar system, with Jupiter having twice the mass of all the other planets combined. The remaining 0.015% of the mass comes from comets, planetary satellites, asteroids, meteoroids, and interplanetary medium.

DEFINITION OF PLANET

On August 24, 2006, the International Astronomical Union redefined the criteria a body must meet to be classified as a planet, stating that the following conditions must be met:

- "A planet orbits around a star and is neither a star nor a moon."
- "Its shape is spherical due to its gravity."
- "It has 'cleared' the space of its orbit."

A **dwarf planet** such as Pluto does not meet the third condition. Small solar system bodies such as asteroids and comets meet only the first condition.

SOLAR SYSTEM

The **solar system** developed about 4.6 billion years ago out of an enormous cloud of dust and gas circling around the sun. Four rocky planets orbit relatively close to the sun. Their inside orbit is separated from the outside orbit of the four, larger gaseous planets by an asteroid belt. Pluto, some comets, and several small objects circle in the Kuiper belt outside Neptune's orbit. The Oort cloud, composed of icy space objects, encloses the planetary system like a shell.

> **Review Video: Solar System**
> Visit mometrix.com/academy and enter code: 273231
>
> **Review Video: The Inner Planets of Our Solar System**
> Visit mometrix.com/academy and enter code: 103427
>
> **Review Video: The Outer Planets of Our Solar System**
> Visit mometrix.com/academy and enter code: 683995

EARTH'S MOON

Earth's **moon** is the closest celestial body to earth. Its proximity has allowed it to be studied since the invention of the telescope. As a result, its landforms have been named after astronomers, philosophers, and other scholars. Its surface has many craters created by asteroids since it has no protective atmosphere. These dark lowlands looked like seas to early astronomers, but there is virtually no water on the moon except possibly in its polar regions. These impact craters and depressions actually contain solidified lava flows. The bright highlands were thought to be continents, and were named terrae. The rocks of the moon have been pounded by asteroids so often that there is a layer of rubble and dust called the regolith. Also, because there is no protective atmosphere, temperatures on the moon vary widely, from 265°F to -255°F.

EARTH'S SUN AND OTHER STARS

A **star** begins as a cloud of hydrogen and some heavier elements drawn together by their own mass. This matter then begins to rotate. The core heats up to several million degrees Fahrenheit, which causes the hydrogen atoms to lose their shells and their nuclei to fuse. This releases enormous amounts of energy. The star then becomes stable, a stage called the **main sequence**. This is the stage our sun is in, and it will remain in this stage until its supply of hydrogen fuel runs out. Stars are not always alone like our sun, and may exist in pairs or groups. The hottest stars shine blue-white; medium-hot stars like our sun glow yellow; and cooler stars appear orange. The earth's sun is an **average star** in terms of mass, light production, and size. All stars, including our sun, have a **core** where fusion happens; a **photosphere** (surface) that produces sunspots (cool, dark areas); a red **chromosphere** that emits solar (bright) flares and shooting gases; and a **corona**, the transparent area only seen during an eclipse.

> **Review Video: The Sun**
> Visit mometrix.com/academy and enter code: 699233

COMETS, ASTEROIDS, AND METEOROIDS

Comets are celestial bodies composed of dust, rock, frozen gases, and ice. Invisible until they near the sun, the heat causes them to emit volatile components in jets of gas and dust. The **coma** is the comet's fog-like envelope that glows as it reflects sunlight and releases radiation. **Solar winds** blow a comet away from the sun and give it a tail of dust or electrically charged molecules. Each orbit of a comet causes it to lose matter until it breaks up or vaporizes into the sun.

Asteroids are irregularly-shaped boulders, usually less than 60 miles in diameter, that orbit the sun. Most are made of graphite; about 25% are silicates, or iron and nickel. Collisions or gravitational forces can cause them to fly off and possibly hit a planet.

Meteoroids are fragments of asteroids of various sizes. If they come through earth's atmosphere, they are called meteors or shooting stars. If they land on earth, they are called meteorites, and create craters on impact (the Barringer Crater in Arizona).

> **Review Video: Meteoroids, Meteors, and Meteorites**
> Visit mometrix.com/academy and enter code: 454866

Chemistry

ATOMIC NUMBER, NEUTRONS, NUCLEON, AND ELEMENT

- **Atomic number** (proton number) — The atomic number of an element refers to the number of protons in the nucleus of an atom. It is a unique identifier. It can be represented as Z. Atoms with a neutral charge have an atomic number that is equal to the number of electrons.
- **Neutrons** — Neutrons are the uncharged atomic particles contained within the nucleus. The number of neutrons in a nucleus can be represented as "N."
- **Nucleon** — This refers collectively to the neutrons and protons.
- **Element** — An element is matter with one particular type of atom. It can be identified by its atomic number, or the number of protons in its nucleus. There are approximately 117 elements currently known, 94 of which occur naturally on Earth. Elements from the periodic table include hydrogen, carbon, iron, helium, mercury, and oxygen.

PAST ATOMIC MODELS AND THEORIES

There have been many revisions to theories regarding the structure of **atoms** and their **particles**. Part of the challenge in developing an understanding of matter is that atoms and their particles are too small to be seen. It is believed that the first conceptualization of the atom was developed by **Democritus** in 400 B.C. Some of the more notable models are the solid sphere or billiard ball model postulated by John Dalton, the plum pudding or raisin bun model by J.J. Thomson, the planetary or nuclear model by Ernest Rutherford, the Bohr or orbit model by Niels Bohr, and the electron cloud or quantum mechanical model by Louis de Broglie and Erwin Schrodinger. Rutherford directed the alpha scattering experiment that discounted the plum pudding model. The shortcoming of the Bohr model was the belief that electrons orbited in fixed rather than changing ecliptic orbits.

> **Review Video: Atomic Models**
> Visit mometrix.com/academy and enter code: 434851

STRUCTURE OF ATOMS

All matter consists of **atoms**. Atoms consist of a nucleus and electrons. The **nucleus** consists of protons and neutrons. The properties of these are measurable; they have mass and an electrical charge. The nucleus is positively charged due to the presence of protons. **Electrons** are negatively charged and orbit the nucleus. The nucleus has considerably more mass than the surrounding electrons. Atoms can bond together to make **molecules**. Atoms that have an equal number of protons and electrons are electrically neutral. If the number of protons and electrons in an atom is not equal, the atom has a positive or negative charge and is an ion.

MODELS OF ATOMS

Atoms are extremely small. A hydrogen atom is about 5×10^{-8} mm in diameter. According to some estimates, five trillion hydrogen atoms could fit on the head of a pin. **Atomic radius** refers to the average distance between the nucleus and the outermost electron. Models of atoms that include the proton, nucleus, and electrons typically show the electrons very close to the nucleus and revolving around it, similar to how the Earth orbits the sun. However, another model relates the Earth as the nucleus and its atmosphere as electrons, which is the basis of the term "**electron cloud.**" Another description is that electrons swarm around the nucleus. It should be noted that these atomic models are not to scale. A more accurate representation would be a nucleus with a diameter of about 2 cm in a stadium. The electrons would be in the bleachers. This model is similar to the not-to-scale solar system model.

ATOM, NUCLEUS, ELECTRONS, AND PROTONS

- **Atom** — The atom is one of the most basic units of matter. An atom consists of a central nucleus surrounded by electrons.
- **Nucleus** — The nucleus of an atom consists of protons and neutrons. It is positively charged, dense, and heavier than the surrounding electrons. The plural form of nucleus is nuclei.
- **Electrons** — These are atomic particles that are negatively charged and orbit the nucleus of an atom.
- **Protons** — Along with neutrons, protons make up the nucleus of an atom. The number of protons in the nucleus determines the atomic number of an element. Carbon atoms, for example, have six protons. The atomic number of carbon is 6. The number of protons also indicates the charge of an atom. The number of protons minus the number of electrons indicates the charge of an atom.

MOLECULES

Electrons in an atom can orbit different levels around the nucleus. They can absorb or release energy, which can change the location of their orbit or even allow them to break free from the atom. The outermost layer is the **valence layer**, which contains the valence electrons. The valence layer tends to have or share eight electrons. **Molecules** are formed by a chemical bond between atoms, a bond which occurs at the valence level. Two basic types of bonds are covalent and ionic. A **covalent bond** is formed when atoms share electrons. An **ionic bond** is formed when an atom transfers an electron to another atom. A **hydrogen bond** is a weak bond between a hydrogen atom of one molecule and an electronegative atom (such as nitrogen, oxygen, or fluorine) of another molecule. The **Van der Waals force** is a weak force between molecules. This type of force is much weaker than actual chemical bonds between atoms.

INTERACTION OF ATOMS TO FORM COMPOUNDS

Atoms interact by **transferring** or sharing the electrons furthest from the nucleus. Known as the outer or **valence electrons**, they are responsible for the chemical properties of an element. **Bonds** between atoms are created when electrons are paired up by being transferred or shared. If electrons are transferred from one atom to another, the bond is ionic. If electrons are shared, the bond is covalent. Atoms of the same element may bond together to form molecules or crystalline solids. When two or more different types of atoms bind together chemically, a compound is made. The physical properties of compounds reflect the nature of the interactions among their molecules.

These interactions are determined by the structure of the molecule, including the atoms they consist of and the distances and angles between them.

MATTER

Matter refers to substances that have mass and occupy space (or volume). The traditional definition of matter describes it as having three states: solid, liquid, and gas. These different states are caused by differences in the distances and angles between molecules or atoms, which result in differences in the energy that binds them. **Solid** structures are rigid or nearly rigid and have strong bonds. Molecules or atoms of **liquids** move around and have weak bonds, although they are not weak enough to readily break. Molecules or atoms of **gases** move almost independently of each other, are typically far apart, and do not form bonds. The current definition of matter describes it as having four states. The fourth is **plasma**, which is an ionized gas that has some electrons that are described as free because they are not bound to an atom or molecule.

MOST ABUNDANT ELEMENTS IN THE UNIVERSE AND ON EARTH

Aside from dark energy and dark matter, which are thought to account for all but four percent of the universe, the two most abundant elements in the universe are **hydrogen** (H) and **helium** (He). After hydrogen and helium, the most abundant elements are oxygen, neon, nitrogen, carbon, silicon, and magnesium. The most abundant isotopes in the solar system are hydrogen-1 and helium-4. Measurements of the masses of elements in the Earth's crust indicate that oxygen (O), silicon (Si), and aluminum (Al) are the most abundant on Earth. Hydrogen in its plasma state is the most abundant chemical element in stars in their main sequences, but is relatively rare on planet Earth.

ENERGY TRANSFORMATIONS

The following are some examples of energy transformations:

- Electric to mechanical: Ceiling fan
- **Chemical to heat**: A familiar example of a chemical to heat energy transformation is the internal combustion engine, which transforms the chemical energy (a type of potential energy) of gas and oxygen into heat. This heat is transformed into propulsive energy, which is kinetic. Lighting a match and burning coal are also examples of chemical to heat energy transformations.
- **Chemical to light**: Phosphorescence and luminescence (which allow objects to glow in the dark) occur because energy is absorbed by a substance (charged) and light is re-emitted comparatively slowly. This process is different from the one involved with glow sticks. They glow due to chemiluminescence, in which an excited state is created by a chemical reaction and transferred to another molecule.
- **Heat to electricity**: Examples include thermoelectric, geothermal, and ocean thermal.
- **Nuclear to heat**: Examples include nuclear reactors and power plants.
- **Mechanical to sound**: Playing a violin or almost any instrument
- Sound to electric: Microphone
- Light to electric: Solar panels
- Electric to light: Light bulbs

RELATIONSHIP BETWEEN CONSERVATION OF MATTER AND ATOMIC THEORY

Atomic theory is concerned with the characteristics and properties of atoms that make up matter. It deals with matter on a *microscopic level* as opposed to a *macroscopic level*. Atomic theory, for instance, discusses the kinetic motion of atoms in order to explain the properties of macroscopic quantities of matter. John Dalton (1766-1844) is credited with making many contributions to the field of atomic theory that are still considered valid. This includes the notion that all matter consists of atoms and that atoms are indestructible. In other words, atoms can be neither created nor destroyed. This is also the theory behind the conservation of matter, which explains why chemical reactions do not result in any detectable gains or losses in matter. This holds true for chemical reactions and smaller scale processes. When dealing with large amounts of energy, however, atoms can be destroyed by nuclear reactions. This can happen in particle colliders or atom smashers.

DIFFERENCE BETWEEN ATOMS AND MOLECULES

Elements from the periodic table such as hydrogen, carbon, iron, helium, mercury, and oxygen are **atoms**. Atoms combine to form molecules. For example, two atoms of hydrogen (H) and one atom of oxygen (O) combine to form one molecule of water (H_2O).

CHEMICAL AND PHYSICAL PROPERTIES

Matter has both physical and chemical properties. **Physical properties** can be seen or observed without changing the identity or composition of matter. For example, the mass, volume, and density of a substance can be determined without permanently changing the sample. Other physical properties include color, boiling point, freezing point, solubility, odor, hardness, electrical conductivity, thermal conductivity, ductility, and malleability. **Chemical properties** cannot be measured without changing the identity or composition of matter. Chemical properties describe how a substance reacts or changes to form a new substance. Examples of chemical properties include flammability, corrosivity, oxidation states, enthalpy of formation, and reactivity with other chemicals.

CHEMICAL AND PHYSICAL CHANGES

Physical changes do not produce new substances. The atoms or molecules may be rearranged, but no new substances are formed. Phase changes or changes of state such as melting, freezing, and sublimation are physical changes. For example, physical changes include the melting of ice, the boiling of water, sugar dissolving into water, and the crushing of a piece of chalk into a fine powder. **Chemical changes** involve a chemical reaction and do produce new substances. When iron rusts, iron oxide is formed, indicating a chemical change. Other examples of chemical changes include baking a cake, burning wood, digesting a cracker, and mixing an acid and a base.

PHYSICAL AND CHEMICAL PROPERTIES AND CHANGES

Both physical changes and chemical reactions are everyday occurrences. **Physical changes** do not result in different substances. For example, when water becomes ice it has undergone a physical change, but not a chemical change. It has changed its form, but not its composition. It is still H_2O. **Chemical properties** are concerned with the constituent particles that make up the physicality of a substance. Chemical properties are apparent when **chemical changes** occur. The chemical properties of a substance are influenced by its electron configuration, which is determined in part by the number of protons in the nucleus (the atomic number). Carbon, for example, has 6 protons

360

and 6 electrons. It is an element's outermost valence electrons that mainly determine its chemical properties. Chemical reactions may release or consume energy.

ELEMENTS, COMPOUNDS, SOLUTIONS, AND MIXTURES

- **Elements** — These are substances that consist of only one type of atom.
- **Compounds** — These are substances containing two or more elements. Compounds are formed by chemical reactions and frequently have different properties than the original elements. Compounds are decomposed by a chemical reaction rather than separated by a physical one.
- **Solutions** — These are homogeneous mixtures composed of two or more substances that have become one.
- **Mixtures** — Mixtures contain two or more substances that are combined but have not reacted chemically with each other. Mixtures can be separated using physical methods, while compounds cannot.

HEAT, ENERGY, WORK, AND THERMAL ENERGY

- **Heat** — Heat is the transfer of energy from a body or system as a result of thermal contact. Heat consists of random motion and the vibration of atoms, molecules, and ions. The higher the temperature is, the greater the atomic or molecular motion will be.
- **Energy** — Energy is the capacity to do work.
- **Work** — Work is the quantity of energy transferred by one system to another due to changes in a system that is the result of external forces, or macroscopic variables. Another way to put this is that work is the amount of energy that must be transferred to overcome a force. Lifting an object in the air is an example of work. The opposing force that must be overcome is gravity. Work is measured in joules (J). The rate at which work is performed is known as power.
- **Thermal energy** — Thermal energy is the energy present in a system due to temperature.

TYPES OF ENERGY

Some discussions of energy consider only two types of energy: **kinetic energy** (the energy of motion) and **potential energy** (which depends on relative position or orientation). There are, however, other types of energy. **Electromagnetic waves**, for example, are a type of energy contained by a field. Another type of potential energy is electrical energy, which is the energy it takes to pull apart positive and negative electrical charges. **Chemical energy** refers to the manner in which atoms form into molecules, and this energy can be released or absorbed when molecules regroup. **Solar energy** comes in the form of visible light and non-visible light, such as infrared and ultraviolet rays. **Sound energy** refers to the energy in sound waves.

CHEMICAL REACTIONS

Chemical reactions measured in human time can take place quickly or slowly. They can take fractions of a second or billions of years. The rates of chemical reactions are determined by how frequently reacting atoms and molecules interact. Rates are also influenced by the temperature and various properties (such as shape) of the reacting materials. **Catalysts** accelerate chemical reactions, while inhibitors decrease reaction rates. Some types of reactions release energy in the form of heat and light. Some types of reactions involve the transfer of either electrons or hydrogen ions between reacting ions, molecules, or atoms. In other reactions, chemical bonds are broken down by heat or light to form reactive radicals with electrons that will readily form new bonds.

Processes such as the formation of ozone and greenhouse gases in the atmosphere and the burning and processing of fossil fuels are controlled by radical reactions.

READING CHEMICAL EQUATIONS

Chemical equations describe chemical reactions. The **reactants** are on the left side before the arrow and the **products** are on the right side after the arrow. The arrow indicates the reaction or change. The **coefficient**, or stoichiometric coefficient, is the number before the element, and indicates the ratio of reactants to products in terms of moles. The equation for the formation of water from hydrogen and oxygen, for example, is $2H_2$ (g) + O_2 (g) → $2H_2O$ (l). The 2 preceding hydrogen and water is the coefficient, which means there are 2 moles of hydrogen and 2 of water. There is 1 mole of oxygen, which does not have to be indicated with the number 1. In parentheses, g stands for gas, l stands for liquid, s stands for solid, and aq stands for aqueous solution (a substance dissolved in water). Charges are shown in superscript for individual ions, but not for ionic compounds. Polyatomic ions are separated by parentheses so the ion will not be confused with the number of ions.

BALANCING EQUATIONS

An **unbalanced equation** is one that does not follow the **law of conservation of mass**, which states that matter can only be changed, not created. If an equation is unbalanced, the numbers of atoms indicated by the stoichiometric coefficients on each side of the arrow will not be equal. Start by writing the formulas for each species in the reaction. Count the atoms on each side and determine if the number is equal. Coefficients must be whole numbers. Fractional amounts, such as half a molecule, are not possible. Equations can be balanced by multiplying the coefficients by a constant that will produce the smallest possible whole number coefficient. $H_2 + O_2 → H_2O$ is an example of an unbalanced equation. The balanced equation is $2H_2 + O_2 → 2H_2O$, which indicates that it takes two moles of hydrogen and one of oxygen to produce two moles of water.

PERIODIC TABLE

The **periodic table** groups elements with similar chemical properties together. The grouping of elements is based on **atomic structure**. It shows periodic trends of physical and chemical properties and identifies families of elements with similar properties. It is a common model for organizing and understanding elements. In the periodic table, each element has its own cell that includes varying amounts of information presented in symbol form about the properties of the element. Cells in the table are arranged in **rows** (periods) and **columns** (groups or families). At minimum, a cell includes the symbol for the element and its atomic number. The cell for hydrogen, for example, which appears first in the upper left corner, includes an "H" and a "1" above the letter. Elements are ordered by atomic number, left to right, top to bottom.

SOLUTIONS

A **solution** is a homogeneous mixture. A **mixture** is two or more different substances that are mixed together, but not combined chemically. Homogeneous mixtures are those that are uniform in their composition. Solutions consist of a solute (the substance that is dissolved) and a solvent (the substance that does the dissolving). An example is sugar water. The solvent is the water and the solute is the sugar. The intermolecular attraction between the solvent and the solute is called solvation. **Hydration** refers to solutions in which water is the solvent. Solutions are formed when the forces of the molecules of the solute and the solvent are as strong as the individual molecular forces of the solute and the solvent. An example is that salt ($NaCl$) dissolves in water to create a solution. The Na^+ and the Cl^- ions in salt interact with the molecules of water and vice versa to overcome the individual molecular forces of the solute and the solvent.

MIXTURES, SUSPENSIONS, COLLOIDS, EMULSIONS, AND FOAMS

A **mixture** is a combination of two or more substances that are not bonded. **Suspensions** are mixtures of heterogeneous materials. Particles are usually larger than those found in true solutions. Dirt mixed vigorously with water is an example of a suspension. The dirt is temporarily suspended in water, but the two separate once the mixing is ceased. A mixture of large (1 nm to 500 nm) particles is called a **colloidal suspension**. The particles are termed dispersants and the dispersing medium is similar to the solvent in a solution. Sol refers to a liquid or a solid that also has solids dispersed through it, such as milk or gelatin. An aerosol spray is a colloid suspension of gas and the solid or liquid being dispersed. An **emulsion** refers to a liquid or a solid that has a liquid dispersed through it. A **foam** is a liquid that has gas dispersed through it.

PROPERTIES OF BASES

When they are dissolved in aqueous solutions, some properties of **bases** are that they conduct electricity, change red litmus paper to blue, feel slippery, and react with acids to neutralize their properties. A **weak base** is one that does not completely ionize in an aqueous solution, and usually has a low pH. **Strong bases** can free protons in very weak acids. Examples of strong bases are hydroxide compounds such as potassium, barium, and lithium hydroxides. Most are in the first and second groups of the periodic table. A **superbase** is extremely strong compared to sodium hydroxide and cannot be kept in an aqueous solution. Superbases are organized into organic, organometallic, and inorganic classes. Bases are used as insoluble catalysts in heterogeneous reactions and as catalysts in hydrogenation.

PROPERTIES OF SALTS

Some properties of **salts** are that they are formed from acid base reactions, are ionic compounds consisting of metallic and nonmetallic ions, dissociate in water, and are comprised of tightly bonded ions. Some common salts are sodium chloride ($NaCl$), sodium bisulfate, potassium dichromate ($K_2Cr_2O_7$), and calcium chloride ($CaCl_2$). Calcium chloride is used as a drying agent, and may be used to absorb moisture when freezing mixtures. Potassium nitrate (KNO_3) is used to make fertilizer and in the manufacture of explosives. Sodium nitrate ($NaNO_3$) is also used in the making of fertilizer. Baking soda (sodium bicarbonate) is a salt, as are Epsom salts [magnesium sulfate ($MgSO_4$)]. Salt and water can react to form a base and an acid. This is called a **hydrolysis reaction**.

UNIQUE PROPERTIES OF WATER

The important properties of **water** (H_2O) are high polarity, hydrogen bonding, cohesiveness, adhesiveness, high specific heat, high latent heat, and high heat of vaporization. It is essential to life as we know it, as water is one of the main if not the main constituent of many living things. Water is a liquid at room temperature. The high **specific heat** of water means it resists the breaking of its hydrogen bonds and resists heat and motion, which is why it has a relatively high boiling point and high vaporization point. It also resists temperature change. Water is peculiar in that its solid state floats in its liquid state. Most substances are denser in their solid forms. Water is *cohesive*, which means it is attracted to itself. It is also *adhesive*, which means it readily attracts other molecules. If water tends to adhere to another substance, the substance is said to be *hydrophilic*. Water makes a good solvent. Substances, particularly those with polar ions and molecules, readily dissolve in water.

> **Review Video: Properties of Water**
> Visit mometrix.com/academy and enter code: 279526

PROPERTIES OF ACIDS

When they are dissolved in aqueous solutions, some properties of **acids** are that they conduct electricity, change blue litmus paper to red, have a sour taste, react with bases to neutralize them, and react with active metals to free hydrogen. A **weak acid** is one that does not donate all of its protons or disassociate completely. **Strong acids** include hydrochloric, hydriodic, hydrobromic, perchloric, nitric, and sulfuric. They ionize completely. **Superacids** are those that are stronger than 100 percent sulfuric acid. They include fluoroantimonic, magic, and perchloric acids. Acids can be used in pickling, a process used to remove rust and corrosion from metals. They are also used as catalysts in the processing of minerals and the production of salts and fertilizers. Phosphoric acid (H_3PO_4) is added to sodas and other acids are added to foods as preservatives or to add taste.

> **Review Video: Properties of Acids**
> Visit mometrix.com/academy and enter code: 645283

PH

The **potential of hydrogen** (pH) is a measurement of the concentration of hydrogen ions in a substance in terms of the number of moles of H^+ per liter of solution. A lower pH indicates a higher H^+ concentration, while a higher pH indicates a lower H^+ concentration. Pure water has a **neutral** pH, which is 7. Anything with a pH lower than water (less than 7) is considered **acidic**. Anything with a pH higher than water (greater than 7) is a **base**. Drain cleaner, soap, baking soda, ammonia, egg whites, and sea water are common bases. Urine, stomach acid, citric acid, vinegar, hydrochloric acid, and battery acid are acids. A pH indicator is a substance that acts as a detector of hydrogen or hydronium ions. It is halochromic, meaning it changes color to indicate that hydrogen or hydronium ions have been detected.

> **Review Video: pH**
> Visit mometrix.com/academy and enter code: 187395

KINETIC THEORY OF GASES

The **kinetic theory of gases** assumes that gas molecules are small compared to the distances between them and that they are in constant random motion. The attractive and repulsive forces between gas molecules are negligible. Their kinetic energy does not change with time as long as the temperature remains the same. The higher the temperature is, the greater the motion will be. As the temperature of a gas increases, so does the kinetic energy of the molecules. In other words, gas will occupy a greater volume as the temperature is increased and a lesser volume as the temperature is decreased. In addition, the same amount of gas will occupy a greater volume as the temperature increases, but pressure remains constant. At any given temperature, gas molecules have the same average kinetic energy. The **ideal gas law** is derived from the kinetic theory of gases.

> **Review Video: Ideal Gas Law**
> Visit mometrix.com/academy and enter code: 381353

INORGANIC COMPOUNDS

The main trait of **inorganic compounds** is that they **lack carbon**. Inorganic compounds include mineral salts, metals and alloys, non-metallic compounds such as phosphorus, and metal complexes. A metal complex has a central atom (or ion) bonded to surrounding ligands (molecules or anions). The ligands sacrifice the donor atoms (in the form of at least one pair of electrons) to the central atom. Many inorganic compounds are **ionic**, meaning they form ionic bonds rather than share electrons. They may have high melting points because of this. They may also be colorful, but this is not an absolute identifier of an inorganic compound. Salts, which are inorganic compounds, are an example of inorganic bonding of cations and anions. Some examples of salts are magnesium chloride ($MgCl_2$) and sodium oxide (Na_2O). Oxides, carbonates, sulfates, and halides are classes of inorganic compounds. They are typically poor conductors, are very water soluble, and crystallize easily. Minerals and silicates are also inorganic compounds.

> **Review Video: Phosphorus Halides**
> Visit mometrix.com/academy and enter code: 590810

HYDROGEN BONDS

Hydrogen bonds are weaker than covalent and ionic bonds, and refer to the type of attraction in an electronegative atom such as oxygen, fluorine, or nitrogen. Hydrogen bonds can form within a single molecule or between molecules. A water molecule is **polar**, meaning it is partially positively charged on one end (the hydrogen end) and partially negatively charged on the other (the oxygen end). This is because the hydrogen atoms are arranged around the oxygen atom in a close tetrahedron. Hydrogen is **oxidized** (its number of electrons is reduced) when it bonds with oxygen to form water. Hydrogen bonds tend not only to be weak, but also short-lived. They also tend to be numerous. Hydrogen bonds give water many of its important properties, including its high specific heat and high heat of vaporization, its solvent qualities, its adhesiveness and cohesiveness, its hydrophobic qualities, and its ability to float in its solid form. Hydrogen bonds are also an important component of proteins, nucleic acids, and DNA.

ORGANIC COMPOUNDS

Two of the main characteristics of **organic compounds** are that they **include carbon** and are formed by **covalent bonds**. Carbon can form long chains, double and triple bonds, and rings. While inorganic compounds tend to have high melting points, organic compounds tend to melt at temperatures below 300° C. They also tend to boil, sublimate, and decompose below this temperature. Unlike inorganic compounds, they are not very water soluble. Organic molecules are organized into functional groups based on their specific atoms, which helps determine how they will react chemically. A few groups are alkanes, nitro, alkenes, sulfides, amines, and carbolic acids.

The hydroxyl group (-OH) consists of alcohols. These molecules are polar, which increases their solubility. By some estimates, there are more than 16 million organic compounds.

Physics

LAWS OF THERMODYNAMICS

The **laws of thermodynamics** are generalized principles dealing with energy and heat.

- The **zeroth law** of thermodynamics states that two objects in thermodynamic equilibrium with a third object are also in equilibrium with each other. Being in thermodynamic equilibrium basically means that different objects are at the same temperature.
- The **first law** deals with conservation of energy. It states that neither mass nor energy can be destroyed; only converted from one form to another.
- The **second law** states that the entropy (the amount of energy in a system that is no longer available for work or the amount of disorder in a system) of an isolated system can only increase. The second law also states that heat is not transferred from a lower-temperature system to a higher-temperature one unless additional work is done.
- The **third law** of thermodynamics states that as temperature approaches absolute zero, entropy approaches a constant minimum. It also states that a system cannot be cooled to absolute zero.

HEAT AND TEMPERATURE

Heat is energy transfer (other than direct work) from one body or system to another due to thermal contact. Everything tends to become less organized and less orderly over time (**entropy**). In all energy transfers, therefore, the overall result is that the energy is spread out uniformly. This transfer of heat energy from hotter to cooler objects is accomplished by conduction, radiation, or convection. **Temperature** is a measurement of an object's stored heat energy. More specifically, temperature is the average kinetic energy of an object's particles. When the temperature of an object increases and its atoms move faster, kinetic energy also increases. Temperature is not energy since it changes and is not conserved. Thermometers are used to measure temperature.

Mass, Weight, Volume, Density, and Specific Gravity

Mass — Mass is a measure of the amount of substance in an object.

Weight — Weight is a measure of the gravitational pull of Earth on an object.

Volume — Volume is a measure of the amount of space occupied. There are many formulas to determine volume. For example, the volume of a cube is the length of one side cubed (a^3) and the volume of a rectangular prism is length times width times height ($l \cdot w \cdot h$). The volume of an irregular shape can be determined by how much water it displaces.

Density — Density is a measure of the amount of mass per unit volume. The formula to find density is mass divided by volume ($D=m/V$). It is expressed in terms of mass per cubic unit, such as grams per cubic centimeter (g/cm^3).

Specific gravity — This is a measure of the ratio of a substance's density compared to the density of water.

Thermal Contact

Thermal contact refers to energy transferred to a body by a means other than work. A system in thermal contact with another can exchange energy with it through the process of heat transfer. Thermal contact does not necessarily involve direct physical contact. **Heat** is energy that can be transferred from one body or system to another without work being done. Everything tends to become less organized and less useful over time (entropy). In all energy transfers, therefore, the overall result is that the heat is spread out so that objects are in thermodynamic equilibrium and the heat can no longer be transferred without additional work.

Models for Flow of Electric Charge

Models that can be used to explain the **flow of electric current, potential, and circuits** include water, gravity, and roller coasters. For example, just as gravity is a force and a mass can have a potential for energy based on its location, so can a charge within an electrical field. Just as a force is required to move an object uphill, a force is also required to move a charge from a low to high potential. Another example is water. Water does not flow when it is level. If it is lifted to a point and then placed on a downward path, it will flow. A roller coaster car requires work to be performed to transport it to a point where it has potential energy (the top of a hill). Once there, gravity provides the force for it to flow (move) downward. If either path is broken, the flow or movement stops or is not completed.

Atomic Structures

Magnetic Fields

The motions of subatomic structures (nuclei and electrons) produce a **magnetic field**. It is the direction of the spin and orbit that indicate the direction of the field. The strength of a magnetic field is known as the **magnetic moment**. As electrons spin and orbit a nucleus, they produce a magnetic field. Pairs of electrons that spin and orbit in opposite directions cancel each other out, creating a net magnetic field of zero. Materials that have an unpaired electron are magnetic. Those with a weak attractive force are referred to as paramagnetic materials, while ferromagnetic materials have a strong attractive force. A diamagnetic material has electrons that are paired, and therefore does not typically have a magnetic moment. There are, however, some diamagnetic materials that have a weak magnetic field.

ELECTRIC CHARGES

The attractive force between the electrons and the nucleus is called the **electric force**. A positive (+) charge or a negative (-) charge creates a field of sorts in the empty space around it, which is known as an **electric field**. The direction of a positive charge is away from it and the direction of a negative charge is towards it. An electron within the force of the field is pulled towards a positive charge because an electron has a negative charge. A particle with a positive charge is pushed away, or repelled, by another positive charge. Like charges repel each other and opposite charges attract. Lines of force show the paths of charges. **Electric force** between two objects is directly proportional to the product of the charge magnitudes and inversely proportional to the square of the distance between the two objects. **Electric charge** is measured with the unit Coulomb (C). It is the amount of charge moved in one second by a steady current of one ampere (1C = 1A × 1s).

> **Review Video: Electric Charge**
> Visit mometrix.com/academy and enter code: 323587

ELECTRIC CURRENT MOVEMENT THROUGH CIRCUITS

Electric current is the sustained flow of electrons that are part of an electric charge moving along a path in a circuit. This differs from a static electric charge, which is a constant non-moving charge rather than a continuous flow. The **rate of flow of electric charge** is expressed using the ampere (amp or A) and can be measured using an ammeter. A current of 1 ampere means that 1 coulomb of charge passes through a given area every second. Electric charges typically only move from areas of high electric potential to areas of low electric potential. To get charges to flow into a high potential area, you must to connect it to an area of higher potential, by introducing a battery or other voltage source.

SIMPLE CIRCUITS

Movement of electric charge along a path between areas of high electric potential and low electric potential, with a resistor or load device between them, is the definition of a **simple circuit**. It is a closed conducting path between the high and low potential points, such as the positive and negative terminals on a battery. One example of a circuit is the flow from one terminal of a car battery to the other. The electrolyte solution of water and sulfuric acid provides work in chemical form to start the flow. A frequently used classroom example of circuits involves using a D cell (1.5 V) battery, a small light bulb, and a piece of copper wire to create a circuit to light the bulb.

MAGNETS

A **magnet** is a piece of metal, such as iron, steel, or magnetite (lodestone) that can affect another substance within its **field of force** that has like characteristics. Magnets can either attract or repel other substances. Magnets have two **poles**: north and south. Like poles repel and opposite poles (pairs of north and south) attract. The magnetic field is a set of invisible lines representing the paths of attraction and repulsion. Magnetism can occur naturally, or ferromagnetic materials can be magnetized. Certain matter that is magnetized can retain its magnetic properties indefinitely and become a permanent magnet. Other matter can lose its magnetic properties. For example, an iron nail can be temporarily magnetized by stroking it repeatedly in the same direction using one pole of another magnet. Once magnetized, it can attract or repel other magnetically inclined materials, such as paper clips. Dropping the nail repeatedly will cause it to lose its charge.

MAGNETIC FIELDS, CURRENT, AND MAGNETIC DOMAINS

A **magnetic field** can be formed not only by a magnetic material, but also by electric current flowing through a wire. When a coiled wire is attached to the two ends of a battery, for example, an electromagnet can be formed by inserting a ferromagnetic material such as an iron bar within the coil. When electric current flows through the wire, the bar becomes a magnet. If there is no current, the magnetism is lost. A **magnetic domain** occurs when the magnetic fields of atoms are grouped and aligned. These groups form what can be thought of as miniature magnets within a material. This is what happens when an object like an iron nail is temporarily magnetized. Prior to magnetization, the organization of atoms and their various polarities are somewhat random with respect to where the north and south poles are pointing. After magnetization, a significant percentage of the poles are lined up in one direction, which is what causes the magnetic force exerted by the material.

MOTION AND DISPLACEMENT

Motion is a change in the location of an object, and is the result of an unbalanced net force acting on the object. Understanding motion requires the understanding of three basic quantities: displacement, velocity, and acceleration.

When something moves from one place to another, it has undergone **displacement**. Displacement along a straight line is a very simple example of a vector quantity. If an object travels from position $x = -5$ cm to $x = 5$ cm, it has undergone a displacement of 10 cm. If it traverses the same path in the opposite direction, its displacement is -10 cm. A vector that spans the object's displacement in the direction of travel is known as a displacement vector.

GRAVITATIONAL FORCE

Gravitational force is a universal force that causes every object to exert a force on every other object. The gravitational force between two objects can be described by the formula, $F = Gm_1m_2/r^2$, where m_1 and m_2 are the masses of two objects, r is the distance between them, and G is the gravitational constant, $G = 6.672 \times 10^{-11}$ N-m^2/kg^2. In order for this force to have a noticeable effect, one or both of the objects must be extremely large, so the equation is generally only used in problems involving planetary bodies. For problems involving objects on the earth being affected by earth's gravitational pull, the force of gravity is simply calculated as $F = mg$, where g is 9.81 m/s^2 toward the ground.

NEWTON'S FIRST TWO LAWS OF MOTION

NEWTON'S FIRST LAW

An object at rest or in motion will remain at rest or in motion unless acted upon by an external force.

This phenomenon is commonly referred to as **inertia**, the tendency of a body to remain in its present state of motion. In order for the body's state of motion to change, it must be acted on by an unbalanced force.

NEWTON'S SECOND LAW

An object's acceleration is **directly proportional** to the net force acting on the object, and **inversely proportional** to the object's mass.

It is generally written in equation form $F = ma$, where F is the net force acting on a body, m is the mass of the body, and a is its acceleration. Note that since the mass is always a positive quantity, the acceleration is always in the same direction as the force.

SIMPLE MACHINES

Simple machines include the inclined plane, lever, wheel and axle, and pulley. These simple machines have no internal source of energy. More **complex or compound machines** can be formed from them. Simple machines provide a force known as a mechanical advantage and make it easier to accomplish a task. The inclined plane enables a force less than the object's weight to be used to push an object to a greater height. A lever enables a multiplication of force. The wheel and axle allows for movement with less resistance. Single or double pulleys allows for easier direction of force. The wedge and screw are forms of the inclined plane. A wedge turns a smaller force working over a greater distance into a larger force. The screw is similar to an incline that is wrapped around a shaft.

FRICTION

Friction is a force that arises as a **resistance to motion** where two surfaces are in contact. The maximum magnitude of the frictional force (f) can be calculated as $f = F_c \mu$, where F_c is the contact force between the two objects and μ is a coefficient of friction based on the surfaces' material composition. Two types of friction are static and kinetic. To illustrate these concepts, imagine a book resting on a table. The force of its weight (W) is equal and opposite to the force of the table on the book, or the normal force (N). If we exert a small force (F) on the book, attempting to push it to one side, a frictional force (f) would arise, equal and opposite to our force. At this point, it is a **static frictional force** because the book is not moving. If we increase our force on the book, we will eventually cause it to move. At this point, the frictional force opposing us will be a **kinetic frictional force**. Generally, the kinetic frictional force is lower than static frictional force (because the frictional coefficient for static friction is larger), which means that the amount of force needed to maintain the movement of the book will be less than what was needed to start it moving.

SOUND

Sound is a pressure disturbance that moves through a medium in the form of mechanical waves, which transfer energy from one particle to the next. Sound requires a medium to travel through, such as air, water, or other matter since it is the vibrations that transfer energy to adjacent particles, not the actual movement of particles over a great distance. Sound is transferred through the movement of atomic particles, which can be atoms or molecules. Waves of sound energy move outward in all directions from the source. Sound waves consist of compressions (particles are forced together) and rarefactions (particles move farther apart and their density decreases). A wavelength consists of one compression and one rarefaction. Different sounds have different wavelengths. Sound is a form of kinetic energy.

PITCH, LOUDNESS, SOUND INTENSITY, TIMBRE, AND OSCILLATION

Pitch — Pitch is the quality of sound determined by frequency. For example, a musical note can be tuned to a specific frequency. A, for instance, has a frequency of 440 Hz, which is a higher frequency than middle C. Humans can detect frequencies between about 20 Hz to 20,000 Hz.

Loudness — Loudness is a human's perception of sound intensity.

Sound intensity — Sound intensity is measured as the sound power per unit area, and can be expressed in decibels.

Timbre — This is a human's perception of the type or quality of sound.

Oscillation — This is a measurement, usually of time, against a basic value, equilibrium, or rest point.

DOPPLER EFFECT

The **Doppler effect** refers to the effect the relative motion of the source of the wave and the location of the observer has on waves. The Doppler effect is easily observable in **sound waves**. What a person hears when a train approaches or a car honking its horn passes by are examples of the Doppler effect. The pitch of the sound is different not because the emitted frequency has changed, but because the received frequency has changed. The frequency is higher (as is the pitch) as the train approaches, the same as emitted just as it passes, and lower as the train moves away. This is because the wavelength changes. The Doppler effect can occur when an observer is stationary, and can also occur when two trains approach and pass each other. **Electromagnetic waves** are also affected in this manner. The motion of the medium can also affect the wave. For waves that do not travel in a medium, such as light waves, it is the difference in velocity that determines the outcome.

WAVES

Waves have energy and can transfer energy when they interact with matter. Although waves transfer energy, they do not transport matter. They are a disturbance of matter that transfers energy from one particle to an adjacent particle. There are many types of waves, including sound, seismic, water, light, micro, and radio waves. The two basic categories of waves are mechanical and electromagnetic. **Mechanical waves** are those that transmit energy through matter. **Electromagnetic waves** can transmit energy through a vacuum. A **transverse wave** provides a good illustration of the features of a wave, which include crests, troughs, amplitude, and wavelength.

ELECTROMAGNETIC SPECTRUM

The **electromagnetic spectrum** is defined by frequency (f) and wavelength (λ). Frequency is typically measured in hertz and wavelength is usually measured in meters. Because light travels at a fairly constant speed, frequency is inversely proportional to wavelength, a relationship expressed by the formula $f = c/\lambda$, where c is the speed of light (about 300 million meters per second). Frequency multiplied by wavelength equals the speed of the wave; for electromagnetic waves, this is the speed of light, with some variance for the medium in which it is traveling. Electromagnetic waves include (from largest to smallest wavelength) radio waves, microwaves, infrared radiation (radiant heat), visible light, ultraviolet radiation, x-rays, and gamma rays. The energy of electromagnetic waves is carried in packets that have a magnitude inversely proportional to the wavelength. **Radio waves** have a range of wavelengths, from about 10^{-3} to 10^5 meters, while their frequencies range from about 10^3 to 10^{11} Hz.

VISIBLE LIGHT

Light is the portion of the electromagnetic spectrum that is visible because of its ability to stimulate the retina. It is absorbed and emitted by electrons, atoms, and molecules that move from one energy level to another. **Visible light** interacts with matter through molecular electron excitation (which occurs in the human retina) and through plasma oscillations (which occur in metals). Visible light is between ultraviolet and infrared light on the spectrum. The wavelengths of visible light cover a range from 380 nm (violet) to 760 nm (red). Different wavelengths correspond to different colors.

REFLECTION AND REFRACTION

Reflection is the rebound of a light wave from a surface back toward the medium from where it came. A light wave that hits a reflecting surface at a 90-degree angle retraces its original path back to its source. Striking the surface at any other angle results in reflection of the wave at an angle in the opposite direction. Reflectance is the amount of light a material reflects; metals have high reflectance. The smoother a surface, the higher its reflectance. **Refraction** is the change in the direction of a light wave when it passes through a transparent medium with a different optical density from the one in which the wave had been traveling. This results in a change in the wave's velocity. The ratio of the sine of the angle of the incoming ray to the sine of the angle of refraction is equal to the ratio of the speed of light in the original medium to the speed of light in the refracting medium.

Science Pedagogy

IMPORTANCE OF STUDYING SCIENCE IN CONTEXT OF PERSONAL AND SOCIAL PERSPECTIVES

Learning must be **relevant**, so when students study science in the context of personal and social perspectives, they see the practical application of the textbook knowledge. They are given an understanding of the issues around them that can be solved by science and the means to act on those issues. Science should be taught within the **social context of history** so that students can see where society has been and how far it has come thanks to scientific advancements related to tools, medicine, transportation, and communication. Students should also understand how these advances developed in response to resources, needs, and values. Students need to review the **process of scientific inquiry** through the centuries to get a sense of the benefits of intellectual curiosity, the inter-relatedness of science, and the development of civilization. Students should question the role science has played in the development of various cultures by considering how computers, refrigeration, vaccines, microscopes, fertilizers, etc. have improved the lives of people.

INQUIRY-BASED SCIENCE

If learning in the science classroom is **inquiry based**, children should see themselves as being involved in the process of learning. They should feel free to express curiosity and skepticism, change ideas and procedures, take risks, and exchange information with their classmates. Inquiry-based learning in science begins with observations of details, sequences, events, changes, similarities and differences, etc. Observations are followed by investigations based on scientific standards and safety that are designed by students. Designs should allow for verification, extension, or dismissal of ideas. Investigations should involve choosing tools, handling materials, measuring, observing, and recording data. The results of an investigation can take the form of a journal, report, drawing, graph, or chart. The summary of the observations and investigation should include explanations, solutions, and connections to other ideas, as well as further questions, an assessment of the quality of the work, a description of any problems encountered, and a description of the strengths and weaknesses of the investigation. Finally, students should reflect together about the lessons learned from the investigation.

RESEARCH-BASED TEACHING STRATEGIES FOR SCIENCE

Research-based teaching strategies for science emphasize student-centered learning and encourage that all new concepts be connected to prior knowledge. Research suggests that having students connect new concepts to prior knowledge allows for new information to be

comprehended more easily and retained more frequently. To ensure that activities are developmentally appropriate, teachers must take into consideration the prior knowledge of students, along with students' maturity and ability levels. Students must be mature enough to handle all necessary materials and must also have the ability to complete the tasks assigned to them, with an appropriate level of scaffolding.

CONSIDERING READING STRATEGIES AND MATHEMATICAL PRACTICES WHEN CHOOSING SCIENCE CONTENT MATERIAL

For students to understand and make sense of science materials, certain **reading and math skills** must be attained. For example, when learning about a new science concept, students must have the ability to identify a main idea, analyze new information, interpret findings, and use decoding strategies (as well as context clues) for unknown words or phrases. During labs, students must have the ability to draw conclusions, identify cause and effect, follow written directions and answer questions. When working through specific science topics, students must use their math skills to make sense of problems, persevere through challenging scenarios, reason abstractly, model their findings, and construct arguments to explain why things happen the way they do. When choosing appropriate science content, teachers must gauge the reading and mathematical abilities of their students to ensure that developmentally appropriate materials are provided.

DIFFERENTIATED SCIENCE INSTRUCTION AND ASSESSMENT

Differentiated instruction is the way in which teachers modify the delivery of lessons and assessment of learning to meet the needs of all ability levels. In a science classroom, all students are exposed to the same concepts; however, the delivery of those concepts may look different for each student. Accelerated learners may be expected to read an excerpt from a science journal and answer questions based on their reading, whereas struggling learners may be given a video to watch or listen to a read-aloud to complete a guided note sheet. As an assessment, accelerated learners may be given a task with written directions and the expectation of written responses and explanations. Struggling learners might demonstrate learning of the same concept through the completion of smaller tasks, broken into more manageable chunks, where responses can be written or sketched.

DEVELOPMENTALLY APPROPRIATE ASSESSMENTS IN SCIENCE CLASSROOM

The three types of assessments in the science classroom are diagnostic, formative, and summative. **Diagnostic assessments** are given at the start of each unit or topic in an effort to determine prior knowledge. This prior knowledge is then used as a way of making a connection to new concepts in a meaningful way. **Formative assessments** are ongoing throughout each unit of study. These assessments are used to track each student's learning and direct future instruction. **Summative assessments** occur at the end of each unit of study to measure each student's comprehension and mastery of the skills and concepts that are being evaluated.

Health Education and Physical Education

Physical Education

ASSESSING PERSONAL FITNESS

Personal fitness is particular to the individual. Some people may be considered fit when they can run for a mile without stopping, while others may be athletic enough to accomplish that feat without really being in shape. Most people will acquire a sense of their own fitness only after spending a great deal of time exercising, setting fitness goals, and working to achieve them. However, those who want more objective data on their physical condition may submit to **testing** at a sports medicine laboratory. There, they will have their muscular and cardiovascular endurance measured on a treadmill, their body fat measured in a submersion tank, and their flexibility tested through a variety of trials.

CARDIOVASCULAR FITNESS

An individual's **cardiovascular fitness** is the ability of his or her heart to pump blood through the body at the necessary rate. Proper cardiovascular fitness can be achieved through **aerobic exercise**: that is, any activity during which the amount of oxygen taken into the body is equal to or more than the amount the body is using. Jogging, walking, or riding a bike are all examples of aerobic activity. The heart also gets an excellent workout during **anaerobic exercise**, in which the body takes in less oxygen than it needs to maintain the activity. Sprinting or swimming fast can be anaerobic exercises, if they leave the person breathless. **Nonaerobic exercise**, like bowling or golf, does not challenge the heart and lungs and therefore will not improve cardiovascular fitness.

MUSCLE STRENGTH AND ENDURANCE

Developing **healthy muscles** is not simply a matter of lifting the heaviest possible object. The ability to use your muscles over and over without getting tired is also an important part of physical fitness. Developing muscular strength and endurance will help make body tissue firmer and more resilient. Well-maintained muscles tend to work more efficiently, and they can withstand more strain. Furthermore, muscular development aids in circulation, with the result that the whole body absorbs and makes use of nutrients in the blood more quickly. Strength and endurance training has also been shown to be one of the most effective ways to lose weight, as developed muscles burn more calories than does fat.

IMPORTANCE OF EXERCISING MUSCLES

Muscles are in a constant state of **change**. If muscles are not used, they will atrophy and weaken; on the other hand, if they are regularly exercised, they will grow stronger and possibly larger. Muscles are best exercised when they are **overloaded** or asked to do more than they usually do. When you are training your muscles, you will need to gradually increase the amount of the weight or the number of repetitions to ensure that your muscles are always receiving a challenge. Many fitness professionals contend that a good muscular workout will be somewhat painful because muscles can only be developed by exceeding their normal requirements. However, not every kind of pain is profitable for a muscular workout, and individuals should be careful to distinguish muscular fatigue from injury, particularly when they are lifting heavy loads.

PHYSICAL EDUCATION

The meaning of the phrase "**physical education**" may seem obvious at first glance, but it is quite possible for individuals to have very distinct ideas of what physical education entails. Physical education, by most accounts, is composed of **exercise** (the use of the body), **play** (the action generated by the exertion of the body), **games** (competitions of any kind), **leisure** (freedom from the responsibilities of work), **recreation** (any activity that refreshes the mind and body after work), **sport** (physical activities performed for pleasure or achievement), and **athletics** (organized, competitive activities). So, a general definition of physical education might be that it is the process whereby an individual improves his or her physical, mental, and social skill through physical activity.

Warming Up and Cooling Down in Exercise

There are important reasons for warming up before and cooling down after exercise. For one thing, performance is always enhanced by **warming up**. Muscles tend to work more effectively when their temperature has been slightly raised; they are also more resistant to strains and tears at a higher temperature. Warming up directs the blood to working muscles and gives the heart time to adjust to the increased demands of the muscles. Warming up also stimulates the secretion of synovial fluid into the joints, which makes them less likely to suffer wear and tear. Warming up should include slow stretching and low-impact cardiovascular exercise. **Cooling down** is important for easing the body's transition to a normal resting condition. By stretching and slowly decreasing cardiovascular workload, the heart is aided in its readjustment.

Physical Education as Recreation Versus Competition

One of the perennial issues facing physical educators is whether activities should be promoted as forms of recreation or as competition. If **competition** is to be the dominant feature, then activities must have explicit rules, a formal way of keeping score, and identifiable winners and losers. When students are taught activities for competition, the emphasis will be on practicing specific skills, and avoiding mistakes as much as possible. When sports are taught as **recreation**, participation is the most important factor for students. Each student should get an equal amount of experience and performance time, regardless of his or her skill level. Although score is typically not kept in strictly recreational activities, students may receive certificates for good sportsmanship or diligent participation.

Aerobic Fitness

A **minimum of aerobic fitness** has been achieved when you are able to exercise three times a week at 65% of your maximum heart rate. The easiest means of achieving this level of fitness is by running for 30 minutes three or four times a week. **Moderate aerobic fitness** is achieved by exercising four or more times a week for at least 30 minutes at a heart rate that is 75% or more of maximum. This level of aerobic fitness is appropriate for athletes who are seeking to play vigorous sports like football or tennis. **Maximum aerobic fitness** can only be achieved by working close to maximum heart rate several times a week and by exercising vigorously almost every day. In order to achieve this level of fitness, you must consistently work beyond your anaerobic threshold. A good way to do this is having interval training or brief, high-intensity workouts.

Lymphatic System

The **lymphatic system** is connected to the cardiovascular system through a network of capillaries. The lymphatic system filters out organisms that cause disease, controls the production of disease-fighting antibodies, and produces white blood cells. The lymphatic system also prevents body tissues from swelling by draining fluids from them. Two of the most important areas in this system are the right lymphatic duct and the thoracic duct. The **right lymphatic duct** moves the immunity-bolstering lymph fluid through the top half of the body, while the **thoracic duct** moves lymph throughout the lower half. The spleen, thymus, and lymph nodes all generate and store the chemicals which form lymph and which are essential to protecting the body from disease.

NERVOUS SYSTEM

The **nervous system** collects information for the body and indicates what the body should do to survive in the present conditions. For instance, it is the nervous system that administers a bad feeling when the body is cold, and then sends a more positive message when a person warms up. These important messages are sent by the nerves, which vary in size and cover the entire body. The **central nervous system** is composed of the brain and spinal cord, and the peripheral nervous system is composed of the rest of the body, including those organs which a person does not voluntarily control. The **peripheral nervous system** is divided into *sympathetic* and *parasympathetic systems*, which counterbalance one another to allow for smooth function.

CARTILAGE

The areas of bones that are close to joints are covered in a shiny connective tissue known as **cartilage**. Cartilage supports the joint structure and protects the fragile bone tissue underneath. Cartilage is susceptible to injury because it is subject to gravitational pressure as well as pressure born of joint movement itself. Long-term stress to cartilage can result in rheumatoid arthritis and osteoarthritis. There are no blood vessels in cartilage; nutrients are delivered by the synovial fluid, and from nearby blood vessels. Cartilage contains a huge number of spongy fibers because it needs to absorb a great deal of shock. Especially resilient cartilage, known as **fibrocartilage**, is found between the vertebrae and in the knees, among other places.

LIGAMENTS

Ligaments are dense bundles of fibers running parallel to one another from one bone in a joint to another. Ligaments are a part of the joint capsule, although they may also connect to other nearby bones that are not part of the joint. Ligaments are not like muscles; they cannot contract. Instead, ligaments passively strengthen and support the joints by absorbing some of the tension of movement. Ligaments do contain nerve cells which are sensitive to position and speed of movement, and so ligaments can hurt. One function of this pain is to alert the person to an unnatural or dangerous movement of the joint. Ligaments may also be strained or rupture if they are placed under unnecessary or violent stress.

MUSCLE TISSUE

Muscle tissue is made up of bundles of fibers which are held in position and separated by various partitions. These partitions range from large (deep fascia, epimysium) to small (perimysium, endomysium), and often extend beyond the length of the muscle and form tendons connecting to a bone. Each muscle cell is extremely long and has a large amount of nuclei. Every muscle cell contains a number of smaller units called **sarcomeres**; these contain thick filaments of the protein myosin and thin filaments of the protein actin. Muscle tissue contracts when a nerve stimulates the muscle and the thin filaments compress within the sarcomere, causing a general muscle contraction.

GROSS MOTOR SKILLS

The three types of fundamental **gross motor skills** include locomotor, balance, and ball skills. **Locomotor skills** involve movement from place to place, such as running, jumping, skipping, or hopping. Teachers can help improve these skills by organizing relay races or obstacle courses for students to compete in. The second type of gross motor skill, **balance**, involves movement where the body remains in place, such as bending, stretching, or twisting. These skills can be improved by providing opportunities for yoga or basic calisthenics. The third gross motor skill, **ball skills**, describes a student's ability to throw, catch, kick, or manipulate a ball or similar item. These skills

can be improved by providing opportunities to partake in sports such as softball, kickball, or bowling. With younger students, equipment such as beanbags or balloons could be substituted.

Health

HEALTH

Quite simply, **health** is the state of being sound in mind, body, and spirit. According to the World Health Organization, health is not only the absence of disease, but the presence of physical, mental, and social well-being. When assessing an individual's health, a professional is likely to examine him or her from a physical, psychological, spiritual, social, intellectual, or environmental standpoint. Although every individual has his or her own standard of health, it is common for people to recognize the following characteristics as healthy: an optimistic outlook in life, the ability to relax, a supportive home life, a clean environment, a satisfying job, freedom from pain and illness, and the energy necessary to enjoy life.

WELLNESS

Health professionals refer to the highest state of health as **wellness**. Wellness has a number of definitions: it may mean enjoying life, or having a defined purpose in life and being able to work towards it, or it may mean deliberately taking the steps necessary to avoid disease and maximize health. Wellness is different from health in that it means actively *enhancing* health, not just *maintaining* good health. Total wellness depends on psychological, physical, and social factors. In the general model for wellness, all of these factors combine to produce the individual's complete level of wellness. Indeed, part of the reason why health professionals promote the idea of wellness is to show people that all the areas of their lives depend on one another.

PSYCHOLOGICAL HEALTH

In order to achieve **psychological health**, you must have an accurate and favorable impression of yourself. Having healthy **self-esteem** does not mean overestimating your talents and value; it means feeling good about your role in life and expecting that you will have the personal resources to deal with any adversity. A person who has a reasonable concept of themselves will be able to tolerate the faults of others, based upon the knowledge gained from self-reflection. Part of establishing a realistic but positive view of the world is accepting that there are many things that you will be unable to change in life, and that rather than making yourself miserable about them, you can direct your attention to those things that are under your control.

VITAL SIGNS

Every individual should be able to identify the **vital signs** and know how to measure them. The four common measures considered to be vital signs are body temperature, blood pressure, pulse rate, and respiration rate. **Body temperature** can be taken with a thermometer and should register between 96º and 99.9º Fahrenheit, depending on the time of day and sex (women tend to have slightly higher temperatures). Measuring **blood pressure** requires some equipment; a normal blood pressure is between 120/70 and 140/90, depending on age and sex. A normal **pulse rate** is about 72 beats per minute. A normal **respiration rate** is between 15 to 20 breaths a minute.

HEALTH EDUCATION AS COMMUNITY SERVICE

In a general sense, all of health education can be seen as **community service**. By teaching positive health behaviors and promoting good health to students, health teachers are improving the **quality of life** for everyone in the community. More specifically, though, the Center for Disease Control has recommended that health educators use their special training to improve health through work outside of school. Many health educators participate in fundraising for health charities, give speeches on health related topics, or work in the community to generate enthusiasm for exercise and nutrition. According to the Code of Ethics for health educators, it is imperative for those with knowledge and skills to advance positive health behaviors whenever possible and, thus, help their community.

GENDER DIFFERENCES

Science has documented that men and women not only have differences in appearance but actually **think** and **sense** in different ways. In most cases, women have stronger senses of hearing, smell, and taste, while men tend to have better vision. Men tend to be stronger, though women often have better fine motor skills. Brain scans have displayed significant differences in the areas of the brain that are more active in men and women. Science has not yet determined whether these differences are entirely physiological or whether upbringing and environment contribute. Most scientists believe that a combination of nature and nurture create the **differences between the genders**.

SMOG

Smog is the informal name given to the combination of smoke, gases, and fog that accumulates in major industrial or metropolitan areas. Most smog is created by motor vehicles, wood-burning stoves, industrial factories, and electric utilities plants. **Gray smog**, which is mainly sulfur dioxide, is common in the eastern United States because of the high concentration of industry. This kind of smog acts like cigarette smoke on the lungs, impairing the ability of the cilia to expel particulates. **Brown smog** comes from automobiles and is mainly composed of nitrogen dioxide. Ozone, one of the other components of brown smog, can impair the immune system. Automobiles are also known to produce carbon monoxide, which diminishes the ability of the red blood cells to carry oxygen.

SKELETAL SYSTEM

The **skeletal system** is composed of about 200 bones which, along with the attached ligaments and tendons, create a protective and supportive network for the body's muscles and soft tissues. There are two main components of the skeletal system: the axial skeleton and the appendicular skeleton. The **axial skeleton** includes the skull, spine, ribs, and sternum; the **appendicular skeleton** includes the pelvis, shoulders, and the various arm and leg bones attached to these. There are few differences between the male and female skeleton: the bones of a male tend to be a bit larger and heavier than those of the female, who will have a wider pelvic cavity. The skeleton does not move, but it is pulled in various directions by the muscles.

> **Review Video: Skeletal System**
> Visit mometrix.com/academy and enter code: 256447

WATER

A person should drink 7 to 10 average sized glasses of **water** daily. Water is probably the most important substance a person can consume. Water carries nutrients throughout the body and regulates body temperature. Water lubricates joints, aids digestion, and helps speed waste matter out of the body. Losing even 5% of the body's water causes immediate physical symptoms, like dizziness, fatigue, and headache; losing 15% of the body's water can be fatal. The normal daily loss is between 64 and 80 ounces of water a day, which is equal to about 9 large glasses of water. Many fruits and vegetables contain helpful water, but people should still consume the recommended amount of water each day. People who are active, live at a high altitude, or travel a great deal should be sure to drink even more water.

FAT

Fats are divided into two main categories: saturated and unsaturated. **Saturated fats** are mostly found in meat, lard, butter, coconut, and palm oil. Doctors consider these fats to be the most hazardous to health because they increase the risk of heart disease and certain kinds of cancer. **Unsaturated fats** include sunflower oil, corn oil, olive oil, and canola oil. The last two oils are called **monounsaturated fats** and are particularly good for the body because they lower cholesterol. Recent research has concluded that the most harmful kinds of fats are **trans fats**, which are formed when liquid vegetable oil is processed to make table spreads and cooking fats. Trans fats have been consistently shown to create buildup in arteries, a process which can impair heart health.

RELATIONSHIP BETWEEN CHOLESTEROL AND FAT

Many fats can increase **cholesterol**, a substance in the body which has consistently been linked with **heart disease**. Cholesterol has many positive uses in the body, like helping the liver operate and helping to form many hormones, but if cholesterol becomes too abundant, it can build up in the arteries and impede the flow of blood. Research has shown that **saturated fats** cause a more significant buildup of cholesterol than unsaturated fats or other foods that contain cholesterol. In order to minimize cholesterol in the diet, individuals should cut back on fats altogether, but especially limit their intake of saturated fats. Monounsaturated fats, like canola and olive oil, are a good, low-cholesterol source of fat.

FIBER

Whole grains, fruits, and vegetables are all excellent sources of **fiber**. Fiber can be either insoluble or soluble. **Insoluble fibers** (cellulose and lignin, for example) speed digestion and can reduce the risk of colon cancer and heart disease. Wheat and corn bran, leafy vegetables, and fruit and vegetable skins are all great sources of insoluble fiber. **Soluble fibers** (pectins and gums, for example) lower cholesterol levels and help manage the level of blood sugar. They can be found in the pulp of fruits and in vegetables, oats, beans, and barley. Doctors warn that most Americans do not eat nearly enough fiber. However, increasing fiber in your diet should be done gradually, as a sudden increase in fiber can result in bloating, cramps, and diarrhea.

ALCOHOLISM

The National Council on Alcoholism and Drug Dependence considers **alcoholism** as a disease that is influenced by social, environmental, and genetic factors. The common features of alcoholism are the inability to control consumption, continued drinking despite negative consequences, and distorted thinking patterns (like irrational denial). It is important to note that alcoholism is not simply the result of a weak will but is a **physiological state** that requires medical treatment so that it can be controlled. Many individuals may have a problem with alcoholism but not realize it if they are still functioning well overall and only drink in social situations. Alcoholics tend to be those who, even when they aren't drinking, place an undue amount of psychological emphasis on alcohol.

DRUG ABUSE

A **drug** is any chemical substance that changes the way a person acts or feels. Drugs may affect a person's mental, physical, or emotional state. Though many drugs are taken to improve the condition of the body or to remedy personal problems, drugs can also undermine health by distorting a person's mind and weakening a person's body. According to the World Health Organization, **drug abuse** is any excessive drug use that is not approved by the medical profession. The use of some drugs in any quantity is considered abuse; other drugs must be taken in large quantities before they are considered to have been abused. There are health risks involved with the use of any drug, legal or illegal, insofar as they introduce a foreign substance into the balanced system of physical health.

POLLUTION

Many people do not consider **pollution** a personal health issue, but polluted air and water can affect every aspect of a person's life. Scientists define pollution as any change in the air, soil, or water that impairs its ability to host life. Most pollution is the byproduct of human acts. Some of the common health problems associated with pollution are nasal discharge, eye irritation, constricted air passages, birth defects, nausea, coughing, and cancer. Environmental agents that change the DNA of living cells are called **mutagens**, and they can lead to the development of cancer. Pollutants that can pass through the placenta of a woman and cause damage to an unborn child are called teratogens.

SAFETY OF OUR WATER SUPPLY

Even though Americans have generally been able to rely on the **water supply**, in recent years some concerns have been raised about the prevalence of potentially dangerous chemicals in water. **Fluoride**, which has greatly improved dental health by strengthening teeth since it was added to the water supply, may be damaging to bone strength if it is consumed in great volume. **Chlorine**, which is often added to water to kill bacteria, may increase the risk of bladder cancer. One of the most dangerous chemicals that can affect water is **lead**, which is known to leach from pipes and enter the drinking supply. High amounts of lead in the body can cause serious damage to the brain and heart.

CANCER

Every **cancer** has some characteristics in common with other cancers, but it may be more or less treatable depending on its particular nature. The most common forms of cancer are carcinoma, sarcoma, leukemia, and lymphoma. **Carcinoma** is the most common kind of cancer; it originates in the cells that line the internal organs and the outside of the body. **Sarcomas** are those cancers that develop in the connective and supportive tissues of the body, namely bones, muscles, and blood vessels. **Leukemias** are cancers that originate in the blood-creating parts of the body: the spleen, bone marrow, and the lymph nodes). **Lymphomas** are cancers that originate in the cells of the lymph system where impurities are filtered out.

TOBACCO AND OTHER CARCINOGENS

By now, most Americans should be aware that the risk of developing cancer is increased more by **cigarette smoking** than by any other single behavior. Not only do cigarettes lead to lung cancer, but they also lead to cancer of the mouth, pharynx, larynx, esophagus, pancreas, and bladder. The risk of developing cancer is not limited to cigarettes: pipes, smokeless tobacco, and cigars all put a person at risk. **Second-hand smoke** has a similar effect; scientists have shown that individuals who are exposed to environmental smoke for more than 3 hours a day are three times more likely to develop cancer than those not exposed. In addition to tobacco, other acknowledged carcinogens are asbestos, dark hair dye, nickel, and vinyl chloride. Individuals should always try to make certain their living and working spaces are well ventilated to reduce the harmful substances in the air.

OBESITY

Obesity is a condition of the body where the individual has increased his or her own body weight significantly beyond what is normally considered healthy, usually by excessive eating. Obesity occurs because the individual takes in more food than his or her body can actually use, and the excess food is stored as fat. Overeating is the primary cause of obesity, but obesity can also be tied to family history, genetic factors, stress and lack of sleep, various illnesses and conditions, and many other causes. An individual who is obese is at a significantly higher risk for certain health problems, including problems with the heart, stomach, muscles, lungs, skin, nervous system, and many other areas of the body. The best way to treat obesity is through a **well-balanced diet** that eliminates excessive food intake and a **rigorous exercise program**. In extreme cases, individuals may also use medication or even surgery to help lower their weight.

IMPROVING HEALTH BY SETTING GOALS

Individuals who are most likely to make positive permanent changes in their health set **realistic goals** along the way. When setting goals, individuals should identify what resources (time, money, and effort) are available to achieve them. Individuals should also identify the potential barriers to success and consider ways to minimize or remove these problems. It is always better to set a number of small, attainable goals rather than goals that may be difficult to achieve.

PHYSICAL FITNESS

Physical fitness is the body's ability to perform all of its tasks and still have some reserve energy in case of an emergency. People who are physically fit can meet all of their daily physical needs, have a realistic and positive image of themselves, and are working to protect themselves against future health problems. Physical fitness has three main components: *flexibility*, *cardiovascular fitness*, and *muscular strength* or endurance. Some other factors, like agility and balance, are also often considered when assessing physical fitness. The benefits of pursuing physical fitness throughout life are not only physical but mental and emotional; regular exercise is proven to reduce the risk of disease and increase life expectancy.

FLEXIBILITY

A person's **flexibility** is his or her *range of motion* around particular joints. An individual's flexibility will vary according to age, gender, and posture. Some individuals may be less flexible because of bone spurs, and some individuals may be less flexible because they are overweight. Typically, an individual's flexibility will increase through childhood until adolescence, at which point joint mobility slows and diminishes for the rest of the individual's life. Muscles and the connective tissue around them (tendons and ligaments) will contract and become tighter if they are not used to their potential. Lack of flexibility can lead to a buildup of tension in the muscles and can increase the risk of injury during exercise.

BENEFITS OF REGULAR EXERCISE

Maintaining physical fitness has a number of advantages besides improving personal appearance. It has been shown time and again that habitual **exercise** is the best way to prevent coronary death. In fact, individuals who don't exercise are twice as likely as active individuals to die of a heart attack. Exercise makes the lungs more efficient, as they are able to take in more oxygen and make better use of it. This provides the body with more available energy. Exercise also benefits the bones. Individuals who do not exercise are more likely to have weak or brittle bones, and they are more prone to osteoporosis, in which bones lose their mineral density and become dangerously soft.

The benefits of **regular exercise** are both physical and mental. It is well documented that frequent exercise improves a person's mood, increases energy, focus, and alertness, and reduces anxiety. In fact, long workouts cause the release of mood-elevating chemicals called **endorphins** into the brain. Exercise also reduces the risk of disease. By aiding in the proper digestion, exercise reduces the risk of colon and rectal cancers. Studies have also indicated that women who exercise are less likely to develop breast cancer. Finally, exercise is beneficial because it helps people lose weight and keep it off. The body's **metabolism** remains elevated for a prolonged period after exercise, which means food is processed more quickly and efficiently. In addition, regular exercise helps suppress the appetite.

NUTRITION AND EXERCISE

For most people, the balanced diet depicted in the USDA's **MyPlate** will supply all the nutrients the body needs to maintain a program of physical fitness. However, individuals who are seriously testing their endurance by exercising for periods of more than an hour at a time will need to increase their intake of **complex carbohydrates**, which keep the level of blood sugar stable and increase the amount of available glycogen. Contrary to popular thought, heavy workouts do not require a diet high in protein, and in fact, consuming too much protein can put a severe strain on the kidneys and liver. Similarly, most health experts discourage the use of dietary supplements and body-building foods unless under supervision because these products can easily result in nutritional imbalances.

WATER AS AN IMPORTANT COMPONENT OF EXERCISE

Water is the most important thing for a person to consume before, during, and after exercise. On hot days, active people can sweat up to a quart of water. If you become **dehydrated**, your heart will have a difficult time providing oxygen and nutrients to muscles. Even sports drinks cannot provide the hydrating effect of cool water because the sodium, sugar, and potassium in them delay their absorption into the body. Salt tablets should be avoided as well; they are potentially dangerous and unnecessary. Although people do lose a bit of sodium when they sweat, this is more than offset by the huge amount of salt in the average American diet.

FIRST-AID

Since it is necessary to act fast when an **emergency** happens, it is a good idea to think ahead and have a **plan** in place. If you are in a public place, you may want to begin by shouting for help to see if a doctor is available. Someone should immediately dial 911. Do not attempt any resuscitation techniques unless you are trained. If you have a car and it is appropriate, you should immediately take the victim to the nearest hospital. Furthermore, every home should have some basic first-aid supplies. A good first-aid kit will include bandages, sterile gauze pads, scissors, adhesive tape, calamine lotion, cotton balls, thermometer, ipecac syrup (to induce vomiting), a sharp needle, and safety pins.

PHYSICAL ADDICTION TO SMOKING

Nicotine is consistently shown to be far more **addictive** than alcohol; whereas only one in ten users of alcohol will eventually become alcoholics, approximately eight of ten heavy smokers will attempt and fail to quit. The method that nicotine uses is similar to that of other addictive substances: it creates an immediate positive feeling when taken; it will cause painful withdrawal symptoms if it is not taken; and it stimulates powerful cravings in the user even after it is removed from the system. Nicotine addiction can become so strong that a heavy smoker will experience withdrawal symptoms a mere two hours after smoking. Persistent tobacco use will also lead to an increased tolerance for nicotine, and so the user will have to consume more and more to achieve the pleasure or avoid the pain.

AVOIDING ALCOHOL ABUSE

There are a few guidelines students should know so that they can avoid chronic **alcohol abuse**. First, never use alcohol as a medicine or as a way to escape personal problems. Always drink slowly, and if possible, alternate alcoholic and non-alcoholic beverages. It is a good idea to eat both before and during drinking so that less alcohol rushes into the bloodstream. Drinking should never be the primary reason for a social function, though individuals should try to avoid drinking alone, as well. At a party, it is a good idea to avoid mixed drinks, as it is often difficult to tell just how much alcohol they contain. Finally, and most importantly, every person should have the self-control to say "no" to a drink without feeling guilty or rude.

PSYCHOLOGICAL AND PHYSICAL DEPENDENCE ON DRUGS

A **psychological dependence on drugs** may begin as a craving for the pleasurable feelings or relief from anxiety that the drug provides. However, this craving can soon turn into a dependency on the drug in order to perform normal mental operations. A **physical dependency**, on the other hand, is said to occur when the individual requires increasing amounts of the drug to get the desired effect. Many drugs, like marijuana or hallucinogens, do not cause withdrawal symptoms; others, like heroin or cocaine, may be extremely painful to stop using. Individuals with a severe chemical dependency will eventually use a drug like this simply to avoid experiencing the effects of withdrawal. Typically, an individual with a severe dependency will try to stop many times without success.

APPETITE

The feeling of **hunger** can be caused by up to 12 different hormones and areas of the brain. There is even some speculation that the size of an individual's fat cells may cause him or her to feel hungry. The **appetite** is the physiological desire to eat, and though it is thought to be the body's means of avoiding failure, it can also be stimulated when the body does not really need food. Humans tend to stop eating when they reach the point of **satiety**, in which they are no longer hungry and feel full. Scientists have advanced the set-point theory of appetite, which contends that each individual has an internal system that is geared to regulate hunger and satiety so as to keep body fat at a certain rate.

RELATIONSHIP BETWEEN EXERCISE AND WEIGHT LOSS

Despite the appeal of quick solutions to obesity, **exercise** remains the best way to reduce weight and maintain weight loss. Many people think that increasing exercise will make them want to eat more; in actuality, frequent exercise tends to reduce the appetite, and since it raises the rate of metabolism, it also helps keep weight off. There are numerous other advantages to exercise in regard to weight; exercise burns off fat reserves and increases muscle mass. Since muscle tends to use calories more quickly than fat, this means it will be more difficult for the individual to put on pounds of fat. In study after study, individuals who exercise regularly are shown to be more likely to lose weight and keep it off.

DIGESTIVE SYSTEM

The **digestive system** is composed of organs that convert food into energy. This process begins with the teeth, which grind food into small particles that are easy to digest. Food is then carried through the pharynx (throat) and esophagus to the stomach. In the stomach, it is partially digested by strong acids and enzymes. From there, food passes through the small and large intestines, the rectum, and out through the anus. On this journey, it will be mixed with numerous chemicals so that it can be absorbed into the blood and lymph system. Some food will be converted into immediate energy, and some will be stored for future use; whatever cannot be used by the body will be expelled as waste.

> **Review Video: Gastrointestinal System**
> Visit mometrix.com/academy and enter code: 378740

MUSCULAR SYSTEM

The **muscles** of the body are attached to the skeleton by tendons and other connective tissues. Muscles exert force and move the bones of the body by converting chemical energy into contractions. Every muscular act is the result of some muscle growing shorter. The muscles themselves are composed of millions of tiny proteins. Muscles are stimulated by nerves that link them to the brain and spinal cord. There are three types of muscles: **cardiac muscles** are found only in the heart and pump the blood through the body; **smooth muscles** surround or are part of internal organs; **skeletal muscles** are those a person controls voluntarily. Skeletal muscles are the most common tissue in the body, accounting for between 25 and 40% of body weight.

> **Review Video: Muscular System**
> Visit mometrix.com/academy and enter code: 967216

ENDOCRINE SYSTEM

The **endocrine system** creates and secretes the hormones that accomplish a wide variety of tasks in the body. The endocrine system is made up of glands. These glands produce chemicals that regulate metabolism, growth, and sexual development. Glands release hormones directly into the bloodstream, where they are then directed to the various organs and tissues of the body. The endocrine system is generally considered to include the pituitary, thyroid, parathyroid, and adrenal glands, as well as the pancreas, ovaries, and testes. The endocrine system regulates its level of hormone production by monitoring the activity of hormones; when it senses that a certain hormone is active, it reduces or stops production of that hormone.

> **Review Video: Endocrine System**
> Visit mometrix.com/academy and enter code: 678939

CIRCULATORY SYSTEM

The **circulatory system** is composed of the heart, the blood vessels, and the blood. This system circulates the blood throughout the body, giving nutrients and other essential materials to the body cells and removing waste products. **Arteries** carry blood away from the heart, and **veins** carry blood back to the heart. Within body tissues, tiny **capillaries** distribute blood to the various body cells. The heart takes oxygenated blood from the lungs and distributes it to the body; when blood comes back bearing carbon dioxide, the heart sends it to the lungs to be expelled. Other organs not always considered to be a part of this system (for instance, the kidneys and spleen) help to remove some impurities from the blood.

HORMONE SYSTEM

Hormones are the chemicals that motivate the body to do certain things. They are produced in the organs that make up the endocrine system. With the exception of the sex organs, males and females have identical endocrine systems. The actions of the hormones are determined by the **hypothalamus**, an area of the brain about the size of a pea. The hypothalamus sends messages to the pituitary gland, which is directly beneath it. The **pituitary gland** turns on and off the various glands that produce hormones. Hormones, once released, are carried to their targets by the bloodstream, at which point they motivate cells and organs to action. Hormones can influence the way a person looks, feels, behaves, or matures.

COMMUNICABLE AND NON-COMMUNICABLE DISEASES

Communicable diseases are those that are caused by microorganisms and can be transferred from one infected person or animal to a previously uninfected person or animal. Although some diseases are passed on by direct contact with an infected individual, many can be spread through close proximity: airborne bacteria or viruses account for most communication of disease. Some examples of communicable disease are measles, smallpox, influenza, and scarlet fever. Some communicable diseases require specific circumstances for transmission; for instance, tetanus requires the presence of infected soil or dirt. Any disease that cannot be transferred from one person or animal to another is considered non-communicable.

INFECTIOUS AND NON-INFECTIOUS DISEASES

Infectious diseases are those that are caused by a virus, bacterium, or parasite. Infectious diseases are distinguished from non-infectious diseases in that they stem from biological causes, rather than from physical or chemical causes (as in the case of burns or poisoning). An infectious disease will always have an **agent** (something that has the disease and spreads it to others) and a **vector** (a way of transmitting the disease). In the case of malaria, for instance, a parasite contains the disease, and it is introduced to the body when a mosquito carrying it places it in the bloodstream. The vector of an infectious disease does not need to be biological; many diseases are transmitted through water, for example.

VIRUSES

Viruses are the smallest of the pathogens, but they are also the most difficult to destroy. Viruses consist of a small bit of nucleic acid (either DNA or RNA) inside a coating of protein. Viruses are unable to reproduce by themselves, so they infest the reproductive systems of cells already in the body and command them to make new viral cells. These new cells are then sent to other parts of the body. Some of the most common viruses are influenza, herpes, hepatitis, and papilloma. It is difficult to treat viruses without also damaging the cells that they are using. Antibiotics, for instance, have no effect on viruses. Special antiviral drugs must be taken, and even these do not entirely eliminate the presence of the virus.

BACTERIA

Bacteria are simple, one-celled organisms and are the most common microorganism and pathogen. Most bacteria do not cause disease; in fact, many bacteria are important to body processes. Bacteria can harm the body when they release enzymes that actually digest other body cells or when they produce toxins. Since bacteria are quite different from the normal body cell, they can usually be effectively treated with antibiotics. However, not just any antibiotic can be used to treat every bacterial infection; a doctor must determine the particular strain of bacteria that is causing the problem before he or she writes a prescription. Over time, bacteria may become resistant to antibiotics, so it is best not to take too much of this effective treatment.

IMMUNE SYSTEM

The body uses a number of different weapons to try to defeat infections. Most obviously, the **skin** repels most invaders. Many substances produced by the body (like mucus, saliva, and tears) also fight against infection. When these methods are ineffective, however, the immune system goes to work. The **immune system** consists of parts of the lymphatic system, like the spleen, thymus gland, and lymph nodes, and vessels called lymphatics that work to filter impurities out of the body. The *spleen* is where antibodies are made, as well as the place where old red blood cells are disposed. The *thymus gland* fortifies white blood cells with the ability to find and destroy invaders. The *lymph nodes* filter out bacteria and other pathogens.

Review Video: Immune System
Visit mometrix.com/academy and enter code: 622899

BASIC IMMUNE RESPONSE

Whenever an **antigen**, or infecting substance, enters the body, the **immune system** immediately goes to work to defeat it. To begin with, the **T cells** fight the antigen, assisted by **macrophages** (cells that scavenge for foreign or weakened cells). While this battle is raging, the **B cells** create **antibodies** to join in. Many pathogens will be transported to the **lymph nodes**, where a reserve store of antibodies will eliminate them. It is for this reason that the lymph nodes often become swollen during cold and flu season. If the antigens find some success, the body will rush a greater blood supply to the infected area, enriching the supply of oxygen and nutrients. In the event that the pathogens are able to contaminate the blood stream, the infection becomes systemic and much more dangerous.

> **Review Video: Antibodies**
> Visit mometrix.com/academy and enter code: 549715

ALLERGIES

An **allergy** is a hypersensitivity or overreaction to some substance in a person's environment or diet; it is the most common kind of immune disorder. There are many different symptoms of an **allergic reaction**, but the most common are sneezing, hives, eye irritation, vomiting, and nasal congestion. In some extreme cases, the person may collapse and even die. Allergic triggers, or **allergens**, can be anything from peanuts to pollen, from insect bites to mold. Although there is no way to reverse or eliminate a personal allergy, science has made progress in treating the allergic reaction. These days, it is possible to be treated for an allergic reaction without becoming drowsy or sluggish.

IMMUNIZATIONS

Despite the overwhelming evidence supporting the use of **immunization** in preventing potentially life-threatening diseases, many Americans still neglect to get the basic immunizations. At present, the American Academy of Pediatrics recommends that every child be immunized against measles, mumps, smallpox, rubella, diphtheria, tetanus, and hepatitis B. Some vaccinations will need to be repeated on a certain schedule. Basically, a vaccination is the intentional introduction of a small amount of an antigen into the body. This stimulates the immune system to learn how to fight that particular antigen. There are certain vaccinations that a pregnant woman should not get, and a person should never be vaccinated if he or she is sick.

COMMON COLD

The **common cold** is one of the most pesky and irritating of viruses, though it is rarely a great risk to long-term health. One reason the cold is so difficult to fight is that there are over 200 varieties of the virus, so the body is never able to develop a comprehensive immunity. The cold virus is typically spread through the air or through contact. There is no completely effective medical treatment, either. Indeed, doctors warn that taking aspirin and acetaminophen may actually suppress the antibodies that the body needs to fight the infection and may therefore contribute to some symptoms. There is also no conclusive evidence to support taking vitamin C in large doses. Antihistamines, which many people credit with relieving the symptoms of the common cold, may make the user drowsy.

CANCER

Cancer is the uncontrolled growth and spread throughout the body of abnormal cells. Cancer cells, unlike the regular cells of the body, do not follow the instructions encoded in the body's DNA. Instead, these cells reproduce themselves quickly, creating neoplasms, or tumors. A **tumor** may be either benign, when it is not considered dangerous, or malignant (cancerous). Unless they are stopped, cancer cells continue to grow, crowding out normal cells in a process called infiltration. Cancer cells can also **metastasize**, or spread to the other parts of the body by entering the bloodstream or lymphatic system. The gradual overtaking of the body by these cancer cells will eventually make it impossible to sustain human life.

HYGIENE
IMPORTANCE

Besides helping you maintain an attractive appearance, **hygiene** is essential for keeping you healthy and free of disease. The body is usually covered with a certain amount of bacteria, but if this number is allowed to grow too high, you may place yourself at risk for disease. Individuals who fail to regularly wash their hair are more likely to have head lice, and those who fail to properly clean their genitals are more susceptible to urinary tract infections. Good hygiene also reduces an individual's contagiousness when sick. Hygiene is especially important when dealing with **food**: failing to wash everything involved in the preparation of a meal can result in the spread of bacterial infections like E. coli and hepatitis A.

BASIC PERSONAL HYGIENE PRACTICES

To stay clean and reduce the risk of disease, students should practice **daily basic hygiene**. Everyone should wash hair and body daily and should wash the hands more frequently than that. Teeth should be brushed between one and three times daily. Always wash hands before eating, avoid spitting or nose-picking, and cover your mouth when sneezing. Try to avoid coming into contact with any bodily fluids, and keep clothes and living space clean. Finally, avoid putting your fingers in your mouth, and try not to touch any animals before eating.

SIMILARITIES BETWEEN BASIC FOOD PREPARATION AND MEDICAL HYGIENE

There are a few basic **hygiene habits** that every individual should practice when preparing food or performing basic medical procedures. Always clean off the areas where food will be prepared, and wash your hands after touching any uncooked foods. Do not use the same tools to prepare different foods. Always refrigerate foods before and after they are used. Label stored food to indicate when it was produced. Dispose of any uneaten food that cannot be stored. When performing basic medical procedures, always use sterile bandages and any necessary protective clothing, like masks, gloves, or eyewear. Always make sure any medical waste, like used bandages, is disposed of securely.

USDA DIETARY GUIDELINES
INCEPTION TO THE EARLY 1990S

The United States Department of Agriculture began issuing **nutrition guidelines** in 1894, and in 1943 the department began promoting the Basic 7 food groups. In 1956, Basic 7 was replaced with the Basic Four food groups. These were fruits and vegetables, cereals and breads, milk, and meat. Basic Four lasted until 1992, when it was replaced with the **Food Pyramid**, which divided food into six groups: 1) Bread, cereal, rice, pasta 2) Fruit 3) Vegetables 4) Meat, poultry, fish, dry beans, eggs, nuts 5) Milk, yogurt, cheese 6) Fats, oils, sweets. The Food Pyramid also provided recommendations for the number of daily servings from each group.

USDA'S MYPLATE

The **USDA's Food Pyramid** was heavily criticized for being vague and confusing, and in 2011 it was replaced with **MyPlate**. MyPlate is much easier to understand, as it consists of a picture of a dinner plate divided into four sections, visually illustrating how our daily diet should be distributed among the various food groups. Vegetables and grains each take up 30% of the plate, while fruits and proteins each constitute 20% of the plate. There is also a representation of a cup, marked Dairy, alongside the plate. The idea behind MyPlate is that it's much easier for people to grasp the idea that half of a meal should consist of fruits and vegetables than it is for them to understand serving sizes for all the different kinds of foods they eat on a regular basis.

Most experts consider MyPlate to be a great improvement over the Food Pyramid, but it has still come under criticism from some quarters. Many believe too much emphasis is placed on protein, and some say the dairy recommendation should be eliminated altogether. The Harvard School of Public Health created its own **Healthy Eating Plate** to address what it sees as shortcomings in MyPlate. Harvard's guide adds healthy plant-based oils to the mix, stresses whole grains instead of merely grains, recommends drinking water or unsweetened coffee or tea instead of milk, and adds a reminder that physical activity is important.

IMPORTANCE OF SELF-IMAGE IN RELATIONSHIPS

One of the most important determinants of how an individual forms relationships with others may be how that individual **perceives him or herself**. If an individual feels unlovable, it may be impossible for him or her to seek affection from others. If a person has confidence in him or herself, he or she should be able to develop honest and open relationships with others. Though the phrase is a bit clichéd, it is nevertheless true that a person cannot love another without loving him or herself. Sadly, studies have shown that individuals who have a negative opinion of themselves tend to establish relationships with people who treat them poorly and thus reinforce their negative self-image.

FAIR PLAY

Fair play is the term used to describe the goal of sportsmanship in physical education. Fair play includes following rules, displaying etiquette, helping others, including everyone, sharing equipment, playing safely, persevering, working collaboratively, and winning without cheating. It also teaches students how to win without gloating or putting down their competitors. Creating an environment of fair play allows physical education to promote physicality while remaining inclusive and sensitive to the needs of all learners.

CONFLICT RESOLUTION

It is inevitable in life that everyone will come into **conflict** with some difficult individuals. Many people persistently spar with others because they have a **personality disorder** based on low self-esteem or illness. For the most part, you will not be close enough to an individual to try and change them in any permanent way. Therefore, in most cases of conflict, health professionals recommend acknowledging the other person's viewpoint and then finding a way to either avoid or circumvent that person. If **confrontation** is necessary, you should state your feelings honestly and politely. If possible, try to avoid making confrontations personal. Sometimes it helps to have a third party mediate an especially contentious dispute.

EFFECTS OF SIBLINGS

Siblings (brothers and sisters) can be almost as important as parents in helping children develop models for their future relationships. **Sibling rivalry**, for example, can have damaging consequences in other relationships if it is taken too far. Likewise, children who feel they were appreciated by their parents less than their brothers or sisters may go through life expecting to be taken for granted. Typically, people grow more distant from their siblings during adolescence, as each tries to assert his or her own independence. Later in life, though, people report much stronger relationships with their brothers and sisters. Siblings may not be as close as friends for some, but they nevertheless occupy a unique and prized place in people's lives.

TYPICAL STATE EDUCATIONAL STANDARDS FOR PHYSICAL EDUCATION CLASSES

A typical state standard in **physical education** is for students to understand the rules for a variety of physical activities, including games and sports. Some examples of the kinds of **benchmarks** that a state education department might specify for this standard are, for third grade: to identify the rules and procedures in specified physical activities, including games; for fifth grade: to demonstrate that they understand the rules that must be followed when participating in specified physical activities, including games; and for high school grades: to demonstrate the rules in complex versions of at least two different categories of movement forms in individual activities, dual activities, cardiorespiratory and aerobic lifetime activities, outdoor activities, team sports, aquatics, self-defense, yoga, martial arts, dance, and strength training and conditioning. For a standard of identifying the rules, procedures, and etiquette in a specified game or physical activity, a typical benchmark for fifth grade might be to demonstrate and explain the rules, procedures, and etiquette to follow when participating in physical activities or games; for eighth grade, to apply safe, effective rules, procedures, and etiquette for specific activities or games; and for high school, to analyze and apply the safe, effective rules, procedures, and etiquette for specific activities or games.

MTTC Practice Test

1. *Sea* and *see*, *fair* and *fare*, are called:

    a. Homophones
    b. Antonyms
    c. Homographs
    d. Twin words

2. In preparation for writing a paper, a high school class has been instructed to skim a number of Internet and print documents. They are being asked to:

    a. Read the documents several times, skimming to a deeper level of understanding each time
    b. Read the documents quickly, identifying those that offer the most specific information
    c. Read the documents quickly, looking for key words in order to gather the basic premise of each
    d. Read the documents carefully, looking for those that offer the most in-depth information

3. Which of the following is the best definition of Information Literacy?

    a. It is the set of skills required for reading and comprehending different information.
    b. It is the cognitive skill set necessary to amass a comprehensive base of knowledge.
    c. It is the skill set required for the finding, retrieval, analysis, and use of information.
    d. It is the set of skills necessary for effectively communicating information to others.

4. Which of the following choices describes the best introduction to a unit on oral traditions from around the world?

    a. Introducing games that practice new sight words, encoding words based on phonics rules, and answering short comprehension questions.
    b. Setting up video-conferencing with a school in Asia so that students can communicate with children from other countries.
    c. Inviting a guest speaker from a nearby Native American group to demonstrate oral story-telling to the class.
    d. Creating a PowerPoint presentation about various types of oral cultures and traditions and characteristics of each.

5. A syllable must contain:

    a. A vowel
    b. A consonant
    c. Both a vowel and a consonant
    d. A meaning

6. A class is reading a 14-line poem in iambic pentameter. There are three stanzas of four lines each, and a two-line couplet at the end. Words at the end of each line rhyme with another word in the same stanza. The class is reading a:

    a. Sonnet
    b. Villanelle
    c. Sestina
    d. Limerick

7. According to MLA guidelines for writing research papers, which of the following is correct regarding citations of Web sources if you cannot immediately see the name of a source's author?

a. Assume the author is not named, as this is a common occurrence on the Web.

b. Do not name an agency or corporation as the author if it is the sponsor of the source.

c. Author names are often on websites but need additional looking to discover.

d. It is not permissible to cite the book or article title in lieu of an author's name.

8. A student says, "We learned that knowledge and understanding of language is important." This is an example of an error in which of these?

a. Phonology

b. Semantics

c. Syntax

d. Pragmatics

9. The purpose of corrective feedback is:

a. To provide students with methods for explaining to the teacher or classmates what a passage was about

b. To correct an error in reading a student has made, specifically clarifying where and how the error was made so that the student can avoid similar errors in the future

c. To provide a mental framework that will help the student correctly organize new information

d. To remind students that error is essential in order to truly understand and that it is not something to be ashamed of

10. A third grader knows he needs to write from left to right and from top to bottom on the page. He knows what sounds are associated with specific letters. He can recognize individual letters and can hear word families. He correctly identifies prefixes, suffixes, and homonyms, and his reading comprehension is very good. However, when he is asked to write, he becomes very upset. He has trouble holding a pencil, his letters are very primitively executed, and his written work is not legible. He most likely has:

a. Dysgraphia

b. Dyslexia

c. Dyspraxia

d. Nonverbal learning disorder

11. Which statement is correct regarding the relationship of your audience profile to the decisions you make in completing a writing assignment?

a. How much time you spend on research is unrelated to your audience.

b. Your audience does not influence how much information you include.

c. The writing style, tone, and wording you use depend on your audience.

d. How you organize information depends on structure, not on audience.

12. A classroom teacher observes that a new ELL student consistently omits the /h/ sound in words. Of these, what is the *first* factor the teacher should consider?

a. The student may have an articulation disorder.

b. The student may be a native Spanish speaker.

c. The student may need a hearing assessment.

d. The student may have a respiratory problem.

13. *Phone, they, church.* The underlined letters in these words are examples of:

   a. Consonant blend
   b. Consonant shift
   c. Continental shift
   d. Consonant digraph

14. **Examples of onomatopoeia are:**

   a. Sink, drink, mink, link
   b. Their, there, they're
   c. Drip, chirp, splash, giggle
   d. Think, in, thin, ink

15. **Which of the following exercises would be the most appropriate tool for helping students evaluate the effectiveness of their own spoken messages?**

   a. Discuss written and oral assignments in class before completing them. Once the assignments are completed, the teacher meets individually with each student to discuss the content and effectiveness of each student's work.
   b. Instruct students to present oral reports in class, which are then "graded" by classmates. A score of 1-10 is assigned based on students' perception of the reports' clarity. The student's average score determines his report's effectiveness.
   c. Ask each student to prepare an oral report and a content quiz that highlights the report's main idea. The student then uses classmates' scores on the reviews to determine his report's effectiveness.
   d. Put students into groups of three. Two students complete a role-playing assignment based on prompts provided by the teacher. The third student gives constructive feedback on how the other two can refine and clarify their speech.

16. **When teaching students relationships between sounds and letters and between letters and words, what practices should teachers best follow?**

   a. Use a variety of instructional techniques, but including only the auditory and visual modes
   b. Incorporate multisensory modalities within a variety of instructional strategies and materials
   c. Always adhere to the same exact instructional method and materials to ensure consistency
   d. Introduce similar-looking letters and similar-sounding phonemes together for discrimination

17. **Which is greater, the number of English phonemes or the number of letters in the alphabet?**

   a. The number of letters in the alphabet, because they can be combined to create phonemes
   b. The number of phonemes. A phoneme is the smallest measure of language sound
   c. They are identical; each letter "owns" a correspondent sound
   d. Neither. Phonemes and alphabet letters are completely unrelated

18. **An understanding of the meanings of prefixes and suffixes such as *dis, mis, un, re, able,* and *ment* are important for:**

   a. Reading comprehension
   b. Word recognition
   c. Vocabulary building
   d. Reading fluency

19. When considering strategies for writing assignments, it helps to know the cognitive (or learning) objective(s) your teacher is aiming to meet with an assignment. If the assignment asks you to "describe," "explain," "summarize," "restate," "classify," or "review" some material you read, what is the cognitive objective?

a. Knowledge recall
b. Application
c. Comprehension
d. Evaluation

20. Among the following, which is NOT a common academic standard for kindergarten students in decoding and identifying words?

a. Showing knowledge that letter sequences correspond to phoneme sequences
b. Understanding that word sounds and meanings change along with word letters
c. Decoding monosyllabic words using initial and final consonant and vowel sounds
d. Matching letters to consonant sounds; reading simple, monosyllabic sight words

21. Which of the following choices will be most important when designing a reading activity or lesson for students?

a. Selecting a text
b. Determining the number of students participating
c. Analyzing the point in the school year at which the lesson is given
d. Determining a purpose for instruction

22. Silent reading fluency can best be assessed by:

a. Having the student retell or summarize the material to determine how much was understood
b. Giving a written test that covers plot, theme, character development, sequence of events, rising action, climax, falling action, and outcome. A student must test at a 95% accuracy rate to be considered fluent at silent reading
c. Giving a three-minute Test of Silent Contextual Reading Fluency four times a year. The student is presented with text in which spaces between words and all punctuation have been removed. The student must divide one word from another with slash marks, as in the following example: The/little/sailboat/bobbed/so/far/in/the/distance/it/looked/like/a/toy. The more words a student accurately separates, the higher her silent reading fluency score
d. Silent reading fluency cannot be assessed. It is a private act between the reader and the text and does not invite critique

23. Which of the following strategies would not be helpful in building the word-identification skills of emergent readers?

a. Allowing for invented spelling in written assignments or in-class work.
b. Reinforcing phonemic awareness while reading aloud.
c. Using dictionaries to look up unfamiliar words.
d. Studying and reviewing commonly used sight words at the students' ability level.

24. According to English Language Arts and Reading, which of the following are students in grades 1-3 expected to do?

a. Regularly read materials at the independent level, i.e., text containing one in 10 or fewer difficult words

b. Select text to read independently using author knowledge, difficulty estimation, and personal interest

c. Regularly read materials at the instructional level, i.e., text containing 1 in 20 or fewer difficult words

d. Read aloud from unfamiliar texts fluently, i.e., with accuracy, phrasing, expression, and punctuation

25. A student is able to apply strategies to comprehend the meanings of unfamiliar words; can supply definitions for words with several meanings such as *crucial, criticism,* and *witness*; and is able to reflect on her background knowledge in order to decipher a word's meaning. These features of effective reading belong to which category?

a. Word recognition

b. Vocabulary

c. Content

d. Comprehension

26. Which of the following was the author of *The Pilgrim's Progress?*

a. John Bunyan

b. William Congreve

c. Daniel Defoe

d. Samuel Butler

27. Which of the following gives an example of a fallacy of inconsistency?

a. "There are exceptions to all general statements."

b. "Please pass me; my parents will be upset if I fail."

c. "He is guilty: there is no evidence he is innocent."

d. "Have you stopped cheating on your assignments?"

28. Which statement accurately reflects a principle regarding self-questioning techniques for increasing student reading comprehension?

a. Asking only what kinds of "expert questions" fit the text's subject matter

b. Asking only those questions that the text raises for the individual student

c. Asking how each text portion relates to chapter main ideas is unnecessary

d. Asking how the text information fits with what the student already knows

29. A student encounters a multisyllabic word. She's not sure if she's seen it before. What should she do first? What should she do next?

a. Locate familiar word parts, then locate the consonants

b. Locate the consonants, then locate the vowels

c. Locate the vowels, then locate familiar word parts

d. Look it up in the dictionary, then write down the meaning

30. In the model known in reading instruction as the Three Cueing Systems, which of these relate most to how sounds are used to communicate meaning?

a. Syntactic cues
b. Semantic cues
c. Phonological cues
d. Pragmatic cues

31. Which choice does not describe a common outcome of reading or writing?

a. Communication of ideas
b. Character development
c. Enjoyment
d. Language acquisition

32. Of the following examples, which one is *not* an open-ended question?

a. "When does the climax of this story occur?"
b. "Is this expression a simile or a metaphor?"
c. "How are similes and metaphors different?"
d. "What are some reasons we have poetry?"

33. *Bi, re,* and *un* are:

a. Suffixes, appearing at the beginning of base words to change their meaning
b. Suffixes, appearing at the end of base words to enhance their meaning
c. Prefixes, appearing at the beginning of base words to emphasize their meaning
d. Prefixes, appearing at the beginning of base words to change their meanings

34. Some experts maintain that teaching reading comprehension entails not just the application of skills, but the process of actively constructing meaning. This process they describe as *interactive, strategic,* and *adaptable*. Which of the following best defines the *interactive* aspect of this process?

a. The process involves the text, the reader, and the context in which reading occurs.
b. The process involves readers' using a variety of strategies in constructing meaning.
c. The process involves readers' changing their strategies to read different text types.
d. The process involves changing strategies according to different reasons for reading.

35. Mr. Harris divides his 3rd-grade English class into two sections each day. Approximately 60% of the class period is spent on phonics and sight word practice, and 40% is spent on learning comprehension strategies. Which statement is most true regarding Mr. Harris' approach?

a. This approach neglects several important components of language instruction.
b. This approach will bore the students and possibly create negative feelings about English class.
c. This approach will provide the best balance of reading instruction for this age group.
d. This approach could be improved by spending equal amounts of time on each component, as they are equally important.

36. After only two or three months into 1st grade, a new substitute teacher gives grades in the 80s to a student who had been receiving 100s from the regular teacher before the teacher had to take emergency leave. The substitute deducts points when the student occasionally reverses a letter or number, or misspells words like *biscuit, butterfly,* and *swallowed.* Which of the following most accurately describes this scenario?

a. The regular teacher should not have given 100s; the substitute grades errors more thoroughly.
b. The student should be evaluated for possible dyslexia because she reverses letters and numbers.
c. The student's writing is developmentally appropriate; the substitute's grading is inappropriate.
d. The student's occasional reversals are not important, but the misspellings need interventions.

37. Collaborative Strategic Reading (CSR) is a teaching technique that depends on two teaching practices. These practices are:

a. Cooperative learning and reading comprehension
b. Cooperative reading and metacognition
c. Reading comprehension and metacognition
d. Cooperative learning and metacognition

38. Which of the following is the most accurate characterization of dialects?

a. They are non-standard versions of any language.
b. They are often seen as less socially acceptable.
c. They include linguistic features that are incorrect.
d. They indicate poor/incomplete language learning.

39. Which of the following choices would be the least effective example of an integrated curriculum that includes language arts instruction?

a. Ms. Smith, a language teacher, confers with Mr. Langston, a history and social studies teacher. Ms. Smith shows Mr. Langston how to model previewing and predicting skills before he introduces a new unit or assignment so that the students build their comprehension skills while reading for information.
b. A science teacher recognizes that the students are having difficulty retaining information from their science textbooks when test time arrives. She creates a study guide with leading questions designed to help jog the students' memory about important concepts before the test.
c. Ms. Shannon, an art teacher, plans a field trip to see the latest exhibit featuring a symbolic artist. A language teacher at her school joins the students at the museum to lead a discussion about the function of symbols and their meanings, as well as different methods of interpreting shared symbols in a society.
d. A 1st-grade teacher uses children's books that introduce mathematical skills. For example, she reads a book weekly that tells a story about children preparing for a picnic, adding and subtracting items they need for the trip along the way. She encourages the children to solve the math questions along with her during the story.

40. A teacher has a student in her class who is not very motivated to write because he finds it difficult. She observes he has a highly visual learning style, does not like reading books but loves graphic novels, and has considerable artistic drawing talent and interest. Which of the following instructional strategies would best address his individual needs, strengths, and interests?

a. Giving him audio recordings to accompany and guide his writing homework
b. Letting him complete all assignments by drawing pictures instead of writing
c. Having him draw the pictures and write accompanying text in graphic novels
d. Providing and assigning him to view animated videos on the topic of writing

41. A reading teacher feels that some of his strategies aren't effective. He has asked a specialist to observe him and make suggestions as to how he can improve. The reading specialist should suggest that first:

a. The teacher set up a video camera and record several sessions with different students for the specialist to review. The presence of an observer changes the outcome; if the specialist is in the room, it will negatively affect the students' ability to read
b. The teacher reflects on his strategies himself. Which seem to work? Which don't? Can the teacher figure out why? It's always best to encourage teachers to find their own solutions so that they can handle future issues themselves
c. They meet to discuss areas the teacher is most concerned about and decide on the teacher's goals
d. The specialist should arrive unannounced to observe the teacher interacting with students. This will prevent the teacher from unconsciously over-preparing

42. Which of the following is an example of a portmanteau?

a. Fax
b. Brunch
c. Babysitter
d. Saxophone

43. Which answer choice describes the best sort of classroom modifications for a 1st grade student with Auditory Processing Disorder?

a. A multi-sensory literacy approach using tactile, kinesthetic, visual and auditory techniques in combination with systematic instruction.
b. Modified lessons that teach concepts without the use of reading skills.
c. Extra practice in reading on a daily basis.
d. Creating engaging activities that will capture Amelia's interest in reading and introducing texts that will motivate her to complete lessons.

44. To measure children's emergent literacy development, an early childhood teacher informally evaluates their performance and behaviors during daily classroom activities. This is an example of what kind of assessment?

a. Formative assessment
b. Summative assessment
c. Both (a) and (b)
d. Neither (a) nor (b)

45. Round-robin reading refers to the practice of allowing children to take turns reading portions of a text aloud to the rest of the group during class. Which of the following statements is <u>least</u> true about this practice?

a. Students have the chance to practice reading aloud with this strategy
b. This practice is ineffective in its use of time, leaving students who are not reading aloud to become bored or daydream
c. Round-robin reading lacks the creativity or engaging qualities that will interest students in building literacy skills
d. This practice helps students feel comfortable with reading aloud due to continuous practice and encouragement from the teacher and peers

46. Which of the following correctly represents the sequence of stages or steps in the writing process?

a. Prewriting, drafting, revising, editing, publishing
b. Prewriting, drafting, editing, publishing, revising
c. Prewriting, editing, drafting, revising, publishing
d. Prewriting, drafting, editing, revising, publishing

47. The words chow, whoosh, and stalk all contain:

a. Blends
b. Digraphs
c. Trigraphs
d. Monoliths

48. Determine the number of diagonals of a dodecagon.

a. 12
b. 24
c. 54
d. 108

49. A dress is marked down by 20% and placed on a clearance rack, on which is posted a sign reading, "Take an extra 25% off already reduced merchandise." What fraction of the original price is the final sales price of the dress?

a. $\frac{9}{20}$
b. $\frac{11}{20}$
c. $\frac{2}{5}$
d. $\frac{3}{5}$

50. The graph below shows Aaron's distance from home at times throughout his morning run. Which of the following statements is (are) true?

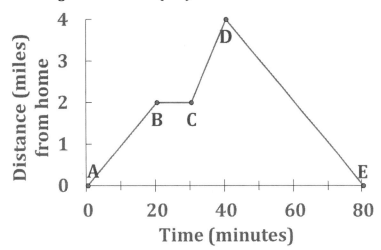

I. Aaron's average running speed was 6 mph.
II. Aaron's running speed from point A to point B was the same as from point D to E.
III. Aaron ran a total distance of four miles.

a. I only
b. II only
c. I and II
d. I, II, and III

51. If a, b, and c are even integers and $3a^2 + 9b^3 = c$, which of these is the largest number which must be factor of c?

a. 2
b. 3
c. 6
d. 12

52. Solve $\frac{x-2}{x-1} = \frac{x-1}{x+1} + \frac{2}{x-1}$.

a. $x = 2$
b. $x = -5$
c. $x = 1$
d. No solution

53. Which of these is NOT a net of a cube?

a.

b.
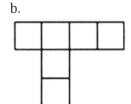

c.
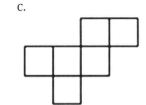

d.
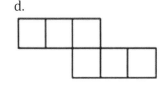

54. If the midpoint of a line segment graphed on the xy-coordinate plane is $(3, -1)$ and the slope of the line segment is -2, which of these is a possible endpoint of the line segment?

    a. $(-1, 1)$
    b. $(0, -5)$
    c. $(7, 1)$
    d. $(5, -5)$

55. A manufacturer wishes to produce a cylindrical can which can hold up to 0.5 L of liquid. To the nearest tenth, what is the radius of the can which requires the least amount of material to make?

    a. 2.8 cm
    b. 4.3 cm
    c. 5.0 cm
    d. 9.2 cm

56. Which of these does NOT simulate randomly selecting a student from a group of 11 students?

    a. Assigning each student a unique card value of A, 2, 3, 4, 5, 6, 7, 8, 9, 10, or J, removing queens and kings from a standard deck of 52 cards, shuffling the remaining cards, and drawing a single card from the deck
    b. Assigning each student a unique number 0-10 and using a computer to randomly generate a number within that range
    c. Assigning each student a unique number from 2 to 12; rolling two dice and finding the sum of the numbers on the dice
    d. All of these can be used as a simulation of the event.

57. Which of the following statements is true?

    a. A number is divisible by 6 if the number is divisible by both 2 and 3.
    b. A number is divisible by 4 if the sum of all digits is divisible by 8.
    c. A number is divisible by 3 if the last digit is divisible by 3.
    d. A number is divisible by 7 if the sum of the last two digits is divisible by 7.

58. A dress is marked down 45%. The cost, after taxes, is $39.95. If the tax rate is 8.75%, what was the original price of the dress?

    a. $45.74
    b. $58.61
    c. $66.79
    d. $72.31

59. Which of the following represents an inverse proportional relationship?

    a. $y = 3x$
    b. $y = \frac{1}{3}x$
    c. $y = \frac{3}{x}$
    d. $y = 3x^2$

60. What linear equation includes the data in the table below?

x	y
−3	1
1	−11
3	−17
5	−23
9	−35

   a. $y = -3x - 11$
   b. $y = -6x - 8$
   c. $y = -3x - 8$
   d. $y = -12x - 11$

61. Tom needs to buy ink cartridges and printer paper. Each ink cartridge costs $30. Each ream of paper costs $5. He has $100 to spend. Which of the following inequalities may be used to find the combinations of ink cartridges and printer paper that he may purchase?

   a. $30c + 5p \leq 100$
   b. $30c + 5p < 100$
   c. $30c + 5p > 100$
   d. $30c + 5p \geq 100$

62. Eric has a beach ball with a radius of 9 inches. He is planning to wrap the ball with wrapping paper. Which of the following is the best estimate for the number of square feet of wrapping paper he will need?

   a. 4.08
   b. 5.12
   c. 7.07
   d. 8.14

63. Which of the following transformations has been applied to $\triangle ABC$?

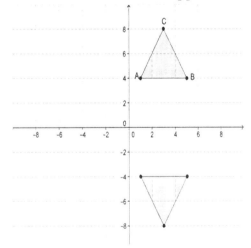

   a. translation
   b. rotation of 90 degrees
   c. reflection
   d. dilation

64. Kayla rolls a die and tosses a coin. What is the probability she gets an even number and heads?

    a. $\frac{1}{6}$

    b. $\frac{1}{4}$

    c. $\frac{1}{3}$

    d. 1

65. Mrs. Miller is teaching a unit on number and operations with her 5th grade class. At the beginning of class, she asks the students to work in groups to sketch a Venn diagram to classify whole numbers, integers, and rational numbers on a white board. Which of the following types of assessments has the teacher used?

    a. Summative assessment
    b. Formative assessment
    c. Formal assessment
    d. Informal assessment

66. Which of the following learning goals is most appropriate for a fourth grade unit on geometry and measurement?

    a. The students will be able to use a protractor to determine the approximate measures of angles in degrees to the nearest whole number.
    b. The students will be able to describe the process for graphing ordered pairs of numbers in the first quadrant of the coordinate plane.
    c. The students will be able to determine the volume of a rectangular prism with whole number side lengths in problems related to the number of layers times the number of unit cubes in the area of the base.
    d. The students will be able to classify two-dimensional figures in a hierarchy of sets and subsets using graphic organizers based on their attributes and properties.

67. Sophia is at the market buying fruit for her family of four. Kiwi fruit is only sold in packages of three. If Sophia would like each family member to have the same number of kiwi fruits, which of the following approaches can Sophia use to determine the fewest number of kiwi fruits she should buy?

    a. Sophia needs to determine the greatest common multiple of 3 and 4.
    b. Sophia needs to determine the least common multiple of 3 and 4.
    c. Sophia needs to determine the least common divisor of 3 and 4.
    d. Sophia needs to determine the greatest common divisor of 3 and 4.

68. A 6th grade math teacher is introducing the concept of positive and negative numbers to a group of students. Which of the following models would be the most effective when introducing this concept?

    a. Fraction strips
    b. Venn diagrams
    c. Shaded regions
    d. Number lines

69. Which of the following problems demonstrates the associative property of multiplication?

    a. $2(3 + 4) = 2(3) + 2(4)$
    b. $(3 \times 6) \times 2 = (4 \times 3) \times 3$
    c. $(2 \times 3) \times 4 = 2 \times (3 \times 4)$
    d. $6 \times 4 = 4 \times 6$

70. Which of the following is the correct solution for x in the system of equations $x - 1 = y$ and $y + 3 = 7$?

    a. $x = 6$
    b. $x = 5$
    c. $x = 4$
    d. $x = 8$

71. Which of the following best describes an isosceles triangle?

    a. A triangle with no sides of equal measurement and one obtuse angle
    b. A triangle with three sides of equal measurement
    c. A triangle with two sides of equal measurement and two acute angles
    d. A triangle with one right angle and two non-congruent acute angles

72. Mr. Amad draws a line with a slope of $-\frac{2}{3}$ on the white board through three points. Which of the sets could possibly be these three points?

    a. (-6, -2) (-7, -4), (-8, -6)
    b. (-4, 7), (-8, 13), (-6, 10)
    c. (-3, -1), (-6, 1), (0, -3)
    d. (-2, -3), (-1, -3), (0 -3)

73. Given this stem and leaf plot, what are the mean and median?

Stem	Leaf	
1	6	8
2	0	1
3	4	
4	5	9

    a. Mean = 28 and median = 20
    b. Mean = 29 and median = 20
    c. Mean = 29 and median = 21
    d. Mean = 28 and median = 21

74. A can has a radius of 1.5 inches and a height of 3 inches. Which of the following best represents the volume of the can?

    a. 17.2 in^3
    b. 19.4 in^3
    c. 21.2 in^3
    d. 23.4 in^3

75. The 5th grade teachers at Washington Elementary School are doing a collaborative unit on cherry trees. Miss Wilson's math classes are making histograms summarizing the heights of black cherry trees located at a local fruit orchard. How many of the trees at this local orchard are 73 feet tall?

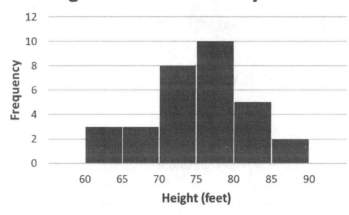

Heights of Black Cherry Trees

a. 8
b. That information cannot be obtained from this graph.
c. 9
d. 17

76. Elementary teachers in one school surveyed their students and discovered that 15% of their students have iPhones. Which of the following correctly states 15% in fraction, decimal, and ratio equivalents?

a. $\frac{3}{20}$, 0.15, 3:20
b. $\frac{3}{25}$, 0.15, 3:25
c. $\frac{15}{10}$, 1.5%, 15:10
d. $\frac{2}{1}$, 1.5%, 2:1

77. Mrs. Vories, a 5th grade teacher, asks her class to use compatible numbers to help her determine approximately how many chicken nuggets she needs to buy for a school-wide party. The school has 589 students and each student will be served nine nuggets. Which student correctly applied the concept of compatible numbers?

a. Madison estimates: $500 \times 10 = 5,000$ nuggets
b. Audrey estimates: $600 \times 5 = 3,000$ nuggets
c. Ian estimates: $600 \times 10 = 6,000$ nuggets
d. Andrew estimates: $500 \times 5 = 2,500$ nuggets

78. The table below shows the average amount of rainfall Houston receives during the summer and autumn months.

Month	Amount of Rainfall (in inches)
June	5.35
July	3.18
August	3.83
September	4.33
October	4.5
November	4.19

What percentage of rainfall received during this timeframe, is received during the month of October?

    a. 13.5%
    b. 15.1%
    c. 16.9%
    d. 17.7%

79. What is the area of the shaded region in the figure shown below?

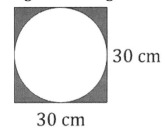

30 cm

30 cm

    a. 177 cm^2
    b. 181 cm^2
    c. 187 cm^2
    d. 193 cm^2

80. What is the perimeter of the trapezoid graphed below?

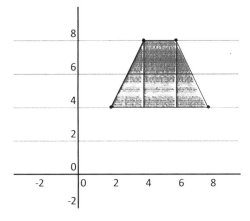

    a. $4 + \sqrt{10}$
    b. $8 + 4\sqrt{5}$
    c. $4 + 2\sqrt{5}$
    d. $8 + 2\sqrt{22}$

81. What is the slope of the leg marked x in the triangle graphed below?

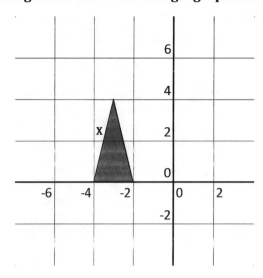

a. 2
b. 3.5
c. 4
d. 4.5

82. $A = \{5, 9, 2, 3, -1, 8\}$ and $B = \{2, 0, 4, 5, 6, 8\}$. What is $A \cap B$?

a. $\{5, 2, 8\}$
b. $\{-1, 0, 2, 3, 4, 5, 6, 8, 9\}$
c. $\emptyset$
d. $\{5, 8\}$

83. In a pack of 20 jelly beans, there are two licorice- and four cinnamon-flavored jelly beans. What is the probability of choosing a licorice jelly bean followed by a cinnamon jelly bean?

a. $\frac{2}{5}$
b. $\frac{8}{20}$
c. $\frac{2}{95}$
d. $\frac{1}{50}$

84. Amy saves $450 every 3 months. How much does she save after 3 years?

a. $4,800
b. $5,200
c. $5,400
d. $5,800

85. Which of the following statements is *not* true regarding English expansionism in the 16th century?

a. England's defeat of the Spanish Armada in 1588 brought a decisive end to their war with Spain.

b. King Henry VIII's desire to divorce Catherine of Aragon strengthened English expansionism.

c. Queen Elizabeth's support for the Protestant Reformation strengthened English expansionism.

d. Sir Francis Drake and other English sea captains plundered the Spaniards' plunders of Indians.

86. During the decolonization of the Cold War years, which of the following events occurred chronologically latest?

a. The Eastern Bloc and Satellite states became independent from the Soviet Union

b. Canada became totally independent from British Parliament via the Canada Act

c. The Bahamas, in the Caribbean, became independent from the United Kingdom

d. The Algerian War ended, and Algeria became independent from France

87. Who negotiates treaties?

a. The President

b. The House of Representatives

c. Ambassadors

d. The Senate

88. How long can members of the Federal Judiciary serve?

a. Four years

b. Eight years

c. For life

d. Six years

89. Guaranteed rights enumerated in the *Declaration of Independence*, possessed by all people, are referred to as:

a. Universal rights

b. Unalienable rights

c. Voting rights

d. Peoples' rights

90. Which of the following statements is *not* true about the Gilded Age in America?

a. The Gilded Age was the era of the "robber barons" in the business world

b. The Gilded Age got its name from the excesses of the wealthy upper-class

c. The Gilded Age had philanthropy Carnegie called the "Gospel of Wealth"

d. The Gilded Age is a term whose origins have not been identified clearly

91. Which of the following exemplifies the multiplier effect of large cities?

a. The presence of specialized equipment for an industry attracts even more business.

b. The large population lowers the price of goods.

c. Public transportation means more people can commute to work.

d. A local newspaper can afford to give away the Sunday edition.

92. Criminal cases are tried under:

    I. State law
    II. Federal law
    III. Civil court

  a. I and III
  b. II only
  c. I only
  d. I and II

93. Which of the following is *not* a true statement regarding the Louisiana Purchase?

  a. Jefferson sent a delegation to Paris to endeavor to purchase only the city of New Orleans from Napoleon.
  b. Napoleon, anticipating U.S. intrusions into Louisiana, offered to sell the U.S. the entire Louisiana territory.
  c. The American delegation accepted Napoleon's offer, though they were only authorized to buy New Orleans.
  d. The Louisiana Purchase, once it was completed, increased the territory of the U.S. by 10% overnight.

94. The idea that the purpose of the American colonies was to provide Great Britain with raw materials and a market for its goods is an expression of:

  a. Free trade.
  b. Most favored nation status.
  c. Mercantilism.
  d. Laissez-faire capitalism.

95. During the early Medieval period in Europe, before the 5th century, where were the main centers of literacy found?

  a. They were in the homes of the wealthy
  b. They were in the churches and monasteries
  c. They were in the local artisan and craft guilds
  d. There were no centers of literacy

96. How must inferior courts interpret the law?

  a. According to the Supreme Court's interpretation
  b. According to the Constitution
  c. However they choose
  d. According to the political climate

97. Which entity in American government is the closest to true democracy?

  a. The Electoral College
  b. The House of Representatives
  c. Committees within the Senate
  d. The Supreme Court

98. Power divided between local and central branches of government is a definition of what term?

    a. Bicameralism
    b. Checks and balances
    c. Legislative oversight
    d. Federalism

99. Virginian _____ advocated a stronger central government and was influential at the Constitutional Convention.

    a. Benjamin Franklin
    b. James Madison
    c. George Mason
    d. Robert Yates

100. Which of the following will result if two nations use the theory of comparative advantage when making decisions of which goods to produce and trade?

    a. Each nation will make all of their own goods
    b. Both nations will specialize in the production of the same specific goods
    c. Each nation will specialize in the production of different specific goods
    d. Neither nation will trade with one another

101. The Presidential veto of legislation passed by Congress illustrates which principal in American government?

    a. Checks and balances
    b. Federal regulation
    c. Freedom of speech
    d. Separation of church and state

102. A filibuster is used to delay a bill. Where can a filibuster take place?

    I. The House
    II. The Senate
    III. Committees

    a. I only
    b. II only
    c. I and II
    d. I, II, and III

103. To be President of the United States, one must meet these three requirements:

    a. The President must be college educated, at least 30 years old, and a natural citizen
    b. The President must be a natural citizen, have lived in the U.S. for 14 years, and have a college education
    c. The President must be a natural citizen, be at least 35 years old, and have lived in the U.S. for 14 years
    d. The President must be at least 30 years old, be a natural citizen, and have lived in the U.S. for 14 years

104. Which of the following is most likely to benefit from inflation?

a. A bond investor who owns fixed-rate bonds
b. A retired widow with no income other than fixed Social Security payments
c. A person who has taken out a fixed-rate loan
d. A local bank who has loaned money out at fixed rate

105. After the Civil War, urban populations increased. This growth was likely due to:

a. An increased reliance on agriculture
b. The Industrial Revolution
c. Prohibition
d. Slavery persisting in some areas

106. As a form of government, what does oligarchy mean?

a. Rule by one
b. Rule by a few
c. Rule by law
d. Rule by many

107. The Trail of Tears was:

a. The forced removal of British soldiers after the American Revolution
b. The forced evacuation of Cherokee peoples into Oklahoma
c. The forced evacuation of freed slaves from the South after the Civil War
d. The tears of Betsy Ross while she sewed the first American flag

108. What is the main reason that tropical regions near the Equator tend to experience relatively constant year-round temperatures?

a. They are usually located near the ocean
b. The angle at which sunlight hits them remains relatively constant throughout the year
c. They are located along the "Ring of Fire"
d. They do not have seasons

109. Which of the following is *not* correct regarding assumptions of mercantilism?

a. The money and the wealth of a nation are identical properties
b. In order to prosper, a nation should try to increase its imports
c. In order to prosper, a nation should try to increase its exports
d. Economic protectionism by national governments is advisable

110. Which scientist first proposed the heliocentric universe instead of a geocentric one?

a. Galileo
b. Ptolemy
c. Copernicus
d. Isaac Newton

111. Congressional elections are held every _____ years.

a. Four
b. Two
c. Six
d. Three

112. All else being equal, which of the following locations is likely to have the coolest climate?

a. A city located at 6,000 feet above sea level
b. A city located at 500 feet above sea level
c. A city that receives less than 10 inches of precipitation per year
d. A city that receives more than 50 inches of precipitation per year

113. Which Italian Renaissance figure was best known as a political philosopher?

a. Dante Alighieri
b. Leonardo Da Vinci
c. Francesco Petrarca
d. Niccolò Machiavelli

114. Scientists often form hypotheses based on particular observations. Which of the following is NOT true of a good hypothesis?

a. A good hypothesis is complex.
b. A good hypothesis is testable.
c. A good hypothesis is logical.
d. A good hypothesis predicts future events.

115. What will happen to light waves as they hit a convex lens?

a. They will be refracted and converge.
b. They will be refracted and diverge.
c. They will be reflected and converge.
d. They will be reflected and diverge.

116. Which of the following animal structures is not paired to its correct function?

a. Muscle System – controls movement through three types of muscle tissue
b. Nervous System – controls sensory responses by carrying impulses away from and toward the cell body
c. Digestive System – breaks down food for absorption into the blood stream where it is delivered to cells for respiration
d. Circulatory System – exchanges gasses with the environment by delivering oxygen to the bloodstream and releasing carbon dioxide

117. What change occurs when energy is added to a liquid?

a. a phase change
b. a chemical change
c. sublimation
d. condensation

118. After a science laboratory exercise, some solutions remain unused and are left over. What should be done with these solutions?

a. Dispose of the solutions according to local disposal procedures.
b. Empty the solutions into the sink and rinse with warm water and soap.
c. Ensure the solutions are secured in closed containers and throw away.
d. Store the solutions in a secured, dry place for later use.

119. If an atom has a neutral charge, what must be true of the atom?

a. The nucleus contains only neutrons and no protons.
b. The atomic mass is equal to the number of neutrons.
c. The atomic number is equal to the number of neutrons.
d. The atomic number is equal to the number of electrons.

120. Which of the following words is not connected to the process of mountain building?

a. Folding
b. Faulting
c. Transform
d. Convergent

121. What laboratory practice can increase the accuracy of a measurement?

a. repeating the measurement several times
b. calibrating the equipment each time you use it
c. using metric measuring devices
d. following SDS information

122. Elements on the periodic table are arranged into groups and periods and ordered according to all of the following except

a. atomic number.
b. refractive index
c. reactivity.
d. number of protons.

123. A gas is held in a closed container and held at constant temperature. What is the effect of increasing the volume of the container by 3 times?

a. The pressure is tripled.
b. The pressure increases by one-third.
c. The pressure decreases by one-third.
d. The pressure remains constant.

124. Which of the following terms describes an intrusion of magma injected between two layers of sedimentary rock, forcing the overlying strata upward to create a dome-like form?

a. Sill
b. Dike
c. Laccolith
d. Caldera

125. Which of the following is needed for an experiment to be considered successful?

a. a reasonable hypothesis
b. a well-written lab report
c. data that others can reproduce
d. computer-aided statistical analysis

126. Which of the following statements about heat transfer is not true?

a. As the energy of a system changes, its thermal energy must change or work must be done.
b. Heat transfer from a warmer object to a cooler object can occur spontaneously.
c. Heat transfer can never occur from a cooler object to a warmer object.
d. If two objects reach the same temperature, energy is no longer available for work.

127. A man accidentally drops his wallet in a swimming pool. He can see his wallet at the bottom of the pool. He jumps in to retrieve it, but the wallet is not where it appeared to be. What is the reason for the optical illusion?

a. The reflection of sunlight off of the water disrupted his view
b. Light is refracted as it exits the water, changing the wallet's apparent location
c. The current at the bottom of the pool caused the wallet to move
d. The heat from the Sun has impaired the man's vision

128. The precision of a number of data points refers to:

a. How accurate the data is
b. How many errors the data contains
c. How close the data points are to the mean of the data
d. How close the actual data is to the predicted result

129. The most recently formed parts of the Earth's crust can be found at:

a. Subduction zones.
b. Compressional boundaries.
c. Extensional boundaries.
d. Mid-ocean ridges.

130. Which type of nuclear process features atomic nuclei splitting apart to form smaller nuclei?

a. Fission
b. Fusion
c. Decay
d. Ionization

131. How does adding a solute to a liquid solvent affect the vapor pressure of the liquid?

a. The vapor pressure increases by an amount proportional to the amount of solute.
b. The vapor pressure increases by an amount proportional to the amount of solvent.
c. The vapor pressure decreases by an amount proportional to the amount of solute.
d. The amount of solute present in a liquid solvent does not have any effect on vapor pressure.

132. What drives weather systems to move west to east in the mid-latitudes?

a. The prevailing westerlies
b. The prevailing easterlies
c. The trade winds
d. The doldrums

133. How are organisms, such as snakes, cacti, and coyotes, able to survive in harsh desert conditions?

a. Over thousands of years, these organisms have developed adaptations to survive in arid climates
b. These organisms migrate out of the desert during the summer months, only living in the desert for a portion of the year
c. Snakes, cacti, and coyotes work together to find sources of food and water
d. Snakes, cacti, and coyotes are all aquatic species that live in ponds and rivers during the hot day

134. In which of the following scenarios is work not applied to the object?

a. Mario moves a book from the floor to the top shelf.
b. A book drops off the shelf and falls to the floor.
c. Mario pushes a box of books across the room.
d. Mario balances a book on his head.

135. Which of the following would not be used as evidence for evolution?

a. Fossil record
b. DNA sequences
c. Anatomical structures
d. Reproductive habits

136. Which of the following is considered a non-renewable resource?

a. Glass
b. Wood
c. Cattle
d. Soil

137. The stream of charged particles that escape the Sun's gravitational pull is best described by which of the following terms?

a. Solar wind
b. Solar flare
c. Solar radiation
d. Sunspots

138. According to Ohm's Law, how are voltage and current related in an electrical circuit?

a. Voltage and current are inversely proportional to one another.
b. Voltage and current are directly proportional to one another.
c. Voltage acts to oppose the current along an electrical circuit.
d. Voltage acts to decrease the current along an electrical circuit.

139. Where are the reproductive organs of a plant?

a. Style
b. Stigma
c. Flowers
d. Sepals

140. What is the definition of work?

a. the amount of energy used to accomplish a job
b. the force used to move a mass over a distance
c. the amount of energy used per unit of time
d. energy stored in an object due to its position

141. Which of the following organelles is/are formed when the plasma membrane surrounds a particle outside of the cell?

a. Golgi bodies
b. Rough endoplasmic reticulum
c. Secretory vesicles
d. Endocytic vesicles

142. Which of the following is not one of the primary elements of art?

a. Dimension
b. Unity
c. Texture
d. Space

143. Drybrush is a technique that is primarily used in

a. watercolor painting.
b. oil painting.
c. acrylic painting.
d. ceramic glazing.

144. An art teacher wants to incorporate the subjects students are learning in their general education classes into his art lesson. Which of the following lessons could be best incorporated into his art class?

a. A social studies lesson on political propaganda
b. A math lesson on equations
c. An English lesson about haiku
d. A science lesson about metabolic efficiency

145. Diminished chords are considered dissonant for which of the following reasons:

a. They sound "sad."
b. They lack a tonal center.
c. They are barely audible.
d. They are viewed with universal disdain and absent from most popular recordings.

146. Which of the following terms refers to the relative lightness or darkness of color in a painting?

a. Hue
b. Intensity
c. Value
d. Texture

147. Which of the following artistic elements is most commonly used to create the illusion of depth in a painting?

a. Balance
b. Line
c. Contrast
d. Symmetry

148. Which of these locomotor activities is most appropriate for children younger than five years old?

a. Blob tag
b. Musical hoops
c. Follow the leader
d. Any of these equally

149. Of the four types of diseases—cancers, cardiovascular diseases, diabetes, and respiratory diseases—that cause the majority of deaths from noncommunicable diseases, which risk factor is not common to all four types?

a. Unsafe water
b. Drinking alcohol
c. Poor diet
d. Smoking tobacco

150. The advantage of drawing with charcoal as opposed to lead pencils is that

a. charcoal can be smudged to create shading.
b. charcoal does not require a fixative.
c. charcoal is available in a variety of hues.
d. charcoal is available in a wide range of different values, ranging from dark and soft to light and hard.

Answer Key and Explanations

1. A: Homophones. Homophones are a type of homonym that sound alike but are spelled differently and have different meanings. Other examples are *two, to,* and *too; their, they're,* and *there.*

2. C: Read the documents quickly, looking for key words in order to gather the basic premise of each. Skimming allows a reader to quickly gain a broad understanding of a piece of writing in order to determine if a more thorough reading is warranted. Skimming allows students who are researching a topic on the Internet or in print to consider a substantial body of information in order to select only that of particular relevance.

3. C: According to the Association of College and Research Libraries, Information Literacy is the set of skills that an individual must have for finding, retrieving, analyzing, and using information. It is required not just for reading and understanding information (A). Information Literacy does not mean learning and retaining a lot of information (B), or only sharing it with others (D), but rather knowing how to find information one does not already have and how to evaluate that information critically for its quality and apply it judiciously to meet one's purposes.

4. C: Oral language is a vital aspect of any language arts instruction. Often, the first concepts of language are transmitted via oral and auditory processes. The first Americans also possessed a rich oral culture in which stories and histories were passed down through generations via storytelling. Inviting a guest speaker who is part of this culture helps students understand more about cultures in their world, as well as the value of oral language and storytelling. This introduction gives students a relevant personal experience with which to connect what they will be learning in class.

5. A: A vowel. A syllable is a minimal sound unit arranged around a vowel. For example, *academic* has four syllables: *a/ca/dem/ic.* It is possible for a syllable to be a single vowel, as in the above example. It is not possible for a syllable to be a single consonant.

6. A: Sonnet. There are three primary types of sonnets. The Shakespearean sonnet is specifically what these students are reading. A Spenserian sonnet is also composed of three four-line stanzas followed by a two-line couplet; however, the rhymes are not contained within each stanza but spill from one stanza to the next (*abab bcbc cdcd ee).* A Petrarchan sonnet divides into an eight-line stanza and a six-line stanza.

7. C: On the Internet, it often occurs that the name of the author of an article or book is actually provided but is not obviously visible at first glance. Web sources frequently include the author's name, but on another page of the same site, such as the website's home page; or in a tiny font at the very end of the web page, rather than in a more conspicuous location. In such cases, students doing online research may have to search more thoroughly than usual to find the author's name. Therefore, they should not immediately assume the author is not named (A). Also, many Web sources are sponsored by government agencies or private corporations and do not give individual author names. In these cases, the research paper *should* cite the agency or corporation name as author (B). Finally, it is much more common for online sources to omit an author's name than it is in print sources. In these cases, it is both permitted and advised by the MLA to cite the article or book title instead (D).

8. C: The example has an error in subject-verb agreement, which is a component of syntax (sentence structure and word order). Phonology (A) involves recognition and production of speech sounds and phonemes, including differentiation, segmentation, and blending. Semantics (B) involves the meanings of words. Pragmatics (D) involves the social use of language to communicate and meet one's needs.

9. B: To correct an error in reading a student has made, specifically clarifying where and how the error was made so that the student can avoid similar errors in the future. A reading teacher offers corrective feedback to a student in order to explain why a particular error in reading is, in fact, an error. Corrective feedback is specific; it locates where and how the student went astray so that similar errors can be avoided in future reading.

10. A: Dysgraphia. Dysgraphic individuals have difficulty with the physical act of writing. They find holding and manipulating a pencil problematic. Their letters are primitively formed, and their handwriting is illegible.

11. C: The kind of audience for whom you are writing, as well as your purpose for writing, will determine what style, tone, and wording you choose. Knowing who your audience is will enable you to select writing strategies, a style and tone, and specific word choices that will be most understandable and appealing to your readers. Knowing the type of audience will also dictate how much time to spend on research (A). Some readers will expect more supporting evidence while others will be bored or overwhelmed by it. Similarly, you will want to include more or less information depending on who will be reading what you write (B). And while the structure of your piece does inform how you organize your information, you should also vary your organization according to who will read it (D).

12. B: In the Spanish language, the letter *h* is typically silent. Because the student is an ELL and the USA has many people—both immigrants and those born here—whose first and/or only language is Spanish, this is the first factor to consider among the choices. An articulation disorder (A) is possible, but the teacher should not assume this first with an ELL student. (An SLP evaluation can determine the difference.) While hearing assessment (C) is always a good idea, if /h/ omission were due to hearing loss the student would likely omit or distort other unvoiced fricatives like /f/, /s/, /ʃ/, and /θ/. If the student had a breathing problem (D), other symptoms would occur in addition to not articulating /h/.

13. D: Consonant digraph. A consonant digraph is a group of consonants in which all letters represent a single sound.

14. C: *Drip, chirp, splash, giggle.* Onomatopoeia refers to words that sound like what they represent.

15. C: Each answer can be an effective tool in teaching students to build oral language skills. The question makes clear that the objective is to help students evaluate their own oral language skills, which will assist them in both spoken and written assignments. The only answer choice that involves the student himself evaluating his message is choice C. When the student prepares a review/quiz based upon important information, he or she will be more able to speak specifically to that information. When classmates complete the review, the student can identify any patterns in the questions' answers that give clues as to how well those main ideas were communicated. In this way, the student can evaluate how effective the oral presentation was, without relying on classmates or the teacher.

16. B: Teachers should apply a variety of instructional techniques to enable students with different strengths, needs, and learning styles to understand sound-letter and letter-word relationships, but they should not restrict the instructional modalities to auditory and visual (A) simply because sounds are auditory and letters are visual. Multisensory modalities (B) are more effective because different students use different senses to learn; redundancy is necessary for learning; and input to multiple senses affords a more multidimensional learning experience, promoting comprehension and retention. While some aspects of this instruction should be consistent (e.g., starting with high-frequency letters and with phonemes children can produce more easily), sticking to only one method and set of materials (C) prevents using variety to reach all students. Visually similar letters and auditorily similar phonemes should *not* be introduced together (D) before students can discriminate among them; teachers should begin with more obvious differences.

17. B: The number of phonemes. A phoneme is the smallest measure of language sound. English-language phonemes, about 40 in number, are composed of individual letters as well as letter combinations. A number of letters have more than one associated sound. For example, "c" can be pronounced as a hard "c" (cake) or a soft "c" (Cynthia). Vowels, in particular, have a number of possible pronunciations.

18. A: Reading comprehension. Prefixes and suffixes change the meanings of the root word to which they are attached. A student who understands that *un* means "not" will be able to decipher the meanings of words such as *unwanted, unhappy,* or *unreasonable.*

19. C: The verbs quoted all refer to interpreting information in your own words. This task targets the cognitive objective of comprehension. Tasks targeting the cognitive objective of knowledge recall (A) would ask you to name, label, list, define, repeat, memorize, order, or arrange the information. Tasks targeting the cognitive objective of application (B) would ask you to calculate, solve, practice, operate, sketch, use, prepare, illustrate, or apply the material. Tasks targeting the cognitive objective of evaluation (D) would ask you to judge, appraise, evaluate, conclude, predict, score, or compare the information.

20. C: Decoding monosyllabic words by referring to the initial and final consonant, short vowel, and long vowel sounds represented by their letters is a common academic standard for 1st-grade students. Typical academic standards for kindergarten students include demonstrating knowledge of letter-sound correspondences (A); understanding the alphabetic principle (B); matching letters to their corresponding consonant (and short vowel) sounds; and reading simple, monosyllabic sight words (D), i.e., high-frequency words.

21. D: It is impossible to include every text desired into the language curriculum—there are simply too many good books, stories, poems, speeches, and media available. Teachers must first think about what skills their students need to acquire, as well as what skills they have already mastered. In designing activities for class, a good teacher will start first with the purpose for instruction (or perceiving oral or visual text such as video or music). For example, purposes of reading can include: reading for information; reading for enjoyment; understanding a message; identifying main or supporting ideas; or developing an appreciation for artistic expression/perception. Once the purpose or intended learning outcome has been identified, the teacher will have a much better idea of which texts, strategies, and activities will support that purpose.

22. C: Giving a three-minute Test of Silent Contextual Reading Fluency four times a year. The student is presented with text in which spaces between words and all punctuation have been removed. The student must divide one word from another with slash marks, as in the following example: *The/little/sailboat/bobbed/so/far/in/the/distance/it/looked/like/a/toy.* The more words a student accurately separates, then the higher her silent reading fluency score. Silent reading fluency can be monitored over time by giving the Test of Silent Contextual Reading Fluency (TSCRF) four times a year. A similar assessment tool is the Test of Silent Word Reading Fluency (TOSWRF), in which words of increasing complexity are given as a single, undifferentiated, and unpunctuated strand. As with the TSCRF, three minutes are given for the student to separate each word from the next. *Itwillcannotschoolbecomeagendaconsistentphilosophysuperfluous* is an example of such a strand.

23. A: Emergent readers are those who are not yet reading fluently (with appropriate speed and accuracy). Choice B refers to the practice of reviewing relationships between letters and sounds, which is vital to building reading skills. Choice C would help students build vocabulary retention by requiring them to find unfamiliar words in the dictionary. This practice causes the student to analyze and retain spelling of unfamiliar words, as well as reinforces dictionary/reference skills. Choice D addresses the fact that many words in the English language are irregularly spelled and cannot be decoded with conventional phonetic instruction. While invented spelling described in Choice A may be permitted in emergent readers, this practice is not likely to build specific reading skills.

24. B: Standards expect 1st- to 3rd-graders to read materials regularly that are at the independent level, which they define as text where approximately one in 20 words or fewer are difficult for the student—not one in 10 (A). Students are also expected to select text to read independently, informed by their knowledge of authors, text genres and types; their estimation of text difficulty levels; and their personal interest (B). They should also read text regularly that is at the instructional level, which they define as including no more than one in 10 words the reader finds difficult—not one in 20 (C). Finally, standards expect students to read aloud fluently from familiar texts, not unfamiliar ones (D).

25. B: Vocabulary. Strategizing in order to understand the meaning of a word, knowing multiple meanings of a single word, and applying background knowledge to glean a word's meaning are all ways in which an effective reader enhances vocabulary. Other skills include an awareness of word parts and word origins, the ability to apply word meanings in a variety of content areas, and a delight in learning the meanings of unfamiliar words.

26. A: John Bunyan (1628-1688) was the author of *The Pilgrim's Progress*, a religious allegory, among many other works. William Congreve (B) (1670-1729) wrote *The Way of the World,* originally a play not successful on the theater stage, but subsequently highly regarded as a literary exemplar of the comedy of manners. Daniel Defoe (C) (circa 1660-1731) is known for *Robinson Crusoe* and other adventure novels, and *The Apparition of Mrs. Veal,* a ghost story later found to be factually based. Samuel Butler (D) (1612-1680), one of the Augustan poets, wrote the burlesque poem *Hudibras.*

27. A: A fallacy of inconsistency exists in a statement that contradicts itself or defeats itself. Saying there are exceptions to all general statements is itself a general statement; therefore, according to the content, this statement must also have an exception, implying there are NOT exceptions to all general statements. Option B is an example of a fallacy of irrelevance: passing or failing is determined by course performance, so asking to pass because parents will be upset if one fails is an irrelevant reason for appealing to a teacher for a passing grade. Choice C is an example of a fallacy of insufficiency: a statement is made with insufficient evidence to support it. A lack of evidence of innocence is not enough to prove one is guilty because there could also be an equal lack of evidence of guilt. Option D is an example of a fallacy of inappropriate presumption: asking someone if s/he has stopped cheating presumes that s/he has cheated in the past. The person being asked this question cannot answer either "yes" or "no" without confirming that s/he has indeed been cheating. If the person being asked has not been cheating, then the person asking the question is making a false assumption.

28. D: When students ask themselves how the information in a text they are reading fits with what they already know, they are relating the text to their own prior knowledge, which increases their reading comprehension. Students should not only ask themselves what kinds of "expert questions" fit the subject matter of the text (A)—e.g., classification, physical, and chemical properties are typical question topics in science; genre, character, plot, and theme are typical of literature questions; sequence, cause-and-effect, and comparison-contrast questions are typical of history— but also what questions the material brings up for them personally (B). It is necessary and important for students to ask themselves continually how each text portion relates to its chapter's main ideas (C) as they read to optimize their reading comprehension and retention.

29. C: Locate the vowels, then locate familiar word parts. Syllables are organized around vowels. In order to determine the syllables, this student should begin by locating the vowels. It's possible to have a syllable that is a single vowel (*a/gain*). It isn't possible to have a syllable that is a single consonant. Once the word has been broken into its component syllables the reader is able to study the syllables to find ones that are familiar and might give her a clue as to the word's meaning, such as certain prefixes or suffixes.

30. C: Phonological cues are based on the speech sounds in words and their alphabetic representations in print. Readers can identify words by knowing sound-to-letter correspondences. Syntactic cues (A) are based on how words are arranged and ordered to create meaningful phrases, clauses, and sentences. Semantic cues (B) are based on the meanings of morphemes and words and how they combine to create additional meanings. Pragmatic cues (D) are based on the readers' purposes for reading and their understanding of how textual structures function in the texts that they read.

31. B: Character development is not a common function of reading and writing; it is a skill set for a specific type of writing. Reading can achieve a variety of purposes. Initially, students learn to read as a form of language acquisition. This process also enables them to learn about various concepts through written texts, both inside and outside of school. Individuals will write and read to share thoughts, stories, and ideas with others. As language develops, many individuals will view reading as a common form of entertainment or enjoyment, regardless of the text's perceived instructional value or content.

32. B: This is an example of a closed question because it asks either/or and the student can only answer "simile" or "metaphor" without needing to elaborate unless asked to explain the answer. In contrast, choice C is an open-ended question because the student must both define simile and metaphor and explain the difference between them. Choice A is an open-ended literature question because the student cannot answer with yes, no, or some other single word or short phrase; s/he has to describe the action or events in a story that represent its climax, which requires understanding story structure, story elements, knowing the definition of a story's climax, reading the story, and understanding it. Choice D is a very open-ended question, as students have considerable latitude in giving the reasons each of them perceives for having poetry.

33. D: Prefixes, appearing at the beginning of base words to change their meanings. Suffixes appear at the end of words. Prefixes are attached to the beginning of words to change their meanings. *Un+happy, bi+monthly,* and *re+examine* are prefixes that, by definition, change the meanings of the words to which they are attached.

34. A: The process of actively constructing meaning from reading is interactive, in that it involves the text itself, the person reading it, and the setting in which the reading is done: the reader interacts with the text, and the text interacts with the reader by affecting him/her; the context of reading interacts with the text and the reader by affecting them both; and the reader interacts with the reading context as well as with the text. Choice B is a better definition of the *strategic* aspect of the process. Options C and D are better definitions of the *adaptable* aspect of the process.

35. A: In order to achieve a balanced language program, a teacher must spend time on many different skills that have been mentioned in previous questions and answers. Language skills cannot be reduced to the process of reading (fluency plus comprehension). Students develop their language skills over a long period of time, and they do so across multiple domains. Students' ability to listen and speak, write, view, respond, synthesize information, and read for a variety of purposes all must be included in daily instruction. By practicing only fluency and comprehension, students will not fully understand the various functions of language skills and may even lack an appreciation for them.

36. C: It is normal for students to reverse letters and numbers occasionally not only in 1st grade but through the end of 2nd grade. Thus, they do not indicate possible dyslexia (B) at this age. The words cited are above 1st-grade spelling level, particularly so early in the school year, so misspelling them is normal, should not be marked incorrect, and does not require intervention (D). Also, teachers should not deduct points for misspelling in written compositions unless the misspelled words are included in weekly class spelling lists. First-graders are frequently in transitional phases of writing when phonetic spelling is not only common but desirable. The student's writing is developmentally appropriate; the substitute's grading is inappropriate. Hence choice A is incorrect.

37. A: Cooperative learning and reading comprehension. Cooperative learning occurs when a group of students at various levels of reading ability have goals in common. Reading comprehension is achieved through reading both orally and silently, developing vocabulary, a reader's ability to predict what will occur in a piece of writing, a reader's ability to summarize the main points in a piece of writing, and a reader's ability to reflect on the text's meaning and connect that meaning to another text or personal experience.

38. B: As linguists have long pointed out, dialects are NOT non-standard versions of a language (A). In linguistics, dialects are *differing* varieties of any language, but these may be vernacular (nonstandard) OR standard versions of a language. They are often considered less socially acceptable, especially in educational, occupational and professional settings, than whichever standard version is most accepted. The linguistic features of dialects are not incorrect (C), but simply different. Their use does not indicate poor or incomplete language learning (D).

39. B: Integrated curriculum is vital to student growth and to fostering a love of learning. In reality, all subject areas are related, and a good teacher will find ways to highlight the connection of concepts across the curriculum. In choice B, the science teacher provides a way to help students study for a test. However, she would probably be better advised to work with the students on comprehension and retention before test time arrives. She could use a variety of previewing and reviewing skills, as well as creative ways to bring the information to life during class discussions and activities. This teacher might also benefit from discussing the situation with a language arts teacher to get ideas on how to build skills in reading for information, main ideas, and supporting concepts.

40. C: Because this student loves reading graphic novels and has both talent and enjoyment in drawing, having him create his own graphic novels is a good way to motivate him to write by using his visual style, ability, and interest to access writing activity. Giving audio recordings (A) to a highly visual student is not as appropriate to his strengths and interests. Letting him substitute drawing pictures for all writing assignments (B) would address his strengths and interests, but not his needs for learning to write. Having him watch animated videos about writing (D) would suit his visual learning style, but would not give him the actual writing practice he needs.

41. C: They meet to discuss areas the teacher is most concerned about and decide on the teacher's goals. In order to best achieve goals, those goals must be understood and established.

42. B: The word "brunch" is a blend of "breakfast" and "lunch". Blends of two or more words are known as portmanteau words. (*Portmanteau* is a French word meaning a suitcase.) "Fax" (A) is an example of clipping, or shortening a word, from its original "facsimile." "Babysitter" (C) is an example of compounding, or combining two or more words into one. "Saxophone" (D) is an example of proper noun transfer: A Belgian family that built musical instruments had the last name of Sax, and this wind instrument was named after them. These represent some of the ways that new words have entered—and still do enter—the English language.

43. A: Most traditional methods teach reading via aural and visual techniques. However, students with auditory processing problems or dyslexia will not learn to read effectively with these methods, no matter how much practice is provided. Therefore, most students with this type of difficulty will benefit from a multi-sensory technique in which they can make use of all their senses. Combined with systematic instruction and a great deal of practice, the multi-sensory technique is very effective in building reading and processing skills in students with this kind of life-long learning difference.

44. A: This is an example of formative assessment, which can be formal or informal but is more often informal; it is conducted during instruction to inform teachers of student progress and enable them to adjust instruction if it is not effective enough; this is done on an ongoing basis. Summative assessment (B) is typically formal; it is conducted after instruction to measure final results for grading, promotion, accountability, etc. and inform changes to future instruction, but does not enable adjusting the current instruction. Therefore, it is not an example of choices C or D.

45. D: Round-robin reading is a common practice in language arts classes and has been for many years. In this process, students take turns reading aloud for their peers. Other students are asked to follow along silently in their texts while a peer is reading. This strategy does provide a way for students to read texts in class and include as many students as possible, which is often the intended outcome. However, this process often creates a boring atmosphere, since only one student at a time is actively engaged. While that student is reading, other students may become distracted by their own thoughts, other school work, or off-task interaction with each another; all of these issues subvert the intended outcome of the process. There is rarely enough time for each student to practice reading aloud to build students' reading fluency or comprehension in significant ways.

46. A: After prewriting (planning, visualizing, brainstorming), the correct sequence of steps in the writing process are drafting, in which the writer takes the material generated during prewriting work and making it into sentences and paragraphs; revising, where the writer explores any changes in what one has written that would improve the quality of the writing; editing, in which the writer examines his or her writing for factual and mechanical (grammar, spelling, punctuation) errors and correcting them; and publishing, when the writer finally shares what he or she has written with others who will read it and give feedback.

47. B: The term "blend" is commonly used to refer to a grapheme consisting of two sounds, such as the /fl/ in *flip*. In this word, the /f/ and /l/ sounds are distinctly audible. However, the words from the question prompt contain phoneme combinations in which a completely new sound is formed.

The /ch/ sound is similar to neither the /c/ nor /h/. This type of combination is called a "digraph," which is a kind of blended sound.

48. C: One strategy is to draw polygons with fewer sides and look for a pattern in the number of the polygons' diagonals.

Polygon	Sides	Diagonals	Δ Diagonals
	3	0	-
	4	2	2
	5	5	3
	6	9	4

A quadrilateral has two more diagonals than a triangle, a pentagon has three more diagonals than a quadrilateral, and a hexagon has four more diagonals than a pentagon. Continue this pattern to find that a dodecagon has 54 diagonals.

49. D: When the dress is marked down by 20%, the cost of the dress is 80% of its original price; thus, the reduced price of the dress can be written as $\frac{80}{100}x$, or $\frac{4}{5}x$, where x is the original price. When discounted an extra 25%, the dress costs 75% of the reduced price, or $\frac{75}{100}\left(\frac{4}{5}x\right)$, or $\frac{3}{4}\left(\frac{4}{5}x\right)$, which simplifies to $\frac{3}{5}x$. So the final price of the dress is three-fifths of the original price.

50. C: Aaron ran four miles from home and then back again, so he ran a total of eight miles. Therefore, statement III is false. Statements I and II, however, are both true. Since Aaron ran eight miles in eighty minutes, he ran an average of one mile every ten minutes, or six miles per hour; he ran two miles from point A to B in 20 minutes and four miles from D to E in 40 minutes, so his running speed between both sets of points was the same.

51. D: Since a and b are even integers, each can be expressed as the product of 2 and an integer. So, if we write $a = 2x$ and $b = 2y$, $3(2x)^2 + 9(2y)^3 = c$.

$$3(4x^2) + 9(8y^3) = c$$
$$12x^2 + 72y^3 = c$$
$$12(x^2 + 6y^3) = c$$

Since c is the product of 12 and some other integer, 12 must be a factor of c. Incidentally, the numbers 2, 3, and 6 must also be factors of c since each is also a factor of 12.

52. B: Notice that choice C cannot be correct since $x \neq 1$. ($x = 1$ results in a zero in the denominator.)

$$\frac{x-2}{x-1} = \frac{x-1}{x+1} + \frac{2}{x-1}$$
$$\frac{x-4}{x-1} = \frac{x-1}{x+1}$$
$$(x+1)(x-4) = (x-1)(x-1)$$
$$x^2 - 3x - 4 = x^2 - 2x + 1$$
$$-5 = x$$

53. B: A cube has six square faces. The arrangement of these faces in a two-dimensional figure is a net of a cube if the figure can be folded to form a cube. Figures A, C, and D represent three of the eleven possible nets of a cube. If choice B is folded, however, the bottom square in the second column will overlap the fourth square in the top row, so the figure does not represent a net of a cube.

54. D: The point $(5, -5)$ lies on the line which has a slope of -2 and which passes through $(3, -1)$. If $(5, -5)$ is one of the endpoints of the line, the other would be $(1,3)$.

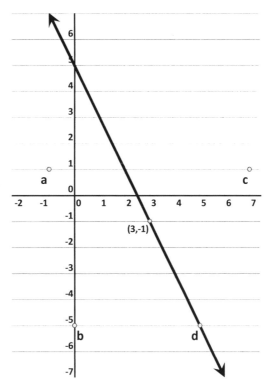

55. B: The manufacturer wishes to minimize the surface area A of the can while keeping its volume V fixed at 0.5 L = 500 mL = 500 cm^3. The formula for the surface area of a cylinder is $A = 2\pi rh + 2\pi r^2$, and the formula for volume is $V = \pi r^2 h$. To combine the two formulas into one, solve the volume formula for r or h and substitute the resulting expression into the surface area formula for r or h. The volume of the cylinder is 500 cm^3, so $500 = \pi r^2 h \rightarrow h = \frac{500}{\pi r^2}$. Therefore, $A = 2\pi rh + 2\pi r^2 \rightarrow 2\pi r\left(\frac{500}{\pi r^2}\right) + 2\pi r^2 = \frac{1000}{r} + 2\pi r^2$. Find the critical point(s) by setting the first derivative equal to zero and solving for r. Note that r represents the radius of the can and must therefore be a positive number.

$$A = 1000r^{-1} + 2\pi r^2$$
$$A' = -1000r^{-2} + 4\pi r$$
$$0 = -\frac{1000}{r^2} + 4\pi r$$
$$\frac{1000}{r^2} = 4\pi r$$
$$1000 = 4\pi r^3$$
$$\sqrt[3]{\frac{1000}{4\pi}} = r \approx 4.3 \text{ cm}$$

So, when $r \approx 4.3$ cm, the minimum surface area is obtained. When the radius of the can is 4.30 cm, its height is $h \approx \frac{500}{\pi(4.30)^2} \approx 8.6$ cm, and surface area is approximately $\frac{1000}{4.3} + 2\pi(4.3)^2 \approx 348.73$ cm^2. Confirm that the surface area is greater when the radius is slightly smaller or larger than 4.3 cm. For instance, when $r = 4$ cm, the surface area is approximately 350.5 cm^2, and when $r = 4.5$ cm, the surface area is approximately 349.5 cm^2.

56. C: When rolling two dice, there is only one way to roll a sum of two (rolling a 1 on each die) and twelve (rolling 6 on each die). In contrast, there are two ways to obtain a sum of three (rolling a 2 and 1 or a 1 and 2) and eleven (rolling a 5 and 6 or a 6 and 5), three ways to obtain a sum of four (1 and 3; 2 and 2; 3 and 1) or ten (4 and 6; 5 and 5; 6 and 4), and so on. Since the probability of obtaining each sum is inconsistent, choice C is not an appropriate simulation. Choice A is acceptable since the probability of picking A, 1, 2, 3, 4, 5, 6, 7, 8, 9, or J from the modified deck cards of cards is equally likely, each with a probability of $\frac{4}{52-8} = \frac{4}{44} = \frac{1}{11}$. Choice B is also acceptable since the computer randomly generates one number from eleven possible numbers, so the probability of generating any of the numbers is $\frac{1}{11}$.

57. A: If a number is divisible by 2 and 3, it is also divisible by the lowest common multiple of these two factors. The lowest common multiple of 2 and 3 is their product, 6.

58. C. The original price may be modeled by the equation:

$$(x - 0.45x) + 0.0875(x - 0.45x) = 39.95$$

which simplifies to $0.598125x = 39.95$. Dividing each side of the equation by the coefficient of x gives $x \approx 66.79$.

59. C: An inverse proportional relationship is written in the form $y = \frac{k}{x}$, thus the equation $y = \frac{3}{x}$ shows that y is inversely proportional to x.

60. C: Using the points $(-3, 1)$ and $(1, -11)$, the slope may be written as $m = \frac{-11-1}{1-(-3)}$ or $m = -3$. Substituting the slope of -3 and the x- and y-values from the point $(-3, 1)$, into the slope-intercept form of an equation gives $1 = -3(-3) + b$, which simplifies to $1 = 9 + b$. Subtracting 9 from both sides of the equation gives $b = -8$. Thus, the linear equation that includes the data in the table is $y = -3x - 8$.

61. A: The inequality will be less than or equal to, since he may spend $100 or less on his purchase.

62. C: The surface area of a sphere may be calculated using the formula $SA = 4\pi r^2$. Substituting 9 for r gives $SA = 4\pi(9)^2$, which simplifies to $SA \approx 1017.36$. So the surface area of the ball is approximately 1017.36 square inches. There are twelve inches in a foot, so there are $12^2 = 144$ square inches in a square foot. In order to convert this measurement to square feet, then, the following proportion may be written and solved for x: $\frac{1}{144} = \frac{x}{1017.36}$. So $x \approx 7.07$. He needs approximately 7.07 square feet of wrapping paper.

63. C: The original triangle was reflected across the x-axis. When reflecting across the x-axis, the x-values of each point remain the same, but the y-values of the points will be opposites.

$$(1,4) \rightarrow (1,-4), \qquad (5,4) \rightarrow (5,-4), \qquad (3,8) \rightarrow (3,-8)$$

64. B: The probability may be written as $P(E \text{ and } H) = P(E) \times P(H)$. Substituting the probability of each event gives $(E \text{ and } H) = \frac{1}{2} \times \frac{1}{2}$, which simplifies to $\frac{1}{4}$.

65. B: This is a formative assessment because she is assessing students while she is still teaching the unit. Summative assessments are given at the end of the unit. Formal assessments are usually a quizzes or tests. Informal assessments include asking individual students questions. Therefore, the correct choice is B.

66. A: Choice A is correct because standards for fourth grade state that students will be able to use a protractor to determine the approximate measures of angles in degrees to the nearest whole number. Choices B, C, and D are stated in the standards for fifth grade. Therefore, the correct choice is A.

67. B: Sophia needs to find multiples of 3 (3, 6, 9, 12, 15...) and multiples of 4 (4, 8, 12, 16,...) and find the least common multiple between them, which is 12. The greatest common divisor of 3 and 4 is 1. The least common divisor between two numbers is always 1. The greatest common multiple can never be determined. Therefore, the correct choice is B.

68. D: Number lines can help students understand the concepts of positive and negative numbers. Fraction strips are most commonly used with fractions. Venn diagrams are commonly used when comparing groups. Shaded regions are commonly used with fractions or percentages. Therefore, the correct choice is D.

69. C: The associative property of multiplication states that when three or more numbers are multiplied, the product is the same regardless of the way in which the numbers are grouped. Choice C shows that the product of 2, 3, and 4 is the same with two different groupings of the factors. Choice A demonstrates the distributive property. Choice B shows grouping, but the factors are different. Choice D demonstrates the commutative property of multiplication. Therefore, the correct choice is C.

70. B: The equation $y + 3 = 7$ is solved by subtracting 3 from both sides to yield $y = 4$.

Substituting $y = 4$ into $x - 1 = y$ yields $x - 1 = 4$. Adding 1 to both sides of this equation yields $x = 5$. Therefore, the correct choice is B.

71. C: Triangles can be classified as scalene, isosceles, or equilateral. Scalene triangles have no equal side measurements and no equal angle measurements. Isosceles triangles have two sides of equal measurement and two angles of equal measurement. Equilateral triangles have three sides of equal measurement and three angles of equal measurement. A right triangle is isosceles only if its two acute angles are congruent. Therefore, the correct choice is C.

72. C: The slope of a line can be found from any two points by the formula $slope = \frac{y_2 - y_1}{x_2 - x_1}$. A sketch of the point in choice C reveals a line with a negative slope. Substituting the last two points into the formula yields $slope = \frac{-3-1}{0-(-6)}$ which reduces to $\frac{-4}{6}$ or $\frac{-2}{3}$. The points in choice A form a line with a positive slope. The points in choice B form a line with a negative slope of $\frac{-3}{2}$. The points in choice D form a horizontal line. Therefore, the correct choice is C.

73. C: The mean is the average of the data and can be found by dividing the sum of the data by the number of data: $\frac{16 + 18 + 20 + 21 + 34 + 45 + 49}{7} = 29$. The median is the middle data point when the data are ranked numerically. The median is 21. Therefore, the correct choice is C.

74. C: The volume of a cylinder may be calculated using the formula $V = \pi r^2 h$, where r represents the radius and h represents the height. Substituting 1.5 for r and 3 for h gives $V = \pi(1.5)^2(3)$, which simplifies to $V \approx 21.2$.

75. B: The histogram only shows that there are eight trees between 70 and 75 feet tall. It does not show the individual heights of the trees. That information cannot be obtained from this graph. Therefore, the correct choice is B.

76. A: To a convert a percent to a fraction, remove the percent sign and place the number over 100. That means 15% can be written as $\frac{15}{100}$, which reduces to $\frac{3}{20}$. To covert a percent to a decimal, remove the percent sign and move the decimal two places to the left. To convert a percent to a ratio, first write the ratio as a fraction, and then rewrite the fraction as a ratio. Therefore, the correct choice is A.

77. C: The number 589 can be estimated to be 600. The number 9 can be estimated to be 10. The number of chicken nuggets is approximately 600×10, which is 6,000 nuggets. Therefore, the correct choice is C.

78. D: The total rainfall is 25.38 inches. Thus, the ratio $\frac{4.5}{25.38}$, represents the percentage of rainfall received during October. $\frac{4.5}{25.38} \approx 0.177$ or 17.7%.

79. D: The area of the square is equal to $(30)^2$, or 900 square centimeters. The area of the circle is equal to $\pi(15)^2$, or approximately 707 square centimeters. The area of the shaded region is equal to the difference of the area of the square and the area of the circle, or 900 cm^2 – 707 cm^2, which equals 193 cm^2. So, the area of the shaded region is about 193 cm^2.

80. B: The perimeter is equal to the sum of the lengths of the two bases, 2 and 6 units, and the diagonal distances of the other two sides. Using the distance formula, each side length may be represented as $d = \sqrt{20} = 2\sqrt{5}$. Thus, the sum of the two sides is equal to $2\sqrt{20}$, or $4\sqrt{5}$. The whole perimeter is equal to $8 + 4\sqrt{5}$.

81. C: The slope may be written as $m = \frac{4-0}{-3-(-4)}$, which simplifies to $m = 4$.

82. A: $A \cap B$ means "A intersect B," or the elements that are common to both sets. "A intersect B" represents "A and B," that is, an element is in the intersection of A and B if it is in A *and* it is in B. The elements 2, 5, and 8 are common to both sets.

83. C: To find the probability of an event, divide the number of favorable outcomes by the total number of outcomes. When there are two events in which the first depends on the second, multiply the first ratio by the second ratio. In the first part of the problem, the probability of choosing a licorice jelly bean is two out of twenty possible outcomes, or $\frac{2}{20}$. Then, because one jelly bean has already been chosen, there are four cinnamon beans out of a total of 19, or $\frac{4}{19}$. By multiplying the two ratios and dividing by a common denominator, one arrives at the final probability of $\frac{2}{95}$.

84. C: There are 36 months in 3 years. The following proportion may be written: $\frac{450}{3} = \frac{x}{36}$. The equation $3x = 16{,}200$, may be solved for x. Dividing both sides of the equation by 3 gives $x = 5{,}400$.

85. A: It is not true that England's defeat of the Spanish Armada in 1588 ended their war with Spain. It did establish England's naval dominance and strengthened England's future colonization of the New World, but the actual war between England and Spain did not end until 1604. It is true that Henry VIII's desire to divorce Catherine of Aragon strengthened English expansionism (B). Catherine was Spanish, and Henry split from the Catholic Church because it prohibited divorce. Henry's rejection of his Spanish wife and his subsequent support of the Protestant movement angered King Philip II of Spain and destroyed the formerly close ties between the two countries. When Elizabeth became Queen of England, she supported the Reformation as a Protestant, which also contributed to English colonization (C). Sir Francis Drake, one of the best known English sea captains during this time period, would attack and plunder Spanish ships that had plundered American Indians (D), adding to the enmity between Spain and England. Queen Elizabeth invested in Drake's voyages and gave him her support in claiming territories for England.

86. A: The latest occurring decolonization event was the Eastern Bloc and Soviet Satellite states of Armenia, Azerbaijan, Estonia, Georgia, Kazakhstan, Kyrgyzstan, Latvia, Lithuania, Moldova, Russia, Tajikistan, Turkmenistan, Ukraine, and Uzbekistan all became independent from the Soviet Union in 1991. (Note: This was the last decolonization of the Cold War years, as the end of the Soviet Union marked the end of the Cold War.) Canada completed its independence from British Parliament via the Canada Act (B) in 1982. In the Caribbean, the Bahamas gained independence from the United Kingdom (C) in 1973. Algeria won its independence from France when the Algerian War of Independence, begun in 1954, ended in 1962 (D). In Africa, Libya gained independence from Italy and became an independent kingdom in 1951.

87. A: The President has the authority to negotiate and sign treaties. A two-thirds vote of the Senate, however, is needed to ratify a treaty for it to be upheld.

88. C: Article III judges are appointed for life and can retire at 65. They can only be removed from their posts by impeachment in the House and conviction in the Senate. Having judges serve life terms is meant to allow them to serve without being governed by the changing opinions of the public.

89. B: "...endowed by their Creator with certain unalienable Rights," is excerpted from the Declaration of Independence. These rights are unable to be taken away from individuals, referring to the colonists' rights that Great Britain could not oppress.

90. D: It is not true that the Gilded Age is a term whose origins have not been identified clearly. In 1873, Mark Twain and Charles Dudley Warner co-authored a book entitled The Gilded Age: A Tale of Today. Twain and Warner first coined this term to describe the extravagance and excesses of America's wealthy upper class (B), who became richer than ever due to industrialization. Furthermore, the Gilded Age was the era of the "robber barons" (A) such as John D. Rockefeller, Cornelius Vanderbilt, J.P. Morgan, and others. Because they accumulated enormous wealth through extremely aggressive and occasionally unethical monetary manipulations, critics dubbed them "robber barons" because they seemed to be elite lords of robbery. While these business tycoons grasped huge fortunes, some of them—such as Andrew Carnegie and Andrew Mellon—were also philanthropists, using their wealth to support and further worthy causes such as literacy, education, health care, charities, and the arts. They donated millions of dollars to fund social improvements. Carnegie himself dubbed this large philanthropic movement the "Gospel of Wealth" (C). Another characteristic of the Gilded Age was the Beaux Arts architectural style, a neo-Renaissance style modeled after the great architectural designs of the European Renaissance. The Panic of 1893 ended the Gilded and began a severe four-year economic depression. The Progressive Era followed these events.

91. A: One example of the multiplier effect of large cities would be if the presence of specialized equipment for an industry attracted even more business. Large cities tend to grow even larger for a number of reasons: they have more skilled workers, they have greater concentrations of specialized equipment, and they have already-functioning markets. These factors all make it easier for a business to begin operations in a large city than elsewhere. Thus, the populations and economic productivity of large cities tend to grow quickly. Some governments have sought to mitigate this trend by clustering groups of similar industries in smaller cities.

92. D: Criminal cases are tried under both state law and federal law. The nature of the crime determines whether it is tried in state court or federal court.

93. D: The Louisiana Purchase actually increased the U.S.'s territory by 100% overnight, not 10%. The Louisiana territory doubled the size of the nation. It is true that Jefferson initially sent a delegation to Paris to see if Napoleon would agree to sell only New Orleans to the United States (A). It is also true that Napoleon, who expected America to encroach on Louisiana, decided to avoid this by offering to sell the entire territory to the U.S. (B). It is likewise true that America only had authority to buy New Orleans. Nevertheless, the delegation accepted Napoleon's offer of all of Louisiana (C). Due to his belief in a strict interpretation of the Constitution, Jefferson did require approval from Congress to make the purchase. When his advisors characterized the purchase as being within his purview based on the presidential power to make treaties, Congress agreed.

94. C: Mercantilism is the economic theory that nations advance the goal of accumulating capital by maintaining a balance of trade such that the value of exports exceeds that of imports. Great Britain maintained colonies to provide an inexpensive source of raw materials while creating markets for the goods manufactured in England. Under free trade, governments refrain from hindering the international exchange of goods and services. Nations that are granted most favored nation status are assured of enjoying equal advantages in international trade. A laissez-faire capitalist economy would theoretically be completely free of government regulation.

95. B: During the early Medieval period (or Middle Ages), Europe was characterized by widespread illiteracy, ignorance, and superstition once the unifying influence of the Roman Empire was lost. Few universities, like the university at Constantinople founded in 2 C.E. and those at Athens, Antioch, and Alexandria around the same time, existed then. Before the 5th and 6th centuries C.E., any education was conducted at cathedral or monastery schools or privately in the homes of wealthy families, which cannot be considered "main centers of literacy." More religious schools were created through Charlemagne's reforms in the 9th century, and early forms of universities began developing in the 11th and 12th centuries.

96. A: The Supreme Court interprets law and the Constitution. The inferior courts are bound to uphold the law as the Supreme Court interprets and rules on it.

97. B: Members of the House of Representatives are elected in proportion to the population of each state. Representation by senators is not based on population and is therefore skewed in electoral weight. The Electoral College can and has contradicted the popular vote in the Presidential election.

98. D: Federalists who helped frame the Constitution believed the central government needed to be stronger than what was established under the Articles of Confederation. Anti-federalists were against this and feared a strong federal government. A system of checks and balances was established to prevent the central government from taking too much power.

99. B: James Madison was a close friend of Thomas Jefferson and supported a stronger central government. George Mason and Robert Yates were both against expanding federal authority over the states. Benjamin Franklin was a proponent of a strong federal government, but he was from Massachusetts.

100. C: When a nation follows the theory of comparative advantage, it specializes in producing the goods and services it can make at a lower opportunity cost and then engages in trade to obtain other goods.

101. A: Presidents may veto legislation passed by both houses of Congress, and in turn, Congress can override a Presidential veto with a 2/3 majority. These governmental practices are a further manifestation that each branch of government is watched by the other branches and, when necessary, can undo a decision it deems ill-advised or unconstitutional.

102. B: The House has strict rules that limit debate. A filibuster can only occur in the Senate where Senators can speak on topics other than the bill at hand and introduce amendments. A filibuster can be ended by a supermajority vote of 60 Senators.

103. C: The President must be a natural citizen, be at least 35 years old, and have lived in the U.S. for 14 years. There is no education requirement for becoming President. Truman did not have a college education, but most Presidents have degrees.

104. C: A person who has taken out a fixed-rate loan can benefit from inflation by paying back the loan with dollars that are less valuable than they were when the loan was taken out. In the other examples, inflation harms the individual or entity.

105. B: Growth of industry was concentrated in urban areas, which cyclically drew laborers into cities, growing the population of cities and increasing efficiency and quality in industry.

106. B: Oligarchy is defined as the rule by few. An example is aristocracy, which in ancient Greece, was government by an elite group of citizens as opposed to a monarchy. In later times, it meant government by the class of aristocrats, a privileged group, as opposed to democracy. The rule of one is called autocracy. Examples include monarchy, dictatorship, and many others. The rule by law is called a republic. Some examples are constitutional republics, parliamentary republics, and federal republics. The rule by many could apply to democracy, which governs according to the people's votes or to the collective leadership form of socialism, where no one individual has too much power.

107. B: The Trail of Tears was the forcible removal of Native American tribes from their homes in the Southeastern US to Oklahoma. The name came due to the high number of Native Americans who died on the journey.

108. B: Tropical regions near the Equator tend to experience relatively constant temperatures year-round because the angle at which sunlight hits them remains relatively constant throughout the year. In regions that are farther north or south, the angle at which sunlight hits them changes much more drastically due to the changing angle of the Earth's axis relative to the Sun. This results in greater variations in the length of daylight and in temperatures. Tropical regions do have seasons (usually a "wet" season and a "dry" season), but temperature fluctuations are less pronounced than those in regions farther from the Equator.

109. B: In order to prosper, a nation should not try to increase its imports. Mercantilism is an economic theory including the idea that prosperity comes from a positive balance of international trade. For any one nation to prosper, that nation should increase its exports (C) but decrease its imports. Exporting more to other countries while importing less from them will give a country a positive trade balance. This theory assumes that money and wealth are identical (A) assets of a nation. In addition, this theory also assumes that the volume of global trade is an unchangeable quantity. Mercantilism dictates that a nation's government should apply a policy of economic protectionism (D) by stimulating more exports and suppressing imports. Some ways to accomplish this task have included granting subsidies for exports and imposing tariffs on imports. Mercantilism can be regarded as essentially the opposite of the free trade policies that have been encouraged in more recent years.

110. C: Copernicus's De Revolutionibus orbium coelestium (On the Revolutions of the Heavenly Spheres) was published in 1543, almost simultaneously with his death. He was the first to contradict the then-accepted belief that the Earth was the center of the universe and the Sun and other bodies moved around it. This geocentric model was associated with Ptolemy and hence called the Ptolemaic system. Galileo Galilei published Siderius Nuncius (Starry Messenger) in 1610. In it, he revealed his observations, made through his improvements to the telescope, which corroborated Copernicus's theory. Sir Isaac Newton (1642–1727) built the first usable reflecting telescope and erased any lingering doubts about a heliocentric universe by describing universal gravitation and showing its congruence with Kepler's laws of planetary motion.

111. B: Members of the House are elected for two-year terms. Senators serve six-year terms, but the elections are staggered so roughly one-third of the Senate is elected every two years.

112. A: A city located at 6,000 feet above sea level is likely to have a cooler climate, all other things being equal. Since air is less dense at higher altitudes, it holds heat less effectively and temperatures tend to be lower as a result. Precipitation is not as strong an indicator of temperature. Some areas that receive moderate or large amounts of precipitation are cooler (temperate and continental climates), while some areas that receive lots of precipitation, like the tropics, are warmer.

113. D: Niccolò Machiavelli, perhaps best known for his book The Prince, was an Italian Renaissance political philosopher noted for writing more realistic representations and rational interpretations of politics. In The Prince, he popularized the political concept of "the ends justify the means." Dante Alighieri was a great poet famous for his Commedia (additionally labeled Divina by contemporary poet and author Bocaccio, who wrote the Decameron and other works) or Divine

Comedy, a trilogy consisting of Inferno, Purgatorio, and Paradiso (Hell, Purgatory, and Heaven). Dante's work helped propel the transition from the Medieval period to the Renaissance. Francesco Petrarca, known in English as Petrarch, was famous for his lyrical poetry, particularly sonnets.

114. A: A good hypothesis is testable and logical, and can be used to predict future events. A good hypothesis is also simple, not complex. Therefore, the correct choice is A.

115. A: They will be refracted and converge. When light waves hit a convex lens they are refracted and converge. A convex lens curves or bulges with the middle being thicker and the edges thinner. A magnifying glass is an example. Light rays are refracted by different amounts as they pass through the lens. After light rays pass through, they converge at a point called the focus. An object viewed with a magnifying glass looks bigger because the lens bends the rays inwards. Choice B would indicate a concave lens as it would cause the light to be refracted and diverge. Light is not reflected in this case, so neither choice C nor D would be applicable.

116. D: Circulatory System – exchanges gasses with the environment by delivering oxygen to the bloodstream and releasing carbon dioxide, is not paired correctly. It is the respiratory system that exchanges gasses with the environment by delivering oxygen to the bloodstream and releasing carbon dioxide. The circulatory system transports nutrients, gasses, hormones, and blood to and away from cells. The muscle system controls movement through three types of muscle tissue. The nervous system controls sensory responses by carrying impulses away from and toward the cell body. The digestive system breaks down food for absorption into the blood stream where it is delivered to cells for respiration.

117. A: The addition of energy causes a phase change. Phase changes are physical changes, not chemical changes. While sublimation is an example of a phase change, it occurs when a solid turns directly into a gas without passing through the liquid state. Condensation, another phase change, occurs when a gas turns to liquid.

118. A: Dispose of the solutions according to local disposal procedures. Solutions and compounds used in labs may be hazardous according to state and local regulatory agencies and should be treated with such precaution. Emptying the solutions into the sink and rinsing with warm water and soap does not take into account the hazards associated with a specific solution in terms of vapors or interactions with water, soap, and waste piping systems. Ensuring the solutions are secured in closed containers and throwing them away may allow toxic chemicals into landfills and subsequently into fresh water systems. Storing the solutions in a secured, dry place for later use is incorrect as chemicals should not be re-used due to the possibility of contamination.

119. D: The atomic number is equal to the number of electrons. An atom has a neutral charge if its atomic number is equal to its number of electrons. The atomic number (Z) of an element refers to the number of protons in the nucleus. If an atom has fewer or more electrons than its atomic number, then it will be positively or negatively charged, respectively. Cations are positively charged ions; anions are negatively charged ones. Choices A and B both describe a nucleus containing only neutrons with no protons. An element of this nature is referred to as neutronium but is theoretical only.

120. C: Transform. Transform is not connected to the process of mountain building. Orogeny, or mountain building, occurs at the Earth's lithosphere or crust. Folding, or deformation, is a process that occurs to make mountains where two portions of the lithosphere collide. One is subducted and the other is pushed upward forming a mountain. This action produces various types of folding. Faulting can be characterized by a brittle deformation where the rock breaks abruptly (compared with folding). Faulting and fault types are associated with earthquakes and relatively rapid deformation. Convergent is a more general term used to describe plates interacting.

121. A: Repeating a measurement several times can increase the accuracy of the measurement. Calibrating the equipment (B) will increase the precision of the measurement. None of the other choices are useful strategies to increase the accuracy of a measurement.

122. B: Refractive Index. The refractive index is an optical property which is not related to the organization of the periodic table. Elements on the periodic table are arranged into periods, or rows, according to atomic number, which is the number of protons in the nucleus. The periodic table illustrates the recurrence of properties. Each column, or group, contains elements that share similar properties, such as reactivity.

123. C: The pressure decreases to one-third. A gas in a closed container at constant temperature will decrease in pressure to one-third when the volume of the container is tripled. The ideal gas law is $PV = nRT$ where P is pressure, V is volume, n is the moles of the gas, R is the gas constant and T is temperature. A variation to solve for pressure is:

$$P = nRT/V$$

Boyle's Law indicates that pressure and volume are inversely proportional. The pressure cannot be increased because that would imply that pressure and volume are directly proportional.

124. C: Laccolith. A laccolith is formed when an intrusion of magma injected between two layers of sedimentary rock forces the overlying strata upward to create a dome-like form. Eventually, the magma cools, the sedimentary rock wears away and the formation is exposed. Sills and dikes are both examples of sheet intrusions, where magma has inserted itself into other rock. Sills are horizontal and dikes are vertical. A caldera is a crater-like feature that was formed from the collapse of a volcano after erupting.

125. C: For an experiment to be considered successful, it must yield data that others can reproduce. Choice A may be considered part of a well-designed experiment. Choices B and D may be considered part of an experiment that is reported on by individuals with expertise.

126. C: Heat transfer can never occur from a cooler object to a warmer object. While the second law of thermodynamics implies that heat never spontaneously transfers from a cooler object to a warmer object, it is possible for heat to be transferred to a warmer object, given the proper input of work to the system. This is the principle by which a refrigerator operates. Work is done to the system to transfer heat from the objects inside the refrigerator to the air surrounding the refrigerator. All other answer choices are true.

127. B: Light travels faster in air than it does in water. When the light travels from the wallet to the man, it will bend as it exits the water. The bending of light is called refraction and creates the illusion of the wallet being next to where it actually is.

128. C: The closer the data points are to each other, the more precise the data. This does not mean the data is accurate, but that the results are very reproducible.

129. D: The most recently formed parts of the Earth's crust can be found at mid-ocean ridges. New crust forms here when magma erupts from these ridges and pushes pre-existing crust horizontally towards the continental plates. Such ridges include the Mid-Atlantic Ridge and the East Pacific Rise.

130. A: Fission. Fission is a nuclear process where atomic nuclei split apart to form smaller nuclei. Nuclear fission can release large amounts of energy, emit gamma rays and form daughter products. It is used in nuclear power plants and bombs. Answer B, Fusion, refers to a nuclear process whereby atomic nuclei join to form a heavier nucleus, such as with stars. This can release or absorb energy depending upon the original elements. Answer C, Decay, refers to an atomic nucleus spontaneously losing energy and emitting ionizing particles and radiation. Answer D, Ionization, refers to a process by which atoms obtain a positive or negative charge because the number of electrons does not equal that of protons.

131. C: The vapor pressure decreases by an amount proportional to the amount of solute. Raoult's law states that the vapor pressure of a solution containing a non-volatile solute is equal to the vapor pressure of the volatile solvent multiplied by its mole fraction, which is basically the proportion of the solution that is made up by solvent. In a liquid, some of the surface particles have higher than average energy and can break away to become a gas, or evaporate. The pressure of this gas right above the surface of the liquid is called the vapor pressure. Increasing the amount of solute in a liquid decreases the number of solvent particles at the surface. Because of this, fewer solvent molecules are able to escape, thus lowering the vapor pressure.

132. A: The prevailing westerlies. The prevailing westerlies drive weather systems to move west to east in the mid-latitudes. The direction refers to that which the wind is coming from. The polar easterlies that travel from the northeast occur between 90-60 degrees north latitude. The ones from the southeast are between 90-60 degrees south latitude. The trade winds refer to those occurring near the equator in the tropics moving east. The doldrums are also in the tropics but refer to an area of low-pressure where frequently the winds are light and unpredictable.

133. A: Many organisms, especially organisms that live in harsh conditions such as deserts or frozen icy areas, have developed specific adaptations that allow them to survive. For example, cacti are able to expand to store large amounts of water, coyotes absorb some water from their food, and snakes can escape the heat by hiding within rocks.

134. D: Mario balances a book on his head. In this example, work is not applied to the book because the book is not moving. One definition of work is a force acting on an object to cause displacement. In this case, the book was not displaced by the force applied to it. Mario's head applied a vertical force to the book to keep it in the same position.

135. D: Reproductive habits. Reproductive habits would not be considered evidence for evolution. Usually, how a species reproduces does not support nor add to the body of evidence for the theory of evolution. Reproduction habits might exemplify how any given organism can adapt to changes in its environment as a way to survive. This does not necessarily show evolution. Fossil record is evidence for evolution as it shows evolutionary change of organisms over time. DNA sequences show that organisms that are related evolutionarily also have related gene sequences. Anatomical structures such as having an internal bony structure provide evidence of descent from a common ancestor.

136. A: Glass. Glass is considered a non-renewable resource. Glass is manufactured and can be recycled, but is considered a non-renewable resource. Wood is considered a renewable resource because with proper management, an equilibrium can be reached between harvesting trees and planting new ones. Cattle are managed in herds and a balance can be achieved between those consumed and those born. Soil is the result of long-term erosion and includes organic matter and minerals needed by plants. Soil found naturally in the environment is renewed. Crops can be rotated to help maintain a healthy soil composition for farming.

137. A: The stream of charged particles that escape the Sun's gravitational pull is called solar wind. Solar wind is comprised primarily of protons and electrons, and these particles are deflected away from the Earth by its magnetic field. When stray particles do manage to enter the atmosphere, they cause the aurorae (Northern and Southern Lights) and geomagnetic storms that can affect power grids.

138. B: Voltage and current are directly proportional to one another. Ohm's Law states that voltage and current in an electrical circuit are directly proportional to one another. Ohm's Law can be expressed as V=IR, where V is voltage, I is current and R is resistance. Voltage is also known as electrical potential difference and is the force that moves electrons through a circuit. For a given amount of resistance, an increase in voltage will result in an increase in current. Resistance and current are inversely proportional to each other. For a given voltage, an increase in resistance will result in a decrease in current.

139. C: Flowers. Flowers are the reproductive organs of a plant. Flowering plants reproduce by sexual reproduction where the gametes join to form seeds. Pollen is sperm. Pollinators help transfer the sperm to the ovule, the egg. The style is the part of the female reproduction system that transports the sperm between the stigma and the ovary, all part of the pistil. The stigma is the sticky tip of the style on which the pollen lands. Sepals are usually small leaves between or underneath the petals and are not as obvious or as large and colorful as the petals.

140. B: Work is defined as the force used to move a mass over a distance. Choice A may be a secular (non-scientific) definition of work. Choice C is the definition of power. Choice D is the definition of potential energy.

141. D: Endocytosis is a process by which cells absorb larger molecules or even tiny organisms, such as bacteria, that would not be able to pass through the plasma membrane. Endocytic vesicles containing molecules from the extracellular environment often undergo further processing once they enter the cell.

142. B: Dimension, texture, and space are all *elements* of art, while unity is one of the *principles* of art. Unity in artwork is achieved when an artist's use of the elements produces a sense of wholeness or completeness in the finished product.

143. A: Drybrush is a technique that is primarily used in watercolor painting. It involves using a fine, nearly dry brush that is dipped in undiluted watercolor paint. It is used to create precise brushstrokes—an effect that is otherwise very difficult to achieve in this medium.

144. A: A social studies lesson on political propaganda could be incorporated into an art class by asking students to evaluate political propaganda posters or create their own. Although the other lessons could possibly be incorporated, such an endeavor would not be particularly useful.

145. B: Because they lack a tonal center. For example, diminished triads consisting of a root, a minor third, and a diminished fifth symmetrically divide the octave. Choice A is incorrect since diminished chords do not necessarily sound "sad" depending on their placement in the chord progression (minor chords typically are considered "sad," anyway). Choice C, they are barely audible, is incorrect, as the word "diminished" refers to the state of the fifth and not the volume of the chord, which can be played at any volume. Finally, Choice D is incorrect, as diminished chords have been used throughout musical history in many famous works.

146. C: Value is the term that refers to the relative lightness or darkness of the colors in a painting. Intensity relates the vibrancy of colors in a painting; high-intensity colors are pure, while low-intensity colors are mixed with other colors to suggest a somber mood. A color's hue refers to the actual pigmentation (red, blue, green, or yellow). Texture is a tactile quality of an artwork's surface, rather than a property of color.

147. B: Line is the artistic element most commonly used to create the illusion of depth in a painting. For instance, an artist could use line to convey depth by incorporating an object, such as a road, that stretches from the foreground to the background of a painting. Balance is a principle of art that involves creating an impression of stability in a work; contrast and symmetry would not function to create the illusion of depth.

148. B: The activity, Musical hoops, is played like musical chairs, except children must jump into hoops instead of sitting on chairs when the music stops. This is appropriate for younger children. Freeze tag or blob tag (A) is more appropriate for children older than 5 years, up to 12 years old. Children must try to tag others while holding hands with those in their blob. This demands higher levels of coordination than younger children have. Follow the leader (C) is better as a warm-up activity for children age 5 to 12 years, as younger children can have difficulty with leading and following and with the variations in leaders and locomotor skills that teachers can use with older children. Therefore, choice D is incorrect.

149. A: Unsafe water is a risk factor for many diseases, but not for all four types of diseases listed. Drinking alcohol (B), poor nutrition (C), and smoking tobacco (D) are all risk factors shared in common by all four types of illnesses that cause the majority of deaths from noncommunicable diseases.

150. A: The advantage of drawing with charcoal as opposed to lead pencils is that charcoal can be smudged to create shading. Because of its loose, chalky texture, charcoal requires a fixative, unlike lead pencil. Neither pencils nor charcoal is available in different hues, but both can be purchased in a range of values.

How to Overcome Test Anxiety

Just the thought of taking a test is enough to make most people a little nervous. A test is an important event that can have a long-term impact on your future, so it's important to take it seriously and it's natural to feel anxious about performing well. But just because anxiety is normal, that doesn't mean that it's helpful in test taking, or that you should simply accept it as part of your life. Anxiety can have a variety of effects. These effects can be mild, like making you feel slightly nervous, or severe, like blocking your ability to focus or remember even a simple detail.

If you experience test anxiety—whether severe or mild—it's important to know how to beat it. To discover this, first you need to understand what causes test anxiety.

Causes of Test Anxiety

While we often think of anxiety as an uncontrollable emotional state, it can actually be caused by simple, practical things. One of the most common causes of test anxiety is that a person does not feel adequately prepared for their test. This feeling can be the result of many different issues such as poor study habits or lack of organization, but the most common culprit is time management. Starting to study too late, failing to organize your study time to cover all of the material, or being distracted while you study will mean that you're not well prepared for the test. This may lead to cramming the night before, which will cause you to be physically and mentally exhausted for the test. Poor time management also contributes to feelings of stress, fear, and hopelessness as you realize you are not well prepared but don't know what to do about it.

Other times, test anxiety is not related to your preparation for the test but comes from unresolved fear. This may be a past failure on a test, or poor performance on tests in general. It may come from comparing yourself to others who seem to be performing better or from the stress of living up to expectations. Anxiety may be driven by fears of the future—how failure on this test would affect your educational and career goals. These fears are often completely irrational, but they can still negatively impact your test performance.

Review Video: 3 Reasons You Have Test Anxiety
Visit mometrix.com/academy and enter code: 428468

Elements of Test Anxiety

As mentioned earlier, test anxiety is considered to be an emotional state, but it has physical and mental components as well. Sometimes you may not even realize that you are suffering from test anxiety until you notice the physical symptoms. These can include trembling hands, rapid heartbeat, sweating, nausea, and tense muscles. Extreme anxiety may lead to fainting or vomiting. Obviously, any of these symptoms can have a negative impact on testing. It is important to recognize them as soon as they begin to occur so that you can address the problem before it damages your performance.

Review Video: 3 Ways to Tell You Have Test Anxiety
Visit mometrix.com/academy and enter code: 927847

The mental components of test anxiety include trouble focusing and inability to remember learned information. During a test, your mind is on high alert, which can help you recall information and stay focused for an extended period of time. However, anxiety interferes with your mind's natural processes, causing you to blank out, even on the questions you know well. The strain of testing during anxiety makes it difficult to stay focused, especially on a test that may take several hours. Extreme anxiety can take a huge mental toll, making it difficult not only to recall test information but even to understand the test questions or pull your thoughts together.

Review Video: How Test Anxiety Affects Memory
Visit mometrix.com/academy and enter code: 609003

Effects of Test Anxiety

Test anxiety is like a disease—if left untreated, it will get progressively worse. Anxiety leads to poor performance, and this reinforces the feelings of fear and failure, which in turn lead to poor performances on subsequent tests. It can grow from a mild nervousness to a crippling condition. If allowed to progress, test anxiety can have a big impact on your schooling, and consequently on your future.

Test anxiety can spread to other parts of your life. Anxiety on tests can become anxiety in any stressful situation, and blanking on a test can turn into panicking in a job situation. But fortunately, you don't have to let anxiety rule your testing and determine your grades. There are a number of relatively simple steps you can take to move past anxiety and function normally on a test and in the rest of life.

Review Video: How Test Anxiety Impacts Your Grades
Visit mometrix.com/academy and enter code: 939819

Physical Steps for Beating Test Anxiety

While test anxiety is a serious problem, the good news is that it can be overcome. It doesn't have to control your ability to think and remember information. While it may take time, you can begin taking steps today to beat anxiety.

Just as your first hint that you may be struggling with anxiety comes from the physical symptoms, the first step to treating it is also physical. Rest is crucial for having a clear, strong mind. If you are tired, it is much easier to give in to anxiety. But if you establish good sleep habits, your body and mind will be ready to perform optimally, without the strain of exhaustion. Additionally, sleeping well helps you to retain information better, so you're more likely to recall the answers when you see the test questions.

Getting good sleep means more than going to bed on time. It's important to allow your brain time to relax. Take study breaks from time to time so it doesn't get overworked, and don't study right before bed. Take time to rest your mind before trying to rest your body, or you may find it difficult to fall asleep.

Review Video: The Importance of Sleep for Your Brain
Visit mometrix.com/academy and enter code: 319338

Along with sleep, other aspects of physical health are important in preparing for a test. Good nutrition is vital for good brain function. Sugary foods and drinks may give a burst of energy but this burst is followed by a crash, both physically and emotionally. Instead, fuel your body with protein and vitamin-rich foods.

Also, drink plenty of water. Dehydration can lead to headaches and exhaustion, especially if your brain is already under stress from the rigors of the test. Particularly if your test is a long one, drink water during the breaks. And if possible, take an energy-boosting snack to eat between sections.

Review Video: How Diet Can Affect your Mood
Visit mometrix.com/academy and enter code: 624317

Along with sleep and diet, a third important part of physical health is exercise. Maintaining a steady workout schedule is helpful, but even taking 5-minute study breaks to walk can help get your blood pumping faster and clear your head. Exercise also releases endorphins, which contribute to a positive feeling and can help combat test anxiety.

When you nurture your physical health, you are also contributing to your mental health. If your body is healthy, your mind is much more likely to be healthy as well. So take time to rest, nourish your body with healthy food and water, and get moving as much as possible. Taking these physical steps will make you stronger and more able to take the mental steps necessary to overcome test anxiety.

Review Video: How to Stay Healthy and Prevent Test Anxiety
Visit mometrix.com/academy and enter code: 877894

Mental Steps for Beating Test Anxiety

Working on the mental side of test anxiety can be more challenging, but as with the physical side, there are clear steps you can take to overcome it. As mentioned earlier, test anxiety often stems from lack of preparation, so the obvious solution is to prepare for the test. Effective studying may be the most important weapon you have for beating test anxiety, but you can and should employ several other mental tools to combat fear.

First, boost your confidence by reminding yourself of past success—tests or projects that you aced. If you're putting as much effort into preparing for this test as you did for those, there's no reason you should expect to fail here. Work hard to prepare; then trust your preparation.

Second, surround yourself with encouraging people. It can be helpful to find a study group, but be sure that the people you're around will encourage a positive attitude. If you spend time with others who are anxious or cynical, this will only contribute to your own anxiety. Look for others who are motivated to study hard from a desire to succeed, not from a fear of failure.

Third, reward yourself. A test is physically and mentally tiring, even without anxiety, and it can be helpful to have something to look forward to. Plan an activity following the test, regardless of the outcome, such as going to a movie or getting ice cream.

When you are taking the test, if you find yourself beginning to feel anxious, remind yourself that you know the material. Visualize successfully completing the test. Then take a few deep, relaxing breaths and return to it. Work through the questions carefully but with confidence, knowing that you are capable of succeeding.

Developing a healthy mental approach to test taking will also aid in other areas of life. Test anxiety affects more than just the actual test—it can be damaging to your mental health and even contribute to depression. It's important to beat test anxiety before it becomes a problem for more than testing.

Review Video: <u>Test Anxiety and Depression</u>
Visit mometrix.com/academy and enter code: 904704

Study Strategy

Being prepared for the test is necessary to combat anxiety, but what does being prepared look like? You may study for hours on end and still not feel prepared. What you need is a strategy for test prep. The next few pages outline our recommended steps to help you plan out and conquer the challenge of preparation.

STEP 1: SCOPE OUT THE TEST

Learn everything you can about the format (multiple choice, essay, etc.) and what will be on the test. Gather any study materials, course outlines, or sample exams that may be available. Not only will this help you to prepare, but knowing what to expect can help to alleviate test anxiety.

STEP 2: MAP OUT THE MATERIAL

Look through the textbook or study guide and make note of how many chapters or sections it has. Then divide these over the time you have. For example, if a book has 15 chapters and you have five days to study, you need to cover three chapters each day. Even better, if you have the time, leave an extra day at the end for overall review after you have gone through the material in depth.

If time is limited, you may need to prioritize the material. Look through it and make note of which sections you think you already have a good grasp on, and which need review. While you are studying, skim quickly through the familiar sections and take more time on the challenging parts. Write out your plan so you don't get lost as you go. Having a written plan also helps you feel more in control of the study, so anxiety is less likely to arise from feeling overwhelmed at the amount to cover.

STEP 3: GATHER YOUR TOOLS

Decide what study method works best for you. Do you prefer to highlight in the book as you study and then go back over the highlighted portions? Or do you type out notes of the important information? Or is it helpful to make flashcards that you can carry with you? Assemble the pens, index cards, highlighters, post-it notes, and any other materials you may need so you won't be distracted by getting up to find things while you study.

If you're having a hard time retaining the information or organizing your notes, experiment with different methods. For example, try color-coding by subject with colored pens, highlighters, or post-it notes. If you learn better by hearing, try recording yourself reading your notes so you can listen while in the car, working out, or simply sitting at your desk. Ask a friend to quiz you from your flashcards, or try teaching someone the material to solidify it in your mind.

STEP 4: CREATE YOUR ENVIRONMENT

It's important to avoid distractions while you study. This includes both the obvious distractions like visitors and the subtle distractions like an uncomfortable chair (or a too-comfortable couch that makes you want to fall asleep). Set up the best study environment possible: good lighting and a comfortable work area. If background music helps you focus, you may want to turn it on, but otherwise keep the room quiet. If you are using a computer to take notes, be sure you don't have any other windows open, especially applications like social media, games, or anything else that could distract you. Silence your phone and turn off notifications. Be sure to keep water close by so you stay hydrated while you study (but avoid unhealthy drinks and snacks).

Also, take into account the best time of day to study. Are you freshest first thing in the morning? Try to set aside some time then to work through the material. Is your mind clearer in the afternoon or evening? Schedule your study session then. Another method is to study at the same time of day that you will take the test, so that your brain gets used to working on the material at that time and will be ready to focus at test time.

STEP 5: STUDY!

Once you have done all the study preparation, it's time to settle into the actual studying. Sit down, take a few moments to settle your mind so you can focus, and begin to follow your study plan. Don't give in to distractions or let yourself procrastinate. This is your time to prepare so you'll be ready to fearlessly approach the test. Make the most of the time and stay focused.

Of course, you don't want to burn out. If you study too long you may find that you're not retaining the information very well. Take regular study breaks. For example, taking five minutes out of every hour to walk briskly, breathing deeply and swinging your arms, can help your mind stay fresh.

As you get to the end of each chapter or section, it's a good idea to do a quick review. Remind yourself of what you learned and work on any difficult parts. When you feel that you've mastered the material, move on to the next part. At the end of your study session, briefly skim through your notes again.

But while review is helpful, cramming last minute is NOT. If at all possible, work ahead so that you won't need to fit all your study into the last day. Cramming overloads your brain with more information than it can process and retain, and your tired mind may struggle to recall even previously learned information when it is overwhelmed with last-minute study. Also, the urgent nature of cramming and the stress placed on your brain contribute to anxiety. You'll be more likely to go to the test feeling unprepared and having trouble thinking clearly.

So don't cram, and don't stay up late before the test, even just to review your notes at a leisurely pace. Your brain needs rest more than it needs to go over the information again. In fact, plan to finish your studies by noon or early afternoon the day before the test. Give your brain the rest of the day to relax or focus on other things, and get a good night's sleep. Then you will be fresh for the test and better able to recall what you've studied.

STEP 6: TAKE A PRACTICE TEST

Many courses offer sample tests, either online or in the study materials. This is an excellent resource to check whether you have mastered the material, as well as to prepare for the test format and environment.

Check the test format ahead of time: the number of questions, the type (multiple choice, free response, etc.), and the time limit. Then create a plan for working through them. For example, if you have 30 minutes to take a 60-question test, your limit is 30 seconds per question. Spend less time on the questions you know well so that you can take more time on the difficult ones.

If you have time to take several practice tests, take the first one open book, with no time limit. Work through the questions at your own pace and make sure you fully understand them. Gradually work up to taking a test under test conditions: sit at a desk with all study materials put away and set a timer. Pace yourself to make sure you finish the test with time to spare and go back to check your answers if you have time.

After each test, check your answers. On the questions you missed, be sure you understand why you missed them. Did you misread the question (tests can use tricky wording)? Did you forget the information? Or was it something you hadn't learned? Go back and study any shaky areas that the practice tests reveal.

Taking these tests not only helps with your grade, but also aids in combating test anxiety. If you're already used to the test conditions, you're less likely to worry about it, and working through tests until you're scoring well gives you a confidence boost. Go through the practice tests until you feel comfortable, and then you can go into the test knowing that you're ready for it.

Test Tips

On test day, you should be confident, knowing that you've prepared well and are ready to answer the questions. But aside from preparation, there are several test day strategies you can employ to maximize your performance.

First, as stated before, get a good night's sleep the night before the test (and for several nights before that, if possible). Go into the test with a fresh, alert mind rather than staying up late to study.

Try not to change too much about your normal routine on the day of the test. It's important to eat a nutritious breakfast, but if you normally don't eat breakfast at all, consider eating just a protein bar. If you're a coffee drinker, go ahead and have your normal coffee. Just make sure you time it so that the caffeine doesn't wear off right in the middle of your test. Avoid sugary beverages, and drink enough water to stay hydrated but not so much that you need a restroom break 10 minutes into the test. If your test isn't first thing in the morning, consider going for a walk or doing a light workout before the test to get your blood flowing.

Allow yourself enough time to get ready, and leave for the test with plenty of time to spare so you won't have the anxiety of scrambling to arrive in time. Another reason to be early is to select a good seat. It's helpful to sit away from doors and windows, which can be distracting. Find a good seat, get out your supplies, and settle your mind before the test begins.

When the test begins, start by going over the instructions carefully, even if you already know what to expect. Make sure you avoid any careless mistakes by following the directions.

Then begin working through the questions, pacing yourself as you've practiced. If you're not sure on an answer, don't spend too much time on it, and don't let it shake your confidence. Either skip it and come back later, or eliminate as many wrong answers as possible and guess among the remaining ones. Don't dwell on these questions as you continue—put them out of your mind and focus on what lies ahead.

Be sure to read all of the answer choices, even if you're sure the first one is the right answer. Sometimes you'll find a better one if you keep reading. But don't second-guess yourself if you do immediately know the answer. Your gut instinct is usually right. Don't let test anxiety rob you of the information you know.

If you have time at the end of the test (and if the test format allows), go back and review your answers. Be cautious about changing any, since your first instinct tends to be correct, but make sure you didn't misread any of the questions or accidentally mark the wrong answer choice. Look over any you skipped and make an educated guess.

At the end, leave the test feeling confident. You've done your best, so don't waste time worrying about your performance or wishing you could change anything. Instead, celebrate the successful

completion of this test. And finally, use this test to learn how to deal with anxiety even better next time.

Important Qualification

Not all anxiety is created equal. If your test anxiety is causing major issues in your life beyond the classroom or testing center, or if you are experiencing troubling physical symptoms related to your anxiety, it may be a sign of a serious physiological or psychological condition. If this sounds like your situation, we strongly encourage you to seek professional help.

How to Overcome Your Fear of Math

The word *math* is enough to strike fear into most hearts. How many of us have memories of sitting through confusing lectures, wrestling over mind-numbing homework, or taking tests that still seem incomprehensible even after hours of study? Years after graduation, many still shudder at these memories.

The fact is, math is not just a classroom subject. It has real-world implications that you face every day, whether you realize it or not. This may be balancing your monthly budget, deciding how many supplies to buy for a project, or simply splitting a meal check with friends. The idea of daily confrontations with math can be so paralyzing that some develop a condition known as *math anxiety*.

But you do NOT need to be paralyzed by this anxiety! In fact, while you may have thought all your life that you're not good at math, or that your brain isn't wired to understand it, the truth is that you may have been conditioned to think this way. From your earliest school days, the way you were taught affected the way you viewed different subjects. And the way math has been taught has changed.

Several decades ago, there was a shift in American math classrooms. The focus changed from traditional problem-solving to a conceptual view of topics, de-emphasizing the importance of learning the basics and building on them. The solid foundation necessary for math progression and confidence was undermined. Math became more of a vague concept than a concrete idea. Today, it is common to think of math, not as a straightforward system, but as a mysterious, complicated method that can't be fully understood unless you're a genius.

This is why you may still have nightmares about being called on to answer a difficult problem in front of the class. Math anxiety is a very real, though unnecessary, fear.

Math anxiety may begin with a single class period. Let's say you missed a day in 6th grade math and never quite understood the concept that was taught while you were gone. Since math is cumulative, with each new concept building on past ones, this could very well affect the rest of your math career. Without that one day's knowledge, it will be difficult to understand any other concepts that link to it. Rather than realizing that you're just missing one key piece, you may begin to believe that you're simply not capable of understanding math.

This belief can change the way you approach other classes, career options, and everyday life experiences, if you become anxious at the thought that math might be required. A student who loves science may choose a different path of study upon realizing that multiple math classes will be required for a degree. An aspiring medical student may hesitate at the thought of going through the necessary math classes. For some this anxiety escalates into a more extreme state known as *math phobia*.

Math anxiety is challenging to address because it is rooted deeply and may come from a variety of causes: an embarrassing moment in class, a teacher who did not explain concepts well and contributed to a shaky foundation, or a failed test that contributed to the belief of math failure.

These causes add up over time, encouraged by society's popular view that math is hard and unpleasant. Eventually a person comes to firmly believe that he or she is simply bad at math. This belief makes it difficult to grasp new concepts or even remember old ones. Homework and test grades begin to slip, which only confirms the belief. The poor performance is not due to lack of ability but is caused by math anxiety.

Math anxiety is an emotional issue, not a lack of intelligence. But when it becomes deeply rooted, it can become more than just an emotional problem. Physical symptoms appear. Blood pressure may rise and heartbeat may quicken at the sight of a math problem – or even the thought of math! This fear leads to a mental block. When someone with math anxiety is asked to perform a calculation, even a basic problem can seem overwhelming and impossible. The emotional and physical response to the thought of math prevents the brain from working through it logically.

The more this happens, the more a person's confidence drops, and the more math anxiety is generated. This vicious cycle must be broken!

The first step in breaking the cycle is to go back to very beginning and make sure you really understand the basics of how math works and why it works. It is not enough to memorize rules for multiplication and division. If you don't know WHY these rules work, your foundation will be shaky and you will be at risk of developing a phobia. Understanding mathematical concepts not only promotes confidence and security, but allows you to build on this understanding for new concepts. Additionally, you can solve unfamiliar problems using familiar concepts and processes.

Why is it that students in other countries regularly outperform American students in math? The answer likely boils down to a couple of things: the foundation of mathematical conceptual understanding and societal perception. While students in the US are not expected to *like* or *get* math, in many other nations, students are expected not only to understand math but also to excel at it.

Changing the American view of math that leads to math anxiety is a monumental task. It requires changing the training of teachers nationwide, from kindergarten through high school, so that they learn to teach the *why* behind math and to combat the wrong math views that students may develop. It also involves changing the stigma associated with math, so that it is no longer viewed as unpleasant and incomprehensible. While these are necessary changes, they are challenging and will take time. But in the meantime, math anxiety is not irreversible—it can be faced and defeated, one person at a time.

False Beliefs

One reason math anxiety has taken such hold is that several false beliefs have been created and shared until they became widely accepted. Some of these unhelpful beliefs include the following:

There is only one way to solve a math problem. In the same way that you can choose from different driving routes and still arrive at the same house, you can solve a math problem using different methods and still find the correct answer. A person who understands the reasoning behind math calculations may be able to look at an unfamiliar concept and find the right answer, just by applying logic to the knowledge they already have. This approach may be different than what is taught in the classroom, but it is still valid. Unfortunately, even many teachers view math as a subject where the best course of action is to memorize the rule or process for each problem rather than as a place for students to exercise logic and creativity in finding a solution.

Many people don't have a mind for math. A person who has struggled due to poor teaching or math anxiety may falsely believe that he or she doesn't have the mental capacity to grasp mathematical concepts. Most of the time, this is false. Many people find that when they are relieved of their math anxiety, they have more than enough brainpower to understand math.

Men are naturally better at math than women. Even though research has shown this to be false, many young women still avoid math careers and classes because of their belief that their math abilities are inferior. Many girls have come to believe that math is a male skill and have given up trying to understand or enjoy it.

Counting aids are bad. Something like counting on your fingers or drawing out a problem to visualize it may be frowned on as childish or a crutch, but these devices can help you get a tangible understanding of a problem or a concept.

Sadly, many students buy into these ideologies at an early age. A young girl who enjoys math class may be conditioned to think that she doesn't actually have the brain for it because math is for boys, and may turn her energies to other pursuits, permanently closing the door on a wide range of opportunities. A child who finds the right answer but doesn't follow the teacher's method may believe that he is doing it wrong and isn't good at math. A student who never had a problem with math before may have a poor teacher and become confused, yet believe that the problem is because she doesn't have a mathematical mind.

Students who have bought into these erroneous beliefs quickly begin to add their own anxieties, adapting them to their own personal situations:

I'll never use this in real life. A huge number of people wrongly believe that math is irrelevant outside the classroom. By adopting this mindset, they are handicapping themselves for a life in a mathematical world, as well as limiting their career choices. When they are inevitably faced with real-world math, they are conditioning themselves to respond with anxiety.

I'm not quick enough. While timed tests and quizzes, or even simply comparing yourself with other students in the class, can lead to this belief, speed is not an indicator of skill level. A person can work very slowly yet understand at a deep level.

If I can understand it, it's too easy. People with a low view of their own abilities tend to think that if they are able to grasp a concept, it must be simple. They cannot accept the idea that they are capable of understanding math. This belief will make it harder to learn, no matter how intelligent they are.

I just can't learn this. An overwhelming number of people think this, from young children to adults, and much of the time it is simply not true. But this mindset can turn into a self-fulfilling prophecy that keeps you from exercising and growing your math ability.

The good news is, each of these myths can be debunked. For most people, they are based on emotion and psychology, NOT on actual ability! It will take time, effort, and the desire to change, but change is possible. Even if you have spent years thinking that you don't have the capability to understand math, it is not too late to uncover your true ability and find relief from the anxiety that surrounds math.

Math Strategies

It is important to have a plan of attack to combat math anxiety. There are many useful strategies for pinpointing the fears or myths and eradicating them:

Go back to the basics. For most people, math anxiety stems from a poor foundation. You may think that you have a complete understanding of addition and subtraction, or even decimals and percentages, but make absolutely sure. Learning math is different from learning other subjects. For example, when you learn history, you study various time periods and places and events. It may be important to memorize dates or find out about the lives of famous people. When you move from US history to world history, there will be some overlap, but a large amount of the information will be new. Mathematical concepts, on the other hand, are very closely linked and highly dependent on each other. It's like climbing a ladder – if a rung is missing from your understanding, it may be difficult or impossible for you to climb any higher, no matter how hard you try. So go back and make sure your math foundation is strong. This may mean taking a remedial math course, going to a tutor to work through the shaky concepts, or just going through your old homework to make sure you really understand it.

Speak the language. Math has a large vocabulary of terms and phrases unique to working problems. Sometimes these are completely new terms, and sometimes they are common words, but are used differently in a math setting. If you can't speak the language, it will be very difficult to get a thorough understanding of the concepts. It's common for students to think that they don't understand math when they simply don't understand the vocabulary. The good news is that this is fairly easy to fix. Brushing up on any terms you aren't quite sure of can help bring the rest of the concepts into focus.

Check your anxiety level. When you think about math, do you feel nervous or uncomfortable? Do you struggle with feelings of inadequacy, even on concepts that you know you've already learned? It's important to understand your specific math anxieties, and what triggers them. When you catch yourself falling back on a false belief, mentally replace it with the truth. Don't let yourself believe that you can't learn, or that struggling with a concept means you'll never understand it. Instead, remind yourself of how much you've already learned and dwell on that past success. Visualize grasping the new concept, linking it to your old knowledge, and moving on to the next challenge. Also, learn how to manage anxiety when it arises. There are many techniques for coping with the irrational fears that rise to the surface when you enter the math classroom. This may include controlled breathing, replacing negative thoughts with positive ones, or visualizing success. Anxiety interferes with your ability to concentrate and absorb information, which in turn contributes to greater anxiety. If you can learn how to regain control of your thinking, you will be better able to pay attention, make progress, and succeed!

Don't go it alone. Like any deeply ingrained belief, math anxiety is not easy to eradicate. And there is no need for you to wrestle through it on your own. It will take time, and many people find that speaking with a counselor or psychiatrist helps. They can help you develop strategies for responding to anxiety and overcoming old ideas. Additionally, it can be very helpful to take a short course or seek out a math tutor to help you find and fix the missing rungs on your ladder and make sure that you're ready to progress to the next level. You can also find a number of math aids online: courses that will teach you mental devices for figuring out problems, how to get the most out of your math classes, etc.

Check your math attitude. No matter how much you want to learn and overcome your anxiety, you'll have trouble if you still have a negative attitude toward math. If you think it's too hard, or just have general feelings of dread about math, it will be hard to learn and to break through the anxiety. Work on cultivating a positive math attitude. Remind yourself that math is not just a hurdle to be cleared, but a valuable asset. When you view math with a positive attitude, you'll be much more likely to understand and even enjoy it. This is something you must do for yourself. You may find it helpful to visit with a counselor. Your tutor, friends, and family may cheer you on in your endeavors. But your greatest asset is yourself. You are inside your own mind – tell yourself what you need to hear. Relive past victories. Remind yourself that you are capable of understanding math. Root out any false beliefs that linger and replace them with positive truths. Even if it doesn't feel true at first, it will begin to affect your thinking and pave the way for a positive, anxiety-free mindset.

Aside from these general strategies, there are a number of specific practical things you can do to begin your journey toward overcoming math anxiety. Something as simple as learning a new note-taking strategy can change the way you approach math and give you more confidence and understanding. New study techniques can also make a huge difference.

Math anxiety leads to bad habits. If it causes you to be afraid of answering a question in class, you may gravitate toward the back row. You may be embarrassed to ask for help. And you may procrastinate on assignments, which leads to rushing through them at the last moment when it's too late to get a better understanding. It's important to identify your negative behaviors and replace them with positive ones:

Prepare ahead of time. Read the lesson before you go to class. Being exposed to the topics that will be covered in class ahead of time, even if you don't understand them perfectly, is extremely helpful in increasing what you retain from the lecture. Do your homework and, if you're still shaky, go over some extra problems. The key to a solid understanding of math is practice.

Sit front and center. When you can easily see and hear, you'll understand more, and you'll avoid the distractions of other students if no one is in front of you. Plus, you're more likely to be sitting with students who are positive and engaged, rather than others with math anxiety. Let their positive math attitude rub off on you.

Ask questions in class and out. If you don't understand something, just ask. If you need a more in-depth explanation, the teacher may need to work with you outside of class, but often it's a simple concept you don't quite understand, and a single question may clear it up. If you wait, you may not be able to follow the rest of the day's lesson. For extra help, most professors have office hours outside of class when you can go over concepts one-on-one to clear up any uncertainties. Additionally, there may be a *math lab* or study session you can attend for homework help. Take advantage of this.

Review. Even if you feel that you've fully mastered a concept, review it periodically to reinforce it. Going over an old lesson has several benefits: solidifying your understanding, giving you a confidence boost, and even giving some new insights into material that you're currently learning! Don't let yourself get rusty. That can lead to problems with learning later concepts.

Teaching Tips

While the math student's mindset is the most crucial to overcoming math anxiety, it is also important for others to adjust their math attitudes. Teachers and parents have an enormous influence on how students relate to math. They can either contribute to math confidence or math anxiety.

As a parent or teacher, it is very important to convey a positive math attitude. Retelling horror stories of your own bad experience with math will contribute to a new generation of math anxiety. Even if you don't share your experiences, others will be able to sense your fears and may begin to believe them.

Even a careless comment can have a big impact, so watch for phrases like *He's not good at math* or *I never liked math*. You are a crucial role model, and your children or students will unconsciously adopt your mindset. Give them a positive example to follow. Rather than teaching them to fear the math world before they even know it, teach them about all its potential and excitement.

Work to present math as an integral, beautiful, and understandable part of life. Encourage creativity in solving problems. Watch for false beliefs and dispel them. Cross the lines between subjects: integrate history, English, and music with math. Show students how math is used every day, and how the entire world is based on mathematical principles, from the pull of gravity to the shape of seashells. Instead of letting students see math as a necessary evil, direct them to view it as an imaginative, beautiful art form – an art form that they are capable of mastering and using.

Don't give too narrow a view of math. It is more than just numbers. Yes, working problems and learning formulas is a large part of classroom math. But don't let the teaching stop there. Teach students about the everyday implications of math. Show them how nature works according to the laws of mathematics, and take them outside to make discoveries of their own. Expose them to math-related careers by inviting visiting speakers, asking students to do research and presentations, and learning students' interests and aptitudes on a personal level.

Demonstrate the importance of math. Many people see math as nothing more than a required stepping stone to their degree, a nuisance with no real usefulness. Teach students that algebra is used every day in managing their bank accounts, in following recipes, and in scheduling the day's events. Show them how learning to do geometric proofs helps them to develop logical thinking, an invaluable life skill. Let them see that math surrounds them and is integrally linked to their daily lives: that weather predictions are based on math, that math was used to design cars and other machines, etc. Most of all, give them the tools to use math to enrich their lives.

Make math as tangible as possible. Use visual aids and objects that can be touched. It is much easier to grasp a concept when you can hold it in your hands and manipulate it, rather than just listening to the lecture. Encourage math outside of the classroom. The real world is full of measuring, counting, and calculating, so let students participate in this. Keep your eyes open for numbers and patterns to discuss. Talk about how scores are calculated in sports games and how far apart plants are placed in a garden row for maximum growth. Build the mindset that math is a normal and interesting part of daily life.

Finally, find math resources that help to build a positive math attitude. There are a number of books that show math as fascinating and exciting while teaching important concepts, for example: *The Math Curse; A Wrinkle in Time; The Phantom Tollbooth;* and *Fractals, Googols and Other Mathematical Tales.* You can also find a number of online resources: math puzzles and games, videos that show math in nature, and communities of math enthusiasts. On a local level, students can compete in a variety of math competitions with other schools or join a math club.

The student who experiences math as exciting and interesting is unlikely to suffer from math anxiety. Going through life without this handicap is an immense advantage and opens many doors that others have closed through their fear.

Self-Check

Whether you suffer from math anxiety or not, chances are that you have been exposed to some of the false beliefs mentioned above. Now is the time to check yourself for any errors you may have accepted. Do you think you're not wired for math? Or that you don't need to understand it since you're not planning on a math career? Do you think math is just too difficult for the average person?

Find the errors you've taken to heart and replace them with positive thinking. Are you capable of learning math? Yes! Can you control your anxiety? Yes! These errors will resurface from time to time, so be watchful. Don't let others with math anxiety influence you or sway your confidence. If you're having trouble with a concept, find help. Don't let it discourage you!

Create a plan of attack for defeating math anxiety and sharpening your skills. Do some research and decide if it would help you to take a class, get a tutor, or find some online resources to fine-tune your knowledge. Make the effort to get good nutrition, hydration, and sleep so that you are operating at full capacity. Remind yourself daily that you are skilled and that anxiety does not control you. Your mind is capable of so much more than you know. Give it the tools it needs to grow and thrive.

Thank You

We at Mometrix would like to extend our heartfelt thanks to you, our friend and patron, for allowing us to play a part in your journey. It is a privilege to serve people from all walks of life who are unified in their commitment to building the best future they can for themselves.

The preparation you devote to these important testing milestones may be the most valuable educational opportunity you have for making a real difference in your life. We encourage you to put your heart into it—that feeling of succeeding, overcoming, and yes, conquering will be well worth the hours you've invested.

We want to hear your story, your struggles and your successes, and if you see any opportunities for us to improve our materials so we can help others even more effectively in the future, please share that with us as well. **The team at Mometrix would be absolutely thrilled to hear from you!** So please, send us an email (support@mometrix.com) and let's stay in touch.

> **If you'd like some additional help, check out these other resources we offer for your exam:**
> **http://MometrixFlashcards.com/MTTC**

Additional Bonus Material

Due to our efforts to try to keep this book to a manageable length, we've created a link that will give you access to all of your additional bonus material.

Please visit
http://www.mometrix.com/bonus948/mttcelemed103 to
access the information.